California Real Estate
Property
Management

Fourth Edition

Cutoff Dates:
Legal editing of this material was
completed September 2006

Copyright ©2007 by first tuesday

Printed in the United States of America

Editorial Staff

Legal Editor/Publisher:
Fred Crane

Managing Editor:
Ai M. Kelley

Project Editor:
Connor P. Wallmark

Contributing Editors:
David F. Crane
Giang Hoang
Sheena Wong

Senior Editorial Assistant:
Joseph Duong

Editorial Assistant:
Sylvia Rodemeyer

Published by
Zyrus Press
PO Box 17810
Irvine, CA 92623
888-622-7823

Table Of Contents

SECTION A

SECTION B

SECTION C

**Rents
and
Deposits**

SECTION D

**Enforcing
Rents;
Forfeiting
Tenancies**

SECTION E

Maintenance and Security

SECTION F

Nonresidential Lease Provisions

SECTION G

SECTION H

Table of Forms

No.	Form Name	Page

Introduction

Written for California brokers, agents, landlords, resident managers and attorneys, **California Real Estate Property Management** is the definitive educational tool needed to understand landlord / tenant relationships in residential and nonresidential properties located in California.

The objective of this book is to fully inform the reader of federal, state and local landlord / tenant rights and obligations, and of the well-developed nature of interests held in real estate by landlords and tenants.

California Real Estate Property Management examines and applies the detailed and exacting rules of leasing and renting for both residential and nonresidential income properties. Hundreds of examples vividly present and resolve landlord / tenant situations encountered by owners, tenants and real estate licensees who manage income property or perform services as leasing agents.

All the forms and notices required by California law, along with detailed explanations of how to use them, are included in this book. These forms are used in California to establish leasing and management agencies, to create, alter and terminate tenancies, and to preserve rent obligations for later enforcement after evictions. Each form and notice reflects relevant codes, judicial decisions and practices in effect on the date of this publication. All forms referenced in this book are developed by **first tuesday**.

SECTION A

Ownership and Possession

Chapter 1

Fee vs. leasehold

This chapter examines the entitlement to possession of real estate held by owners of different interests in a parcel of real estate.

A matter of possession

A parcel of real estate is located by circumscribing its *legal description* on the "face of the earth." Based on the legal description, a surveyor locates and sets the corners and **surface boundaries** of the parcel.

The legal description is contained in deeds, subdivision maps or government surveys relating to the property.

However, a parcel of real estate is three dimensional, reaching beyond the surface boundaries. In addition to the surface area within the boundaries, real estate consists of the soil below the surface to the core of the earth as well as the air space above it to infinity.

All permanent structures, crops and timber within this *inverse pyramid* are also a part of the parcel of real estate.

A **parcel of real estate** is often mistakenly thought of as a plot of unimproved land. Also mistaken is the notion any improvements can be treated as personal property, unless they are to be removed from the land.

Real estate, sometimes legally called *real property*, consists of:

- the land;

- the improvements and fixtures attached to the land; and

- all rights incidental or belonging to the property. [Calif. Civil Code §658]

Real estate includes buildings, fences, trees, watercourses and easements within the parcel's boundaries.

Anything below the surface, such as water and minerals, or above the surface in the air space, such as crops and timber, is part of the real estate.

The rental of a boat slip includes the water and the land below it, both of which comprise the real estate. Thus, landlord/tenant law controls the rental of the slip. [**Smith** v. **Municipal Court of San Mateo County** (1988) 202 CA3d 685]

In the case of a condominium unit, the air space enclosed within the walls is the real estate conveyed and held by the owner of the unit. The structure, land and air space outside the unit are the property of the homeowners' association, creating what is called a *common interest development (CID)*. [CC §1351(f)]

Possessing interests in real estate

The **ownership interests** a person may hold in real estate are called *estates*. Four kinds of estates exist in real estate:

- fee estates, also known as inheritance or perpetual estates;

- life estates;

- leasehold estates, sometimes called estates for years; and

- estates at will. [CC §761]

In practice, these estates are separated into three categories: fee simple estates, leasehold estates and life estates. Estates at will are part of the leasehold estates controlled by landlord/tenant law.

A **life estate** terminates on the death of the owner of the life estate or the death of another person named in the deed which conveys or reserves the life estate to the owner.

Leasehold interests in the real estate exist for a specific period of time. The interest will terminate when the period of time expires.

An **estate at will**, unlike a leasehold, is not conveyed in an exchange for value, called *consideration* or rent. Estates at will terminate at the discretion of the fee owner, subject to proper advance notice. Possession of real estate under leasehold interests and estates at will is controlled primarily by landlord/tenant law.

Fee ownership

A fee owner has the right to possess and control his property indefinitely. A fee owner's possession is exclusive and absolute. Thus, the owner has the right to deny others permission to cross his boundaries. No one can be on the owner's property without his consent, otherwise they are trespassing. The owner may recover any money losses caused by the trespass.

A fee owner has the exclusive right to use and enjoy the property. As long as local ordinances such as building codes and zoning regulations are obeyed, a fee owner may do as he pleases with his property. A fee owner may build new buildings, tear down old ones, plant trees and shrubs, grow crops or simply leave the property unattended.

A fee owner may *occupy, sell, lease* or *encumber* his parcel of real estate, give it away or pass it on to his heirs or to anyone he chooses on his death. The fee estate is the interest in real estate transferred in a real estate sales transaction, unless a lesser interest is noted.

A fee owner is entitled to the land's surface and anything permanently located above or below it. [CC §829]

The ownership interests in one parcel may be separated into several fee interests. One person may own the mineral rights beneath the surface, another may own the surface rights, and yet another may own the rights to the air space. Each solely owned interest is held in fee in the same parcel.

Underground oil and gas reserves have a tendency to flow from one place to another. However, the right to extract oil and gas can be separately conveyed by the fee owner of the real estate. The drilling rights separated from the fee ownership are called *profit a prendre*. [**Gerhard** v. **Stephens** (1968) 68 C2d 864]

Profit a prendre is the right to remove profitable materials from property owned and possessed by another.

Consider a fee owner who grants separate fee interests in his property to two individuals. One individual receives the land's surface and air space rights. The other individual receives the subsurface oil and mineral rights.

The surface owner claims the title to the entire parcel of real estate should be vested — *quieted* — in his name.

The subsurface owner objects, claiming the surface owner's real estate interest is less than the entire fee estate in the property.

Here, the surface owner's fee interest in the parcel of real estate is separate from the subsurface ownership and possession of the oil and mineral rights. Also, they are not co-owners of the real estate. Both owners hold an individual fee estate in mutually exclusive and divided portions of the same parcel. [**In re Waltz** (1925) 197 C 263]

In most cases, one or more individuals own the entire fee and lease the subsurface rights to others to remove underground oil or minerals.

Thus, a fee owner can convey a leasehold interest in the oil and minerals while retaining the fee interest.

Life estates and the life tenant

A life estate is an interest in a parcel of real estate lasting the lifetime of the *life tenant*. Life estates are granted by a deed entered into by the fee owner, an executor under a will or by a trustee under an inter vivos trust.

Life estates are commonly established by a fee owner who wishes to provide a home or financial security for another person during that person's lifetime, called the *controlling life*.

Life estates terminate on the death of the controlling life. Life estates may also be terminated by agreement or by merger of different ownership interests in the property.

For example, an owner of a vacation home has an elderly aunt who needs a place to live. The owner grants her a life estate in the vacation home for the duration of her lifetime. The aunt may live there for the rest of her life, even if she outlives the fee owner who granted her the life estate.

Although the aunt has the right to exclusive possession of the entire parcel of real estate, the owner retains title to the fee. Thus, the conveyance of a life estate transfers a right to possession which has been "carved out" of the fee, comparable to possession under a leasehold interest since it is conveyed out of a fee. Unlike a lease, a life estate does not require rent to be paid.

On the aunt's death, possession of the property *reverts* to the fee owner, his successors or heirs since the right to possession under the life estate is extinguished on the aunt's death.

The holder of a life estate based on his life has the right of possession until death, as if he were the owner in fee. The holder of a life estate is responsible for taxes, maintenance and a reasonable amount of property assessments. [CC §840]

However, the holder of a life estate may not impair the fee interest. [CC §818]

For instance, the holder of a life estate may not make alterations which decrease the property's value, such as removing or failing to care for valuable plants or demolishing portions of the improvements or land.

Conversely, the owner of the life estate has the right to lease the property to others and collect and retain all rents produced by the property during the term of the life estate. Profit on the sale of the life estate can be taken in addition to rental income.

For example, a life estate tenant enters into a lease with a logging company allowing it to remove trees from the property.

The property value increases after the trees are removed since the property's best use is as a farm. Additional crops can be planted on the cleared land, making the parcel more productive and able to generate greater rents.

The fee owner claims the life tenant did not have the right to remove the trees, which were improvements.

However, the life tenant did not injure the fee interest by diminishing its value, called *impairment*. The life estate tenant is entitled to the profits from selling any timber located on the parcel, provided the property's value is not impaired by the removal of the trees. [**Sallee** v. **Daneri** (1942) 49 CA2d 324]

Also, a life tenant is entitled to be reimbursed by the fee owner for the fee owner's share of the costs to improve the property.

For example, a city inspector notifies a life tenant the city will order the property demolished unless the property is renovated to bring it up to health and safety codes.

The life tenant has a duty, owed to the fee owner, not to impair the property's value.

Thus, the life tenant must prevent the demolition of the property.

To do so, the life tenant improves the property, satisfying code requirements and increasing the property's value, all at considerable expense.

Here, the fee owner is liable to the life tenant for any increase in the value of the fee ownership in the property resulting from the improvements made by the life tenant. [**Eastman** v. **Peterson** (1968) 268 CA2d 169]

The rights of a life tenant as against a fee owner are quite different from those of a leasehold tenant against a fee owner (landlord).

Leasehold interests held by tenants

Leasehold interests are the result of rights *conveyed* to a tenant by a fee owner (or life estate tenant or master lessee) to possess a parcel of real estate. Leaseholds are created when the landlord and the tenant enter into a lease or a rental agreement that conveys a possessory interest in the real estate to the tenant.

The tenant becomes the owner of a leasehold with the right to possess and use the entire property until the lease expires. The title to the fee interest in the property remains with the landlord (or his successor) throughout the term of the leasehold, subject to the tenant's right to possession, which is carved out of the fee on the fee owner's entry into the lease agreement.

In exchange for the right to occupy and use the property, the landlord is entitled to rental income from the tenant during the period of the tenancy.

Types of leaseholds

Four types of leasehold interests exist and can be held by tenants. The interests are classified by the length of their term:

- a fixed-term tenancy, simply known as a *lease* and legally called an *estate for years*;

- a periodic tenancy, usually referred to as a *rental*;

- a tenancy-at-will; and

- a tenancy-at-sufferance, commonly called a *holdover tenancy*.

A **fixed-term tenancy** lasts for a specific length of time agreed to in a lease between a landlord and tenant.

On expiration of the lease, the tenant's right to possession automatically terminates unless an agreement, such as an option which is exercised, extends the expiration date or renews or establishes an entirely new tenancy.

Periodic tenancies also last for a specific length of time, such as for a week or a month. However, in the creation of a periodic tenancy, the landlord and tenant agree to automatic successive rental periods of the same length of time, such as in a month-to-month tenancy.

A **tenant-at-will** has the right to possession of property with the consent of the owner. Tenancies-at-will can be terminated at any time by an advance notice from either party or as set by agreement. Tenancies-at-will do not have a fixed duration, are usually not in writing and a rent obligation generally does not exist.

Leaseholds conveying special uses

In addition to the typical residential and non-residential leases, leases exist which serve special purposes.

Oil, gas, water and **mineral leases** convey the right to use mineral deposits below the earth's surface.

The purpose of an oil lease is to discover and produce oil or gas. The lease is a tool used by the property owner to develop and realize the wealth of his land. The tenant provides the money and machinery for exploration and development.

The tenant pays the landlord rent, called a *royalty*, and keeps any profits from the sale of oil or minerals he extracts from beneath the surface of the parcel.

A **ground lease** on a parcel of real estate is granted to a tenant in exchange for the payment of rent. Rent is based on the rental value of the portion of the parcel called land, whether the parcel is vacant or improved. The lease is a financing tool for fee owners of vacant, unimproved land to induce others in acquiring an interest in the property and developing the property.

Ground leases are common in more densely populated areas. Developers often need financial assistance from owners to avoid massive cash outlay to acquire unimproved parcels. Also, owners of developable property often refuse to sell, choosing to become landlords for the long-term rental income they will receive.

An original tenant under a ground lease constructs his own improvements. Typically, the tenant encumbers his ground lease with a trust deed lien to provide security for a construction loan.

Master leases benefit owners who want the financial advantages of renting fully improved property, but do not want the day-to-day obligations and risks of managing the property.

For instance, an owner of a shopping center and a prospective owner-operator agree to a master lease.

As the master tenant, the owner-operator will collect rent from the many subtenants, address their needs and concerns and maintain the property. The master tenant is responsible for the rent due the landlord under the master lease, even if the subtenants do not pay their rents to the master tenant.

The master lease is sometimes called a *sandwich lease* since the master tenant is "sandwiched" between the fee owner (the landlord on the master lease) and the many subtenants with their possession under subleases.

The **master lease** is a regular, nonresidential lease agreement form with the deletion of any clause prohibiting assignments and subletting. A **sublease** is also a regular, nonresidential lease agreement with an additional clause referencing the attached master lease and declaring the sublease subject to the terms of the master lease. [See **first tuesday** Form 552]

Another type of special-use lease is the **farm lease**, sometimes called *cropping agreements* or *grazing lease*. Here, the tenant operates the farm and pays the landlord either a flat fee for rent or a percentage of the value of the crops or livestock produced on the land.

Chapter 2

License
to use land

This chapter distinguishes a license to use land from a tenant's leasehold and an easement on land.

A personal right to use another's property

The purpose of a *license*, like an easement and a lease, is to grant the right to use property owned by another person. A **license** is similar in this essential purpose to an easement and a lease, yet it is neither.

Similar to an easement or a lease, a license is an agreement. Instead of being placed in writing, a license is often oral. Unlike an easement, a license does not have a perpetual life, nor does it have a specific expiration date like a lease.

Also similar to an easement, a property burdened with a license is referred to as the *servient tenement*. Unlike an easement, which benefits the owner of another (adjacent) parcel of real estate, called the *dominant tenement*, and is an appurtenant right transferred with the conveyance of that property, a license has no **dominant tenement** (adjacent property) which benefits from the license. A license is not appurtenant to any property since it is personal, called *in gross*.

Unlike an easement or a lease, a license is a **personal privilege** held by an individual, not an appurtenant right remaining with a property for future owners to use. Since a license is not an appurtenant right and does not benefit a property, the right given by the license cannot be transferred to another individual.

A holder of a license does not typically pay rent for the right to use the burdened property. If consideration for the license exists, it is in the form of an expenditure of time and money by the licensee to improve or maintain the use authorized on the burdened property, such as an irrigation ditch, roadway, fence, etc.

Due to the fact that there is no right to exclusive possession of a burdened property (the **servient tenement**) for an authorized use, a license, like an easement and unlike a lease, permits only the nonexclusive use of the property by the licensee.

Unlike either a lease agreement or an easement deed, which are conveyances of an interest in real estate, a license agreement **conveys no interest** in real estate. The right to use a property granted by a license is a mere personal privilege, held by an individual under an agreement with the owner of the burdened property. The license is **revocable** by the owner of the burdened property at any time, unless revocation would be unfair to the holder of the privilege, called a *licensee*.

Typically, a license agreement arises between a property owner and a neighbor or friend as the result of a property owner's acceptance of an informal offer by an individual to jointly or separately make use of the owner's property for a specific activity. The individual given the license generally agrees to maintain or improve the property for the agreed-to use.

Use as a personal privilege

A broker wants to increase the exposure of his business to the public by billboard advertising.

The broker has a friend and business acquaintance who owns vacant property adjacent to a highway. The property owner is willing to allow the broker to place a billboard on his vacant land.

The broker and property owner enter into an oral understanding allowing the broker to put up a billboard for his use only. It is agreed the broker may enter and exit the property at his will to install and maintain the billboard.

A time limitation is not specified for maintaining the billboard on the property, nor is any fee or other compensation established. However, the property owner does not relinquish any control over the real estate since he does not give the broker any other right to use the property.

Have the broker and property owner established a landlord/tenant relationship or an easement?

Neither! The broker has only been given a **license** to use the owner's property.

Unlike a landlord/tenant relationship or an easement, a license to use real estate is a **personal privilege**, unattached to any property owned by the broker. Thus, the use is generally non-assignable to others by the broker and, unless agreed to the contrary, is revocable by the property owner at any time.

A license to use

A license is the **nonexclusive right** given to an individual to use a space or area within a parcel of real estate, or its improvements, that belong to another person. The right to use is held by an individual under an agreement, without the rights to assign or to privacy. A license is subject to termination by the owner of the burdened property at will, unless it has become irrevocable.

Consider a property owner who contracts for development work to be done on his property. The owner allows the construction company to store excess dirt on vacant lots he owns until they can haul it away.

While the dirt remains on the vacant lots, an adventurous dirtbiker enters the property and is injured. The injured dirtbiker claims the construction company is a licensee who is not in possession of the real estate and thus is liable for his injuries. The construction company claims they have a recreational use immunity since they have an interest in the property as a licensee with a right to use it for the agreed-to purpose.

In this example, the holder of any interest in the property is exempt from liability for injuries incurred by others arising out of the **recreational use** of private property. The property interest exempt from liability can be either possessory or nonpossessory.

Since a licensee has a nonpossessory interest in the property, he also has recreational user immunity even though the owner remains in possession and control of the land and the licensee has only a nonexclusive personal right to use the property. [Calif. Civil Code §846]

Thus, the construction company is not liable for injuries which occur during the dirtbiker's recreational use of the property since the construction company holds an interest in the property under their license to use.

License vs. lease

A license is often confused with a lease. A **lease** conveys a possessory interest in real estate which allows the tenant to **exclusively occupy** the leased premises in exchange for rent, called a *leasehold estate* or a *lease*. [CC §761]

A **license-to-use** another person's real estate, called a *servient tenement*, is a personal privilege held by an individual. A license is neither personal property nor real property, and it is neither owned by a person nor is it an appurtenance to adjoining real estate. Thus, a license, not being property or capable of ownership, cannot be transferred to the licensee's successors or assignors. [**Beckett** v. **City of Paris Dry Goods Co.** (1939) 14 C2d 633]

Characteristics which distinguish a license from a lease include:

- no writing to formalize the agreement;

- no rental payments;

- no specific location on or within the property where the use will occur;

- no intent to convey a leasehold estate;

- no right to exclude others;

- no termination date; and

- termination at the owner's will, unless the license is irrevocable.

In our previous example, the broker can use his business acquaintance's property to set up his billboard and leave it in place on the property. Also, the broker (or his representative) has the right to go back and forth across the property to maintain or repair the billboard. Thus, the property is a **servient tenement** subject to the terms of the license held by the broker. However, no **dominant tenement** exists since no property benefits from the license; only the broker benefits as the licensee.

Thus, the owner of the property can demand removal of the broker's billboard from the property at any time, and the broker must immediately remove it.

A common thread which runs through both a lease and license is the right to use the property. The glaring distinction between the two is that the license does not include the **right to exclude** any other person from possession as does a lease.

Continuing with our example, the broker cannot fence off, lock out or quarantine in any way the ground under or around his billboard from the property owner or any other person. The license affords the broker no greater right to be on the property than anyone else the owner might allow to concurrently use his property.

License distinguished from a lease

When an agreement with a property owner gives another person exclusive right to possession of the property against all others, includ-ing the owner, it is a lease agreement or periodic rental agreement — a leasehold estate, not a license.

Conversely, when the agreement confers only the privilege to use property which remains under the owner's day-to-day control, it is a **license**. [**Von Goerlitz** v. **Turner** (1944) 65 CA2d 425]

For example, an owner of a packing company enters into an agreement to purchase raw materials from a wholesale merchant. The wholesale merchant is to supply the packing company with raw materials over a three-year period. In exchange, the packing company will pay the agreed-to price for the materials, as well as allow the wholesale merchant the right to use an unlocked storage unit for temporary stockpiling of his materials and desk space in an office at the packing facility to conduct business.

The agreement does not designate the exact spaces to be used by the merchant. Also, the packing company will concurrently use the same space to be used by the merchant.

Two years into the arrangement, the packing company is sold. The new owner demands the wholesale merchant to move out immediately. The wholesale merchant claims a lease existed between himself and the previous owner, allowing him to remain on the property until the lease expires.

However, no dollar rental amount had been established. Also, the wholesale merchant did not have exclusive possession of the spaces he occupied.

Instead of a lease, the wholesale merchant held a license agreement to use space under which the packing company had a superior possessory right to the premises. Thus, the wholesale merchant's use of unlocked space, concurrently occupied by the original owner, was not a lease.

The mere permission of an owner to let someone use and occupy unidentified space in a structure in a **non-exclusive manner** when the owner retains possession and total control over the premises constitutes a license. [**Caldwell** v. **Gem Packing Co.** (1942) 52 CA2d 80]

Terms implying a lease

The stated intentions in a written agreement between an owner and another person may be to enter into a license agreement. However, the actual language and provisions of the agreement may render it a lease which is improperly titled as a license.

For example, an optometrist enters into a written agreement with an operator of a store to establish an optical department on the premises. The written agreement is entitled a license.

The agreement allows the store to determine the space the optometrist will occupy, set the rent at a percentage of the optometrist's total sales and require the optometrist to make nightly deposits of receipts with the store's cashier. Also, the optometrist has the exclusive right to manage and operate his trade within his space. The agreement prohibits the optometrist from assigning his business and the occupancy to another without the store's consent.

The agreement is for a term of three years, at which time the optometrist agrees to surrender the premises in good condition.

Two years after commencement of the agreement, the store hands the optometrist a notice of cancellation of their agreement (rather than a three-day notice to perform or quit) for his failure to deposit his daily cash receipts with the store cashier.

The optometrist refuses to vacate, claiming he is a tenant of the store under the written agreement. The store contends the agreement was a license, terminable at any time and the optometrist must leave.

However, the terminology in their agreement and the payment of rent is more in line with a lease than a license, indicating the parties created a landlord/tenant relationship by their arrangements.

Similar to a lease, the provision **prohibiting assignment** is only applicable to the ownership of an interest in real estate since a license is non-assumable as nothing is actually owned for the licensee to assign. Also, the optometrist was given **exclusive possession** of a designated space within the store for a fixed period of time which eliminates the owner's right to enter the optometrist's space at any time.

Thus, the arrangement by the content of the written agreement was a lease. The right to exclude others from entry for a stated term, coupled with assignment rights and rent, are characteristics of a landlord/tenant relationship, not a license. [Beckett, *supra*]

If an occupancy agreement contains words or phrases like **lease, rental, demise** or **good tenantable condition**, the agreement will be construed to be a lease rather than a license.

Consider a corporation which owns 150 units in a resort condominium and sells time-share memberships in the resort. A member can purchase up to four one-week time share interests.

However, a member is not entitled to reserve any particular unit in advance of occupancy. The assignment of units for actual occupancy during the time period selected is left up to the discretion of the corporation's board of directors.

A *restraining order* is issued by the Department of Real Estate (DRE) stopping sales of these time-share memberships because a permit and a public report to sell **fractional interests in real estate** was not first obtained from the DRE by the corporation.

The corporation contends the memberships are mere licenses held by the members to use unidentified space and are not a lease or other conveyance of space to the members which would require a permit and public report. The corporation further contends the members do not hold an interest in the real estate since they do not have exclusive right to the possession of any specific unit.

However, the occupancy rights held by the members constitute a lease. The units to be occupied are identical, the duration of occupancy is specific and each member has the right to **exclusive occupancy** of a unit. [**Cal-Am Corporation** v. **Department of Real Estate** (1980) 104 CA3d 453]

Recharacterization of a license

A *license* is usually oral with very few terms agreed to except the permission to use or conduct an activity on a property while the owner remains in actual possession and retains the right to exclude others, including the licensee. Above all else, a **license** does not carry with it the right to exclude anyone from the property.

However, with every additional condition agreed to between an owner and user, a license begins to recharacterize itself more and more into a lease.

For example, a broker has an office with unoccupied desks. The broker wants to operate alone and avoid commitments to manage and supervise associate licensees. However, he is willing to share space in the office with other brokers.

The broker offers another broker the use of an office, desk space, a telephone line and secretarial services. The brokers orally agree each will pay their own proportionate share of utilities, secretarial services and rent.

A time period for the use is not specified. The office space selected by the other broker is unlocked and open to the entire office.

In this instance, the original broker may terminate this "rent-a-space" relationship at any time without prior notice or cause since the other broker has been given no more rights than a licensee to use office space.

Conversely, when a broker offers space in his office under a written agreement providing for lockable office space and a specific period for occupancy, the agreement is a lease. With a lease (or a month-to-month rental agreement) in hand, the broker has created a landlord/tenant relationship, not a license.

By specifying more and more terms regarding the right to exclude others — such as the locked door prohibiting entry by others for a period of time — what started out as a mere license to use has been restructured to constitute a lease.

A license coupled with a lease

On some occasions, a **license and a lease co-exist** and are held by the same person.

A person can be a tenant with exclusive occupancy to part of the space on the premises of a shopping center and hold a license to use an adjacent portion of the premises as well.

For example, a retail tenant leases space in a shopping center. The tenant has exclusive possession of his store space controlling who may enter. However, the tenant shares use of the sidewalks and parking lots with other shopping center tenants and all the customers of the shopping center.

The tenant has no right to exclusive possession of the sidewalk and parking area, only the space enclosed within his unit. Thus, the tenant holds a license for access and non-exclusive use of the parking area and a lease for the space within the shopping center.

An irrevocable license

When an individual makes substantial expenditures to improve or maintain his use of another person's property for a long period of time in reliance on his oral agreement with the owner of that property, the license becomes *irrevocable* and cannot be terminated at will by the property owner.

An **irrevocable license** grants an individual the right to enter and use property as long as the specific activity for which the license was granted is feasible.

For example, if a neighbor expends money, or its equivalent in labor, on the on-going maintenance of a road (which provides access from his property to a main road) through the property owned by another person in reliance on an oral agreement with that property owner, the neighbor by his agreement has an irrevocable license to use the road. [**Cooke** v. **Ramponi** (1952) 38 C2d 282]

Consider the construction of a privacy wall along the entire length of a common property line between adjacent lots. The lots are located on a hillside, one above the other. Each lot is flat with a graded slope between them to adjust for the difference in the elevation. Each lot is improved with a residence.

The boundary between the lots is located at the bottom of the slope. However, for a wall to give the owner of each lot privacy, the wall must be located at the top of the slope, entirely on the uphill parcel and several feet from the boundary line.

The owner of the uphill lot agrees to allow the neighbor below to construct a masonry wall with its foundation on the top of the slope. The owner and the neighbor agree on the height of the wall and that the neighbor may **use the slope** between the wall and the property line.

The owner orally agrees to an easement for the encroachment, which is never reduced to writing so no easement was created.

The neighbor constructs the masonry wall at the top of the slope. He also builds a gazebo within the slope area between the fence and property line.

The owner of the uphill lot sells the property to a buyer. The buyer surveys the lot and demands the neighbor to remove the wall and gazebo since they encroach on what is now the buyer's property.

The neighbor claims he has an irrevocable license to maintain the encroachments and use the slope since he spent considerable time and money to construct the encroaching structure in reliance on the prior owner's oral agreement which allowed him to build the wall and use the top of the slope.

The buyer claims he should not be estopped from revoking the license since he had no notice the license existed and the use was not reduced to an enforceable easement.

However, the license became irrevocable since substantial effort or expenditures were made in reliance on the oral agreement with the property owner allowing the use. Further, the buyer — as a successor owner of the property burdened with the use allowed by the oral license agreement — need not have any knowledge of the **irrevocable license** to be barred from denying the neighbor's continual use to maintain the existing wall and gazebo under the oral agreement. [**Noronha** v. **Stewart** (1988) 199 CA3d 485]

Chapter 3

Types of tenancies

This chapter discusses the different types of tenancies and how each is established.

Know your tenancy or lose time

A landlord and tenant enter into a lease agreement without including an option to renew or extend the term of the occupancy on expiration of the lease.

Several months before the lease expires, they begin negotiations to enter into a new lease agreement extending the term of occupancy. An agreement is not reached before the original tenancy expires. The tenant remains in possession on expiration of the lease — an unlawful detainer of the premises, commonly called a holdover, unless agreed to.

The landlord and tenant continue lease negotiations. Meanwhile, the tenant pays monthly rent at the same rate he was paying when the lease expired, which the landlord accepts.

Ultimately, they fail to agree on the terms for a new lease. The landlord then serves a 30-day notice on the tenant to either **stay and pay** a substantially higher monthly rent or **vacate** and forfeit the right to possession. [See **first tuesday** Forms 569, 571 or 579; see Chapter 29]

The tenant does neither; he remains in possession and does not pay the increased rent.

Can the landlord file an unlawful detainer (UD) action and proceed to evict the tenant on expiration of the 30-day notice and without further notice?

Yes! The tenant went from a fixed-term tenancy (the lease) to a tenancy-at-sufferance on expiration of the lease (a holdover) to a periodic (month-to-month) tenancy on the landlord's acceptance of rent for occupancy after the lease expired. The right to possession under the periodic tenancy ended due to the expiration of the notice and the tenant's failure to pay rent (set by the notice).

However, the type of notice to quit used when the landlord decides to terminate the tenant's right to possession will change depending on the **type of tenancy** that exists and the purpose of the notice.

Tenancies as leasehold estates

Tenancies are possessory interests in real estate, called *leasehold estates*.

Four types of tenancies exist:
1.   Fixed-term tenancies.
2.   Periodic tenancies.
3.   Tenancies-at-sufferance.
4.   Tenancies-at-will.

To initially establish a tenancy, a landlord must somehow **transfer to the tenant** — either in writing, orally or by his conduct — the right to occupy the real estate. If the landlord does not transfer the right to occupy, the occupant who takes possession is a *trespasser*.

All tenancies have an agreed-to termination date or are capable of termination by notice. Termination of a fixed-term tenancy held by the tenant, which was conveyed by the **lease-agreement**, occurs on the expiration date stated in the lease and without further notice.

A month-to-month rental agreement conveys an automatically renewable periodic tenancy, which is terminated by service of a 30-day notice to vacate at any time or a 3-day notice to vacate on a breach of the rental agreement. [See Chapters 26 and 29]

A tenant's possessory interest in real estate can shift from one type of tenancy to another due to:

- a notice;

- expiration of a lease; or

- by conduct.

Thus, before a landlord can file a UD action and proceed with the eviction process based on an unlawful detainer of the premises by the tenant, the tenant's **right to possession** under his tenancy must be terminated by the proper notice to vacate (quit), unless the tenant holdover is under an expired lease.

In our opening example, the tenant traversed three types of **tenancies**:

- *fixed-term* (lease);

- *sufferance* (no agreed-to holdover); and

- *month-to-month* (acceptance of monthly payments), also called a *periodic tenancy*.

The tenant entered into his occupancy under a fixed-term tenancy, a leasehold estate commonly called a *lease*. During the term of the lease, the tenant can only be evicted for cause — and then only after the service of a 3-day notice to cure the breach or vacate (quit) the property. [See **first tuesday** Form 576]

On expiration of a lease, the tenant who remains in possession without an agreement or acceptance of rent by the landlord for the extended occupancy becomes a holdover tenant, legally called a *tenant-at-sufferance*. The landlord does not have to serve a notice to vacate on the holdover tenant before filing a UD action to evict the tenant. [Calif. Code of Civil Procedure §1161(1)]

However, if the landlord accepts monthly rent from a tenant in payment for his continued occupation after expiration of the lease, a month-to-month tenancy is established on the terms and conditions of the expired lease agreement, unless a renewal or extension option exists. When an option to renew or extend exists, the lease is renewed or extended by the post-expiration acceptance of the rent called for in the option. [Calif. Civil Code §1945]

To terminate a month-to-month tenancy which was created by acceptance of monthly rent after expiration of a lease which is not in default, the landlord must serve the tenant with a 30-day notice to vacate before filing a UD action. [**Colyear** v. **Tobriner** (1936) 7 C2d 735]

Fixed-term tenancy

A **fixed-term tenancy**, also known as an *estate for years* or more commonly as a *leasehold*, is the result of an agreement between the landlord and the tenant for a fixed time period, typically called a *lease*. [CC §761]

The occupancy under a lease agreement must have a beginning date, called the *commencement date*, and an ending date, called the *expiration date*. If the rental period is longer than one year, the lease arrangements must be in writing and signed by the landlord and tenant to be enforceable, called a *lease agreement*, and sometimes loosely referred to as *the lease*. [CC §1624]

In a fixed-term tenancy, the tenant has an exclusive right to possession of the premises for the term of the occupancy stated in the lease agreement. On expiration of the lease, the tenancy automatically terminates. The tenant is not entitled to any notice to vacate other than the notice provided by the tenancy's expiration date stated in the lease agreement. [CCP §1161(1)]

For example, a landlord and tenant orally agree to a six-month lease. At the end of six months, the landlord and tenant orally agree to another six-month lease.

At the end of the second term, the tenant refuses to vacate. The tenant claims the landlord must first serve him with a notice to vacate.

Here, the tenant is not entitled to any further notice beyond the agreed-to termination date. The oral occupancy agreement was not a periodic tenancy, such as a month-to-month rental agreement, even though it contained monthly rent payments. Instead, the occupancy agreement was a fixed-term lease with a set expiration date.

Thus, the tenant's right to possession terminates on expiration of the orally agreed-to six-month period. The oral lease agreement is enforceable since it was for a term of less than one year. [**Camp** v. **Matich** (1948) 87 CA2d 660]

A **fixed-term tenancy** provides a tenant with several advantages:

- the right to occupy for the fixed term;

- a predetermined rental amount; and

- limitations on termination or modification.

However, some disadvantages also exist for the fixed-term tenant:

- the tenant is liable for the total amount of rent due over the entire term of the lease (subject to the landlord's duty to mitigate losses); and

- the tenant may want to vacate prior to expiration of the leasing period and assign or sublet the premises to a new tenant to cover rent obligations, but cannot due to prohibitions in the lease against his transfer of possession, called *restraints on alienation*.

Periodic tenancy

If the landlord finds a fixed-term tenancy too restrictive or inflexible for his financial purposes or use requirements, a periodic tenancy may be more suitable.

A periodic tenancy automatically continues for **successive periods**, each for the same length of time, until terminated by a notice to vacate. The length of each successive period of time is determined by the interval between scheduled rental payments.

Examples of **periodic payment** intervals include:

- annual rental payments, indicating a year-to-year tenancy;

- monthly rental payments, indicating a month-to-month tenancy; and

- weekly rental payments, indicating a week-to-week tenancy.

Consider a property manager who rents an apartment to a tenant under a fixed-term lease. At the end of the leasing period, the tenant retains possession and continues to pay rent monthly, which the property manager accepts.

Later, the tenant is served with a 30-day notice to vacate. On the running of the 30 days, the tenant refuses to vacate. The tenant claims he is now a tenant-at-will and entitled to an additional 3-day notice to vacate before he is unlawfully detaining the property since the notice to vacate served on him merely terminated his right to possession and made him a tenant-at-will on expiration of the notice.

However, an occupancy agreement for an **indefinite term** with a monthly rent schedule is a month-to-month tenancy. Thus, a tenant is only entitled to one notice to vacate before a UD action may be filed to evict him. [**Palmer** v. **Zeis** (1944) 65 CA2d Supp. 859]

The flexibility of a periodic tenancy allows the landlord and the tenant to terminate a month-to-month tenancy by giving the appropriate notice to vacate to the other party. [CC §1946; see Chapter 29]

Also, the operator of a **residential hotel** may not require a resident to change units or to check out and re-register in order to avoid creating a month-to-month tenancy and falling under landlord/tenant law. A residential hotel operator violating this rule is liable for a $500 civil penalty and attorney fees. [CC §1940.1]

Tenancy-at-sufferance

When a fixed-term (lease) or periodic (month-to-month) tenancy terminates by prior agreement or notice, the tenant who remains in possession — a *tenant-at-sufferance* — unlawfully detains the property from the landlord.

A tenant-at-sufferance is more commonly called a *holdover tenant*. A holdover tenant retains possession of the premises without any contractual right to do so, a situation called an *unlawful detainer*.

A **holdover tenant** no longer owes rent under the expired lease or terminated rental agreement since he no longer has the right to possession. However, the rental or lease agreement usually calls for a penalty rate of daily rent owed for each day the tenant holds over. Without a holdover rent provision, the tenant owes the landlord the *reasonable rental value* of the property, a daily rate owed for each day the tenant holds over in possession after expiration of his tenancy.

Holdover rent is due **after** the tenant vacates or is evicted, when the holdover period is known and the amount owed can be determined.

The landlord's acceptance of "holdover" rent **prior** to the tenant vacating or being evicted establishes a periodic tenancy on receipt of the rent.

For example, a tenant with a fixed-term lease holds over after the lease agreement expires. The lease agreement contains no provisions for the amount of rent due during any holdover period.

On the tenant's failure to vacate, the landlord serves the tenant a 30-day notice to either pay a rent amount substantially higher than rental market rates or vacate. The tenant refuses to pay any rent or vacate.

The landlord files a UD action seeking payment of rent at the rate stated in the notice to pay or quit since the tenant did not vacate.

At the UD hearing, the landlord is awarded the reasonable market rental value for the entire time the tenant held over, not the higher rent demanded in the notice to pay or quit. The tenant never paid nor agreed to pay any amount of rent after the lease expired. Thus, a periodic tenancy was not established.

The higher rental amount demanded in the notice to pay or quit was not accepted by the holdover tenant since he refused to pay it. Thus, a UD court will only award a reasonable rental value for the time period the tenant held over since he is a tenant-at-sufferance in unlawful possession of the property. Also, the notice to (pay or) quit was not needed to evict the tenant on expiration of the lease. [**Shenson** v. **Shenson** (1954) 124 CA2d 747]

Expired first refusal becomes a holdover

Now consider a tenant who enters into a fixed-term lease for the second floor of a building.

Without a charge for additional rent, the tenant will also take and retain possession of the third floor until the landlord secures a *bona fide* tenant. The tenant has the **right of first refusal** to rent the third floor should the landlord find a tenant. If the tenant does not exercise his right of first refusal to rent the third floor, his right to possession of the third floor ends.

The tenant moves into the second and third floors of the building. Later, the landlord locates a prospective tenant to rent the third floor.

The landlord notifies the tenant he must immediately exercise his right of first refusal or vacate the third floor.

The tenant does not exercise his right of first refusal and refuses to move. The tenant claims he is a tenant-at-will with the right to receive a notice to vacate before his right to occupancy can be terminated.

However, the tenant's lease of the third floor had a *specific termination date* — the date the tenant fails to exercise his right of first refusal. Thus, he is a tenant for a fixed-term and not a tenant-at-will since his occupancy ended on expiration of his right of first refusal.

The tenant, now a holdover, becomes a *tenant-at-sufferance* on expiration of his right of first refusal. Thus, the tenant is not entitled to any further notice to quit before his unlawful detainer of the premises is established. The tenant's notice of the date of termination of the occupancy was his failure to exercise his right of first refusal prior to its expiration. [**Vandenbergh** v. **Davis** (1961) 190 CA2d 694]

For the tenant with a right of first refusal to also be entitled to an additional period of lawful occupancy and a notice to vacate after expiration of a lease, a provision so stating must be included in the lease agreement or the right of first refusal agreement.

A **tenancy-at-sufferance** also arises when a resident manager's compensation includes the right to occupy a unit rent-free. When the landlord terminates the employment and the resident manager fails to vacate immediately, a tenancy-at-sufferance exists.

For example, a landlord hires a caretaker to do general maintenance work around an apartment complex in exchange for rent-free possession of a unit in the complex.

Several months later, during a dispute with the landlord, the tenant refuses to work, which results in his dismissal as an employee.

The landlord delivers a notice to the tenant to immediately pay rent (as demanded in the notice) or quit. The tenant does neither and the landlord files a UD action.

The tenant contends he is a tenant-at-will, entitled to a notice to vacate before the landlord can establish an unlawful detainer and file his UD action.

However, the tenant's right to occupancy ended when his employment ended, the expiration of a fixed-term lease. Thus, the tenant became a **holdover tenant** who was not entitled to notice, other than the notice from the landlord terminating the employment, before the landlord could commence a UD action to evict him. [**Karz** v. **Mecham** (1981) 120 CA3d Supp. 1]

If the employee is to receive notice and time to pay or vacate on termination of his employment (and right to occupancy), his employment agreement must provide for it.

Under rent control ordinances, a tenant-at-sufferance must receive a notice to vacate. However, courts in rent-controlled areas have exempted employee-tenants from rent control protection by classifying them, for purposes of rent control, as licensees rather than tenants.

Yet, employee-tenants clearly are not licensees (for any other purpose) since they have exclusive rights to occupy the unit assigned to them. [**Chan** v. **Antepenko** (1988) 203 CA3d Supp. 21]

Tenancy-at-will

The characteristics of a *tenancy-at-will* include:

- possession delivered to the tenant with the landlord's knowledge and consent;

- possession for an indefinite and unspecified period; and

- no provision for the payment of rent.

For a **tenancy-at-will**, a written notice to vacate or pay rent is required to make any change in the right to occupy the premises. However, the parties can always agree to a shorter or longer notice period. [CC §§789, 1946]

For example, an owner-occupant agrees to sell his office building under a purchase agreement providing for him to retain the **free use and possession** of the property after closing until he can occupy an office building he is constructing. Thus, a tenancy-at-will is created.

The buyer agrees in the purchase agreement to give the seller a 90-day written notice to either vacate the property or pay rent.

The buyer resells the property to a new owner. The new owner demands the tenant-seller pay rent or vacate immediately. The new owner claims he is not subject to the prior owner's **unrecorded agreement** to give a 90-day notice.

However, the new owner acquired the property subject to the rights held by the tenant in possession. Thus, the new owner is charged with *constructive knowledge* of the unrecorded agreement regarding notices and took title subject to the terms of the agreement.

Until the tenant-at-will receives the appropriate notice to vacate, he is not unlawfully detaining the property and the owner/landlord cannot proceed with a UD action to recover possession. [**First & C. Corporation** v. **Wencke** (1967) 253 CA2d 719]

However, a tenancy-at-will is automatically terminated if the tenant **assigns or sublets** his right to occupy the property to another tenant. The new tenant becomes a tenant-at-sufferance or a trespasser. [**McLeran** v. **Benton** (1887) 73 C 329]

Also, the tenancy-at-will terminates on the **death** of either the landlord or tenant, unless an agreement to the contrary exists. [**Dugand** v. **Magnus** (1930) 107 CA 243]

Other situations giving rise to a tenancy-at-will include:

- when a tenant with the right to indefinitely occupy the property in exchange for making improvements fails to make the improvements [**Carteri** v. **Roberts** (1903) 140 C 164];

- when a tenant takes possession of the property under an unenforceable lease agreement (e.g., the written lease with terms orally agreed to was never signed by any of the parties) — unless rent is accepted, which establishes a periodic tenancy [**Psihozios** v. **Humberg** (1947) 80 CA2d 215]; or

- when a tenant is given possession of the property without the payment of rent while negotiations on the lease provisions are still in progress. [**Miller** v. **Smith** (1960) 179 CA2d 114]

Terminating a tenancy

A landlord's primary concern when terminating a tenancy is the type of notice to vacate he must deliver to establish an unlawful detainer under the different **types of tenancies**, including:

- a *fixed-term tenancy*, in which case the landlord does not need to deliver any notice to vacate prior to commencing a UD action against a holdover tenant after expiration of the lease since the tenancy automatically expires by the terms of the lease [CCP §1161(1)];

- a *periodic tenancy*, in which case the notice to vacate must be for a period at least as long as the interval between scheduled rental payments, but need not exceed 30 days. [CC §1946; see Chapter 29];

- a *tenancy-at-sufferance*, in which case the holdover tenant is not entitled to any further notice prior to commencing eviction proceedings since a lease has expired or a periodic tenancy has been terminated by notice [CCP §1161];

- a *tenancy-at-will*, in which case a 30-day notice to vacate or otherwise alter the tenancy-at-will is required [CC §789; see Chapter 29];

- a rent-controlled tenancy of *residential property*, in which case termination of the right to possession is restricted by local ordinances; and

- a *tenancy-at-will in a mobilehome park*, in which case a 60-day written notice is required to be delivered to the tenant. [CC §798.55(b)]

Further, a landlord and tenant by agreement can establish a shorter or lengthier notice period, but not less than seven days, industrial and commercial tenants typically require three months minimum notice due to the time lost receiving and responding to a notice since it must first go through multiple tiers of corporate management. [CC §1946]

Changing the type of tenancy

A landlord, by using an improper notice, can end up with a different tenancy relationship from the one he initially conveyed to a tenant. When an existing tenancy is altered, in writing or by conduct, the tenancy may have been converted into another type of tenancy.

A classic example involving a change in the type of tenancy arises when a holdover tenant (a tenancy-at-sufferance) becomes a month-to-month tenant (a periodic tenancy).

A landlord who accepts any rent from a holdover tenant under an expired lease, in payment for a period of occupancy after the lease expired, has elected by his conduct to treat the continuing occupancy as a periodic tenancy. [**Peter Kiewit Sons Co.** v. **Richmond Redevelopment Agency** (1986) 178 CA3d 435]

Thus, a proper notice to vacate, a requisite to a UD eviction, must be served on the holdover tenant who paid rent for the continued occupancy, which was accepted by the landlord. [Colyear, *supra*]

When the tenant holds over after a fixed-term tenancy expires and the landlord accepts rent for the holdover period while the tenant is in possession, the expired lease agreement is *renewed* on the same terms except for the period of occupancy, which is now periodic. [CC §1945]

On expiration of a fixed-term lease, the landlord's continued acceptance of rental payments does not **renew** the tenancy for another term equal to the term of the original lease. Rather, the tenancy is extended as a periodic tenancy for consecutive periods equal to the interval between rent payments — being one month if rent is paid monthly. [CC §1945]

For example, a landlord and tenant agree in writing to a three-year lease with rent paid annually in advance. At the end of the three-year lease, the tenant holds over without further agreement. The tenant tenders an annual rent payment which the landlord accepts.

The landlord's acceptance of rent extends the expired three-year lease for a period of one year since the rent paid was for an annual period. Without a written agreement to the contrary, the tenancy is extended only for the period of the prepaid rent even though the term of the original lease, which controlled the terms of the extended one-year occupancy, was for a three-year period. [**Hagenbuch** v. **Kosky** (1956) 142 CA2d 296]

Transient occupancies and removals

An occupant of a vacation property, hotel, motel, inn, boardinghouse, lodginghouse, tourist home or similar sleeping accommodation for a period of 30 days or less is classified as a **guest**, also called a *transient occupant*.

A transient guest occupies property known as *lodging, accommodation* or *unit*. The property is not called a rental which is a landlord/tenant characterization of their relationship.

The guest's occupancy of the accommodations contracted for is labeled a *stay*, not possession. During a guest stay in the lodging, the owner or manager of the property is entitled to enter the unit at check-out time even though the guest may not yet have departed.

The contract entered into for the lodging is usually called a **reservation agreement**, but never a rental agreement or lease agreement. [See **first tuesday** Form 593]

Also, guests pay a **daily rate**, not a daily or weekly rent, and they *arrive* at a pre-set date and time for *check-in*, not for commencement of possession. Likewise, guests *depart* at an hour on a date agreed to as the *check-out time*. Unlike a tenant, a guest does not vacate the premises, they check out.

When a guest fails to depart at the scheduled check-out hour on the date agreed, no holdover tenancy is created as occurs under a tenancy for occupancy conveyed by a rental agreement or lease. Thus, a UD action or court involvement is not required to remove the guest. [CC §1940(b)]

However, for the owner or manager to avoid the UD eviction process, the guest, when checking in, must have signed a notice stating:

- the unit is needed at check-out time for another guest who has been promised the unit; and

- if he has not departed at check-out time, the owner or manager may enter, take possession of the guest's property, re-key the doors and clean up the unit for the next guest. [CC §1865; see **first tuesday** Form 593]

To **remove a guest** who fails to timely depart the unit and remains in the unit after a demand has been made to leave, the police can be called in by the manager if his own intervention might cause a breach of the peace, called self-help. The police or the sheriff will assist, without the need for a court order, to remove the guest and prevent a danger to persons or property during the re-keying, removal of possessions and clean up for the arrival of the next guest. [Calif. Penal Code §§602(r); 803.1(a)(3)]

Transient occupancies include all occupancies that are taxed as such by local ordinance or could be taxed as such by the city or by the county. Taxwise, the occupancy is considered a *personal privilege*, not a tenancy. Time share units, when occupied by their owners, are not transient occupancies and are not subject to these ordinances and taxes. [Calif. Revenue and Taxation Code §7280]

Transient units do not include *residential hotels* since the occupants of residential hotels treat the dwelling they occupy as their *primary residence*. Also, the occupancy of most individuals in residential hotels is for a period of more than 30 days.

A broker or any other person or entity who manages "vacation rental" occupancies for owners of single-family homes, units in a common interest development (condominium project), units in an apartment complex or any other residence subject to a local transient occupancy tax, must maintain **accounting records**.

Further, the property manager must send a monthly accounting statement to each owner he represents and make the records available for inspection and reproduction by the owner, as well as comply with the transient occupancy tax regarding collection, payment and record keeping. [CC §1864]

Chapter 4

Landlord's right to enter

This chapter addresses resolutions to conflicts between a tenant's right to privacy within his rented space and the landlord's need to access the space.

Conflict with tenant's right to privacy

Unknown to a residential landlord, a tenant changes the locks on the door to his unit. Several months later, the tenant is arrested by law enforcement officers as he steps out of his apartment. The tenant is hastily escorted away, leaving on lights and his pet inside, but locking the door.

The landlord becomes aware of the tenant's dilemma. Fearful the gas stove was also left on, he attempts, but is unable to enter with his passkey.

The landlord **calls the police** and asks them to witness his entry so he can inspect the apartment to make sure it is in a safe and secure condition. The landlord then enters the apartment through a window. The police are let in to observe the landlord's conduct. They proceed to make a visual inspection of the apartment.

Unfortunately for the tenant, the police find illegal possessions in plain view casually lying around the kitchen and dining area of the apartment.

Did the landlord have the right to enter the apartment? Did he have the right to allow the police to come in?

Yes to both! The landlord had the right to enter since he reasonably believed the safety of his other tenants and the building could have been in jeopardy.

Also, the officers were present at the **request of the landlord** to act as an eyewitness so the tenant could not legitimately claim the landlord removed any of his possessions. [**People** v. **Plane** (1969) 274 CA2d 1]

In contrast, consider the landlord who permits the police to enter and search a tenant's garage at the **request of the police,** but without a warrant. The police have reason to believe the tenant is manufacturing drugs, an illegal use of the premises and of concern to the landlord.

May a landlord collaborate and allow the police to enter a tenant's garage?

No! The landlord has no right to possession when the tenant's right to possession has not expired or been terminated, even though the tenant has vacated and only a day remains under a 30-day notice to vacate. Thus, the landlord has no possessory right allowing him to enter the property or let the police enter the premises since he has leased it to the tenant, even if he suspects the tenant of using the premises to commit a crime. The police must first obtain a search warrant to legally authorize them to come onto the premises occupied by the tenant when the landlord has no right to entry. [**United States** v. **Warner** (9th Cir. 1988) 843 F2d 401]

However, a landlord does have the right to allow police to enter a unit abandoned or vacated by the tenant as determined by state law rules of abandonment or surrender since the tenancy has been terminated. [**United States** v. **Sledge** (9th Cir. 1981) 650 F2d 1075; see Chapter 31]

Further, "lock-box" entry by the police in collaboration with a multiple-listing service (MLS) member to check out a crime is prohibited without a warrant. The entry violates the purpose of a listing broker's agency and his lock-box authority. The broker may enter only to show the premises to prospective tenants who accompany him (or other authorized agents), not the police since they are not prospective tenants. [**People** v. **Jaquez** (1985) 163 CA3d 918]

Landlord's right to enter

A landlord's right to enter a residential or non-residential unit during the period of the tenant's right to occupy the premises is severely limited. The possessory rights to occupy the property have been **conveyed to the tenant** and are no longer held by the landlord, until a *reversion* of possession occurs on termination of the tenancy.

For example, a residential landlord may enter the tenant's actual dwelling space during the lease or rental term only in limited circumstances, namely:

- in an emergency;

- to make repairs, alterations, improvements, or supply services that are either necessary or previously agreed to by the tenant;

- to complete a pre-termination inspection for deficiencies which would result in a deduction from the security deposit [See Chapter 19];

- to show the unit to prospective or actual buyers, lenders, tenants or repairmen and contractors;

- when the tenant has vacated the premises and his right to occupy terminated by *surrender* or *abandonment*; or

- under a court order allowing entry. [Calif. Civil Code §1954]

A property manager's entry into a tenant's unit out of concern for the safety of the property or other tenants constitutes an *emergency* allowing entry without the tenant's knowledge and permission. The property manager may properly enter the unit for the limited purpose of dealing with the emergency. [Plane, *supra*]

Consider a nonresidential lease agreement that prohibits any tenant violations of government laws and regulations.

The landlord asks the tenant for permission to come onto the property to conduct tests and investigate whether the leased property contains any contamination from hazardous waste. The tenant refuses to give the landlord permission to conduct the investigation, claiming the landlord does not have a right to determine whether contamination exists until the lease expires.

Here, the landlord, on advance notice to the tenant, has the right to access the property to determine if contamination has or is occurring on the property since hazardous waste contamination is a **violation of law** and a breach of the lease provision prohibiting unlawful activities adversely affecting the value of the property. [**Sachs** v. **Exxon Company, U.S.A.** (1992) 9 CA4th 1491]

Notice of entry for repairs

Before a residential landlord proceeds with any maintenance or services which require entry into a tenant's unit, the tenant must be given a **written notice** of the landlord's intent to enter. Maintenance includes all routine or non-emergency repairs, decorations, alterations, improvements, replacements or services, whether or not agreed to by the tenant. [CC §1954; see Form 567 accompanying this chapter]

The written notice must give the tenant a **reasonable period of time** in which to prepare for the entry. A 24-hour notice is considered reasonable, unless extenuating circumstances known to the landlord or his property managers, such as the tenant's vacation or business trip, indicate the tenant needs more time to actually receive the notice and prepare for the entry.

NOTICE OF INTENT TO ENTER DWELLING

DATE:_____, 20_____, at _____, California.

NOTICE: A landlord may enter a tenant's unit during normal business hours after giving twenty-four (24) hours prior notice of intent to enter. [Calif. Civil Code §1954]

Items left blank or unchecked are not applicable.

FACTS:

1. You are a Tenant under a rental or lease agreement

　1.1　dated: _____, at_____California,

　1.2　entered into by _____, Tenant,

　　　and _____, Landlord,

　1.3　regarding real estate referred to as: _____

　　　_____.

NOTICE TO TENANT:

2. The landlord will enter the above premises at or about the normal business hour of _____, on _____, 20_____ for the following checked purposes:

　2.1　☐ To make necessary or agreed repairs of _____

　　　_____

　2.2　☐ To decorate the unit by _____

　　　_____

　2.3　☐ To alter or improve the unit by _____

　　　_____

　2.4　☐ To supply necessary or requested services of _____

　　　_____

　2.5　Other _____

　　　_____

3. You are not required to be on the premises during this entry. A passkey will be used in the event of your absence.

Date: _____, 20_____

Landlord/Agent: _____

Signature: _____

Address: _____

_____

Phone: _____

Fax: _____

E-mail: _____

FORM 567　　　09-02　　©2007 **first tuesday**, P.O. BOX 20069, RIVERSIDE, CA 92516 (800) 794-0494

Service of a 24-hour **notice of entry** in advance of the entry is accomplished by any one of the following methods:

- handing a written notice to the tenant personally;

- handing the notice to an occupant of the unit who appears of suitable age and discretion to relay the notice to the tenant; or

- posting the notice on or near the usual entry door or under the door so it will be discovered by the tenant on his return.

Alternatively, the notice may be mailed, but at least six days must pass after mailing before the intended entry can be scheduled to occur. [CC §1954]

The time of day for the entry must only be during normal business hours, emergencies excepted. If the entry is after business hours, the tenant's consent must be obtained "at the time of entry," even if previously arranged to occur after business hours.

The notice of entry procedures should never be used to harass a tenant in a retaliatory or abusive manner. [CC §1954]

A tenant in a community apartment project or a homeowner in a condominium project, collectively called *common interest developments* (CIDs), must receive at least 15 days but no more than 30 days written notice when the management or association needs the occupants to vacate the project in order to treat termites. [CC §1364(d)(2)]

Entry for pre-termination inspection

A residential landlord may enter a tenant's unit when the tenant requests a joint pre-termination inspection of the premises in response to the landlord's mandatory notice to the tenant of the tenant's right to request the joint inspection. [See Chapter 19]

The purpose of the pre-termination inspection prior to expiration or termination of the tenancy is to advise the tenant of any deficiencies in the condition of the premises so the tenant can correct or eliminate them before vacating. Thus, the tenant may take steps to avoid deductions from the security deposit.

Before the residential landlord may enter to conduct the agreed-to pre-termination inspection, the tenant must be given a 48-hour written notice stating the date and time for the inspection. [CC §1950.5(f)(1)]

Service of the 48-hour notice of entry is accomplished in the same manner as for the 24-hour notice of advance entry to complete repairs. However, the tenant may waive the 48-hour notice if both he and the landlord sign a written waiver. [CC §1950.5(f)(1)]

Entry during "For Sale" period

Real estate brokers who list residential or non-residential property for sale which is **occupied by a tenant**, called a *rental*, need to inform the seller about the **seller's right** to coordinate inspections of the property by buyers under one of two notice procedures. [CC §1954]

To avoid surprises when the tenant is contacted and advised to prepare the premises for an inspection by a prospective buyer, two procedures exist for the **listing agent** to enter the unit with the buyer.

A **24-hour advance written notice** of the intended entry may be served by the seller or his manager:

- on the tenant personally; or

- on an occupant of the unit of suitable age and ability to inform the tenant of the notice; or

- by posting the notice on or near the entrance to the unit or leaving it under the door. [CC §1954(d)(1)]

If instead it is mailed by regular or certified mail, six days must pass before the time for entry can occur. [CC §1954; see **first tuesday** Form 567]

The seller's alternative to the 24-hour written notice is a **120-day "For Sale" notice**. The "For Sale" notice may be given to the tenant personally or by regular mail at any time after the seller enters into a listing to sell the property. [CC §1954(d)(2); see Form 116 accompanying this chapter]

The "For Sale" notice commences a 120-day period during which the seller or the seller's listing agent may, on a 24-hour **notice by phone** to the tenant, enter the unit during normal business hours with a prospective or actual buyer to conduct an inspection of the unit.

Prior to the time for entry, the tenant must receive no less than **24 hours advance notice by phone** or in person of the actual entry date and time. The actual entry is conditioned on the listing agent leaving a written note in the unit regarding the entry and completion of the inspection.

Here, the giving of the 24-hour notice by phone, during the 120-day period following service of the written "For Sale" notice, is exclusively the right of the seller and his listing agent. The agent representing a buyer must arrange for the listing agent to give the 24-hour advance telephonic notice. The buyer's agent may not be given authority to notify the tenant, unless he is also the listing agent.

Thus, on taking a listing to sell property occupied by tenants, the listing agent needs to inform the seller of the two notice procedures for entry to present the unit to prospective buyers or buyers under contract. Once resolved as to which notice procedure, if any, the seller is willing to authorize in the listing agreement, the information is shared with buyer's agents through the MLS publication of information on the listed property under "showing instruc-

tions," such as "call the listing office (LO) or listing agent (LA) to arrange for 24-hour telephonic (or alternative written) notice of entry."

The purpose of the advance notice of entry is to eliminate the element of surprise which would leave the tenant unprepared to ready the unit for inspection and to deal with the inspection on a later 24-hour telephonic notice.

Once informed of the procedure for entry and inspection, some sellers may restrict inspections of the property to **qualified buyers** who have entered into a purchase agreement. Thus, sellers might not allow prospective buyers to preview the premises until they have entered into a purchase agreement and been financially qualified as capable buyers.

Sellers often do not feel tenants should be involved in the marketing process. The weaker the real estate market, with its lessened likelihood of a sale and abundance of units for rent, the greater the seller's concern will be to keep the tenant uninvolved until the agents have a buyer under contract who is ready to conduct his due diligence investigation before closing escrow.

Entry on surrender or abandonment

A landlord or his manager may enter a unit when the tenant has vacated the unit and his right to possession has been terminated by expiration of a lease (or rental agreement by a 30-day notice to vacate), surrender, notice of abandonment or 3-day notice containing a declaration of forfeiture.

Neither a surrender nor an abandonment of the tenant's right to possession, called the lease, ever automatically takes place simply because the tenant vacates the unit. The landlord must react to the vacating by terminating the tenant's leasehold right to possession — by establishing a surrender, abandonment or forfeiture of possession.

By a *surrender*, the tenant who breaches the lease and vacates the premises while conducting himself in a manner which indicates to the landlord the tenant's desire to both:

- **terminate possession** by a return of the premises to the landlord; and

- **cancel the lease agreement** obligations owed to the landlord.

If the landlord agrees to the termination of the tenant's possession and a cancellation of the rental or lease agreement, or if the landlord's conduct on taking possession constitutes his acceptance of the tenant's offer to vacate in exchange for canceling the lease agreement, a *surrender* has occurred. Thus, the tenancy is terminated (and the lease agreement canceled). The landlord may then enter and take possession of the unit, by mutual agreement or conduct. [See Chapter 30]

As an alternative to accepting possession and canceling the lease agreement and any right to collect future rents by a surrender, the landlord may serve the tenant with a 3-day notice to pay or quit and **declare a forfeiture** of the tenant's right to possession. Thus, on expiration of the 3-day notice, the tenant's right to possession has been eliminated.

If the tenant has vacated the property and the 3-day notice expired, the landlord or his agents may then enter and reoccupy or relet the premises since the right to **possession reverted** to the owner. In the process, the lease agreement remains fully enforceable, except for the occupancy provisions.

An *abandonment* requires the premises to be vacated by the tenant and a **breach** of the lease agreement. Like a surrender, an **abandonment** requires that the tenant never intends to return to the premises. However, a tenant intending to abandon the leased premises cannot unilaterally terminate (reconvey) his leasehold right of possession to the landlord. The transfer of possession to the landlord requires the landlord to act before the right to possession is terminated by abandonment.

However, unlike the cancellation of the lease agreement when both the tenant and the landlord agree to a surrender, the lease agreement is *not canceled* on the landlord's notice of abandonment (or forfeiture on a 3-day notice to quit). Only the leasehold interest (right to possession) in the real estate is terminated.

Abandonment versus forcible entry

To establish an **abandonment** by a tenant who has breached his lease agreement and vacated, the landlord must serve the tenant with a *notice of abandonment*. On expiration of the notice and without the tenant denouncing the abandonment, the tenant's leasehold interest is terminated without need for the landlord's further action. Importantly, the landlord retains the right to collect future rents due under the unexpired (and uncancelled) rental or lease agreement. [See Chapter 31]

Without proof of the termination of the tenancy by the process of abandonment (or an alternative process) by expiration of the statutory notice of abandonment served on the tenant, the landlord taking possession could be faced with an angry tenant claiming *forcible entry* — and money damages — or a financially detrimental surrender with its elimination of the lease agreement.

For example, a manager rents an apartment to a couple who are expecting a child.

The husband, needing further training for his job, moves to another county for several months. His wife remains in the apartment, intending to live their until her husband returns.

Later, the expectant wife leaves the unit and travels to visit her husband. She posts a note on the unit's front door. It is addressed to her brother who checks in on her from time to time. The note states her destination, but makes no mention whether she will return. The payment of rent is not delinquent. The manager reads the note, misconstrues its meaning and re-rents the unit on removing the tenant's possessions.

DATE:_____, 20_____, at _____, California.

Items left blank or unchecked are not applicable.

FACTS:

1. You are a Tenant under a rental or lease agreement
    1.1 Dated: _____, at_____,California.
    1.2 entered into by _____, Tenant,
         and _____, Landlord,
    1.3 regarding real estate referred as: _____
         _____

NOTICE TO TENANT:

2. You are hereby advised the premises you occupy has been placed on the real estate market "For Sale".

3. During the period of 120 days following the date of this notice, the landlord or his authorized listing agent for the sale of the property may need to enter your unit during normal business hours for the purpose of exhibiting the premises for review by prospective or actual buyers.

4. At lease 24 hours prior to entry for this purpose, you will be given telephonic or personal notice of our intent to enter.

5. You are not required to be present on the premise during the entry and review. A passkey will be used should you be absent.

6. On departing the premises, the real estate agents will leave a written note identifying themselves and indicating they have entered and completed their exhibiting of the unit to the buyers.

Date:_____, 20_____

Landlord: _____

Listing Agent:_____

Signature: _____

Address:_____

_____

Phone: _____

Fax: _____

E-mail: _____

On the wife's return she discovers new tenants living in the unit and confronts the manager. The wife is reduced to retrieving the family possessions from the storage unit where the resident manager placed them. Shortly afterwards, she suffers pregnancy-related medical complications from the physical and emotional stress of relocating.

Here, the property manager's entry into the unit and the subsequent re-renting was unjustified. The tenant's right to continued possession had not been terminated by the landlord or his manager. Thus, the property manager, as well as the landlord, is liable for all losses caused by the property manager's actions, called a *forcible entry*. [**Richardson** v. **Pridmore** (1950) 97 CA2d 124]

Alternatives to abandonment include:

*   acceptance of a surrender terminating the possession and canceling the rental or lease agreement; or

- service of a 3-day notice to cure the breach (pay) or quit (vacate) with a provision declaring the forfeiture of the right to possession.

On expiration of the notice of abandonment or the statutory 3-day notice and the vacating of the space by the tenant, the landlord or his agents may enter and occupy or relet the vacated premises. By this process, the landlord retains the right to collect future rents due under the rental or lease agreement breached by the tenant.

Entry by court order

A landlord often has the right to recover possession of the premises due to a forfeiture declared in a 3-day notice to quit or expiration of the rental or lease agreement. However, he may only enforce his right to recover possession from the tenant who remains on the property by using **legal** means to evict the tenant — self-help is absolutely unacceptable.

For example, in an unlawful detainer (UD) action, a landlord obtains an unlawful detainer judgment against a tenant due to the tenant's failure to promptly answer the UD lawsuit. Before the eviction is carried out under the court order, the court "sets aside" the judgment. The court-ordered eviction order is now invalid.

The landlord acts on what he now knows is an *invalid* eviction order. The landlord privately enlists two uniformed county marshals who, without knowing the eviction order is invalid, appear at the tenant's door demanding the tenant vacate the unit.

The tenant leaves the unit immediately and the landlord takes possession. Later, the tenant seeks a money judgment against the landlord claiming the conduct of the landlord was a *forcible entry and detainer* of the premises.

The landlord claims his conduct cannot be considered a forcible entry and detainer since his method for evicting the tenant did not lie entirely outside the law. The landlord obtained a court order (although he knew it was invalid) and did not personally evict the tenant (he used law enforcement officers instead).

However, the landlord is liable for forcible entry and detainer. He caused the tenant to be evicted by using a judgment which he knew to be invalid. The landlord's use of uniformed law officials to carry out the entry and removal of the tenant does not excuse his use of a known invalid eviction order. Thus, the landlord is still using self-help methods to attain access to and possession of the premises since the eviction was not court ordered. [**Bedi** v. **McMullan** (1984) 160 CA3d 272]

Now consider a nonresidential landlord who obtains a **money judgment** against his tenant for unpaid rent. A *writ of possession* is erroneously issued by the clerk of the court and the tenant is evicted by the sheriff.

The tenant now seeks to recover possession since the money judgment did not award the landlord possession of the premises or include an eviction order. The court later recalls the writ as having been erroneously issued, but refuses to order the landlord to surrender possession of the property to the tenant.

The tenant seeks to recover his money losses for the eviction claiming the landlord is liable for forcible entry and detainer since the landlord had him removed without his consent under an invalid writ of possession.

The landlord claims he is not liable for forcible entry or detainer since he relied on court authorization — the writ of possession erroneously issued by the clerk of the court — to evict the tenant and recover possession of the premises.

Here, the landlord is not liable for the tenant's money losses since imposing liability on landlords relying on a properly issued court order which is erroneous and later recalled, would undermine the *public policy* favoring orderly judicial process (instead of self-help) by opening up landlords to liability when acting under the authority of the court. [**Glass** v. **Najafi** (2000) 78 CA4th 45]

Tenant's right to privacy

Rental and lease agreements occasionally contain an unenforceable provision giving the landlord the *right of re-entry* for the purpose of **retaking possession** of the premises should the tenant breaches any provision in the rental or lease agreement. However, a default alone does not constitute a **forfeiture** or **conveyance** of the leasehold and its possessory rights to the landlord.

For example, a tenant **defaults** in rent under a lease agreement, with or without a provision allowing the landlord to take possession on a default in rent.

Statutory notice requirements of service and expiration of a 3-day notice to pay or quit, together with a declaration of forfeiture of the lease, must be completed while a tenant occupies the space in order to terminate the tenant's right to possession (except for a holdover on expiration of a lease). Self-help by the landlord's taking possession without the tenant's consent at or after the time of the breach constitutes a forcible entry, imposing liability on the landlord for the tenant's money losses. [**Lamey** v. **Masciotra** (1969) 273 CA2d 709]

A tenant's right to possession arises out of his ownership of a leasehold estate in the property, often also called a *lease*. To have an enforceable transfer of the right of possession before it is terminated or expires, the tenant's possessory interest (the leasehold) must be voluntarily *conveyed* by the tenant at or after the time of the breach in exchange for cancellation of the lease (or some other consideration for its conveyance), such as occurs by a surrender or under a deed-in-lieu of foreclosure on a fee simple ownership interest in a property. [CC §1953(a)(l)]

Consider an owner who goes on an extended overseas vacation. He rents his home for the duration of his trip. The rental agreement provides for the tenant to vacate immediately on the owner's return.

The owner returns from his trip, but the tenant refuses to immediately relinquish possession of the house. While the tenant is at work, the owner enters the house, removes the tenant's belongings and retakes possession of the property based on the authority given him by a right of re-entry provision in the rental agreement.

Can the owner use self-help to dispossess the tenant?

No! The tenant's occupancy includes the tenant's right to exclude others from possession, including the owner, as exists for all occupancies granting an exclusive right to possession, such as held by a tenant under a rental or lease agreement. An owner, even though entitled to possession by agreement, cannot re-enter the premises without first obtaining a court order when the tenant wrongfully denies the owner possession.

Forcible entry

Forcible entry by a landlord or property manager is conduct consisting of:

- peaceable entry by open doors, windows or other parts of the premises *without permission, prior notice*, or *justification*;

- entry by any kind of *violence* or *threat of terror*; or

- entry by peaceable means, *after which threats, force* or *menacing conduct* is used to dispossess the tenant. [Calif. Code of Civil Procedure §1159]

Actions by a landlord, property manager or resident manager construed as forcible entry include:

- entry resulting from any physical acts of force or violence;

- entry through a window and removal of the tenant's belongings in the occupant's absence [**Bank of California** v. **Taaffe** (1888) 76 C 626];

- entry under the false pretense of making an inspection and then taking over possession from the tenant [**White** v. **Pfieffer** (1913) 165 C 740];

- entry by unlocking the door of the unit in the tenant's absence [**Winchester** v. **Becker** (1906) 4 CA 382];

- entry accomplished by a locksmith who opens the door during the tenant's absence [**Karp** v. **Margolis** (1958) 159 CA2d 69]; and

- entry by breaking locks. [**Pickens** v. **Johnson** (1951) 107 CA2d 778]

Tenant's possessions as security

Some lease agreements contain an unenforceable clause purporting to give the landlord the right to take or hold the tenant's **personal property as security** should the tenant default in the payment of money owed to the landlord under the agreement.

For example, a tenant enters into a lease agreement and occupies the unit. The agreement authorizes the landlord to re-enter the unit on the tenant's default in the payment of rent and take the tenant's personal possessions as security until the rent is paid.

The tenant fails to pay rent and it becomes delinquent. To enforce the security provision in the lease, the landlord uses his key to enter the unit in the tenant's absence and remove the tenant's possessions. The landlord then refuses to allow the tenant to re-enter the unit until the rent is paid.

Here, the landlord may not enter or interfere with the tenant's continued access to the premises based on the tenant's default on the lease agreement without first obtaining a court order, no matter how peaceably the entry is accomplished, called *forcible entry and detainer*. [**Jordan** v. **Talbot** (1961) 55 C2d 597]

Forcible entry by others

Forcible entry into premises leased to a tenant occurs whenever **anyone enters** the tenant's premises without the tenant's *present consent*.

Consider a hotel operator who encumbers his leasehold interest in a hotel with a trust deed to provide security for a loan. The trust deed states the lender may appoint a trustee to take possession of the real estate and operate and manage the hotel should the hotel operator default on repayment of the loan.

The operator defaults on the loan. The lender appoints a trustee in compliance with the trust deed provisions. The trustee goes to the hotel to remove the hotel operator from the premises as agreed by a provision in the trust deed.

The trustee, although not entering the premises by force, breaks and replaces locks on the storage cabinets, raids cash registers and threatens to harm the hotel operator if he refuses to relinquish possession of the hotel.

Is the trustee guilty of forcible entry onto the property even though the trustee was appointed under a trust deed provision agreed to by the operator and used non-violent means to enter onto the premises?

Yes! The trustee holds the same status as the secured lender and has no more right to possession than the lender, in spite of prior agreements granting authority to the trustee to take possession on default. Thus, the trustee's right to possession, like that of a landlord, could only be lawfully obtained by judicial process — a receivership or foreclosure (judicial or by trustee's sale) — against the interest in the property encumbered by the trust deed, and a UD action following service and expiration of a notice to vacate. [**Calidino Hotel Co. of San Bernardino** v. **Bank of America Nat. Trust & Savings Ass'n** (1939) 31 CA2d 295]

Forcible entry by the tenant

Even a tenant can be guilty of a forcible entry.

Consider a prospective tenant who enters into a rental agreement but since it is presently occupied does not first inspect the condition of the premises.

When he is to take possession, he discovers the physical condition of the premises is unacceptable and refuses to take possession. As a result, the landlord does not give the tenant a key or any other means of access to the premises.

The landlord, realizing he will not be able to rent the property until the premises is restored, renovates the improvements. On the landlord's completion of the renovations, the would-be tenant climbs through an open window in the landlord's absence and takes possession of the premises, claiming he holds a rental agreement granting him the right to possession of the unit.

Here, the tenant did not have authority from the landlord to occupy the premises. The rental agreement he entered into has been previously canceled by the tenant's conduct when he refused to accept delivery of possession and was not given access to the premises. The tenant's occupancy was gained only by his unauthorized and peaceful entry, legally called *forcible entry*. [**McNeil** v. **Higgins** (1948) 86 CA2d 723]

Landlord as co-tenant

Consider the owner of a single-family residence who rents rooms to individuals, called *roommates*.

Soon, the owner spends less and less time residing on the property. However, the owner continues to maintain his mailing address at the residence.

After a week-long absence, the owner returns and discovers the locks on all the doors have been changed. He breaks a window and enters the property. The roommates claim the owner is guilty of forcible entry since he broke into the property.

Did the owner's roommates have the exclusive right to possession barring the owner from entering the property without prior notice?

No! The owner was not attempting to regain possession. Rather, he was a co-occupant in **actual possession** of the premises with others at the time of his entry.

The owner and his roommates had joint possession. No one roommate had been given exclusive possession against any other roommate. As a joint possessor with the right to occupy the premises concurrently with others, the owner is not liable for forcible entry. [**Bittman** v. **Courington** (1948) 86 CA2d 213]

Losses due to wrongful dispossession

A tenant wrongfully removed from his premises by a landlord or property manager is entitled to be returned to possession of the premises for the duration of the lease, called *restitution*. The tenant also has additional remedies against the landlord and the property manager. [CCP §1174(a), (b)]

Besides recovery of possession, a tenant may recover all money losses caused by the landlord's wrongful entry. However, the amount of money the tenant may collect is limited to losses incurred during the time period the tenant was dispossessed but retained a legal right to possession, prior to the expiration or termination of his tenancy under a rental or lease agreement. [**Orly** v. **Russell** (1921) 53 CA 660]

For example, a nonresidential tenant is served a 30-day notice to vacate to terminate his month-to-month tenancy.

Later, prior to the expiration of the notice to vacate and due to a default, the landlord bars the tenant from entry to his premises. The tenant is unable to continue operating his business from the property. The tenant does not regain possession of the premises before his right to possession is terminated by the expiration of the notice to vacate.

The tenant wants to recover for the landlord's unlawful detention of the property and for loss of business income.

However, recovery of the tenant's losses is limited to the net operating income (NOI) which could have been earned during the balance of the unexpired term. [Orly, *supra*]

Damages to the *goodwill* of a tenant's business are also evaluated. If the tenant has built up goodwill with the customers of his business, the remaining days of his period of tenancy are used to advise customers of his expired lease and new location.

The landlord who forcibly enters the leased premises during the remaining period of the tenancy is liable for the tenant's money losses due to lost earning power when the tenant is deprived of transferring customers to his new location, called *business goodwill*. [**Schuler** v. **Bordelon** (1947) 78 CA2d 581]

A tenant whose possession has been interfered with can recover his money losses due to:

- lost profits [**Stillwell Hotel Co.** v. **Anderson** (1935) 4 C2d 463];

- rental value of the lost use of the premises [Stillwell Hotel Co., *supra*];

- loss of **business goodwill** (earning power of the business) [Schuler, *supra*]; and

- emotional distress caused by the landlord or property manager's conduct towards the tenant. [**Newby** v. **Alto Riviera Apartments** (1976) 60 CA3d 288]

Also, the tenant may collect up to three times his actual money losses for the landlord's wrongful entry as punishment judicially inflicted on the landlord, if the landlord willfully or maliciously took possession from the tenant, called *punitive damages*.

For example, a landlord seeking to collect a debt owed by his tenant bars his tenant's employees from the leased premises, changes the locks and refuses to allow the tenant access to records and personal property.

Here, the landlord is acting with malice and the tenant has the right to recover trebled damages. [**Civic Western Corporation** v. **Zila Industries, Inc.** (1977) 66 CA3d 1]

Additionally, a landlord or property manager using actual force or violence to enter a leased unit is guilty of a misdemeanor. [Calif. Penal Code §418]

Chapter 5

Leasehold improvements

This chapter discusses improvements made by a tenant on leased property and the landlord's rights regarding them.

Real estate or trade fixtures

A retail business owner enters into a nonresidential lease agreement to occupy commercial space as a tenant. The leased premises does not contain *tenant improvements* (TIs) since the building is nothing more than a shell.

The tenant agrees to make all the **tenant improvements** needed for him to occupy the premises and operate his business (i.e., walls, flooring, carpeting, lighting, plumbing, telephone and electronic wiring, etc.). The tenant will also install *trade fixtures* on the premises.

The lease agreement provides for the property to be delivered to the landlord on expiration of the lease "in the condition the tenant received it", less normal wear and tear.

However, no other provision in the lease agreement addresses whether tenant improvements will remain with the property or if the property is to be restored to its original condition when the lease expires.

On expiration of the lease, the tenant strips the premises of all improvements he made and vacates. The building is returned to the landlord in the condition it was found by the tenant, an empty shell, less wear and tear. In order to relet the space, the landlord replaces nearly all the tenant improvements that were removed.

Is the tenant liable for the landlord's costs to replace the tenant improvements for the next tenant?

Yes! Improvements made by a tenant that are **permanently affixed** to real estate become part of the real estate to which they are attached. Improvements remain with the property on expiration of the tenancy, less normal wear and tear, unless the lease agreement provides for the property to be *restored* to its original condition by removal of tenant improvements. [Calif. Civil Code §1013]

However, the landlord's right to improvements added to the property by the tenant depends upon:

- the permanent or temporary nature of the tenant improvements (i.e., built-in or free standing); and

- any provisions in the lease agreement relating to the tenant's removal of improvements and restoration of the premises.

With the exception of **trade fixtures**, improvements attached to the building become part of the real estate. [CC §660]

Examples of improvements that become part of the real estate include:

- built-ins (i.e., central air conditioning or heating, cabinets and stairwells);

- fixtures (i.e., electrical and plumbing);

- walls, doors and dropped ceilings; and

- attached flooring (i.e., carpeting, tile or linoleum).

Leasehold improvement provisions

Nonresidential lease agreements typically contain a *further-improvements* provision allowing the landlord to either:

- retain tenant improvements and alterations made by the tenant; or

- require restoration of the property to its original condition on expiration of the lease. [See **first tuesday** Form 552 §9]

Further-improvement provisions usually include clauses stating:

- who will make the improvements (landlord or tenant);

- who will pay for the improvements (landlord or tenant);

- the landlord's consent is required before the tenant makes improvements;

- any mechanic's liens due to improvements contracted by the tenant will be removed;

- the condition of the premises on expiration of the lease; and

- whether the improvements are to remain or be removed on expiration of the lease.

Failure to make improvements

Consider a landlord who, under a lease agreement, obligates himself to make improvements. Once agreed to, the landlord must complete the improvements in a *timely* manner so the tenant may use them or the tenant may cancel the lease agreement. [See **first tuesday** Form 552 §10]

For example, a landlord agrees to make all the improvements necessary to convert a ranch into a dairy farm for a tenant who operates a dairy.

The landlord obligates himself to construct a barn and several sheds that are essential to the operation of the tenant's dairy business.

The tenant moves into the property before the improvements begin. Several months pass and the landlord does not begin construction on the promised improvements. The tenant vacates the property since it is impossible to conduct his dairy business without the dairy barn.

Here, the landlord's failure to make the promised improvements is a breach of the lease agreement.

Since the landlord has breached an essential provision of the lease, the tenant may vacate the property and cancel the lease agreement without obligation to pay further rent. [**Souza v. Joseph** (1913) 22 CA 179]

Now consider a landlord who agrees to construct the shell of a building for a tenant. The tenant agrees to install all other improvements and fixtures required to occupy and use the property.

Before the building is completed by the landlord, the building code is changed to require the installation of a sprinkler system. The tenant demands the landlord pay the cost of installing the sprinkler system since he cannot occupy the premises without the sprinkler system.

The landlord refuses to pay the additional cost to install the sprinkler system, claiming the lease agreement calls for him to build the structure, not to make it ready for occupancy.

Is the tenant responsible for the cost of the sprinkler system?

Yes! It is the tenant's responsibility to make the alterations or improvements required to bring the building into compliance with use (occupancy) ordinances since the tenant agreed to make all improvements within the structure needed to take occupancy. [**Wong v. DiGrazia** (1963) 60 C2d 525]

Conversely, lease agreement provisions can obligate a tenant to improve vacant, unimproved property with buildings, such as occurs with ground lease arrangements.

Improvements promised by the tenant

A tenant must complete improvements he has agreed to construct or install on the leased premises within the time period agreed to in the lease agreement, or within a reasonable period of time if no commencement or completion date for construction is specified in the lease agreement. [CC §1657]

However, if the tenant fails to make or complete mandated improvements prior to expiration of the lease and the improvements were to remain with the property, the tenant is liable to the landlord for the cost incurred by the landlord to complete the agreed-to improvements.

For example, a tenant agrees to construct additional buildings on a leased property in lieu of paying rent for one year. When the lease expires, the improvements will remain with the property since the lease agreement does not call for restoration of the premises.

The tenant fails to construct the buildings during the term of the lease. The tenant claims the lease provision calling for construction is *permissive*, not mandatory, since he only had to build if he needed to do so for the operation of his business.

Here, the improvements were agreed to in exchange for rent. Accordingly, the tenant is required to make the improvements since the landlord **bargained for them** in the lease agreement. Thus, the landlord is entitled to recover an amount equal to the cost of the improvements the tenant failed to construct. [**Simen** v. **Sam Aftergut Co.** (1915) 26 CA 361]

Additionally, if the tenant agrees to but does not complete the construction of improvements that are to remain with the property on expiration of the lease, the landlord may complete those improvements. The tenant is then financially responsible for the landlord's expenditures to construct the improvements the tenant agreed to construct. [**Sprague** v. **Fauver** (1945) 71 CA2d 333]

The landlord is also entitled to recover lost rent and expenses arising after the expiration of a lease resulting from the tenant's failure to construct the improvements as promised.

Consider a landlord who enters into a lease agreement calling for the landlord to construct a building on the leased property. After the foundation is laid, the landlord and tenant orally modify the construction provisions. The tenant agrees to finish construction of the building in exchange for the landlord forgoing his construction profit.

The tenant then breaches the *oral modification* of the written lease agreement by failing to complete the construction. The breach places the landlord in financial jeopardy as he now must complete the building himself. The landlord terminates the tenant's right to occupancy, evicts the tenant and completes the construction promised by the tenant.

Here, the tenant is not only responsible for the landlord's costs of construction, he is also liable for future rents under the lease agreement and any expenses the landlord incurs to relet the property since the landlord's conduct did not cancel the lease agreement. [**Sanders Construction Company, Inc.** v. **San Joaquin First Federal Savings and Loan Association** (1982) 136 CA3d 387]

Landlord's consent to improvements

Lease provisions often allow a tenant to make improvements to the leased premises. However, further-improvement provisions typically call for the landlord to approve the planned improvements before construction is commenced.

For example, a tenant wishes to add a room to the premises he leased for use in the operation of his business. The tenant begins construction without the landlord's prior approval as mandated in the lease agreement. The addition is located in space outside the area described as the leased premises in the lease agreement, an encroachment of the tenant's improvements on other land owned by the landlord.

In the past, the landlord had approved tenant improvements. This time, however, the landlord refuses to give consent and complains about the construction the tenant has begun and the encroachment.

The landlord continues to accept rent while he negotiates with the tenant regarding the approval of the addition and the modification of the lease agreement to include use of the area subject to the encroachment.

Ultimately, after a few years of negotiations without resolution, the landlord declares a *forfeiture of the lease* based on both the breach of the provision requiring his prior consent to construction and the encroachment of the unapproved improvements.

The tenant now claims the landlord *waived* his right to declare a forfeiture of the lease since the landlord continued to accept the rental payments after the breach of the tenant-improvement provision and encroachment.

As long as negotiations to resolve the breach continue, a landlord may accept rent from the tenant without waiving his right to consent to additional improvements. [**Thriftimart, Inc.** v. **Me & Tex** (1981) 123 CA3d 751]

Likewise, when a tenant with an option to buy makes improvements with the expectation of ultimately becoming the owner of the property under the option to buy, and the lease agreement requires approval of the improvements by the landlord, the landlord's consent is needed before any improvements can be made since the tenant is not yet the owner.

Further, the tenant is not entitled to reimbursement for the cost of his improvements, whether or not the landlord consents to the improvements. The improvements will not become the tenant's unless he exercises his option to buy and becomes the owner of the property. [**Whipple** v. **Haberle** (1963) 223 CA2d 477]

Permissive improvements by the tenant

Some lease agreement provisions allow a tenant to make improvements as deemed necessary by the tenant, but do not specifically mandate that he do so or do so in lieu of rent, called *permissive improvements*. Here, the tenant has not obligated himself to make the improvements, but is merely authorized to do so without the need for further consent from the landlord.

For example, a landlord and tenant sign a long-term lease agreement. Its further improvements provision authorizes the tenant to demolish an existing building located on the property and construct a new one in its place without first obtaining the landlord's consent. The rent is based solely on the current value of the premises.

The further-improvements provision does not state a specific time period for demolition or construction.

The tenant makes no effort to tear down the old building or erect a new one. Ultimately, the landlord claims the tenant has breached the lease agreement for failure to demolish the existing building and construct a new one.

Here, the tenant has not breached the lease agreement. The agreement contained **no promise** by the tenant to build and the rental amount was not based on the construction. The tenant was not obligated to build and was merely authorized to build without need for the landlord's approval.

Thus, the tenant was granted a privilege to make improvements. Further improvements on the tenant's part were not mandatory, they were permissive. [**Kusmark** v. **Montgomery Ward and Co.** (1967) 249 CA2d 585]

A further-improvements provision that requires a tenant to construct improvements on a vacant parcel he leases, at a rental rate reflecting the value of the land, has different consequences. If a date is not specified for completion of the improvements, the tenant must complete construction within a reasonable period of time since construction of improvements is mandated to occur.

For example, a landlord leases unimproved land to a developer who is obligated to build improvements, contingent on obtaining a construction loan. A time period is not set for commencement or completion of the construction. However, a cancellation provision gives the tenant/developer the right to cancel the lease agreement within one year if financing is not found to fund the construction. No provision authorizes the landlord to terminate the lease if the required construction is not completed.

The tenant is unable to arrange financing within the one-year period but he does not exercise his right to cancel the lease agreement and avoid payment of future rents. Instead, the tenant continues his good faith effort to locate and qualify for construction financing. Ultimately, financing is not located and construction is not commenced.

The landlord terminates the lease a few years later, claiming the lease agreement has been breached since the promised construction was not completed.

The tenant claims the landlord cannot terminate the lease as long as the tenant continues his good faith effort to locate financing and remains solvent to qualify for the financing.

Here, the tenant has breached the lease agreement. He failed to construct the intended improvements within a *reasonable period of time*. The original purpose of the lease was to have buildings erected without specifying a completion date. Following the expiration of the right to cancel, the landlord gave the tenant/developer a reasonable amount of time in which to commence construction before terminating the lease.

When the original purpose for the lease was the development of the land by the tenant, a landlord cannot be forced to leave the property unimproved forever. [**City of Stockton** v. **Stockton Plaza Corporation** (1968) 261 CA2d 639]

Surrender of improvements

All tenant improvements are to remain with the leased property on termination of a lease unless a provision in the lease agreement **permits** or **mandates** their removal by the tenant as a restoration of the premises.

Most lease agreements merely provide for the property to be returned in *good condition*, minus ordinary wear and tear for the years of the tenant's occupancy.

Thus, the tenant is not required to **restore** the property to its actual condition when he took possession. A provision calling for ordinary care of the premises during the lease does not mean the tenant must remove his improvements or renovate the improvements to eliminate deterioration, obsolescence and normal wear and tear due to the use permitted to the tenant. [**Kanner** v. **Globe Bottling Co.** (1969) 273 CA2d 559]

Now consider a landlord and tenant who enter into a lease of nonresidential property. The lease agreement contains a provision requiring the tenant, if the landlord at his option so demands, to **restore the premises** to the original condition received by the tenant, less normal wear and tear.

The tenant makes all the tenant improvements necessary to operate his business, such as installation of a concrete vault, the removal of partitions and a stairway, and the closing of two entrances into the premises.

On expiration of the lease, the tenant vacates the premises. The landlord exercises his right to require removal of tenant improvements by making a demand on the tenant to **restore** the premises, which the tenant rejects.

The landlord incurs costs to prepare the premises for reletting to a new tenant.

The landlord claims the tenant is liable for the costs he incurred to restore the premises since the tenant's improvements radically altered the premises and made it unrentable to others.

The tenant claims he is not liable for the landlord's costs to remove the improvements and restore the premises to its original condition since the alterations became part of the real estate and were beneficial to the property.

Is the tenant liable for the landlord's costs to restore the premises to a rentable condition?

Yes! On expiration of the lease, the tenant becomes obligated to restore the premises to its original condition, less normal wear and tear, when the landlord exercised his option to call for removal of the improvements since the lease agreement provides for restoration by the tenant on a demand from the landlord. The tenant improvements made the premises less desirable and unsuitable for other occupants. On the tenant's failure to restore the premises, the landlord was forced to incur restoration costs to relet the premises. The tenant is liable for the landlord's expenditures to restore and relet the premises to a new tenant. [**Masonic Temple Ass'n. of Sacramento** v. **Stockholders Auxiliary Corporation** (1933) 130 CA 234]

In another example, a lease agreement states a tenant will return the property in *good repair* and *restore the premises* to its original condition, less normal wear and tear.

The tenant modifies the premises to operate his business. After the lease expires, the tenant moves out and leaves all his improvements and structural modifications on the property. As a result, the landlord is unable to relet the premises in the condition left by the tenant.

Here, the tenant is liable for the reasonable costs incurred by the landlord to restore the premises to its original condition and for lost rental income for the period of time required to make the repairs.

Lease provisions calling for **restoration** of the premises to its original condition require the tenant to remove his improvements and restore the property to its original condition, minus any normal deterioration due to the passage of

time and use of the premises as permitted. [**Iverson** v. **Spang Industries** (1975) 45 CA3d 303]

If a lease does not require the tenant to **restore the property** to the condition it was in when received, the tenant may only remove his personal improvements, called trade improvements or trade fixtures.

The tenant only needs to leave the property and tenant improvements in good condition. [**Formosa Corp.** v. **Rogers** (1951) 108 CA2d 397]

Reimbursement for TIs on eviction

What compensation may be due to a tenant who has improved the property and is evicted prior to expiration of a lease?

A tenant who is evicted is entitled to reimbursement for the **rental value** of his improvements for the remainder of his unexpired lease term. The tenant is not, however, entitled to reimbursement for the market value or cost of the improvements. Without reimbursement, the landlord receives a windfall profit for his use of the tenant's improvements until they would have reverted to the landlord on expiration of the original lease.

Thus, an evicted tenant is limited to collecting the reasonable value for the landlord's use of the improvements during the remainder of the term on the original lease. [**Asell** v. **Rodrigues** (1973) 32 CA3d 817]

Real estate fixtures vs. trade fixtures

Two types of fixtures exist distinguishing improvements installed on a building located on a parcel of real estate:

- *real estate fixtures*; and

- *trade fixtures*.

A **real estate fixture** is personal property that is **attached** to the real estate. It becomes part of the real estate it is attached to and is conveyed with the property. [CC §§660; 1013]

For example, if a tenant rents an office and builds bookshelves into the wall rather than merely anchoring them to the wall, the bookshelves become part of the improvements located on the real estate.

When the lease expires, real estate fixtures become the landlord's property. The landlord takes possession of the real estate fixtures as part of the real estate forfeited or surrendered to the landlord, unless the lease agreement provides for restoration or permits removal by the tenant. The passage of real estate fixtures from tenant to landlord on expiration of the lease is a conveyance called *reversion*. [**City of Beverly Hills** v. **Albright** (1960) 184 CA2d 562]

Conversely, **trade fixtures** do not revert to the landlord on expiration of the lease. A trade fixture is an improvement that is attached to the real estate by the tenant and is unique to the operation of his business, not the use of the building.

Consider a tenant who leases property to operate a beauty salon. The tenant moves in work-related furnishings (i.e., mirrors, salon chairs, wash stations and dryers), necessary to run the business. The items are attached to the floor, walls, plumbing and electrical leads.

On expiration of the lease, the tenant removes the fixtures that were used to render the services offered by the business. The landlord claims the fixtures are improvements to his property and cannot be removed since they became part of the real estate when installed.

However, furnishings unique to the operation of a business are considered trade fixtures even though the furnishings are attached and built into the structure. Trade fixtures are removable by the tenant.

A tenant may, at the end of or anytime during the lease term, remove any fixture used for trade purposes if the removal can be done without damaging the premises. [**Beebe** v. **Richards** (1953) 115 CA2d 589]

Fixtures that have become an integral part of the building structure due to the way they are attached or the general purpose they serve cannot be removed. Examples of fixtures not used to render services include toilets, air conditioners, vent conduits, sprinkler systems and lowered ceilings. [CC §1019]

Trade fixtures as security

Lease agreements often contain a default provision prohibiting the tenant from removing the trade fixtures when the agreement is breached. The tenant (and his unsecured creditors) no longer have a right to the trade fixtures under a default provision.

Consider a tenant who signs a commercial lease agreement to use the premises to operate a frozen packaging plant. The lease agreement states all fixtures, trade or leasehold, belong to the landlord if the lease is terminated due to a breach by the tenant.

The tenant later encumbers his existing trade fixtures by borrowing money against them. The tenant then defaults on his lease payments. While in default on the lease, the tenant surrenders the property to the landlord, including all trade fixtures.

Does the lender on the loan secured by the trade fixtures have a right to repossess them?

No! The tenant lost his ownership right to remove the trade fixtures under the terms of the lease agreement that was entered into before he encumbered the trade fixtures. Any right to the fixtures held by the secured lender is similarly lost since the lender is junior in time and thus subordinate to the landlord's interest in the fixtures under the lease agreement.

However, if the trade fixtures installed by the tenant are owned by a third party, or if a third party had a lien on them at the time of their installation, the landlord has no more right to them than the tenant. [**Goldie** v. **Bauchet Properties** (1975) 15 C3d 307]

Notice of Nonresponsibility

A landlord may find himself paying for improvements made by the tenant if he does not:

- **post** a notice on the premises of his intention to avoid subjecting his property to a lien for the improvements, called a *Notice of Nonresponsibility*; and

- **record** the notice with the county recorder. [See Form 597 accompanying this chapter]

Tenants occasionally contract for improvements to be constructed on the premises they have leased. Any mechanic's lien by a contractor for nonpayment initially attaches to the tenant's leasehold interest in the property. [CC §3128]

However, the mechanic's lien for unpaid labor and materials may also attach to the *fee simple* interest held by the landlord if:

- the landlord or his property manager learns the construction is taking place; and

- fails to post and record a Notice of Nonresponsibility.

A **Notice of Nonresponsibility** is a written notice that must be:

- posted in a conspicuous place on the premises within ten days after the landlord (or his agent) initially learns of the construction; and

- recorded with the county recorder's office within the same ten-day period. [CC §3094]

A landlord who becomes aware of the construction and fails to post and record the Notice of Nonresponsibility does not become personally liable to the contractor. Rather, the contractor can only lien the landlord's interest in the real estate and then foreclose on his lien to collect for unpaid labor and materials delivered to improve the property under contract with the tenant. [**Peterson** v. **Freiermuth** (1911) 17 CA 609]

Further, a mechanic's lien can attach to the landlord's interest even when he has posted and recorded a Notice of Nonresponsibility if the lease agreement requires the tenant to make improvement — mandatory improvements.

For example, a lease agreement requires the tenant to make certain improvements as a condition of renting the property. Since the improvements are not permissive, the tenant is deemed to be the **landlord's agent** when he contracts for the construction of the mandated improvements.

Since the lease mandated the tenant to construct improvements, the mechanic's lien incurred by the tenant will attach to both the tenant's and the landlord's interest in the property despite any posting and recording of a Notice of Nonresponsibility. [**Los Banos Gravel Company** v. **Freeman** (1976) 58 CA3d 785]

Had the lease agreement merely *authorized* the tenant to make permissive improvements, whether they may be made with or without the landlord's prior consent, the tenant is not acting as an agent for the landlord. Thus, the landlord's interest in the property will not be subject to a mechanic's lien if the Notice of Nonresponsibility is timely posted and recorded on discovery of the tenant improvements. [**Baker** v. **Hubbard** (1980) 101 CA3d 226]

Also, a **mechanic's** lien cannot be recorded against the landlord if the improvements are removed by the contractor recording the lien.

For example, a tenant contracts to have air conditioning installed in the building. The contractor sells the equipment to the tenant on a conditional sales contract. The contractor retains title to the equipment as security until monies due on the sales contract are paid by the tenant.

RECORDING REQUESTED BY

AND WHEN RECORDED MAIL TO

Name

Street
Address

City &
State

⌐   ⌐

└   ┘

SPACE ABOVE THIS LINE FOR RECORDER'S USE

NOTICE OF NONRESPONSIBILITY
(Civil Code §3094)

DATE:_____, 20_____, at _____, California.

NOTICE IS HEREBY GIVEN:

1. _____ is the vested and legal owner of
   real property located in the County of _____, State of California, identified as:

   1.1   Common address:_____

   1.2   Legal description:

2. _____ is:

   2.1   ☐ The buyer of the property under a purchase agreement, option or land sales contract, or

   2.2   ☐ The tenant under a lease of the property.

3. Within 10 days before the posting and recording of this notice, the undersigned owner or agent of the owner obtained knowledge that a work of improvement has commenced on the site of the property involving ☐ construction, ☐ alteration, or ☐ repair.

4. The owner will not be responsible for any claim arising out of this work of improvement.

5. I declare under penalty of perjury under the laws of the State of California that the foregoing is true and correct.

Date:_____, 20_____   Signature:_____

                                      ☐ Owner, or ☐ Agent of the owner.

STATE OF CALIFORNIA
COUNTY OF_____
On _____ before me,
_____
                    (name of notary public)
personally appeared _____
                                                          ,
                    (name of principal)
personally known to me (or proved to me on the basis of satisfactory evidence) to be the person(s) whose name(s) is/are subscribed to the within instrument and acknowledged to me that he/she/they executed the same in his/her/their authorized capacity(ies), and that by his/her/their signature(s) on the instrument the person(s), or the entity upon behalf of which the person(s) acted, executed the instrument.
WITNESS my hand and official seal.

Signature: _____
              (Signature of notary public)   *(This area for official notarial seal)*

FORM 597   06-06   @2007 **first tuesday**, P.O. BOX 20069, RIVERSIDE, CA 92516 (800) 794-0494

The landlord's consent to the improvements is not obtained by the tenant, but the landlord has knowledge the work has commenced. The landlord does not post a Notice of Nonresponsibility.

Later, after the air conditioning units are installed, the tenant vacates the property.

The contractor is not paid and files a mechanic's lien against the landlord's fee interest in the property. Further, the contractor repossesses the air conditioning units and resells them at a loss, which he now seeks to recover under his lien.

However, by his election to repossess the units, the contractor waived his right to enforce the mechanic's lien and foreclosure since his equipment is no longer a **fixture** on the real estate. Whether the air conditioning units are considered a removable fixture due to the financing or a property improvement permitting the recording of a mechanic's lien is no longer an issue once they have been removed by the contractor.

As authorized by the conditional sales contract, the contractor removed the air conditioning units and chose to treat the units as personal property, not real estate fixtures. Thus, the con-tractor lost his lien rights against the real estate for nonpayment. [**Cornell** v. **Sennes** (1971) 18 CA3d 126]

Consider a tenant who leases a property with tanks for holding gasoline. The tenant negotiates a reduced rental payment in exchange for installing fuel pumps free of any liens.

The tenant purchases the pumps on credit and the pumps are installed. The supplier of the pumps does not receive a UCC-1 financing statement from the tenant, and thus does not file a UCC-1 with the Secretary of State, a requisite to perfecting the supplier's lien on the pumps.

Later, the pump supplier claims title to the pumps due to an unpaid installation debt and seeks to repossess them.

However, the landlord owns the pumps as fixtures that became part of the real estate when they were installed since he gave consideration in the form of reduced rent to acquire the pumps and the pump supplier failed at the time the pumps were installed to perfect its lien with a UCC-1 to establish his priority interest in the pumps. [**Southland Corp.** v. **Emerald Oil Company** (9th Cir. 1986) 789 F2d 1441]

Chapter 6

Options to buy and the right of first refusal

This chapter distinguishes the tenant's exercisable right to buy under the owner's irrevocable offer to sell from the tenant's preemptive right to buy should the owner decide to sell.

Purchase rights held by tenants

A prospective tenant is negotiating to lease a single-user property. An offer to lease or letter of intent (LOI) is prepared by the tenant's leasing agent calling for the owner to grant the tenant an **option to purchase** the property, an irrevocable right to later buy the property at the *tenant's discretion*. If the owner agrees to grant an option to buy, he will be obligated to sell the property on the terms of the option if the tenant decides to buy.

However, the owner rejects the offer to lease because he is not willing to sell the property.

While negotiating a counteroffer with the landlord, the leasing agent discovers the owner is willing to grant the tenant a **right of first refusal** for the term of the lease, called a *preemptive right*. Thus, if the owner decides to sell the leased premises before the lease expires, the tenant could exercise the right to buy the property.

To exercise the right of first refusal, the tenant must accept the terms of sale the owner presents or match an offer made by another buyer.

Should the tenant decide not to exercise his right of first refusal, the lease remains in effect and he retains possession. If the property is sold to another person, however, ownership is transferred subject to the tenant's leasehold interest. On the owner's completion of the sale, the lease agreement will no longer include the preemptive right to acquire the property since the right of first refusal expired unexercised. [**Manasse** v. **Ford** (1922) 58 CA 312]

Option to buy vs. right of first refusal

An owner and tenant may agree to a tenant's option to buy the property under provisions that grant the tenant either:

- an **irrevocable right to purchase** the property within a specific time period, called an *option to buy*; or

- a **pre-emptive right to purchase** the property if the owner later decides to sell the property, called a *right of first refusal*.

The option to buy is typically evidenced by an agreement separate from the lease agreement, since the option includes the terms of purchase which are unrelated to the lease. The option to buy is usually referenced in the lease and attached as an addendum. [See **first tuesday Form 161** accompanying this chapter]

Conversely, the right of first refusal is a provision included in the body of the lease agreement, or by an addendum, since the provision rarely contains the terms of a sale. [See Form 579 accompanying this chapter]

Unlike the right of first refusal, an **option to buy** must contain all terms needed to form an enforceable agreement to sell the real estate. The tenant holding an option to buy has the discretionary right to buy or not to buy on the sales terms stated in the option, and to do so within an agreed-to time period. No variations are allowed.

To buy the property under an option, the tenant *exercises* his right to buy through acceptance of the *irrevocable offer to sell* granted by the option. Thus, the decision to buy or not to buy the property rests at all times with the tenant, the owner having already agreed to sell.

Conversely, when an owner grants his tenant a **right of first refusal**, the tenant only acquires the right to buy or not to buy the property if the owner later decides to sell. However, once the tenant is notified of the owner's intent to sell, the right of first refusal becomes an option to buy on the terms offered by the landlord.

When the owner presents his offer to sell, the tenant has the right to accept the offer and buy the property within the fixed period of time for exercise by the right of first refusal provision. [See Form 579 §3.1]

The owner's motives

An owner who desires to sell his property often uses the option to buy or a right of first refusal to induce a tenant to buy the property, rather than rent it.

The timing of a sale by the use of options and the right of first refusal provisions may reflect:

- the tenant's present inability to buy;

- the tenant's desire to buy;

- the owner's inability to find a buyer; or

- the owner's desire to sell later, not now.

The owner's motives for delaying the decision to sell the leased property when the prospective tenant would rather buy include:

- tax benefits, available by delaying the sale and reporting profit in a year when profit taxes will be lower or the profit can be offset by losses on the sale or operations of other properties;

- financial incentives flowing from delaying the sale to obtain the highest price possible in a rising market, the elimina-

tion of neighborhood obsolescence, the re-zoning of the property, or avoiding locked-in financing on property which prohibits a current sale;

- legal problems hindering the sale (and value) of the property, such as a *lis pendens* or toxic cleanup;

- personal concerns interfering with any desire to sell the property due to health, estate planning or family considerations.

Also, an owner may grant a right of first refusal even though he has no intention of ever selling the property. The tenant may request a right of first refusal on theory that the owner may change his mind or die and the successor will sell.

The right of first refusal serves the same purpose for the owner as an option serves for the tenant — to avoid entering into an enforceable commitment to, respectively, sell or buy real estate.

Consideration for granting an option

To create an enforceable option to buy or right of first refusal agreement, a condition called *mutuality of obligation* must exist between the owner and the tenant. The owner and the tenant must legally commit themselves to one another in some way before the tenant can enforce the agreement against the owner. [**Kowal** v. **Day** (1971) 20 CA3d 720]

The **owner commits** to be bound by the agreement by *signing* a document granting the tenant the option to buy or the right of first refusal. To create an enforceable option to buy or right of first refusal, the tenant must make a commitment in return. These commitments to one another are called *consideration*.

When the option or right of first refusal is negotiated concurrently as an addendum to the lease, the **tenant's commitment** is his promise to pay rent and perform under the lease he *signs* concurrent with receiving the option or right of first refusal.

RIGHT OF FIRST REFUSAL TO BUY
Addendum

DATE:_____, 20_____, at _____, California.

Items left blank or unchecked are not applicable.

FACTS:

1. This is an addendum to a lease/rental agreement

    1.1   dated _____, 20_____, at_____, California,

    1.2   entered into by: _____and_____

    1.3   regarding real estate referred to as: _____

        _____

AGREEMENT:

In addition to the terms of the above referenced agreement, the undersigned agree to the following:

Right of first refusal to buy:

2. Landlord hereby grants tenant a right of refusal to purchase the leased premises, for a term commencing _____, 20_____, and expiring _____, 20_____, or ☐ on termination of the right of occupancy.

3. Should landlord decide to sell the premises during the term of the tenant's right of first refusal, landlord shall notify tenant of the terms on which landlord is willing to sell.

    3.1   Tenant shall have the option for a period of _____days after receiving written notice to purchase the premises on terms stated in the notice.

    3.2   Should tenant fail to exercise the option within the option period, landlord shall have the right to sell the premises to a third party on the same terms stated in the notice to tenant.

    3.3   Any sale on different terms reinstates the tenant's right of first refusal.

4. If the landlord has not closed a sale of the property within six (6) months after tenant's receipt of notice, the tenant's right of first refusal is reinstated.

5. _____

      _____

      _____

      _____

      _____

Tenant: I agree to the terms stated above.	**Landlord: I agree to the terms stated above.**
Date:_____, 20_____	Date:_____, 20_____
Name: _____	Name: _____
Signature: _____	Signature: _____
Name: _____	Name: _____
Signature: _____	Signature: _____

FORM 579   06-06   ©2007 **first tuesday**, P.O. BOX 20069, RIVERSIDE, CA 92516 (800) 794-0494

However, if the option to buy or right of first refusal is later added to an existing lease, additional consideration must be negotiated and delivered to the owner since the tenant is not committing himself to do anything new or different in exchange for the new rights. Here, the **tenant's commitment** could be agreeing to a modification of the terms in the existing lease, the settlement of a dispute with the landlord or the payment of a sum of money.

The option agreement

Under an option agreement, the tenant is not obligated to buy the leased property. The tenant is merely given the right to buy if he so chooses, a type of *call option*.

For the option to be enforceable, the purchase price of the property and terms of payment on exercise of the option must be included in the option agreement. Therefore, if not set as a dollar amount, the purchase price may be stated as the fair market value of the property at the time the option is exercised.

The right to buy must be exercised by the tenant within a specified time period, called the *option period*. The option period often runs until the right to occupy (lease) expires or is terminated. [See Form 161 §4]

If the option is not exercised precisely as agreed during the option period, the option period expires of its own accord. Thereafter, the option no longer exists and the tenant has no right to acquire the property. [**Bekins Moving & Storage Co.** v. **Prudential Insurance Company of America** (1985) 176 CA3d 245]

When options to renew or extend are included in the lease, the **expiration** of the option to buy is tied by agreement to either:

- the expiration of the initial lease term; or

- the expiration of any renewal or extension.

For example, a tenant rents space under a ten-year lease with an **option to extend** the term of the lease. The tenant also holds an option to buy the leased property. The option references the lease term — until expiration or termination of the lease — as the period for exercise of the option to buy.

If the lease is later extended, the option period is automatically extended with the extension of the lease since the option to buy allows the tenant to exercise the option *during the lease term*, the period of occupancy provided by the lease agreement. [**In re Marriage of Joaquin** (1987) 193 CA3d 1529]

Now consider a lease agreement which contains an **option to renew**, not to extend. The renewal option requires the preparation and signing of a new lease agreement on *identical terms* to the original lease agreement. The initial lease agreement, by way of a referenced attachment, provided the tenant with an **option to buy** which can be exercised *prior* to the expiration of the lease.

On renewal of the lease agreement, the tenant must ensure the option to buy is not left to expire at the end of the initial lease term. The new lease agreement must also reference the option to buy (as part of the identical terms of the original lease) since a new lease is not an *extension* of the original lease. [In re Marriage of Joaquin, *supra*]

Right of first refusal

To trigger the tenant's right of first refusal, the owner does not need to first agree to sell the leased property by entering into a purchase agreement with another person, with the provision it is "subject to the tenant's right of first refusal."

Any indication of the owner's decision to sell the property is sufficient to activate the right to buy, including:

- listing or advertising the property for sale;

- offering the property to a buyer;

- accepting an offer or making a counteroffer involving a buyer; and

- granting a purchase option to another person.

For example, a buyer of income property contacts the owner of leased commercial property to acquire it. The buyer is informed the major tenant holds the right to buy the property under a right of first refusal provision in the lease.

The buyer attempts to circumvent the right of first refusal by negotiating an option to buy the property, exercisable only after the tenant's right of first refusal expires. The owner grants the buyer an option to buy the property. The granting of the option now binds the owner unconditionally to sell the property if the option is exercised.

Here, the owner's granting of the option to sell the property is a clear indication of his intention to sell, triggering the right of first refusal. The tenant is now allowed to purchase the property on the same terms as contained in the option. [**Rollins** v. **Stokes** (1981) 123 CA3d 701]

*Editor's note — The right of first refusal is not triggered by conveyance of the property to the owner's heirs on his death. The heirs take title subject to the right of first refusal. However, the right of first refusal is triggered by a sale of the property ordered by the probate court or entered into by the heirs. To exercise the right of first refusal, the tenant must match the highest offer submitted in open bidding and approved by the court, or the listing or sale of the property by an executor. [**Estate of Patterson** (1980) 108 CA3d 197]*

Once the owner's decision to sell is manifested, the right of first refusal becomes an option to buy. Control of the transaction then passes to the tenant holding the right of first refusal, converting the tenant position under the right of first refusal to that of an optionee.

The owner may not now retract his decision to sell the property without breaching the right of first refusal provision.

Matching the back-up offer

The owner subject to a **right of first refusal** held by a tenant is obligated to notify the tenant of the terms of any sales listing, option to buy, offer to purchase, counteroffer or acceptance of an offer to purchase which triggers the tenant's right to buy under the right of first refusal provision.

The tenant must then agree to match the sales terms within the time period set in the right of first refusal provision or he has waived the right to buy for failure to *exercise* the right.

Consider a tenant who holds a right of first refusal on the industrial property he leases. A buyer makes an offer to purchase the property. The terms for the payment of the price in the buyer's offer include cash and an assumption of the existing first trust deed on the property.

The property is also encumbered with a nonrecourse second trust deed (carried back by a prior owner) to be paid off and reconveyed on closing under the terms of the buyer's offer. The owner accepts the offer and notifies the tenant, giving the tenant the opportunity to match the buyer's offer under the right of first refusal provision in the lease agreement.

The tenant exercises his right of first refusal by agreeing to purchase the property at the same price, but by assuming both the existing first trust deed and nonrecourse second, paying the remainder of the price in cash.

The owner rejects the tenant's conditions and refuses to sell to the tenant.

STANDARD OPTION TO PURCHASE
Irrevocable Right-to-Buy

DATE:_____, 20_____, at _____, California.

Items left blank or unchecked are not applicable.

1. OPTION MONEY:

Optionor herewith receives from Optionee option money in the amount of $_____ evidenced by ☐ cash, ☐ check, or ☐ _____, given in consideration for this option to purchase real property.

2. REAL PROPERTY UNDER OPTION:

Address:_____

_____

Legal description/Assessor's parcel number: _____

_____

3. ADDITIONAL CONSIDERATION:

As further consideration for this option, Optionee is to obtain at his expense and deliver to Optionor prior to expiration of this option the following checked items regarding the property:

☐ Property survey report by licensed California surveyors.

☐ Architectural plans and specifications.

☐ Zoning ordinance request.

☐ On-site engineering plans.

☐ Application for a parcel map or waiver.

☐ Off-site improvement plans.

☐ Soil engineer's report.

☐ Land use study.

☐ Application for a conditional use permit.

☐ _____

4. OPTION PERIOD:

Optionor hereby grants to Optionee the irrevocable option to purchase the Optionor's rights, title and interest in the property on the terms stated, for a period commencing with the acceptance of this option and expiring _____, 20_____, or ☐ on termination of the optionee's leasehold interest in the property.

5. EXERCISE OF OPTION:

Optionee may exercise this option during the option period by:

5.1 Signing escrow instructions, identical in provisions to those attached as **Exhibit A**, and delivering the instructions to escrow [ft Form 401]; and

5.2 Depositing cash in escrow of $_____; and

5.3 Delivering an escrow certified copy of the signed escrow instructions to Optionor, within the option period, in person or by both certified and regular mail.

6. ESCROW CONTRACT:

In the event this option is exercised, the transaction shall be escrowed with:_____

_____

Escrow shall close within _____ days after exercise.

7. DELIVERY OF TITLE:

On Optionee's exercise of this option, Optionor shall timely place all documents and instruments into escrow required of the Optionor as necessary for escrow to close as scheduled.

8. BROKERAGE FEE:

Optionor agrees to pay a brokerage fee of $_____, or _____ percent of the selling price, IF:

8.1 This option is exercised;

8.2 Within one year after expiration of option period and any extension or renewal, Optionor enters into an agreement to option, sell, lease or exchange with Optionee, or their assigns; or

8.3 Optionor wrongfully prevents the exercise of this option,

8.4 Payable to Broker:_____

Address: _____

_____

Phone:_____ Fax: _____

9. SALE TERMS:

Price of $_____ payable as follows:

9.1 ☐ All cash.

9.2 Cash down payment in the amount of $_____.

9.3 ☐ Take title subject to, or ☐ Assume, an existing first trust deed note held by_____ with an unpaid principal balance of $_____, payable $_____ monthly, including interest not exceeding _____%, ☐ ARM, type _____, plus a monthly tax/insurance impound payment of $_____.

    a. At closing, loan balance differences per beneficiary statement(s) to be adjusted into:
       ☐ cash, ☐ carryback note, or ☐ sales price.

    b. The impound account to be transferred: ☐ charged, or ☐ without charge, to Optionee.

9.4 ☐ Take title subject to, or ☐ Assume, an existing second trust deed note held by _____ with an unpaid principal balance of $_____, payable $_____ monthly, including interest not exceeding _____%, ☐ ARM, type _____, due _____, 20_____.

9.5 A NOTE for the balance of the purchase price in the amount of $_____ to be executed by Optionee in favor of Optionor and secured by a trust deed on the property junior to the above referenced financing, payable $_____ monthly, or more, beginning one month after closing, including interest at _____% per annum from closing, due _____ years after closing.

    a. This note and trust deed to contain provisions to be provided by Optionor for:
       ☐ due-on-sale, ☐ prepayment penalty, ☐ late charges, ☐ _____

    b. ☐ The attached Carryback Disclosure Statement is an addendum to this agreement (mandatory on four-or-less residential units). [**ft** Form 300]

    c. ☐ Optionee to provide a Request for Notice of Delinquency to senior encumbrancers. [**ft** Form 412]

10. GENERAL PROVISIONS:

10.1 ☐ **See attached addendum for additional provisions.** [**ft** Form 250]

10.2 Attached as addenda are the following checked provisions mandated on four-or-less residential units:

    a. ☐ Condition of Property (Transfer) Disclosure statement [**ft** Form 304]

    b. ☐ Natural Hazard Disclosure Statement [**ft** Form 314]

    c. ☐ Disclosure of sexual predator database [**ft** Form 250]

    d. ☐ Hazard Disclosure Booklet, and related Optionor disclosures, containing Environmental Hazards, Lead-based Paint and Earthquake Safety. [**ft** Forms 313 and 315]

    e. ☐ Documentation on any Homeowners' Association involved.

    f. ☐ Notice of Supplemental Property Tax Bill [**ft** Form 317]

10.3 Possession of the property to be delivered on:
☐ close of escrow, or ☐ see attached Occupancy Agreement. [**ft** Forms 271 and 272]

10.4 Both parties reserve their rights to assign, and agree to cooperate in effecting an Internal Revenue Code §1031 exchange prior to close of escrow, on either party's written notice.

10.5 **Expiration of Option:**

This offer to sell shall be deemed expired if not accepted by exercise during the option period.

    a. This option contract shall automatically terminate by expiration on _____, 20_____.

I hereby grant this option and agree to the terms stated above.	I hereby accept this option and agree to the terms stated above.
Date:_____, 20_____	Date:_____, 20_____
Optionor: _____	Optionee:_____
Signature: _____	Signature: _____
Signature: _____	Signature: _____
Address: _____	Address: _____
_____	_____
Phone:_____ Fax:_____	Phone:_____ Fax:_____
E-mail: _____	E-mail: _____

FORM 161   10-01   ©2007 **first tuesday**, P.O. BOX 20069, RIVERSIDE, CA 92516 (800) 794-0494

Here, the owner must comply with the tenant's terms for payment of the price since they are the financial equivalent of the proposed sale. The tenant need merely provide the **same net financial result** to the owner as the offer being matched — a cash-out of the owner's equity in the property. The tenant's performance under the right of first refusal does not need to be identical in all aspects to the buyer's offer.

Thus, the owner must sell on the tenant's exercise of his right of first refusal since the owner's net proceeds, economic benefits and liabilities resulting from the sale on terms set by the tenant would be the same as those he would experience under the purchase offer which triggered the right of first refusal. [**C. Robert Nattress & Associates** v. **CIDCO** (1986) 184 CA3d 55]

Now consider a buyer who offers to purchase property leased under a right of first refusal held by the tenant. The terms of purchase include a cash down payment and a note executed by the buyer for the balance of the owner's equity which is secured by a trust deed on other property which has adequate value as security. The owner accepts the offer and notifies the tenant, who agrees to match the buyer's offer.

However, the value of the property offered by the tenant as security is inadequate, causing the owner to refuse to accept it.

Here, due to the inadequate value of the security offered by the tenant for an identical note, the tenant's offer is not **financially equivalent** to the terms of the buyer's offer since the risk of loss on default has been increased. The landlord is not obligated to accept the tenant's deficient exercise of his preemptive right, which constitutes a waiver of the tenant's right to buy. The owner may now sell the property to the buyer — but only on the same terms. [**McCulloch** v. **M & C Beauty Colleges** (1987) 194 CA3d 1338]

Reinstatement of the right of first refusal

A right of first refusal provision automatically carries with it the *reinstatement* of the right when:

- the owner agrees to sell the property on terms different from those terms offered to the tenant; or

- the property remains unsold after the running of an agreed-to period of time following the tenant's waiver of the right to buy. [See Form 579 §4]

Consider an owner who, under a right of first refusal, notifies his tenant of the purchase terms on which he has listed the property for sale. The tenant chooses not to exercise his option to buy at the price and on the terms offered.

The owner later modifies the listing by lowering the sales price or altering the terms for payment of the price.

The price reduction or modification of terms automatically **reinstates** the tenant's right of first refusal obligating the owner to notify of the new terms for purchase of the property. The tenant only waived his right of first refusal for a sale based on the terms originally given to him by the owner, not on the different price or set of terms.

Should a buyer purchase the property on terms other than those offered to the tenant, the buyer takes title subject to the tenant's preemptive right to purchase which is reinstated due to the sale on different terms. Thus, the buyer must sell to the tenant on the same price and terms he paid since the buyer is on notice of the tenant's rights to acquire the property due to the tenant's possession.

SECTION B

Property Management and Agency

Chapter 7

Property management licensing

This chapter reviews the licensing requirements for property managers and resident managers, and their employees.

When is a DRE license required?

An individual owns and operates income-producing real estate. As the owner-operator, he locates and qualifies tenants, prepares and signs occupancy agreements, contracts for property maintenance, collects rent, serves any notices and initiates any unlawful detainer (UD) actions to evict tenants.

Does the owner-operator need a real estate broker's license to perform these activities?

No! The owner of income-producing real estate does not need a real estate broker license to operate **as a principal**. The owner-operator is not acting **on behalf of someone else** as an agent when he is managing his own property. [Calif. Business and Professions Code §10131(b)]

On the other hand, if the owner-operator decides to hire an individual to take over the general management of the apartment complex, the individual he employs to act as his property manager must be licensed as a California real estate broker.

A real estate broker license must be held by an individual or corporation that, with expectation of a fee, offers to or performs any of the following services *for another individual*:

- list real estate for rent or lease;

- market listed property and locate prospective tenants;

- list prospective tenants for the rental or lease of real estate;

- locate property to rent or lease;

- sell, buy or exchange existing leasehold interests in real estate;

- manage income-producing properties; or

- collect rents from tenants of real estate. [Bus & P C §10131(b)]

An individual employed by the broker to act as his agent to perform any of the **services requiring a license** must also be licensed by the Department of Real Estate (DRE), either as a broker or sales agent, with the exception of agents employed by a broker to handle **residential units**. [Bus & P C §10131.01(a)(3)]

For licensing purposes, the activities of an individual employed by a real estate broker to act as his agent in the rental and leasing of **residential complexes**, other than single units, are categorized as either:

- *licensed employee activities*, such as **landlord-related** solicitations, listings and rental or lease negotiations, care and maintenance of the property, marketing of the listed space and accounting; or

- *unlicensed employee activities*, such as **tenant-related** negotiations, such as showing properties, giving out leasing information and screening applications, and accepting rental or lease agreements, rent and deposits.

For **licensed employee activities** performed by an agent of the broker who solicits or has entered into a property management agreement or a leasing agent agreement, the agent must also be licensed as a broker or sales agent. Activities requiring licensing relate to contacts with the owner, not the tenant, and decisions about the leasing, care of the property and accounting.

Unlicensed employee activity

While under the supervision and control of a licensed broker, administrative and **non-discretionary duties** carried out by employees on behalf of the broker who is managing transient housing or apartment complexes are *exempt* from real estate licensing requirements. [Bus & P C §10131.01(a)]

Tenant negotiations that can be performed by unlicensed agents on behalf of a broker who has been retained to manage an apartment complex building, complex or court include:

- showing rental units and facilities to prospective tenants;

- providing prospective tenants with information about rental rates and rental and lease agreement provisions;

- providing prospective tenants with rental application forms and answering questions regarding their completion;

- accepting tenant screening fees;

- accepting signed lease and rental agreements from tenants; and

- accepting rents and security deposits. [Bus & P C §10131.01(a)(1)]

Power-of-attorney exemption

Also exempt from licensing is an individual who has been given authority to act as an "attorney in fact" under a power of attorney to **temporarily manage** an owner's property. [Bus & P C §10133(a)(2); see **first tuesday** Form 447]

However, a power of attorney cannot be used as authority to continuously manage real estate and cannot substitute for a broker's license.

Consider a landlord who can no longer handle the responsibilities of managing his property due to illness. The landlord grants a power of attorney to a friend to manage the property.

The landlord pays his friend for performing property management tasks, including locating tenants, negotiating leases and collecting rent.

After the landlord's recovery from his illness, he continues to employ his friend to perform these management tasks.

Does the landlord's friend need a real estate broker's license to perform property management tasks on a regular, on-going basis in exchange for a fee, even though the landlord has given him a power of attorney?

Yes! The power-of-attorney exemption may only be used in situations where the landlord is compelled by necessity, such as a vacation or illness, to authorize another person to complete a specific or isolated transaction.

Any person receiving a fee for the continuous performance of property management tasks requiring a broker's license cannot rely on the power-of-attorney exemption to avoid licensing requirements. [**Sheetz** v. **Edmonds** (1988) 201 CA3d 1432]

Apartment resident managers

Apartment building management has special licensing rules distinguishing resident managers from nonresident property managers.

A resident manager is employed by either the landlord or the broker who is the property manager of the apartment building or complex. The resident manager lives on the premises as a requirement of his employment.

A resident manager and his employees do not need a real estate license to manage the apartment complex. [Bus & P C §10131.01(a)(1)]

However, a resident manager of one apartment complex is barred from being the property manager of a separate apartment complex unless he is licensed, even if both properties are owned by the same landlord. The resident manager would be a nonresident property manager of the other complex. Thus, he would need to be licensed. [Bus & P C §10131(b)]

Other licensing exceptions

A person is not required to have a real estate broker's license when he is acting:

- as an attorney performing management as part of his legal services [Bus & P C §10133(a)(3)]; or

- under court appointment, such as a receiver or bankruptcy trustee. [Bus & P C §10133(a)(4)]

These exceptions are usually short-term and refer to specific properties. A person whose business is advertised or held out as including property management for others must comply with the licensing laws.

Individuals managing property without a license and without qualifying for an exemption will not be able to enforce collection of the fee they were to receive. [Bus & P C §10137]

Contingent fees and bonus awards

If a landlord is a corporation, limited liability company (LLC) or partnership, any officer of the entity may manage the entity's property without a broker's license. However, the unlicensed officer may not receive any contingent fees or extra compensation based on achievement, production or occupancy factors during his management of the property. [Bus & P C §10133(a)(1)]

For example, a corporation owns a shopping mall managed by an officer of the corporation. The officer's duties include maintaining the premises, locating tenants and collecting rents.

As the manager, the corporate officer is paid an annual salary as a base pay. Whenever a vacancy occurs in the mall, the manager locates a new tenant and negotiates the lease for the corporation. For each new tenant, the manager receives an *incentive fee* over and above his corporate salary, a **bonus** for his successful efforts.

Here, the manager must be licensed as a broker even though he is an officer and employee of the corporation that is the owner of the property. His earnings include extra compensation based on his performance of real estate management activities requiring a license.

The manager's receipt of an incentive bonus payment for leasing space, called a *contingency fee*, establishes that the manager is acting as a broker, not merely as a salaried officer of the corporate owner. If the corporation holds a DRE corporate license, then the individual only needs to be a licensed salesperson employed in writing by the corporation as his broker. The exclusion of employees from licensing in residential rentals for tenant-related contacts does not apply to nonresidential leasing.

Similarly, where a LLC owns the property, the manager of the LLC does not need to be licensed to manage the property — provided fees are not paid based on the quantity of leases he negotiates or the LLC's rental income. [Bus & P C §10133(a)(1)]

If the LLC manager receives a percentage of gross rents as compensation, the compensation is considered a *contingent fee* unless all the members of the LLC receive the same percentage.

A property manager paid on a **contingent fee** basis, or any other employee or officer whose pay is structured as a contingency fee, of an office building, shopping center, industrial park, apartment building or other income property will need a broker's license if his duties include recruiting tenants, negotiating leases or collecting rents. However, employees of a broker dealing exclusively with prospective tenants for units in apartment complexes are not required to possess a license. [Bus & P C §10131(b)]

Bonus, award, commission, incentive or contingency fee programs in excess of a base salary require the person receiving them to be licensed by the DRE, whether they are resident managers, assistant resident managers or maintenance personnel. Examples of these programs include:

- a flat dollar fee for each month without a UD filing;

- a flat dollar fee for each new tenant;

- a monthly flat dollar fee for keeping operating expenses below projections;

- a percentage fee based on increases in rents; and

- a percentage of monthly gross rents if rents collected for the month exceed a percentage (for example, 97%) of scheduled income.

Chapter 8

Property management agreement

This chapter discusses the function of a property management agreement and the landlord's and property manager's rights and responsibilities under the agreement.

Authority to operate the rental property

A property manager's authority to take control of income-producing real estate and manage its leases, rents and expenses in expectation of a fee is established in a property management agreement. [See Form 590 accompanying this chapter]

A property management agreement sets out the specific rights, responsibilities and expectations of both the property manager and the landlord, including authorized activities, performance standards and expense limitations.

Landlord responsibilities include handing the property manager the information and files necessary in managing the property and its tenants, such as all rental or lease agreements, service and maintenance contracts and utilities. Information on hazard and worker's compensation insurance is also needed to cover the activities of the property manager and his employees.

The management agreement **authorizes** the property manager to locate tenants, enter into leases and rental agreements, collect rents, incur operating expenses and disburse funds to pay expenses, loan payments and management fees.

Further, the management agreement includes written authorization that is required for the property manager to enter into and sign leases and bind the landlord to leases for a term of over one year. [Calif. Civil Code §1624(a)(3)]

Short-form vs. long-form agreements

Brokers who manage property should enter into highly detailed property management agreements, not generalized "short-form" management agreements.

Short-form agreements neither specifically identify nor clarify the performance and expectations of both the property manager and the landlord. Instead, short-form agreements *imply industry customs* will be followed — whatever those customs might be or become.

These implied standards, while familiar to the broker, are often misunderstood or unknown to the landlord. Disputes usually result when landlords have high expectations and then receive less than they believe they bargained for when they employed the property manager.

Management obligations detailed in a long-form agreement, which spells out what conduct the landlord can expect from his broker, more fully protect a broker from claims he has breached his duties to the landlord. Surprises are eliminated and client expectations are more realistic.

Property managed "as is"

Some landlords want their property maintained at a below-standard level. A broker taking on the management must document the maintenance he recommends by using either an addendum to the management agreement or estoppel letters sent from time to time stating the situation and his recommendations with a request for authority to act on the recommendations.

For example, a property manager should document a landlord's refusal to trim back overgrown and top-heavy landscaping needed to prevent damage from occurring to the structure or injury to the tenants.

Also, a property manager should note any advice given, explained and then rejected by the landlord regarding the installation or maintenance of security systems, lighting or other maintenance or installation work needed to eliminate dangerous conditions.

Handling rents and expenses

Property management agreements authorize the property manager to handle, on behalf of the landlord, all income received and expenses incurred in the operation of the property.

The property manager's responsibilities regarding the property's income and expenses include:

- collecting rents and other amounts due, such as common area maintenance charges (CAMs) and assessments for property insurance and real estate taxes;

- collecting, accounting for and refunding security deposits;

- paying expenses and loans owed by the landlord from rent paid by tenants; and

- complying with any local rent control ordinances.

A written management agreement spells out which operating expenses, insurance premiums, utilities, loan payments and taxes are to be paid by the property manager, and which are to be paid by the landlord.

Trust accounts

The receipt and accounting for cash reserves, security deposits, rent and other amounts received from tenants and coin-operated machines will be handled as *trust funds* owned by the landlord. **Trust funds** of this nature must be deposited into a trust account in the name of the property manager.

Accounting provisions in the management agreement:

- authorize the property manager to pay, out of the income and reserve funds held in the trust account, obligations incurred in the management and ownership of the property;

- specify the bank to be used; and

- call for remaining funds held on behalf of the landlord to be disbursed to him periodically and on termination of the property management agreement.

The management agreement sets the amount of cash reserves the landlord will deposit in the property manager's trust account as a minimum balance to cover operating expenses and fees.

Periodic accounting by the manager

A landlord is entitled to a *statement of accounting* at least once a quarter and when the property management agreement is terminated. [Calif. Business and Professions Code §10146]

The management agreement sets forth the time periods for when the property manager must deliver the **statement of accounting** to the landlord.

The accounting provision indicates the property manager will disburse to the landlord, with each accounting, any funds exceeding the minimum balance to be held for reserves.

The property manager's authority to withdraw his management fee from the trust account is included.

PROPERTY MANAGEMENT AGREEMENT

DATE:_____, 20_____, at_____, California.

Items left blank and unchecked are not applicable.

1. RETAINER PERIOD:

1.1 Owner hereby retains and grants Broker the exclusive right to lease, rent, operate and maintain the property as property manager, commencing _____, 20_____, and continuing for one year and thereafter until terminated.

2. RECEIPT OF SECURITY DEPOSITS:

2.1 Owner hands $_____ to Broker for deposit into the trust account towards Owner's security deposit obligation to tenants.

3. RECEIPT OF CASH RESERVE:

3.1 Owner hands $_____ to Broker as a deposit towards Owner's obligation under the agreement.

3.2 Owner to maintain a minimum cash reserve, in addition to any security deposits, in the amount of $_____. On request from Broker, Owner will advance additional funds to maintain this minimum balance.

3.3 The cash reserve may be used to pay costs diligently incurred by Broker or due Broker in fulfilling Broker's obligations.

4. BROKERAGE FEE:

NOTICE: The amount or rate of real estate fees is not fixed by law. They are set by each broker individually and are negotiable between Owner and Broker.

4.1 Broker compensation to be:

a. _____% of all rents collected and deposited by Broker during the month, except for any first month's rent for which a broker fee is paid under §4.1 b as follows;

b. _____% of the first month's rent collected and deposited under ☐ rental agreements, and ☐ leases;

c. All sums remaining from credit check fees in excess of credit report expenses; and

d. ☐ Late payment charges and returned check charges paid by a tenant.

5. TRUST ACCOUNT:

5.1 Broker will place Owner's deposit for costs and security deposits into ☐ Broker's trust account, or ☐ separate trust account for Owner, maintained with _____ at their _____branch.

a. This account shall be ☐ non-interest bearing, or ☐ interest bearing.

5.2 All funds received by Broker for the account of Owner will be placed in the trust account.

5.3 Amounts to pay and satisfy the obligations incurred by Broker may be disbursed from the account after payment is due.

5.4 On termination of this agreement, Broker will return to Owner all remaining trust funds belonging to Owner.

6. PERIODIC ACCOUNTING:

6.1 Within ten days after each calendar ☐ month, or ☐ quarter, and on termination of this agreement, Broker will deliver to Owner a Statement of Account for all receipts and expenditures, together with a check to Owner for any funds in excess of minimum reserves under §3.2.

6.2 Amounts to compensate Broker under §4 may be withdrawn from the trust account.

6.3 Each Statement of Account delivered by Broker shall include no less than the following information for the period:

a. Amount of security deposits received or refunded.

b. Amount of rent or receipts, itemized by unit.

c. An itemized description of disbursements.

d. End of month balance of the income, expense and security deposit trust accounts.

6.4 ☐ Broker to reserve and disburse from the trust account any property and employee taxes, special assessments, insurance premiums, loan payments and other payments required to be made by the owner.

6.5 Advertising costs incurred to locate new tenants to be: ☐ paid by Owner, or ☐ paid by Broker.

— — — — — — — — — — — *PAGE ONE OF THREE — FORM 590* — — — — — — — — — — — — — —

7. TITLE CONDITION AND LOANS:

7.1   The property is referred to as: _____
_____
_____
_____

7.2   Owner's interest in the property is:
☐ Fee simple, ☐ Other_____.

7.3   Loan payments are to be timely disbursed by Broker to:
a. Lender:_____
Address:_____
_____
_____
Phone: _____
Payment of $_____, due on the _____ day and delinquent on the _____ day of each month.

b. Lender:_____
Address:_____
_____
_____
Phone: _____
Payment of $_____, due on the _____ day and delinquent on the _____ day of each month.

8. BROKER AGREES TO:

8.1   Use diligence in the performance of this employment.

8.2   Continuously maintain a California real estate broker's license.

8.3   Collect all rents, security deposits or other charges and expenses due Owner, and timely refund tenants' security deposits, less allowable deductions and including any interest due tenants.

8.4   Prepare and place advertisements for prospective tenants.

8.5   Show property to prospective tenants, obtain credit reports and confirm creditworthiness of tenants before executing leases or rental agreements.

8.6   Execute, renegotiate or cancel rental agreements or leases with tenants.
No lease to exceed _____ months.

8.7   Serve rent collection and other notices, file unlawful detainer and money damage actions, recover possession of premises or settle with delinquent tenants.

8.8   Inspect the property monthly and each unit when tenants vacate.

8.9   Maintain and periodically confirm the inventory of personal property on premises.

8.10 Evaluate leases and rental agreements periodically for income, expense and provision updates.

8.11 Contract for utilities, services and equipment to operate and maintain the property and safeguard the tenants.

8.12 Contract for any repairs, maintenance or improvements needed to lease or rent the property. Owner to approve all repairs in excess of $_____.

8.13 Obligate Owner to no unauthorized agreement or liability.

8.14 Protect and enhance the goodwill of Owner's rental business and keep confidential and secure any knowledge of Owner's business activities acquired during this employment.

8.15 Hire, supervise and discharge: ☐ a resident manager, and ☐ an assistant resident manager.

8.16 Inspect and take any action necessary to comply with federal, state, county or municipal safety and building codes affecting the property.

8.17 Notify Owner of any potential hazards to the tenants or property, and Owner to respond within seven (7) days. Should an emergency situation arise placing the tenants or property in jeopardy, Broker may immediately remedy the situation without further authority from Owner.

9. OWNER AGREES TO:

9.1 Hand Broker all keys and entry codes to the property, and copies of leases and rental agreements with existing tenants.

9.2 Hand Broker (if Broker is to disburse) loan payment coupons/envelopes, property tax bills, insurance premium billings and _____.

9.3 Indemnify Broker for the expense of any legal action arising out of Broker's proper performance of this agreement.

9.4 Provide public liability, property damage and worker's compensation insurance sufficient in amount to protect Broker and Owner, naming Broker as an additional insured.

Owner's insurance agent is: _____

9.5 _____

10. TERMINATION:

10.1 This agreement shall continue until terminated by mutual written agreement or until either party, for legally justifiable cause, serves a written Notice of Termination.

10.2 Owner may terminate this agreement at any time during the initial one-year term by paying Broker a fee equal to three times Broker's management fee earned during the month preceding termination.

10.3 On termination, Owner will assume the obligation of any contract entered into by Broker under this agreement.

11. GENERAL PROVISIONS:

11.1 Broker is authorized to place a for rent/lease sign on the property and publish and disseminate property information.

11.2 Owner authorizes Broker to cooperate with other brokers and divide with them any compensation due.

11.3 The authorized agent-for-service is ☐ Broker, ☐ Owner, ☐ _____

11.4 If an action is instituted to enforce this agreement, the prevailing party shall receive reasonable attorney fees.

11.5 ☐ **See attached addendum(s) for additional terms.**

11.6 _____

Broker: I agree to render services on the terms stated above.	Owner: I agree to employ Broker on the terms stated above.
Date:_____, 20_____	Date:_____, 20_____
Broker: _____	Owner:_____
By: _____	Signature: _____
Address: _____	Address: _____
Phone:_____	Phone:_____
Fax: _____	Fax: _____
E-mail: _____	E-mail: _____

FORM 590   10-00   ©2007 **first tuesday**, P.O. BOX 20069, RIVERSIDE, CA 92516 (800) 794-0494

Brokerage fee enforcement

Property managers cannot enforce collection of their management fees without a written agreement.

When the landlord and property manager orally agree to the payment of management fees, the property manager is unable to enforce collection of his fees for services rendered if the landlord fails to pay. [**Phillippe** v. **Shapell Industries Inc.** (1987) 43 C3d 1247]

Thus, the property management agreement sets forth the fees due the property manager.

An accounting is provided at the end of the employment period, usually each month, since trust account balances for each client must be reconciled by the broker at least once a month. [Department of Real Estate Regulations §2831.2]

A property manager who fails to give the landlord a timely and accurate accounting faces loss of his real estate broker's license. [**Apollo Estates Inc.** v. **Department of Real Estate** (1985) 174 CA3d 625]

The property manager must also keep all documents, such as his management and accounting files, for each activity connected with any transaction requiring a real estate broker's license for three years. [B & P C §10148]

Management of CIDs

Brokers may be retained by condominium homeowners' associations (HOAs) or other common interest developments (CIDs) to manage membership, exercise control over the common areas and structures and account for assessment revenues, expenses and reserves. Brokers seeking such employment are called *prospective managing agents*.

Before a broker acting as a prospective managing agent enters into a management agreement with a CID, the broker must disclose:

- the names and addresses of the owners of the brokerage company if it is an entity;

- the relevant licensing of the owners, such as for architectural design, construction, engineering, real estate or accounting, and the effective dates of the licensees; and

- the relevant professional designations held by the owners, what organizations issued the designation, the issuance dates and any expiration dates. [CC §1363.1]

The benchmark professional certification is called the Certified Community Association Manager and is issued by the California Association of Community Managers.

Funds received by the managing agent belong to the HOA. If the HOA does not have a bank account, the manager will maintain a separate trust fund account as trustee for the HOA. Extensive statutory controls are placed on the handling of the trust fund account held for CIDs. [CC §1363.2]

Chapter 9

Property manager's responsibilities

This chapter examines a property manager's responsibilities in his management of income property on behalf of an owner.

An evolving standard of conduct

Property management is an economically viable and personally rewarding real estate service an individual can provide to others. Serious brokers and agents often turn their interests from residential sales to the specialized industry of property management.

A broker's primary objective as a property manager is to oversee the maintenance of rental property, rent to suitable tenants, collect rent and account to the owner. Thus, a property manager must have time to actively oversee all rental properties entrusted to his management.

To conduct business in California as a property manager acting on behalf of others for a fee, an individual must hold a valid California real estate broker's license. [Calif. Business and Professions Code §§10130, 10131(b)]

The duty of care a property manager owes an owner is the same duty of care a broker in real estate sales owes his sellers and buyers. As a property manager, the broker is an agent acting as a trustee on behalf of the owner. Sales agents acting on behalf of the broker perform property management services as authorized by the broker.

A property manager's real estate license may be revoked or suspended if he demonstrates negligence or incompetence in performing his management tasks, including the supervision of his employees, such as his agents. [Bus & P C §§10177(g), 10177(h)]

Requisite competence to manage

To be successful in the property management field, a broker must first acquire the minimum knowledge and experience required to successfully perform his tasks. His level of competence must be equivalent to or exceed the competence an owner could expect of a broker who holds himself out as a property manager in the community where the property is located.

A broker acquires a property manager's expertise through:

- courses required to qualify for and maintain a real estate license [Bus & P C §§10153.2, 10170.5];

- on-the-job training as an agent;

- experience as a landlord;

- practical experience in the business management field; or

- exposure to related or similar management activities.

Owners should view the aptitude of a broker's management skills as the measure of how capable, and thus successful, a broker will be at handling their properties. Most owners look to hire an experienced property manager with well-earned credentials who will hopefully perform to the owner's expectations.

Indicators an owner might best rely on to determine whether a property manager can successfully handle rental property include:

- prior experience handling and reporting trust account activities;

- an adequate computer system to record and track activity on each property to be managed by the property manager; and

- a competent staff to perform office and field duties and to quickly respond to both the landlord's and the tenants' needs.

Management obligations

A property manager's obligations to a landlord include:

- holding a broker's license;

- diligently performing his employment;

- handling and accounting for all income and expenses produced by the property;

- contracting for services, repairs and maintenance on the property;

- monitoring utility services provided by the landlord;

- advertising for prospective tenants;

- showing the property and qualifying tenants;

- negotiating and executing rental and lease agreements;

- responding in a timely manner to the needs of the tenants;

- evaluating rental and lease agreements periodically;

- serving notices on tenants and filing unlawful detainer (UD) actions as needed;

- performing regular periodic property inspections; and

- keeping secure any personal property.

In addition to these tasks, the property manager must also:

- confirm or obtain general liability and workers' compensation insurance sufficient to protect the landlord, naming himself as an additionally insured;

- obligate the landlord to only authorized agreements;

- maintain the property's earning power, called *goodwill*;

- hire and fire resident managers and other on-site employees as needed;

- comply with all applicable codes affecting the property; and

- notify the landlord of any potentially hazardous conditions or criminal activities affecting the health and safety of individuals on or about the property.

The "prudent investor" standard

A property manager must employ a higher standard of conduct regarding the operation of a property than a typical resident owner or investor might apply. This standard is called the *prudent investor standard*.

A **prudent investor** is a person who has the knowledge and expertise to determine the wisest conduct for reasonably managing his property. The *prudent investor standard of conduct* is the minimum level of competency which can be expected of a property manager by a landlord, whether or not the landlord would apply the standard or even know about it.

The standards exemplified by resident owners may not necessarily be based on obtaining the maximum rental income and incurring only those minimal expenses needed to maintain the income flow from rents.

A resident owner is more apt to maintain the property in a condition which satisfies himself, not necessarily sound economic principles. Also, resident owners are not often concerned about the effect of the marketplace on their property's value until it is time to sell or refinance.

Likewise, the resident owner may not have the knowledge or expertise to effectively manage the property himself. Most owners of rental income property pursue unrelated occupations which leave them very little time to concentrate on the management of their properties.

However, the property manager is employed to manage the property as his primary occupation. A landlord's primary business reason for hiring a property manager is to have the property manager maintain the condition of his investment and income.

Thus, decisions regarding the property should be made by the property manager based on the need to generate a reasonable income from the property and incur expenses necessary to preserve the habitability of the property, provide a safe and secure environment for persons on the property and maintain the property's condition so it will support the income.

Property analysis

To conduct property operations in compliance with the **prudent investor standard of care**, a property manager should consider the following factors at the outset of employment:

- the type of the property and its niche in the market;

- the socioeconomic mix in the area surrounding the property's location;

- the competition currently existing in the local market;

- the current physical condition of the property; and

- the existing financing on the property, called *capitalization*.

The competition in the marketplace includes the manager's ability to locate ready, willing and able tenants to rent at rates sought by the manager.

For example, if there are more tenants seeking space than units available to rent, the property manager can increase the rent and still maintain occupancy levels, excluding residential units covered by rent control ordinances.

Conversely, if the number of rental units or spaces available exceeds the quantity of tenants available in the area to occupy them, a property manager may have to initiate programs to better retain tenants and attract new ones to keep his units at optimum levels of occupancy.

The current physical condition of the property — known as *curb appeal* — reflects the attitude of the ownership towards tenants. A property manager must analyze the repairs, maintenance, landscaping and improvements presently needed so the property's visual appearance and ambiance has a positive impact on tenants.

A prospective tenant's immediate concern when viewing rental property will be the lure of the landscaping, the freshness of interior and exterior paint and the overall care and tidiness of the premises. More importantly, existing tenants stay or leave based on these observances.

Liens affect nonresidential tenants

Along with the condition of the property, a property manager on nonresidential property must take a close look at the landlord's trust deed liens on the property. Both the property manager and the tenants are ultimately affected by the burden existing financing places on the landlord's cash flow.

A property manager cannot perform economic miracles for a landlord when payments on the financing encumbering the property interfere with the property's capacity to generate a positive cash flow or, worse yet, to maintain the premises or pay management fees.

Further, a prudent property manager, aware of the existing financing on the property, will apprise the landlord when the opportunity arises to refinance the property with more advantageously structured loans. The property manager can charge an additional fee for soliciting or arranging such financing.

As for a tenant, his right to possession of the property is usually junior and subject to the existing lender's right to foreclose on any default by the owner on the lender's trust deed. A non-residential tenant's move-in costs and tenant improvements are at risk of loss if the pre-existing lender forecloses.

Title profile analysis

It is in the property manager's best interest to do a cursory title check on the property he intends to manage.

A title check, commonly called a *property profile* is obtained from a title company and will confirm:

- how ownership is vested and who has authority to retain management;

- all outstanding liens and encumbrances on the property; and

- any use restrictions affecting tenants.

Any discrepancy in information provided by the landlord and a property profile report should be cleared up with the owner prior to taking over management of the property.

Due diligence and the paper trial

A property manager's efforts to locate tenants should be documented on a **file activity sheet** maintained for each property. The paper trail a property manager leaves shows he has diligently pursued activities leading to the renting of the property. Thus, the property manager reduces the risk that claims will be made that he failed to diligently seek tenants for the property.

For example, any advertisements placed by the property manager should focus on and clearly identify the property to be rented. Since the advertisement identifies the property, the owner can be properly billed for the expense of the advertisement. Whenever an advertisement is placed, a purchase order should be prepared, whether or not it is given to the publisher or printer.

As in any business, a purchase order will contain the dates the advertisement is to run, the advertising copy, which vendor (newspaper or printer) it was placed with and the property to be charged. When the billing is received referencing the purchase order, the property manager has it as a written reminder of his activity and which owner to charge. Computer programs for bookkeeping provide for the entry, control and printout of this data.

The goal in property management is to make a diligent effort to locate a tenant and rent the property as quickly as possible.

Therefore, marketing nonresidential property by remaining in the office or failing to set or keep appointments to meet with prospective tenants is inexcusable negligence. As prospective tenants respond to an advertisement, the property manager must make himself available to show them the property, unless the property has a resident or on-site manager.

When the property manager cannot timely perform or complete the management tasks undertaken, he needs to delegate some of his work load to employees or resident managers, keeping in mind he must maintain constant oversight as their supervisor and employer.

Handling UD actions

A property manager may file a small claims action on behalf of the owner to recover amounts due and unpaid under a lease or rental agreement, such as rent or late charges, if:

- the owner has not retained the property manager under a property management agreement solely to represent the owner in small claims court; and

- the claim relates to the rental property. [Calif. Code of Civil Procedure §116.540(h)]

A property manager may also file small claims actions on behalf of a homeowners' association (HOA) created to manage a common interest development (CID). [CCP §116.540(i)]

However, in order for the property manager to represent the owner in a small claims action, the court requires property managers to file a declaration stating the property manager:

- is authorized by the owner to appear on his behalf under a property management agreement; and

- is not employed solely to represent the owner in small claims court. [CCP §116.540(j)]

Consider a licensed real estate broker who operates his property management business as a sole proprietorship, not as a corporation.

The broker manages an apartment complex for an owner under a property management agreement.

The management agreement gives the broker all care and management responsibilities for the complex, including the authority to:

- enter into leases and rental agreements as the landlord;

- file UD actions; and

- hire an attorney to handle evictions, if necessary.

The broker signs all lease and rental agreements in his own name **as the lessor** since his management contract gives him this authority. The owner's name does not appear on any lease or rental agreement.

A tenant of the complex fails to pay his rent under a rental agreement entered into with the

broker. A 3-day notice to pay rent or quit the premise is served on the tenant by the broker. [See **first tuesday** Form 575]

The tenant does not pay the delinquent rent within three days and remains on the premises. The broker files a UD action to recover possession by an eviction of the tenant, **naming himself** as the plaintiff on the UD complaint.

The tenant defends against the eviction by claiming the broker cannot maintain a UD action to evict him since the broker is not the owner of the real estate or the owner's attorney.

Can the broker file and maintain a UD action against the tenant in his own name?

Yes! The broker may file the UD action even though he is not the owner. The broker entered into the lease agreement and delivered possession as the lessor, and is now recovering possession from the tenant in his own name. [**Allen** v. **Dailey** (1928) 92 CA 308]

As the lessor under the lease, the property manager has the **greater right to possession** of the premises than the tenant, even though the owner is known to be the true landlord, a situation legally entitled *jus tertii*.

Thus, as the lessor named on the lease, the property manager can maintain the UD action against the tenant and recover possession of the premises.

Property inspections by the manager

A property manager's frequent, well-documented inspections of property he manages are nearly as important as his accurate accounting of income and expenses through his trust account. Inspections determine the physical condition of the property, availability of habitable units or commercial spaces and the use of the leased premises by existing tenants.

Several key moments when a property manager should make an inspection include:

1. *When the property manager and land-lord enter into a property management agreement.*

   Any deferred maintenance or defects which would interfere with the renting of the property should be discussed with the landlord. Resolve the discrepancy by either correcting the problem or noting it is to be left "as is," except for conditions which would endanger the health and safety of tenants and their guests.

2. *When the property manager rents to a tenant.*

   A walk-through should be conducted with a new tenant prior to giving them occupancy. The property's condition should be noted on a condition of premises addendum form and signed by the tenant. [See **first tuesday** Form 560]

3. *During the term of the lease.*

   While the tenant is in possession, the property should be periodically inspected by the property manager to make sure it is being properly maintained. Notes on the date, time and observations are made in the property management file. File notes are used to refresh the property manager's memory of his last inspection, order out maintenance and evidence his diligence.

4. *Two weeks prior to the tenant vacating.*

   Residential property must be inspected prior to termination of possession if the tenant requests a joint pre-termination inspection after receiving the mandatory landlord's notice of right to a wear and tear analysis. [See Chapter 22]

5. *When the tenant vacates.*

   The property's condition should be compared against its condition when first occupied by the tenant. Based on differences in the property's condition as documented by the property manager, the reasonable amount of deductions from the tenant's security deposit for corrective repairs can be documented when accounting for the return of the deposit.

6. *When the broker returns management of the property back to the landlord or over to another management firm.*

   Documenting all property inspections helps avoid disputes with the landlord or tenants regarding just what was the condition of the property when possession or management was transferred to and from the property manager.

The property's condition should be noted on a form, such as a condition of property disclosure and be approved by the property manager and the landlord. Also, the property manager should keep a copy in the property's file as part of the paper trail maintained on the property. [See **first tuesday** Form 304]

Inspections at the time of key events help to establish who is responsible for any deferred maintenance and upkeep, or for any damage to the property.

Periodic review of the leases

On entering into a **management agreement**, a broker and landlord should conduct a comprehensive review of all rental and lease agreement forms used by the landlord, including proposed changes and the use of other forms.

Also, the property manager must be aware of the dates of all lease expirations, rent adjustments, tenant sales reports, renewal or extension deadlines, and grace periods for rent payments and late charges. Computer programs have made this tracking easier.

Periodic evaluations by the property manager of his existing rental and lease agreements is important. Vacant units should be evaluated to determine the type of tenant and tenancy desired (periodic versus fixed-term), how rents will be established and which units consistently underperform.

The amount of rental income receipts is directly related to the property manager's evaluation of the rents charged and implementation of any changes. A **re-evaluation** of rents includes the consideration of factors which influence the amount to charge for rent, including:

- market changes, such as a decrease or increase in tenants competing for a greater or lesser availability of units;

- the physical condition and appearance of the property; and

- the property's location, such as its proximity to employment, shopping, transportation, schools, financial centers, etc.

A property manager must keep abreast of the market changes which might affect the property's rental rates in the future, then make the necessary changes when negotiating leases and rental agreements. The more curious and perceptive the property manager is about future trends, the more protection his landlord's investment will likely receive against loss.

Maintenance and repairs

Obtaining the highest rents available requires constant **maintenance and repair** of the property. The property manager is responsible for all the maintenance and repairs on the property while he is managing it, whether he retains or delegates responsibility to tenants in lease agreements.

Thus, the property manager's knowledge of the property's condition prior to entering into a management agreement is a must in order to properly ascertain what maintenance and repairs need to be made or will be deferred.

The responsibility for maintenance includes:

- determining necessary repairs and replacements;

- contracting for repairs and replacements;

- confirming completion of repairs and replacements;

- paying for completed repairs and replacements; and

- advising the landlord about the status of repairs and replacements in the monthly report.

Different types of property require greater or lesser degrees of maintenance and upkeep.

A commercial or industrial tenant who occupies the entire (nonresidential) property may agree in their lease to perform all maintenance and upkeep of the property. The broker, as the property manager, then has a greatly reduced role in the care and maintenance of the property — that of oversight to confirm the tenant is caring for the property and otherwise fully performing the terms of the lease agreement.

On the other hand, if the property manager is responsible to an owners' association (HOA), he will exercise a high degree of control over the maintenance and upkeep of the property and the security of the occupants.

Usually, landlords set a ceiling on the dollar amount of repairs and maintenance the property manager has authority to incur on behalf of the landlord. The property manager should not exceed this dollar ceiling without the landlord's consent even though the landlord receives a benefit from the expenditure.

Profits from all sources disclosed

If maintenance or repair work is done by the property manager's staff or he stands to additionally benefit financially by the materials purchased or services performed, the property manager must disclose his financial involvement to the landlord.

Thus, the property manager should prepare a **repair and maintenance disclosure addendum** and attach it to the management agreement to cover information such as:

- types of repairs and maintenance his staff will perform;

- hourly charges for jobs performed;

- costs of workers' compensation and method for charging the landlord;

- any service or handling charges for purchasing parts, materials or supplies (usually a percentage of the cost);

- whether the staff will perform work when they are available and qualified, in lieu of contracting the work out (i.e., no bids will be taken); and

- to what extent repairs and maintenance will generate net revenue for the management company so as to constitute additional income to the property manager.

Due to the risk of accepting *undisclosed profits*, the property manager must give written disclosure of any ownership interests or fee arrangements he may have with vendors performing work, such as landscapers, plumbers, etc. Any undisclosed profit received for work performed by the property manager or others on the landlord's property is improperly received and must be returned to the landlord.

Additionally, the landlord can recover any other brokerage fees he has already paid when the property manager improperly or intentionally takes an undisclosed profit while acting as his agent. [**Terry** v. **Bender** (1956) 143 CA2d 198]

Goodwill as value

A property and how it is operated develops a reputation among tenants, called *goodwill*. Economically, goodwill equates to the earning power of the property. A property manager in the ordinary course of managing property will concentrate on increasing the intangible image — goodwill — of the property.

Goodwill is maintained, and hopefully increased, when the property manager cares for the appearance of the property, maintains an appropriate tenant mix (without employing prohibited discriminatory selection) and gives effective and timely attention to the tenants' concerns.

A prudent property manager makes recommendations to the landlord about maintaining the property to eliminate any accumulated wear and tear, deterioration or obsolescence. Thus, he helps enhance the property's "curb appeal."

The manager who fails to promptly complete necessary repairs or correctly maintain the property may be impairing the property's goodwill built up with tenants and the public. Allowing the property or the tenancies to deteriorate will expose the property manager to liability for the decline in revenue.

Reserves for the trust account

To accommodate the flow of income and expenditures from the properties he manages, the property manager maintains a trust account in his name, as trustees, at a bank or financial institution. [10 Calif. Code of Regulations §2830]

Generally, a property manager receives a cash deposit from the owner, which includes a "start-up" fee, a cash reserve for costs and the tenants' security deposits.

A **start-up fee** is usually a flat, one-time management fee charged by the property manager. The **cash reserves** are used to pay the operating expenses preliminarily incurred on the property.

The **cash reserve** is a set amount of cash the owner agrees to maintain as a minimum balance in the broker's trust account. The cash reserve will be used to pay costs incurred should costs and loan payments exceed income. Security deposits are in addition to the client's cash reserves.

The property manager should insist all **security deposits** previously collected from existing tenants are handed over to him for his control and management through his trust account. Eventually, due to legislation, interest must be paid on some security deposits, comparable to interest paid by lenders on escrow accounts for impound advances by property owners.

The security deposit should, but does not need to be accounted for separately from other funds in the trust account. Security deposits belong to the tenant and must be used or returned to a residential tenant with an accounting within 21 days after the tenant's departure, or 30 days for nonresidential occupancies. [Calif. Civil Code §1950.5(g)(1); 1950.7(c)(1)]

On receipt of security deposits, rents, cash reserves, start-up fees, etc., the property manager is required to deposit these funds into a trust account within three business days. [Bus & P C §10145(a); Department of Real Estate Regulations §2832]

Separate ledger for each landlord

All accounts must be maintained in accordance with standard accounting procedures. These standards are best met by using computer software designed for property management. [DRE Reg. §2831]

Also, withdrawals from the trust fund account cannot be made by the landlord, only by the property manager.

However, the property manager can give written consent to make withdrawals from the trust account to a licensed agent under his employ or to an unlicensed employee who is bonded. [DRE Reg. §2834(a)]

No matter who the property manager authorizes to make the withdrawal, he alone is responsible for the accurate daily maintenance of the trust account. [DRE Reg. §2834(c)]

The property manager's bookkeeping records for **each trust account** maintained at a bank or thrift must include entries of:

- the amount, date of receipt and source of all trust funds deposited;

- the date the trust funds were deposited in his trust account;

- the date and check number for disbursements of trust funds previously deposited in the trust account; and

- the daily balance of the trust account. [DRE Reg. §2831(a)]

Entries in the **general ledger** for the overall trust account must be in chronological order and in a column format. Also, the ledgers may be maintained in a written journal or one generated by a computer software program. [DRE Reg. §2831(c)]

In addition to the general ledger of the entire trust account, the property manager must maintain a separate **subaccount ledger** for each owner he represents, to account for all trust funds deposited to or disbursed from his trust account for their accounts.

Each separate, individual subaccount ledger must identify the parties to each entry and include:

- the date and amount of trust funds **deposited**;

- the date, check number and amount of each related **disbursement** from the trust account;

- the date and amount of any **interest earned** on funds in the trust fund account; and

- the total amount of trust **funds remaining** after each deposit or disbursement from the trust account. [DRE Reg. §2831.1]

Like the general ledger for the entire trust account, entries in each client's subaccount record must also be in chronological order on a written, columnized journal/ledger or one generated by a computer software program. [DRE Reg. §2831.1(b)]

Manager's trust account supervision

Any behavior on the part of the property manager or his employees to delay the proper maintenance of the trust account places the property manager's broker license at risk of loss or suspension for violation of his duty to the landlord to maintain the trust account.

To avoid activities that may jeopardize the status of the property manager's license due to his handling of the trust account, the property manager must:

- deposit the funds received, whether in cash, check or other form of payment, within three business days [DRE Reg. §2832];

- keep trust fund account records for three years after the transaction [Bus & P C §10148];

- keep a separate ledger or record of deposits and expenditures itemized by each transaction and for each landlord [DRE Reg. §2831.1]; and

- keep accurate trust account records for all receipts and disbursements. [DRE Reg. §2831]

Handling of trust account funds

When a property manager places funds into his trust account, he must then **diligently manage** the account to avoid claims of mishandling, misappropriation or commingling of the landlord's funds with his personal funds.

Consider a landlord who hires a broker to act as his property manager. In addition to paying for expenses and costs incurred, the property manager is instructed and authorized to pay the monthly mortgage payments.

The property manager locates a tenant and collects the initial rent and security deposit.

After depositing the funds in his bank trust account, but prior to disbursing the loan payment, the property manager withdraws both his leasing fee for locating the tenant and his monthly property manager's fee. Both fees are due the property manager for work completed under his property management contract.

However, the withdrawal of the property manager's fees leaves insufficient funds in the trust account that are needed to make the loan payment. The property manager then issues a check on funds held in one of his personal accounts to make the landlord's mortgage payment. However, this account also has insufficient funds.

Meanwhile, the lender sends the landlord a late payment notice for the delinquency. The landlord immediately contacts the property manager regarding the delinquent payment. The property manager says he will cover it and does so.

Three months later, the landlord informs the broker he no longer wants him to manage the property. The property management agreement is terminated by the landlord.

The property manager sends a closing statement on the account containing some erroneous deductions.

Prior to the closing statement, the landlord received no other accounting since retaining the broker.

More than three months passed between collecting funds and sending an accounting. After discussion with the landlord, the property manager corrects the errors, issues the landlord a check for the remaining balance, closes the account and destroys (deletes) the landlord's file.

Later, the landlord files a complaint with the Department of Real Estate (DRE) regarding the property manager.

The DRE contends the property manager breached his agency duties. The property manager issued a check for a loan payment from an account other than the trust account, an activity that automatically constitutes *commingling* of the property manager's personal funds with trust funds. Also, the property manager knew he had insufficient funds when he issued the check, a dishonest act.

In addition, the property manager failed to accurately, and no less than quarterly, account for funds taken in or expended by him on behalf of the landlord.

Finally, the property manager destroyed the records prior to the three-year limitation. Thus, it is proper for the DRE to revoke the property manager's real estate broker license. [**Apollo Estates Inc.** v. **Department of Real Estate** (1985) 174 CA3d 625]

Accounting to the landlord

Tied to the property manager's duty to properly maintain his trust account is the duty to account to the landlord.

All landlords are entitled to a *statement of accounting* no less than at the end of each calendar quarter (i.e., March, June, September and December).

The **accounting** is to include the following information:

- the name of the property manager;
- the name of the landlord;
- a description of the services rendered;
- the identification of the trust fund account credited;
- the amount of funds collected to date;
- the amount disbursed to date;
- the amount, if any, of fees paid to field agents or leasing agents;

- the overhead costs; and
- a breakdown of the advertising costs, a copy of the advertisement, the name of the newspaper or publication and the dates the advertisement ran.

Also, the property manager must give a full accounting when the management agreement expires or is terminated. Any discrepancy or failure by the property manager to properly account for the trust funds will be resolved against him and in favor of the landlord. Even if the property manager's only breach is sloppy or inaccurate accounting, he is responsible as though **misappropriation** and **commingling** occurred.

Although the property manager is only required to account each calendar quarter, a monthly accounting should be undertaken. He may then rightly collect his fee at the end of each month after he has fully performed and his fee is due. In this way, the property manager can avoid the receipt of advance fees for which the use of a DRE-approved form is required. [Bus & P C §10146]

Management fees

Property managers structure management fee schedules in several different ways:

1. *A percentage of the rents collected.*

   The property manager is entitled to charge a set percentage of the rents collected as a fee (customarily between 5% to 10%), usually payable monthly. The percentage fee is not paid on security deposits since deposits are not rents. A percentage fee is a proper method for establishing the amount of fees.

2. *Fixed fee.*

   The property manager and landlord agree in advance to a set dollar amount to be charged monthly for the management services. The amount stays constant whether or not the units are rented. This method, while proper, lacks the motivational incentive to induce the property manager to generate maximum rental income.

3. *Fixed fee per unit.*

   Usually applied to large apartment complexes or condominium associations, a set dollar amount is charged for each unit in the complex managed by the property manager. In addition to the basic fee, property managers often charge a one-time fee each time a unit is re-rented.

4. *A percentage of the first month's rent.*

   A front-end fee paid to the property manager is called a leasing or origination fee. If the landlord agrees, a fee can be charged for exercise of an option to renew or extend, or when a new lease is entered into with an existing tenant.

Fees are to be negotiated and set between each individual property manager and landlord. [Bus & P C §10147.5]

However, no matter how customary and prevalent it is in the real estate industry to charge a particular percentage fee, fees may not be set by agreement **between brokers** or as a result of *conscious parallelism* and peer pressure among brokers to maintain equivalent fees; conduct which still permeates the brokerage industry. [**People** v. **National Association of Realtors** (1984) 155 CA3d 578]

Conflicts with sales operations

A broker who operates a real estate sales office, in conjunction with a property management operation, has a potential conflict of interest that may need to be disclosed to his clients.

For example, a creditworthy prospective tenant might be swayed by the broker's sales staff to purchase a residence instead of renting. Sales fees are typically greater than leasing fees for the time spent. Conversely, sales fees are one-shot fees, not continuously recurring fees.

Any active attempt to convert a prospective tenant to a buyer when the prospect has responded to a rental advertisement that has been paid for by a landlord or provided as part of the property management services, suggests improper conduct. The broker's conduct may range from "bait and switch" techniques to diverting the landlord's business opportunities (tenants) established through efforts expended on behalf of landlords he represents.

A broker must be careful to keep his sales and management operations sufficiently separate from one another and to diligently pursue leases or rental agreements with creditworthy tenants who apply to rent.

The landlord comes first; the broker's concern for greater fees comes second.

Chapter
10

Resident
managers

This chapter discusses the hiring of a resident manager, the pay and reporting regulations and the termination of the resident manager's employment and occupancy.

Employees: not independent contractors, not tenants

A broker, retained as a property manager, hires an individual as an on-site resident manager to handle the daily operations of an apartment building comprising 16 or more residential units. The resident manager enters into an employment contract with the property manager. [See Form 591 accompanying this chapter]

Under the **employment contract**, the resident manager:

- acknowledges he is an employee of the property manager; and

- agrees to vacate the property on termination of employment.

The resident manager's job is to show vacant units, run credit checks, negotiate and sign leases, collect rents, supervise repairs and maintenance, serve three-day and 30-day notices, etc.

In exchange for his services, the resident manager receives the use of an apartment rent-free.

Later, the property manager terminates the resident manager's employment.

The landlord demands the resident manager immediately vacate the premises and relinquish possession of the unit to the property manager.

However, the resident manager claims he is a tenant and does not need to vacate until he is served a notice to vacate, not just a notice terminating his employment. [See Chapter 29]

Is a resident manager who holds the right to occupy and use a residential unit as compensation for managing an apartment complex entitled to a notice to vacate?

No! A resident manager who occupies a unit after termination of employment is a *tenant-at-sufferance* — a holdover tenant who does not have a right to a notice to vacate since the term of his occupancy was fixed in the resident manager agreement until the date of termination of employment. [**Roberts** v. **Casey** (1939) 36 CA2d Supp. 767]

On termination of employment, a resident manager is not entitled to retain possession of the unit since the term of **occupancy expires** on termination of his employment. Possession of the unit is part of his compensation and the compensation ends, as agreed, with the employment.

Also, the resident manager who is being evicted by an unlawful detainer (UD) action cannot defend his possession by asserting a good cause must exist for terminating his employment or by relying on local rent control ordinances. [**Tappe** v. **Lieberman** (1983) 145 CA3d Supp. 19]

The property manager may begin eviction proceedings against the resident manager on termination of the employment without serving any notices, other than the notice terminating the employment which then terminates the occupancy as agreed in the resident manager employment agreement.

However, occupancy is not terminated if the resident manager employment agreement provides for the creation of tenancy following the

RESIDENT MANAGER AGREEMENT

DATE:_____, 20_____, at _____, California.

Items left blank or unchecked are not applicable.

1. RETAINER PERIOD:

1.1 Employer hereby employs _____, Employee, as Resident Manager of the rental property referred to as:

_____

located at _____ in _____
California, commencing _____, 20_____ and continuing until terminated.

2. EMPLOYEE AGREES TO:

2.1 Collect all rents, security deposits or other charges due the Owner and maintain collection records.

2.2 Advertise available rental units.

2.3 Screen and select tenants.

2.4 Show rental units to prospective tenants.

2.5 Negotiate, execute or cancel lease/rental agreements with tenants. No lease is to exceed _____ months.

2.6 Serve three-day notices as needed.

2.7 Clean, repair and maintain the rental real estate, inside and outside, as needed to promote the occupancy of the units.

2.8 Inspect daily the structure, grounds, parking lots, garages, and vacant units of the rental property for cleanliness and repairs.

2.9 Maintain receipt books, key racks and petty cash records in good order.

2.10 Conduct all minor maintenance and repairs not exceeding $_____ in cost. All materials to be purchased out of petty cash.

2.11 Contact the material and labor suppliers retained by the Employer to conduct all major repairs and maintenance. Employer to approve all repairs in excess of $_____.

2.12 Notify Employer immediately of any potential hazards to the tenants or property. Should an emergency situation arise placing tenants or property in jeopardy, Employee may immediately take action without further authority from Employer.

2.13 Conduct no other business on the premises nor solicit the tenants for any business other than the rental of the property.

3. BANKING:

3.1 Employee will place all rents, security deposits, and other funds received for the benefit of the Owner into an account maintained by Employer with _____
at their _____ branch.

3.2 On depositing funds into the Employer's Account, Employee shall deliver to Employer a copy of the bank deposit identifying the itemized deposits by the unit from which they were collected.

4. COMPENSATION OF EMPLOYEE AND HOURS WORKED:

4.1 As compensation for services, Employee shall be paid a total monthly salary, from all sources, of $_____.

4.2 In part, Employee's salary shall be in the form of possession to rental unit _____, which must be occupied as a condition of employment. The rental credit is $_____. The fair monthly rental value of the unit is $_____. The utilities including gas, electricity, and trash removal ☐ are, ☐ are not, included with the occupancy.

4.3 The balance of the Employee's salary shall be paid ☐ monthly, ☐ semi-monthly, on the _____ of each calendar month.

4.4 Employee will not work more than _____ hours per day and _____ hours per week.

4.5 Employee to have _____ days off weekly being the weekdays of _____.

4.6 Employee agrees to obtain Employer's consent if the hours required to carry out duties exceeds the agreed-to hours.

4.7 Employee will notify Employer within 48 hours of additional hours worked in an emergency situation.

4.9 Employee acknowledges he is not a tenant, but is an employee for purpose of occupancy of the unit provided for his on-site residency.

4.10 _____

_____

_____

_____

_____

_____

5. EMPLOYER AGREES TO:

5.1 Hand Employee all keys and entry codes to the property, and copies of leases/rental agreements with existing tenants.

5.2 Provide public liability, property damage and worker's compensation insurance sufficient in amount to protect the Employee and Employer.

5.3 Hand to Employee $_____ to be accounted for as petty cash to pay costs incurred in performing Employee's duties, and to replenish this amount on Employee's request.

5.4 Withhold all Employee's social security, federal and state income taxes, and disability insurance from cash salary paid.

5.5 Pay all federal and state unemployment insurance, worker's compensation and Employer's social security payments.

EMPLOYEE:

I agree to perform on the terms stated above.

Date:_____, 20_____

Employee: _____

Address:_____

_____

Phone: _____

Fax: _____

E-mail: _____

By: _____

EMPLOYER:

I agree to employ on the terms stated above.

Date:_____, 20_____

Employer:_____

Address:_____

_____

Phone: _____

Fax: _____

E-mail: _____

By: _____

FORM 591   06-06   ©2007 **first tuesday**, P.O. BOX 20069, RIVERSIDE, CA 92516 (800) 794-0494

termination of employment, as a monthly payment of rent after termination. [Calif. Code of Civil Procedure §1161(1)]

Resident manager activities

A resident manager is a person who lives in a residential unit, on either residential rental property or nonresidential property, as an employee managing the **daily operations** of the property, including:

- screening tenants and negotiating leases;

- cleaning vacated units;

- supervising landscaping, maintenance and repairs;

- serving notices; or

- attending to tenant inquiries.

Apartment buildings with 16 or more units must have an owner, resident manager or responsible caretaker living on the premises to manage the property. [25 Calif. Code of Regulations §42]

Resident managers do not need to be licensed as a real estate broker to negotiate leases or collect rents. However, the nonresident property manager, other than the landlord himself, must be a licensed real estate broker. [Calif. Business and Professions Code §10131.01; see Chapter 6]

Hiring a resident manager

Brokerage activities of concern to a property manager when employing an on-site resident manager include:

- selecting and hiring the resident manager;

- overseeing the resident manager; and

- terminating the resident manager's employment.

The resident manager's status as an employee is established in the employment agreement.

Any family members of the resident manager should be listed in the employment agreement as living with the resident manager, noting they are not tenants. They are employees **required to reside** in a unit on site.

References to the parties in the employment agreement identify the property manager/landlord as "employer" and the resident manager as "employee." [See Form 591 §4.9]

Payment for services

Depending on the size of the complex, the resident manager may receive occupancy of a unit in the complex as **compensation** for his services based on:

- a reduced rent in exchange for the value of the resident manager's services;

- free rent for services; or

- free rent plus a monthly salary.

On the resident manager employment agreement, the **salary** paid to the resident manager is stated as a monthly amount. The fair rental value of the resident manager's unit is deducted from his salary. After the rent deduction, the resident manager is paid the balance of his salary. Utilities may also be included as part payment for the resident manager's services and as a deduction from the agreed-to salary. [See Form 591 §4]

As an **employer**, the property manager/landlord has the responsibility to withhold all proper federal and state income taxes, as well as to make required payments for social security, unemployment insurance and disability insurance. [Calif. Unemployment Insurance Code §13020]

The property manager or landlord must carry workers' compensation insurance to cover resident manager injuries on the job.

As a result of the degree of control the property manager retains over a resident manager, a resident manager does not qualify as an independent contractor to avoid tax withholding, employer contributions and workers' compensation premiums.

Rental value is not income

Consider the property manager who hires a resident manager to run a large apartment complex. As part of his salary, the resident manager receives a unit rent-free plus a fixed monthly salary.

Is the value of the unit occupied by the resident manager in exchange for services considered **taxable income** which the resident manager must declare for state or federal tax reporting?

No! Taxwise, the value of the apartment is not income to the resident manager and is not declared as income when the unit occupied by the resident manager is:

- located on the premises managed;

- for the property manager's or landlord's convenience; and

- occupied by the resident manager as a condition of his employment. [Revenue Regulations §1.119-1(b)]

Minimum wage requirements

A resident manager's employment is subject to minimum wage laws even though the portion of the wages paid by a reduction in rent or free rent is not taxable as income. [Calif. Labor Code §1182.8]

Strict minimum wage requirements apply to resident managers since they **carry out the instructions** of the property manager or landlord, rather than having the authority to make their own independent decisions about management policies. [8 CCR §11050(1)(B)(1)]

A **rent credit** may be used as all or part of the wages received per hour of work performed by a resident manager to establish the amount earned per hour for minimum pay requirements. However, a cap exists limiting the rent credit toward hourly wages at two thirds of the fair rental value of the unit, not to exceed $381.20 per month. Should a couple be employed as resident managers, the rent credited toward hourly pay cannot exceed $563.90 per month. [8 CCR §11050(10)(C)]

The property manager should require the resident manager to prepare time cards, limit the number of hours per week the resident manager may work so wages per hour do not drop below the minimum, and make provisions for the payment of any overtime permitted.

Weekly work reports by the resident manager and a review of the reports by the property manager or landlord are to confirm the total compensation exceeds the minimum wages for time spent on the job. These reports will help avoid any resident manager's claim he worked excessive hours in relation to his salary and maximum rent credit. [See Form 591 §4]

Thus, all work requiring additional hours, except emergency work, must be approved by the property manager prior to being performed by the resident manager.

For example, a resident manager who is provided with a base salary, plus a unit, is required to **remain on the premises** at all times, but only performs five hours of daily work as limited by the resident manager employment agreement.

The resident manager claims he is entitled to overtime pay for the hours he is required to be on the premises.

However, the resident manager is only entitled to receive compensation for the time he actually performed work agreed to in the resident manager employment agreement, not for the time he was required to remain on the premises doing no work at all. [**Brewer** v. **Patel** (1993) 20 CA4th 1017]

Mismanaged managers

A resident manager is an employee of the property manager or the landlord who hires him.

As an employer, it is the landlord or property manager who is liable to others who are injured due to the improper conduct (negligence) of the resident manager in the course and scope of the resident manager's employment. [Calif. Civil Code §2338]

To avoid liability for negligent violations of law or personal injuries to others, the conduct of resident managers must be **closely supervised** by the property manager or landlord.

Termination

A resident manager employment agreement creates an agency with the property manager or landlord, which is an *at-will* relationship. Thus, the employment of the resident manager may be terminated at any time and without prior notice.

While a landlord or property manager does not need to have a good reason to terminate a resident manager, they may not have an improper reason.

For instance, a resident manager has managed a large complex for many years as an agent for the property manager. The resident manager is over 62 years of age.

The property manager hires a new, younger resident manager and relegates the old resident manager to a lesser position.

The property manager constantly suggests to the older manager that he should retire and demotes him to even lesser positions while dramatically reducing his compensation.

Has the property manager discriminated against the older resident manager?

Yes! The property manager's basis for demoting the older resident manager was not substandard performance, but age.

As a result, the property manager is responsible for money damages for emotional distress and attorney fees. A property manager or landlord cannot terminate the resident manager or otherwise harass him because of race, creed, color, gender or age. [**Stephens** v. **Coldwell Banker Commercial Group, Inc.** (1988) 199 CA3d 1394]

Terminating the occupancy

Consider a resident manager employment agreement that provides for a property manager to receive immediate possession of the unit occupied by the resident manager on termination of his employment.

The resident manager employment agreement must avoid creating any landlord/tenant relationship in the resident manager's occupancy of a unit, or requiring that prior notice be given to the resident manager before his occupancy can be terminated.

For example, the owner of an apartment complex hires a resident manager to run the complex. In exchange for his services, the resident manager receives an apartment rent-free and a monthly salary.

Under the resident manager's employment agreement, he agrees to vacate the apartment unit on termination of his employment. Thus, the right to possession is extinguished on being terminated.

The owner terminates the resident manager's employment. The owner then serves the resident manager with notice to **immediately vacate** and relinquish possession of the unit, or **stay and pay** monthly rent.

The resident manager remains in possession of the apartment, but fails to pay the monthly rent called for in the notice to vacate. Without further notice, the owner begins UD proceedings to regain possession of the apartment from the terminated resident manager.

The resident manager claims he is now a tenant and the owner must serve him with a notice to vacate to establish his unlawful detainer of the unit.

The landlord claims the resident manager is a holdover tenant who has been unlawfully detaining the premises since the termination of his employment.

Is the resident manager entitled to a notice to vacate?

Yes! The resident manager's occupancy was converted to a month-to-month tenancy when the owner served the resident manager with a notice to vacate that included an offer to remain in possession, which the former resident manager did.

Here, the resident manager's continued occupancy of the apartment constituted **acceptance** of the new tenancy offered by the owner. Thus, the failure to pay rent is a breach of the new tenancy agreement noted in the notice to stay and pay. The owner's UD action cannot be filed until a three-day notice to vacate is given to terminate the resident manager's new tenancy for failure to pay rent. [**Karz** v. **Mecham** (1981) 120 CA3d Supp. 1; CC §1946]

On termination of his employment, the resident manager should not have been served any notice to pay or vacate. If the terminated resident manager remains in possession, he is unlawfully detaining the property and can be evicted.

Neither the landlord nor the property manager should at any time enter into a separate lease/rental agreement with a resident manager.

Rather, the occupancy arrangement should be written as part of the resident manager employment agreement, even if the management services do not equal the unit's rental value and the resident manager pays the difference as a reduced monthly rent charged for the unit. [Form 591 §4]

To avoid creating a tenancy that continues on termination of the resident manager's employment, the resident manager employment agreement must state:

- possession is incidental to his employment;

- possession automatically ends concurrent with termination of his employment; and

- failure to perform managerial duties constitutes a breach of the employment agreement and is grounds for immediate termination and eviction.

Chapter 11

Identification of landlord or property manager

This chapter addresses the disclosures required to be given to residential tenants identifying the landlord or the landlord's agent-for-service, his property manager and the resident manager.

Notice to tenant of agent-for-service

A residential landlord, under a property management agreement, employs a broker to manage his property. The broker will manage and care for the property, as well as assume all contact with the tenants, which includes the decision to enter into all future rental and lease agreements.

One of the landlord's objectives is to become as anonymous as possible and avoid giving the tenants any personal information.

The landlord is advised he can avoid being identified to the tenants by appointing another individual to act as his *agent-for-service of process*, such as the broker or the landlord's attorney. The **agent-for-service**, acting on behalf of the landlord, will accept service of legal documents and notices initiated by tenants. [Calif. Civil Code §1962(a)(1)(B)]

Here, when the landlord appoints an agent-for-service, the landlord's name and address do not need to be disclosed to any tenant, even if the tenant demands it to sue the landlord. Serving the agent-for-service with the lawsuit is the same as serving the landlord. [CC §1962(a)(1)(B)]

Editor's note — The identity of a landlord is easily located by a search of the county records. If title to the property is vested in the name of a limited liability company (LLC), corporation, or other entity, a review of other records with the Secretary of State may be required to locate the manager of the entity.

Appointing the agent-for-service

A landlord may himself accept service of notices and legal documents from a tenant. However, a residential landlord may appoint any individual, including his property manager or his attorney, to be his agent-for-service and avoid personal service on himself.

The property manager may be appointed as the landlord's agent-for-service by including an **agent-for-service clause** in the property management agreement employing the broker. [See Figure 1 accompanying this chapter]

As the landlord's *agent-for-service*, the broker accepts personal service of legal documents on behalf of the landlord, such as notices and lawsuits initiated by tenants. However, both the broker and the landlord must first consider whether the broker should act as the landlord's agent-for-service.

The broker's additional responsibility of accepting service of tenant complaints on the landlord's behalf conflicts with his main responsibilities of managing and caring for the landlord's property. Litigation could result from the broker's purported mismanagement of the property. A landlord might prefer to appoint an attorney as his agent-for-service to avoid the potential conflict of interest.

Who is identified to the tenant?

The names and addresses of the following individuals must be disclosed to all residential tenants:

- the landlord or other individual appointed by the landlord as his agent-for-service;

CHANGE OF OWNER OR PROPERTY MANAGER
Addendum To Rental Or Lease Agreement

DATE:_____, 20_____, at _____, California.

To Tenant: _____

Items left blank or unchecked are not applicable.

FACTS:

1. This is an addendum to the ☐ lease, ☐ rental agreement dated _____,
   at_____, California, entered into by

   1.1 Landlord _____, and

   1.2 Tenant(s)_____

   1.3 recorded on _____, as Instrument No. _____ in
   _____County Records, California,

   1.4 regarding real estate referred to as: _____
   _____

AGREEMENT:

2. This notice is to advise you of a change in ownership or management of the premises you occupy as checked below:

   2.1 ☐ The ownership of the real estate you lease or rent has been transferred.

   2.2 The new property management broker is: _____
   Address: _____
   Phone: _____

   2.3 The new resident manager is: _____
   Address: _____
   Phone: _____

3. Beginning _____, 20_____, your monthly rent due is to be paid by ☐ check, ☐ credit card, ☐ cash, or ☐ cashier's check, made payable to: _____.

   3.1 Rent may be tendered by ☐ mail, or ☐ personal delivery,
   to:

   _____
   (Name)

   _____
   (Address)

   _____

   _____
   (Phone)

   a. Personal delivery of rent will be accepted during the hours of _____ am to _____ pm on the following days: _____

   3.2 Rent may also be paid by deposit into account number _____
   at: _____
   (Financial Institution)

   _____
   (Address)

   _____

   3.3 If rent is to be paid by credit card, the credit card number is _____/_____/_____/_____
   issued by _____ which landlord will charge each month for the rent due.

   3.4 Your current monthly rent is $_____.

   3.5 Your rent has been paid up to and including _____, 20_____.

4. Your security deposit of $_____

   4.1   has been transferred to the new owner.

   4.2   has been transferred to the new property manager.

5. No breach of your lease or rental agreement by Landlord or Tenant currently exists, except: _____

6. Any notices or demands on the owner by Tenant, including service of process, may be served on:

   Name: _____

   Address:_____

   Phone: _____

7. All terms and conditions of your lease and rental agreement remain in effect.

I agree to the terms stated above.	**I agree to the terms stated above.**
Date:_____, 20_____	Date:_____, 20_____
Landlord: _____	Tenant:_____
Agent: _____	Tenant:_____
Signature: _____	Signature: _____
Address: _____	Signature: _____
_____	Address: _____
Phone:_____	_____
Fax: _____	Phone:_____
E-mail: _____	Fax: _____
	E-mail:_____

FORM 554   02-02   ©2007 **first tuesday**, P.O. BOX 20069, RIVERSIDE, CA 92516 (800) 794-0494

- any property managers; and

- any resident managers. [CC §1962(a)]

The addresses given for the manager and agent-for-service must be *street* addresses where legal notices can be **personally** served on the individual. A post office box will not suffice. [CC §1962(a)(1)]

The individual responsible for making the disclosures is:

- the landlord; or

- the individual authorized to enter into rental and lease agreements on behalf of the landlord, such as the property manager or resident manager. [CC §1962(a)]

Delivery of the notice

The names and addresses of the landlord's manager and agent-for-service may be disclosed in:

- the rental and lease agreements entered into with tenants; or

- a notice posted on the property. [CC §§1962(a); 1962.5(a)]

When the disclosure notice is posted, the notice must be posted in two conspicuous places on the property. [CC §1962.5(a)(2)]

If the rental property contains an elevator, the written notice must be posted in:

- every elevator in the building; and

- one other conspicuous place on the property. [CC §1962.5(a)(1)]

An oral residential rental or lease agreement requires a written statement containing the name and address of the manager and agent-for-service to be provided to tenants. [CC §1962(b)]

Change in ownership and management

The landlord, property manager or resident manager responsible for entering into rental and lease agreements must notify all tenants of the name and address for service of a notice or complaint initiated by the tenant and do so within 15 calendar days after any change in:

- the manager(s) of the property;

- the owner(s), unless the new owner appoints an agent-for-service; or

- the landlord's agent-for-service. [CC §1962(c); see Form 554 accompanying this chapter, *ante*]

To disclose a change in ownership or management, the broker or resident manager responsible for leasing should:

- prepare the notice of change of ownership or property management as an addendum to each existing rental or lease agreement and provide it to each tenant to sign and return [See Form 554]; or

- post the property with the name and address of the manager and landlord's agent-for-service.

The notice must also include information regarding how and when rent will be paid.

Failure to give notice

A broker, acting as property manager for a residential landlord, or the landlord's resident manager responsible for leasing, must disclose the name and address of the landlord or agent-for-service.

If the name and address of the landlord or his agent-for-service is not disclosed, then the individual who enters into rental agreements on behalf of the landlord:

- automatically becomes the landlord's agent-for-service of process and agent for receipt of all tenant notices and demands [CC §1962(d)(1)]; and

- will be treated as the landlord and be liable for performing of all obligations described under rental and lease agreements with tenants. [CC §1962(d)(2)]

When the person signing the rental or lease agreement for the landlord fails to make the disclosures, the tenant may have no indication the person signing is not the landlord.

However, the landlord is not relieved of any liability to tenants if the name and address of the owner or agent-for-service is not disclosed. [CC§1962(e)]

Chapter 12

Exclusive authorization to lease

This chapter discusses a broker's right to collect his fee from a nonresidential landlord who employs the broker as his exclusive leasing agent.

Leasing agent's bargain for fees

A nonresidential property is offered for lease by an owner, also called the landlord. A broker makes an appointment with the owner to discuss the possibility of becoming his leasing agent.

During the discussion, the broker explains he can best help lease the property if he is operating under a signed exclusive authorization to lease, also called a *listing*. Under the listing, the broker, on the owner's behalf, will be able to:

- market the space and locate prospective tenants, called *users*, as the owner's sole representative [See Form 110 §1 accompanying this chapter];

- disclose the terms under which a user can actually lease and occupy the space [See Form 110 §10];

- assure other brokers the owner has agreed to pay a fee that can be shared in cooperation with brokers who represent users [See Form 110 §5.2]; and

- conduct negotiations with users and their brokers, and accept deposits with offers to lease the space. [See Form 110 §5.3]

The broker will not be managing the property, only locating prospective tenants and leasing space.

Right to compensation for services

The exclusive authorization listing assures the broker he will receive a fee for his efforts if anyone procures a tenant during the listing period, either on:

- the leasing terms sought in the listing; or

- other terms accepted by the owner.

However, the owner is reluctant to give up his ability to lease the property himself. Further, he would like to avoid employing the broker and paying a brokerage fee.

On the other hand, the owner feels he has a better chance of finding a tenant on acceptable terms in the current market if he is represented by a member of the local brokerage community of leasing agents.

Ultimately, the owner orally agrees to employ the broker. He confirms he will work exclusively with the broker to market the space and locate a user. The owner does not, however, believe it is necessary to have a written agreement — a handshake and his word should do the job.

The broker explains an exclusive authorization must be written and signed by the owner for the broker to be entitled to collect a fee — no signed writing, no services.

Is the broker correct in his analysis?

Yes! A written agreement in writing signed by the client is the only way a broker can protect his right to compensation for services and strengthen his resolve to perform, whether representing a tenant or a landlord.

An oral fee agreement between a broker and his client, be he a tenant or an owner, **without a later writing** signed by the client, is unenforceable by the broker.

Oral fee agreements to lease space are unenforceable even when the broker documents the oral agreement by referencing the fee and terms of payment in written correspondence sent to and acted on by the client. [**Phillippe** v. **Shapell Industries, Inc.** (1987) 43 C3d 1247]

Thus, a broker best protects his right to collect a fee for acting on behalf of an owner by entering into an exclusive authorization, signed by the owner, before performing any services.

Editor's note — If a broker is employed to renegotiate an existing lease (rather than originate one), his employment agreement does not need to be in the form of a signed written agreement. Fees promised a broker for his negotiation of modifications, space expansions, extensions or renewals of existing leases are not required to be written to be enforceable since the lease has already been created. [**Shell** v. **Darnell** (1984) 162 CA3d 957]

Exclusive authorization

An exclusive authorization to lease operates like an exclusive right-to-sell listing agreement.

The leasing agent is employed to "sell the use," a leasehold interest, by **locating a user** for the owner's property, rather than "sell the ownership" by locating a buyer for the property.

The broker owes the same obligations and duties to the owner under an exclusive leasing authorization as he would owe to a seller under an exclusive right-to-sell listing. The primary obligation owed an owner seeking tenants is the broker's duty to use diligence in his effort to continuously and conscientiously market the property and locate qualified tenants.

Conversely, a broker's performance under an open listing requires only his **best efforts**, not constant diligence in the search for a tenant as is required under an exclusive listing.

An open listing sets the leasing agent in competition with the owner and other brokers to be the **first to locate** a tenant and be entitled to collect a fee.

To best secure his time, energy and money invested (and provide incentive) to locate a tenant and lease the premises on behalf of an owner, a leasing agent uses an exclusive authorization to lease form. [See Form 110]

The provision in an exclusive authorization to lease calls for a fee schedule to be prepared and attached. The fee schedule references leasing situations which trigger the earning of formulated fees, such as 5% of the total rents for the first five years and 3% of the total rents for the balance of the lease. The schedule includes fees for extensions, renewals and other continuing leasehold and purchase arrangements which might be entered into in the future by the tenant and the owner. [See **first tuesday** Form 113]

The fee amount established in the fee schedule is **earned and due** on the occurrence of any one of the following events:

- an exclusive *right-to-collect* clause assures payment of the agreed-to fee if the broker, another broker, the owner or anyone else procures a tenant on the terms stated in the listing or on any other terms accepted by the owner [See Form 110 §4.1a];

- an *early-termination option* assures payment of the fee should the owner withdraw the property from the rental market during the listing period [See Form 110 §4.1b];

- a *termination-of-agency* clause assures payment of the fee if the owner cancels the employment without cause before it expires under the listing [See Form 110 §4.1c]; and

EXCLUSIVE AUTHORIZATION TO LEASE PROPERTY

DATE:_____, 20_____, at _____, California.

Items left blank or unchecked are not applicable.

1. RETAINER PERIOD:

1.1 Landlord hereby retains and grants to Broker the exclusive and irrevocable right to solicit prospective tenants and negotiate for the lease of the property for the period:
beginning on _____, 20_____ and terminating on _____, 20_____.

1.2 Broker to use diligence in the performance of this agreement.

2. ADDENDUMS to this agreement:

a. ☐ Title Report, or ☐ Title Policy

b. ☐ Work Authorization [**first tuesday** Form 108] (Also see §3.1b)

c. ☐ Property Operating Data [**ft** Form 562]

d. ☐ Agency Law Disclosure Addendum [**ft** Form 305]
(Mandated for one-to-four residential units if lease exceeds one year.)

e. ☐ Lead-based Paint Disclosure [**ft** Form 557]
(Mandated for one-to-four residential units constructed before 1978.)

f. ☐ _____

g. ☐ _____

h. ☐ _____

3. LANDLORD'S DEPOSIT:

3.1 Landlord hands $_____ to Broker for deposit into Broker's trust account for application to obligations under this agreement and the following attachments:

a. ☐ Advance Fee Addendum [**ft** Form 106]

b. ☐ Advance Cost Addendum [**ft** Form 107] (Also see §2b)

4. BROKERAGE FEE:

NOTICE: The amount or rate of real estate fees is not fixed by law. They are set by each Broker individually and may be negotiable between the Client and Broker.

4.1 Landlord agrees to pay Broker ☐ see attached fee schedule [**ft** Form 113], or

☐ _____ as compensation for services rendered, IF:

a. Anyone procures a tenant on the terms stated in this agreement, or any other terms acceptable to Landlord, during the period of this agreement.

b. The property is withdrawn from the rental market or made unmarketable by Landlord during the period of this agreement.

c. The Landlord terminates this employment of the Broker during the period of this agreement.

d. Within one year after termination of this agreement, Landlord or his agent commences negotiations which later result in a transaction contemplated by this agreement with a tenant with whom the Broker, or a cooperating broker, negotiated during the period of this agreement. Broker to identify prospective tenants by written notice to the Landlord within 21 days after termination of this agreement. [**ft** Form 122]

4.2 Should this agreement terminate without Landlord becoming obligated to pay Broker a fee, Landlord to pay Broker the sum of $_____ per hour of time accounted for by Broker, not to exceed $_____.

4.3 If Broker procures a tenant who purchases the property during the term of tenant's lease or any modification, extension or renewal of the lease or other continuing occupancy of leased property, Landlord agrees to pay Broker a fee of ☐ see attached fee schedule [**ft** Form 113], or

☐ _____.

5. GENERAL PROVISIONS:

5.1 Broker is authorized to place a For Lease sign on the property and publish and disseminate property information to meet the objectives of this employment.

5.2 Landlord authorizes Broker to cooperate with other agents and divide with them any compensation due.

5.3 Broker is authorized to receive, on behalf of any tenant, an offer and deposit.

5.4 The Landlord's acceptance of any tenant's offer to lease to be contingent on approval of the tenant's creditworthiness and management capabilities.

5.5 In any action to enforce this agreement, the prevailing party shall receive attorney fees.

5.6 This agreement will be governed by California law.

6. REAL ESTATE:

6.1 Type: _____

Address: _____

Described as: _____

_____

_____

_____

_____

_____

Vesting: _____

6.2. Encumbrances of record:

a. A first loan in the amount of $_____ payable $_____ per month until paid, including interest at _____%, ☐ ARM, type _____, impounds being $_____ monthly.

Lender: _____

b. A second loan in the amount of $_____ payable $_____ per month, including interest at _____%, due_____, 20_____.

Lender: _____

c. Other encumbrance, bond, assessment or lien in the amount of $_____.

d. Any defaults: _____

7. PERSONAL PROPERTY INCLUDED:

7.1 Described as: _____

_____

_____

_____

_____

8. CONDITION OF TITLE:

8.1 Landlord's interest in the property is:

☐ Fee simple

☐ Leasehold

☐ _____

8.2 Landlord warrants there are no unsatisfied judgments or actions pending against him, no condemnation/eminent domain proceedings or other actions against the property, and no unrecorded deeds or encumbrances against the property.

9. LEASE TERMS:

9.1 The lease term sought is for a period of _____.

9.2 Occupancy to be available _____, 20_____.

9.3 Initial rent shall be $_____ payable on the _____ day of each month, with annual adjustments based on _____.

9.4 A total deposit of $_____, being $_____ advance rents and $_____ security deposit.

9.5 A late charge of $_____ to be incurred _____ days after the rent is due, plus interest at _____% per annum beginning from the due date for the delinquent rent.

9.6 Tenant to pay for and maintain:

☐ Water

☐ Gas

☐ Electricity

☐ Heat/Air Conditioning

☐ Public liability insurance

☐ Property damage insurance

☐ Plate glass insurance

☐ Other: _____

9.7 Landlord to maintain: _____

_____

9.8 Tenant may not assign, lease or sublet any portion of the property without written consent of the Landlord.

9.9 The lease form sought to be used by Landlord is form #_____ published or drafted by _____.

9.10 Other terms: _____

_____

_____

_____

_____

I agree to render services on the terms stated above.	I agree to employ Broker on the terms stated above.
Date:_____, 20_____	Date:_____, 20_____
Broker:_____	Landlord: _____
By: _____	Signature: _____
Signature: _____	Address: _____
Address: _____	_____
_____	Phone:_____
Phone:_____	Fax: _____
Fax: _____	E-mail:_____
E-mail:_____	

- a *safety clause* assures payment of the fee if, within a year after termination of the exclusive authorization, the owner enters into negotiations resulting in the leasing or selling of the property to a prospective tenant the broker negotiated with during the listing period. [See Form 110 §4.1d]

Ready, willing and able tenant

Now consider a broker who is employed by a landlord under an *exclusive authorization* to lease.

The **authorization** states the landlord will pay the broker a fee if the broker, or anyone else including the landlord, produces a tenant ready, willing and able to lease the property on the same terms specified in the exclusive authorization agreement. [See Form 110 §4.1a]

The broker produces a creditworthy tenant who is financially capable of leasing the premises on the terms set forth in the exclusive authorization agreement. [See Form 110 §10]

The broker prepares and submits the tenant's offer to lease on terms substantially identical to the leasing terms in the authorization, called a full listing offer. [See **first tuesday** Form 556]

The landlord refuses to accept the offer, disclosing to the broker he now wants a higher rental rate.

The broker claims he is entitled to his fee since he produced a tenant who is ready, willing and able to lease the property on the terms stated in the exclusive authorization agreement.

The landlord claims the broker is not entitled to a fee since the property was never leased.

Here, a written fee agreement exists under which the broker only needs to **locate a tenant** ready, willing and able to lease the landlord's property *on the terms listed* for the broker to earn and be entitled to immediate payment of his fee. [**Twogood** v. **Monnette** (1923) 191 C 103]

An exclusive right to collect

Now consider a broker whose **exclusive authorization** to lease contains a fee provision that states he is entitled to a fee if the landlord rents the space during the listing period, called a right-to-collect clause. It is the right-to-collect clause which makes an exclusive listing exclusive. The clause states "a fee is due if anyone procures a tenant." [See Form 110 §4.1a]

The broker, as part of his efforts to locate a tenant, places a "For Lease" sign on the premises. The sign is seen by a prospective tenant.

Without contacting the broker, the prospective tenant contacts the landlord of the premises.

Before the exclusive authorization period expires, the prospective tenant and landlord enter into a lease agreement, though the terms are different from those specified in the broker's exclusive authorization.

Even though the landlord's broker had no contact with the prospective tenant (other than the sign exposure), the broker is earned to his fee. A tenant's offer to lease was accepted by the landlord during the exclusive authorization period.

Further, the broker receives his fee even though the final terms agreed to by the landlord and the tenant differed from the terms of the listing since the tenant's terms were accepted by the landlord during the exclusive authorization period. [**Carlsen** v. **Zane** (1968) 261 CA2d 399]

Early termination by landlord

A typical exclusive authorization agreement contains boilerplate wording in the fee provision stating the landlord will pay the broker the agreed-to fee if the property is:

- withdrawn from the rental market;

- transferred or conveyed;

- leased without the broker's consent; or

- made unrentable by the landlord, called an *early-termination clause*. [See Form 110 §4.1b]

An early-termination clause protects the broker from loss of his time and money spent in a diligent effort to locate a tenant should the landlord's conduct actually or effectively remove the property from the rental market before the listing expires. When the landlord interferes with the objective of the employment of the broker — to produce a ready, willing and able tenant on the terms stated — a fee has been earned and is immediately due.

Consider a broker and a landlord who enter into an exclusive authorization to lease that expires in six months. The agreement contains a fee provision with an **early-termination clause**.

The broker diligently attempts to locate a tenant for the landlord's property.

During the listing period, the landlord notifies the broker the property is no longer for lease. The broker is instructed to stop marketing the property. In compliance with his client's instructions, the broker takes the property off the market.

The broker then makes a demand on the landlord for a full listing fee. The broker claims the early-termination clause in the exclusive listing provides for payment of the broker's fee by the landlord when the landlord withdraws the property from the rental market before the listing period expires.

The landlord claims the broker cannot collect a fee under the early-termination clause since it calls for a lump sum payment on the landlord's breach of the employment agreement, called a *liquidated damages provision*.

Is the broker entitled to his fee on the client's termination of the broker's employment?

Yes! The broker is entitled to his fee since the early-termination clause gives the landlord the **option to cancel** the exclusive authorization agreement in exchange for paying the broker a fee instead of allowing the listing to expire without interference with the broker's marketing efforts. The landlord exercises the right to cancel by conduct which interferes with the broker's ability to lease the property, such as taking the property off the market.

The landlord does not breach the exclusive authorization to lease when he withdraws the property from the rental market. He merely exercises his option to do so as provided by the early-termination clause. Thus, the amount due is not liquidated damages for a breach. [**Blank v. Borden** (1974) 11 C3d 963]

However, the landlord did ultimately breach the exclusive authorization agreement. The landlord failed to compensate the broker for the fee earned and due when he exercised his option to take the property off the market.

*Editor's note — See **first tuesday** Form 121 for an agreement to cancel an exclusive authorization during the listing period.*

Safety clause covers prospects

A landlord's broker needs to provide protection for his time and effort spent locating a tenant during the listing period when the effort produces results after the listing expires. The inclusion of a safety clause in the fee provisions of an exclusive authorization to lease assures this result. [See Form 110 §4.1d]

The **safety clause** commits the landlord to pay the broker the scheduled fee if, within **one year after** the exclusive authorization expires, the landlord enters into negotiations during the safety clause period (one year) which later result in a lease of the premises to a tenant who was located and exposed to the property by the broker or his agents during the listing period.

Consider a broker and a landlord who enter into an exclusive authorization to lease containing a fee provision with a safety clause.

On expiration of the listing period, the broker, as agreed in the safety clause, supplies the landlord with the **names of tenants** he has had contact with and who **received information** regarding the property, an activity called *negotiations* even though no proposal or offer is submitted by the prospective tenant.

Thus, the name of each prospective tenant contacted by the broker or a cooperating broker, who was provided with information about the property, is "registered" with the landlord. [See **first tuesday** Form 122]

After the listing expires, the landlord employs a second broker without discussing the terms of the prior listing.

Within the one-year period after expiration of the first broker's authorization, the second broker arranges a lease of the premises to a tenant registered by the first broker, but without the first broker's participation in negotiations or the fee.

Here, the landlord owes the first broker the entire amount of the agreed-to fee even though the property was leased while listed exclusively with another broker.

The exclusive authorization entered into by the landlord and the first broker promised the first broker his fee if, within one year after expiration of the listing, the landlord **enters into negotiations** which result in a lease with a prospective tenant located and registered by the first broker. [**Leonard** v. **Fallas** (1959) 51 C2d 649]

As a "safety net" for brokerage services rendered, the clause discourages the landlord from attempting to avoid payment of the broker's fee by:

- waiting until the exclusive authorization agreement expires and then directly or indirectly approaching a prospective tenant located and solicited by the broker; or

---

Residential agency disclosures

Before a landlord enters into an exclusive authorization to lease residential property, a property manager or leasing agent is required to hand a landlord a Rules-of-Agency Disclosure if:

- the lease will be for a term of more than one year; and

- the premises is a one-to-four unit residential property or a mobilehome. [Calif. Civil Code §2079.13(j)]

The rules-of-agency should be disclosed by attaching an Agency Disclosure Addendum to the exclusive authorization. [See **first tuesday** Form 305]

If the broker fails to make the rules-of-agency disclosure prior to signing the exclusive authorization:

- the fee agreement is unenforceable; and

- the broker is not entitled to a fee even if agency disclosures are made later with the offer to lease or in the lease. [**Huijers** v. **DeMarrais** (1992) 11 CA4th 676]

- making special fee arrangements with another broker which re-ignite negotiations with a prospective tenant located and exposed to the property by the broker.

Contingency fees

Offer-to-lease forms typically contain a provision stating the broker's fee is payable on the transfer of possession to the tenant, called a *contingency fee clause*. [See Form 556 §15]

Sometimes, the lease agreed to in the offer to lease is never entered into by the landlord and prospective tenant. Without a lease, the agreed-to change of possession triggering payment of the fee earned by the broker does not occur due to a breach of the offer to lease by the landlord. As a result, the earned brokerage fee is not paid. The condition for payment of the fee — occupancy — did not occur.

However, a broker may recover contingency fees contained in offers to lease even when, due to a breach by either the landlord or the tenant, the lease agreed to in the offer is not later entered into and possession is not transferred.

Consider a landlord who accepts an **offer to lease** submitted by a broker on behalf of a prospective tenant. The signed offer to lease contains a fee provision which states the broker's fee is payable by the landlord on change of possession.

Later, the landlord wrongfully refuses to enter into a lease agreement and convey the leasehold estate (occupancy) as agreed in the offer to lease. The broker makes a demand on the landlord for payment of a fee.

The landlord claims the broker is not entitled to receive a fee since the right to possession was never conveyed to the prospective tenant, i.e., the lease agreement contracted for in the offer to lease was never entered into.

Is the broker entitled to his fee?

Yes! The landlord cannot avoid paying the fee the broker has **already earned** by claiming the transfer-of-possession contingency was not satisfied (no lease). Here the **landlord's breach** of the agreement to lease prevented the transfer of occupancy to the tenant. The landlord failed to deliver the lease and possession as agreed to in the offer to lease. Thus, the failure to enter into the lease triggers payment of the fee previously earned when the landlord accepted the tenant's offer to lease.

The contingency fee provision included in the offer to lease merely **designates the time** for payment of a fee which the broker previously earned on locating a tenant or the acceptance of the tenant's offer. The contingency fee provision in the offer does not defeat the broker's right to be compensated simply because the landlord later wrongfully refused to enter into the agreed-to lease. [**Steve Schmidt & Co.** v. **Berry** (1986) 183 CA3d 1299]

The contingency fee provision in an agreement to lease, as in a purchase agreement, shifts the **time for payment** of the fee from the time the fee is earned (and due) under an exclusive authorization agreement to the time a lease is entered into in the agreement to lease.

Also, unless the listing broker approves, the landlord cannot include and enforce a fee provision in the offer to lease that is unacceptable to the broker and contrary to the terms of the fee schedule agreed to by the landlord and the broker in the exclusive authorization agreement.

For instance, the landlord cannot unilaterally insert and enforce a provision in a leasing document for the broker's fee to be paid in installments unless the broker agrees. Under the exclusive authorization or offer to lease, the broker has only agreed to accept payment of his fee in cash at the time an offer or lease is entered into by the landlord. [**Seck** v. **Foulks** (1972) 25 CA3d 556]

Additional fees on extension of lease

Exclusive authorization agreements have fee schedules attached which contain formulas for calculating the brokerage fee earned based on the length of the lease negotiated with the tenant. Further, they usually state the broker will receive an **additional fee** for any extension, renewal or modification of the tenant's occupancy under the original lease. [See **first tuesday** Form 113]

For example, a broker operating under the authority of a written listing procures a tenant who signs a ten-year lease. The broker is paid the fee called for in the listing agreement fee schedule.

The fee schedule also provides for a percentage fee to be paid on any future leasehold arrangements entered into between the landlord and the tenant for **continued occupancy** of the premises on the expiration of the original lease.

On expiration of the original lease, the landlord and tenant negotiate a new lease for the tenant's **continuing occupancy and use** of the premises. A brokerage fee is not paid for the tenant's continued occupancy.

The broker makes a demand for an additional fee under the original listing agreement claiming the new lease, which he did not negotiate, earned him a fee.

The landlord claims he does not owe the broker a fee since the new lease is a separate agreement, not an extension, renewal or modification of the original lease.

However, the landlord must pay the broker the additional fee agreed to in the original listing based on a percentage of the total rent due under the new lease since the new lease constitutes a renewal of the original lease.

Here, the tenant located by the broker **continued in possession and use** of the premises on expiration of the original lease. The listing agreement stated the broker was to be paid a fee on this event. The form of documentation (new lease agreement) was used to permit the continued occupancy of the premises is of no importance. [**John B. Kilroy Company** v. **Douglas Furniture of California, Inc.** (1993) 21 CA4th 26]

Chapter 13

Exclusive authorization to locate space

This chapter explains the benefits enjoyed by a broker and a prospective nonresidential tenant when the tenant employs the broker to locate space under an exclusive authorization listing.

A broker and his nonresidential tenant

An owner of a nonresidential property holds an open house attended by brokers who are leasing agents to encourage them to locate tenants for his vacant space.

Leasing agents who are in attendance and representing tenants are handed the owner's brochure on available space. The information includes a schedule of brokerage fees the owner will pay if a broker procures a tenant for the property, called a *user*. The informational handout also includes a tenant registration form.

One of the brokers who received a brochure inspects the property with a prospective tenant.

The broker completes the tenant registration form which identifies the broker and the prospective tenant. The registration form does not reference the fee schedule or any amount payable to the broker as a fee.

The registration form is handed to the owner, or the owner's employee, who signs it and returns a copy to the broker.

Later, the broker prepares an **offer to lease**, which is signed by the tenant and submitted to the landlord. The offer to lease form contains a provision stating the tenant will pay the brokerage fee in the event the landlord does not agree to pay the broker a fee. [See Form 556 §15]

The offer to lease is not accepted by the landlord. The landlord does not make a counteroffer. However, without contacting the broker, the landlord and the tenant engage directly in lease negotiations. Later, they enter into a lease which does not provide for a fee to be paid to the broker. In the lease, the landlord agrees to be responsible for payment of any brokerage fee due as a result of the lease, called a *hold harmless provision*.

On discovering the tenant's occupancy, the broker seeks payment of his fee from the tenant, not the landlord. The broker claims the tenant breached the brokerage fee provision in his offer to lease by failing to provide for payment of the fee he earned when the tenant leased the property.

The tenant claims he is not liable for payment of the brokerage fee since the landlord agreed to pay the brokerage fee under the hold harmless provision in the lease.

Can the broker recover his fee from the tenant?

Yes! The offer to lease **signed by the tenant** contains a fee provision which states the broker will receive compensation for his efforts if the tenant leases the premises.

Thus, the broker is able to enforce collection of a fee from the tenant. The tenant signed an offer regarding the leasing of the property. The offer contained a **brokerage fee provision** calling for the broker to be paid a fee. The buyer breached that fee provision in the offer, and in doing so incurred liability for the fee. [**Rader Company** v. **Stone** (1986) 178 CA3d 10]

Conversely, a broker who does not have an agreement signed by a tenant containing provisions for the payment of a fee if the tenant leases property — such as a tenant listing agreement or offer to lease — is unable to enforce collection of a fee from the tenant. An oral agreement to pay a brokerage fee is unenforceable against the client making the oral promise. [**Phillippe** v. **Shapell Industries, Inc.** (1987) 43 C3d 1247]

Written fee agreements

A leasing agent has the opportunity to enter into a written fee agreement signed by either the tenant or the landlord on at least four occasions during lease negotiations:

1. When the leasing agent solicits a **nonresidential landlord** for authorization to represent the landlord as his leasing agent to locate users and negotiate a lease agreement acceptable to the landlord, called an *exclusive authorization to lease*. [See **first tuesday** Form 110; see Chapter 12]

2. When the leasing agent solicits (or is solicited by) a **nonresidential tenant** for authorization to act as the tenant's leasing agent to locate suitable space and negotiate a lease agreement acceptable to the tenant, called an *exclusive authorization to locate space*. [See Form 111 accompanying this chapter]

3. When the leasing agent prepares a **tenant's offer to lease** by including a brokerage fee provision in the offer.

4. When the leasing agent prepares the **lease agreement** by including a fee provision.

These opportunities are listed in the order of a leasing agent's declining ability to negotiate.

The employment agreement

A broker approached by a prospective tenant to locate space should ask for and enter into an **employment agreement** with the tenant before analyzing the tenant's needs, locating space or exposing the tenant to available space not listed with the broker. [See Form 111]

The exclusive authorization assures the broker he will be paid for his time and effort spent locating and investigating available space if the tenant ultimately leases space of the type and in the area noted in the authorization. Through the exclusive authorization, the tenant commits himself to work with the broker to accomplish the objective of the employment — to rent space.

The exclusive authorization form is similar in structure and purpose to a buyer's listing agreement and includes:

- the term of the retainer period;

- the formulation for calculating the broker's compensation [See **first tuesday** Form 113];

- a description of the type and location of space or property sought by the tenant; and

- identification of the broker as the agent and the tenant as the client.

The description of the property in the exclusive authorization specifies the space requirements, location, rental range, terms and other property conditions sought by the tenant.

Based on the fee provisions in an exclusive authorization to locate space, the broker has earned a fee if the tenant enters into a lease agreement for space similar to the space sought under the exclusive authorization. The fee is collectible no matter who — the tenant's broker, another broker or the tenant himself — negotiates the lease agreement, due to the *exclusive clause* in the lease agreement. [See Form 111 §5.1a]

Also, a fee provision containing a *safety clause* allows the broker to collect a fee if property located by the broker and disclosed to the tenant during the retainer period is later leased by the tenant in negotiations commenced during the one-year period after the exclusive authorization expires.

EXCLUSIVE AUTHORIZATION TO LOCATE SPACE

DATE:_____, 20_____, at _____, California.

Items left blank or unchecked are not applicable.

1. RETAINER PERIOD:

1.1 Tenant hereby retains and grants to Broker the exclusive right to locate space of the type described below and to negotiate terms and conditions for its rental acceptable to the Tenant, for a retainer period beginning on _____, 20_____, and terminating on _____, 20_____.

2. BROKER'S OBLIGATIONS:

2.1 Broker to use diligence in the performance of this employment.

2.2 ☐ Attached is the Agency Law Addendum. [**first tuesday** Form 305]

3. TENANT'S DEPOSIT:

3.1 Tenant hands $_____ to Broker for deposit into Broker's trust account for application to Tenant's obligations under this agreement and the following attachments:

    a. ☐ Advance Fee Addendum [**ft** Form 106]

    b. ☐ Advance Cost Addendum [**ft** Form 107]

4. GENERAL PROVISIONS:

4.1 In any action to enforce this agreement, the prevailing party shall receive attorney fees.

4.2 Tenant authorizes Broker to cooperate with other agents and divide with them any compensation due.

4.3 This agreement will be governed by California law.

5. BROKERAGE FEE:

NOTICE: The amount or rate of real estate commissions is not fixed by law. They are set by each broker individually and may be negotiable between the Tenant and the Broker.

5.1 Tenant agrees to pay Broker ☐ see attached fee schedule [**ft** Form 113], or ☐ _____ _____ of the rental price of the space located, IF:

    a. Tenant, or any person acting on Tenant's behalf, leases space located during the retainer period.

    b. Tenant terminates this employment of the Broker during the retainer period.

    c. Within one year after termination of this agreement, Tenant or his agent commences negotiations which later result in a transaction contemplated by this agreement with a landlord with whom the Broker, directly or indirectly, negotiated during the period of this agreement. Broker to identify prospective properties by written notice to Tenant within 21 days after termination of this agreement. [**ft** Form 123]

5.2 Should this agreement terminate without Tenant becoming obligated to pay Broker a fee, Tenant to pay Broker the sum of $_____ per hour of time accounted for by Broker, not to exceed $_____.

5.3 Should the Landlord of space leased to Tenant agree to pay a fee acceptable to the Broker, Tenant's obligation to pay a brokerage fee will be satisfied.

TYPE OF SPACE SOUGHT:

GENERAL DESCRIPTION:_____

SIZE: _____

LOCATION: _____

RENTAL AMOUNT AND TERMS: _____

_____

_____

I agree to render services on the terms stated above.	**I agree to employ Broker on the terms stated above.**
Date:_____, 20_____	Date:_____, 20_____
Tenant's Broker: _____	Tenant:_____
By: _____	Signature: _____
Address: _____	Address: _____
_____	_____
Phone:_____ Fax:_____	Phone:_____ Fax:_____
E-mail: _____	E-mail: _____

FORM 111   10-00   ©2007 **first tuesday**, P.O. BOX 20069, RIVERSIDE, CA 92516 (800) 794-0494

If the tenant decides not to lease space during the exclusive authorization period, the fee provision is structured so the broker can include payment of a fee on an hourly basis for the time spent locating rental property, called a *consultation fee*.

Benefits of exclusive authorization

An exclusive authorization to locate space is mutually beneficial to a prospective tenant and a broker since it commits a nonresidential tenant and broker to work together to accomplish a single objective — the leasing of space.

Typically, an unrepresented tenant is at the mercy of the leasing agent employed by the owner. Agents employed by owners owe the employing owner an **agency duty** to use diligence in seeking the most qualified tenant and negotiating terms for a lease most favorable to the landlords.

Conversely, only a **general duty** is owed to a non-client tenant to avoid misleading the tenant when making disclosures by including all material facts about the property, without explanation, which might adversely affect its rental value.

The exclusive authorization to locate space is an *employment agreement*. It imposes on the broker an agency duty to use diligence in locating suitable space and negotiating the best leasing terms available for the tenant in exchange for a fee — even though the fee may be paid by the owner.

The prospective tenant who exclusively authorizes a competent broker to locate space is saving time and money since he has retained a professional advisor to conduct the search and handle negotiations to lease property on his behalf.

With property information readily available, the tenant's broker will be able to locate qualifying properties for review with the tenant.

However, a the tenant who works directly with an owner's broker will initially (and properly) only be shown space the broker has been employed by the owner to lease.

In a rising market, owners have superior negotiating power. Thus, it is in the tenant's best interest to employ a broker as his exclusive representative.

Curiously, when the market allows owners to control negotiations in real estate transactions and when prospective tenants and buyers most need representation, brokers tend to avoid entering into employment agreements with prospective tenants and buyers. It seems to be easier, during periods of rapidly rising prices and rents, to list property and wait for the inevitable user to contact the owner's broker, instead of the reverse activity of locating property on behalf of a prospective tenant or buyer.

However, in a falling market, when tenants and buyers have more negotiating power than owners due to the increasing availability of space and properties, brokers are prevented from easily obtaining written employment agreements from prospective tenants than during periods of short supply of space.

Also, when the market position of owners weakens, owners become more flexible in lease negotiations and are more apt to employ brokers to locate tenants and fill vacant space, particularly builders and developers.

Interference with economic advantage

Consider a nonresidential landlord who **orally promises** a broker he will pay a fee if the broker locates a prospective tenant who leases space. A prospective tenant is located by the broker. The tenant is orally advised by the broker that the landlord has agreed to and will pay his fee.

The tenant, after seeing the property and before signing an offer, contacts the landlord directly to negotiate a lease. Ultimately, the tenant and

Residential agency rules and confirmation of representation

A broker acting on behalf of a residential tenant is required to provide both the tenant and the landlord with a Rules-of-Agency Disclosure if:

- the lease will be for a term of more than one year; and

- the premises is a one-to-four unit residential property or a mobilehome. [Calif. Civil Code §§2079.13(j), 2079.14]

The rules-of-agency form is to be handed to the tenant prior to the tenant's signing of an offer to lease for more than one year by attaching a Rules-of-Agency Disclosure to an offer to lease residential property. [CC § 2079.14(d); see **first tuesday** Form 305]

If the tenant's broker did not prepare the offer to lease himself, the broker should provide the tenant with the rules-of-agency no later than the next business day after the tenant hands him the signed offer to lease. [CC §2079.14(d)]

The landlord is to be provided with the rules-of-agency when the prospective tenant's offer to lease is presented. [CC §2079.14(b)]

If a residential landlord's broker fails to deliver the Rules-of-Agency Disclosure prior to or concurrent with signing the exclusive authorization to lease for more than one year:

- the authorization is unenforceable; and

- the broker is not entitled to a fee. [**Huijers** v. **DeMarrais** (1992) 11 CA4th 676]

Further, when a tenant signs an offer to lease a residence for a period exceeding one year, the broker must provide the tenant with an Agency Confirmation Statement. [See **first tuesday** Form 306]

The Agency Confirmation Statement discloses any agency relationships the broker may have with the landlord or the prospective tenant, disclosing whether the agency is exclusive, dual or nonexistent.

landlord enter into a lease agreement. The documentation does not contain provisions for a brokerage fee.

Here, the broker cannot enforce collection of his fee from the landlord who orally promised to pay.

Thus, the broker makes a demand on the tenant for the brokerage fee claiming the tenant knew about the landlord's oral promise to pay him and interfered.

The tenant claims the broker is not entitled to recover anything from him since a written fee agreement does not exist to evidence the fee agreement with the landlord.

Is the tenant liable for payment of the broker's fee which was known by the tenant to be orally agreed to by the landlord?

Yes! The tenant is liable for the brokerage fee the landlord promised to pay since the tenant:

- was actually aware the landlord had promised to pay the broker a fee if the broker located a tenant; and

- excluded the broker from lease negotiations with the intent of avoiding payment of the fee. [**Buckaloo** v. **Johnson** (1975) 14 C3d 815]

When a tenant (successfully) induces a landlord not to pay the brokerage fee agreed to by the landlord, the tenant becomes liable for the fee the landlord promised to pay the broker whether or not the employment agreement between the broker and the landlord is **oral or written**. The broker does not pursue the person who orally agreed to pay the fee. [**Della Penna** v. **Toyota Motor Sales, U.S.A., Inc.** (1995) 11 C4th 376]

Understanding dual agency

Now consider a broker engaged in locating space for a prospective tenant. The broker does not ask for and is not employed under an exclusive authorization to locate space. The broker extends his search to space that he does not have listed.

The broker locates space acceptable to the tenant. However, it is space the owner does not have listed with a broker.

To assure payment of a fee, the broker enters into a so called "one-time" or "one-party" listing agreement with the owner.

The broker does not advise the owner about his agency relationship with the prospective tenant, which was established due to his efforts to locate suitable space on behalf of the tenant.

On listing the property, the broker presents the owner with the tenant's signed offer or letter of intent (LOI) to lease. The owner rejects the offer or LOI by making a counteroffer. Again, no disclosure or *confirmation* of the agency relationship with the tenant is made to the owner.

Negotiations conducted by the broker between the tenant and the owner ultimately result in an agreement to lease. The agreement contains a provision stating the brokerage fee will be paid by the owner.

The owner then discovers the broker was also acting as an agent on behalf of the tenant, a dual agency relationship which was not disclosed to the owner when he was induced to employ the broker under the listing. The owner refuses to pay the broker his fee.

The broker makes a demand on the owner for payment of the agreed-to fee claiming he acted as the exclusive agent of the tenant at all times and undertook no agency duty to act on behalf of the owner by entering into the "one-party" listing required to collect a fee.

The owner claims the broker is not entitled to his fee since the broker failed to disclose he was representing both parties as a *dual agent*.

Can the broker enforce collection of his fee?

No! The broker is not entitled to a fee. He was an **undisclosed dual agent** in the transaction.

The broker became the **tenant's agent** when he undertook, by an oral agreement, the task of locating and submitting all available space to the tenant, including space not listed with the broker, which might be suitable for the tenant.

On entering into the listing agreement with the owner, the broker also became employed as the **owner's agent**. The result was a conflicting employment, i.e., control over the negotiations on behalf of both parties, which imposed a duty to disclose the resulting dual agency to both the owner and tenant. [**L. Byron Culver & Associates** v. **Jaoudi Industrial & Trading Corporation** (1991) 1 CA4th 300]

To avoid losing the right to collect a fee on the transaction, the broker should have asked the tenant, rather than the owner, to enter into a written employment agreement before undertaking the agency duty of locating space on behalf of the tenant.

Thus, an agency relationship with the owner would not have arisen had the tenant's offer to lease been submitted without first entering into a listing with the owner. The owner may agree to pay the fee in an LOI, offer to lease or the lease agreement without ever employing the broker as his agent. Thus, the issue of a dual agency does not arise.

No written authorization from tenant

Now consider a broker who represents a tenant without the tenant's written authorization. The broker locates space and prepares an LOI or an offer to lease. The space is listed with another broker.

Here, the broker should first enter into a written or oral *cooperative fee-splitting agreement* with the owner's broker. [See **first tuesday** Form 105]

A cooperative fee-splitting agreement assures the broker he will receive a fee on any lease his tenant may enter into for the space listed with the other broker. **Oral agreements** between brokers to share fees are enforceable. [**Century 21 Butler Realty, Inc.** v. **Vasquez** (1995) 41 CA4th 888]

Brokers all too often undertake the agency duty to locate space on behalf of a nonresidential tenant without first asking for and obtaining a written authorization granting the broker the right to represent the prospective tenant.

However, without a signed, written authorization to act as the agent for a prospective tenant, the broker has no assurance he will be paid by the owner or the tenant for his services rendered on behalf of the tenant until either the tenant or the owner signs a document calling for someone to pay his fee.

Chapter 14

Cost of operating in leased space

This chapter analyzes the leasing agent's use of a property's operating costs data as a disclosure to assist prospective tenants in the selection of suitable space.

Disclosures by leasing agents

The availability of a property's data and the advice brokers give to assist prospective tenants, also called *users*, who are making decisions about leasing property, has increased dramatically since these data are now more readily accessible on inquiry.

As a result, consumer expectations when leasing property have risen. Unlike other industries, competition among brokers for clientele has not been the primary force behind rising consumer expectations.

Industry-wide, consumers have taken hits for failure to receive property information. This failure has prompted the legislature to take action pressuring brokers into making more disclosures of known and knowable facts about a property which adversely affect its value. Brokers are charged with knowing readily available features comprising the property they are marketing. [**Jue** v. **Smiser** (1994) 23 CA4th 312]

A greater burden which requires investigation and advice is placed on brokers who represent **users** as opposed to the lesser burden carried by an owner's broker when dealing with perspective tenants. A user's broker must know his client's needs and capacities if the broker is to make better use of his time spent locating space best suited to meet his client's needs and objectives.

Upon locating a qualifying property, disclosures and representations about the property provided by the user's broker must be based on that broker's investigations, not conjecture, unless the representations are credited to another

source and not known or believed in any way to be false by the owner's broker. [**Field** v. **Century 21 Klowden-Forness Realty** (1998) 63 CA4th 18]

As new expectations are placed on brokers by users of real estate, the issue as to whether brokers have a **duty to respond** to the consumer's expectations is judicially resolved. Resolution is based on the agency environment surrounding the gathering and delivery of information to the prospective user, and the degree of availability of the information to brokers.

Also, as the expectations of real estate consumers are reviewed by the courts, the *level of competency* imposed on brokers and the extent to which landlords and brokers must disclose information (and its source) becomes clearer.

As couriers of information and the "gatekeepers" for almost all real estate transactions, brokers are retained by consumers to inform them of relevant conditions surrounding a property.

As for an owner and his broker, their role in marketing space has been reduced to avoiding misleading disclosures. The duty owed to users by the owner's broker to **avoid misleading** a user does not include enlightening prospective users by also advising them about the consequences of the disclosed facts. The advice about the **risks and uncertainty** surrounding the disclosed facts is for the user to seek out so he can make an informed decision when selecting the premises best suited from all available properties.

It is the role and burden of the user's leasing agent, as his duty owed to the user, to ascertain a property's essential facts (or advise the tenant on what they should do to get the facts), and make relevant recommendations to assist the tenant to meet his goals.

The factual information available to brokers about properties and the assistance brokers can offer to users who are leasing space fall into three general categories for analysis:

1. The property's **physical aspects** (square footage, shipping facilities, utilities, HVAC units, tenant improvements, sprinkler system, condition of the structure, soil, geologic hazards, toxic or noise pollution, parking, etc.);

2. The conditions affecting the **use and enjoyment** of the property, i.e., facts available on request from title companies (CC&Rs, trust deeds and vesting), planning departments (uses permitted), redevelopment agencies, business tax rates, police and fire departments (response times), security, natural hazards and conditions of the neighborhood surrounding the location; and

3. The **cost of operating** the leased premises when put to the expected use.

Operating costs disclosed

A property's operating costs are part of the property's signature. Operating costs distinguish the property from other available properties. A property's operating costs are gathered and set forth on the *occupant's cost sheet* which is handed to perspective users to induce them to rent the space. [See Form 562 accompanying this chapter]

Property related expenditures which will be incurred by a user during the leasing period, other than the payment of rent and any tenant debt the tenant secures by the leasehold, fall into two categories:

- recurring operating expenses; and

- nonrecurring deposits or charges.

Users, their leasing agents and property managers **compare the costs** a user will incur to occupy and operate in a particular space against the costs to operate in other available space, a type of *comparative cost analysis*.

The user's cost analysis is even more relevant to negotiations during periods of economic slowdown when vacancy levels increase due to overbuilding or a decline or consolidation in the number of users who traditionally occupying this type of space.

When users search for space without the pressure of high occupancy levels with the attendant scarcity of space experienced during periods of peak economic activity, they are more likely to compare properties based on operating costs or the cost of improvements the owner or tenant will provide, rather than rent alone.

Also, owners renting for less than the competition should be subjected to requests for information and history on the operating costs the user will incur in addition to the rent. The below-market rent may be suspect due to the excessive operating costs or local taxes the tenant will pay, security, requirements, etc.

The nondisclosure of a property's operating costs a user will incur under a net or modified *gross rent* lease agreement leaves the perspective user to speculate on what will be the amount of monthly operating costs (in addition to rent) he will experience.

The nondisclosure of operating costs is more likely to occur during tight rental markets when owners and their brokers are less responsive (or uncooperative) in the release of information to users and their leasing agents.

At the very least, the user's leasing agent has the obligation to **bring the availability** of the data to the user's attention. Then, if the user wants the information, it can be obtained during negotiations or to clear contingencies before taking occupancy. At his best, the user's

OCCUPANT'S OPERATING EXPENSE SHEET
Ongoing Operating Costs

DATE:_____, 20_____, at _____, California.

Occupant (Buyer or Tenant): _____

Property type: _____

Address: _____

Items left blank or unchecked are not applicable.

FACTS:

This cost sheet demonstrates the cash expenditures the Occupant should initially experience while owning or leasing the property.

These amounts are: ☐ figures currently experienced operating the property.

☐ estimates and not amounts confirmed by the owner or former occupant.

OPERATING EXPENSES:

Electricity. . . . . $_____

Gas. . . . . $_____

Water . . . . $_____

Rubbish. . . . . $_____

Sewage and misc. included . . . . $_____

CATV . . . . $_____

Phone . . . . $_____

DSL/T1/Cable modem, etc.. . . . . $_____

Insurance . . . . $_____

Taxes . . . . $_____

General obligation bonds . . . . . . $_____

Lawn/Gardening. . . . . $_____

Pool/Spa . . . . $_____

Janitorial/Maids . . . . $_____

Maintenance and repair . . . . $_____

Common Area Maintenance . . . . $_____

Other_____ $_____

Other:_____ . . $_____

DEPOSITS:

Rental Security Deposit . . . . $_____

Water Deposit . . . . $_____

Sewage and Rubbish Deposit. . . $_____

Gas Service Deposit. . . . . $_____

Phone Service Deposit. . . . . $_____

Other:_____ . . $_____

Other:_____ . . $_____

TOTAL Deposits . . . . **$_____**

Total Operating Expenses . . . . **$_____**

Monthly Loan or Lease Payment . **$_____**

TOTAL Monthly Expenditures. . **$_____**

I have read and approve this information:

Date:_____, 20_____

Seller/
Landlord: _____

Seller/
Landlord: _____

Date Prepared: _____, 20_____

Broker:_____

Agent: _____

Phone: _____

Fax: _____

I have read and received a copy of this estimate.

Date: _____, 20_____

Occupant's Signature: _____

Occupant's Signature: _____

FORM 562   10-00   ©2007 **first tuesday**, P.O. BOX 20069, RIVERSIDE, CA 92516 (800) 794-0494

leasing agent not only advises, but investigates and reports to his client on the data he collects, and provides analysis and recommendation.

The owner either knows, or can easily obtain from his property manager, the actual costs of operating his property for the intended use. Thus, property's operating data is readily available to the owner. If the owner or the owner's broker refuses to supply the data to the user, the user's broker can research the history of expenses the prior users have experienced.

Leases on nonresidential properties often include charges for common area maintenance (CAMs) — expenses incurred by the owner and paid by the user as additional rent to the base rent, adjustments and percentages. The prospective user and his agent should insist on the seller providing an operating cost sheet estimating the monthly charge for the user's share of the CAMs he would incur in this space.

Since information about the amount of CAMs paid by the prior occupant of the space might affect the user's negotiations and rental commitment, it is a *material fact* essential to the user's decision-making process. During a tight leasing market with reduced availability of unoccupied space, owners increase their net income by adding fixed amounts of CAM charges instead of directly raising rents. Thus, they fractionalize the rent to distract the prospective user from what initially appears to be the rent.

A broker has a duty to disclose all conditions or aspects of a property which might affect a user's decision to lease, called *material facts*. [**Ford** v. **Cournale** (1973) 36 CA3d 172]

Accurate estimates by brokers

Disclosing the costs the user will incur while occupying and operating the property imposes on the user's broker a duty to disclose the actual costs which have been incurred in the space. If not available and estimates are prepared and provided by the user's broker, they must be reasonably accurate and state they are estimates — they cannot be guesstimates.

Also, the user's broker must **identify the source** of the data provided to the user and the reliability of the source as known to the broker. If a need exists for confirmation of the data due to questionable or unknown reliability, the offer to lease needs to include a further-approval contingency. The contingency provision allows the user time to check out and confirm his expectations brought about by the disclosure or cancel the offer for their failure to be verified. [Ford, *supra*]

The proper brokerage activity for disclosing the operating costs and deposits incurred to occupy and operate leased space include:

- the preparation of an operating cost sheet by the owner (or property manager) of each available space, with or without the assistance of a leasing agent, which is **signed** by the owner;

- a comparison by the user and the user's broker of the costs to operate in this space against the cost of operating in other space; and

- a review of the economic (cost) impact of the rent and other operating expenses for this space against operating costs and rent incurred in other qualifying space.

With documentation and a comparative analysis of rent and operating costs completed, the user and the user's broker can intelligently negotiate the best lease arrangements for the user.

Occasionally, a property owner may want to be "tight-lipped" about the operating data due to various different arrangements with numerous tenants. Thus, the owner (or his broker) will insist a **confidentiality agreement** be entered into by the prospective tenant before any data is released.

Chapter 15

Tenant profiles

This chapter details a tenant's needs and desires to be considered by a broker when locating space for the tenant.

Get the negotiations rolling

A broker negotiating a nonresidential lease on behalf of a client needs to possess a high level of knowledge and expertise regarding the aspects of leasing, including:

- the economic and financial attributes of lease agreements;

- the legal consequences of each document affecting the right to possession, called the *lease*; and

- the tax implications of the lease transaction.

These aspects of leasing arrangements are separate but in addition to the physical condition or operating costs a tenant incurs.

The level of the broker's **technical expertise** sets his ability to ascertain the needs and requirements of a client to attain the client's objectives, whether the client is a landlord or a tenant. On comprehension of the objectives, the broker can either locate a suitable tenant, called a *user*, or property, called *space* or *premises*, and begin lease negotiations.

Most nonresidential tenants are completely consumed by their business. They usually do not have sufficient time to devote to the decisions to be made in real estate leasing transactions. Further, the amount of rent a tenant pays for space is generally between 1.5% and 4% of their gross revenue, with the exception of high-traffic retail locations.

Most landlords are concerned primarily with efforts to get vacant space rented. Consequently, landlords and tenants rely on brokers as their leasing agents to put the lease package together, consisting of property data and lease documents.

The final lease agreement negotiated by a leasing agent will be the result of:

- the relative bargaining strength of the landlord and tenant in the current market conditions;

- the time the landlord and tenant are willing to devote and the urgency given to negotiating the leasing details;

- the expertise exercised and attention given to details by their respective leasing agents; and

- local market conditions affecting demand for the property and rent amounts.

The broker typically gets the negotiations started with a an offer or letter of intent (LOI). Once negotiations are underway, the broker's advice helps shape the final terms. The broker generally drafts the LOI, the lease agreements and closes the transaction. Landlords with larger leasing operations often prepare their own documents "in house," or retain legal counsel to do so.

A leasing agent best determines the **tenant's intentions** for leasing property by preparing:

- a *tenant lease worksheet* to assess the tenant's space requirements and, with financial statements, the financial condition of the tenant's business [See Form 555 accompanying this chapter]; and

- an *offer to lease* to commit the tenant so an acceptance by the landlord will bring about an enforceable contract set by the terms of a lease agreement. [See **first tuesday** Form 556]

A LOI will probably precede the tenant's actual offer in an effort to "feel out" the landlord.

List the tenant

With or without a written retainer agreement with a tenant, the leasing agent who undertakes the task of locating space for the tenant assumes **agency obligations** to act on behalf of, and in the best interest of, the tenant.

However, without a written agreement, the prospective tenant is not obligated to the leasing agent (broker) to pay, or see to it he is paid, a brokerage fee. [**Phillippe** v. **Shapell Industries, Inc.** (1987) 43 C3d 1247]

Thus, the prudent leasing agent only undertakes the duty to represent a tenant when the tenant enters into and signs an exclusive authorization to locate space. [See **first tuesday** Form 111]

Under a tenant's exclusive authorization to locate space, the broker is formally retained as the tenant's representative. Thus, the broker will be paid a leasing fee, either by the landlord or the tenant, if the tenant enters into a lease for the type of property described in the tenant's exclusive authorization agreement.

Tenant conferences

A leasing agent should investigate and confirm for himself **why the tenant wants to move** if he is to better understand the user's needs.

For example, the tenant's existing space may have become too large or too small for his current or future needs. Alternatively, the tenant may be arguing with his current landlord over:

- the rent, common area maintenance charges (CAMs) or assessments when renewing a lease;

- the tenant's current space requirements that conflict with space provided for under an option to renew or extend; or

- a lease assignment or sublease of a portion of the leased space.

By uncovering the precise reasons for moving, the broker is better able to find a suitable new location and premises, or negotiate a renewal or extension of the tenant's current lease.

When a prospective tenant is starting a new business, the leasing agent must get information on the tenant's **business projections** at the outset. A tenant's new business projections may be overly optimistic. He may want space that is simply too large or in too expensive a location. The tenant may have to settle for incubator space in a less desirable location which accepts "start-up" business tenants. Rent might be paid by the landlord accepting a fractional participation in the ownership of the tenant's business.

Conversely, a tenant may underestimate the potential future growth of his business. The premises he favors may be too small to absorb his growth, frustrating later attempts to expand. The tenant will be forced to relocate again prematurely. Options or the right of first refusal on additional space, or a lease cancellation or buyout provision to vacate the premises, may be the answer.

Also, overprojection of the potential income of a business under a percentage-rent lease will reduce the landlord's projected rental income. Unless the leasing agent considers the space needs and gross income of a user, the leasing agent's long-term service to either the landlord or tenant is limited. Thus, the leasing agent needs to develop a system to match up the right landlord with the right tenant.

TENANT LEASE WORKSHEET

1. GENERAL INFORMATION:
Tenant's name: _____
Business Address: _____
Phone: _____ Fax: _____
E-mail: _____
Type of business: _____

2. Information on space presently occupied by tenant:

2.1 Type of building: ☐ Multi-tenant ☐ Free-standing

2.2 Location: ☐ Good ☐ Poor ☐ Adequate

2.3 Suitability to business: ☐ Good ☐ Poor ☐ Adequate

2.4 Square feet:_____ determined by: _____

2.5 Tenant utility costs:
- a. ☐ Lighting/electrical . . . . $_____
- b. ☐ Gas . . . . $_____
- c. ☐ Water . . . . $_____
- d. ☐ Other:_____ . . . . . $_____

    Total . . . . $_____

2.6. Tenant operating costs:
- a. ☐ CAMs . . . . $_____
- b. ☐ Casualty insurance . . . . $_____
- c. ☐ Use fees . . . . $_____
- d. ☐ Real property taxes . . . . $_____
- e. ☐ Maintenance . . . . $_____
- f. ☐ Assessments . . . . $_____
- g. ☐ Property management . . . . $_____
- h. ☐ Janitorial services . . . . $_____
- i. ☐ Parking . . . . $_____
- j. ☐ Fire insurance . . . . $_____
- k. ☐ Other:_____ . . . . . . $_____
- l. ☐ Other:_____ . . . . . . $_____

    Total . . . . $_____

2.7 Rooms/offices:
- ☐ Offices . . . . _____
- ☐ Reception area . . . . _____
- ☐ Storage rooms . . . . _____
- ☐ Kitchen . . . . _____
- ☐ Conference rooms . . . . _____
- ☐ Lab/R&D rooms . . . . _____
- ☐ Rest rooms . . . . _____
- ☐ Dressing rooms . . . . _____
- ☐ Computer rooms . . . . _____
- ☐ Hallways . . . . _____
- ☐ Lunch room . . . . _____
- ☐ Other _____

2.8 Tenant improvements and trade fixtures: _____
_____

3. Information on space sought by tenant:

3.1 Type of building: ☐ Multi-tenant ☐ Free-standing

3.2 Location preference: ☐ Downtown ☐ Suburbs ☐ Rural

City: _____ County: _____

3.3 Access needed:

☐ Residential	☐ Legal/civic centers	☐ Shopping centers
☐ Agricultural	☐ Hotels	☐ Restaurants
☐ Industrial	☐ Libraries	☐ Redevelopment areas
☐ Mountain areas	☐ Universities/colleges	☐ Government-state
☐ Freeways	☐ Financial services	☐ Government-federal
☐ Public transit	☐ Warehouses	☐ Publishing houses
☐ Parking	☐ Office centers	☐ Manufacturing centers
☐ Airports	☐ Convention centers	☐ Disposal facilities
☐ Coastal	☐ Sports facilities	☐ Trains
☐ Shipyards	☐ Near competition	☐ Other
☐ Trucking	☐ Medical/hospital	

3.4 Space needs:

a. Square feet: _____

b. Rooms/offices:

☐ Offices	_____	☐ Storage rooms	_____
☐ Conference rooms	_____	☐ Rest rooms	_____
☐ Computer rooms	_____	☐ Lunch rooms	_____
☐ Reception area	_____	☐ Kitchen	_____
☐ Lab/R&D rooms	_____	☐ Dressing rooms	_____
☐ Hallways	_____	☐ Other	_____

3.5 Physical plant needs:

☐ Signs	_____	☐ Ceilings	_____
☐ Stairwells	_____	☐ Walls	_____
☐ Finishing	_____	☐ Floors	_____
☐ Partitions	_____	☐ Painting	_____
☐ Carpeting	_____	☐ Ramps/parking	_____

3.6 Utility needs:

☐ Lighting/electrical	_____	☐ Computer	_____
☐ Water	_____	☐ Gas	_____

4. Tenant business goals:

4.1 Short term (3-5 years):

_____

_____

_____

_____

4.2 Long term (5-10 years):

_____

_____

_____

_____

5. Lease terms on space now occupied by tenant:

5.1 Type: ☐ Office ☐ Shopping center ☐ Retail

☐ Industrial ☐ Light business

5.2 Term: _____ Expiration date: _____/_____/_____

5.3   Base rent $_____ payable_____

5.4   Current rent $_____ payable _____

5.5   Rent based on: ☐ Per sq. ft.   ☐ Percent gross sales

5.6   Rental adjustments based on: ☐ CPI   ☐ Other index

                             ☐ Graduated   ☐ Fixed   ☐ Reappraisal

5.7   Security deposit:. . . . . $_____

5.8   Prepaid rent: . . . . $_____

5.9   Options to renew/extend: ☐ Yes   ☐ No

5.10 Option to buy: ☐ Yes   ☐ No

5.11 Option to lease additional space: ☐ Yes   ☐ No

5.12 Lease assignment: ☐ Freely   ☐ Landlord consent

5.13 Other terms: _____

5.14 Landlord's name:_____

         Business address:_____

         Phone:_____ Fax:_____

         Agent's name: _____

         Phone:_____ Fax:_____

6. Lease terms sought:

6.1   Desired monthly base rent: $_____

6.2   Rent based on: ☐ Per sq. ft.   ☐ Percent gross sales

6.3   Rental adjustments based on:

                             ☐ CPI   ☐ Other index

                             ☐ Graduated   ☐ Fixed   ☐ Reappraisal

6.4   Landlord responsibility for utilities:

                             ☐ Lighting/electrical   ☐ Gas

                             ☐ Water   ☐ Other

6.5   Landlord responsibility for operating costs:

                             ☐ Maintenance   ☐ Insurance

                             ☐ Property mgmt. ☐ Parking

                             ☐ Use fees   ☐ Janitorial

                             ☐ Taxes   ☐ Other

6.6   Common area maintenance provision cap:

                             ☐ _____ per sq. ft.   ☐ _____% per year

6.7   Security deposit: . . . . $_____

6.8   Prepaid rents: . . . . $_____

6.9   Options to renew: ☐ Yes   ☐ No

6.10 Option to buy: ☐ Yes   ☐ No

6.11 Option to lease additional space: ☐ Yes   ☐ No

6.12 Lease assignment: ☐ Freely   ☐ Landlord consent

6.13 Miscellaneous information: _____

         _____

         _____

         _____

FORM 555   10-01   ©2007 **first tuesday**, P.O. BOX 20069, RIVERSIDE, CA 92516 (800) 794-0494

Using a tenant lease worksheet

Consider a tenant who runs an insurance agency that has more employees and files than the premises it now occupies will accommodate. The tenant has three agents and a support staff of eight people, including secretaries, an office manager and a full-time computer technician and webmaster.

The tenant expects the business to continue to grow and require a larger space to meet his present and expanding needs.

The tenant contacts a leasing agent to locate a new facility with tenant improvements suitable for his staff to occupy the space. The leasing agent explains he is the leasing agent for a number of landlords in the area and should be able to find suitable space for the tenant. If needed, planners are available to design the use of the space and specify the tenant improvements for occupancy.

The leasing agent prepares a *tenant lease worksheet*. [See **first tuesday** Form 555]

The **worksheet** itself covers three key areas the leasing agent must consider and analyze:

- the tenant's current lease conditions and existing space;

- the tenant's current and future needs for leased space; and

- the tenant's financial condition and creditworthiness.

Regarding the tenant's existing space, the leasing agent will determine:

- the type of building;

- the square footage;

- the monthly operating and utility costs; and

- the tenant improvements and trade fixtures.

A necessary review of the tenant's current lease includes:

- the expiration date;

- monthly rent and period adjustments and assessments;

- the obligation to continue to occupy the premises;

- the obligation to restore the premises or remove fixtures;

- options to extend or renew the lease or buy the premises;

- the tenant's ability to assign or sublease; and

- the amount of the security deposit.

These facts will help the leasing agent determine the tenant's rights and obligations under his present lease. When representing the tenant, the leasing agent must point out and explain, to the best of his ability, his knowledge of the beneficial or detrimental effect any lease provisions have on the tenant.

When representing an owner, the leasing agent will advise him which **terms** the tenant is unhappy with and which lease provisions are "throw away" clauses, designed for negotiations, since they are of little or no concern to the owner and are used as bargaining chips.

Locating new space

Next, the leasing agent ascertains the tenant's needs and goals for the new space.

Regarding the space requirements, the leasing agent will need to uncover the tenant's:

- current square footage needs;

- future square footage needs;

- phone, utilities and computer facility needs;

- heating and air conditioning requirements;

- parking, docking, turn-around and shipping requirements;

- access to freeways, airports and other public transportation;

- access to civic, financial, legal, governmental or other "downtown" facilities;

- response time for police and fire departments;

- access to housing areas; and

- any needs peculiar to the tenant.

Some tenants may focus on specific **geographic locations** in the business market or population centers. Others may need the **lowest rent** possible, regardless of location.

On completing a tenant lease worksheet, the leasing agent discovers the tenant wants to:

- stay in the same community because of his many strong business and social ties to the area;

- keep his rent fixed or have predictable (fixed) annual adjustments over the next three to five years; and

- move closer to the freeway for quick access to customers in outlying areas.

The tenant currently needs 4,000 square feet to accommodate:

- four private offices;

- a computer room;

- a reception area;

- a conference room;

- a storage room;

- restrooms;

- a lunch room; and

- areas for sales staff and secretaries.

Financially, the business is profitable, but the tenant wants to keep rent at a minimum. Additionally, the tenant is concerned future inflation will mount. Thus, he does not want his rent adjustments tied to the Consumer Price Index (CPI). If they must be, then a ceiling needs to be set on any annual rise in the CPI.

Also, the leasing agent might suggest negotiating for an **option to lease** additional space if the tenant's business increases, requiring more space for expansion (and an additional fee for the leasing agent if exercised).

Finally, the leasing agent and the tenant need to discuss the rental terms available in the leasing market. Several provisions in leases have a financial impact, favorable or not, on the landlord and the tenant. **Financial provisions** in a lease agreement include:

- base monthly rent;

- periodic rental adjustments (CPI, percentage or rollover);

- responsibility for maintenance expenses (CAMs);

- assessments of real estate taxes and insurance premiums;

- government ordered retrofitting;

- structural, roofing and HVAC maintenance;

- lease assignability and subletting authority;

- options to renew or extend, or to buy;

- personal guarantees or letters of credit; and

- tenant improvements.

Chapter 16

Offers to lease

This chapter discusses the importance of written negotiations when entering into a nonresidential lease.

Negotiating the nonresidential lease

Once a leasing agent locates suitable premises for a prospective tenant, the agent must bring the landlord and tenant together through negotiations to develop the terms of a lease acceptable to all.

The role the broker plays in negotiations and his duties as a leasing agent depends on who he represents in the transaction: the landlord, the tenant or both. How aggressive a role a broker may play depends on the bargaining power given to the landlord or tenant during the current phase of the cyclical market conditions.

When representing the tenant, the broker must initially determine his client's need for space and the rental amount he is willing and able to pay for the space. This information is gathered on the tenant lease worksheet reviewed and prepared when first interviewing the tenant. [See **first tuesday** Form 555; see Chapter 16]

When representing the landlord, the broker must know the rental terms and leasing conditions sought by the landlord to rent the space. Usually, this data is set out in the exclusive authorization to lease property. [See **first tuesday** Forms 110 and 590]

The offer to lease

Whether a broker represents the tenant or the landlord, the broker initiates negotiations most efficiently by preparing an **offer to lease** form for the tenant to review and consider for signing. [See Form 556 accompanying this chapter]

The tenant enters into the offer to lease much like a buyer reviews and signs an offer to purchase real estate.

For example, a **tenant** under an offer to lease, which is accepted by a landlord, acquires a right to possession which the landlord agrees to *convey* to the tenant for a set period of time under the lease.

Likewise, a **buyer** of a real estate interest under a purchase agreement acquires either an existing leasehold (held by and being sold by an existing tenant) or fee title (from the owner), which will be conveyed to the buyer by an assignment or deed.

Thus, like a sales transaction, the arranging of a lease transaction has two phases:

- the offer and acceptance (agreement to lease); and

- the drafting and signing of the lease agreement and delivery of funds and possession (the conveyance of the leasehold interest on closing).

In the leasing situation, the broker, the landlord or the landlord's attorney prepares and handles all the closing instruments, such as the lease agreement and transfer of funds.

Leasing is usually accomplished without the benefit of a formal escrow. If documents are to be recorded, such as occurs in a long-term leasing transaction, a title officer and title insurance company become involved with a title search and issuance of a policy of leasehold title insurance.

OFFER TO LEASE
And Receipt of Deposit

DATE:_____, 20_____, at _____, California.

Items left blank or unchecked are not applicable.

Received from _____

the sum of $_____ evidenced by ☐ check, or_____ ☐,payable to _____,

to be held undeposited until acceptance of this offer as a deposit toward the leasing of the following premises:

_____

The following checked addendums are part of this offer to lease:

☐ Plat of the premises   ☐ Tenant's credit application [**ft** Form 302]   ☐ Tenant's financial statements

☐ Right of first refusal to buy   ☐ lease agreement form   ☐ Option to renew/extend [**ft** Form 565]

☐ Option to buy [**ft** Form 161]   ☐ _____

TERMS:

1. The commencement date of the lease to be _____, 20_____, and the expiration date to be _____, 20_____.

2. The monthly rent to be payable in advance as follows:

   2.1 ☐ Monthly rent to be fixed at $_____ until expiration of the lease. Holdover rent to be $_____ daily.

   2.2 ☐ Monthly rent to be adjusted from a monthly base rent for the first year of $_____. On each anniversary date of the lease, the monthly base rent shall be adjusted upward only based on the annual increase in the Consumer Price Index for All Urban Consumers (CPI-U) for:

   ☐ Los Angeles-Anaheim-Riverside   ☐ San Diego   ☐ Other index _____

   ☐ San Francisco-San Jose-Oakland   ☐ National   ☐ Capped at a _____ % annual increase

   2.3 ☐ Monthly rent to be graduated on each anniversary under the following schedule:

   a. Base year monthly rent of $_____, and on each anniversary month an upward adjustment, to the monthly rent of _____% over the prior year's monthly rent; or _____

   _____

   b. Base Year: $_____   Second Year:$_____   Third Year: $_____

   Fourth Year: $_____   Fifth Year: $_____   Sixth Year: $_____

   2.4 ☐ Rent to be the greater of _____% of monthly gross sales/receipts or the total of other rents, taxes insurance and common area maintenance (CAMs) checked in this offer.

   2.5 ☐ Monthly base rent to be adjusted upward to current market rental value every _____ years.

3. The utility expenses for the space leased to be paid as follows:

   Tenant to pay: _____

   Landlord to pay: _____

4. ☐ Common Area Maintenance (CAMs) costs for maintaining and operating of the common areas are to be paid by Tenant based on his proportionate share of the total space leased on the premises, or _____% of the CAMs. The CAMs charge shall be assessed: ☐ monthly, or ☐ quarterly, and payable within 10 days. The CAM change will not exceed ☐ _____% of the rent; ☐ _____ cents per square monthly, or _____.

5. Real estate taxes and assessments on the real estate shall be paid by ☐ Landlord, or ☐ Tenant.

   5.1 Any taxes and assessments paid by Tenant to be capped at a _____% annual increase.

6. A security deposit of $_____ to secure the performance under Tenant's lease to be paid on signing of the lease.

7. ☐ Tenant to have the option to renew or extend the lease as set forth in the attached option to renew/extend. [**ft** Form 565]

8. Tenant may assign, sublet or encumber the leasehold interest subject to Landlord's consent:

9. Tenant's intended use of the premises includes:_____

_____

10. Landlord to make improvements prior to the time Tenant is to take possession as follows:
_____
_____

11. Tenant to make improvements as follows:_____
_____
_____

12. Tenant may exercise the right to lease additional space from Landlord as follows (note the premises, rent, terms, and period): _____
_____

13. Tenant to maintain insurance on the premises to cover any casualty loss in the amount of $_____.

14. Landlord and Tenant to sign a lease to be prepared by ☐ Tenant, or ☐ Landlord on a form entitled _____ published by _____

15. Parties to pay Broker(s) a fee of ☐ see attached fee schedule [**ft** Form 113], or ☐ _____
_____, as follows:
Landlord to pay the brokerage fee on transfer of possession. The party wrongfully preventing a examples of possession to pay the brokerage fee. Landlord's Broker and Tenant's Broker, respectively, to share the brokerage fee _____:_____.

16. This offer shall be deemed revoked unless accepted in writing and personally delivered to Tenant or Tenant's Broker on or before _____, 20_____.

17. _____
_____
_____
_____
_____
_____
_____
_____
_____

Landlord's Broker: _____	Tenant's Broker: _____
By: _____	By: _____
Is the agent of: ☐ Landlord exclusively, or	Is the agent of: ☐ Tenant exclusively, or
☐ both Landlord and Tenant.	☐ both Landlord and Tenant.
I agree to the terms stated above.	**I agree to the terms stated above.**
Date:_____, 20_____	Date:_____, 20_____
Landlord: _____	Tenant:_____
Agent: _____	Tenant:_____
Signature: _____	Signature: _____
Address: _____	Signature: _____
_____	Address: _____
Phone: _____	_____
Fax: _____	Phone:_____
E-mail: _____	Fax: _____
	E-mail: _____

Contents of the offer

An *offer to lease* sets forth the crucial elements of the leasing arrangements. [See Form 556]

An **offer to lease**, like an offer to purchase, contains four sections:

1. Identification of the parties and premises.

2. Rental payment schedules and period of occupancy.

3. Property maintenance and terms of possession (use).

4. Signatures of the parties.

The identification section names the contracting parties, describes the premises and acknowledges receipt of any good faith deposit. A floor plan or common description of the premises is usually attached by a reference to it in the identification section.

The tenant should be asked to include a good faith deposit as would be asked of a fee simple buyer under a purchase agreement. The check for the deposit should be made payable to a broker involved, not the landlord.

The section of the offer setting forth the rental payment schedule is a **checklist** of various rental arrangements which can be selected by the tenant to pay rent, including:

- the duration/term of the initial leasing period;

- the monthly base rent for the first year;

- any rental adjustments during the leasing period for inflation and appreciation;

- responsibility for payment of utilities;

- any common area maintenance charges (CAMs);

- any assessment for insurance or taxes;

- the amount of the security deposit; and

- options to renew or extend the leasing period or to buy the property.

It is good brokerage practice to reference and attach a copy of the proposed lease agreement form to the offer as it includes boilerplate provisions covering:

- the **responsibility** for property operating and maintenance expenses;

- the **right to sell**, sublet or encumber the lease; and

- **default remedies**.

In the offer's miscellaneous leasing provisions, the tenant and landlord further agree to other terms peculiar to leasing, including:

- the tenant's proposed use;

- the lease agreement form to be used;

- responsibility for tenant improvements;

- any alterations by the tenant;

- brokerage fees; and

- the time and manner for accepting the offer to lease.

Some landlords initially present prospective tenants with fully prepared but unsigned lease agreements, a condition which generally works to the landlord's advantage. The parties then orally negotiate the final terms.

To better clarify negotiations, the broker should write up the offer to lease (and counteroffers) and, within the offer-counteroffer context, develop acceptable terms based on signed offers and counteroffers. Expectations are properly reached and negotiations are memorialized in writing to avoid later conjecture (and litigation).

The final section of the offer to lease is the signature section where the landlord and tenant sign and agree to the terms stated in the offer.

Offers to lease vs. proposals

By signing an offer to lease prepared by a broker, a prospective tenant initiates the negotiations in earnest. The landlord's acceptance concludes the search for space.

The key difference between an offer and a **proposal to lease** or letter of intent (LOI) is that the offer can be *accepted* to form a binding contract and the proposal is a mere *solicitation* and inquiry into the landlord's intentions binding on no one.

Solicitations, such as a proposal or LOI sent to the landlord or his leasing agent by the tenant's agent, require the landlord, should he respond, to "negotiate with himself" or to clarify his previously announced terms and conditions. No offer exists for the landlord to accept or counter. If the landlord responds, he should make an offer in writing, which forces the leasing agents to submit the offer to lease to the tenant for an acceptance, counteroffer or rejection.

A proposal merely evidences a tenant's or landlord's intent to gather and provide leasing information. The tenant and the landlord are not yet ready to make a binding commitment, otherwise an offer would be submitted by one or the other.

Leasing agents who use their accumulated knowledge and skills can and should do better than proposals, unless the tenant is not yet ready to be bound due to concurrent negotiations with other landlords.

Counteroffers focus on negotiations

To form a binding agreement to lease, an offer or counteroffer must be accepted in its entirety and without qualification or alteration. [Calif. Civil Code §1582]

When the landlord or tenant conditions his acceptance of an offer to lease by changing or adding specific terms, acceptance does not occur and a binding agreement to lease is not formed. [CC §1585]

The added conditions or changes establishes a rejection of the offer and creates a *counteroffer*. To avoid alteration of a signed document (the offer or lease), a counteroffer form referencing the signed document should be prepared, signed and submitted for the other party to then accept, reject or further counter.

Thus, if the offer to lease is not acceptable to the landlord (or the tenant), he can counter by using a counteroffer form to state terms which are acceptable. [See **first tuesday** Form 180]

As the negotiations in writing continue, an acceptable set of terms develops by the use of counteroffer forms. Written counteroffers keep the parties focused on the remaining unnegotiated details and demonstrate serious consideration by all — as indicated by a deposit and credit application delivered with the offer.

After acceptance of the offer or counteroffer to lease, only the preparation of the lease agreement (and other closing documents), transfer of possession and the payment of the security deposits and initial rent remain to close the lease transaction (tenant improvements notwithstanding).

Interference with negotiations

Consider a landlord who is currently negotiating with the CEO of a company to enter into a lease agreement. A competing landlord (or his broker) actively solicits officers and board members of the company to lease space from him instead.

Ultimately, the company enters into a lease agreement with the competing landlord.

The landlord who lost out seeks to recover lost rent from the competing landlord, claiming the competing landlord *intentionally interfered* with his prospective economic advantage. The landlord claims the competing landlord induced the officers and board members to consider and accept the competing landlord's proposal while he was **completing negotiations** with the company's CEO.

However, a competing landlord has a right to solicit a tenant who he knows is negotiating with another landlord as a *privilege of competition*. The competing landlord did not engage in unlawful interference since the company had not yet finalized negotiations by entering into an enforceable agreement to rent space from another landlord.

A landlord who has not yet entered into a binding offer to lease or lease agreement does not hold an economic advantage (in the form of a binding contract) with which a competing landlord may not interfere. [**San Francisco Design Center Associates** v. **Portman Companies** (1995) 41 CA4th 29]

SECTION C

Rents and Deposits

Chapter 17

Residential tenant credit checks

This chapter delves into the background check a landlord or property manager should complete to analyze a prospective tenant's creditworthiness.

Protection for landlords and brokers

A landlord's and property manager's initial analysis of the capability and willingness of a prospective residential tenant to meet obligations imposed by a rental or lease agreement is based on information obtained by:

- a completed **credit application** from the tenant [See Form 302 accompanying this chapter];

- a **credit clearance** through a credit reporting agency as authorized on the credit application; and

- an **unlawful detainer (UD) clearance** through a consumer reporting agency.

Besides relying solely on financial ratios and formulas to analyze the suitability of an individual as a tenant, a residential landlord on receipt of an application to rent should:

- call prior landlord(s) to confirm the amount of the prospective tenant's prior rent, payment history and personal conduct as an occupant on the premises;

- call the current employer to confirm the employment data on the application;

- confirm other sources of income, expenses and amount of indebtedness disclosed in the credit application; and

- determine whether the prospective tenant can afford the payments.

The investigation and analysis of the credit information received on prospective tenants is critical to a landlord's or property manager's successful operation of residential rentals in the high mobility environment of California rental residents, especially when they lack longevity in the community or with an employer.

Collecting relevant information

Accurate credit and background information is needed on each prospective tenant to properly analyze the business risk of collecting payments from the prospective tenant and that the tenant will properly use and maintain the property.

Owners and property managers of income-producing property need information to make decisions to accept or reject prospective tenants, such as the existence of prior evictions, late rent payments, bounced checks or other breaches of lease agreements.

A conclusion on creditworthiness is drawn from the tenant's **credit history** and **financial statements**.

Credit information is easily and inexpensively obtained. While readily available, it does take some time and concentration to collect and confirm the information.

A property manager in the course of his brokerage business makes decisions and advises landlords on the ability (income) and willingness (payment history) of tenants to pay rent and care for the premises.

Property managers advising landlords on the creditworthiness of tenants will find it necessary to subscribe to the services available from a *credit reporting agency* (CRA). Apartment owners' associations obtain credit information for their membership from the same private tenant screening services directly available to landlords.

CREDIT APPLICATION
Individual

DATE:_____, 20_____, at _____, California.

THIS CREDIT APPLICATION is for the amount of $_____, for ☐ rental, ☐ purchase, or ☐ borrowing.

Property address: _____

Received from Applicant(s) $_____, ☐ cash, or ☐ check, for a consumer credit report which is a non-refundable cost and not a deposit.

Received from Applicant(s) $_____, ☐ cash, or ☐ check, as a deposit toward the first month's rent on landlord's acceptance of the applicant's creditworthiness.

Applicant(s):

Applicant 1: _____
    (Last Name)   (First Name)   (Middle Name)   (Sr., Jr., etc.)

    Social Sec.#: _____ Drivers Lic.#:_____State:_____

Applicant 2: _____
    (Last Name)   (First Name)   (Middle Name)   (Sr., Jr., etc.)

    Social Sec.#: _____ Drivers Lic.#:_____State:_____

Additional Occupant(s): Name: _____

                 Name: _____

Rental History: Have you ever been party to an eviction? ☐ Yes ☐ No   Filed bankruptcy? ☐ Yes ☐ No

Present Address:_____

    City: _____ Zip:_____

    Length of Residency:_____ Monthly Rent $_____

    Landlord/Agent: _____

    Address:_____

    City:_____ Zip:_____ Phone:_____

    Reason for Moving: _____ Moving Date ____/____/____

Previous Address: _____

    City: _____ Zip:_____

    Length of Residence:_____ Monthly Rent $_____

    Landlord/Agent: _____

    Address:_____

    City:_____ Zip:_____ Phone:_____

Employment:

Applicant 1:

    Employer:_____

    Address:_____

    City:_____ Zip:_____ Phone:_____

    Length of Employment:_____ Position:_____Wages:_____

    Pay Period:_____ Union: _____

    Previous Employer:_____

    Address:_____

    City:_____ Zip:_____ Phone:_____

— — — — — — — — — — — — *PAGE ONE OF TWO — FORM 302* — — — — — — — — — — — — —

Applicant 2:

Employer:_____

Address:_____

City:_____ Zip:_____ Phone: _____

Length of Employment:_____ Position:_____ Wages:_____

Pay Period:_____ Union: _____

Previous Employer:_____

Address:_____

City:_____ Zip:_____ Phone: _____

Additional Income: Amount $_____ Source _____

Recipient: _____

General Credit Information:

Automobile 1 Make: _____

Year:_____ Model:_____ Lic.#/State: _____

Lender:_____

Automobile 2 Make: _____

Year:_____ Model:_____ Lic.#/State: _____

Lender:_____

Bank/branch: _____

Check Acc.#:_____ Savings Acc.#: _____

Bank/branch: _____

Check Acc.#:_____ Savings Acc.#: _____

Credit References

1: _____

Address:_____

Account #:_____ Balance due: $_____ Phone: _____

2: _____

Address:_____

Account #:_____ Balance due: $_____ Phone: _____

Personal Reference: _____

Address:_____ Phone: _____

Personal Reference: _____

Address:_____ Phone: _____

Nearest Relative (name/relationship): _____

Address:_____ Phone: _____

We declare all information given in this application is true and correct. We authorize your credit reporting agency to obtain and verify a complete consumer report and supply the information obtained to you. This information is not privileged.

Date:_____, 20_____

Name: _____

Signature: _____ (Applicant 1)

Name: _____

Signature: _____ (Applicant 2)

I acknowledge receipt of a copy and accompanying payment.
Landlord:_____
Signature: _____
Phone: _____

FORM 302   06-00   © 2007 **first tuesday**, P.O. Box 20069, RIVERSIDE, CA 92516 (800) 794-0494

One such service is the **Tenant Screening Center, Inc.** at 140 Wikiup Drive, Santa Rosa, CA 95403, 1-800-523-2381, info@tsci.com.

An initial subscription fee and a minimum charge for credit reporting services is common. In any event, the cost is passed on to the tenant either in an up-front nonrefundable credit screening fee or as a cost of doing business covered by the monthly rent.

Acquiring credit data

A credit report on an individual does not guarantee performance of the rental or lease agreement entered into by the prospective tenant or establish the prospect's ability to pay rent in the future.

However, it does reveal the prospect's previous performance in paying debts he has incurred, such as money owed on finance contracts, utility services or professional services, and whether he has incurred late penalty charges on consumer credit accounts, or been subjected to judgments or tax liens. Thus, the report gives an indication as to whether the tenant will pay rent, and do so timely.

Property managers seeking credit information must identify themselves to the credit reporting agency (CRA), state their purpose for seeking the information and certify to the CRA that the information will be used for no other purpose than stated. [Calif. Civil Code §1785.14(a)]

Even if a broker is approved by a CRA, the agency will not provide a broker credit information on just anyone. A broker seeking information on a prospective tenant will be refused service unless the tenant signs a release form for the information. [See Form 302]

The requirement that the tenant authorize the release of credit information is often waived if the broker is a member of an agency's credit association. Membership is open only to applicants who allow the agency to make a full investigation of their own creditworthiness and professional integrity. Abuse of the credit reporting service leads to termination of the service.

For a one-time membership fee and minimum monthly billing, an agency provides its members with credit reports at a pre-set cost per request.

Credit report contents

Consumer credit reports are limited to specific factual information on a prospective tenant's creditworthiness standing or capacity. **Consumer credit reports** are used to establish eligibility for:

- credit to be used for personal, family or household purposes;

- employment purposes; and

- the rental of a dwelling unit. [CC §1785.3(c)]

A *telecredit check* reviews the tenant's check writing history. The broker will be informed if the tenant has written checks on insufficient funds in the past.

The credit report includes references to the status of existing liens, loan and finance contracts, charge accounts, delinquencies, rental histories and payments, skips, damages and monies owed landlords and other creditors.

Information not available on a credit report includes:

- bankruptcies pre-dating the report by more than ten years;

- judgments pre-dating the report by the longer of seven years or the governing statute of limitations;

- unlawful detainer (UD) actions in which the landlord did not receive a *final judgment* by default, summary judgment or trial;

- paid tax liens and accounts on collection pre-dating the credit report by more than seven years; and

- criminal activity or other adverse information pre-dating the report by more than seven years. [CC §1785.13(a)]

UD reporting services

A prudent property manager uses a service which provides records on unlawful detainer (UD) actions in which the landlord prevailed by receiving a final judgment.

Some specialty credit services constantly obtain UD information from the municipal courts and landlords who subscribe to their service. These credit reporting agencies (CRAs) sell landlords information gathered from public records regarding UD evictions, and from landlords on particular tenants who have had adverse relationships with the landlords. The broker obtains more information on these tenants by contacting the landlord giving the adverse activity to the CRA.

In the early 1990s, CRAs were singled out and prohibited from disclosing the UD information needed by the landlords to analyze their risks. The prohibition was based on the claim the state had an interest in maintaining the availability of rental housing to all individuals, despite their adverse credit history. However, without the information, landlords are unable to analyze the risk they undertake by renting to a particular prospect.

Today, credit agencies may collect and report UD evictions since the statute prohibiting credit agencies from reporting UD actions is unenforceable since it violates the First Amendment rights of landlords. [**U.D. Registry, Inc.** v. **State** (1995) 34 CA4th 107]

However, a tenant, on request, is entitled to a clarification by the agency of the disposition of the UD action if the initial report, while technically true, is misleading or incomplete. [**Cisneros** v. **The U.D. Registry, Inc.** (1995) 39 CA4th 548]

Investigative reports go further

Investigative consumer reports provide information on a tenant's character, reputation, personal characteristics and mode of living.

This information is obtained through personal interviews with neighbors, friends and associations of the tenant.

Investigative consumer reports can be used for:

- insurance or employment purposes; and

- the rental of a dwelling unit. [CC §1786.12(d)]

Editor's note — Investigative consumer reports are commonly used by landlords when hiring a property manager or resident manager, or entering into a percentage lease with a tenant. Before obtaining an investigative consumer report, a landlord must notify and receive written permission from the prospective employee or tenant to retrieve and use the investigative consumer report for employment or leasing purposes. [CC §1786.12; 15 USC §1681b]

Prior rental history inquiries

Additional information on the tenant's creditworthiness and character is readily available to property managers by contacting the tenant's previous landlord. Critical questions to be asked of the prior landlord include:

1. Did the tenant cause any damage to the rental property?

2. Was the rent paid on time every month? Were partial payments made?

3. Were any late charges incurred, and if so, were they demanded and did the tenant pay the late charges?

4. Was the tenant ever served a 3-day notice?

5. Did the tenant leave on friendly terms?

6. Did the tenant care for and maintain the premises?

7. Did the tenant abide by restrictions in the lease (i.e., pets, guests, building policy, etc.)?

8. Did the tenant interfere with or endanger other tenants?

If, after investigating a prospective tenant's background, it seems likely the tenant will mismanage his use of the property, damage or contribute to the deterioration of its physical appearance or otherwise diminish its value for other tenants, a prudent landlord or property manager may not be willing to lease to the prospect or consent to his assumption of an existing lease.

Evaluating credit information

Once a property manager has obtained the necessary credit information on the tenant, the data must be **evaluated**.

Information provided on forms filled out by the tenant, brokers and landlords must not be used to discriminate against any tenant based on his race, color, religion, sex, sexual orientation, marital status, national origin, ancestry, familial status or disability. [Calif. Government Code §12955]

However, when applying **income-to-debt** or **income-to-rent** ratios as guidelines to determine a tenant's creditworthiness, each tenant should be treated individually. A tenant who does not meet an income ratio is not necessarily a credit risk if they have a strong balance sheet (assets and net worth).

However, a landlord or property manager may analyze a prospective tenant's capability to pay the amount of rent sought by the landlord by applying a ratio or formula, such as a "three-to-one" income-to-rent ratio, as the only basis for determining the tenant's creditworthiness. [**Harris** v. **Capital Growth Investors XIV** (1991) 52 C3d 1142]

Income-to-debt ratios and percentage income-to-rent standards assume all prospective tenants who do not meet the ratio or percentage are unable to pay simply because they do not meet an arbitrary mathematical formula adopted by the landlord or property manager. However, the exclusive use of qualifying ratios to qualify prospective tenants sacrifices a thoughtful review of a prospective tenant's ability to pay rent and maintain the premises.

A more thorough review based on the tenant's financial statements and occupancy history, rather than a quick, mechanical test of the tenant's financial ability, will often yield tenants of better financial capacity than those who are merely employed.

Denied due to bad credit

Any tenant refused occupancy or subjected to increased rent or security deposit due to the risks posed by the information contained in a credit report must:

- be **told** so by the landlord or property manager relying on the credit report; and

- be given the **name of the service** who issued the credit report. [CC §1787.2]

Any consumer who is denied credit, i.e., refused as a tenant for lack of creditworthiness, must be informed he is entitled to a written statement from the landlord or property manager of the reasons for the denial. [CC §1787.2(b)(2)(i)]

Nonrefundable fees for credit reports

A residential landlord may charge a prospective tenant a nonrefundable *credit screening fee* to cover the costs of obtaining information about the prospective tenant. [CC §1950.6(a)]

The information requested by the landlord for which the fee may be charged includes personal reference investigative and credit reports.

The amount of the applicant **screening fee** may not exceed $38.97 (for 2007) or the lesser amount of:

- out-of-pocket costs for gathering the information; and

- the costs of the landlord's time in obtaining the information. [CC §1950.6(b)]

The screening fee ceiling is adjusted annually based on increases in the Consumer Price Index (CPI). The base year is 1997 and the amount was set at $30. The CPI figure for 1997 is 158.7 (from December 1996).

For the year 2007, the maximum amount of the applicant screening fee is $38.97, a 29.9% increase from the amount set for 1997. This amount reflects the increase in the CPI from 1997 (158.7) to the figure of 206.2 from December 2006 used to compute the 2007 maximum screening fee amount. The West Urban CPI is used in this example although the statute does not specify which CPI a landlord or property manager must use. [CC §1950.6(b)]

The landlord has an affirmative duty to provide the prospective tenant with an itemized receipt of the out-of-pocket expenses and the time spent to obtain and process the tenant's credit information. [CC §1950.6(d)]

If a personal reference check is not performed or a consumer credit report is not ordered, the landlord must refund any amount of the screening fee not used. [CC §1950.6(e)]

Further, **on request** from the prospective tenant, the landlord must provide the prospective tenant with a copy of the consumer report obtained by the landlord. [CC §1950.6(f)]

An applicant screening fee may not be charged when a rental unit is presently unavailable or will not be available within a reasonable period of time. [CC §1950.6(c)]

Editor's note — A reasonable time is probably the time period required to notice the termination of a tenancy, such as under a notice to vacate.

Chapter 18

Nonresidential tenant screening

This chapter explores the inquiry a landlord or property manager should make into a prospective nonresidential tenant's background before agreeing to let space.

Qualified to stay and pay

An owner's leasing agent, when reviewing an application to rent from a prospective nonresidential tenant, has a duty to the owner to review the tenant's qualifications from much the same standpoint a commercial lender would review a person's qualifications to borrow money.

Like lending money, leasing real estate is an extension of credit. Rent paid for the use of property is comparable to interest paid for the use of money. Both financial arrangements have the same economic function since each generates a rate of return — one called rent, the other called interest.

Further, the owner conveys to the tenant the right to use the property, comparable to a lender advancing money for use by a borrower. Both are on loan. Finally, property let to a tenant must be returned to the owner, just as money lent to a borrower must be returned to the lender.

Thus, the leasing agent and landlord analyze the creditworthiness of the prospective tenant as if they were arranging and making a commercial loan for the same period of time. In other words, is the prospective tenant *qualified* to take possession of the property, pay for its use in a timely manner and return it undiminished as agreed?

A *credit report* provides only partial information on a nonresidential tenant's creditworthiness, information which is publicly available. Credit reports do not evaluate the tenant's managerial ability to successfully operate his trade or business, nor do they consider the ten-

ant's assets (net worth) or the profitability of the business. However, *investigative reports* carry this type of information.

A tenant, on inquiry from a leasing agent, can provide *financial statements* on his company. The tenant's business income, expenses and net operating income (NOI) are disclosed in the tenant's *profit and loss statement*, a type of **financial statement**. The tenant's *balance sheet* is a separate financial statement which sets forth the tenant's net worth (assets) and liabilities (debts).

In the unlikely event a tenant does not have a computer generated financial statement for his company, such as occurs with a start up company, financial statement forms are available from institutional lenders and publishers of forms for tenant's to fill out.

The information contained in financial statements supplied voluntarily by the tenant should be confirmed by the owner or his leasing agent. Most credit agencies will perform this activity for a fee. The credit application usually supplies the name and address of banks and creditors of the tenant's company.

Leasing agents can also check out the property currently occupied (leased or owned) by nonresidential tenants to see if a failure to care for or maintain the property occurred during the tenant's occupancy. A diminished property value on the tenant's return of possession is what an owner wants to avoid. Investigating the tenant's behavior before entering into a leasing agreement will help establish a better level of certainty about what risk the tenant poses for the owner.

For managers of nonresidential property, the added dimension of the tenant's business operations and conduct must be considered. The tenant's business acumen and style of marketing from the premises will have an affect on occupants of adjacent space.

Also, the leasing agent's review of a substitute tenant who is seeking the owner's consent to allow him to assume an existing tenant's nonresidential lease and occupy the premises must be given the same review the owner would give a prospective tenant negotiating a new lease on the space.

Tenants who seek possession of a property under a sublease or by an assignment of an existing lease which contains an alienation provision calling for the owner's consent "on the condition it will not be unreasonably withheld," must be subjected to no different standards for consent to assume the lease than are used to qualify new tenants.

The use of different qualifying standards represents an unreasonable interference with the nonresidential tenant's right to sell his business and transfer the leasehold with the right of the substitute tenant to continue to occupy the premises for the remaining term.

Purpose of background checks

A nonresidential manager, leasing agent or owner conducts a **background check** on a new tenant to determine his:

- credit history (evidence of debt and payment as agreed);

- financial status (income, expenses, disposable income, assets, liabilities and net worth);

- business track record and proposed business plans;

- compatibility in terms of the tenant's business conduct with other tenants and class of clientele; and

- ability to manage his business and maintain the property's value.

Credit and financial history

Before a prospective tenant's credit and financial history can be analyzed by the owner, the prospective tenant must complete a *credit application*, also called an *application to rent*. On receiving the tenant's **credit application**, the owner and his leasing agent can begin the process of verifying the tenant's payment history based on the information supplied by the tenant and reports ordered out from credit agencies. [See **first tuesday** Form 302; see Chapter 20]

Specifically, the owner or his leasing agent should contact the tenant's past landlords to ascertain the tenant's:

- rental payment record;

- day-to-day upkeep and appearance of the leased space;

- clientele profile and compatibility with clientele of other tenants; and

- ability to cooperate with other tenants.

Any possible adverse information, such as foreclosures, bankruptcies, tax liens, evictions, violations of use ordinances or records of arrests, should be given weight when analyzing the tenant's acceptability. Litigious and troublesome tenants are to be shunned since they come with baggage and attitudes adverse to problem-free landlord-tenant relationships.

Business track record

Extensive financial data on the prospective tenant's business is readily available to the owner on an inquiry of the tenant. Financial information on the tenant's business operations are typically provided through financial statements, including:

- profit and loss, income and operating statements for the current and preceding year; and

- a balance sheet for the last day of the prior month to the application to rent.

Attention should be focused on the tenant's:

- prior work experience;

- business or professional licenses;

- familiarity with his proposed use of the property;

- degree of responsibility;

- managerial skills;

- vocational or educational experience;

- business acumen and survivability;

- name recognition and length of time in the community; and

- civic and community involvement.

The prospective nonresidential tenant's income statement and balance sheet statement should be examined for:

- income, expenses and net operating income (NOI) ratios;

- ability to maintain or increase sales;

- budget and income projections (and rent percentage of gross income);

- net cash flow;

- age of accounts payable;

- amortization periods and due dates of debts;

- cash reserves;

- ownership and control; and

- product performance and service satisfaction.

Future plans and business goals

The **tenant's future plans** for the space they have applied for to lease and their business objective or goal to be accomplished by the relocation are legitimate concerns of an owner. Some entrepreneurial owners become so involved they actually participate in the business of a prospective tenant by accepting stock or other share ownership in the tenant's company in lieu of rent for the leased space, particularly with business start-ups.

Regardless of the form in which rent will be paid, questions arise about the nature and substance of the **tenant's operations**, including:

1. Is the tenant consolidating or expanding his operations?

2. Do his income and expense projections make sense?

3. Does the business require the infusion of capital to relocate to new space?

4. Does the tenant need to increase or reduce his debt or annual debt service?

5. For tenants who are a corporation or limited liability company (LLC), is a stockholder or a member willing to personally guarantee the lease agreement or provide security?

6. Will the activities of the tenant pose any zoning, ordinance or insurance coverage problems?

7. Will the tenant's operations and the type of clientele it attracts enhance or impair the future value of the real estate?

Chapter 19

Security deposits and pre-expiration inspections

This chapter discusses the variety of rules for residential and nonresidential landlords who receive and refund security deposits, and the residential tenant's right to a pre-expiration inspection.

Residential and nonresidential rules

An investor in nonresidential income-producing properties acquires his first residential rental property. The residential rental property is a large apartment complex consisting of furnished and unfurnished units.

The investor retains a broker with experience managing apartment buildings of comparable size and quality in the local rental market. As the property manager, the broker makes an initial **inspection** of the units. The impact of the local residential rental market on rents and security deposits in this property are reviewed with the investor.

As a result, rents and security deposits to be charged are re-established based on the size of the units, the maximum number of occupants for the various sizes of units, amenities each unit offers, the unit's location within the complex and whether or not the units are furnished.

The investor is aware he must rent to families with children whose credit and background qualify them as tenants. However, the investor is concerned about the excessive wear and tear children could cause to the units. The investor is advised any excessive wear and tear brought on by a tenant which remains unrepaired when the tenant vacates is a breach of the lease, called a *default*. Any additional clean-up expenses incurred by the landlord are recoverable from that tenant.

If a unit will be occupied by a family with children whose family size or background check indicates they will likely place an excessive burden on the unit, the broker can recommend either the unit not be rented to them or the rent be adjusted upward to cover the additional wear and tear brought about by the burdensome increase in the number of occupants.

However, the investor would like to impose a larger security deposit equal to one-half month's rent for each child who will occupy a unit since the increased deposit would either discourage large families from renting or provide funds to restore the unit for re-renting when they vacate.

The property manager informs the investor that security deposits charged to tenants of residential units who fall into a *protected class* of people, such as families, are controlled by statute and call for *nondiscriminatory, equal treatment*.

Thus, the investor is cautioned he cannot require higher security deposits for tenants with children than for tenants without children. Any increase in a security deposit for larger versus smaller families is a prohibited **discriminatory** practice. [Calif. Government Code §12955(a); 24 Code of Federal Regulations §100.65; see Chapter 44]

Also, other limitations are placed on the tenant's upfront advance for rent and security deposits. In addition to the collection of one month's advance rent, the **further amount** which a residential tenant may be required to pay as a **security deposit** to cover defaults during the period of occupancy is limited to an amount equal to:

- two months' rent for unfurnished units; and

- three months' rent for furnished units. [Calif. Civil Code §1950.5(c)]

If permitted by competition in the local rental market, the investor may require all tenants in an unfurnished unit an advance payment of no more than:

- the first month's rent and the last month's rent and a security deposit equal to one month's rent; or

- the first month's rent and a security deposit equal to two months' rent.

The property manager informs the investor a security deposit equal to one month's rent, together with one month's advance rent, is all the market will currently sustain for his units. If he demands more, the units will not readily rent since prospective tenants will likely be unwilling or unable to pay that amount up front.

Security against nonperformance

Both nonresidential and residential landlords traditionally require tenants to deposit funds with the landlord in addition to the first month's rent. [See **first tuesday** Forms 550 §1.1 and 552 §1.2]

The additional funds provide **security** for the tenant's future performance of those obligations he agrees to in the rental or lease agreement if the tenant defaults. Tenant obligations include paying rent, reimbursing the landlord for expenses incurred due to the tenant's conduct, maintaining the premises during the occupancy and returning the premises in the same level of cleanliness existing when leased to the tenant, less ordinary wear and tear.

For **residential rentals**, all monies paid to the landlord in addition to the first month's rent, screening fee and waterbed administrative fee is considered a security deposit. **Security deposits** include any funds received for the purpose of covering defaults by the tenant under the rental or lease agreement, no matter the

name given to the funds by the landlord, such as a nonrefundable deposit, cleaning charge or last month's rent. [CC §§1940.50, 1950.5(b), (c); 1950.6]

Thus, any funds legally recharacterized as a security deposit are **refundable** when the tenant vacates, less deductions for unpaid rent and recoverable costs incurred by the landlord for the repair of damages caused by the tenant or for the cleaning of the premises to return cleanliness to its condition when leased to the tenant. [CC §§1950.5(b), 1950.7(c)]

For nonresidential tenancies, a small services firm may pay an amount equal to one month's rent as a security deposit, while a photography studio which uses chemicals in its film processing may be asked to pay an amount equal to two month's rent.

Editor's note — A photography studio tenant or other users of chemicals must also be required to provide **insurance coverage.**

In a market downturn, aggressively competitive landlords are less likely to require a security deposit in exchange for maintaining current rental income (occupancy), exposing themselves to an increased risk of loss if the tenant defaults.

Like all other terms in a nonresidential lease, the amount of the security deposit is negotiated between the nonresidential landlord and the tenant prior to entering into the lease.

Unlike nonresidential tenants, residential tenants, as a matter of public policy, are perceived as lacking bargaining power when they negotiate a lease or rental agreement. Thus, limits are imposed by law on the amount of security deposit a residential landlord may require.

The problematic last month's rent

When the availability of unfurnished residential units is low, residential landlords often require prospective tenants to advance the maximum permissible amount of rent and security deposit allowed. For unfurnished units the maximum advance payment includes the first and last month's rent, plus a security deposit equal to one month's rent. The landlord's do so to eliminate the less solvent tenants from renting their units.

Editor's note — Payment of the first and last month's rent is recharacterized on residential rentals as one month's advance rent for the first month of the occupancy and a security deposit equal to the amount paid for the last month's rent, plus any advances called a security deposit. [CC §1950.5(c)]

Nonresidential landlords also typically require an advance payment of both the first and last month's rent on a lease, the last month's prepayment being a security deposit until the last month arrives.

Now consider a residential tenant who pays the first month's rent and a security deposit equal to one month's rent on entering into his lease or rental agreement.

When the last month's rent becomes due, the tenant does not pay it. The tenant knows the defaulted payment of rent will be deducted from his security deposit, a permissible use of the security deposit by the landlord.

On expiration of the lease, the tenant vacates the unit. Due to excess wear and tear on the unit inflicted by the tenant, repairs and replacements are required before the unit can be re-rented.

However, after deducting the unpaid last month's rent from the security deposit, no security deposit remains to reimburse the landlord for the cost of the repairs.

The recovery of the **repair costs** is limited to a demand on the tenant for payment, and if unpaid, a small claims court action to enforce collection.

A similar demand for payment of repair costs occurs when the landlord requires advance payment of the first and last month's rent, but no security deposit.

Residential deposits

A residential landlord must require the same security deposit for all units, such as an amount equal to one month's rent, or base the amount of the security deposit on each tenant's creditworthiness.

Editor's note — A landlord should set the amount of the security deposit based on a tenant's creditworthiness — the greater or lesser risk of a loss posed by the prospective tenant's likely failure to perform on lease provisions. However, clear and precise standards for setting the different levels of creditworthiness and equal application of each level's creditworthiness standard to all prospective tenants who fall into that level of credit must exist. Lenders set levels of creditworthiness and charge different rates of interest for each level. [24 CFR §100.60(b)(4)]

Any money handed to a residential landlord by a tenant on entering into a lease or rental agreement must be **characterized** as one of the following:

- a *tenant screening fee* for processing an application; [See Chapter 19]

- a *waterbed administrative fee*; [See Chapter 53]

- *rent*; or

- a *security deposit*. [CC §§1940.5(g), 1950.5(b), 1950.6(b)]

A residential landlord has limited authority to require an additional **pet deposit** if the tenant is permitted to keep one or more pets in the unit.

However, the total amount of advance funds received from a tenant **with a pet** may not ex-

Deferring the first month's rent

Consider a landlord who locates a creditworthy tenant for his residential property.

In addition to the advance payment of the first month's rent, the landlord requires a security deposit equal to one month's rent.

The tenant asks the landlord if he can pay half the security deposit up front and the other half with the second month's rent.

The tenant is unable to pay the security deposit in full until he receives his security deposit refund from his current landlord.

The landlord wants this applicant as a tenant, and is willing to arrange further credit.

However, the landlord structures receipt of the funds as payment of the entire security deposit and half of the first month's rent.

The tenant will pay the remaining half of the first month's rent with payment of the second month's rent.

Thus, should the tenant fail to pay the second month's rent, or the remainder of the first month's rent:

- the landlord may serve a three-day notice to pay rent or quit; and

- the amount can be deducted from the security deposit, as a source of last resort.

Conversely, consider a landlord who allows a tenant to allocate his funds first to rent and spread payment of the security deposit over two or more months.

A tenant's failure to pay the second installment of the security deposit will not be a material breach, which is necessary for an eviction based on service of a three-day *notice to perform*. A security deposit is not rent.

A tenant's breach must be material and go to the root of the lease or rental agreement, such as a failure to pay rent, to justify service of a three-day notice. A **minor breach** of the lease will not justify serving a three-day notice to forfeit the tenant's right to possession. [**Baypoint Mortgage Corp.** v. **Crest Premium Real Estate Investments Retirement Trust** (1985) 168 CA3d 818]

ceed one month's rent plus an amount equal to two month's rent for an unfurnished unit or three month's rent for a furnished unit. [See Chapter 43]

However, these security deposit limitations may be exceeded when a tenant maintains a **waterbed on the premises**. The residential landlord of an unfurnished unit may then require, in addition to the first months' rent:

- an amount equal to **one-half month's rent**, in addition to the maximum security deposit; and

- a **reasonable fee** to cover administrative costs of processing the waterbed arrangements. [CC §1940.5(g); see Chapter 53]

Also, if the term of a residential lease is six months or more, the landlord and tenant may then agree to an advance payment of six months' rent, or more, instead of one month's rent. [CC §1950.5(c)]

Thus, advance payment of an amount equal to only two to five months' rent is prohibited.

Should the landlord and tenant agree to an advance payment of six months' rent on the lease of an unfurnished unit, the landlord may also require the maximum security deposit of two months' rent.

Holding security deposits

Funds advanced by a tenant and held by residential and nonresidential landlords to cover defaults in the tenant's performance of his obligations on the lease or rental agreement, are called security deposits. The funds belong to the tenant who advanced them to the landlord. [CC §§1950.5(d), 1950.7(b)]

However, while the security deposit belongs to the tenant, a landlord may **commingle** the funds with other monies in a general business account. No trust relationship is established when a landlord holds a tenant's security deposit. [**Korens** v. **R.W. Zukin Corporation** (1989) 212 CA3d 1054]

Without a trust relationship, the landlord's receipt of a security deposit does not obligate him to pay **interest** on the security deposit for the period held. However, some local rent control ordinances require residential landlords to pay interest to tenants on their security deposits — and the legislature is contemplating extending this to all residential landlords.

For example, the city of San Francisco requires residential landlords to pay simple interest to tenants on security deposits held by the landlord for one year or more as long as the rent is not subsidized by any government agency. [San Francisco Administrative Code §49.2]

Joint pre-expiration inspection

A residential landlord must **notify a tenant** in writing of the tenant's **right to request** a joint inspection of his unit within two weeks prior to the date the tenancy expires due to:

- expiration of the lease term; or

- a 30-day notice to vacate initiated by either the landlord or the tenant. [CC §1950.5(f)(1); see Form 567-1 accompanying this chapter]

The requirement of notice does not apply to tenants who are unlawfully remaining in possession after the expiration of a 3-day notice to pay/perform or quit for failing to pay rent, failing to perform terms and conditions of the rental agreement, or committing waste or a nuisance on the property,

The purpose for the **joint pre-expiration inspection**, legally called an *initial inspection*, is to require the landlord to advise the tenant of the repairs or conditions the tenant needs to perform to **avoid deductions** from the security deposit.

If a residential tenant requests the pre-expiration inspection in response to the notice of his right to the inspection, the landlord or his agent must complete the inspection no earlier than two weeks before the tenant is to vacate the unit.

Ideally, the notice advising the tenant of his right to a joint inspection is given to the tenant at least 30 days prior to the end of the lease term or, in the case of a lease agreement, immediately upon receiving or serving a 30-day notice to vacate. A period of 30 days will allow the tenant time to request the inspection and provide two full weeks to prepare for the inspection and then two weeks to remedy any repairs or uncleanliness the landlord observes during the inspection which might constitute a deduction from the security deposit.

NOTICE OF RIGHT TO REQUEST
A JOINT PRE-EXPIRATION INSPECTION

DATE:_____, 20_____, at _____, California.

> **NOTICE:** Residential tenants may request a joint pre-expiration inspection of the premises they occupy. At the inspection they will receive a statement of deficiencies itemizing the repairs and cleaning necessary to be remedied or eliminated by the tenant to avoid a deduction of their costs from the security deposit. [Civil Code §1950.5(f)]

To Tenant: _____

Items left blank or unchecked are not applicable.

FACTS:

1. You are a Tenant under a rental or lease agreement
    1.1 dated _____, at_____, California,
    1.2 entered into by _____, Tenant,
        and _____, Landlord,
    1.3 regarding real estate referred to as: _____
    1.4 which tenancy expires _____, 20_____.

NOTICE:

2. You are hereby advised of your right to request and be present at a pre-expiration inspection of the premises you occupy, and at the time of the inspection, be given the Landlord's itemized statement of deficiencies specifying repairs and cleaning which will be the basis for deduction from your security deposit.

    2.1 The purpose for the inspection and the statement of deficiencies is to give you the opportunity to remedy or eliminate the itemized deficiencies before vacating to avoid a deduction of their cost from your security deposit.

    2.2 The inspection, if requested by you, may be scheduled no earlier than two weeks before the expiration of your tenancy, and is separate from the Landlord's final inspection and accounting for your security deposit within 21 days after you vacate.

    2.3 If you do not request a pre-expiration inspection, no inspection will be made prior to the final inspection after you vacate.

3. You may request an inspection at any time after you are given this notice by preparing the form attached to this notice and giving it to the Landlord or his agent.

    3.1 On the Landlord's receipt of your request, the Landlord will attempt to set a mutually agreeable date and time for the inspection.

    3.2 On the Landlord's receipt of your request, you will be given a written 48-hour notice of entry advising you of the date and time scheduled by the Landlord for the inspection.

4. On completion of the scheduled inspection, whether or not you are present, the Landlord or his agent will hand you or leave on the premises a copy of an itemized statement of deficiencies specifying repairs and cleaning which will be the basis for deductions from your security deposit, unless you remedy or eliminate them prior to your vacating on or before your tenancy expires.

    4.1 Once you have requested an inspection you may withdraw the request at any time prior to the inspection.

Date:_____, 20_____

Landlord/Agent:_____

Signature: _____

Address: _____

_____

Phone:_____

Fax: _____

E-mail:_____

REQUEST FOR JOINT PRE-EXPIRATION INSPECTION

DATE:_____, 20_____, at _____, California.

To Landlord:

1. I, the Tenant, hereby request an inspection at the earliest possible date and time during the two-week period prior to the expiration or expiration of my tenancy.

2. The dates I prefer for an inspection during normal business hours include: _____
   _____

3. I understand you will give me a 48-hour notice prior to the inspection.

   Address of the premises: _____

   Tenant's name: _____

   Signature:_____

   Daytime telephone number:_____

FORM 567-1   02-02   ©2007 **first tuesday**, P.O. BOX 20069, RIVERSIDE, CA 92516 (800) 794-0494

On the landlord's receipt of the tenant's request for an inspection, the landlord must serve a written 48-hour **notice of entry** on the tenant stating the purpose of entry, date and time of the pre-expiration inspection. If the date and time cannot be mutually agreed to, they are to be set by the landlord.

However, if a mutually acceptable time for the inspection is within 48 hours, a written waiver of the notice of entry must be signed by both the landlord and tenant. [CC §1950.5(f)(1); see **first tuesday** Form 567-2]

When the waiver is signed, the landlord may proceed with the inspection, whether or not the tenant is present at the premises, unless the tenant has previously withdrawn his request for the inspection.

On completion of the pre-expiration inspection, the landlord must give the tenant an itemized statement of deficiencies specifying any repairs or cleaning necessary to be completed

by the tenant to avoid deductions from his security deposit. Also, itemized statement of deficiencies must contain the contents of subdivisions (b) and (d) of Civil Code §1950.5. [See Form 567-3 accompanying this chapter]

The landlord's **pre-expiration inspection statement** must be delivered to the tenant by either:

- handing the statement directly to the tenant if he is present at the inspection; or

- leaving the statement inside the premises at the time of the inspection if the tenant is not present. [CC §1950.5(f)(2)]

The purpose for the inspection and statement of deficiencies in repairs or cleanliness is to give the tenant time in which to remedy the identified repairs before vacating the premises.

Alternatively, the tenant may choose not to request a pre-expiration inspection, in which case

STATEMENT OF DEFICIENCIES
ON JOINT PRE-EXPIRATION INSPECTION

DATE:_____, 20_____, at _____, California.

To Tenant: _____

Items left blank or unchecked are not applicable.

FACTS:

1. On this date, a pre-expiration inspection was conducted by the Landlord on the premises and appurtenances which are the subject of a rental agreement or lease agreement.

    1.1 dated _____, at _____, California,

    1.2 entered into by _____, Tenant(s),

    and_____, Landlord,

    1.3 regarding real estate referred to as: _____

    _____

    1.4 ☐ The Tenant was present and given a copy of this statement prepared and signed by the Landlord or his agent.

    1.5 ☐ The Tenant was not present and a copy of this statement prepared and signed by the Landlord or his agent was left inside the premises.

2. The tenancy under the rental agreement or lease expires on _____, 20_____ by which date you are to vacate the premises.

3. **NOTICE TO TENANT:**

    3.1 You have until the date for expiration of your tenancy to remedy or eliminate the repairs and cleaning specified in this Statement of Deficiencies to avoid the deduction from your security deposit of the cost to repair and clean the identified deficiencies.

    3.2 Unobservable conditions or conditions which occur after the pre-expiration inspection, requiring repair and cleaning will be deducted from your security deposit after the final inspection by the landlord or his agent.

STATEMENT OF DEFICIENCIES:

4. The following itemized list of identified deficiencies in repairs and cleaning will be the basis for deductions from your security deposit, unless remedied or eliminated by you prior to vacating and later confirmed by the Landlord or his agent during a final inspection after you vacate.

    4.1 Damage to the premises and appurtenances caused by the Tenant or their guests, other than ordinary wear and tear, which needs to be repaired are listed as follows:_____

    _____

    _____

    _____

    _____

    _____

    _____

    _____

    4.2 Cleaning which needs to be performed to bring the premises up to the level of cleanliness which existed on commencement of the tenancy is listed as follows: _____

    _____

    _____

    _____

    _____

    _____

    _____

— — — — — — — — — — — — — — *PAGE ONE OF TWO — FORM 567-3* — — — — — — — — — — — — — —

5. The following recitals are excerpts from Civil Code §1950.5 regarding security deposits:

5.1 1950.5(b) As used in this section, "security" means any payment, fee, deposit or charge, including, but not limited to, any payment, fee, deposit, or charge, except as provided in Section 1950.6, that is imposed at the beginning of the tenancy to be used to reimburse the landlord for costs associated with processing a new tenant or that is imposed as an advance payment of rent, used or to be used for any purpose, including, but not limited to, any of the following:

(1) The compensation of a Landlord for a Tenant's default in the payment of rent.

(2) The repair of damages of the premises, exclusive of ordinary wear and tear, caused by the Tenant or by a guest or licensee of the tenant.

(3) The cleaning of the premises upon termination of the tenancy necessary to return the unit to the same level of cleanliness it was in at the inception of the tenancy. The amendments to this paragraph enacted by the act adding this sentence shall apply only to tenancies for which the Tenant's right to occupy begins after January 1, 2003.

(4) To remedy future defaults by the Tenant in any obligation under the rental agreement to restore, replace, or return personal property or appurtenances, exclusive of ordinary wear and tear, if the security deposit is authorized to be applied thereto by the rental agreement.

5.2 1950.5(d) Any security shall be held by the Landlord for the Tenant who is party to the lease or agreement. The claim of a Tenant to the security shall be prior to the claim of any creditor of the Landlord.

Date:_____ , 20_____

Landlord/Agent: _____

Signature: _____

Address: _____

_____

Phone: _____

Fax:_____

the landlord or his agent will not have to conduct an inspection or prepare and give the tenant a statement of deficiencies before the tenancy expires and the tenant vacates. However, the notice of the tenant's right to request a pre-expiration inspection **must** be given to the tenant.

If the tenant chooses to withdraw his request for an inspection after submitting it, the landlord should send a memo to the tenant confirming the tenant's decision to withdraw. [See **first tuesday** Form 525]

Editor's note — The completion of a pre-expiration inspection statement by the landlord does not bar the landlord from deducting other costs from the security deposit for:

- *any damages noted in the joint pre-expiration inspection statement which are not cured;*

- *any damages which occurred between the pre-expiration inspection and termination of the tenancy; or*

- *any damages not identified during the pre-expiration inspection due to the tenant's possessions being in the way. [CC §1950.5(f)]*

Regardless of whether the tenant requests a pre-expiration inspection, the final inspection after the tenant vacates and the itemized statement for the refund of the security deposit (less any deductions) must still be completed and mailed within 21 days after the **tenant vacates** the residential unit. [CC §1950.5(g)]

Residential refund requirements

Within a window period of **21 days** after a residential tenant vacates, but not before 60 days prior to the expiration of the lease or before the notice of termination under a rental agreement, the residential landlord must:

- refund the security deposit, less reasonable deductions; and

- provide the tenant with an **itemized statement of deductions** taken from the security deposit. [CC §1950.5(g); see Form 585 accompanying this chapter]

Also, the landlord must **attach copies** of receipts, invoices and/or bills to the itemized statement showing charges incurred by the landlord and deducted from the security deposit. [CC §1954]

If landlord repairs are not completed and the costs are unknown within 21 days after the tenant vacates, the landlord may deduct a **good faith estimated amount** of the cost of repairs from the tenant's security deposit. This estimate is stated on the itemized security deposit refund statement, disclosing the name, address and telephone number of any person or entity providing repair work, materials or supplies. [CC §1954]

Within 14 days after the **completion of repairs** or the receipt of bills, invoices and/or receipts for the repairs and materials, the landlord must deliver the final itemized security deposit refund statement with attached receipts and invoices to the tenant. [CC §1954]

It is not necessary for the landlord to provide copies of receipts, bills and/or invoices for repair work or cleaning to the tenant if:

- the total deduction from the security deposit to cover the costs of repairs and cleaning does not exceed $125; or

- the tenant signs a waiver of his right to receive bills at the time or after notice to terminate his tenancy is given. [CC §1954]

A residential tenant may request copies of receipts, bills or invoices for repair work or cleaning within 14 days after receipt of the itemized security deposit refund statement, and the landlord is to provide copies of the documents within 14 days after the tenant's request [CC §1954].

Reasonable deductions from a residential tenant's security deposit include:

- **delinquent rent**;

- **costs to clean** the premises after the tenant vacates — if the tenant agreed to and failed to leave the unit in the same level of cleanliness as existed when he took occupancy;

- **costs of repairs** for damages caused by the tenant, excluding ordinary wear and tear; and

- **costs to replace or restore** furnishings provided by the landlord if agreed to in the lease. [CC §1950.5(b)]

Unpaid late charges incurred on a proper demand may be deducted from the security deposit since they are a **form of rent** in that they are **amounts due** the landlord under the lease agreement. [See Chapter 15]

The landlord may not deduct from a tenant's security deposit the costs he incurs to repair defects in the premises which existed prior to the tenant's occupancy. [CC §1950.5(e)]

Tenants seeking to recover security deposits retained by landlords may make unfounded claims that the excessive wear and tear existed when they took possession of the property. To best avoid claims of pre-existing defects, a

SECURITY DEPOSIT DISPOSITION
ON VACATING RESIDENTIAL PREMISES

DATE:_____, 20_____, at _____,California.

NOTICE: This itemized statement of the security deposit's disposition, including documentation of charges deducted, must be given to the tenants by the landlord within 21 days after a tenant vacates residential property. [California Civil Code §1950.5(f)]

Use of this form in a timely and proper fashion avoids landlord liability for 2% monthly penalty on any portion of the security deposit wrongfully retained.

To Tenant: _____

Items left blank or unchecked are not applicable.

FACTS:

1. This is notice to the tenant of any Landlord deductions from the security deposit under the following agreement:
    ☐ Residential lease agreement   ☐ Occupancy agreement
    ☐ Month-to-month residential rental agreement ☐ Other:_____
    1.1 dated _____,20_____, at _____,California,
    1.2 entered into by _____,Landlord,
    and _____, Tenant,
    1.3 regarding residential premises referred to as: _____

DISPOSITION OF DEPOSIT:

2. Under the above referenced agreement, Tenant handed Landlord a security
    deposit in the amount of . . . . $_____
3. The following deductions have been made by Landlord from the security deposit:
    3.1 Repair of damages   Cost
        a. _____ $_____
        b. _____ $_____
    3.2 Necessary cleaning of the premises   Cost
        a. _____ $_____
        b. _____ $_____
    3.3 Delinquent or holdover rent   Amount
        a. From:_____To:_____ $_____
    3.4 Replacement/repair of lost or damaged furnishings   Cost
        a. _____ $_____
    3.5 TOTAL deductions from security deposit . . . . (-)$_____

4. **BALANCE DUE TENANT:**
    4.1 Balance of security deposit remaining after deductions (line 2 less line 3.5) . . . . $_____
    4.2 Interest on the security deposit from _____ to _____
        at _____% per annum . . . . (+)$_____
    4.3 Balance due Tenant herewith refunded is the amount of (line 4.1 plus 4.2) . . . . $_____
        by Landlord/Agent's check #_____.

5. ☐ **AMOUNT DUE LANDLORD:**
    5.1 The amount due Landlord after deductions (line 2 less line 3.5). . . . . $_____
    5.2 Less interest on the security deposit from _____ to _____
        at _____% per annum . . . . (-)$_____
    5.3 Tenant to hand or mail Landlord/Agent the balance due of (line 5.1 less line 5.2) . . . . $_____

This statement is true and correct:
Date:_____, 20_____
Landlord/Agent: _____
Signature: _____
Address: _____
_____
Phone:_____ Fax: _____
By: _____

FORM 585   10-01   ©2007 **first tuesday**, P.O. BOX 20069, RIVERSIDE, CA 92516 (800) 794-0494

joint inspection of the unit (landlord and tenant) and written documentation of any defects should be completed **before possession** is given to the tenant. [See **first tuesday** Form 560]

Itemized security deposit statements

When a residential tenant vacates, the landlord itemizes the deductions from the tenant's security deposit on a security deposit disposition statement. [See Form 585]

If a landlord is required by local rent control ordinances (or state law) to pay interest on security deposits, the landlord may also use the itemized statement to account for interest accrued on the security deposit. [See Form 585 §3.2]

A residential landlord who, in bad faith, fails to comply with security deposit refund requirements may be subject to statutory penalties of up to twice the amount of the security deposit. [CC §1950.5(l)]

A residential or nonresidential landlord also delivers an itemized statement to tenants on the **sale of the property**, indicating the amount of the security deposits, any deductions and the name, address and telephone number of the buyer. The notice shifts liability for the future return of the security deposit to the buyer. [CC §§1950.5(h), 1950.7(d); see **first tuesday** Form 586]

Nonresidential refund requirements

A nonresidential lease does not need to set forth:

- the circumstance under which a tenant's security deposit will be refunded; and

- a time period within which a landlord will refund a tenant's security deposit.

Other than its receipt, a nonresidential lease does not even need to contain a provision addressing when the security deposit will be returned. [See **first tuesday** Form 552]

If a refund period is not agreed to and the nonresidential landlord does not take any deductions from the security deposit, the landlord must refund the security deposit within a reasonable time period.

A nonresidential landlord must return the remainder of the security deposit within **30 days** from the date he receives possession including any permissible deductions from the security deposit for unpaid rent, cost of cleaning or repairs. Thirty days is considered a reasonable refund period since the landlord is allotted 30 days to determine whether repairs are needed. After 30 days, no good reason exists to continue to hold the deposit.

However, if the security deposit **exceeds** the combined amount of the first and last month's rent and the only deduction from the deposit is delinquent rent, the landlord must, within two weeks after he takes possession of the property, return the remaining amount of the security deposit after deducting delinquent rent and an additional amount equal to one month's rent. The additional amount retained must be returned within 30 days after the landlord takes possession. [CC §1950.7]

Unlike the residential landlord, the nonresidential landlord is not required to provide tenants with an itemized statement of deductions when the security deposit is refunded. However, a prudent nonresidential landlord provides tenants with an itemized statement when they vacate, unless a full refund is made.

An accounting avoids the inevitable demand for documentation which arises when a tenant does not receive a full refund of his security deposit. A nonresidential landlord who, in bad faith, fails to comply with the refund requirements is liable to the tenant for up to $200 in statutory damages. [CC §1950.7(f)]

Chapter 20

Recovery of residential turnover costs

This chapter reviews how rent is a residential landlord's sole source for funds to pay for tenant turnover costs.

The security deposit plays no role

A landlord of an apartment complex is determined to reduce or offset the costs of tenant turnover by shifting the costs to tenants.

An increasing number of his tenants are staying for ever shorter periods of time. On vacating, the units are re-renting quickly, keeping lost rent due to "turn-around" at a minimum.

However, each tenant turnover requires expenditures to:

- **refurbish** the unit to eliminate the cumulative effect of normal wear and tear, such as painting the walls, deep-cleaning the carpet and dry-cleaning the drapery;

- **advertise** the unit's availability to locate a tenant;

- pay for time and effort spent **showing** the unit and clearing prospective tenants; and

- pay the property manager's **tenant-origination fee**.

Since the rate of tenant turnovers is exceeding normal expectations, the landlord's *net operating income* (NOI) is being reduced by the excessive refurbishing and reletting costs. [See **first tuesday** Form 352]

From the landlord's point of view, the NOI consists of the remaining amounts of rental income generated by the property after deducting expenses incurred in operating the property — prior to deductions for interest paid on purchase and improvement loans and depreciation as well as principal reduction on the loans.

The landlord is concerned about the economics used since the *value* of the property for establishing its net worth (equity), maximum loan amount and sales price is based on the NOI. Also, *spendable income* slips due to increasing turnover costs.

To increase the property's NOI and net spendable income, the landlord chooses to add a *stay-or-pay* clause to his month-to-month rental agreements.

The **stay-or-pay clause** calls for the residential tenant to forego a return of his security deposit if he moves within six months after taking occupancy. [See Figure 1 accompanying this chapter]

The landlord believes the stay-or-pay clause will dissuade month-to-month tenants from moving for at least six months.

If a tenant is unpersuaded and vacates the premises within the first six months, the stay-or-pay clause states the landlord can recover his "prematurely incurred" turnover costs from the tenant's security deposit.

Can the landlord enforce the stay-or-pay clause in his rental agreements claiming they are based on sound economic policies?

No! The stay-or-pay clause is unenforceable. It is an illegal forfeiture of the security deposit.

If the tenant has not breached the lease or rental agreement and on expiration of proper notice returns the unit in the condition it was received, normal wear and tear excepted for the use allowed, the security deposit must be fully refunded, regardless of how long the unit remains vacant.

The security deposit **may not** be used to cover rent lost for the period of the vacancy or costs incurred to eliminate normal wear and tear and refurbish the unit for the next tenant. [Calif. Civil Code §1950.5(e)]

Thus, the landlord cannot use the stay-or-pay clause in tandem with the security deposit to provide more revenue (rent) to cover his operating costs. Revenue for operating expenses must come from rents, not a one-time lump sum advance payment, a *cost-plus* (profit) pricing imperative.

Classifying the receipt of tenant funds

Funds received from a tenant by a **residential landlord** fall into only four classifications of receipts:

- tenant screening fees;

- waterbed administration fees;

- rent; and

- security deposits.

The amount of the **tenant screening fee** may not exceed $38.97 for 2007 as annually adjusted from an original statutory amount of $30 in 1997 based on the Consumer Price Index (CPI).

Further, the tenant screening fee is limited to:

- the out-of-pocket cost (money) for gathering the information; and

- the cost of the landlord's or property manager's time spent obtaining the information and processing an application to rent. [CC §1950.6(b)]

Rent is compensation, usually periodic, received as revenue by a landlord in exchange for the tenant's use, possession and enjoyment of the property. [**Telegraph Ave. Corporation** v. **Raentsch** (1928) 205 C 93]

Rent also includes the tenant's payment of any late charges agreed to and demanded on the delinquent payment of periodic rent. [**Canal-Randolph Anaheim, Inc.** v. **Moore** (1978) 78 CA3d 477]

A charge for any purpose other than rent, a tenant screening fee or a waterbed administration fee is, by elimination, a refundable security deposit, regardless of any other name or form given to the funds received. [**Granberry** v. **Islay Investments** (1984) 161 CA3d 382]

A **security deposit** is any advance payment designed to be used as security for the tenant's future performance of his obligations agreed to in a rental agreement or lease.

Security deposit deductions

When one month's rent is collected in advance from a residential tenant, the **security deposit is limited** to an amount equal to:

- two months' rent for an *unfurnished unit*; or

- three months' rent for a *furnished unit*. [CC §1950.5(c)]

A residential landlord may deduct from the security deposit those amounts reasonably necessary to:

Figure 1   *(an unenforceable provision)*

A stay-or-pay clause minimum tenancy

If the tenancy is terminated during the six-month period following commencement of this agreement, tenant shall forfeit tenant's security deposit.

- cure tenant defaults in the payment of rent;

- repair damages to the premises caused by the tenant;

- clean the premises except for normal wear and tear; and

- dispose of abandoned personal property. [CC §1950.5(b)]

Any amount of security deposit remaining after taking allowable deductions must be refunded to the residential tenant within three weeks after the tenant moves out. [CC §1950.5(g)(1)]

A residential landlord's retention of any portion of a security deposit in violation of the deduction rules subjects the landlord to statutory penalties of up to twice the amount of the security deposit, in addition to actual damages. [CC §1950.5(l)]

Is it extra rent or a screening fee?

A landlord funds the care and maintenance expenses of a property from rents, not from an initial lump sum amount paid in addition to rent.

Consider a residential landlord who requires new tenants to prepay one month's rent and a refundable security deposit in an amount equal to one month's rent before entering into a lease or rental agreement.

The landlord also charges an additional one-time, nonrefundable, new-tenant fee, membership fee or tenant application expense reimbursement fee.

The purported purpose of the **nonrefundable fee** is to cover administrative expenses and services related to **processing** the tenant's application to rent the unit.

A tenant seeks to recover the one-time extra charge, claiming it is a nonrefundable security deposit since the one-time, lump-sum charge covers expenses that must be recovered through amounts collected as rents, thus making it a security deposit.

Can the tenant recover the one-time extra charge imposed by the landlord as a masked security deposit?

No, not as a security deposit! The one-time charge for administrative costs incurred by the landlord to process the tenant's rental application is not a security deposit. A security deposit is imposed and collected to secure the landlord against future tenant defaults under the lease or rental agreement by providing a source of recovery for any loss caused by the default. [**Krause** v. **Trinity Management Service, Inc.** (2000) 23 C4th 116; CC §§1950.5, 1950.6]

However, a "nonrefundable upfront fee" is controlled by the tenant screening fee statute which limits the amount of the application processing fee to $38.97 for 2007. The difference is refundable as an excess screening fee charge which is neither rent nor a security deposit.

Unenforceable liquidated damages

Consider a residential landlord who includes a *liquidated damages* provision in the rental agreement in an effort to reduce or offset his tenant turnover costs. [See Figure 2 accompanying this chapter]

In addition to the first month's rent, the landlord properly collects a security deposit from the tenant in an amount equal to one month's rent to cover any future breach of the rental agreement by the tenant.

Before the completion of six months, a tenant hands the landlord a 30-day notice to vacate and then vacates the unit.

Within **21 days after vacating**, the landlord sends the tenant an itemized accounting for the security deposit, deducting one month's rent as the liquidated damages owed agreed as due to the early (and proper) termination of the month-to-month rental agreement.

The tenant claims he is entitled to a refund of the security deposit since a **liquidated damages** provision in a rental agreement or lease is unenforceable as a *forfeiture penalty*.

Is the liquidated damages provision unenforceable?

Yes! A liquidated damages provision is unenforceable in residential rental agreements and leases. The amount of recoverable losses a residential landlord incurs when a tenant vacates a unit, such as the lost rent and the maintenance costs of labor and materials to cover excess wear and tear, is readily ascertainable. [CC §1671(d)]

A liquidated damages provision may only be enforced when conditions make it extremely difficult or impracticable to determine the amount of actual money losses. This is never the case in real estate rentals. [CC §1671(d)]

Further, liquidated damages do not represent a recovery of **actual money losses** incurred by the landlord, losses which without calling for a forfeiture may be deducted from the security deposit. The purpose of the landlord's liquidated damages provisions is not to recover money lost due to unpaid rent owed or excessive wear and tear, but to increase his NOI and spendable income.

Even if the landlord does not deduct the liquidated damages amount agreed to from the security deposit, he will not be able to recover the liquidated damages from the tenant in a civil action.

Covering tenant turnover costs

Recovery of a landlord's turnover costs must come from the periodic rents bargained for and received from his tenants — an expense of operations deducted from income.

The costs of refurbishing a unit to eliminate normal wear and tear so it can be re-rented in a "fresh" condition are known, or readily available on inquiry, in advance. Financially, the amount of the refurbishing costs must be amortized over the length of each tenant's probable occupancy period so the costs can be recovered as a component of the periodic rent charged to a tenant.

However, since the local rental marketplace determines rent ceilings, a landlord is limited in the amount he can charge for rent and successfully compete for tenants.

Thus, a landlord's most logical cost recovery approach is to stretch out each tenant's term of occupancy to an optimal length of time to reduce the frequency of tenant turnover and increase net spendable income.

The lease reduces costs

The landlord's best method for recovering turnover costs is to rent to creditworthy tenants on a lease agreement with a one year term or

---

Figure 2   *(an unenforceable provision)*

A liquidated damages minimum tenancy provision

Should the tenant choose to terminate this tenancy during the six-month period beginning on commencement of this tenancy, the tenant shall pay as liquidated damages, and not as a penalty or forfeiture, an amount equal to one month's rent in consideration for exercising the right to vacate prematurely.

longer, local rental market permitting. Rent may require a reduction to induce the longer period of occupancy.

A lease agreement allows the landlord to amortize the **anticipated costs of refurbishing** the unit over the maximum term negotiable. Also, a lease agreement reduces the frequency of move-outs and provides a schedule for turnover maintenance since tenants under a lease agreement tend to remain in possession until the lease term expires.

Although the market limits the amount a landlord can charge for rent, different rental rates exist for rental and lease agreements in most local markets.

Month-to-month tenancies typically give the landlord less time over which he can amortize his turnover costs. A landlord with month-to-month tenants must also deal with the likelihood of frequent turnovers requiring the investment of his time and effort to constantly re-rent vacant units.

As compensation, a landlord is able to charge **higher rents** for month-to-month tenancies which reflects the cost-push of higher and more frequent turnover expenses than occur under a lease.

In contrast, a lease agreement locks a tenant into a fixed period of occupancy, such as one year or longer. Lease agreements reduce the **tenant turnover rate**, and in turn, reduce operating costs and lost rent due to vacancies. Thus, the landlord can amortize his anticipated turnover costs over a greater period of time.

As a result, the lower rent usually received on lease agreements is a reflection of lower overall refurbishing expenses, reduced annual vacancy rates, less management time and effort, and usually less risk of lost rents.

Tiered rents for time in occupancy

A rental or lease agreement structured with tiered rents for future periods of occupancy provide for a slightly higher rent for months included in the first-tier period — such as the first six months of the periodic tenancy — than in the following months should the tenant remain in possession.

If the month-to-month tenant continues in occupancy after the first-tier period, the rental agreement calls for a lower rent during a second-tier period or for the remainder of the occupancy, both rates being consistent with the marketplace.

Tiered rents which decrease after a period of time encourage tenants to stay longer since their rent will be lower.

As a result, the landlord's turnover costs are fully amortized and "reserved" through the higher periodic rent charged during the first tier.

If the month-to-month tenant does vacate on 30 days notice before the period of higher first-tier rent ends, less of the landlord's turnover costs prematurely incurred due to the early vacancy are left unamortized.

However, tiered rents will only avoid the security deposit limitations if:

- a security deposit of a customary amount to cover credit risks is charged;

- the higher monthly rent is consistently charged over a long enough period so as not to be characterized as a disguised or delayed receipt of a security deposit, application processing (screening) fee, cleaning fee or forfeiture; and

- the tenancy is month-to-month.

It is not certain that tiered rents will never be construed as a disguise for a nonrefundable security deposit, but it has become far less likely. [Krause, *supra*]

The same economics and amortization logic applies to the cost of **tenant improvements** (TIs) made by a nonresidential landlord (or a tenant himself). For example, if the TIs are recovered by the landlord over the first four years of a lease as part of the rent amount, the rent thereafter (second tier) could be reduced to an amount which reflects the elimination of the TI charges in order to induce the tenant to stay for a greater period of time.

Chapter 21

Accepting partial rent

This chapter distinguishes the rights held by residential and nonresidential landlords to file or continue an unlawful detainer (UD) action after receipt of partial rent.

Rights of residential and nonresidential landlords

A **nonresidential tenant**, also called a *commercial or industrial tenant*, experiences cash flow difficulties due to a business downturn. As a result, the tenant becomes delinquent in the payment of rent.

Discussions between the landlord and tenant follow. To enforce collection of the rent, the landlord eventually serves the tenant with a **3-day notice** to pay rent or quit the premises. [See **first tuesday** Form 575]

Prior to the filing of an unlawful detainer (UD) action, the tenant offers to hand the landlord a *partial payment* of the delinquent rent. Further, the tenant wants to pay the balance of the delinquent rent by a specific date if the landlord will agree in writing to defer any filing of a UD action, called a **partial payment agreement**. [See Form 558 accompanying this chapter]

The partial payment agreement specifies the amount of **deferred rent** remaining unpaid, the date for its payment and the consequences of nonpayment — eviction by a UD action without further notice. If the deferred rent is not paid as rescheduled, the nonresidential landlord has the agreed-to **right to file** a UD action to evict the tenant without repeating the 3-day notice requirement for filing a UD action.

Here, the partial payment agreement has only temporarily delayed the nonresidential landlord from moving forward with the eviction process commenced by the service of the 3-day notice on the tenant.

Under the partial payment agreement, the nonresidential landlord retains his right to proceed, based on the service of the 3-day notice, by filing a UD action to evict the tenant if the deferred payment for the balance of the delinquency is not received as rescheduled.

The tenant fails to pay the deferred balance of the delinquent rent on the date scheduled for payment. Without further notice to the tenant, the landlord files a UD action.

The nonresidential tenant seeks to prevent the landlord from proceeding with the UD action, claiming the landlord's acceptance of the partial rent payment invalidates the 3-day notice since the notice now states an amount of rent which is no longer due.

Can the nonresidential landlord accept a payment of partial rent after serving a 3-day notice and later file a UD action against the tenant without serving another 3-day notice for the remaining unpaid rent?

Yes! A **nonresidential landlord** can accept a partial payment of rent after serving a 3-day notice and before filing a UD action. Without further notice to the tenant, the nonresidential landlord can commence a UD action and evict the tenant. [Calif. Code of Civil Procedure §1161.1(b)]

Further, on accepting a partial payment of delinquent rent, a nonresidential landlord does not need to agree to a due date for the remaining rent. He also does not need to enter into any agreement regarding his acceptance of the partial payment if the tenant has previously received a reservation of rights from the landlord, called a *nonwaiver provision* (which appears as a provision in nonresidential leases). [See **first tuesday** Form 552 §22]

However, the nonresidential landlord who memorializes his acceptance of the partial rent payment and the due date for payment of the unpaid balance eliminates any conflicting claims the tenant may make in a UD action concerning the tenant's expectations based on the landlord's acceptance of partial payment of rent.

Residential property distinguished

Consider the same situation involving residential property instead of nonresidential property. As for serving a 3-day notice and later accepting partial payment of the delinquent rent, a huge distinction exists in the separate unlawful detainer rules for residential and nonresidential tenancies.

A **residential landlord** who accepts any amount of rent from a tenant after serving a 3-day notice waives his right to file a UD action based on that 3-day notice. A residential landlord must re-serve the tenant a notice for the amount now remaining unpaid. [**EDC Associates, Ltd.** v. **Gutierrez** (1984) 153 CA3d 167]

Residential vs. nonresidential landlords

Acceptance of a **partial payment** toward delinquent rent is within the discretion of the landlord. A landlord may be willing to accept partial payments when:

- the partial payment is at least equal to the rent accrued at the time the tenant offers the payment;

- the tenant is creditworthy;

- the tenant has an adequate payment history; and

- the tenant is one the landlord wants to retain.

Both residential and nonresidential landlords may accept a partial payment of delinquent rent, then immediately serve the tenant with a 3-day notice demanding payment of the balance due or quit.

However, a landlord could agree in a partial payment agreement not to serve a 3-day notice after receipt of the partial payment of rent on the condition the balance will be received on or before a specified date. [See Forms 558 and 559 accompanying this chapter]

Residential rent paid after notice

If a **residential landlord** files a UD action and later accepts a partial payment of rent, the UD action cannot go forward to eviction. The reason lies in the different amounts of rent demanded in the notice to pay and the amount actually remaining delinquent at the UD hearing. In residential UD actions the amounts must be the same. This rule does not apply to nonresidential tenancies.

Once the residential landlord accepts a partial payment of delinquent rent, the 3-day notice served on the tenant and used to prove up a UD action no longer states the correct amount which must be paid by the tenant to avoid losing his right to possession.

Any 3-day notice served on a residential tenant overstating the amount of delinquent rent due at the **time of trial** on the UD action is invalid. The UD action in a residential eviction based on an overstated amount in the 3-day notice must fail. [**Jayasinghe** v. **Lee** (1993) 13 CA4th Supp. 33]

Upon acceptance of a partial payment of rent, the residential landlord must serve another 3-day notice demanding payment of the remainder due on unpaid delinquent rent, and, if not paid, file a new UD action.

Nonresidential nonwaiver requirements

However, should a **nonresidential landlord** file a UD action and later accept a partial payment of rent, he must then provide or have previously provided the tenant with notice that the acceptance of rent does not waive the landlord's rights, called a *nonwaiver of rights provision* or *reservation of rights*. When the ten-

PARTIAL PAYMENT AGREEMENT
Nonresidential

DATE:_____, 20_____, at _____, California.
Items left blank or unchecked are not applicable.

FACTS:
This partial payment agreement pertains to the collection of past due rent under a nonresidential rental or lease agreement
dated _____, at _____, California,
regarding leased premises referred to as: _____
_____

AGREEMENT:

1. Tenant has not paid delinquent rent for the periods of_____.

2. Landlord hereby accepts partial payment on delinquent rent in the amount of . . . . $_____

3. The balance of the delinquent rent owed is . . . . $_____

   3.1 Plus late charge for delinquency of . . . . $_____

   3.2 Plus a deferred rent processing charge of . . . . $_____

   3.3 **Total deferred rent** due, including additional charges, is the sum of . . . . $_____

4. Tenant to pay the total deferred rent on or before _____, 20_____.

   4.1 Rent to be paid by ☐ cash, ☐ check, or ☐ cashier's check, made payable to Landlord.

   4.2 Rent may be tendered by ☐ mail, or ☐ personal delivery, to:

      _____ (Name)
      _____ (Address)
      _____ (Phone)

      a. Personal delivery of rent will be accepted during the hours of _____am to _____pm on the following
      days:_____.

   4.3 Rent may also be paid by deposit into account number _____
      at: _____
      _____ (Financial Institution)
      _____ (Address)
      _____

   4.4 No grace period for payment of the deferred rent is granted to Tenant.

   4.5 Delinquent payment of the deferred rent incurs a late charge of $_____

5. If deferred rent is paid when due, any outstanding three-day notice to pay rent or quit is no longer valid.

6. If the deferred rent is not paid when due, Landlord reserves the right to:
   (Check one box only)

   6.1 ☐ Serve Tenant with a three-day notice to pay the remaining balance of the rent due or quit the premises.
      (Check if a three-day notice has not been served)

   6.2 ☐ Commence, without further notice, an unlawful detainer action to evict Tenant from the premises.
      (Check if a three-day notice has been served)

   6.3 ☐ Continue with the unlawful detainer action on file to evict Tenant from the premises.
      (Check if unlawful detainer action has been filed)

7. No provision of the lease agreement or rental agreement is affected in this agreement.

8. _____
   _____

I agree to the terms stated above.	I agree to the terms stated above.
Date:_____, 20_____	Date:_____, 20_____
Landlord: _____	Tenant:_____
Agent: _____	Tenant:_____
Signature: _____	Signature: _____
Phone: _____	Signature: _____
Fax: _____	Phone:_____Fax: _____

ant receives a nonwaiver of rights on or before the landlord's acceptance of partial rent, the landlord may continue with the UD action and recover possession of the premises. [CCP §1161.1(c)]

Nonresidential lease agreements include the necessary **nonwaiver of rights** provision, stating the landlord's acceptance of partial rent does not constitute a waiver of the landlord's right to enforce any remaining breach of the lease. [See Form 552 §22]

Now consider a nonresidential tenant who defaults on a rent payment under a lease agreement containing a nonwaiver provision. He is served with a 3-day notice to pay or quit, but fails to pay the rent before it expires. The 3-day notice to pay does not contain a provision for nonwaiver of rights on acceptance of rent.

The nonresidential landlord files a UD action. He then accepts a partial payment of rent without entering into any agreements, except to receive the amount paid as rent.

The tenant now claims the landlord cannot proceed with a UD hearing since neither the 3-day notice nor the landlord's receipt of the partial rent payment include a nonwaiver of rights provision.

Here, the nonresidential landlord may proceed with the UD action after receipt of partial rent. The nonwaiver provision in the lease agreement gives the tenant notice that the landlord's acceptance of any rent does not waive the landlord's rights. One such right is the right to proceed with a previously filed UD action. [**Woodman Partners** v. **Sofa U Love** (2001) 94 CA4th 766]

A nonwaiver provision in a 3-day notice or partial payment agreement provides the landlord with the same right to proceed with the UD action as though the provision existed in the lease agreement.

On accepting a partial payment of rent after a UD action has been filed, the nonresidential landlord amends the UD complaint to reflect the partial payment received and the remaining amount now due from the tenant. [CCP §1161.1(c)]

Get it in writing

Without a written partial payment agreement, the tenant could claim the landlord who accepted partial rent:

- treated acceptance of partial rent as an *accord and satisfaction* of all the rent due in a purported dispute over the amount of rent actually owed;

- by his conduct *waived* the right to continue eviction proceedings, sometimes called *estoppel*; or

- permanently *modified* the lease agreement, establishing a semi-monthly rent payment schedule.

When a residential or nonresidential landlord accepts a partial payment of rent, the use of the partial payment agreement is evidence that bars the tenant from later claiming the landlord waived valuable rights by accepting rent.

Residential partial payment agreement

The partial payment agreement entered into by a residential landlord and tenant on acceptance of a portion of the rent due memorializes:

- the landlord's receipt of partial rent;

- the tenant's promise to pay the remainder of the rent on or before a rescheduled due date; and

- notification of the landlord's right to serve a 3-day notice on failure to pay the remaining balance. [See Form 559]

While the partial payment agreement does state the amount of the deferred portion of the delin-

PARTIAL PAYMENT AGREEMENT
Residential

DATE:_____, 20_____, at_____, California.

Items left blank or unchecked are not applicable.

FACTS:

This partial payment agreement pertains to the collection of past due rent under a residential rental or lease agreement dated _____, at _____, California, regarding leased premises referred to as:_____

_____

AGREEMENT:

1. Tenant has not paid the full rent due for the months of _____.

2. Landlord hereby accepts partial payment on the past due rent in the amount of .... $_____

3. The balance of the unpaid rent owed by Tenant is .... $_____

   3.1 Plus a late charge for delinquency of...................... $_____

   3.2 Plus a deferred rent processing charge of .... $_____

   3.3 **Total deferred rent** due, including additional charges, is the sum of .... $_____

4. Tenant to pay the total deferred rent on or before _____, 20_____.

   4.1 Rent to be paid by ☐ cash, ☐ check, or ☐ cashier's check, made payable to Landlord.

   4.2 Rent may be tendered by ☐ mail, or ☐ personal delivery,
      to: _____ (Name)
           _____ (Address)
           _____
           _____ (Phone)

      a. Personal delivery of rent will be accepted during the hours of _____ am to _____ pm on the following days: _____.

   4.3 Rent may also be paid by deposit into account number _____
      at: _____(Financial Institution)
           _____(Address)
           _____
           _____(Phone)

   4.4 No grace period for payment of the deferred rent is granted to Tenant.

   4.5 Delinquent payment of the deferred rent incurs a late charge of $_____

5. If the deferred rent is not paid when due, a three-day notice to pay rent or quit may be served at any time.

6. No provision of the lease agreement or rental agreement is affected by this agreement.

7. _____
_____
_____

I agree to the terms stated above.	**I agree to the terms stated above.**
Date:_____, 20_____	Date:_____, 20_____
Landlord:_____	Tenant:_____
Agent:_____	Tenant:_____
Signature:_____	Signature:_____
Address:_____	Signature:_____
_____	Address:_____
Phone:_____	_____
Fax:_____	Phone:_____
	Fax:_____

FORM 559   2-02   ©2007 **first tuesday**, P.O. BOX 20069, RIVERSIDE, CA 92516 (800) 794-0494

quent rent owed by the tenant and the date it is to be paid, the notice is not what is required to establish an unlawful detainer and evict the tenant.

Consider a **residential tenant** who informs the landlord he will be unable to pay the monthly rent within the grace period after it is due, before the payment becomes delinquent. The tenant offers to pay part of the rent prior to delinquency and the remainder ten days later.

Since the tenant is creditworthy, has not been seriously delinquent in the past and the landlord wishes to retain the tenant, the residential landlord agrees to accept the partial payment.

However, to **avoid disputes** regarding the amount of remaining rent due and when it will be paid, the residential landlord prepares and the tenant signs a partial payment agreement formalizing their understanding.

Now consider a residential landlord who serves a 3-day notice and then accepts a partial payment of rent before the notice expires. By accepting a partial payment, the residential landlord has rendered the 3-day notice invalid.

When the rent was accepted the residential landlord required the tenant to enter into a partial payment agreement stating the date the balance owed was due. The partial payment agreement will avoid any claims by the tenant about when the balance is due and when a 3-day notice can be served if the balance is not paid.

Nonresidential partial payment agreement

The eviction rights reserved by a nonwaiver provision allowing a nonresidential landlord to accept partial rent are far less restricted by law than for a residential landlord.

Before service of a 3-day notice to pay rent or quit on a **nonresidential tenant** who is delinquent in his rent payment, the nonresidential landlord can:

- accept partial payment of rent; and

- then or later serve a 3-day notice, or agree not to serve a 3-day notice unless the remainder of the rent is not paid as rescheduled. [See Form 558 §6.1]

When a 3-day notice has been served on a nonresidential tenant and the landlord later accepts a partial payment of rent, the partial payment agreement they enter into to acknowledge receipt of partial rent contains:

- the due date for payment of the delinquent rent remaining unpaid; and

- notice of the nonresidential landlord's right to file a UD action on nonpayment.

More importantly, a nonresidential landlord who **files a UD action** and later accepts a partial payment of rent under a partial payment agreement notifies the tenant that the landlord has not waived his right to continue the UD action and recover possession under the existing UD action in spite of the payment of rent. As a variation, the nonresidential landlord could agree to reinstate the tenant's right to possession if the remainder of the delinquent rent is paid prior to the UD hearing date.

However, no agreement is necessary on acceptance of partial rent from a nonresidential tenant to preserve the landlord's rights. The landlord can accept partial payment and immediately proceed with his next step in the eviction process — service of a 3-day notice, filing of the UD action or the UD hearing — if a nonwaiver provision is in a prior document, such as the lease agreement.

Chapter 22

Changing terms on a month-to-month tenancy

This chapter reviews the requirements for a landlord's 30-day notice to alter the terms in a tenant's month-to-month rental agreement.

Landlord's 30-day notice

A landlord and tenant enter into a month-to-month tenancy under a rental agreement which contains an option to purchase the property. The option **expires on termination** of the tenancy.

Later, the landlord serves the tenant with a 30-day Notice of Change in Rental Terms, stating the option to purchase will now expire in 30 days, unless exercised by the tenant. [See Form 570 accompanying this chapter]

After the 30-day notice expires, the tenant, who is still in possession, attempts to exercise the option. However, the landlord refuses to sell the property under the option, claiming the tenant's right to exercise the option to purchase no longer exists as the option expired due to the 30-day notice.

The tenant claims the option to purchase is binding for the duration of the tenancy, and the month-to-month rental agreement has not been terminated.

Can the tenant enforce the option to purchase?

No! The option expired unexercised on the running of the 30-day notice of change in rental terms which altered its expiration date.

The option to purchase was part of the rental agreement. Thus, on expiration of the 30-day notice canceling the option, the option — as a set of terms in an addendum attached to the month-to-month rental agreement — was eliminated.

Like any other provision contained or referenced in a month-to-month rental agreement, the option to purchase is part of the month-to-month tenancy, subject to change on 30 days' written notice from the landlord. [**Wilcox** v. **Anderson** (1978) 84 CA3d 593]

30-day notice to change rental terms

All covenants and conditions in a residential or nonresidential month-to-month rental agreement, also called *provisions, clauses, terms, conditions, addendums, etc.*, may be changed on 30 days' written notice by the landlord. [California Civil Code §827]

For example, a residential or nonresidential landlord under a month-to-month rental agreement can increase the rent or shift repair and maintenance obligations to the tenant by serving a 30-day Notice of Change in Rental Terms. [See Form 570]

To be enforceable, the 30-day notice must be served in the same manner as a 3-day notice to pay rent or quit. [See Chapter 28]

However, only the landlord may unilaterally change the terms in a rental agreement. [CC §827]

A month-to-month tenant has no ability to alter the terms of his rental agreement, other than to terminate the tenancy and vacate. [CC §1946]

In rent control communities, a landlord or property manager must be fully apprised of how rent control ordinances affect their ability to alter provisions in leases and rental agreements.

30-day notice to increase rents

A landlord or property manager may serve a notice of change in rental terms under a periodic (month-to-month) rental agreement on **any day** during the rental period.

Once a notice of change in rental terms is served on a month-to-month tenant (or other periodic tenancy), the new terms stated in the notice immediately become part of the tenant's rental agreement. [CC §827]

However, the new rental terms stated in the notice do not take effect until expiration of the 30-day notice.

For example, a property manager prepares a 30-day notice of change in rental terms to be served on a month-to-month tenant to **increase the rent**. The due date for the payment of rent is the first day of each month.

The tenant is properly served with the 30-day notice on the 10th of June. The tenant intends to remain in possession at the new rental rate.

Since June 11th is the first day of the 30-day notice period, the rent will not **begin to accrue** at the increased rate until July 11th — the day after the 30-day notice expires. However, rent for all of July is payable **in advance** on the first of the month, including the number of days (21) affected by the rent increase.

The rent due and payable in advance for the calendar month of July is prorated as follows:

- the old rate for the first ten days of the month; and

- the new rate for the remaining 21 days in the month of July.

Pro rata rent will be determined based on the number of days in the calendar month, unless the rental agreement contains a provision prorating rent on a 30-day month. [CC §14]

Tenant's response to a change

On being served with a 30-day notice of a change in rental terms, the month-to-month tenant has three options:

- remain in possession and comply with the new rental terms;

- serve the landlord with a 30-day notice of intent to vacate and pay pro rata rent on the next due date for days remaining unpaid during the month through the end of the 30-day period to vacate; or

- remain in possession, refuse to comply with the rental terms and raise defenses, such as retaliatory eviction, in the resulting unlawful detainer (UD) action.

Editor's note — To prevail on a defense of retaliatory eviction, circumstances showing retaliation for the exercise of rights must exist.

Consider the tenant who receives the landlord's notice but does not wish to comply with changes in the rental terms. Accordingly, the tenant serves the landlord with a 30-day Notice of Intent to Vacate. [See **first tuesday** Form 572]

If the change in terms is a rent increase, the tenant is liable for pro rata rent at the new rate for the days after the rent increase becomes effective until the tenant's notice to vacate — payable in advance on the due date for the next scheduled payment of rent, usually the first.

Rent control restrictions

Most rent control ordinances allow a landlord or property manager to increase the rent to:

- obtain a fair return on his investment;

- recover the cost of capital improvements to the property; and

- pass through the cost of servicing the debt on the property.

30-DAY NOTICE OF CHANGE IN RENTAL TERMS

DATE:_____, 20_____, at _____, California.

> **NOTICE:** A landlord must furnish the tenant with a written 30-day notice of any change in the terms of a month-to-month tenancy. If rent is raised more than 10% within a 12-month period on a residential tenant, a 60-day notice of the increase is required. [Calif. Civil Code §827; See **first tuesday** Form 574]

To Tenant: _____

Items left blank or unchecked are not applicable.

FACTS:

You are a Tenant under a rental agreement or expired lease

dated_____, at _____, California,

entered into by _____, as the Tenant,

and_____, as the Landlord,

regarding real estate referred to as: _____
_____

NOTICE:

Thirty (30) days after service of this notice on you, the terms of your tenancy on the real estate are hereby changed as indicated below:

1. Rent shall be $_____ payable ☐ monthly, or _____,
    in advance, and due on the _____ day of the month.

    1.1   Rent to be paid by ☐ cash, ☐ check, or ☐ cashier's check, made payable to Landlord.

    1.2   Rent may be tendered by ☐ mail, or ☐ personal delivery,

          to: _____ (Name)

          _____ (Address)

          _____ (Phone)

          a. Personal delivery of rent will be accepted during the hours of _____ am to _____ pm on the following
              days: _____.

    1.3   Rent may also be paid by deposit into account number _____

          at: _____ (Financial Institution)

          _____ (Address)

2. The common area maintenance charge shall be $_____ per month, payable with each payment of rent.

3. Utilities now paid by Landlord to be paid by Tenant as checked:

    ☐ Gas ☐ Electricity ☐ Sewage and Rubbish ☐ Water ☐ Cable TV

4. ☐ Tenant to maintain and properly care for the lawns, gardens, tree, shrubs and watering system.

5. An additional security deposit of $_____ is payable with the next rent payment.

6. _____
    _____

7. **This notice affects no other terms of your tenancy.**

Date:_____, 20_____

Landlord/Agent: _____

Signature:_____

Phone: _____

Fax: _____

E-mail: _____

Thus, without further authority from the rent control board, a landlord can make general adjustments to rents in one of three ways:

- increase rent by the maximum percentage set by ordinance;

- increase rent by the maximum percentage of the consumer price index (CPI) as set by ordinance; or

- increase rent by the maximum amount previously set by the rent control board.

Landlords of newly constructed units or individual units (single family residences/condos) held out for rent may establish their own rental rates, within limitations, if they are subject to rent control ordinances established prior to 1995. [See Chapter 57]

Chapter 23

Lease guarantees and small claims actions

This chapter discusses the use of lease guarantees and limitations on small claims court awards against a guarantor.

Recovery amount limited

Three young prospective tenants are seeking to rent their first apartment as roommates. The prospective tenants lack any rental history or independent source of income.

A landlord agrees to lease to the tenants on the condition a creditworthy parent of one of the tenants signs a *lease guarantee agreement*. A **lease guarantee** is entered into by the parents of one of the tenants. Under the lease guarantee, the parents are responsible for all monies due the landlord on the lease agreement to be entered into by the tenants should the tenants fail to pay. [See Form 439-L §3 accompanying this chapter]

The tenants enter into a one-year lease. However, before the lease expires, the tenants stop paying rent.

A 3-day notice to pay rent or quit is served on the tenants.

A copy of the notice is sent to the guarantor as required to enforce the guarantee agreement, called a *condition precedent*. [See Form 439-L §3.1]

The rent remains unpaid and the landlord files an unlawful detainer (UD) action. As a result, the tenants are evicted.

When the landlord regains possession, he discovers the tenants and their guests have damaged the property. The walls have holes, the carpet and drapes are destroyed, screens are missing, a window is broken, the kitchen formica is burned, parts are missing from the range and oven, door jambs are broken, a bathroom fixture is cracked, and the carport assigned to the tenants has been damaged by a vehicle.

The landlord incurs $4,500 in losses due to the cost of preparing the unit for leasing and rents lost before reletting the unit.

Since the recovery sought under the lease agreement is less than $5,000 and possession is no longer an issue, the landlord files a small claims court action against the tenants who signed the lease agreement and the parents who signed the guarantee.

However, at trial, the small claims judge advises the landlord that any award against the parents who guaranteed the lease is limited to $2,500. The landlord is then asked if he wants:

- a $2,500 judgment against the guarantors, which would bar any further recovery from the guarantors; or

- a dismissal of the case against the guarantors, which would allow the landlord to file a superior court action against the guarantors to recover on the guarantee.

Is the small claims court judge correct in limiting the landlord's recovery from the parents under the guarantee agreement?

Yes! The small claims court only has **jurisdiction over a person** who is liable as a guarantor for the obligations of another if the amount awarded is $2,500 or less. [Calif. Code of Civil Procedure §116.220(c)]

Thus, if the landlord wants a judgment against the guarantors for the full amount of his losses, the landlord must dismiss the small claims action against the parents (or never file it against the guarantors in the first place) and seek recovery on the guarantee agreement in a superior court action.

GUARANTEE AGREEMENT
For Lease

DATE:_____, 20_____, at _____, California.

Items left blank or unchecked are not applicable.

FACTS:

1. This Guarantee Agreement (Guarantee) is entered into by:

   1.1 _____, Guarantor,

   1.2 and _____, Landlord,

   1.3 as an addendum to a Lease Agreement for real estate dated:_____, 20_____

   between _____, Lessee,

   and _____, Landlord,

   for real estate described as: _____
   _____.

2. The Lease Agreement is entered into by Landlord in reliance on this Guarantee and the financial statements provided by Guarantor.

3. **LANDLORD AGREES:**

   3.1 To notify Guarantor of any notices served on Lessee for proceedings to enforce the Lease.

   3.2 To apply to the Lease Agreement obligations, in any reasonable manner and in its sole discretion, any payments or recoveries from Lessee or from Guarantor.

   3.3 Any refund to Lessee by Landlord of any payment received by Landlord on the guaranteed Lease Agreement shall remain fully guaranteed.

   3.4 Any recovery by Landlord from any other Guarantor or an insurer shall first be credited to the portion of the indebtedness of Lessee to Landlord which exceeds the maximum liability under this Guarantee.

4. **GENERAL PROVISIONS:**

   4.1 Any communication or notice under this Guarantee is to be in writing and is effective only if delivered by personal service or mailed by registered or certified mail, postage prepaid return receipt requested.

   4.2 This Guarantee is binding on Guarantor, his successor and assigns and inures to the benefit of Landlord and its successors and assigns.

   4.3 No provision of this Guarantee or right of Landlord can be waived, nor can Guarantor be released from his obligations except in writing signed by Landlord.

   4.4 If Guarantor is a corporation or partnership, each individual executing this Guarantee on behalf of Guarantor represents and warrants he is duly authorized to execute this Guarantee on its behalf.

   4.5 In any action to enforce this agreement, the prevailing party shall receive attorney fees.

   4.6 This Guarantee shall be governed by the laws of California.

5. **GUARANTOR AGREES:**

   5.1 To guarantee to Landlord the payment of rent or any other monetary obligation arising under the Lease Agreement.

   5.2 To continue liability under this Guarantee, notwithstanding:

   a. Any modification of the Lease Agreement;

   b. Any waiver or failure to enforce the Lease Agreement;

   c. Any release or modification of any security for the Lease Agreement, including other guarantees for performance of the Lease Agreement;

   d. Any unenforceability of part or all of the provisions of the Lease Agreement.

   5.3 To file all claims against Lessee in bankruptcy or other proceeding on any indebtedness of Lessee to Guarantor, and to assign to Landlord all Guarantor's rights on any such indebtedness. If Guarantor fails to file any claim, Landlord is authorized to do so in the name of Guarantor or as Guarantor's attorney-in-fact.

   5.4 To subordinate any of Guarantor's claims against Lessee to the Lease Agreement obligations of Lessee to Landlord.

   5.5 ☐ The Guarantee is secured by a trust deed.

— — — — — — — — — — — — — — — PAGE ONE OF TWO — FORM 439-L — — — — — — — — — — — — — — —

6. GUARANTOR WAIVES:

6.1 All right of subrogation to Landlord's rights against Lessee.

6.2 All notices to Guarantor or other persons of the creation, modification, renewal or accrual of any obligations under the Lease Agreement or any other related matter, except under §3.1 of this Guarantee Agreement.

6.3 Any failure to timely enforce the Lease Agreement.

6.4 Any statute of limitations.

6.5 Any duty of Landlord to disclose to Guarantor any facts known or discovered about Lessee which materially increase Guarantor's risks of liability.

6.6 Any circumstances which constitute a legal or equitable discharge of Guarantor.

6.7 The right to require Landlord to first proceed against Lessee and enforce Lessee's obligations under the Lease Agreement or to pursue any remedy or to enforce any right before proceeding on this Guarantee.

6.8 Any Lessee defenses to Landlord's exercise of any of its rights under the Lease Agreement.

I agree to the terms stated above.	I agree to the terms stated above.
Date:_____, 20_____	Date:_____, 20_____
Landlord's Signature: _____	Guarantor's Signature:_____
Landlord's Signature: _____	Guarantor's Signature:_____
Address: _____	Address: _____
_____	_____
Phone: _____	Phone: _____
Fax:_____	Fax:_____
E-mail:_____	E-mail:_____

FORM 439-L   10-00   ©2007 first tuesday, P.O. BOX 20069, RIVERSIDE, CA 92516 (800) 794-0494

If the landlord had known the small claims court limitations from the beginning, he could have considered seeking recovery against the guarantor and the tenants in a superior court action by either representing himself, called *in pro per*, or being represented by an attorney licensed in California. Under some property management situations, the broker managing the property can handle the court action to recover possession and money losses. [See Chapter 9]

Partners and officers as guarantors

Now consider a corporate tenant who enters into an agreement to lease an office building to be occupied by the corporation. The president of the corporation signs the lease agreement on behalf of the corporation, acting in his agency capacity as its president as authorized by the board of directors, to bind the corporation to the lease agreement.

In conjunction with the lease agreement, the corporate vice president agrees to personally guarantee, as an individual, the corporation's performance under the lease agreement. The guarantee agreement to be signed by the vice president identifies the guarantor as an individual. The guarantee agreement does not contain a description of the guarantor's relationship to the corporation as a corporate officer.

Further, the guarantee agreement describes the obligation of the guarantor as a personal obligation. The vice president also supplies the landlord with a financial statement itemizing his personal assets.

The vice president signs the guarantee agreement and places the words "Vice President" next to his signature.

The corporation breaches the lease agreement and files for bankruptcy. The landlord then seeks to enforce the guarantee agreement against the vice president, as an individual, to collect his money losses under the lease agreement.

The vice president claims the guarantee agreement cannot be enforced against him personally since, by identifying himself as the vice president of the corporation on the guarantee agreement, he was executing the guarantee on behalf of the corporation which entered into the lease agreement, not himself.

In this example, the guarantee agreement contains words which bind the vice president personally. The fact the words "Vice President" were entered along with his signature does not change the character of the person signing the guarantee agreement.

The words "Vice President" were merely a description of the individual as a corporate officer and the guarantee agreement did not indicate he was acting as an agent of the corporation, rather than on his own behalf, when he signed it.

The nature of the guarantee agreement identifying the individual and the inclusion of his personal financial statement indicated the vice president was binding himself personally as an individual. [**Sebastian International, Inc.** v. **Peck** (1987) 195 CA3d 803]

Had the vice president signed the guarantee agreement on behalf of the corporation (as the guarantor of its obligation to pay on the lease agreement), the guarantee agreement would be redundant and surplusage. The corporation is already bound by the terms of the lease agreement.

Co-signers on the lease

Now consider a landlord who insists on a creditworthy *co-signer* on a lease agreement before he will lease property to a couple who lack sufficient credit and net worth. He wants a third party to hold him harmless if the actual tenant defaults.

A **co-signer** signs the lease agreement but may or may not be identified in the lease agreement as an additional lessee to whom the leasehold is conveyed. The co-signer does not sign a separate guarantee agreement. However, the co-signer is not listed as a tenant who will occupy the unit. The co-signer does not occupy the unit or receive any benefit from the landlord or the property for signing the lease agreement.

The tenants default and vacate the property. The landlord now seeks to recover more than

$2,500 in damages and unpaid rent from the co-signer. The landlord files a small claims court action against the co-signer to collect lost rent and the cost to repair excess wear and tear to the unit.

The co-signer claims the landlord's recovery is limited to $2,500 since the co-signer was not intended to be a tenant, did not take possession of the property and received no benefit from the leasing transaction.

Here, the co-signer signed the lease agreement merely to assure payment of the rent owed by the tenants. Thus, the co-signer claims he is liable for the actions of the tenants as a *guarantor*.

While case law does not exist regarding the co-signer's guarantor defense, state law does limit a small claims recovery to $2,500 from a defendant who is required to respond to claims by paying for losses based on the default, actions or omissions of another person.

The negotiations prior to entering into the lease agreement establish the separate legal nature of the co-signer's involvement in the leasing transaction as that of a **guarantor**. Negotiations demonstrate the purpose of the co-signer's involvement was to assure payment of the prospective tenants' commitment to pay rent, not to enforce possession or other benefit for the landlord conveying a leasehold interest to the tenants.

Editor's note — The co-signer argument is similar to the co-signer of a note who receives no benefit from the loan proceeds and merely co-signs the note.

*As a corollary to the co-signing of a note, the co-signer on a lease agreement would claim his activity of co-signing the lease agreement creates a contact obligation similar to an **accommodation party** under California's Commercial Code, and thus, assures payment of a debt (rent) owed by another person (the occupying tenant).*

Under the Commercial Code, an accommodation party is an individual who:

- *signs a note to include liability for a debt evidenced by the note; and*

- *receives no direct benefit from the debt. [Calif. Commercial Code §3419(a)]*

The co-signer would claim the lease agreement should be viewed as a note since it is evidence of a debt (rent) owed for letting the premises, a debt economically equivalent to interest owed on principal lent (and evidenced by a note). Also, due to the fact the co-signer was not to take possession under the lease agreement, the co-signer is not primarily liable for payment of the rent and should be considered the equivalent of an accommodation party. [Com C §3419]

An accommodation party's liability is secondary and similar to a guarantor's. Thus, the co-signer would argue the landlord's recovery in a small claims court action is limited to $2,500.

In spite of the reference in the lease agreement to the co-signer as a (non-occupying) tenant, the intent and sole purpose behind the co-signer's execution of the lease was to assure payment of the rent owed by others — the occupying tenants. Thus, the co-signer entered into a guarantee agreement on signing the lease agreement.

Further, and to distinguish the landlord's obligations owed to a guarantor when co-signing the lease agreement versus those owed under a guarantee agreement, the guarantor under a guarantee agreement waives his rights to notices and consent to material changes in the lease agreement allowing the landlord to terminate the tenancy and pursue collection from the tenant before ever making a demand on the guarantor. [See Form 439-L §6]

SECTION D

Enforcing Rents; Forfeiting Tenancies

Chapter 24

Forfeiture of the lease

This chapter discusses the effect a termination of the right to occupy, the lease, has on the tenant's obligation to pay future rent under a residential or nonresidential lease agreement.

Lease agreement obligations survive

A tenant occupies real estate under a lease agreement with a *default remedies provision* stating that once the tenant's right to possession — the lease — is terminated due to a default by the tenant, the landlord may collect rents for the remaining unexpired term of the lease. [See **first tuesday** Forms 551 and 552 §23]

The tenant fails to pay the rent, but does not vacate the premises. The landlord serves the tenant with a 3-day notice to pay rent or quit.

In the notice, the **landlord declares** the lease to be *forfeited* if the tenant does not pay rent by expiration of the third day following service. If the tenant fails to pay during the three-day period, his right to possession, the lease, is forfeited and the tenant must vacate or he will be evicted in an unlawful detainer (UD) action. [See **first tuesday** Form 575 §3]

The tenant does not pay the rent within the three-day period and remains in possession of the property, called a *holdover occupancy* or *UD* . The tenant's leasehold, called the *lease*, has been **terminated** due to the expiration of three days after service without payment since the 3-day notice included a **forfeiture declaration**. [Calif. Civil Code §1174(a)]

The landlord does not file a UD action to regain possession of the property, even though the tenant's continued possession is now unlawful and the tenant pays no further rent.

Editor's note — The landlord may benefit by choosing not to evict the tenant when no other tenant is immediately available to occupy the space. The rent earned during the holdover is the holdover rate set in the lease agreement, which usually greatly exceeds the current rental rate for the space. Further, occupancy is often required by insurance carriers to qualify for hazard coverage.

The tenant later voluntarily vacates the property prior to expiration of the lease.

The landlord then files a civil action against the tenant to **collect rent** for:

- the period prior to termination of the right to possession by forfeiture as declared in the 3-day notice;

- the holdover (unlawful detainer) period after the forfeiture of possession and prior to vacating; and

- the remaining period under the lease agreement after the tenant vacated until *expiration* of the lease.

The tenant claims the landlord cannot collect rent called for in the lease agreement for any period after expiration of the 3-day notice since:

- the election to forfeit the lease contained in the 3-day notice to pay or quit canceled the lease agreement, not just terminated the right to occupancy (the lease); and

- the landlord's failure to evict the tenant on cancellation of the lease agreement converted the tenant's continued occupancy into a periodic month-to-month tenancy — for which only reasonable rent is due, not the scheduled rent for a holdover as called for in the lease agreement.

Can the landlord collect all rent unpaid during the tenant's occupancy as well as future rent due during the remaining term of the lease even though the lease was forfeited in the 3-day notice?

Yes! A 3-day notice to pay or quit that declares an election to forfeit the lease on failure to pay rent does not also cancel the lease agreement. The **forfeiture election** only terminates the tenant's **right to possession** under the lease that was conveyed to the tenant by the landlord upon entering into the lease agreement. [**Danner** v. **Jarrett** (1983) 144 CA3d 164]

Here, a distinction must be made between the **lease** held by the tenant, called a *leasehold*, and the **lease agreement** which is a contract also occasionally referred to as *the lease*.

Further, the holdover occupancy does not convert the unlawful possession after expiration of the 3-day notice into a month-to-month tenancy, unless monthly rent is **tendered and accepted** by the landlord for occupancy during the holdover period.

Also, a landlord need not first evict the holdover tenant in a UD action before filing a separate money action to recover future rents called for in the lease agreement. The right to possession, inherent in the lease conveyed to the tenant, and the rights and obligations agreed to in the lease agreement are separately enforceable.

However, the tenant's leasehold **right to possession** must first be terminated, which occurs under the forfeiture declaration and expiration of the 3-day notice (or by an eviction in a UD action or abandonment), before the landlord can demand and recover holdover rents and **unearned future rents** under the lease agreement. [**Walt** v. **Superior Court** (1992) 8 CA4th 1667]

First terminate the lease on default

"Termination of the lease" by forfeiture refers to the termination of the tenant's *right to possession* conveyed to the tenant when he entered into the lease agreement with the landlord.

If a breach of the lease agreement by the tenant is curable, the landlord terminates the tenant's right to possession on expiration of a 3-day notice period (without performance by the tenant) by including a *forfeiture-of-lease clause* in the 3-day notice served on the tenant. [**In re Windmill Farms Inc.** (9th Cir. 1988) 841 F2d 1467]

The tenant's possession becomes unlawful when the tenant continues in possession without permission after the leasehold has been terminated by forfeiture, called an *unlawful detainer (UD), holdover tenancy* or *tenancy at sufferance.*

With the right to possession terminated by the declaration of forfeiture in the 3-day notice, the landlord may file a UD action and recover possession without concern for the tenant *reinstating* the lease and being *restored* to possession after trial. [Calif. Code of Civil Procedure §§1161.2, 1174(c)]

One purpose of the UD action is for a court to determine whether the termination of the right to possession under the 3-day notice was proper. If proper, the landlord is awarded possession and the tenant evicted.

But what if a declaration of forfeiture does not exist in the notice? Without a declaration of forfeiture, the lease is not terminated — forfeited — until a *five-day reinstatement period* has passed after entry of judgment. If the terms of the UD judgment are not met for reinstatement, the lease is forfeited and the tenant evicted. [CC §1174(c); see Chapter 22]

Rent earned and unpaid up to the time of entry of the UD judgment may be awarded in the UD action along with an eviction order. The UD award for money due from rent applies only to periods before the UD trial, including:

- the period before termination of the lease for delinquent, unpaid rent at the rate set by the lease agreement; and

- during the holdover period after termination of the lease up to trial for rent of a **reasonable amount** which is set by the court, not by prior agreement under a holdover rent provision.

A UD award may not include future, unearned rent. Future rents are only collectible through a separate money action, filed after the tenant has been evicted and mitigation of losses undertaken.

3-day notice without a forfeiture

A landlord who needs to evict a tenant by a court order in a UD action is entitled to recover possession based on either:

- terminating the lease by a declaration of forfeiture in the 3-day notice; or

- leaving the lease intact by excluding the forfeiture declaration from the 3-day notice and leave it to the court to terminate the lease on expiration of the five-day reinstatement period following a UD award. [CC §1174(a),(c)]

On termination of the lease and all tenant rights to the unexpired term of the tenancy, the landlord can reoccupy the property for his own account (if the tenant has vacated or been evicted). The tenant has no continuing right to occupy the real estate after the 3-day notice expires due to the declaration of forfeiture. [CCP §1174(a)]

However, the landlord may not want to terminate the tenancy on evicting the tenant. The landlord might rather retake possession on the tenant's behalf, acting as the tenant's agent to relet the property for the account of the tenant, not himself.

Here, the landlord omits, by deletion, the declaration of forfeiture from the 3-day notice since the tenant's lease is to remain intact and the landlord will take possession on behalf of the tenant. Although dispossessed, the tenant still **owns the leasehold** estate under the unexpired lease, now managed by the landlord on the tenant's behalf.

Also, a landlord with a tenant under an unexpired lease whose only breach is the **failure to pay rent** may want to give the tenant every opportunity, including the five-day reinstatement period, to bring the rent current and remain the otherwise good tenant he has been.

Faced with delinquent rent (and failed promises to bring the rent current), the landlord can serve the tenant with a 3-day notice to pay rent or quit from which the declaration of forfeiture provision has been deleted.

Relief from forfeiture

When a lease with an original term of **more than one year** is declared to be forfeited in a 3-day notice and the landlord is awarded possession in a UD action, the tenant who wishes to remain in possession must, within 30 days of the forfeiture, make an application on a petition to the court for *relief from forfeiture*. If granted, the tenant's right to possession under the lease is *restored*. [CCP §1179]

The **relief from forfeiture** is sought primarily by nonresidential tenants who have long-term leases and are prepared to cure any defaults.

Only a court order, or a mutual agreement with the landlord, can **restore** the tenant's right to possession since the declaration of forfeiture in the 3-day notice **terminated** the tenant's lawful right to possession on expiration of the three days without the tenant curing the breach. The tenant has no ability to unilaterally restore his right to possession under the lease after the lease has been terminated by forfeiture.

A tenant's relief from forfeiture and the court ordered reinstatement of the lease are based on the degree of *hardship* the tenant would suffer if evicted. The application for relief and reinstatement of the lease agreement and restoration of the tenant to possession can be filed anytime within 30 days after termination of the tenancy and before the removal of the tenant by the sheriff and the return of possession to the landlord.

The court's grant of the tenant's petition for relief from forfeiture will be:

- conditioned on the payment of all amounts due the landlord, including **full payment** of the rent due; and

- **full performance** of all rental or lease agreement conditions, whether oral or written.

Also, whether the right to possession has already been terminated by a declaration of forfeiture in the 3-day notice does not concern the court when hearing the tenant's petition for relief from forfeiture. [CCP §1179]

If an attorney appears on behalf of the tenant seeking relief from the forfeitures, a copy of the application for relief and petition for the hearing must be served on the landlord or property manager filing the UD action at least five days prior to the hearing. [CCP §1179]

At the UD trial, the landlord needs to be prepared to defend against a motion for relief of forfeiture (i.e., why relief from the forfeiture would be unfair to the landlord, and if fair, the amounts owed and lease/rental conditions to be cured, etc.). The court in a UD action may initiate an inquiry on its own into whether the tenant is entitled to relief from forfeiture.

If the tenant is *in proper*, the tenant can make an oral request of the court at the UD trial in the presence of the landlord (or other plaintiff) to be relieved of the forfeiture and allowed (on conditions) to remain in possession.

The obligation to pay future rent

On termination of the tenant's lease under a declaration of forfeiture in any 3-day notice or at trial by statute, the landlord is entitled to:

- file a UD action to physically remove the defaulting tenant from actual possession, called *eviction*, and enforce collection of rent earned and unpaid through entry of the UD judgment; and

- file a separate action to recover money due during the remaining term of the lease, called *future rents*, and any prior unpaid rent earned but not included in the UD judgment.

The landlord's right to collect rent for the remaining unexpired period of the lease after the tenant has been evicted is **independent and separate** from the issue of whether the tenant has the right to occupy the property. One is a *contract right* (to collect money) and the other is a *real property right* (to occupy the property). Different rules of law apply and each right is separately enforced. [Walt, *supra*]

In a money action to **collect future rents**, the landlord is entitled to recover:

- all unpaid rent earned under the lease agreement up until the right to possession is terminated [CC §1951.2(a)(1)];

- reasonable per diem rent from the termination of the right to possession, until entry of the judgment for rent [CC §1951.2(a)(2)];

- all unearned rent called for in the lease agreement for the remaining unexpired term of the lease, subject to *loss mitigation*, default remedies in the lease agreement, the prior reletting of the premises, and the discounted *present worth* of the future rent [CC §1951.2(a)(3)];

- costs incurred by the landlord as a result of the tenant's breach [CC §1951.2(a)(4)]; and

- attorney fees incurred if the lease agreement contains an attorney fees provision. [CC §1717]

The separate money action to recover future rents can be filed immediately after the tenant has vacated or been evicted and his right to possession terminated.

Of course, double recovery of rent is not allowed. If the landlord, in his UD action, is awarded (or denied) rents accrued prior to the UD award, the landlord cannot again seek to recover those amounts in the separate money action for rents.

For the landlord to recover future rents under a lease agreement after an early termination of possession, the landlord must either:

- have **reserved his right** to collect future rent payments by a provision in the lease agreement, called a *default remedies clause* [See Figure 1 accompanying this chapter]; or

- **relet the property** in good faith prior to being awarded the future rent if the lease agreement does not contain a default remedies clause, called a *statutory recovery*. [CC §1951.2(c)]

Collecting future rents after eviction

Now consider a tenant who breaches the lease agreement by failing to pay the rent when due.

The lease agreement contains a **default remedies clause** stating the landlord may collect all remaining unpaid rents due under the lease agreement after an early termination of possession. [See Figure 1]

The landlord serves the tenant with a 3-day notice to pay rent or quit that includes a forfeiture provision. On expiration of the three days and failure of the tenant to either pay or quit, the landlord brings a UD action to evict the tenant. The landlord is awarded possession. The UD judgment also includes an award for rent earned and unpaid for the periods prior to entry of the UD judgment, and attorney fees.

The landlord later brings a separate money action to recover the unpaid rent due over the remaining term of the lease.

The tenant claims the landlord is barred from recovering the unpaid rent since a forfeiture of the lease was declared.

However, the declaration of the forfeiture only terminates the tenant's right to cure the breach after the 3-day notice expires, unless the tenant can show *hardship* and fully performs on the lease agreement. [CCP §§1174.5, 1179]

Here, even if the lease agreement does not contain a default remedies clause, statutory provisions permit the landlord to recover future rents after termination of the tenant's right to possession. However, without a default remedies clause, the landlord must first **relet the premises** before seeking recovery of the future rent. [CC §1951.2(a)(3), (c)]

Loss mitigation affects future rents

With or without a default remedies clause in a lease agreement, the landlord who seeks to recover future rents is compelled to *mitigate his loss* of rent after the tenant vacates or is evicted.

If the landlord does not act to reduce his loss of future rental income, a tenant has the right to offset any future rent due under his lease by the amount of rent the landlord could have reasonably collected by reletting the space. [CC §1951.2(c)]

Consider the tenant who fails to pay rent as scheduled in the lease agreement.

Ultimately, a UD judgment is entered in the landlord's favor, and the tenant is evicted by the sheriff under a *writ of possession* issued by the court.

Having repossessed the property, the landlord, in an effort to mitigate his losses, takes steps to relet the property. The property is listed with a real estate broker to locate a tenant for the property.

During the effort to relet, the evicted tenant offers to lease the property at the old rental rate. The owner refuses the evicted tenant's offer, opting to relet the property to a more credit-worthy tenant at a lower rental rate.

The landlord then seeks to recover his money losses from the evicted tenant for the difference between the lesser amount of rent the new tenant has agreed to pay — the offset — and the greater amount of rent due and unpaid through the expiration of the evicted tenant's lease.

The evicted tenant claims the landlord is barred from collecting any unpaid future rent since the landlord could have recovered the full amount of rental payments if the landlord had accepted his offer to lease.

Is the evicted tenant liable for the deficiency created by the difference between all rent remaining unpaid on his lease and the amount of rent the new tenant has agreed to pay?

Yes! The tenant owes the deficiency remaining in future rents on the terminated lease after reletting the premises. The landlord's effort to mitigate the loss of rents by reletting the property was in good faith and reasonable.

The reasonableness of the landlord's conduct undertaken to relet the space is determined based on the **actions actually taken** by the landlord, not by evaluating available courses of action the landlord could have taken to mitigate damages (such as re-renting to the evicted tenant).

Here, the landlord actively sought a new tenant and was unable to get the full amount of the rent the evicted tenant had agreed to pay through the expiration of his lease. [**Zanker Development Co.** v. **Cogito Systems, Inc.** (1989) 215 CA3d 1377]

A landlord must pursue a course of action that is likely to reduce the amount of future rent the tenant owes under the lease agreement after the tenancy (lease) is terminated.

Otherwise, the tenant is permitted to offset future rents by showing the landlord's efforts (or lack thereof) to relet the property were unreasonable efforts to *mitigate* the loss of rent.

Discounted future rent and interest

The landlord who is entitled to recover **future rent** under an unexpired lease agreement will only be awarded the *present value* of the unearned future rents.

To determine the **present value** of unearned rent at the time of the court's money award, the future rents will be **discounted** (to their present value) at the annual rate of 1% over the Federal Reserve Bank of San Francisco's discount rate. The bank's discount rate during late 2006 was 6.25%. Thus, the discount rate for calculating the present worth of future rent on an award at that time would be 7.25%. [CC §1951.2(b)]

From the time the tenant defaults on the payment of rent to the time the unpaid rent is awarded, the landlord is entitled to **recover interest** on unpaid amounts of back rent.

The interest accrued prior to judgment is calculated at the rate agreed to in the lease agreement. If the interest rate is not stated in the lease agreement, the interest will accrue at 10%

Figure 1   *Excerpt from **first tuesday** Form 552 — Nonresidential Lease Agreement*

23.   Default Remedies:

23.1 If the Tenant breaches any provision of this lease, the Landlord may exercise its rights, including the right to collect future rental losses after forfeiture of possession.

per annum from the date of default to entry of the money judgment. After judgment is awarded for back rent or discounted further rent, interest accrues at 10% on the money judgment until paid. [CC §§1951.2(b), 3289]

Costs to relet

Since the landlord has a duty to mitigate rental losses over the remaining term of a lease following abandonment or eviction, the landlord is also entitled to recover all **reasonable costs** he incurs to relet the property in his effort to mitigate the loss of rental income after the tenant is no longer in possession. [CC §1951.2(a)(4)]

Costs are expenses incurred to relet the property, including:

- costs to clean up the property;

- brokerage and legal fees to find a new tenant;

- permit fees to construct necessary improvements or renovations; and

- any other money losses incurred as a result of the tenant's breach, such as depreciation of the property's market value. [**Sanders Construction Company, Inc. v. San Joaquin First Federal Savings and Loan Association** (1982) 136 CA3d 387]

Cancellation of the lease agreement

Future rents will become uncollectible if the landlord and tenant agree the right to possession (under real estate law) and the tenant's obligation to pay rent (under contract law) are **both terminated**, called a *surrender* or *cancellation* of the lease agreement. [See Chapter 30]

Conversely, *termination of the lease* refers only to the landlord's or court forfeiture of the tenant's right to possession under the leasehold conveyed to the tenant by the landlord on entering into the lease agreement.

To avoid a surrender, the landlord must ensure all 3-day notices and other communication, including those of his agents, state the landlord's only intent is to declare a *forfeiture* of the lease (leasehold), not a *cancellation* of the lease agreement.

A cancellation of the lease agreement results in a termination of the tenant's contract obligation to pay future rent. The cancellation is comparable to an owner's deed-in-lieu of foreclosure, giving ownership and possession to a lender, in exchange for the lender's cancellation of the debt owed on a trust deed note.

Chapter 25

Delinquent rent and the 3-day notice

This chapter discusses the requirements and consequences for the use of the 3-day notice to pay rent or quit in residential and nonresidential income properties.

Forfeit possession in three days

A tenant, residential or nonresidential, fails to pay the agreed rents on the *due date* and prior to expiration of the *grace period*. The rent is now *delinquent*. The property manager *serves* the tenant with a 3-day notice to pay rent or quit the premises. [See Form 575 accompanying this chapter]

The 3-day notice states the **exact amount** of delinquent rent and any other amounts owed the landlord that are delinquent, the **monetary aspect** of the rental or lease agreement entered into by the tenant. [See Chapter 20]

Further, the notice contains a **lease forfeiture clause** stating the landlord had *elected to forfeit the lease*, the tenant's possessory interest in the property granted by the rental or lease agreement held by the tenant. In the event the tenant fails to pay the delinquent rent before the notice expires, the landlord is entitled to recover possession of the property.

After the 3-day notice expires, the tenant remains in possession and tenders payment of the delinquent rent to the landlord, attempting to cure the default in the lease agreement. The landlord refuses to accept the payment. The tenant refuses to voluntarily vacate.

The landlord files an unlawful detainer (UD) action seeking to evict the tenant and regain possession of the premises. The landlord claims the tenant's possessory right to the property was terminated by the expiration of the 3-day notice and election to forfeit the tenant's right to occupy the property and, as a result, the lease cannot now be *reinstated* by the tenant's tender of delinquent rent.

Can the landlord evict the tenant even though the tenant tendered the delinquent rent in full after expiration of the 3-day notice and before the UD trial?

Yes! The tenant's **right to possession** was terminated by expiration of the 3-day notice since the notice contained a declaration of the landlord's **election to forfeit** the lease (that's the occupancy, not the lease agreement). Thus, the tenant's occupancy became unlawful on expiration of the 3-day notice containing the declaration of forfeiture. [Calif. Code of Civil Procedure § 1174(a)]

On expiration, the landlord is no longer obligated to accept delinquent rent payments and allow the occupancy and the **rental or lease agreement** to be *reinstated* when:

- the landlord **does not actually receive payment before** the notice expires; and

- the landlord declares in the 3-day notice his **election to forfeit** the tenant's right to possession on expiration of the notice. [CCP §§ 1161(2), 1174(a); see **first tuesday** Form 575 §4]

Default, notice, cure or vacate

A tenant *defaults* on his rental or lease agreement by failing to:

- pay rent and any other **amounts due** called for in the rental or lease agreement; or

- perform nonmonetary obligations called for in the rental or lease agreement.

On a tenant's default, the landlord may make a demand on the tenant to cure the default or quit (vacate) the premises.

However, only a *material breach* allows for the landlord to forfeit of the tenancy.

Failure to pay rent or perform other significant obligations called for in the rental or lease agreement is a *material breach*. Conversely, the tenant's failure to pay late charges, interest penalties, bad check charges or security deposits are *minor breaches*,which alone do not justify a demand to cure or quit under a 3-day notice. [**Keating** v. **Preston** (1940) 42 CA2d 110]

A failure to increase the security deposit by paying an additional sum as agreed is not a failure to pay *rent*. Rent must be delinquent before a 3-day notice can be served to collect all other dollar amounts due and unpaid which are minor breaches. A security deposit is *security* for the payment of rent. A security deposit is not rent. Thus, failure to make a security deposit payment is not a basis for a 3-day notice since it is not rent.

Some nonmonetary defaults by a tenant cannot be cured, such as waste to the premises, alienation of the leasehold or significant criminal activity which has occurred on the property, called *incurable breaches*. The landlord's remedy for an incurable breach is to serve notice on the tenant to quit the premises within three days after service, leaving no alternative but to vacate. Here, a lease forfeiture clause accompanying the 3-day notice is unnecessary and ineffective since the failure cannot be cured and the tenancy cannot be reinstated. [CCP §1161(4)]

Three days between notice and UD

When a tenant does not *timely pay* rent, the landlord may serve the tenant with a written notice demanding the tenant pay all amounts due or vacate the premises within three days, called a *3-day notice to pay rent or quit.*

A tenant has three calendar days, day one being the **day after service** of the notice, in which he may pay the delinquent rental amounts and avoid forfeiture of his possession and eventual eviction. [Calif. Civil Code §10]

The tenant cures the default, retaining his right to possession by paying the amount stated before the 3-day notice expires. [CCP §1161.5]

During the three-day notice period, the tenant may **tender payment** of the rent and cure the default in the same manner the tenant made past rental payments — by personal or company check, money order, cashier's check, cash or electronic transfer. [**Strom** v. **Union Oil Co.** (1948) 88 CA2d 78]

A tenant's rent that is paid by check and received on time by the landlord sometimes becomes delinquent when the check is returned to the landlord due to the tenant's lack of sufficient funds with his bank. Since the rent is delinquent, the landlord can now serve a 3-day notice to pay or quit. However, he cannot now limit his demand for payment to cash or a money order in the 3-day notice since the tenant has been paying rent by check.

A rent check received by the landlord during the 3-day notice period must be paid by the tenant's bank to cure the delinquency. If it is returned for lack of sufficient funds (or otherwise), the delinquent rent has not been paid, the notice has expired and the tenant's right to possession terminated by reason of the declaration of forfeiture.Thus, the landlord may file a UD action if the tenant remains in possession.

Editor's note — Consider a tenant under a month-to-month rental agreement whose rent checks are returned due to insufficient funds. To modify the method of payment, the landlord must serve the tenant with a written 30-day notice advising the tenant he now is to pay rent by cash or cashier's check. [CC §827]

THREE-DAY NOTICE TO PAY RENT OR QUIT
With Rent-Related Fees

DATE:_____, 20_____, at _____, California.

> **NOTICE:** A tenant who fails to pay the amounts due under a lease/rental agreement, must, within three (3) days after service of written notice of the breach, either pay the amount due or vacate and deliver possession of the premises to the landlord. [California Code of Civil Procedure §1161(2)]

To Tenant: _____

Items left blank or unchecked are not applicable.

FACTS:

1. You are a Tenant under a rental or lease agreement
    1.1 dated _____, at_____, California,
    1.2 entered into by _____, Tenant,
    and _____, Landlord,
    1.3 regarding real estate referred to as: _____
    _____

NOTICE:

2. You are in breach of the payment of amounts due under the lease or rental agreement.
3. Within three (3) days after service of this notice you are required to either:
    3.1 Pay rent and other amounts now due and unpaid in the **Total Amount** of . . . . $_____
    representing rent for the periods of:

    _____, 20_____ to _____, 20_____ . . . . . Amount $_____
    _____, 20_____ to _____, 20_____ . . . . . Amount $_____
    _____, 20_____ to _____, 20_____ . . . . . Amount $_____

    and amounts due for:
    ☐ returned check fees of . . . . $_____
    ☐ late charge fees of . . . . $_____
    ☐ common area maintenance of . . . . $_____
    ☐ association assessments of . . . . $_____
    ☐ property taxes of . . . . $_____
    ☐ interest on delinquent rent of . . . . $_____

    The **Total Amount** due may be paid in one of the following manners:
    a. By personal delivery to: _____ (Name)
    _____ (Address)
    _____ (Phone)
    Personal delivery of the Total Amount due which will be accepted at the above address during the hours of _____a.m. to _____p.m. on the following days:_____
    b. By deposit into account number _____
    at: _____ (Financial Institution)
    _____ (Address)
    c. By the electronic funds transfer previously established between Landlord and Tenant.

OR

    3.2 Deliver possession of the premises to the Landlord or _____
    _____

4   If you fail to pay the Total Amount due, or to deliver possession of the premises within three (3) days, legal proceedings will be initiated against you to regain possession of the premises and to recover the amounts owed, treble damages, costs and attorney fees.
5. The Landlord hereby elects to declare a forfeiture of your Right to Possession if you fail to pay the Total Amount demanded above.
    5.1 Landlord reserves the right to pursue collection of any future loss of rent allowed by Civil Code §1951.2.

Date:_____, 20_____
Landlord/Agent:_____
Signature: _____
Address: _____
Phone:_____ Fax:_____

FORM 575   07-02   ©2007 **first tuesday**, P.O. BOX 20069, RIVERSIDE, CA 92516 (800) 794-0494

One year rent limitation

Unpaid rents that **became due** more than one year before service of a 3-day notice may not be included in the 3-day notice. If delinquent rents due for more than one year are included in the 3-day notice, the notice is defective and will not terminate the right to possession. More rent has been demanded than will be awarded by a court in a UD action. Thus, any UD action based on a notice demanding rent for delinquencies more than one year on will fail. [**Bevill** v. **Zoura** (1994) 27 CA4th 694]

However, the landlord may recover those rents and other amounts delinquent for more than one year by pursuing collection in a separate civil action, but not in an eviction (UD) action. The time period for a landlord's recovery of due and unpaid amounts in a separate money action from a UD action is four years, due to a *statute of limitations*. [CCP §337]

Before a landlord or his property manager serves a tenant with a 3-day notice to pay rent or quit, the following questions must be answered:

- Is the rent delinquent?

- What amounts are due and unpaid?

- When can rent earned be estimated in the 3-day notice?

- What is a reasonable estimate of delinquent rent?

- When does the 3-day notice expire?

- When does the tenant's right to possession terminate? and

- How are subtenants evicted?

When is the rent delinquent?

Rent must be *delinquent* before a 3-day notice to pay or quit may be served.

Rent becomes **delinquent**:

- the day following the last calendar day of the *grace period* established in the rental or lease agreement; or

---

The holdover tenant

When a lease contains a holdover provision, the landlord's failure to evict the tenant after serving a three-day notice does not create a month-to-month tenancy with rent due as stated in the holdover provision. [**Walt** v. **Superior Court** (1992) 8 CA4th 1667]

Similarly, a three-day notice is not required once a 30-day notice to vacate served on a tenant has expired since a 30-day notice also establishes an unlawful detainer. [CC §1946]

A holdover occurs when a tenant remains in possession after the agreed lease term expires, not when the three-day notice expires. When a tenant holds over, the landlord may immediately file a UD action without serving any notice. [CCP §1161(1)]

However, a landlord under an expired lease should only seek to recover possession, not rent, in a UD action filed against the holdover tenant.

Then in a separate action, the landlord can recover money losses under the holdover provision for the period of the tenant's unlawful detainer.

Typically, holdover rent exceeds fair rental value and will not be the basis for rent awards in a UD action.

- the day following the due date, when the rental or lease agreement does not provide for a *grace period*.

However, when the last day scheduled for payment of rent falls on a legal holiday, the payment may be *tendered* on the **next business day**. A *legal holiday* is every Saturday, Sunday and any other day designated by the state as a holiday, which includes federal holidays. [CCP §§10, 12a]

Likewise, if the last day of a *grace period* for payment of past due rent (which could be the due date) falls on a Saturday, the tenant's rent payment is not delinquent if it is received by the landlord on the first business day following the legal holiday, which would be Monday unless it is designated a federal holiday. [CCP §13; Calif. Government Code §6706]

Thus, when the final day of the 3-day notice falls on a holiday such as a Saturday, Sunday or legal holiday, the 3-day notice expires on the next business day. [**Lamanna** v. **Vognar** (1993) 17 CA4th Supp. 4; CCP §12a]

Unlike the service of documents in civil actions, mailing of the 3-day notice for failure of attempts at personal service does not extend the three-day notice period an additional five days. [**Losornio** v. **Motta** (1998) 67 CA4th 110]

To initiate the **rent collection process** against a tenant who is in possession, the landlord serves the tenant with a 3-day notice to pay rent or quit. The notice may be served on any day after the grace period has expired without receipt of the rent, called a *delinquency*.

A **grace period** is stated in a rental or lease agreement as a set time period following the due date during which rent may be paid without incurring a *late charge*. While rent may be unpaid and past due, it is not *delinquent* until the grace period expires and a late charge may be demanded.

Consider a landlord and tenant who enter into a lease agreement that states rent is due on the first day of each month, the *due date*. The lease agreement also contains a **late charge provision** imposing an additional charge if rent payments are not *received* on or before the tenth of the month. A grace period is not mentioned in the lease agreement.

Each month, the tenant pays his rent after the date for incurring a late charge. The landlord accepts the tenant's late rental payments every month, but makes no demand for payment of the late charge. [See **first tuesday** Form 569]

Finally, on receipt of yet another late payment, the landlord informs the tenant all future rent payments, including the next month's rent which is due in a few days, must be received by the landlord prior to the date for incurring a late charge.

The next month, the late charge period runs and rent has not been paid. On the day the late charge is incurred, the 11th, the landlord serves the tenant with a 3-day notice to pay rent or quit that includes a declaration of forfeiture provision. The tenant does not pay rent before the 3-day notice expires. The landlord files a UD action.

As in the prior months, the tenant tenders the rent payment to the landlord after the late charge period has expired. However, unlike in prior months, the landlord refuses to accept the payment, claiming the tenant is now unlawfully occupying the premises.

Has the landlord established an unlawful detainer on expiration of the 3-day notice?

No! The 3-day notice is premature and useless. The tenant's rent had not yet become **delinquent**. Rent is not delinquent until the grace period — including *extensions* authorized by the conduct of the landlord's prior acceptance of late payments— has run.

When the lease agreement called for an additional charge after the tenth, a **grace period** was established since, by agreement, payments received after the tenth are delinquent. Further, the conduct of the landlord by consistently accepting rent payments after the grace period *without demanding the late charge* by notice, extended the grace period. [**Baypoint Mortgage** v. **Crest Premium Real Estate Investments Retirement Trust** (1985) 168 CA3d 818]

Thus, the tenant's tender of rent after the written grace period ran, but on or before the extended date set by the landlord's conduct, was timely.

For the landlord to **re-establish his ability** to enforce the grace period provision in the rental or lease agreement, the landlord must first give the tenant 30-days' advance notice of the change in terms of payment to reinstate and enforce the written grace period. [See **first tuesday** Form 570]

The 30-day notice of a change in terms used to reinstate the grace period should state all rent payments due following the expiration of the 30 days must be received within the written grace period, prior to delinquency. If payment is not received, a 3-day notice will be served and the late charge imposed for the agreed-to amount.

Editor's note — For payments made on loans secured by single-family, owner-occupied residential dwellings:

- *the borrower is given a statutory ten-day grace period; and*

- *the amount of the late charge is limited to the greater of 6% of the installment due or $5. [CC §2954.4(a)]*

No statutory grace period or late charge limitations exist for rent payments made by tenants. The legislature should provide residential tenants with similar statutory protection (and landlord guidance) to establish consistent expectations among residential tenants and their landlords in California.

Collecting late charges

Late charges demanded and unpaid are properly included in a three-day notice to pay rent or quit since delinquent late charges are sums due under the lease. [**Canal-Randolph Anaheim, Inc.** v. **Moore** (1978) 78 CA3d 477]

However, in a UD action, many municipal court judges, as a matter of discretion, will declare invalid a three-day notice which includes any late charges. [See Chapter 28]

Conversely, a UD action based solely on the failure to pay late charges, bad check fees, accrued interest or the deposit of additional security will not stand. [See Chapter 28]

To collect unpaid late charges other than by a deduction from the security deposit, the landlord may file a small claims or municipal court action. A UD action based solely on the delinquency of late charges will not stand. [See Chapter 23]

A property manager retained by a landlord to manage his residential or nonresidential rental property may represent the landlord in small claims court to recover money due under a rental or lease agreement related to the property managed. [CCP §116.540(h)]

However, no such representation has been extended to UD actions.

Accurate residential rent demands

To be valid, the 3-day notice to pay rent or quit served on a **residential tenant** must state the *exact amount* of money due which has not been paid. Conversely, **nonresidential rent** may be *estimated* when the exact amount cannot be accurately ascertained.

A residential tenant is not required to pay more than the amount due and unpaid to retain his possessory right under his rental or lease agreement. Likewise for nonresidential tenants, even if the rent they pay is erroneously estimated at a higher amount than the amount due.

However, if the amount stated in a 3-day notice served on a **residential tenant** exceeds the amounts actually due and unpaid at the time of the UD trial, the notice is invalid. [**Jayasinghe** v. **Lee** (1993) 13 CA4th Supp. 33]

For both residential and nonresidential tenants, if the amount stated in the 3-day notice is less than the actual amount due and unpaid, the tenant may pay the amount stated and avoid eviction. To collect any amounts omitted in a 3-day notice, the landlord must serve another 3-day notice to pay the balance or quit.

Estimated nonresidential rent

When the property leased is nonresidential, the 3-day notice may include an *estimate* of the amounts due if:

- the notice states the amount due is an estimate; and

- the amount estimated is reasonable. [CCP §1161.1(a)]

Failure to indicate in the 3-day notice that an estimate of the amount due is **an estimate** renders the 3-day notice invalid.

Further, if the landlord knows the **exact amount** of the delinquent rent and other monies owed, and then states a different amount as the amount due in the 3-day notice and de-

clares it an estimate, the landlord will be unable to evict the tenant. The notice is defective for terminating the tenant's right to possession since the exact amount of the delinquency is known to the landlord.

Also, including amounts in the 3-day notice that are not yet due, such as unbilled common area maintenance expenses (CAMs), is not a reasonable estimate of *delinquent amounts*. [**WDT-Winchester** v. **Nilsson** (1994) 27 CA4th 516]

An estimate of rent owed in a 3-day notice is **considered reasonable** if:

- the actual amount owed is truly in question; and

- the delinquent amount demanded is neither 20% **more or less** than the amount determined due at the UD hearing. [CCP §1161.1(e)]

Estimating known amounts

Consider a tenant who leases nonresidential property. The lease agreement states the tenant will pay his proportionate share of the property taxes and assessments to reimburse the landlord for his payment of the taxes.

Rent provisions in the lease agreement state the landlord will first pay all property taxes and assessments on the premises before making a written demand on the tenant for reimbursement of the tenant's proportionate share.

Before the landlord pays the property taxes, he makes a written demand on the tenant for payment of the tenant's portion of the unpaid property taxes. The tenant does not pay his share of the taxes demanded by the landlord and also fails to make his regular monthly rental payment.

The landlord serves the tenant with a 3-day notice to pay rent or quit. The 3-day notice states the amount due includes unpaid rent and the tenant's proportionate share of the property taxes. The total amount does not exceed 20% of the periodic rent payment, and the notice indicates the amount is an **estimate**.

The tenant neither pays the amount stated in the notice nor vacates the premises. The landlord files a UD action.

The tenant claims the 3-day notice is invalid and does not terminate his possessory interest and establish an unlawful detainer since he did not yet owe property taxes on the date the notice was served. The landlord claims the 3-day notice is valid since the estimated amount was within 20% of the actual amount due — the rent.

Is the 3-day notice valid?

No! The 3-day notice to pay rent or quit is invalid. It is not reasonable for the landlord to estimate rents when he knows the **exact amount** owed by the tenant. [WDT-Winchester, *supra*]

Further, the portion of taxes demanded from the tenant as additional rent was not yet due, much less delinquent. The landlord had not yet paid the property taxes and billed the tenant, an agreed-to requisite to a demand for reimbursement.

(Guess)timating unknown amounts

Now consider a nonresidential tenant who takes possession of property on entering into a percentage lease agreement.

The rent provisions in the lease agreement state:

- the rent is payable annually on the anniversary of the commencement of the lease in an amount equal to 20% of the gross sales proceeds; and

- the tenant is to provide the landlord with the amount of his gross sales proceeds.

The tenant fails to furnish the landlord with the amount of sales proceeds or make the annual rental payment. The landlord serves the tenant with a 3-day notice to pay rent or quit. The notice states:

- the amount of rent which is due and unpaid in an amount equal to 20% of the tenant's gross sales proceeds; and

- only the tenant knows the amount of the sales proceeds.

The tenant does not pay the rent before the 3-day notice expires. The landlord files a UD action. The tenant claims the 3-day notice is invalid since the notice did not state the dollar amount of rent due.

Can the landlord evict the tenant even though the 3-day notice did not state the dollar amount of the unpaid and delinquent rent?

Yes! The tenant cannot prevent the landlord from enforcing his right to receive rent or recover possession by failing to provide the landlord with the means needed — the amount of his sales proceeds — to determine the rental amount and then claim the 3-day notice is defective.

The purpose of a 3-day notice is to give a tenant the opportunity to avoid forfeiture of his leasehold estate by paying the delinquent rent. [**Valov** v. **Tank** (1985) 168 CA3d 867]

Rent estimates by nonresidential tenants

On receiving a 3-day notice stating the rental amount due is an estimate, the nonresidential tenant may respond by tendering the amount of rent the **tenant estimates** is due. [CCP §1161.1(a)]

If the amount the tenant estimates and tenders is equal or greater than the rent due, the tenant will retain his right to possession in a UD action. Likewise, when the amount estimated and tendered by the tenant is less than the amount actually due and was a reasonable estimate, the tenant retains possession by paying the additional amount and other sums awarded the landlord within five days after entry of the UD judgment. [CCP §1161.1(a)]

Subtenant evictions by the owner

For an owner to regain possession when the (master) tenant defaults and a subtenant occupies the premises, the 3-day notice must also **name** the subtenant as a tenant in default and be served on the subtenant. [CCP §1161]

Serving a subtenant with a copy of the 3-day notice that only names the master tenant will result in the subtenant retaining his right to possession. [**Briggs** v. **Electronic Memories & Magnetic Corporation** (1975) 53 CA3d 900]

Conversely, an owner who wishes to evict a defaulting master tenant but retain the subtenant may do so. The owner is not required to serve the subtenant with a 3-day notice when only the master tenant is being evicted. [**Chinese Hospital Foundation Fund** v. **Patterson** (1969) 1 CA3d 627]

For example, an owner consents to a sublease which contains an *attornment provision*. Should the master tenant default and his right to possession be forfeited, the owner may enforce the sublease after his exercise of the attornment clause. [See Chapter 59]

Under the sublease's **attornment provision**, the subtenant has agreed to recognize the owner as his landlord in lieu of the master tenant if the owner elects to forfeit the master tenant's leasehold and recognize the subtenant as the owner's tenant.

However, a subtenant who takes possession of the premises after the master tenant has been served with a 3-day notice will be evicted on the owner's successful completion of a UD action. [CCP §1164]

Chapter 26

Three-day notices to quit

This chapter reviews the proper 3-day notice to serve on a tenant for a material breach of a lease, other than for past due amounts of money.

Curable and incurable nonmonetary breaches

On a routine inspection of an apartment complex, the property manager observes a pet in one of the units. All the rental and lease agreements with tenants residing in the complex prohibit housing of a pet on the premises.

As a courtesy, the tenant of the unit is asked, both orally and by a personal note left with the tenant, to remove the pet. However, the tenant retains the pet. [See Chapter 28]

To enforce the pet provision in the tenant's lease agreement, the property manager prepares a 3-day notice to **perform or quit**. The notice is served on the tenant. The notice gives the tenant an ultimatum — either remove the pet (the performance required) or vacate the unit within three days (the alternative performance). [See Form 576 accompanying this chapter]

The tenant fails to remove the pet from the premises and remains in the unit after the 3-day notice expires.

Can an unlawful detainer (UD) action be maintained to evict the tenant for failure to either remove the pet or vacate under the 3-day notice?

Yes! On expiration of the 3-day notice to perform by removing the pet or vacating, the tenant may be evicted if one of the alternative conditions has not been met. The tenant has breached the provision in his lease agreement that prohibits keeping a pet on the premises. [Calif. Code of Civil Procedure §1161(3)]

However, had the tenant breached a provision in his rental or lease agreement that the tenant could not perform within three days, the landlord or property manager would serve a 3-day **notice to quit** the premises, giving no alternative to perform and remain on the premises. [CCP §1161(3)]

Types of 3-day notices

The 3-day notice served on a tenant must be the correct type before the tenant's unlawful detainer, holdover, of a premises can be established and the tenant evicted.

Depending on the nature and extent of the tenant's breach, one of the following types of **3-day notices** may be served:

- a 3-Day Notice to **Pay Rent or Quit** [See **first tuesday** Form 575];

- a 3-Day Notice to **Perform or Quit** [See Form 576 accompanying this chapter]; or

- a 3-Day Notice to **Quit**. [See Form 577 accompanying this chapter]

When a tenant's breach is the **failure to pay** rent or other money obligation which is due, the tenant is served with a 3-day notice *to pay rent or quit*.

When the lease provision breached is not for rent or other money obligation, called a *nonmonetary breach*, and the breach can still be quickly corrected by the tenant, the tenant is served with a 3-day notice *to perform or quit*. [See Form 576]

However, a tenant who is in default on both the payment of money and a curable nonmonetary provision in the lease, such as the obligation to maintain the landscaping, a 3-day notice to perform or quit is used. The demand to pay rent is listed as an additional (monetary) breach to be cured under the notice to perform or quit.

A 3-day notice *to quit* containing no alternative and requiring the tenant to vacate is served on a tenant when the tenant's breach is:

- impossible to cure in three days [**Matthew** v. **Digges** (1920) 45 CA 561]; or

- a statutory breach, such as an unauthorized subletting of the premises, nuisance or unlawful use of the premises. [CCP §1161(4); see Form 577]

Notice to perform or quit

The 3-day notice to **perform or quit** requires the tenant to either:

- **perform** under the breached lease provision; or

- **vacate** the premises. [CCP §1161(3)]

The tenant's breach of the rental or lease agreement must be a *significant breach*, called a *material breach*, to justify serving a 3-day notice to perform or quit. A minor or trivial breach by the tenant will not support a 3-day notice. [**Baypoint Mortgage** v. **Crest Premium Real Estate Investments Retirement Trust** (1985) 168 CA3d 818]

In order for the tenant to avoid a forfeiture of his right to occupy the property, he must be given an opportunity to *reinstate* the rental or lease agreement — if the breach can be cured in three days.

The 3-day notice to perform or quit will specify the provision breached and the action required to cure the breach. When the tenant cures the breach before the 3-day notice expires, the rental or lease agreement is *reinstated* and possession continues as though no breach occurred.

To eliminate the tenant's right to also **reinstate** the rental or lease agreement after the 3-day notice expires, a reinstatement period to avoid eviction that runs on the fifth day after the UD trial, the notice must clearly state the landlord's **election to terminate** the tenant's right to possession if the tenant fails to perform, called a *lease forfeiture clause*. [CCP §1174(a)]

The tenant who vacates instead of performing forfeits his **possessory right** to occupy the leased premises. Further, the tenant cannot reinstate the right to possession after expiration of the 3-day notice to perform or quit when the landlord declares his election to terminate possession by declaring a forfeiture in the notice. [See Form 576 §4]

In spite of the forfeiture of the right to possession, the lease agreement, including provisions imposing obligations on the tenant to pay money, remains fully enforceable by the landlord after the tenant's leasehold interest is terminated. The lease agreement was not canceled.

The tenant's failure to either cure the breach by performance or vacate within the three days following service of a notice and election to forfeit allows the landlord to initiate a UD action and have the tenant removed without the right to reinstate possession after the 3-day notice expires. [CCP §1161(3)]

Curable nonmonetary breaches

A tenant operates a retail business on leased premises. The lease agreement requires the tenant to periodically provide the landlord with a list of his sales merchandise in inventory. Also, the landlord is permitted to examine the tenant's business records.

Upon the landlord's request, the tenant does not provide the inventories or permit the landlord to examine his business records.

The landlord serves the tenant with a 3-day notice to quit the premises — no alternative per-

THREE-DAY NOTICE TO PERFORM OR QUIT

DATE:_____, 20_____, at _____, California.

> **NOTICE:** A tenant who fails to perform any terms of the rental or lease agreement which can be performed or rectified must within three (3) days after service of written notice of the breach either cure the breach or vacate and deliver possession of the premises to the landlord. [California Code of Civil Procedure §1161(3)]

To Tenant: _____

Items left blank or unchecked are not applicable.

FACTS:

You are a Tenant under a rental agreement or expired lease agreement

dated _____, at _____, California,

entered into by _____, Tenant,

and _____, Landlord,

regarding real estate referred to as _____

_____

NOTICE:

1. You are in breach of the terms of your rental or lease agreement as follows:_____
_____
_____

2. Within three (3) days after service of this notice, you are required to either:

   2.1 Perform or rectify the breach by _____
   _____

   OR

   2.2 Deliver possession of the premises to Landlord or _____
   _____

3. If you fail to cure the breach or to deliver possession within three (3) days, legal proceedings may be initiated to regain possession of the premises and recover the rent owed, treble damages, costs and attorney fees.

4. Landlord hereby elects to declare a forfeiture of your lease if you fail to cure the breach noted above.

   4.1 Landlord reserves the right to pursue collection of any future rental losses allowed by Civil Code §1951.2.

Date:_____, 20_____

Landlord/Agent:_____

Signature: _____

Address: _____

_____

Phone:_____

Fax:_____

E-mail:_____

formance is given to allow the tenant to rectify the failures and stay. The tenant does not vacate the premises.

The landlord files a UD action, seeking to evict the tenant since he breached a material lease obligation.

The tenant claims he cannot be evicted since the 3-day notice did not give the tenant the alternative to perform under the rent provisions by delivering inventory lists and records to avoid a forfeiture of possession.

Can the landlord maintain a UD action against the tenant based on the 3-day notice to quit?

No! The 3-day notice served on the tenant must be in the alternative — perform or quit — since the tenant could have handed over an inventory to the landlord and given the landlord access to the business records, all within three days. [**Hinman** v. **Wagnon** (1959) 172 CA2d 24]

A landlord must allow a tenant to cure a material breach, monetary or nonmonetary, within three days after notice when the tenant is capable of performing under the breached lease provision within three days. [CCP §1161(3)]

Notice to quit; no alternatives

If the lease provision violated by the tenant calls for or prohibits an activity that constitutes a material breach and cannot be performed or rectified within three days, the tenant may be served with a 3-day notice to quit. No alternative activity need be stated in the notice as nothing can or remains to be done which the tenant can do (or stop doing) within three days. [CCP §1161(3); see Form 577]

For example, possession can be recovered by service and expiration of a 3-day notice to quit based on **statutory forfeitures** when a tenant:

- maintains a *nuisance* on the premises;

- uses the premises for an *unlawful purpose*; or

- *assigns, sublets* or *commits waste* to the premises in breach of a lease provision. [CCP §1161(4)]

The 3-day notice to quit does not need to indicate the provision breached or the activity of the tenant constituting the breach, such as an unlawful use, nor does it need to include a lease forfeiture declaration by the landlord. The right to possession — the lease — is *automatically forfeited* by the breach, not by the running of the 3-day notice. The tenant's right to possession may not be reinstated unless the landlord chooses to waive the forfeiture.

The landlord serves a 3-day notice to quit only because the notice is a requisite to the recovery of possession in a UD action, as a forfeiture of the lease has already occurred by statute due to these enumerated events. [CCP §1161(4)]

Quit! The breach cannot be undone

Consider a tenant who leases agricultural property. The lease agreement states the tenant's use of the property is limited to grazing sheep. However, the tenant plants a crop on the property, a breach of the use provision in the lease agreement.

Based on the tenant's **unauthorized use** of the premises, the landlord initiates the eviction process by serving a 3-day notice to quit on the tenant.

The tenant's use of the property to raise a crop, instead of the single agreed-to use as a pasture, is an *incurable nonmonetary breach* of the lease agreement. The tenant cannot reverse the effects of raising the crop on the soil since the activity has already occurred. [**Harris** v. **Bissell** (1921) 54 CA 307]

Consider a tenant of agricultural property improved with an orchard of trees. The lease obligates the tenant to poison squirrels on the property to control the agricultural pest.

THREE-DAY NOTICE TO QUIT

DATE:_____, 20_____, at_____, California.

> **NOTICE:** A tenant must vacate and deliver possession to the landlord within three (3) days after service of written notice for breach of any terms of the rental or lease agreement which cannot be performed or rectified. [California Code of Civil Procedure §1161(4)]

To Tenant: _____

Items left blank or unchecked are not applicable.

FACTS:

You are a Tenant under a rental and lease agreement

dated _____, at _____, California,

entered into by _____, Tenant,

and _____, Landlord,

regarding real estate referred to as: _____

_____

NOTICE:

1. You are in breach of the terms of your rental or lease agreement as follows:

   _____
   _____
   _____
   _____
   _____
   _____
   _____
   _____
   _____

2. Within three 3-day after service of this notice you are required to vacate and deliver possession of the premises to Landlord or: _____

3. If you fail to vacate and deliver possession of the premises within three (3) days, legal proceedings may be initiated to regain possession of the premises and to recover the rent owed, treble damages, costs, and attorney fees.

4. Landlord hereby elects to declare a forfeiture of your lease.

   4.1 Landlord reserves the right to pursue collection of any future rental losses allowed by Civil Code §1951.2

Date:_____, 20_____

Landlord/Agent: _____

Signature: _____

Address: _____

_____

Phone: _____

Fax: _____

E-mail: _____

FORM 577   10-01   ©2007 **first tuesday**, P.O. BOX 20069, RIVERSIDE, CA 92516 (800) 794-0494

The tenant does not poison the squirrels as required by the lease agreement and the premises becomes infested with squirrels.

The landlord serves the tenant with a 3-day notice to quit the premises based on the tenant's failure to eradicate the squirrels with poison.

The tenant does not vacate the premises. The landlord files a UD action to evict the tenant. The tenant claims he cannot be evicted since the proper notice to serve for the failure to poison the squirrels is a 3-day notice to perform or quit, allowing the tenant to cure his breach.

However, the 3-day notice to quit is the proper notice. The elimination of squirrels by poisoning could not be performed within three days — before the 3-day notice to quit would expire. [Matthews, *supra*]

Breach of statutory prohibitions

A tenant may be evicted for maintaining a *nuisance or unlawful use* of the premises, even if these activities are not prohibited by the lease agreement. [CCP §1161(4)]

A **nuisance** includes anything which:

- is *injurious to health*, such as contamination of the property's soil;

- is *offensive to the senses*, such as excessive noise levels or obnoxious fumes; or

- *obstructs the use and enjoyment* of surrounding property. [Calif. Civil Code §3479]

For example, a tenant in a multi-unit property maintains a nuisance on the premises, such as excessive late-night noise, which interferes with another tenant's **use or enjoyment** of his premises. As a result, the landlord may serve a 3-day notice to quit on the interfering tenant.

Also, a tenant who illegally sells, grows or manufactures controlled substances on the premises, has by his actions, triggered an *automatic forfeiture* of the leasehold. The tenant may be served with a notice to quit for **maintaining a nuisance**, and if he does not vacate, be evicted by a UD action. [CCP §1161(4)]

A tenant's **unlawful use** of the premises under the statute includes violations of local laws or ordinances affecting the property, such as noncompliance with zoning ordinances restricting the use of the premises. Again, the leasehold is forfeited automatically due to the violation. The 3-day notice is required only as a requisite to a UD action should the tenant remain in possession. [**Haig** v. **Hogan** (1947) 82 CA2d 876]

However, before the unlawful use **justifies** service of a notice to quit, the use must:

- threaten the physical safety of the property;

- stigmatize the premises; or

- impair the landlord's continued receipt of rent.

For example, a tenant's lease agreement contains a provision stating the tenant will not use the premises for any unlawful purpose or to violate any laws, a provision that restates the statute.

The tenant's business, which is authorized to operate on the premises, is penalized for conducting the pricing of its services and goods in violation of federal anti-trust laws. The landlord seeks to evict the tenant for unlawful use of the premises in violation of the lease.

Here, the landlord may not evict the tenant. The tenant's violation of anti-trust laws is the unlawful conduct of his **lawful business**, not an unlawful use of the premises. [**Deutsch** v. **Phillips Petroleum Co.** (1976) 56 CA3d 586]

When a tenant's activity is considered a nuisance or an unlawful use, a 3-day notice to quit may be served on the tenant even if the tenant is able to cure the breach by terminating or eliminating the activity within three days. The mere occurrence of the unlawful and endangering activity **automatically forfeits** the lease, leaving nothing for the tenant to do except vacate or be evicted based on the 3-day notice to quit.

Forfeiture on assigning or subletting

Consider a lease provision prohibiting the tenant from *assigning* the lease or *subleasing* the premises without first obtaining the landlord's written consent. Unknown to the landlord or his property manager, the tenant subleases the premises. The property manager discovers the premises is occupied by a subtenant.

The property manager names and serves both the **tenant and subtenant** with a 3-day notice to quit. The subtenant does not vacate the premises, and a UD action is filed to regain possession from both the tenant and the subtenant.

The tenant claims his leasehold interest cannot be terminated by the 3-day notice to quit since the landlord cannot unreasonably withhold his consent to a sublease of the premises.

Can the landlord serve a 3-day notice to quit on a tenant who subleased without his consent and evict the tenant?

Yes! The landlord can proceed to evict the subtenant based on a 3-day notice to quit. The tenant failed to request the landlord's consent prior to subletting the premises. Thus, the tenant breached the lease agreement, immediately forfeiting his right to possession without the landlord's need to declare the forfeiture.

The tenant cannot avoid the forfeiture of his leasehold due to the subletting by claiming the landlord cannot unreasonably withhold consent when the landlord was not given the opportunity to grant or withhold his consent. [**Thrifty Oil Co.** v. **Batarse** (1985) 174 CA3d 770]

When provisions in a lease agreement prohibit assignment of the lease or subleasing by the tenant without the landlord's consent, and the tenant assigns or subleases without obtaining

consent, a 3-day notice to quit may be served on the tenant to recover possession. By statute, the act is an incurable activity that terminates the lease, leaving no alternative to vacating. [CCP §1161(4)]

However, the landlord need not consider the lease terminated when the tenant assigns the lease or sublets the premises or assigns the lease without the landlord's consent. The landlord can waive the statutory forfeiture of possession.

Thus, a 3-day notice to **perform or quit** may be served on the tenant requiring the tenant to remove the subtenant from the premises — within three days — and retain his right to possession. [CCP §1161(3)]

Waste forfeits the lease

Waste to the leased premises by a tenant is a breach that cannot be cured. Thus, the right to possession has been terminated. The tenant must vacate if the landlord serves a 3-day notice to quit.

However, *waste* is grounds for eviction only when the **value** of the leased premises is substantially or permanently y diminished — *impaired* — due to the tenant's conduct.

Waste occurs when a tenant:

- *intentionally damages* or destroys the leased premises; or

- neglects the premises and *impairs its value* by failing to care for and maintain it as agreed.

Consider a tenant in an office building. The tenant's lease agreement obligates the tenant to follow all building rules. The building rules prohibit tenants from adjusting the temperature controls. The tenant's employees adjust the temperature controls, resulting in damage to the thermostat.

The landlord serves the tenant with a 3-day notice to quit the premises. The tenant does not vacate. The landlord then files a UD action, claiming the tenant committed waste to the premises since adjusting of the temperature controls damaged the building's thermostat.

The tenant cannot, however, be evicted for waste. The damage to the thermostat was minor and reparable within three days. Also, the landlord was unable to demonstrate the tenant's conduct *substantially diminished* the property's market value. [**Rowe** v. **Wells Fargo Realty, Inc.** (1985) 166 CA3d 310]

Now consider a landlord who discovers a tenant's pets have damaged the wooden floors, doors and plastered walls of the tenant's apartment unit. Unsanitary conditions also exist in the unit.

A 3-day notice to quit is served based on the tenant's waste to the unit.

Again, the landlord is unable to evict the tenant for waste. The tenant's failure to maintain the unit has not significantly nor permanently lowered the market value of the unit. The damage created by the tenant's pets could be repaired, and the unit quickly returned to a marketable condition. Thus, a 3-day notice to perform or quit was appropriate. [**Freeze** v. **Brinson** (1991) 3 CA4th Supp. 1]

Waiver of breach by conduct

Consider a tenant of nonresidential property who wants to add further improvements to the leased premises. The lease agreement requires the landlord's written consent before the tenant may make improvements to the premises.

The tenant submits a request to the landlord for approval of additional improvements he wants to make. The landlord does not respond to the tenant's request.

Without the landlord's consent, the tenant begins construction of the improvements. The landlord is aware of the construction. Further, the landlord knows the construction extends beyond the area of the leased premises and encroaches onto other property owned by the landlord.

The landlord demands the tenant remove the improvements he has constructed. As a result, the landlord and tenant commence lease negotiations to expand the leased premises to include the property on which the improvements now encroach.

During negotiations, the landlord accepts all rent payments made by the tenant. Ultimately, the landlord and tenant are unable to reach an agreement and the unauthorized construction remains unresolved. The landlord then serves a 3-day notice to quit followed by a UD action to evict the tenant.

The tenant claims the landlord's acceptance of rent payments waived the landlord's right to terminate the tenant's possession based on the tenant's failure to obtain the landlord's consent before improving the property.

Can the landlord evict the tenant?

Yes! The landlord did not waive his right to terminate the tenant's possession by accepting rent addressed in the lease agreement since the landlord **continuously objected** and never acquiesced to the construction of the improvements.

While the landlord accepted rent payments, the landlord demonstrated to the tenant that he did not intend for the tenant to construct the improvements and continue to occupy the premises on the terms of the existing lease agreement. [**Thriftimart, Inc.** v. **Me & Tex** (1981) 123 CA3d 751]

Many lease agreements contain an enforceable provision that states a waiver by the landlord of a tenant's breach of the lease is not a waiver of similar, subsequent breaches or other breaches by the tenant, called a *nonwaiver provision*. [See Chapter 28]

Covering your bases with alternatives

A tenant's failure to comply with building rules or to maintain the premises in a clean and sanitary manner are breaches of a lease agreement which generally can be performed within three days.

The landlord who serves a 3-day notice to **perform or quit** provides the tenant with the opportunity to comply with building rules or clean the premises and stay. Should the tenant's breach remain uncured after three days and the tenant remain in possession, the landlord may file a UD action to evict the tenant if he so chooses.

For example, the tenant whose authorized pets damage his unit may be unable to replace wood floors and replaster walls within three days. If the tenant fails to perform, the landlord can evict him.

Consider again the tenant who could not be evicted for waste since his failure to follow building rules did not permanently lower the market value of the premises.

A tenant whose breach results from the failure to follow building rules may stop the activity constituting a violation on receiving a 3-day notice to perform or quit. Should the tenant perform the notice to comply with building rules within the three-day period, the tenant cannot be evicted.

However, the tenant might later resume the breaching activity. The tenant's repeat conduct may then constitute a *nuisance*, perhaps obstructing the ability of the landlord or other tenants to enjoy the use of the building due to the constant interference.

The tenant will likely contest a 3-day notice to quit for nuisance. The landlord will then be forced to show how the tenant's conduct constitutes a *continuing nuisance*.

A 3-day notice to quit results in a forfeiture of the tenant's right to possession, as no alternative exists — a harsh result courts do not favor.

Thus, if the tenant's breach is non-statutory and can be cured within three days, a 3-day notice to perform or quit is the proper notice to serve.

When uncertainty exists whether or not the breach can be cured within three days or a tenant's conduct meets the requirements for serving a 3-day notice to quit, a 3-day notice to perform or quit will either:

- cause the tenant to cure the breach within three days; or

- support the landlord's UD action to evict the tenant.

When a **nonwaiver provision** is in the lease agreement, the landlord's acceptance of rent does not constitute a waiver of his right to evict the tenant for a separate later breach of the provision, such as a further assignment of the lease. [**Karbelnig** v. **Brothwell** (1966) 244 CA2d 333]

Consider a tenant who operates a concession stand on leased property. The lease agreement prohibits camping on the premises and contains a nonwaiver provision.

The tenant is unable to stop campers from using the premises. The tenant installs a sign stating camping is not allowed and erects fences to keep overnight campers off the premises. On a demand from the landlord, the tenant takes down the sign and fences.

On removal of the fence, the tenant advises the landlord of his inability to prevent campers from using the premises without maintaining the sign. The landlord does not respond, but continues to accept rent.

After an extended time, the landlord serves a 3-day notice to quit for breach of the lease agreement provision prohibiting camping on the premises. The landlord files a UD action to evict the tenant.

Can the landlord evict the tenant?

No! When a landlord's conduct leads a tenant into believing the **breaching conduct** is no longer a concern of the landlord, the landlord is prevented from processing an eviction based on tenant activity authorized by the landlord, even if the lease agreement contains a nonwaiver provision. [**Salton Community Services District** v. **Southard** (1967) 256 CA2d 526]

Once the tenant's actions breaching a lease agreement provision have been condoned by the landlord, the landlord has *waived* the nonwaiver provision and must take reasonable steps if he intends to *reinstate* the nonwaiver provision so he can enforce it.

A reasonable step to reinstate enforceability would be a written 30-day notice to the tenant stating the landlord intends to enforce the nonwaiver provision in the lease agreement on expiration of the 30-day notice, if 30 days is sufficient time to provide a reasonable opportunity for the tenant to cure the breach. [See **first tuesday** Form 570]

If the tenant continues to breach after expiration of the period for reinstating the provision, the landlord may serve a 3-day notice to perform or quit.

For example, the due date and grace period for rent payments are waived by the landlord when he consistently accepts late payments without demanding a late charge or serving a 3-day notice to pay or quit. A waiver of the late charge provision occurs in spite of the existence of a nonwaiver provision in the lease.

Thus, the late charge provision must be reinstated by a 30-day notice of change in terms before it can be enforced. The landlord's conduct acting inconsistent with written provisions in the lease agreement sets tenant expectations which can be returned to the terms of the written agreement by the notice.

Service of notice

Statutory requirements must be strictly followed when preparing and serving a 3-day notice. [See Chapter 24]

If the 3-day notice is incorrectly or inaccurately prepared, or improperly served on the tenant, the notice is invalid. To evict the tenant, a new 3-day notice must be correctly prepared and properly served. [**Lamey** v. **Masciotra** (1969) 273 CA2d 709]

A proof of service form must be filled out and signed by the person who serves the 3-day notice. Without a proof of service, a UD action cannot be maintained. [See **first tuesday** Form 580]

Concurrent service of two notices

When concurrently serving both a 3-day notice to pay (perform) or vacate and a 30-day notice to vacate or change the terms of a month-to-month tenancy under an expired rental or lease agreement, the notices must not be attached to one another and must be served separately from one another. If attached to one another or combined in any way other than in time, they may be reasonably confused as one. The confusion would properly defeat any UD action based on the 3-day notice.

Also, each notice must be accompanied by its own separate *proof of service* to clarify their independent existence. [See **first tuesday** Form 580]

For example, a tenant on a month-to-month tenancy again breaches his obligation to maintain the premises. The landlord concurrently serves the tenant with both a 3-day **notice to perform** or quit and a 30-day notice to vacate. Each notice stands alone, unattached to the another, and is separately, but concurrently, handed to the tenant. Each service is returned by the server accompanied by a separate proof of service.

The tenant fails to maintain the premises under the 3-day notice to perform and remains in possession. The landlord files a UD action based on the service of the 3-day notice and it's proof of service.

At the UD hearing, the tenant claims he thought he did not have to vacate within three days since the 30-day notice did not mention a breach and gave him 30 days to vacate.

The court, under the "reasonable man" analysis, on examining the content of the separate notices, grants the tenant **relief from forfeiture** of possession under the 3-day notice to perform. Confusion may have caused the tenant not to protect his interest in the property. The tenant is allowed to stay, **on the condition** he immediately perform the maintenance addressed in the 3-day notice. [CCP §1179]

Thus, regardless of any confusion he may have, the tenant will either:

- retain the right to possession after the UD proceedings on the 3-day notice (subject to the outstanding 30-day notice to vacate) on the condition he immediately perform the maintenance called for in the notice; or

- be evicted from the property if he fails to perform the maintenance called for in the notice.

Now consider a tenant who is at the same time served with both a 3-day notice and a separate 30-day notice, each with its own proof of service statement.

The **3-day notice** to pay or quit requires the tenant to pay amounts due and delinquent, within three days after service of written notice of the breach, or vacate and deliver possession to the landlord.

The **30-day notice** to vacate states the tenant is required to vacate and deliver possession of the premises to the landlord within 30 days after service of the notice. [See Chapter 21]

The 30-day notice does not request that the tenant pay any delinquent rent which is due, only the amount which will become due within 30 days on the first of the next calendar month. The tenant pays the rent before the three-day period expires.

Later, at the end of the 30-day period, the tenant refuses to leave. The landlord initiates a UD action on the 30-day notice to vacate. At the UD hearing, the tenant claims he believed that when he paid the delinquent rent under the 3-day notice, the 30-day notice no longer was applicable, since the notices all related to his difficulty in paying rent on time.

Again, the court will apply the *reasonable man test* — examining the contents of both notices and determining if confusion could occur in the mind of the tenant.

The court also must enforce the *legislative scheme* to make sure the landlord followed all statutory requirements regarding the contents and service of the notice. If the landlord is in compliance, the court must award the landlord the relief available under the **legislative scheme**.

Here, the contents of the notices show they are mutually exclusive of one another. The 30-day notice makes no mention of the delinquent rent owed or, that if rent is paid, that the tenancy will continue beyond 30 days.

Also, while served concurrently, the landlord did serve the notices separate from one another. Both notices followed their respective statutory schemes:

- one for collecting delinquent rent; and

- the other for terminating the month-to-month tenancy.

Thus, a court should find that the tenant's purported confusion is not a legal excuse for failing to vacate.

Retaliatory eviction

A landlord concurrently serves a tenant with a 3-day notice to pay or quit and a 30-day notice to vacate — merely because the tenant continuously fails to timely pay rent and is again delinquent. The tenant claims the 30-day notice was served to terminate his tenancy **in retaliation** for being late with the rent, which is true,

although the reason for the termination of the occupancy was not and need not be stated in the 30-day notice.

However, a **retaliatory eviction** does occur in residential properties when the tenant:

- exercises his right to file a complaint with an appropriate agency regarding the *habitability* of the premises;

- orally complains to the landlord about the *habitability* of the premises;

- files documents to initiate a judicial or arbitration proceeding regarding the *habitability* of the premises;

- *organizes or participates* in a tenant association or an association for tenant's rights; or

- lawfully exercises any rights, such as the refusal to authorize credit reports or personal investigation after vacating the premises. [CC §1942.5]

Here, the tenancy was not terminated in retaliation for complaints about the habitability of the premises or for a legal right exercised by the tenant. Instead, the tenant was being evicted for his delinquency in rent payments — a breach by the tenant of the month-to-month rental agreement.

A landlord convicted of a retaliatory eviction is liable for punitive damages up to $2,000 for each act of retaliation. [CC §1942.5]

Chapter 27

Proof of service

This chapter explains the proper service of a 3-day notice, or other notice, on a tenant.

Diligence to locate a tenant is not required

Rent owed by a residential tenant under a rental or lease agreement has become delinquent. In a final effort to collect the delinquent rent, the landlord (or property manager or unlawful detainer (UD) service) prepares a **3-day notice** to pay rent or quit for *service* on the tenant.

The individual serving the notice, called a *process server*, attempts to personally serve the tenant at the tenant's residence. The tenant is not present at the residence and the tenant's place of business is unknown to the landlord.

However, a 16-year-old who responds to the **process server** at the premises is handed the 3-day notice. The process server believes the 16-year-old is of suitable age and discretion to accept service of the notice and pass it along to the tenant without the process server having to post the notice on the property.

A copy of the 3-day notice is also mailed on the same day to the tenant at the residence address since a business address is unknown.

The 3-day notice expires without the tenant paying the delinquent rent or vacating. A UD action is filed to evict the tenant.

At the UD hearing, the tenant defends his occupancy, by claiming the 3-day notice was improperly served. The tenant claims he cannot be evicted since a person of suitable age and discretion to accept service must be at least 18 years old.

Is handing a copy of a 3-day notice to an apparently intelligent 16-year-old on the premises and mailing a copy to the tenant proper service to terminate the occupancy and establish an unlawful detainer of the property on its expiration?

Yes! The tenant's unlawful detainer is established without personal service of the notice on the tenant. After an attempt at personal service, *substituted service* is authorized. Proper **substituted service** of a 3-day notice includes delivery of a copy to an intelligent and mature 16-year-old on the leased premises. Thus, having been served, the tenant can be evicted. [**Lehr** v. **Crosby** (1981) 123 CA3d Supp. 1]

If the tenant is not available for personal service at his residence, or his place of business if known to the landlord, the 3-day notice may be:

- handed to any person who is of **suitable age and discretion** at either location; and

- copied and mailed to the tenant at his residence. [Calif. Code of Civil Procedure §1162(2)]

The rules for serving a 3-day notice do not specify a person of suitable age and discretion must be at least 18 years old.

A younger person who appears to be of suitable age and discretion, such as a guest or family member at the tenant's residence or an employee at his place of business, is a person who may be handed the notice as part of the substituted service on the tenant.

Editor's note — A person of suitable age and discretion to accept substituted service of a 3-day notice must, on questioning, be able to understand their responsibility to hand the notice to the tenant. If the responsibility is not understood, then the process server must post the notice at the property and mail a copy to the tenant.

Serving a 3-day notice

To establish the UD of a tenant or subtenant, a requisite to a UD action, statutory requirements must be strictly followed when **preparing and serving** a 3-day notice. [**Lamey** v. **Masciotra** (1969) 273 CA2d 709]

Both residential and nonresidential property are subject to the same 3-day notice and service rules.

When a rental or lease agreement is breached, one of the following statutory 3-day notices is **served on the tenant**, depending on the type of activity or inaction which is the breach:

- a 3-Day Notice to Pay Rent or Quit [See **first tuesday** Form 575];

- a 3-Day Notice to Perform or Quit [See **first tuesday** Form 576]; or

- a 3-Day Notice to Quit. [CCP §1161; see **first tuesday** Form 577]

Service by elimination of methods

The 3-day notice can be served on the tenant by:

- **personal service**;

- **leaving a copy** with a person of suitable age and discretion at the premises **and mailing** a copy to the premises if the tenant is not personally served at his residence or place of business, called *substituted service*; or

- **posting** the notice on the leased premises **and mailing** a copy to the premises if the tenant is not available for personal service at his place of business or residence address if known, or a person could not be found to be served at the tenant's residence or place of business. [CCP §1162]

The **first attempt** at serving a 3-day notice must be by personal delivery of a copy to the tenant, called *personal service*. [CCP §1162(1)]

Personal delivery can be made wherever the tenant can be located. Personal service must be attempted at both the tenant's residence and place of business, if known. These two attempts to personally serve the notice are a prerequisite to an attempt at substituted service.

Secondly, if the attempt to personally serve the tenant fails because he is absent from both his residence and place of business (if known), a copy of the 3-day notice may then be:

- handed to a person of suitable age and discretion at either the tenant's residence or place of business; and

- mailed to the tenant at his residence, called *substituted service*. [CCP §1162(2)]

Thirdly, if both the tenant's residence and place of business are unknown, which is rare, or the tenant cannot be found for personal service at either the residence or business addresses, or a person of suitable age and discretion cannot be found for substituted service at either place, the 3-day notice may be:

- posted on the leased premises; and

- mailed to the tenant at the address of the leased premises, loosely deemed service by *nail and mail*. [CCP §1162(3)]

Typically, a landlord's resident manager or property manager is responsible for preparing and serving a 3-day notice as part of their employment by the landlord. [See **first tuesday** Forms 590 and 591]

The attorney or UD service handling the anticipated eviction often prepares and causes the notice to be served.

Documenting service

The individual who serves the 3-day notice must complete a form confirming he served the notice and the type of service completed, called a *proof of service*. [See Form 580 accompanying this chapter]

If a UD action is filed to evict a tenant, a completed proof of service must be produced at trial, evidencing service of the 3-day notice.

If the 3-day notice is **personally served** on the tenant, the individual serving the notice must verify he made the personal service at the address served. [See Form 580 §5.1]

When the server completes a **substituted service**, he verifies:

- his attempts to personally serve the tenant at both addresses were unsuccessful;

- the notice was handed to a person of suitable age and discretion at the tenant's residence or business address; and

- the 3-day notice was mailed to the tenant at his residence. [See Form 580 §5.2]

If the notice is served by **posting** on the premises, the server verifies:

- no person of suitable age or discretion was available at the tenant's residence and business addresses, or the addresses are unknown; and

- the 3-day notice was mailed to the tenant at the address of the leased premises. [See Form 580 §5.3]

Full compliance on each attempt

When serving a 3-day notice, the landlord must first attempt to personally serve the tenant before resorting to substituted service. [**Nourafchan** v. **Miner** (1985) 169 CA3d 746]

Personal service occurs when the 3-day notice is handed to the tenant, whether or not the notice is:

- accepted by the tenant; or

- dropped at the tenant's feet after the tenant refuses to accept the notice.

Failure to attempt **substitute service** at both the tenant's residence and place of business, if known, before service of the notice by posting the property results in defective service. The landlord will be unable to maintain a UD action against the tenant should the tenant challenge the service of the 3-day notice.

When attempting substituted service, merely showing, and not handing, a copy of the 3-day notice to a person on the premises and mailing a copy to the address is not proper service. [**Kwok** v. **Bergren** (1982) 130 CA3d 596]

When leaving a copy with a suitable person or posting a 3-day notice on the leased premises, service is completed only if the notice is also mailed to the tenant. [**Jordan** v. **Talbot** (1961) 55 C2d 597]

The notice, when required to be mailed, may be mailed by first-class, registered or certified mail.

However, the **lone mailing** of a 3-day notice is not itself a proper service. For service to be effective when mailed, the notice must first (following attempts at personal service) be either handed to an individual of suitable age and discretion or, if such an individual is not available, posted on the premises. [**Liebovich** v. **Shahrokhkhany** (1997) 56 CA4th 511]

No diligence required to locate

Personal service must first be attempted before resorting to substituted service, but *reasonable diligence* is not required in the attempt to locate the tenant so he can be personally served.

For example, consider a property manager of an apartment building who prepares a 3-day notice for service on a tenant. The property manager is unaware of any business address for the tenant. No business address is listed on the application to rent.

The property manager attempts to serve the 3-day notice on the tenant at his unit.

The property manager receives no response after ringing the doorbell and knocking on the door of the premises. Thus, no personal or substituted service can be made. The property manager posts the 3-day notice to the door with tape (or a nail) and mails another copy addressed to the tenant at the apartment unit by first-class mail.

The tenant does not pay the delinquent rent or vacate before the 3-day notice expires. A UD action is filed and served on the tenant.

The tenant claims improper service of the 3-day notice since the property manager made no effort to locate the tenant's business address in order to personally serve him before serving the 3-day notice by posting the property and mailing him the notice.

However, the property manager is not required to use diligence, much less investigate the location of the tenant when attempting personal service of a 3-day notice. A review of the property management files and personal knowledge will suffice.

The property manager's use of the post-and-mail alternative for service was proper. When the landlord or property manager is unaware of any address for the tenant other than the leased premises:

- no attempt to ascertain the tenant's other address is necessary; and

- service by posting the premises and mailing to the leased premises is sufficient when no suitable person for substituted service is found at the premises. [**Hozz** v. **Lewis** (1989) 215 CA3d 314]

Consider an individual who leases space in a retail center to operate his business.

The tenant fails to pay his rent, and the property manager prepares a 3-day notice for service on the tenant. The property manager does not know the tenant's residential address.

The property manager attempts to personally serve the tenant with the 3-day notice at the leased premises, his place of business, but the tenant is absent from the business.

The property manager hands the 3-day notice to an employee of the tenant and mails a copy to the tenant at the premises.

Is the method of service used by the property manager proper?

Yes! Since reasonable diligence is not required when attempting personal service, the property manager need not make a second effort, such as returning to the premises or looking in a directory or voting records, to discover the tenant's residential address. [Nourafchan, *supra*]

Personal receipt of certified mail

Even if the attempted service is defective, the tenant's **admitted receipt** of the 3-day notice establishes *personal service*. Thus, the defective service is no longer an issue. [**Valov** v. **Tank** (1985) 168 CA3d 867]

For example, a property manager sends a 3-day notice by certified mail. It is the property manager's only attempt to notify the tenant. No personal service is attempted, no copy of the notice is left with a person of suitable age and discretion on the premises, and no notice is posted on the premises.

PROOF OF SERVICE

1. I am over 18 years of age.

2. On _____, 20_____, at _____, California.
   I served the following checked items:

   ☐ 3-Day Notice to Pay Rent or Quit

   ☐ 3-Day Notice to Perform or Quit

   ☐ 3-Day Notice to Quit for Breach

   ☐ 30-Day Notice to Terminate/Vacate

   ☐ 30-Day Notice of Change in Rental Terms

   ☐ 60-Day Notice of Change in Rental Terms

   ☐ Other:_____

3. Regarding tenancy of property commonly known as: _____

   _____

4. On Tenants (name):_____

5. Manner of service (check the proper box):

   5.1 ☐ By personally delivering a copy to each named Tenant;

       a. ☐ at Tenant's residence;
       b. ☐ at Tenant's place of business.

   5.2 ☐ By delivering a copy to a person of suitable age and discretion;

       a. ☐ at the Tenant's residence; or
       b. ☐ at Tenant's place of business, as the named Tenant was absent from each location;

       and

       mailing [by first-class postage prepaid] a copy to each named Tenant at his residence.

   5.3 ☐ By posting a copy for each named Tenant in a conspicuous place on the property described in the notice as no person of suitable age or discretion was found at the Tenant's residence or place of business;

       and

       mailing [by first-class postage prepaid] a copy to each named Tenant at the address of the leased property.

I declare under penalty of perjury that the foregoing is true and correct.

Date:_____, 20_____

Name:_____

Signature:_____

FORM 580   10-00   ©2007 **first tuesday**, P.O. BOX 20069, RIVERSIDE, CA 92516 (800) 794-0494

However, the tenant personally signs the postal receipt accepting the certified mail. Thus, the tenant personally receives the 3-day notice on the date he acknowledges receipt. The tenant's acknowledgement of receipt confirms he has been **personally served** (by the post office) with the 3-day notice on the date he acknowledged receipt.

The mailing of the notice by the property manager did not constitute service of the 3-day notice on the tenant — even though certified mail was used. However, the **tenant's signing** of the postal receipt is proof the tenant was handed the 3-day notice by a post office employee — which is personal service.

The tenant who fails to pay the delinquent rent within the three-day period following acknowledgment of his receipt of the 3-day notice by mail is unlawfully detaining the premises and can be evicted.

Editor's note — If any person other than the tenant signs acknowledging the receipt of the mail, personal service is not accomplished. [Liebovich, *supra*]

An evasive tenant might not pick up certified mail addressed to him when his rental payment is delinquent.

If personal service cannot be accomplished, the three-day notice period begins to run the day the notice is either served by substituted service and mailed, or posted and mailed. The day following service is day one of three. If the third day is a Saturday, Sunday or holiday, the 3-day period continues through the first business day which follows.

Chapter 28

Other amounts due under 3-day notices

This chapter discusses the inclusion of amounts of money due the landlord under a lease agreement other than "rent" in a 3-day notice to pay or quit.

Know what the judge will allow

A lease agreement between a landlord and his tenant contains a rent provision with a clause calling for the **accrual of interest** on any amount of rent from its due date if the payment becomes delinquent, a type of *late payment clause*.

The tenant fails to pay rent before it becomes delinquent. The landlord then prepares a 3-day notice to pay or quit and serves the notice on the tenant. [See **first tuesday** Forms 575 and 575.5]

The 3-day notice itemizes the amounts of delinquent rent and daily interest accrued that are due and unpaid on the date the notice is prepared. The tenant fails to pay or quit during the 3-day period. The landlord files an unlawful detainer (UD) action asking the court to order the removal of the tenant from the premises.

At the UD hearing, the tenant claims the landlord cannot terminate his possession of the premises under the 3-day notice since the notice demands payment of an amount greater than the **rent due** under the lease agreement, and thus is defective as the demand includes *other amounts due* the landlord.

May the 3-day notice include amounts due under monetary provisions in the lease agreement in addition to the rent itself?

Yes! **Monetary amounts due** under rent provisions in the rental or lease agreement that may be demanded in the 3-day notice to pay or quit are not limited to the scheduled amount of periodic rent which is delinquent.

While the notice to pay may not be served until rent is delinquent, the notice itself is all-inclusive allowing it to state the *total amount which is due*, not only the delinquent amount entitled rent. Thus, the notice may include all sums of money which are **due and unpaid** under the rental or lease agreement at the time the notice is served, including the delinquent rent. [**Canal-Randolph Anaheim, Inc.** v. **Moore** (1978) 78 CA3d 477]

Examples of amounts of money due periodically under a rental or lease agreement, in addition to scheduled rent, include:

- common area maintenance charges (CAMs);

- association charges;

- pro rata insurance premiums, property taxes and assessments;

- late payment and bad check charges;

- expenses incurred by the landlord to cure waste or failure to maintain the property, called *future advances*; and

- other amounts of money properly due as compensation or reimbursement of expenses arising out of the occupancy.

A 3-day notice to pay or quit form provides for the itemization of rent and other amounts due which are unpaid and delinquent. [See **first tuesday** Form 575]

Lump sum late charges

Under a nonresidential lease agreement entered into by a tenant, rent is typically due and payable on the first day of each month, called the *due date*. The lease agreement contains a late charge provision stating the tenant agrees to pay a charge in the amount of $150 if the rent is not **received by** the landlord on or before the fifth day of each month, called a *grace period* [See **first tuesday** Form 552 §3.9]

Under the lease agreement, rent is *delinquent* the day after the grace period runs, the sixth day of the month. The delinquency triggers the landlord's right to demand payment of the late charge, or do nothing and waive it.

The lease agreement also provides for the tenant to pay $25 for each rent check returned for insufficient funds (NSF). [See **first tuesday** Form 552 §3.10]

During one month, the landlord receives the rent after the grace period expires. As he must, the landlord accepts the rent since the right to possession, the lease, has not been terminated by a declaration of forfeiture or expiration of the lease. The landlord then notifies the tenant in writing that he is imposing a late charge, payable with the following month's rent, as provided in the lease agreement. [See Form 569 accompanying this chapter]

The following month the landlord receives the regularly scheduled rent within the grace period. However, the tenant does not also tender the late charge the landlord demanded due to the prior month's delinquent payment.

Landlord's options for collection

On the tenant's failure to pay additional charges, the landlord's options to enforce payment, viable or not, include:

- returning the rent check to the tenant as insufficient payment for the total amount due;

- serving the tenant with a 3-day notice to pay or quit;

- deducting the additional charge from the security deposit on written notice to the tenant; or

- filing an action against the tenant in small claims court to collect the late charge.

Returning the rent check to the tenant will result in one of the following scenarios:

- The tenant will submit another check which includes rent and payment of the late charge (which payment will be delinquent and arguably incur another late charge); or

- The tenant will retain the rent check as having been properly tendered and therefore legally paid, and do nothing more until he sends a check for the following month's rent.

A tenant who fails to pay rent or otherwise *materially breaches* the lease agreement, may be served with the appropriate 3-day notice. The 3-day notice based on a material breach properly includes a demand for late charges and any other monetary *amounts past due* [Canal-Randolph Anaheim, Inc., *supra*]

If the tenant fails to cure the breach within three days following service of the notice and remains in possession, the landlord may file an unlawful detainer (UD) action to regain possession. [Calif. Code of Civil Procedure §1161]

However, a landlord will not succeed in a UD action when the landlord's refusal to accept the tenant's timely tender of a rent check is based solely on the tenant's refusal to pay late charges. Failure to pay the agreed late charge after notice is a *minor breach*. [Canal-Randolph Anaheim, Inc., *supra*]

Thus, the landlord has two **viable options** for the collection of unpaid late charges from the tenant:

- accept the rent check, deduct the amount of the unpaid late charge from the security deposit and advise the tenant of the deduction; or

- accept the rent check and file an action in court for the unpaid late charge amounts.

The financially practical action the landlord can take when the tenant refuses to pay a demand for a late charge is to accept the rent and deduct the late charge from the tenant's security deposit.

A UD action cannot be maintained if the sole existing breach of the lease agreement is the failure to pay the late charges. A *material breach* is required to support a UD action, such as a delinquency in the scheduled rent and other scheduled periodic compensation for occupancy and use of the property. A late charge is properly sought when pursuing delinquent rent, but alone, a late charge (or bounced check charge) is a *minor breach* and will not independently support a UD action. [**Baypoint Mortgage** v. **Crest Premium Real Estate Investments Retirement Trust** (1985) 168 CA3d 818]

Late charges

To be enforceable, late charges must be *reasonably related* to:

- the actual costs of collecting the delinquent rent (the time and effort involved); and

- the delay in its receipt (loss of use, such as interest).

A lump sum late charge becomes an unenforceable *liquidated damages provision* if the amount of the late charge is significantly greater than the actual **out-of-pocket losses** suffered by the landlord due to the tenant's late payment of rent, in which case the charge is labeled a penalty and is unenforceable. [**Garrett** v. **Coast and Southern Federal Savings and Loan Association** (1973) 9 C3d 731]

Editor's note — Some may argue any lump sum late charge on residential property is void as a liquidated damage since out-of-pocket money losses due to a late payment are readily ascertainable, especially in a residential real estate transaction.

A **liquidated damages** provision in a residential lease is void, unless the loss covered is impracticable or nearly impossible to calculate (which it is not), or the amount agreed to is a reasonable estimate of the landlord's out-of-pocket expenses for the collection effort. [Calif. Civil Code §1671(d)]

When setting the amount of a late charge for a residential tenant's failure to timely pay rent under a rental or lease agreement, consider charging an amount equivalent to the late charge allowed by the legislature on a residential loan since the amount is a good indicator of *reasonableness*.

The late charge amount allowed for a delinquent payment on a loan secured by residential property is controlled by statute. This is not the case for rent.

For example, the lump sum late charge allowed on a loan secured by an owner-occupied, single-family residence cannot exceed 6% of the delinquent payment (principal and interest only). [CC §2954.4(a)]

Rent is the *economic equivalent* of interest. For purposes of late charges, rent payments should be treated no differently than interest payments.

Late charges as liquidated damages

A lump sum late charge set forth as a dollar amount in a lease agreement is a *liquidated damages* provision. The charge is a one-time, predetermined fixed amount intended by its nature to reimburse the landlord for the **delay in receipt** of the rent money and his **costs and effort** spent to collect the delinquent amount. [CC §1951.5]

A late charge provision calling for *interest to accrue* at a predetermined annual percentage rate on amounts earned and unpaid (delinquent rent) is not a liquidated damages provision and is fully enforceable. [Canal-Randolph Anaheim, Inc., *supra*]

However, some landlords wrongfully view late charges as a means for **coercing tenants to pay** rent on time. Thus, landlords set the late charge at an amount exceeding his actual losses, a **penalty assessment** that is unenforceable.

A lump sum late charge provision in a nonresidential lease agreement is valid unless the tenant can show the amount of the late charge is an unreasonable reimbursement for the delay in receipt of the rent and costs of collection efforts. [CC §1671(b)]

A late charge is unenforceable if the charge is so great in comparison to actual losses that it *imposes a penalty* on the tenant for his late rent payment. [Garrett, *supra*]

An appropriate late charge provision in a lease agreement for single-user residential or nonresidential property encumbered by a loan is the amount of the late charge imposed on the owner when a monthly payment on the loan is delinquent. The owner is simply "passing through" the loss incurred by his late receipt of the tenant's rent payment.

However, in a residential lease agreement, a late charge provision setting a fixed amount is void unless the losses suffered by the landlord due to late payment are impracticable to calculate. [CC §1671(d)]

Editor's note — Determining money losses suffered due to late payments in any real estate transaction, especially in a residential lease, is not impracticable to calculate since it is merely an accounting of known amounts incurred as expenses in the collection and lost use of the funds until received.

Imposing the late charge

A late charge is **not automatically due** and payable by the tenant when the landlord fails to receive the rent payment within the grace period.

The landlord must first make a **written demand** on the tenant for payment of the late charge and include the date when the charge is payable before the collection can be enforced.

Thus, a written billing demanding payment of the late charge with the next month's rent is delivered to the tenant to ensure the late charge agreed to is imposed. [See **first tuesday** Form 568]

The **late charge notice** advises the tenant the landlord is entitled to enforce collection of the unpaid late charge by:

- deducting the unpaid late charge amount from the tenant's security deposit; or

- filing a small claims or municipal court action for unpaid late charge amounts.

Too late to collect

Within one year from the date rent became delinquent, or some other *material breach* of a monetary provision in the lease or rental agreement occurred, the landlord must serve a 3-day notice on the tenant to be able to enforce collection of the amounts sought in a UD action. [CCP §1161(2)]

As an alternative to seeking a recovery of money in a UD action with its one-year limitation, the landlord can file a separate money action within four years of the breach to collect unpaid late charges, returned check handling charges and any other amounts due under the lease agreement. [CCP §337]

Ultimately, the landlord can deduct the late charges from the tenant's security deposit as payment of unpaid amounts due the landlord under the lease agreement. [CC §§1950.5(b)(1), 1950.7(c)]

The UD court problem

While the enforcement of lump sum late charges for the recovery of collection efforts has not been the subject of reported cases, the court in *Canal-Randolph Anaheim, Inc.* ruled an interest-rate late charge on delinquent rent to cover the loss of use of the payment can be included as *amounts due* under a rental or lease agreement.

Canal-Randolph Anaheim, Inc. clarified that a landlord may include any sums due under the lease as **amounts due** in the 3-day notice.

Also, no statutes exist that forbid (or limit) the collection of a late charge in a rental or lease agreement. However, cases do limit the charge to an amount reasonably calculated to cover the losses inflicted by late payment. [Garrett, *supra*]

Further, not all trial judges will concede late charges are part of the *amount due* under a 3-day notice. Despite the holding of *Canal-Randolph Anaheim, Inc.*, some judges declare late charges are not *rent*, the delinquency of which triggers use of a 3-day notice to pay or quit. [CCP §1161(2)]

These judges hold a late charge or bad check charge cannot be included in the 3-day notice as part of the *amount due*. If included, the demand would bar an eviction before those judges.

Before a landlord or a property manager includes any late charge (or other *amounts due* besides technical rent) in a 3-day notice as part of the total amount due, it should first be determined if the judge presiding over UD actions in the landlord or property manager's jurisdiction will allow a demand for late charges.

Judges vary in their approach to late charges:

- some allow *masked late charges* cloaked as a forgiveness of 6% to 10% of the scheduled rent, if paid before the rent (including the masked late charge) is considered delinquent — within five to 10 days after it is due;

- some allow a late charge of up to 6% of the delinquent rent as a reasonable amount;

- some disallow late charges as an unenforceable penalty for being delinquent;

- some disallow late charges as a forfeiture of money (since the amount exceeds the costs of collection); and

- some just disallow late charges altogether as an exercise of their discretion.

Information on the treatment given by the local trial court judge can be obtained from an attorney or other landlords who have experience appearing in front of the judge in question.

If the judge will not allow the late charge as part of the amount due from the tenant, the landlord should leave it out of the 3-day notice. Instead, either deduct the late charge from the security deposit (if any remains when refunded), or pursue collection in a separate action for money, both of which avoid the issue of demands placed in the 3-day notice. Investigate the judge's behavior first to eliminate the risk of getting an erroneous judicial determination that late charges or other amounts due were improperly included in the 3-day notice and therefore a denial of the eviction requiring an appeal or renewal of the 3-day notice and UD process without the late charge.

*Editor's note — An obvious solution to the inconsistent rules applied to late charges would be **public policy** legislation defining the nature of late charges and acceptable limits on time and amounts for recovery of the cost of collecting delinquent rent — guidance for all involved in the UD process.*

Late charges for rent should be treated like late charges on mortgages. Both serve the same economic function — recovery of costs incurred due to the delay of receipt of funds and resulting collection efforts. Also, the number of homeowners with mortgage payments is almost equal to the number of renters with rental payments in California. Both mortgage payments and rental payments are part of the cost of occupancy and entitled to equivalent legislative controls.

Chapter 29

Notices to vacate

This chapter presents the 30-day notice to vacate used by landlords and tenants to terminate month-to-month tenancies other than by use of 3-day notice to quit.

Termination of periodic tenancies

A tenant enters into occupancy of a single family residential property under a lease agreement obligating the tenant to maintain the property's landscaping.

The landlord soon receives complaints from surrounding property owners about excessive noise and a high number of visitors at the property late at night. On more than one occasion, the police have responded to calls from neighbors regarding the noise. Also, the city ordinance compliance department has given notice for the removal of disabled vehicles from the property. On a drive-by inspection, the landlord discovers the landscaping and lawn have deteriorated since the tenant has not watered.

Although the tenant consistently pays the rent on time, the landlord feels the tenant must be evicted even though several months remain on the term of the lease. The tenant is creating a *nuisance* by interfering with his neighbors' use and enjoyment of their property and *waste* by failing to maintain the leased premises, both are justification to terminate the tenancy.

The landlord prepares and serves the tenant with a 30-day **notice to vacate** to avoid stating his reasons for terminating the tenancy. [California Civil Code §1946; see Form 569 accompanying this chapter]

The tenant remains in occupancy of the premises after the 30-day notice expires and tenders the next rent payment on time. The landlord refuses to accept the rent payment and files an unlawful detainer (UD) action to evict the tenant.

Can the landlord, subject to an unexpired lease that the tenant has breached, evict the tenant from the premises with a 30-day notice to vacate?

No! The tenant occupies the property under an unexpired lease. The landlord cannot terminate the tenant's right to possession by using a notice to vacate, much less use the notice to vacate to establish an unlawful detainer when an unexpired lease exists.

A residential or nonresidential 30-day notice to vacate the premises is only effective when used by a landlord or tenant to terminate a periodic tenancy, such as a month-to-month tenancy or a continuing occupancy after a lease expires. The term of the periodic tenancy (weekly, monthly, annually) does not matter, unless the property is **nonresidential** and the rental agreement calls for a greater or lesser period for notice than 30 days, but not less than seven days. [CC §1946]

If agreed, a provision in a residential or nonresidential lease agreement may allow the tenant to terminate his occupancy prior to expiration of the lease on 30 days' notice, or any other period for notice, conditioned on the payment of a penalty for canceling the lease agreement and vacating prematurely, sometimes called a *cancellation provision*.

Periodic tenancies extended/terminated

Unlike the extension of a lease, the 30-day rental period under a **month-to-month rental agreement** is *automatically extended* for the same period and on the same terms, until the right to extend is terminated by a 30-day notice to vacate.

Any landlord under a month-to-month rental agreement (or for any other period) may **interfere at any time** with the automatic renewal of the rental agreement and terminate the tenancy by serving a 30-day notice to vacate on the tenant.

Likewise, any tenant under a month-to-month rental agreement may, at any time, stop the automatic renewal process and terminate the tenancy by giving the landlord a 30-day notice of the tenant's intent to vacate the premises. [CC §1946; see Form 572 accompanying this chapter]

A notice to vacate on a month-to-month tenancy, whether given by the tenant or the landlord, establishes a tenant's unlawful detainer (UD) when it expires and the tenant remains in possession. [**Palmer** v. **Zeis** (1944) 65 CA2d Supp. 859]

Once the notice to vacate expires and the tenant does not vacate, the landlord may file a UD action to evict the month-to-month tenant without further notice. [Code of Civil Procedure §1161(5)]

Lease becomes a periodic tenancy

Consider a tenant entering into a one-year lease of a unit in a residential or nonresidential building. After expiration of the lease, the tenant remains in possession of the unit, an unlawful detainer of the premises. However, the tenant continues to pay rent monthly, which the landlord accepts.

Later, the landlord serves the tenant with a 30-day notice to vacate the property and the tenant refuses. The landlord files a UD action to evict the tenant.

The tenant claims he cannot be evicted based on a 30-day notice to vacate since he holds possession of the unit under a lease agreement, which was automatically extended for the same period as the term of the original lease by the landlord's acceptance of rent after the lease expired.

Here, the 30-day notice to vacate is effective to terminate possession and the tenant can be evicted. The landlord's acceptance of monthly rent after the lease expired, when the lease agreement does not provide the tenant with an option to renew or extend the lease, establishes a month-to-month tenancy on the same conditions stated in the lease agreement. [CC §1945]

Landlord's intent to evict

A landlord, residential or nonresidential, terminates a month-to-month tenancy by preparing and serving the tenant with a 30-day notice to vacate. However, if a **material breach** exists in the payment of amounts due or performance of provisions in the occupancy agreement, a 3-day notice to quit is used. [See **first tuesday** Forms 571 and 579; see Chapter 26]

A 30-day notice to vacate form used by a landlord contains:

- the name of the tenant;

- the address of the premises;

- a reference to the rental agreement or expired lease;

- a statement that the unit must be vacant within 30 days after service of the notice;

- the dollar amount of pro rata rent to be paid when rent is next due;

- a statement regarding the security deposit and its disposition; and

- a statement informing the tenant of his right to request a joint inspection of the premises in order to avoid deductions from his security deposit.

A *forfeiture provision* is not properly included in any 30-day notice to vacate since no right to possession exists to be forfeited on expiration of the rental agreement — the tenancy merely terminates by its own terms when the notice expires.

30-DAY NOTICE TO VACATE
From Tenant

DATE:_____, 20_____, at _____, California.

> **NOTICE:** Unless otherwise agreed, a Tenant may terminate a month-to-month tenancy by giving thirty (30) days written notice to the landlord. [California Civil Code §1946]

To Landlord: _____

Items left blank or unchecked are not applicable.

FACTS:

1. I am a Tenant under a rental agreement or expired lease agreement
    1.1 dated _____, at _____, California,
    1.2 entered into by_____, Tenant,
    and _____, Landlord,
    1.3 regarding real estate referred to as: _____
    _____

NOTICE:

2. Within thirty (30) days after service of this notice, I will vacate and deliver possession of the premises to Landlord or_____.

3. This notice is intended as a Thirty-Day Notice to terminate my month-to-month tenancy.

4. I understand:
    4.1 I will owe prorated daily rent for any days in the 30-day period I have not prepaid rent.
    4.2 I have previously given Landlord a security deposit of $_____.
    a. I acknowledge, if I am a residential tenant, that I have the right to request an inspection of the premises, and be present, to be conducted within two weeks of expiration of this notice to vacate for the purposes of the landlord providing me with an itemized statement of deductible charges for repairs and cleaning to allow me the opportunity to remedy these deficiencies and avoid a deduction from my security deposit. [California Civil Code §1950.5(f)]
    b. Within 21 days after I vacate, Landlord will furnish me a written statement and explanation of any deductions from the deposit, and a refund of the remaining amount. [California Civil Code §1950.5(g)]
    4.4 Landlord may deduct only those amounts necessary to:
    a. Reimburse for Tenant defaults in rental payments;
    b. Repair damages to the premises caused by Tenant (ordinary wear and tear excluded);
    c. Clean the premises, if necessary;
    d. Reimburse for Tenant loss, damage or excessive wear and tear on furnishings provided to Tenant.
    4.5 Landlord may show the premises to prospective tenants by giving reasonable notice as called for in the rental or lease agreement. Twenty-four (24) hours will be presumed to be reasonable notice. Showings will only occur during normal business hours.

5. The reason for termination is _____.

6. I have served this notice on Landlord or Manager ☐ personally, or ☐ by certified or registered mail.
    (optional)

This statement is true and correct.	**For Landlord/Agent's use:**
Date:_____, 20_____	Date Received _____:
Tenant:_____	
Signature: _____	
Forwarding Address:_____	
_____	
Phone:_____	
Fax: _____	
E-mail: _____	

FORM 572   08-06   @2007 **first tuesday**, P.O. BOX 20069, RIVERSIDE, CA 92516 (800) 794-0494

Due to its contents, the landlord's 30-day notice to vacate eliminates any confusion as to the amount of pro rata rent to be paid and when the rent is due. [See Form 571 §3]

Tenant's intent to vacate

A tenant, residential or nonresidential, who intends to vacate and avoid further liability under a month-to-month rental agreement or expired lease must give 30-days advance notice to the landlord of the **tenant's termination** of the tenancy. The notice may be in the form of a letter personally delivered to the landlord or his agent, or sent by certified or registered mail. [CC §§1946]

Some landlords are willing to accept oral notice of the tenant's intent to vacate without reducing the notice to a writing signed by the tenant.

However, both the tenant and the landlord are better served when the landlord hands the tenant a 30-day Notice to Vacate form when entering into a rental agreement or, at worst, when the tenant gives oral notice of his vacating the space. The tenant will then have the correct paperwork to complete and deliver documentation to the landlord or property manager. Use of a form lends certainty to the tenant's understanding of a critical event. [See **first tuesday** Form 572]

A tenant's 30-day notice to vacate acknowledges:

- the tenancy is terminated on expiration of 30 days after service of the notice on the landlord or his manager;

- the tenant's intent to pay pro rata rent;

- the amount of the security deposit and the tenant's right to request a pre-termination inspection and receive an itemized statement of maintenance and cleaning deficiencies for any potential deductions from the security deposit; and

- a security deposit statement and refund based on any deductions for cleaning and repairs on a final review of the premises by the landlord or property manager; and

- the landlord's right to show the premises to a prospective tenant on 24 hour notice.

Service of the notice to vacate

A 30-day notice to vacate may be served at any time during the month.

However, a **nonresidential landlord** and tenant may limit the right to serve the notice at any time by agreeing in the rental agreement that the 30-day notice to vacate cannot be served during the last six days of the month. This is not true for residential tenancies since service can occur at any time to begin the 30-day period. [CC §§1946]

To be effective, the 30-day notice to vacate from a **nonresidential tenant or landlord** must be served:

- in the same manner as a 3-day notice (in person, by substitution or post and mail); or

- by certified or registered mail, a method of service not available for 3-day notices to quit. [CC §1946; see Chapter 26]

Conversely, a **residential landlord or tenant** must serve a 30-day notice to vacate by:

- personally delivering the notice to either the landlord or tenant; or

- **leaving a copy** of the notice either at the residence or the tenant's place of business with a person of appropriate age, **posting the notice** in a conspicuous place on the property and mailing, by certified or registered mail, a copy addressed to the tenant in the unit. [CCP §§ 1161a, 1162]

The date of service to a nonresidential tenant is the date the notice is first:

30-DAY NOTICE TO VACATE

(For Use by Residential Landlord)

DATE:_____, 20_____, at _____, California.

> **NOTICE:** A residential landlord may terminate a month-to-month tenancy by giving at least thirty (30) days' written notice to the tenant unless the tenant has resided on the property for one year or more. [Calif. Civil Code §§1946,1946.1]

To Tenant: _____

Items left blank or unchecked are not applicable.
FACTS:

1. You are a Tenant under a rental agreement or expired lease agreement
   1.1 dated _____, at _____,California,
   1.2 entered into by _____, Tenant,
   and _____, Landlord,
   1.3 regarding real estate referred to as: _____
   _____

NOTICE:

2. This notice is intended as at least a thirty (30) day notice prior to termination of your month-to-month tenancy.

3. On or before _____, 20_____, a date at least thirty (30) days after service of this notice, you will vacate and deliver possession of the premises to Landlord or:_____
   _____

4. Rent due prior to the date to vacate includes prorated rent of $_____, payable on or before _____, 20_____.

5. Landlord acknowledges the prior receipt of $_____ as your security deposit.
   5.1 Notice: You have the right to request an inspection of the premises, and be present, to be conducted within two weeks of expiration of this notice to vacate for the purposes of providing you with an itemized statement of deductible charges for repairs and cleaning and allowing you the opportunity to remedy these deficiencies and avoid a deduction from your security deposit. [Calif. Civil Code §1950.5(f)(i)]
   5.2 Within 21 days after you vacate, Landlord will furnish you with a written statement and explanation of any deductions from the deposit, and a refund of the remaining amount. [Calif. Civil Code §1950.5(g)(i)]
   5.3 Landlord may deduct only those amounts necessary to:
   a. Reimburse for Tenant defaults in rental payments;
   b. Repair damages to the premises caused by Tenant (ordinary wear and tear excluded);
   c. Clean the premises, if necessary;
   d. Reimburse for Tenant loss, damage or excessive wear and tear on furnishings provided to Tenant.

6. Landlord may show the leased premises to prospective tenants during normal business hours by first giving you written notice at least 24 hours in advance of the entry. The notice will be given to you in person, by leaving a copy with an occupant of suitable age and discretion, or by leaving the notice on or under your entry door.

7. If you fail to vacate and deliver possession of the premises by the date set for you to vacate, legal proceedings may be initiated to regain possession of the premises and to recover rent owed, treble damages, costs and attorney fees.

8. The reason for termination is _____
   _____
   (required by rent control ordinance or Section 8 housing)

Date:_____, 20_____

Landlord/Agent: _____

Signature: _____

Address:_____

_____

Phone: _____

Fax: _____

- personally served;

- handed to a person of suitable age and discretion and mailed;

- posted on the leased premises and mailed; or

- mailed by certified or registered mail.

The 30-day minimum period within which the tenant must vacate begins to run the day after the date of service, which is day one of the 30-day period. [CC §10]

If the day for expiration of the notice is a Saturday, Sunday or federal holiday, the tenant is not required to vacate until the next business day. [CCP §12a]

Most notice to vacate forms, when filled out by the property manager, give a **specific date** by which the tenant must vacate, at least 30 days after service of the notice. Thus, the day is not left to chance and, as a practical matter, not set as a weekend day or holiday.

Rent control limitations on eviction

When a residential rental property is located in a **rent control community**, the landlord is limited in his discretionary ability to terminate the tenancy and evict the tenant on a 30-day notice.

Typically, the termination of a tenancy and evictions are allowed in rent control communities when:

- the tenant fails to pay rent or otherwise materially breaches the lease agreement;

- the tenant creates a nuisance;

- the tenant refuses to renew a lease;

- the tenant uses the residence for an illegal purpose; or

- the landlord or a relative will occupy the unit.

A landlord and property manager for properties subject to rent control and his property manager must make themselves aware of the local restrictions imposed on the eviction of tenants.

Good reason to evict exception

A landlord is not required to state his reasons in a notice to vacate, or even have good cause, for evicting a month-to-month tenant. [CC §1946]

Rent control and Section 8 housing are exceptions to the general rule that does not require good cause. The exceptions require the giving of a good-cause condition as the reason for terminating these tenancies. Thus, the tenant is given notice so he can prepare his defense to avoid eviction.

However, under no condition may a landlord evict a tenant for the wrong reason.

The landlord terminating a tenancy for the wrong reason may find himself not only unable to evict the tenant, but defending against the tenant's claim the eviction is:

- **retaliation** for the tenant making official complaints about the property or against the landlord;

- based on **discriminatory reasons**, such as the tenant's ethnicity or marital status; or

- **improper** because of the failure to maintain the property in a habitable condition.

When a tenant's rent is subsidized by the Department of Housing and Urban Development's (HUD) Section 8 housing program, the landlord must set forth *good cause* as the reason for the termination in the 30-day notice to vacate. [**Mitchell** v. **Poole** (1988) 203 CA3d Supp. 1]

Chapter 30

Surrender cancels the lease agreement

This chapter explains the differences in the right to collect future rent between a surrender and other landlord remedies when a tenant breaches and voluntarily vacates the leased premises.

Lost ability to recover future rents

Before a nonresidential lease expires, the tenant closes out his business operations and vacates the premises, paying no further rent. The landlord serves the tenant with a 3-day notice to pay rent or quit. [See **first tuesday** Form 575]

The notice includes a forfeiture clause declaring a *forfeiture of the lease* if the tenant fails to pay rent within three days following service of the notice.

The tenant responds to the notice by letter, stating he elects not to pay future rent and accepts the landlord's offer to terminate the lease. The key to the premises is returned to the landlord with the letter.

The landlord responds by letter stating:

- neither the landlord nor the tenant owe each other any further obligations under the lease; and

- the tenant is to pay all rent due up to the date the tenant returned the key to the landlord.

The landlord then attempts to relet the premises, but without success.

Later, the landlord makes a demand on the tenant for payment of rents called for in the lease agreement for the entire remaining term of the lease since the landlord declared a **forfeiture of the lease** in the 3-day notice which terminated the tenant's right to possession but did not **cancel the lease agreement**.

The tenant claims the landlord is not entitled to any future rents called for in the lease agreement since the landlord agreed to a **surrender of the premises** by their communications, waiving any rights the landlord had to collect future rents otherwise allowed on the declaration forfeiting the lease.

The landlord claims entitlement to collect all future rents due under the lease agreement after the tenant vacated, since his right to future rents is preserved by the declaration of forfeiture in the 3-day notice and he undertook reasonable efforts to relet the premises and mitigate his loss of rent.

Can the landlord recover future rents from the tenant based on the lease agreement, notices and letters?

No! The lease agreement was no longer enforceable having been canceled by the communications agreeing to terminate all obligations under the lease agreement **in exchange for possession**, called a *surrender*. [**Desert Plaza Partnership** v. **Waddell** (1986) 180 CA3d 805]

The tenant's letter "electing to pay no future rent" coupled with the return of the key (possession) to the landlord initiated a surrender, an implied **offer to cancel** the lease agreement.

The landlord's letter in response foregoing future rents released the tenant from further liability on the lease agreement. The landlord's conduct constitutes **acceptance** of the *offer to surrender* initiated by the tenant. The landlord failed to stand on his right to collect rents remaining due for the duration of the uncancelled lease agreement, rights statutorily reserved to him by use of the lease forfeiture clause in the 3-day notice. [Calif. Civil Code §1951.2]

The tenant forfeited his right to possession, the *lease*, by not paying the rent within three days. However, he negotiated a cancellation of the lease agreement that would have remained enforceable after forfeiture of the lease.

Surrender on failure to forfeit

A *surrender* also occurs when the tenant breaches the lease agreement and voluntarily vacates without being served with a notice to quit and election to forfeit, and then the landlord acts inconsistently with the tenant's unforfeited right to possession.

A **surrender** results in the:

- **termination** of the tenant's right to possession; and

- **cancellation** of the lease agreement.

When a breaching tenant vacates the premises, the landlord may fail to **declare a forfeiture** of the tenant's right to possession, or lease, for the period remaining on the lease which he can accomplish by service of either a 3-day notice to pay or quit with election to forfeit the lease or a notice of abandonment.

If the landlord then takes possession and relets the premises, he is acting inconsistent with the tenant's outstanding right to possession that has not been terminated. Thus, the landlord has acted to **cancel the lease agreement** — the landlord's right to recover future rents under the lease agreement is eliminated by his own adverse conduct.

Any rent lost due to the landlord's inability to relet the premises after a surrender is not collectible from the former tenant, and becomes part of the market risks any landlord assumes as the owner of vacant rental property. [Desert Plaza Partnership, *supra*]

Editor's note — Only ownership of real estate and personal property may be forfeited. Conversely, a lease agreement is not property, it is a contract (as well as a conveyance). A contract is evidence of rights and obligations and is not subject to forfeiture.

Vacated space and a breached lease

When a tenant breaches his lease agreement and vacates the premises without service of a 3-day notice to quit, the **landlord responds** in one of four ways:

1. Terminate the tenant's right to occupancy and cancel the lease agreement by a *surrender*, then relet or occupy the premises himself.

2. Terminate the tenant's leasehold by a declaration of *forfeiture* (3-day notice or notice of abandonment) and relet the premises to mitigate losses.

3. Take possession of the premises and relet it on the *tenant's behalf*.

4. Enforce any *tenant-mitigation* provision in the lease agreement, leaving the tenant in possession to relet the premises.

Surrender is an interaction between the tenant and the landlord, residential or nonresidential, causing a termination of the tenant's right to possession and cancellation of the lease agreement.

A **surrender** occurs and cancels the lease agreement by either:

- *mutual consent* of the landlord and the tenant [CC §1933(2)]; or

- *operation of law*, a surrender implied due to the conduct of the landlord.

Surrender by mutual consent

Consider a tenant who makes a written offer to his landlord to surrender the premises — to vacate and return possession in exchange for cancellation of the tenant's obligations under the lease agreement.

The landlord believes a new tenant, who will pay more rent for the space than the current tenant, can be easily located.

Still, the landlord demands an early-termination penalty equal to three months' rent to cancel the lease agreement. The tenant pays the fee and the landlord cancels the lease. A surrender has occurred.

*Editor's note — Mid-term leases sometimes contain an **early-termination provision** for a surrender, allowing the lease agreement to be canceled in exchange for a fee, usually in the amount of two to six months' unearned rent — a type of prepayment penalty or contract liability limitation provision.*

Here, a surrender functions like a deed-in-lieu of foreclosure that conveys the real estate to the lender (possession returned to the landlord) in exchange for the lender's cancellation of the note obligations (cancellation of the lease agreement).

Surrender by operation of law

Now consider a tenant on a lease with a ten-year term. A few years after entering into the lease agreement, the tenant vacates the premises. The tenant removes all of his personal property and returns the key to the landlord. The tenant has no intention of returning and has breached the lease agreement by failing to pay rent.

Knowing a surrender would cancel his right to future rents due under the lease agreement, the landlord informs the tenant he will not accept the tenant's return of possession to the premises as a surrender. He will enforce the collection of future rent called for in the lease agreement.

Without prior notice to the tenant, the landlord retakes possession, refurbishes the vacated space and re-rents it to a replacement tenant. A lease agreement is entered into with the replacement tenant at a lower rental rate for the unexpired term remaining on the breached lease. The landlord notifies the prior tenant he has leased the premises to mitigate his loss of rent.

The landlord makes a demand on the prior tenant for the payment of rent, the amount being the difference between:

- the total amount of rents remaining unpaid over the remaining unexpired term of the prior tenant's lease; and

- the amount of rent to be paid during the same period under the new lease by the replacement tenant.

Can the landlord recover the lost rent from the prior tenant who vacated the premises and returned possession to the landlord?

No! Before entering the space to prepare for reletting the premises, the **landlord failed** to:

- *terminate the tenancy* by serving a 3-day notice with a declaration of forfeiture or a notice of abandonment; or

- *notify the tenant* he was taking possession of the premises as an agent acting on the tenant's behalf.

The conduct of the landlord at the time he unilaterally took possession to relet the premises violated the **tenant's unforfeited right** to possession. Although the landlord did not intend to accept a surrender, he acted to take possession on his own behalf without first forfeiting the tenant's leasehold or advising the tenant of the landlord's intent to act on the tenant's behalf to relet the premises.

A surrender by *operation of law* occurred due to the landlord's actions adverse to the tenant's right to possession. Taking possession without authority to do so is inconsistent with the tenant's remaining possessory interest under his lease (which had not been terminated) and constituted an acceptance of an implied offer to surrender initiated by the tenant's vacating the premises. The landlord's activities, inconsistent with the tenant's outstanding right to reoccupy, terminated the tenancy and canceled the lease agreement as a *surrender*. [**Dorcich** v. **Time Oil Co.** (1951) 103 CA2d 677]

Re-possession on the tenant's behalf

To act on behalf of the tenant when the tenant's right to possession has not been terminated, the landlord who intends to take possession and act on the tenant's behalf to relet the premises as his agent must twice notify the tenant:

- once before taking possession of the premises; and

- again when the premises is relet.

Even though a tenant fails to pay rent, removes all of his personal property, vacates the leased premises and has no intention of returning, the tenant does not and cannot *unilaterally terminate* his right to possess the premises, the leasehold, or escape his rent obligations under the lease agreement.

Until the tenant's right to possession is terminated on a declaration of forfeiture by the landlord, no person other than the tenant has the right to occupy the premises, unless the landlord acts as the tenant's agent or to preserve the landlord's reversionary interest from waste.

Thus, a landlord interferes with the tenant's right to possession and cancels the lease agreement by a surrender when the landlord takes possession of the vacated premises before either:

- terminating the tenancy by forfeiture or abandonment; or

- notifying the tenant he is taking possession to relet the premises as an agent acting on behalf of the tenant. [**Respini** v. **Porta** (1891) 89 C 464]

Inconsistent behavior while reletting

Consider a landlord notifying a tenant who has breached the lease agreement and vacated the premises that the landlord will enter the premises, take possession and relet the premises as an agent acting on the tenant's behalf.

The landlord relets the premises for **less rent** and for a period extending **beyond the expiration** of the term remaining on the tenant's lease. The landlord notifies the tenant he has relet the premises on the tenant's behalf.

A demand is made on the tenant for the loss in rent resulting from the reletting of the premises at a reduced rent. The tenant refuses to pay, claiming a surrender occurred, canceling the lease agreement since the terms and conditions of the new lease agreement exceeded the term of the tenant's remaining right to possession under the breached lease agreement.

Here, a tenant's right to possession runs only until the expiration of the period fixed by his lease agreement. Had the vacating tenant sought to sublet the premises himself, the term of the sublease could not extend beyond the date set for expiration of the tenant's right to occupy the property.

Thus, the landlord who does not terminate the tenant's lease and then acts to relet the premises as the tenant's agent for a **longer term** than the unexpired term remaining on the lease:

- is not renting the premises on behalf of the tenant; and

- has worked a *surrender* — a cancellation of the lease agreement — since his conduct is inconsistent with the vacating tenant's unexpired and unterminated right to possession. [**Welcome** v. **Hess** (1891) 90 C 507]

Now consider a landlord who, on notice to a vacating tenant, takes possession on behalf of the tenant. The landlord maintains and cares for the vacated premises while attempting to relet the premises.

The tenant claims the landlord's care and maintenance of the property constitutes a surrender since the landlord exercised independent control over the premises by his maintenance activity.

Here, the landlord's care and maintenance is conduct entered into on the tenant's behalf. Care and maintenance of the property is activity consistent with the landlord's agency duty owed the tenant, when acting on the tenant's behalf, to perform the tenant's obligation under the lease agreement to care for and maintain the property.

As the agent of the vacated tenant, the landlord must make a good faith effort to lease the premises, called *mitigation of losses*. The landlord, as would the tenant, will be unable to lease the premises in a dilapidated, ill-maintained condition. [**B.K.K. Company** v. **Schultz** (1970) 7 CA3d 786]

In an attempt to avoid all these adverse legal consequences (for failure to know or abide by the rules), some lease agreements contain a remedies provision with a clause stating a surrender can occur only if the tenant enters into a written cancellation and waiver agreement. [See **first tuesday** Form 552 §20]

However, the landlord's **improper conduct** in response to a tenant's breach of the lease agreement and vacating of the premises, acting alone and without a writing, results in a cancellation of the lease by surrender. The landlord's conduct supersedes the lease agreement provisions requiring a written agreement to cancel the lease. Landlord/tenant law controls the result, barring application of contract law principles that would have ignored the landlord's conduct.

Chapter 31

Notice of belief of abandonment

This chapter presents the notice procedure by which a landlord confirms a tenant has abandoned the premises and terminates the tenant's right to possession.

An alternative forfeiture

A tenant who is **delinquent** in rent payments due under his lease agreement has vacated the premises. The tenant has not been served a notice to quit. Here, the landlord may respond in one of several ways, including:

- treat the tenant's right to possession as terminated and the lease agreement as canceled, called a *surrender*;

- treat the tenant's right to possession as terminated by service of a *3-day notice to pay or quit* and a *declaration of forfeiture of the right of possession*, or service of an **abandonment notice**, and proceed to enforce the tenant's financial obligations for rent and other amounts due under the lease agreement;

- take possession on notice, without terminating the lease, to relet the property as the tenant's agent; or

- treat the lease as continuing, if the lease agreement contains a statutory *tenant-mitigation* provision, and recover rent as it becomes due without repossessing or reletting the property. [Calif. Civil Code §§1941.2; 1951.4]

Statutory abandonment notice

The abandonment rules, like surrender rules, apply to both residential and nonresidential property. The commonality between surrender and abandonment is the tenant's breach of the lease and vacating of the premises. They differ, however, on the methods for termination of the tenant's possessory rights and cancellation of contract rights regarding future rent. A surrender is a mutual termination and an abandonment is a unilateral termination by forfeiture delivered by the landlord.

Further, abandonment is to be distinguished from a 3-day notice and forfeiture declaration, as methods of retaining the lease agreement and terminating the tenant's right to possession, by the difference in time after serving the notices until the landlord can retake possession.

An abandonment can be processed when a tenant:

- **voluntarily vacates** the leased premises with no intention to reoccupy; and

- **fails to pay rent** with no intention to further perform his obligations on the lease agreement.

However, the tenant's act of breaching the lease and vacating the premises **does not terminate** the tenant's leasehold ownership in the property or his obligations under the lease agreement. Thus, the landlord must act to terminate the leasehold in response to the **breach and vacating** of the property by the tenant if the landlord is to retake possession.

For the landlord to proceed with the abandonment process, he must confirm the tenant's *intent to abandon* the property and terminate his right to possession. The landlord confirms the tenant's intent by serving a statutory abandonment notice on the tenant. [See Form 581 accompanying this chapter]

A **Notice of Belief of Abandonment** may be served on a tenant only when:

- the tenant has vacated the premises;

- the tenant's rent payment is due and unpaid (no receipt of any amounts) for a period of at least 14 days prior to service of the Notice of Belief of Abandonment [CC §1951.3(b)]; and

- the landlord reasonably believes the tenant has abandoned the premises.

If the tenant's rent is due on the first of the month and has become delinquent and no portion has been paid in the interim, the landlord may serve the notice on the 15th day of the month if the tenant no longer occupies the premises. (A 3-day notice would have already terminated the tenancy and allowed the landlord to enter and take possession of the space.)

The notice of abandonment may be served on the tenant by either:

- personal service; or

- by first-class mail sent to the tenant's last known address and any other addresses known to the landlord where the tenant might reasonably receive the notice. [CC §1951.3(c)]

If the abandonment notice is **personally served** on the tenant, the tenant has 15 days after the date of service to respond before the notice expires. If the abandonment notice is **served by mail**, the notice expires 18 days after the date the notice is deposited in the mail. [CC §1951.3(b)]

When personal service cannot be made, the service requirements for the Notice of Belief of Abandonment are different from service requirements for 3-day notices. [See Chapter 27]

Once served, the notice of abandonment will expire in 15 days unless in the interim:

- the tenant tenders all or partial payment of rent; or

- rejects the abandonment in writing.

On expiration of the notice, in 15 or 18 days, depending on the type of service, the tenant's right to **possession is terminated**.

Having terminated the tenancy by expiration of the abandonment notice, the landlord may:

- enter the premises to **remove** any personal property left behind by the tenant and **relet** the premises as the landlord [CC §1954]; and

- collect past and future rents from the tenant as provided in the lease agreement. [CC §1951.2(a)]

Tenant's response ends abandonment

After the tenant has been served with a notice of abandonment, the tenant may reoccupy the premises. After service of the notice, reoccupying at any time will not stop the abandonment procedure or avoid termination of the tenant's right to possession on expiration of the notice. Once served, further steps must be taken by the tenant to nullify the abandonment procedure. [CC §1951.3(e)]

After an abandonment notice has been served, the tenant can only **disavow an abandonment** and avoid the termination of his right to possession by doing one of the following:

- showing the landlord could not justifiably believe the tenant had abandoned the premises when the notice was served;

- proving rent was not due prior to 14 days before service of the notice or, if due, was not yet delinquent at the time the notice was served;

- proving some or all of delinquent rent was received by the landlord during the 14-day period preceding the service of the notice;

- paying some or all of the past due rent prior to expiration of the notice; or

- handing a written notice to the landlord before the abandonment notice expires stating the tenant has no intention to abandon the premises and including an address for service on the tenant by certified mail of an unlawful detainer (UD) action. [CC §1951.3(e)]

Thus, if a portion or all of the delinquent rent is tendered, or a statement of no intent to abandon is delivered to the landlord by the tenant prior to the expiration of the abandonment notice, a UD action based on abandonment must fail.

Once the notice is served and the tenant reoccupies the premises, before or after expiration of the notice and without payment of rent or a statement of no intent to abandon, the tenant can be evicted by a UD action on expiration of the abandonment notice.

Concurrent service with 3-day notice

Both a 3-day notice to pay or quit (with forfeiture election) and a notice of abandonment may be served **concurrently** under separate proof of service statements. [See Chapter 26]

Since both notices terminate the leasehold on their expiration, a tenant who **reoccupies** or, on a nonresidential property tenders only a partial payment of rent that the landlord accepts, can be dealt with quickly by filing a UD action on expiration of the 3-day notice.

However, under a UD action based on a 3-day notice, the **landlord must prove** his case for eviction, loosely referred to as "having the burden of proof."

Conversely, at a UD trial based on a notice of abandonment where the tenant has reoccupied, the **tenant must prove** he may remain on the premises by showing:

- no delinquency existed when the notice was served;

- A portion or all of the rent was paid within four weeks prior to the expiration of the notice; or

- he delivered the landlord a written statement of his intent to occupy.

Abandoned personal property

Tenants who vacate the leased premises occasionally leave significant personal property behind. When a landlord is confronted with a unit or space vacated by the tenant, but loaded with abandoned personal property, he may find the notice of abandonment an efficient way to terminate the tenant's right to possession. Thus, he can take possession on termination of the tenancy without concern for claims by the tenant.

Before serving a notice of abandonment, a residential landlord may **temporarily enter** the vacated premises to establish his reasonable belief the tenant abandoned the premises. [CC §1954(c)]

Even if the tenant has left personal items behind, a landlord's observations while inside the unit or space may lead him to *reasonably believe* the premises is abandoned. [CC §1951.3(e)(2)]

If the landlord exercises his right to temporarily enter the unit when a tenant appears to have abandoned it, the landlord may **inventory the personal property** so it can be itemized in the abandonment notice. [CC §1983]

Abandoned personal property poses a problem regarding its removal (by the landlord) and recovery (by the tenant). When personal property is left behind by a tenant who has vacated, the landlord is responsible for notifying the tenant of his *right to reclaim* the personal property. [CC §1983]

Notice of the tenant's right to claim personal property can be included in the notice of abandonment. [CC §1991; see Form 581]

When combined in one form, the notice of right to reclaim personal property and the abandonment notice expire simultaneously.

The combined abandonment and right to reclaim property notices are appropriate when the landlord chooses to leave the tenant's personal property on the premises until abandonment of the real estate and the personal property is established by expiration of the notices.

Thus, moving the tenant's belongings twice, or even once if the tenant picks them up, is avoided by the abandonment notice, rather than by preparing both a 3-day notice to pay and a later notice to reclaim personal property.

On termination of the tenancy by expiration of the notice of abandonment, the landlord is entitled to possession of the premises. The landlord may then **enter the unit** to take possession, refurbish it and relet it to a new tenant without concern for the tenant's terminated possessory rights. [CC §1954]

The landlord must not remove personal items, begin refurbishing the premises or relet the premises during the unexpired term of the rental or lease agreement **without first terminating** the tenant's right to possession by a 3-day notice, 30-day notice to vacate or abandonment notice. If the tenant's right to possession is not first terminated, the landlord has interfered with the leasehold estate held by the tenant to occupy the space or unit.

Thus, the landlord who does not first act to terminate the unexpired tenancy before removing personal items or reletting the premises may find himself on the wrong end of a viable forcible detainer action. [Calif. Code of Civil Procedure §1160]

Tenant-mitigation provision

If the tenant's lease agreement, residential or nonresidential, contains a statutory *tenant-mitigation provision*, the landlord may:

- treat the lease rights as continuing without the landlord taking possession; and

- enforce his right to recover rent as it becomes due under the lease agreement. [CC §1951.4]

When a residential or residential tenant breaches his lease agreement and vacates the leased premises, the **tenant-mitigation remedy** can be enforced if:

- the tenant-mitigation remedy is included as a provision in the lease agreement; and

- the assignment and subletting (alienation) provision in the lease agreement does not prohibit the tenant's subletting or assignment of the leasehold interest. [CC §1951.4(b)]

The landlord may treat the lease as continuing and recover rent as it becomes due if the lease agreement contains a provision worded substantially as follows:

"The lessor has the remedy described in California Civil Code Section 1951.4 (lessor may continue lease in effect after lessee's breach and abandonment and recover rent as it becomes due, if lessee has right to sublet or assign, subject only to reasonable limitations)." [CC §1951.4(a)]

A landlord's use of the tenant-mitigation remedy **shifts the responsibility** for mitigating his losses under the lease agreement to the tenant when the tenant vacates the premises and breaches the lease agreement. Instead of the landlord mitigating his loss of rents by reletting the space as a requisite for qualifying to collect future rents, the tenant must take steps to **mitigate his liability** to the landlord.

NOTICE OF BELIEF OF ABANDONMENT

(Residential or Nonresidential Property)

DATE:_____, 20_____, at _____, California.

To Tenant: _____

Items left blank or unchecked are not applicable.

FACTS:

You are a Tenant under the rental or lease agreement
dated _____, entered into by

_____, Tenant,

and _____, Landlord,

regarding real estate referred to as: _____

_____

> **NOTICE:** If the tenant does not respond to this notice and the notice expires, the property, real and personal, has been abandoned and the tenancy terminated. The landlord may then dispose of itemized unclaimed property. [CC §§1951.3; 1991]

YOU ARE HEREBY INFORMED:

Rent on the leased property has been due and unpaid for 14 consecutive days or more, **AND** Landlord believes you have abandoned the property. Personal property remains on the premises as described in Section 5.

NOTICE:

1. This notice expires unless you respond by _____, 20_____, which date is at least:

   ☐ 15 days after this notice was personally served on you; or

   ☐ 18 days after this notice was sent by first class mail, postage prepaid, to your last known address.

2. On expiration of this notice, the property will be considered abandoned, your right to possession terminated, and all remaining personal property will be disposed of [under Section 7 below].

   2.1 Landlord reserves the right to collect future rent losses allowed by California Civil Code §1951.2.

3. **YOU MAY AVOID THIS NOTICE,** if before it expires and at the address below, Landlord receives your written notice stating:

   3.1 Your intent not to abandon the real estate, **AND**

   3.2 An address where you may be served by certified mail in any action for unlawful detainer of the real property.

4. **YOU MAY AVOID DISPOSAL OF PERSONAL PROPERTY** by doing the following before expiration of this notice:

   4.1 Pay the reasonable cost of storage for all the personal property, **AND**

   4.2 Take possession of the personal property.

5. The personal property remaining is described as:_____

   _____

   _____

6. The personal property may be claimed at:_____

   _____

7. **The personal property to be claimed or disposed of is valued as:**

   7.1 ☐ Worth more than $300. If you fail to reclaim the property, it will be sold at a public sale after published notice of the sale. You have the right to bid on the property at this sale. After the property is sold and the cost of storage, advertising and sale are deducted, the remaining money will be handed to the county. You may claim the remaining money within one year after the county receives the money.

   7.2 ☐ Worth less than $300. This property is believed to be worth less than $300. Therefore, it may be kept, sold or destroyed without further notice if you fail to reclaim it prior to expiration of this notice. [CC §1988]

8. You are required by agreement to pay past due rent. Failure to pay can lead to court proceedings against you.

Date:_____, 20_____

Landlord/Agent: _____

Signature:_____

Address: _____

_____

Phone: _____   Fax: _____

When the landlord chooses to enforce the tenant-mitigation remedy, **landlord activities** that do not constitute a termination of the tenant's right to possession or a surrender of the lease agreement include:

- maintenance to preserve the premises from waste;

- appointment of a receiver (by a court) to protect the tenant's interest; or

- the reasonable withholding of consent to an assignment or subletting. [CC §1951.4(c)]

The landlord who includes the tenant-mitigation remedy clause in his lease agreement usually is an absentee owner who enters into long-term, triple-net leases with creditworthy, well-established users.

The landlord entering into a long-term triple net or pure-net lease intends to receive his rent payments without expending time and energy managing the property.

Assignment or subletting restrictions

Now consider a nonresidential lease agreement containing the statutory **tenant-mitigation provision**.

The lease agreement also contains a subletting or assignment provisions calling for the landlord's **consent**, which will not be unreasonably withheld. The assignment provision also calls for the payment of money as a condition for the landlord's consent.

A lease cancellation provision in the lease agreement permits the landlord to cancel the lease agreement on his receipt of a request from the tenant to consent to an assignment.

The tenant stops paying rent and vacates the property.

The landlord elects the remedy available to him under the statutory tenant-mitigation provision in the lease agreement.

The tenant, being responsible for reletting the premises, locates a replacement tenant. The tenant notifies the landlord of his intent to assign the lease and requests the landlord's consent.

On receiving the request for consent to assign, the landlord sends the tenant a notice canceling the lease agreement under the lease cancellation provision.

The tenant claims the landlord cannot terminate the lease since the landlord's ability to refuse consent by exercising his option to terminate the tenant's right of possession is subject to a standard of reasonableness due to the tenant-mitigation provision.

However, the landlord's cancellation of the lease under the lease cancellation provision is neither reasonable nor unreasonable. The lease cancellation provision, when exercised by the landlord on receipt of a request to assign, **relieves the tenant** who has vacated the premises and breached the lease of any further responsibility under the tenant-mitigation provision in the lease. Cancellation of the lease agreement terminates the tenant's right to possession and with it his ability to assign his leasehold interest, a "catch-22" for the tenant. [**Carma Developers, Inc.** v. **Marathon Development California, Inc.** (1992) 2 C4th 342]

Chapter 32

Personal property reclaimed by tenant

This chapter explains the procedural steps residential and nonresidential landlords must take when confronted with personal property left by a tenant who has vacated.

Reclaim it or lose it on notice

A tenant vacates a rental property, residential or nonresidential, leaving behind personal belongings.

The tenant's right to possession of the premises has been **forfeited** by notice from the landlord due to the tenant's breach of the lease agreement. The space is immediately re-rented and needs to be made ready for the new tenant.

The landlord removes the tenant's belongings from the leased space and stores them in a place of safekeeping. The value of the personal property is determined by the landlord to be less than $300.

The landlord immediately mails the tenant a notice, called a *Notice of Right to Reclaim Personal Property*, which:

- describes each item or lot of personal property left on the premises; and

- advises the tenant that the personal property will be discarded if not reclaimed by the tenant within 18 days of mailing the notice. [Calif. Civil Code §1983; see Form 584 accompanying this chapter]

The tenant does not respond to the notice and it expires. The landlord and his property manager dispose of the tenant's belongings.

Later, the tenant sends the landlord a letter requesting the landlord arrange for him to pick up the property. The landlord ignores the tenant's late response and does nothing. The tenant then demands payment for the value of the items left behind.

Here, the landlord is not liable for the value of the personal property left in the unit and unclaimed by the tenant. The landlord followed the statutory procedure for notice and disposal of property estimated to be worth less than $300. [CC §§1982, 1984]

The **statutory notice** procedure:

- provides the tenant with time in which to reclaim his personal property; and

- protects the landlord from liability on disposition of the personal property if the tenant fails to respond prior to expiration of the notice to reclaim.

Removal of personal property

Before removing a tenant's personal property from a vacant unit, a landlord must first be legally entitled to enter and take possession of the unit.

The landlord can enter, take possession and dispose of a tenant's personal property when the tenant has vacated and the tenant's right to possession of the premises has been *terminated*. [See Chapters 29 and 32]

Returning personal property

Two separate statutory procedures exist for the return of personal property left on the premises by a tenant. One is initiated by the landlord, the other by the tenant.

Residential and nonresidential landlords may initiate (and control) the process of returning or disposing of the tenant's personal property. A notice prepared by the landlord is personally served or mailed to the tenant who vacated and left the personal property advising him of his right to **reclaim or abandon** the personal property, called the *landlord-initiated disposition procedure*. [See **first tuesday** Form 581 and Form 584]

The other procedure allows a residential tenant acting within 18 days of vacating the premises to initiate a return of personal property he left behind by handing or mailing to the landlord or the property manager a *request to surrender* personal items he left behind, called the *tenant-initiated recovery procedure*. [CC §1965; see Form 582 accompanying this chapter]

The landlord is not required to use the landlord-initiated procedure when confronted with the disposition of the tenant's personal property. [CC §1981]

However, a landlord who sells or disposes of a tenant's personal property by any procedure other than established by these two procedures can be challenged for his handling of the belongings by the tenant. The statutory procedures are sometimes called *safe harbor rules*.

For example, a tenant claims his personal property was left behind inadvertently, not abandoned. Thus, the landlord would not be entitled to sell or dispose of the property unless the landlord first establishes the tenant's actual intent is not to reclaim the property, but to abandon it.

On the tenant's abandonment of property, the preferred method for establishing the tenant's intent not to reclaim property left behind, so the landlord may dispose of the property, is the landlord-initiated disposition procedure. The tenant is notified of his right to reclaim the property he left behind and his need to respond to avoid its disposal. [See **first tuesday** Form 581 and Form 584]

Residential tenant-initiated recovery

Only a residential tenant may deliver to the landlord or the landlord's agent a written re-

quest for the return of personal property left in the vacated unit, called a *Notice to Landlord to Surrender Personal Property*. [See Form 582]

The **tenant's request** for the release of his belongings by the landlord, called *surrender*, must:

- be written;
- be mailed or handed to the landlord within 18 days after he vacates the unit;
- include the tenant's current mailing address;
- contain an identifiable description of the personal property left behind;
- be received by the landlord while the landlord or his agent is in control or possession of the personal property; and
- be received by the landlord or his agent before they have mailed to him a notice to reclaim the personal property, commencing the landlord-initiated disposition. [CC §1965(a)]

In response to receipt of the tenant's notice of surrender, the **landlord's response** must be a written demand on the tenant for reasonable removal and storage costs that:

- the landlord will mail or hand to the tenant within five days after the landlord receives the tenant's request to surrender the property; and
- itemizes any costs for removal and storage to be paid before the tenant can remove the property. [CC §1965(a)(3); see **first tuesday** Form 588]

It is then incumbent upon the tenant to contact the landlord and arrange a mutually agreeable date, time and location for the tenant to claim and remove his personal property. However, the tenant or the tenant's agent must remove the personal belongings within 72 hours **after the tenant pays** storage charges demanded by the landlord. [CC §1965(a)(4)]

NOTICE TO LANDLORD TO SURRENDER PERSONAL PROPERTY

(For Use by Residential ‚Tenants Only)

DATE:_____, 20_____, at _____, California.

To Landlord:

Items left blank or unchecked are not applicable.

FACTS:

I am a former Tenant under a residential rental or lease agreement dated _____, at _____

_____, California,

entered into by _____, Tenant,

and _____, Landlord,

regarding real estate referred to as: _____

_____

> **NOTICE:**
> If the landlord has not initiated the abandonment remedy, the tenant by this request may reclaim personal property from vacated residential rental premises within 72 hours after payment of removal and storage fees. [Calif. Civil Code §1965]

NOTICE:

1. Within eighteen (18) days prior to mailing or handing this notice to the Landlord, I vacated and delivered possession of the premises to Landlord or

2. This notice is a request for Landlord to surrender to me or personal property not owned by Landlord and described below which was left on the vacated premises.

3. I understand:

   3.1 This notice must be mailed within eighteen (18) days after I vacated the premises.

   3.2 Landlord or the landlord's manager must have control or possession of the personal property at the time the Landlord actually receives this notice.

   3.3 I will pay all reasonable costs actually incurred by Landlord for the removal and storage of the personal property as a condition for the release and return of the personal property.

   3.4 Landlord will provide a written itemized demand for payment of reasonable removal and storage fees within five (5) days of actual receipt of this notice unless the property is first returned. The demand for payment of removal and storage fees will be mailed to the address given below or handed to me personally.

   3.5 I will claim and remove the personal property at a reasonable time mutually agreed upon by Landlord and myself to occur within 72 hours after my payment of reasonable removal and storage fees demanded by landlord.

4. Description of personal property to be reclaimed: _____

_____

_____

_____

_____

_____

_____

This statement is true and correct.

Date:_____, 20_____

Tenant:_____

Signature: _____

Current mailing address: _____

_____

Phone:_____

Fax: _____

E-mail: _____

For Landlord/Manager's use:

Date Received:_____

By: _____

FORM 582   09-02   ©2007 **first tuesday**, P.O. BOX 20069, RIVERSIDE, CA 92516 (800) 794-0494

After a tenant mails the landlord a request to surrender personal property, the landlord might receive **another request** for the same items from the tenant's roommate, a secured creditor or other person with an interest in the property.

The first request received by the landlord controls the return of the property left behind. [CC §1965(d)]

The landlord is not obligated to the roommate or anyone else who makes a later request for the same personal belongings.

Which process controls

The tenant-initiated process for residential rentals does not apply if the **landlord first mails** or personally delivers the notice to reclaim personal property to the tenant before he receives the tenant's notice to surrender. [CC §1965(c)]

But what if the landlord's notice to reclaim property and the tenant's request to surrender the property pass in the mail?

Here, the landlord-initiated process begins the moment the landlord deposits the notice of the tenant's right to reclaim property in the mail (first-class, postage prepaid). The tenant-initiated process does not begin until the landlord or his agent personally receives the tenant's request.

The landlord who neglects to mail the notice before actually receiving a tenant's request must respond to the tenant's request since, under abandonment rules, the landlord no longer controls disposition.

Conversely, if the landlord can show he or his agent deposited either the Notice of Belief of Abandonment or the notice to reclaim personal property in the mail before they actually received the tenant's notice to surrender, the tenant must abide by the landlord-initiated disposition procedure.

Residential landlord violations

Consider a residential tenant who has vacated and timely hands the landlord a notice to surrender personal items he left behind without the landlord acting first.

The landlord makes a demand on the tenant to pay removal and storage costs. The tenant promptly pays the removal and storage costs.

Should the landlord fail to hand over the items within 72 hours after the tenant (or tenant's agent) pays storage and removal fees, the landlord is liable for:

- damages for the value of the personal items;
- $250 for each violation; and
- attorney fees. [CC §1965(e)]

This tenant-initiated procedure is entirely avoided if the landlord merely sends by first-class mail either the notice of abandonment (both real estate and personal property) or a notice to reclaim personal property before he receives the tenant's notice to surrender the property. [See **first tuesday** Form 581 and Form 584]

Landlord-initiated abandonment

On mailing or personally delivering the notice of abandonment to the tenant, and any other possible **owner or creditor known** to have an interest in the belongings, a residential or non-residential landlord commences the landlord-initiated disposition process. [See **first tuesday** Form 581]

The notice to dispose of the tenant's property must be delivered to the tenant by either:

- personal service; or
- first-class mail to the tenant's last known address with a duplicate notice mailed to the address of the vacated premises. [CC §1983(c)]

NOTICE OF RIGHT TO RECLAIM PERSONAL PROPERTY

(To Tenant After Termination of Tenancy)

DATE:_____, 20_____, at _____, California.

TO FORMER TENANT:

Name:_____

Address:_____

_____

Items left blank or unchecked are not applicable.

FACTS:

You were a Tenant under a rental or lease agreement

dated _____, at _____, California,

entered into by _____, Tenant,

and _____, Landlord,

regarding real estate referred to as: _____

_____

> **NOTICE:**
> This notice may be given to a residential and nonresidential tenant who left personal property on the premises which remains after he vacated the premises and his tenancy terminated. On expiration of this notice, the landlord may dispose of the unclaimed property. [CC §1983]

NOTICE:

1. This notice expires unless you respond by _____, 20_____, which date is at least:
   - ☐ 15 days after this notice was personally served, or
   - ☐ 18 days after this notice was deposited in the mail.

2. When you vacated the premises referenced above, the following personal property remained:

   _____

   _____

   _____

   _____

3. You may claim the personal property at: _____

   _____

4. **YOU MAY AVOID DISPOSAL OF PERSONAL PROPERTY** by doing the following before expiration of this notice:
   - 4.1 Pay the reasonable cost of removal and storage of all the personal property; **AND**
   - 4.2 Take possession of the personal property.

5. **The personal property to be claimed or disposed of is valued as:**
   - 5.1 ☐ Worth more than $300. If you fail to reclaim the property, it will be sold at a public sale after published notice of the sale. You have the right to bid on the property at this sale. After the property is sold and the cost of storage, advertising and sale are deducted, the remaining money will be handed to the county. You may claim the remaining money within one year after the county receives the money.
   - 5.2 ☐ Worth less than $300. This property is believed to be worth less than $300. Therefore, it may be kept, sold or destroyed without further notice if you fail to reclaim it prior to expiration of this notice.

This statement is true and correct.

Date:_____, 20_____

Landlord/Agent: _____

Signature: _____

Address:_____

_____

Phone: _____

Fax: _____

E-mail: _____

Notice should be given promptly on termination of the tenancy, but may be given at any time after the tenant has vacated the premises. [CC §1983]

As a matter of practice, the tenancy should first be terminated before entering the premises and determining whether the tenant left personal property, unless the abandonment procedure is used. [See Chapter 31]

Abandonment notices

A landlord may combine the abandoned personal property notice with the notice of abandonment of the premises. [See Chapter 23]

The landlord combines the two notices when he believes the tenant has abandoned both the personal property and the premises, and the landlord **chooses to terminate** the tenant's right to possession by establishing an abandonment of the premises in stead of using a 3-day notice and declaration of forfeiture. [CC §1991; see **first tuesday** Form 581]

Both abandonment notices from the landlord to the tenant must include:

- a description of each item;

- notice that reasonable storage costs will be charged;

- the location where the property may be reclaimed;

- expiration of the notice — the date by which the tenant must reclaim his property;

- notice the property will be kept, sold or destroyed if the value is estimated at less than $300; and

- notice the property will be sold by public sale if it is worth $300 or more and is not reclaimed. [CC §§1983(b), 1984(b)]

If the notice is personally served on the tenant, the notice may expire no less than 15 days after service. If the notice is mailed, the notice may expire no less than 18 days after posting in the mail. [CC §1983(b)]

When personal property worth less than $300 is not reclaimed by a tenant before the notice expires, the landlord may keep, sell or destroy the property without further notice to the tenant. [CC §1984]

Notice to third-party owners

Under the landlord-initiated procedure, the landlord must also notify any other persons he **reasonably believes** may have any ownership interest in the personal property left on the premises. [CC §1983(a); see Form 587 accompanying this chapter]

For example, if a landlord is aware a co-tenant or guest left behind some personal property, the landlord must notify the co-tenant or guest as well as the tenant.

The *reasonable belief* of ownership of the abandoned personal property imposed on a landlord means the **actual knowledge** a prudent person in the landlord's (or property manager's) position would have without making an investigation, unless such an investigation is of probable value and reasonable cost. [CC §1980(d)]

The landlord is not required to investigate public records unless it is likely he will find information pertinent to locating the owner of the personal property.

Also, if a landlord notices a name or phone number inscribed on the personal items, such as a furniture rental company, the landlord will not be protected from liability for failure to investigate the name or phone number.

Identification of personal property

First, the identification of the personal property in notices to reclaim initiated by the landlord should list every significant item or "lot of items" left behind.

NOTICE OF RIGHT TO RECLAIM PERSONAL PROPERTY

(To Others with an Interest in Property Left by Tenant)

DATE:_____, 20_____, at_____, California.

TO: Name: _____

Address: _____

_____

Items left blank or unchecked are not applicable.

NOTICE:

1. This notice to claim personal property you may have an interest in expires on _____, 20_____, which date is at least:

    ☐ 15 days after this notice was personally served on you; or

    ☐ 18 days after this notice was sent by first class mail, postage prepaid, to your last known address.

2. When our former tenant named _____,

    vacated premises known as _____,

    _____,

    the following personal property remained:_____

    _____

    _____

    _____

    _____

    _____.

3. If you have an interest in any of this personal property, you may claim it at:

    _____

    _____

4. You must pay the cost of storage on or before taking possession of the personal property you claim. [**first tuesday** Form 588]

5. Unless you take possession of the personal property you have an interest in prior to the expiration of this notice, the personal property not claimed will be sold at a public sale by competitive bidding. [CC §1988]

NOTICE:

This notice may be given to persons who are believed to own or hold a security interest in personal property left on residential or nonresidential premises by a tenant who has vacated and whose tenancy has been terminated. On expiration of this notice, the landlord may dispose of itemized unclaimed property [CC §1983]

This statement is true and correct.

Date:_____, 20_____

Landlord/Agent:_____

Signature: _____

Address: _____

_____

Phone:_____

Fax: _____

E-mail: _____

Although the landlord may choose to describe only a portion of the personal property left behind, he is protected from liability only for those items he identifies.

A landlord may identify items as simply as a "bundle," a "lot" or a "box" of items, or the landlord may look inside the bundle or boxes to determine the contents and their worth. The **total value** of the bundled, boxed or lot of similar items will determine the method the landlord must employ to dispose of them.

The landlord, property manager or resident manager should use a witness to inventory the items and confirm their estimated worth. The witness will assist the landlord should the tenant claim the landlord confiscated or damaged items.

The landlord may use his reasonable belief to estimate the value of the items.

Storage and release of property

As in the tenant-initiated procedure for reclaiming items, the landlord may charge the tenant for the **cost of removal and storage** of the property. The landlord may store the personal property in the unit, or remove it to another place of safekeeping, for which he may charge a fee.

While the landlord must exercise care in storing the property, he may be held liable only for damages caused by his intentional or negligent treatment of the items when removing and storing them. [CC §1986]

The landlord **must release** the personal property to the tenant, or the person who first notifies the landlord of his right to reclaim, within 72 hours of payment of the storage costs.

The tenant or owner reclaiming the personal items is responsible for storage costs. Any owner other than the tenant is responsible only for the storage costs of property he claims. The landlord may not, however, charge more than one party for storage of any one item. [CC §1990]

Sale of the abandoned property

If the total worth of the abandoned personal items is $300 or more, they must be sold at a public sale by the landlord. [CC §1988(a)]

If the abandoned personal property notice states the property (because of its value) is **subject to public sale**, the landlord must surrender the personal property to the tenant any time prior to the sale, even after the date specified for expiration in the notice of abandonment. [CC §1987]

However, the tenant or the owner must then pay advertising and sale costs in addition to storage costs. [CC §1987]

The landlord must advertise the public sale prior to its scheduled date in a local county newspaper of general circulation. [CC §1988(b)]

The **notice of sale** must appear twice — once each week for two consecutive weeks. The last advertisement may not be later than five calendar days before the date of the public sale. The notice of sale must specify the date, time and location of the sale. Also, the notice of sale must sufficiently describe the personal property to allow the owner to identify the property as his.

The timetable before the sale becomes the combination of the 15 or 18-day period for the notice of abandonment and the 12 days of advertising. The highest bidder (including the tenant or landlord) may buy the property.

Any proceeds from the sale, minus the costs of sale, advertising and storage, are given to the county treasurer within 30 days of the sale. Once the remaining proceeds have been given over to the county treasurer, the tenant or owner of the personal property has one year to claim the proceeds. [CC §1988]

Chapter 33

Constructive eviction cancels the lease

This chapter reviews the tenant's remedies when a landlord breaches a nonresidential lease agreement.

Interference forces tenant to vacate

A nonresidential tenant occupies a building in which he operates his restaurant business. The tenant's lease agreement obligates the landlord to make all necessary repairs to the exterior walls and roof during the term of the lease.

During the tenancy, the roof begins to leak. The tenant notifies the landlord about the leaks and the need for repairs. The landlord makes several personal attempts to repair the roof. However, the roof is never properly repaired and the leaks persist each year during the rainy season.

The leaking water damages the interior walls. During rain storms, water runs along beams and down walls, forming puddles on the floors creating hazardous conditions for employees and patrons.

Fed up, the tenant **vacates the premises**.

The tenant then makes a demand on the landlord to recover his security deposit and business losses. The tenant's losses include lost income from business operations, loss of goodwill, relocation expenses, employee medical expenses and water damage to furnishings and equipment.

Also, the tenant claims the lease agreement has been **canceled** due to the landlord's interference with the tenant's occupancy since the landlord failed to meet his contractual obligation by repairing the roof, resulting in untenantable conditions and caused him to vacate the leased premises, called a *constructive eviction*.

The landlord claims his failure to repair the roof was not conduct so intrusive as to result in a constructive eviction, but was merely an inconvenience to the tenant for which the tenant is only entitled to money for his losses, not a cancellation of the lease agreement and obligation to pay rent.

Here, the landlord's failure to meet his obligation to repair the roof under the terms of the lease agreement was conduct that *terminated* the tenant's right to possession and *canceled* the lease agreement. The leaking roof significantly interfered with the tenant's ability to use the premises to operate a restaurant as stated in the lease agreement.

Collectively, the landlord's **failure to maintain** the property and the tenant **vacating the premises** in response constituted a *constructive eviction* allowing the tenant to recover the security deposit and any money losses caused by the landlord's interference with possession. [**Groh** v. **Kover's Bull Pen, Inc.** (1963) 221 CA2d 611]

A tenant is not obligated to continue to occupy the premises and pay rent if the premises can no longer be used as intended due to the landlord's conduct.

Conversely, if the landlord's **failure to repair** the premises does not *substantially deprive* the tenant of his intended use of the premises, the tenant's right to possession and obligations under the lease agreement remain intact, including the obligation to pay rent.

Further, the tenant's recovery of his money losses incurred due to the landlord's failure to repair or correct conditions that do not significantly interfere with the tenant's use of the premises, sufficient to justify vacating as a constructive eviction, or if they do and the tenant does not vacate, must be pursued in a separate action, not as an offset to rent.

Editor's note — The constructive eviction could easily have been avoided in Groh *had the landlord hired a competent contractor to promptly and properly repair the roof.*

Landlord's breach terminates possession

Both the landlord and the tenant must perform their contractual obligations under the provisions contained or implied in their lease agreement. If either the landlord or tenant fail to fully perform, they breach the lease. A breach by the landlord or tenant for failure to perform as agreed is either a *minor breach* or a *material breach*.

A **minor breach** of a lease agreement provision by either the landlord or the tenant is not a justifiable basis for terminating the lease. Examples of minor breaches include the landlord's failure to maintain landscaping or tenant's failures which could be corrected under a 3-day notice to perform or quit, or the refusal to pay late charges.

However, a **material breach** of the lease agreement by either the tenant or landlord justifies a termination of the tenant's right to possess the premises — his lease in the property.

A landlord's failure to meet significant obligations imposed on him by the lease agreement which substantially interfere with the occupancy is a material breach and **allows the tenant** to:

- terminate his possession of the leased premises, causing his possessory interest in the property to revert to the landlord; and

- cancel the lease agreement, including all future rent obligations.

Constructive eviction

A **constructive eviction** occurs when:

- the landlord or his agent *substantially interferes* with the tenant's use and enjoyment of the premises during the term of the tenancy held by the tenant as intended by the lease purpose provision; and

- the *tenant vacates* the premises due to the interference.

A constructive eviction due to the landlord's interference does not occur until the tenant vacates. An eviction does not exist when the tenant remains in possession.

Examples of **substantial interference** by the landlord that justify the tenant's vacating the premises include:

- a material breach of the lease, such as failing to repair and maintain the leased premises to accommodate and avoid interference with the use intended by the lease [Groh, *supra*];

- extensive alteration of the leased premises that is not authorized in the lease agreement or by the tenant and interferes with the intended use [**Reichhold** v. **Sommarstrom Inv. Co.** (1927) 83 CA 173];

- the sale of adjacent property owned by the landlord without reserving the tenant's parking and water rights given to the tenant as part of the lease [**Sierad** v. **Lilly** (1962) 204 CA2d 770]; or

- the failure to abate a sanitation, noise or safety nuisance over which the landlord, but not the tenant, has control. [**Johnson** v. **Snyder** (1950) 99 CA2d 86]

In a constructive eviction, neither a 3-day notice nor an unlawful detainer (UD) action is used to force the tenant to vacate. [Reichhold, *supra*]

Tenant's losses and remedies

Every month-to-month rental and lease agreement contains an **implied covenant**, an unexpressed lease provision, prohibiting the landlord from interfering with the tenant's agreed use and possession of the property, called the *covenant of quiet enjoyment*. [Calif. Civil Code §1927]

When a landlord breaches the *implied covenant of quiet enjoyment*, or other significant provision in the lease agreement, the tenant can:

- **vacate** the leased premises, recover his money losses incurred and cancel the lease agreement along with his obligation to pay future rents based on his constructive eviction; or

- **retain possession**, continue to pay rent and sue for any income lost or expenses incurred due to the landlord's interference.

The **losses** a tenant may recover when the tenant vacates due to a constructive eviction include:

- advance payments of rent and security deposits [Groh, *supra*];

- the cost of removing trade fixtures [Reichhold, *supra*];

- relocation expenses; and

- loss of business goodwill. [Johnson, *supra*]

The breaching landlord's remedies

A tenant who fails to pay rent and later vacates the premises due to a constructive eviction owes the landlord rent for the period of occupancy prior to vacating.

However, any unpaid back rent the landlord is entitled to collect is offset by money losses the tenant incurs due to the constructive eviction. [**Petroleum Collections Incorporated** v. **Swords** (1975) 48 CA3d 841]

Breach of anti-competition clause

The landlord's breach of an anti-competition provision in the lease agreement is a material breach. The tenant may respond by vacating the premises as a constructive eviction.

Consider a nonresidential lease containing an *anti-competition clause* stating the landlord will not lease other space in the commercial complex to competitors of the tenant.

The lease agreement also contains a *remedies provision* stating the landlord may relet the premises **without notifying** the tenant should the tenant vacate prior to the lease expiration date.

Later, the tenant holds a sale to liquidate his stock. The tenant closes down his business operations, vacates the premises and returns the keys to the landlord with instructions to find another tenant. The tenant's lease does not expire for a few years.

The landlord does not respond by entering into an agreement to cancel (surrender) the lease, nor does he take possession of the premises. Further, the landlord does not take **steps to forfeit** the tenant's right to possession (by an abandonment or 3-day notice).

The tenant pays no further rent and the landlord makes no demand on the tenant for delinquent rent. The landlord tries to locate a new tenant, but is unable.

Several months after closing the business, the tenant re-enters the premises and prepares to reopen for business since his lease of the premises has not been terminated. Meanwhile, the landlord leases another space in the building to a competitor of the tenant.

On discovering a competitor will now occupy the same commercial complex, the tenant vacates the premises. The landlord is notified the tenant has elected to cancel the lease since the landlord breached the anti-competition clause in the lease agreement by renting another space in the building to his competitor.

The landlord makes a demand for all rents due until the expiration of the lease agreement, claiming the obligation to pay rent has not been canceled.

The tenant claims he is liable only for the rents due prior to his vacating the premises (the second time) since the landlord's breach of the anti-competition provision in the lease agreement constituted a constructive eviction.

Can the tenant cancel the lease agreement and terminate his obligation to pay rent for the remaining term of the lease?

Yes! The tenant's right to possession under the lease has been terminated and the tenant's obligation to pay rent under the lease agreement canceled due to the **landlord's interference** with the tenant's use of the premises and the **tenant vacating** the premises. The landlord's breach of the anti-competition clause is a material breach of the lease agreement, justifying the tenant vacating the premises and canceling the lease agreement. [**Kulawitz** v. **Pacific Woodenware & Paper Co.** (1944) 25 C2d 664]

Failure to forfeit may lead to a breach

The landlord in the prior scenario failed to terminate the tenant's right to occupy the premises by declaring a forfeiture of the leasehold estate when the tenant first vacated the premises and became delinquent on rent payments. Due to the landlord's administrative error, the tenant retained all his leasehold interests and lease agreement contract rights.

The landlord could have terminated the lease when the tenant closed his business and delivered the keys to the landlord by:

- a surrender (accepting the possession of the premises in exchange for cancellation of the lease agreement and loss of the right to future rents); or

- a 3-day notice to pay rent or quit with a declaration of forfeiture of the leasehold (or a notice of abandonment).

Without a termination of the tenant's leasehold rights, the tenant's right to possession as agreed to in the lease agreement remained in effect throughout the delinquency and while out of possession.

Since the tenant's right to possession (use of the property) had not been terminated, the landlord's obligation to the tenant to abide by the anti-competition clause in the lease agreement remained in effect.

A landlord cannot reasonably expect to recover rents remaining due for the unexpired duration of a lease agreement that he has breached, causing the tenant to vacate as a constructive eviction.

Independent obligations to perform

Now consider a tenant who leases a gas station. A modular sign on the premises advertising the service station can be seen from a nearby freeway.

However, the sign was previously installed without a permit. The city orders the removal of the sign since its proximity to the gas tanks constitutes a fire hazard.

The landlord removes the sign, replacing it with a billboard that cannot be seen from the freeway. The tenant demands the landlord provide a sign visible from the freeway, and of comparable likeness to the one removed.

When the landlord fails to provide a similar sign, the tenant stops paying rent, but remains in possession of the premises. Months later, the lease agreement is canceled by the mutual agreement of the landlord and tenant. The tenant then vacates the premises.

The landlord now makes a demand on the tenant to pay rent for the months the tenant did not pay rent prior to vacating the premises.

The tenant claims he is not liable for rent during his period of occupancy after removal of the sign since the landlord's conduct of removing the sign constructively evicted him from the premises, a breach of the covenant of quiet enjoyment and use of the property as contemplated by the use provision in the lease agreement.

Is the tenant liable for the unpaid back rent during the period he remained in occupancy?

Yes! The tenant is liable for the agreed-to rent for the period of his occupancy. A constructive eviction — which relieves the tenant of his rent obligation by canceling the lease agreement — cannot occur until the tenant **actually vacates** the premises (and thus owes no more rent). [Petroleum Collections Incorporated, *supra*]

While the landlord's failure to replace the sign that could be seen from the freeway with a similar sign significantly interfered with the tenant's use of the property as intended by the lease agreement, the fact the tenant remained in possession after the breach without first negotiating a modification of the lease agreement obligated the tenant to pay rent.

A tenant owes rent under the lease agreement in exchange for his use and possession of the leased premises. Rent at the agreed price is due even though the use may be diminished by the landlord's interference.

Thus, when the tenant remains in possession and **fails to pay rent**, the interfering landlord who himself has breached the lease may forfeit the tenant's right to occupy the property by use of a 3-day notice to pay rent and declaration of forfeiture.

Quiet enjoyment waiver

A tenant leases space in a retail center under a nonresidential lease agreement containing a **remedies provision** stating:

- the tenant may not terminate the lease agreement on any failure of the landlord to fully perform on the lease; and

- the tenant may only recover money losses if the landlord breaches the lease.

The landlord leases the adjoining space to a dry cleaning business. The dry cleaning business emits fumes that enter the ventilation system and permeate the tenant's premises, negatively impacting his employees and business operations. The landlord is notified of the interference but fails to remedy the ventilation problems over which he has control.

The tenant stops paying rent and vacates the premises, claiming the dry cleaning fumes were noxious and endangered his employees' health.

The landlord makes a demand on the tenant to pay rent for the remainder of the lease term. The tenant rejects the demand, then seeks to recover his lost profits, relocation expenses and employee medical expenses from the landlord.

The tenant claims the landlord's failure to prevent the fumes from invading his leased premises is a breach of the implied covenant of quiet enjoyment and constitutes a constructive eviction, canceling the lease agreement when he vacated.

The landlord claims the tenant is liable for the remaining rent whether or not the tenant vacated since the lease contains a remedies provision, waiving the tenant's right to terminate the lease.

Is the tenant liable for the rent due for the remaining term of the lease?

Yes! The nonresidential tenant is liable for the rent remaining unpaid on the lease. Here, the tenant was constructively evicted. However, he remains liable for all future unpaid rent under the lease agreement since the tenant contracted to limit his remedies on the landlord's material breach to a demand for money. The tenant's claim for money losses is separate from the rent due under the lease. [**Lee** v. **Placer Title Company** (1994) 28 CA4th 503]

Thus, the tenant is obligated by the **remedies provision** in his lease agreement to:

- remain in possession (and care) of the premises even though he has been constructively evicted;

- continue paying the agreed rent for the entire duration of the lease; and

- sue the landlord to recover any money losses caused by the landlord's breach of the lease agreement.

Editor's note — For residential tenants, any waiver or limitation on the remedies for breach of the covenant of quiet enjoyment is void as against public policy; not so for nonresidential tenants. [CC §1953]

However, when the landlord's conduct prevents, not just interferes with, the tenant from operating his business on the property and forces him to vacate, then the value of the tenant's leasehold interest has been completely diminished.

While the nonresidential tenant waived his right to terminate the lease on the landlord's breach of the covenant of quiet enjoyment, he may vacate the property and sue for money, including:

- a 100% offset against future rents due on the lease for money losses occurring after the breach and until the landlord performs or the lease term expires; and

- lost profits, relocation expenses, rent for the replacement space and loss of goodwill.

Landlord interference with subtenants

A tenant may convey a portion of his leasehold rights to possess part or all of the leased premises to a subtenant by entering into a *sublease*. However, most lease agreements held by single-user tenants prevent the tenant from subleasing (or assigning) without the landlord's permission.

On entering into a sublease agreement, the subtenant becomes a third-party beneficiary to the lease agreement entered into by the landlord, referred to as the *master lease*. The benefits received by the subtenant under the master lease include the implied covenant of quiet enjoyment, when:

- the master lease agreement permits subleasing; or

- the landlord consents to a sublease under a restraint on alienation provision in the master lease agreement.

The master lease agreement should be attached to the sublease agreement as an exhibit, as the rights of the subtenant are limited by the terms of the master lease.

*Editor's note — Both the master lease and the sublease are of the same form and thus contain the same provisions, except the lease agreement with the subtenant references the lease agreement held by the tenant. [See **first tuesday** Form 552 § 1.3]*

Thus, when a landlord's conduct interferes with the subtenant's use of the premises under the sublease agreement (as limited by the referenced master lease), the subtenant may vacate and recover losses from the landlord for a constructive eviction. [**Marchese** v. **Standard Realty and Development Company** (1977) 74 CA3d 142]

When a subtenant has been constructively evicted by the landlord, the **master tenant** may:

- vacate the entire premises, cancel the lease agreement and recover losses from the landlord for a constructive eviction of the master tenant; or

- remain in possession and recover money losses for breach of the implied covenant of quiet enjoyment.

Constructive eviction vs. the warranty of habitability

Constructive eviction of either a residential or nonresidential tenant is distinct from the implied warranty of habitability enforceable only against residential landlords. Constructive eviction requires the tenant to vacate or pay the entire rent; the warranty of habitability requires neither.

Both residential and nonresidential lease agreements contain written conditions that, if breached by the landlord, result in termination of the tenant's possession — constructive eviction.

However, the warranty of habitability is not a written provision, it is implied; it is judicially and legislatively considered to exist in all residential rental and lease agreements.

The implied warranty of habitability requires a landlord to maintain safe and sanitary conditions in his residential units. On the landlord's failure to maintain habitable conditions, the residential tenant may remain in possession and pay a reduced rent that will be set by the court. Thus, a constructive eviction has not taken place since the residential tenant remains in possession. [**Green** v. **Superior Court of the City and County of San Francisco** (1974) 10 C3d 616; Calif. Code of Civil Procedure §1174.2; see Chapter 37]

However, both residential and nonresidential tenants can vacate the premises based on the landlord's significant interference with possessory rights and recover any losses from their landlords that flow from the constructive eviction.

Consider a nonresidential landlord who fails to meet his obligations under a lease agreement to maintain the property for the intended use. The nonresidential tenant retaliates by refusing to pay rent. However, the tenant does not vacate the premises.

The landlord files a UD action to evict the tenant for his failure to pay rent after service of a 3-day notice to pay or quit. At trial, the tenant is unable to raise the defense of a breach of the implied warranty of habitability since his lease is nonresidential. Thus, the nonresidential tenant is without a legal excuse for his failure to pay rent for the period of his actual occupancy, and will be evicted in spite of the landlord's material breach of lease agreement provisions. [**Schulman** v. **Vera** (1980) 108 CA3d 552]

Chapter 34

Retaliatory
eviction defense

This chapter discusses a landlord's attempt to evict a tenant in retaliation for the tenant's exercise of his legal rights to the detriment of the landlord.

Shackling vengeful wayward landlords

A tenant occupies a residential unit under a month-to-month rental agreement.

The unit has many defects which are in need of elimination. The tenant requests that the landlord make repairs to correct the defects. The landlord does not make the requested repairs.

The tenant complains to the landlord several more times about the need for repairs and the lack of suitable living conditions in his unit. Finally, the tenant threatens to exercise his right to perform the **repairs and deduct** the costs from the rent. [See Chapter 37]

Before any repairs are made, the landlord serves the tenant with a notice to vacate the premises. [See **first tuesday** Form 569 and 569.5]

The tenant remains in possession after the notice expires. Rent is tendered but refused by the landlord. The landlord files an unlawful detainer (UD) action to evict the tenant.

The tenant defends against the UD action, claiming the landlord seeks to evict him in retaliation for his repeated requests for repairs and the complaints about the habitability of the unit.

The landlord claims the tenant cannot raise the defense of retaliatory eviction since the tenant did not file a complaint with a government agency regarding the habitability of the unit or undertake to make the repairs himself under the statutory repair and deduct remedy.

To successfully defend against a UD action, must the tenant first file a complaint with a government agency or make the repairs himself before claiming the UD action is a retaliatory eviction?

No! The tenant need not file a complaint regarding the habitability of his residential unit or repair the defects himself as a prerequisite to raising the defense of retaliatory eviction in the UD action.

Here, the residential landlord is prevented from evicting the tenant. The landlord's conduct indicated he sought to evict the tenant in retaliation for complaining about the need for repairs. [**Kemp** v. **Schultz** (1981) 121 CA3d Supp. 13]

The retaliatory eviction defense

A landlord's sole purpose for filing an unlawful detainer (UD) action is to recover possession from a tenant.

In addition to the landlord's recovery of possession from the tenant, the **UD award** against the tenant may include:

- any unpaid delinquent amounts of rent accrued prior to the forfeiture of possession by a declaration in the 3-day notice to quit or as granted at the UD trial;

- the reasonable rental value of the premises during the tenant's unlawful detainer which follows the date of forfeiture of the right to possession; and

- up to $600 in addition to the rent for the tenant's malicious behavior. [Calif. Code of Civil Procedure §1174(b)]

Accordingly, UD proceedings are intended to be brief — from the use of notices to quit or vacate to establish an unlawful detainer to the inability of the tenant to bring up frivolous defenses.

Thus, **residential tenants** are allowed to raise only two defenses in a UD action:

- a breach of the warranty of habitability [CCP §1174.2; see Chapter 37]; and

- retaliatory eviction.

Residential tenants include mobilehome owners who rent or lease space in a mobilehome park. [**Rich** v. **Schwab** (1998) 63 CA4th 803]

For **nonresidential tenants**, the only defense allowed in a UD action is the defense of retaliatory eviction. [**Custom Parking, Inc.** v. **Superior Court of the County of Marin** (1982) 138 CA3d 90]

A claim of retaliatory eviction is allowed as a **tenant's defense** in nonresidential evictions, not based on the statutory defense which exists for residential tenants, but on the equivalent, long-standing common law defense of retaliatory eviction. The public policy enforced by courts entitles all tenants to exercise their legal rights against a landlord since the activity outweighs the public's interest in preserving the summary nature of UD hearings provided for landlords. [**Barela** v. **Superior Court of Orange County** (1981) 30 C3d 244]

Further, a residential tenant may sue the landlord to recover money losses incurred due to a landlord's retaliatory acts, such as an unfair rent increase. [**Aweeka** v. **Bonds** (1971) 20 CA3d 278]

Under a notice to vacate, a landlord may evict a tenant for any reason, or no reason at all (except rent control and Section 8 properties), but he may not evict a tenant for an improper reason. [**S.P. Growers Association** v. **Rodriguez** (1976) 17 C3d 719]

In rent control communities, ordinances require a residential landlord to state his reasons for evicting a tenant in the notice to vacate. Also, a landlord providing Section 8 housing must state a good reason in a notice to vacate before he can evict the tenant. [**Mitchell** v. **Poole** (1988) 203 CA3d Supp. 1]

Retaliatory reaction to complaints

Actions by a residential landlord to increase rent, decrease tenant services or evict are considered **retaliatory acts** if initiated by the landlord after a tenant:

- complains to the landlord or a government agency regarding the habitability of the premises;

- exercises the statutory repair and deduct remedy [Calif. Civil Code §1942.5(a)(1)];

- organizes or becomes a member of a tenants' association or tenants' rights group [CC §1942.5(c)]; or

- exercises any other legal rights held by the tenant, such as notifying the police about the landlord's criminal activity. [CC §1942.5(c); Barela, *supra*]

*Editor's note — If a landlord fails to make repairs within 30 days after the tenant notifies him of the need for repairs, the tenant may make the repairs himself and deduct the cost from the rent, called the **repair and deduct remedy**. [CC §1942; see Chapter 37]*

In addition, a residential landlord is **prohibited** from increasing the rent, decreasing tenant services or requiring the tenant to vacate **within 180 days** after any of the following events:

- the tenant's notice to the landlord of the need for repairs, or complaint to the landlord about the habitability of the premises;

- the tenant's filing of a written or oral complaint with a government agency regarding the habitability of the premises;

- an inspection or issuance of a citation resulting from the tenant's complaint to a government agency;

- the filing of documents to initiate an action involving the habitability of the premises; or

- the entry of a judgment or issuance of an arbitration award adverse to the landlord. [CC §1942.5(a)]

Enforcing the 180-day protection rule

Consider a residential tenant holding possession under a month-to-month rental agreement who prevails in an unlawful detainer (UD) action brought by a landlord. The tenant is permitted by the court to remain in possession of his unit.

Four months (120 days) after the UD judgment, the landlord serves the tenant with a notice to vacate. The notice will expire before the 180-day protective period has run.

The tenant tenders an amount of rent on the next due date representing rent due for a rental period extending beyond the expiration of the notice to vacate. The landlord refuses to accept the rent and returns it undeposited. The tenant remains on the premises after the notice to vacate expires.

The landlord next files a UD action to evict the tenant since the tenant retained occupancy after the notice to vacate expired. The UD trial is set for a date more than 180 days after the date of the prior UD trial at which the tenant prevailed.

As a defense to the current UD action, the tenant claims the landlord is barred from evicting him since a notice to vacate cannot be served within 180 days after the tenant prevailed on the prior UD judgment.

The landlord claims he is not barred from evicting the tenant since the current UD trial occurs after the 180-day protective period expired.

In this example, the UD action is barred. The tenant **cannot be required to vacate** the premises within the 180-day protection period. Since the UD action is based on the expiration of a notice to vacate, and under the notice the tenant is required to vacate during the 180-day protection period or be guilty of unlawfully detaining the premises, the landlord cannot use a UD action to evict the tenant. The date set for the return of the premises by a notice to vacate was within the 180-day protection period. [**Kriz** v. **Taylor** (1979) 92 CA3d 302]

However, the landlord is not barred from serving a notice to vacate or a notice of change in rental terms within the 180-day period, as long as the notice does not expire within that period. Thus, the tenant confronted with a hostile landlord has 180 days after exercising lawful rights which antagonize the landlord to voluntarily relocate and avoid the seemingly inevitable notice to vacate or change in terms of the occupancy.

Nonresidential retaliatory eviction

Consider a nonresidential tenant who occupies property under a month-to-month tenancy. The rental agreement (or expired lease) requires the landlord to care for and maintain the exterior walls and roof of the building during the occupancy.

The roof leaks, causing damage to the tenant's personal property. On more than one occasion, the tenant notifies the landlord of the leak, and requests that the landlord repair the roof.

Several months later, the roof leaks again, and the tenant suffers more losses. The tenant repairs the roof himself and makes a demand on the landlord for reimbursement. The landlord rejects the demand.

The tenant does not deduct the cost of the repairs from the monthly rent since the space rented is nonresidential and the "repair and deduct" remedy available to residential cannot be used by nonresidential tenants. The tenant pays the rent as it becomes due.

The tenant sues the landlord to recover the cost of repairing the roof. The landlord immediately serves the tenant with a 30-day notice to vacate. The tenant remains in possession after the 30-day notice expires, and the landlord files an unlawful detainer (UD) action to evict the tenant.

The nonresidential tenant defends the UD action, claiming the landlord is attempting to evict him for an improper reason — in retaliation for the tenant's enforcement of the landlord's obligations by suing the landlord to enforce the rental agreement (or expired lease).

The landlord claims the tenant cannot raise the defense of retaliatory eviction since the defense is statutory and available only to residential tenants. [CC §1942.5]

Here, the common law retaliatory eviction defense, equivalent to the statutory residential tenant defense, is available to the nonresidential tenant as a matter of *public policy* enforced by the courts. The eviction sought by the landlord is in retaliation against the tenant because the tenant exercised a legal right.

Simply put, when a landlord has an improper motive to evict a tenant, the tenant, residential or nonresidential, may raise the common law defense of retaliatory eviction. [Custom Parking, Inc., *supra*]

A nonresidential tenant has a legal right to recover money due from a landlord who has breached the lease agreement causing the tenant to incur expenses. However, when the landlord refuses to voluntarily reimburse the tenant after a demand, the tenant must proceed with litigation and obtain a money judgment, not deduct the expense from the rent due the landlord.

Losses recovered by tenant

Occasionally, a residential landlord will include a provision in his lease or rental agreements in which the residential tenant purports to waive his right to raise the defense of retaliatory eviction, or sue a landlord for retaliatory acts. However, a waiver of legal rights by a residential tenant is void. [CC §1942.5(d)]

If a residential landlord is attempting to evict a tenant in retaliation for any lawful activity by the tenant, the tenant is entitled to recover:

- the tenant's actual money losses incurred due to the landlord's retaliatory activity [CC §1942.5(f)(1)]; and

- punitive damages of no less than $100 and no more than $1,000 for each retaliatory act where the landlord or his agent is guilty of fraud, oppression or malice with respect to the retaliation. [CC §1942.5(f)(2)]

More financially frightening for a residential landlord whose conduct subjects him to statutory punitive damages is the tenant's right to bring a class action suit to recover for the landlord's retaliatory act of increasing the rents on all tenants who participate in forming a tenant association to prevent rental increases and petition the city for rent control. [**Rich** v. **Schwab** (1984) 162 CA3d 739]

Further, the prevailing party in an action brought by a residential tenant seeking to recover losses from a landlord for retaliatory eviction is entitled to reasonable attorney fees. [CC §1942.5(g)]

SECTION E

Maintenance and
Security

Chapter 35

Defective building components

This chapter analyzes a landlord's lack of liability for injuries caused by defects in components installed on the property that were supplied by manufacturers, distributors and retailers.

Liability for neglect, not strict liability

A tenant of a residential rental unit slips and falls in the bathtub, sustaining injuries. The bathtub does not have an anti-skid surface and is very slippery when wet.

The tenant claims the landlord is liable for his injuries since the bathtub without an anti-skid surface is defective.

Is the landlord liable to the tenant for the injuries caused by the defective bathtub surface?

No! Landlords are not liable for tenant injuries caused by a defective bathtub surface. To be liable for another's injuries without concern for fault, called *strict liability*, the landlord must be part of the **chain of distribution** for the installation of the equipment or fixture that caused the injury.

It is unreasonable to extend strict liability to hotel operators and residential landlords for defects in products that are used in the construction of the property, but are manufactured and marketed by others. [**Peterson** v. **Superior Court** (1995) 10 C4th 1185]

Strict liability

Strict liability for an injury caused by a product applies primarily to the manufacturer of the product, since it is the manufacturer who places the product on the market and knows it will not be inspected for defects before it is used. Thus, the manufacturer is liable for defects.

The primary **social purpose** of strict liability is to impose on the manufacturer, not the injured user, the costs of injuries caused by its products when used as intended.

Strict liability for defect-related injuries also extends to distributors and retailers who are part of the "stream of commerce" in marketing products for use by the end user, the customer. Distributors and retailers are considered to be in the best position to **assert influence** over the manufacturer to create a product that is free of defects.

Strict liability is imposed on retailers and distributors since the added liability exposure is considered an incentive for their attention to the safety of the products retailers and distributors purchase from manufacturers for resale to the public.

However, the social goal of imposing strict liability on all involved in the manufacturing, distribution and resale of a product to the consumer is not to **ensure the safety** of the product. The goal is to distribute the risks and costs of injury due to **lack of safety** in the product's use among those most able to bear the burden of the costs.

Previous strict liability rulings

The *Peterson* case barring tenants from pursuing landlords and hotel operators for strict liability for injuries resulting from dangerous and defective construction materials and fixtures overruled a previous California Supreme Court decision. The court previously held a residential landlord was strictly liable for injuries caused by hidden defects in components that were part of the construction of the property. [**Becker** v. **IRM Corporation** (1985) 38 C3d 454]

In *Becker*, a tenant slips in the shower and is injured when the shower door shatters — the door was defective since it was made from untempered glass.

The tenant claims the landlord's use of the product caused his injuries and, under the strict liability doctrine, the landlord is responsible.

The landlord claims he is not liable for the injuries since the defect in the shower door was hidden, and the accident unforeseeable since similar accidents had not occurred, putting the landlord on notice of the defect.

In *Becker*, which is no longer law, the landlord was held strictly liable for the tenant's injuries caused by the latent (hidden) defects in materials and fixtures installed in the unit, regardless of whether the landlord was aware of the defect, since the landlord was in the business of renting property.

However, *Peterson* overruled *Becker*. The *Peterson* court held the theory of strict liability could not be extended to residential landlords. Landlords are not distributors or retailers. Landlords and hotel operators, unlike distributors and retailers, cannot exert influence over the manufacturer to make a product safe. For the most part, landlords and hotel operators are not builders and do not have a business relationship with the manufacturer or the suppliers of the defective product.

Once the product is purchased and installed by the builder, the product leaves the stream of commerce — distribution and resale has come to an end. The later use of the product by occupants, be they tenants or guests, does not transform the landlord and hotel operator into a retailer of the product.

Editor's note — Peterson refused to decide whether strict liability can be imposed on a landlord or a hotel operator who participates in the construction of the building. Specifications established by planners, designers and construction contractors will play a role in deciding whether strict liability will be imposed on owner-builders of rental and hotel units.

Duty to correct known defects

It is the residential landlord's inaction when confronted with a **known dangerous** condition, called *negligence*, that gives rise to liability for injury to others. Thus, a residential landlord who fails to cure known dangerous defects will be liable under general *tort principles of negligence* for injuries caused by the breach of his duty to correct known defects.

Tenants should be able to rely on the landlord's inspection of the rented space and his correction of all visible and known defects. Residential landlords are in the business of leasing property for human occupancy.

The residential landlord must provide a clean, safe and habitable premises during the term of the lease. Further, the landlord is obligated to repair all known patent or latent defects, unless the tenant agrees to undertake repairs and maintenance. [Calif. Civil Code §1942]

Thus, the residential landlord is personally liable to the tenant for injuries occurring on the rental property as a result of the landlord's **failure to inspect**, locate and repair defective and dangerous property conditions that are known or should be known to the landlord. [CC §1941]

The residential landlord is obligated to repair uninhabitable conditions which could affect the tenant's health and safety, and to make these repairs immediately. [See Chapter 37]

Editor's note — The tenant will be able to recover from the landlord if the tenant can show the landlord could have reasonably foreseen the accident.

A landlord or hotel operator who is aware of injuries caused by latent defects in products used on the premises will be liable if other similar latent defects are not cured, since it is reasonably foreseeable injuries caused by similar defects throughout the project will occur. **[Sturgeon v. Curnutt (1994) 29 CA4th 301]**

Chapter 36

Care and maintenance of property

This chapter outlines the respective duties of the landlord and tenant to care for and maintain leased property, and the tenant's remedies if the landlord fails to perform.

Tenant's obligations and remedies

A landlord and a tenant enter into a lease agreement for a furnished unit in an apartment complex. The lease agreement contains a provision stating the landlord will maintain the premises and common areas in a **safe and sanitary condition**, and comply with all applicable ordinances and regulations. [See **first tuesday** Form 550 §6.2]

The lease agreement further provides for the tenant to keep the unit clean and sanitary, and properly operate all electrical, gas and plumbing fixtures. [See **first tuesday** Form 550 §§5.3, 5.4]

Before the tenant takes possession, the resident manager and the tenant conduct a "walk-through" of the unit. They agree on the condition of the premises. The tenant and the resident manager complete a condition of premises form which is attached as an addendum to the lease agreement and signed by the tenant. [See Form 560 accompanying this chapter]

On the condition of premises form, the tenant notes any defects existing on the premises. For example, the tenant marks if appliances are dented, screens have holes or are missing from windows, plumbing fixtures are broken or leaking, linoleum is peeling or damaged, carpeting has stains, chipped paint, etc.

Since the unit is furnished, the tenant and the resident manager also complete a condition of furnishings addendum during the "walk-through." [See Form 561 accompanying this chapter]

The tenant records any defects in the furniture on the condition of furnishings form, such as tears or burns in upholstery or scratches in wood furniture.

No minor or major defective conditions are observed by the tenant or the landlord during the "walk-through."

Later, before the tenant vacates the unit, the tenant and the resident manager will conduct a **pre-expiration inspection** to determine if the unit and the furnishings have sustained any damage other than normal wear and tear during the tenant's occupancy. The tenant will be handed a **statement of deficiencies**, listing any conditions which must be corrected to avoid a deduction of the corrective costs from the security deposit. [See Chapter 19]

The purpose of the condition of premises and condition of furnishings forms is to determine if any defective conditions exist in the rental unit and to repair them before the tenant takes possession.

When the tenant vacates, the landlord wants to be able to recover the cost of any damage to the unit or the furnishings caused by the tenant. The completed forms **document the condition** of the unit and its furnishings at the time of occupancy.

On the other hand, the tenant wants to avoid liability for damage he did not cause.

Tenant's duty to maintain

A tenant must repair all deterioration and damage to the premises caused by his failure to use ordinary care in his use of the premises. Thus,

CONDITION OF PREMISES ADDENDUM

DATE:_____, 20_____, at _____, California.

Items left blank or unchecked are not applicable

FACTS:

This is an addendum to the following referenced document:

☐ Lease agreement
☐ Rental Agreement
☐ Occupancy agreement

dated:_____, 20_____

entered into by_____,Landlord,

and_____,Tenant,

regarding real estate premises referred to as:

_____

_____

_____

AGREEMENT:

1. Landlord and Tenant have jointly inspected the premises and common areas and agree the premises and unchecked items such as fixtures, appliances, and furnishings are in a satisfactory and sanitary condition.

2. Check only those items which are unsatisfactory and state why in "REMARKS."

EXTERIOR/COMMON AREAS:

☐ Garage/parking lot	☐ Garbage facilities	☐ Storage area	☐ TV antenna
☐ Pool/spa	☐ Satellite dish	☐ Patio/decks	☐ CATV hookup
☐ Stairs/railings	☐ Garage door openers	☐ Hallway/lobby	☐ Laundry area
☐ Fencing	☐ Roof	☐ Exterior lighting	☐ Eaves/gutters
☐ Sprinklers/hose	☐ Mailbox	☐ Walkways	☐ _____

ENTRY:

☐ Door	☐ # of keys _____	☐ Doorbell/knocker	☐ Closet
☐ Intercom/security	☐ Shelves	☐ Locks	☐ _____

KITCHEN:

☐ Range	☐ Trash compactor	☐ Oven	☐ Water purifier
☐ Refrigerator	☐ Counters/laminate	☐ Garbage disposal	☐ Cabinets/drawers
☐ Exhaust fan(s)	☐ Pantry/shelves	☐ Dishwasher	☐ Tile/linoleum
☐ Microwave	☐ Sink/faucets		

BATHROOM:

☐ Sink	☐ Tile/linoleum	☐ Faucets/hardware	☐ Closet/shelves
☐ Toilet	☐ Exhaust fan(s)	☐ Shower	☐ Shower enclosure
☐ Tub	☐ Medicine cabinet		

ELECTRICAL:

☐ Outlets	☐ Lighting	☐ Switchplates	☐ Thermostat
☐ Fixtures	☐ Furnace	☐ Smoke detectors	☐ Ventilation
☐ Air conditioning	☐ _____		

PLUMBING:

☐ Water heater	☐ Washer	☐ Hot/cold water	☐ Dryer
☐ Gas hookups	☐ _____		

INTERIOR:

☐ Wall coverings	☐ Floor coverings	☐ Ceilings	☐ Walls
☐ Draperies	☐ Rods/tracks	☐ Glass doors	☐ Windows
☐ Doorknobs	☐ Fireplace	☐ Hardware/fittings	☐ Paint
☐ Floors	☐ Baseboards/trim	☐ Doors	☐ Shades
☐ Closets	☐ Screens	☐ Sills/jambs	☐ Kickplates/stops
☐ Chimney/flue	☐ _____		

— — — — — — — — — — — — *PAGE ONE OF TWO — FORM 560* — — — — — — — — — —

REMARKS:

_____
_____
_____
_____
_____
_____
_____
_____
_____
_____
_____

REPAIRS PROMISED:

1. _____
   _____

   Completion date: _____

2. _____
   _____

   Completion date: _____

I agree to the terms stated above.	**I accept the premise as stated above.**
Date:_____, 20_____	Date:_____, 20_____
Landlord/Manager: _____	Tenant:_____
Signature: _____	Signature: _____
Address: _____	Signature: _____
_____	Address: _____
Phone:_____	_____
Fax: _____	Phone:_____
E-mail: _____	Fax: _____
	E-mail: _____

FORM 560   10-00   ©2007 **first tuesday**, P.O. BOX 20069, RIVERSIDE, CA 92516 (800) 794-0494

normal wear and tear on the unit need not be avoided or eliminated by the tenant. [Calif. Civil Code §1929]

Further, a residential tenant has a **duty of care** and maintenance in the use of the leased premises which includes:

- keeping the premises occupied by the tenant clean and sanitary;

- disposing of all rubbish, garbage and waste in a sanitary manner;

- properly operating all electrical, gas and plumbing fixtures, and keeping them clean and sanitary;

- allowing no person who is on the premises with the tenant's permission to intentionally destroy, damage, waste or remove any part of the premises or the facilities, equipment or appurtenances; and

- occupying and using the premises for the purpose it is intended to be used. [CC §1941.2]

The landlord can agree to be responsible for the cleanliness of the common areas, and the disposal of garbage and rubbish, for example the hiring of a sanitation service. [CC §1941.2(b)]

The tenant breaches his duty to care for and maintain the premises when the tenant:

- contributes substantially to the dilapidation of the premises; or

- substantially interferes with the landlord's duty to maintain the premises. [CC §1941.2(a)]

For example, a tenant does not notify his landlord of a leak in the roof that is causing damage to the ceiling of the rental unit. Eventually, the ceiling falls down, causing damage to the tenant's personal property, the walls and the floor coverings.

Here, the tenant interfered with the landlord's duty to maintain the property since the tenant failed to:

- notify the landlord of the leak in the roof; or

- repair the leak himself.

Also, the landlord is not liable for any damage to the tenant's personal property resulting from the falling ceiling, since the **tenant neglected to report** the water seepage. Conversely, the tenant is liable for the cost of the damage to the rental unit for failure to report the need for repairs on the first sign of leakage.

A landlord can recover the cost of repairs made to correct excessive wear and tear by deducting the cost of repairs from the security deposit and demanding payment for any deficiency in the deposit to cover the expenses. [CC §1950.5(b)]

If the tenant fails to pay any charges remaining unpaid after deductions from the security deposit, the landlord can file an action against the tenant to recover amounts not covered by the security deposit. [CC §1950.5(m)]

Landlord's duty to maintain

A residential landlord has a *general obligation* to:

- put a residential unit in a condition fit for occupancy **prior to leasing**; and

- repair all unsafe and unsanitary conditions that occur **during occupancy** that would render the unit uninhabitable. [CC §1941]

Further, all residential rental and lease agreements automatically contain an implied *warranty of habitability*. The unwritten warranty imposes a contractual duty on a landlord to repair and maintain his residential units so the units are fit for human occupancy at all times. [**Green** v. **Superior Court of the City and County of San Francisco** (1974) 10 C3d 616; see Chapter 32]

Both the landlord's statutory obligation to maintain his residential units and the implied warranty of habitability require the landlord to correct **major defects** interfering with the tenant's ability to live on the property, such as a lack of hot water or a leaky roof.

While the residential landlord has an obligation to care for and maintain all major and structural components of residential rental units, the landlord is further obligated to repair **minor defects**. Minor defects include such conditions as leaky faucets, faulty electrical switches and failed locks or latches. Typically, a residential landlord agrees in the rental or lease agreement to care for and maintain the property, which includes the repair of minor defects. [See **first tuesday** Form 550 §6.2]

The landlord's failure to repair or replace minor defects constitutes a breach of provisions in the rental or lease agreement. The landlord who breaches the lease agreement by failing to make minor repairs must reimburse the tenant for reasonable costs incurred by the tenant to cure the defects.

CONDITION OF FURNISHINGS ADDENDUM
and Inventory

DATE:_____, 20_____, at _____, California.

FACTS:

This is an addendum to the following:

- ☐ Lease agreement
- ☐ Rental agreement
- ☐ Occupancy agreement
- ☐ Other

dated: _____, 20_____

entered into by:

Landlord: _____

Tenant: _____

regarding real estate referred to as: _____

_____

AGREEMENT:

1. Landlord and Tenant have jointly inspected the furniture and furnishings, and agree they are in satisfactory and sanitary condition.

2. Only those items checked are unsatisfactory and explained under "REMARKS."

3. The quantity of furnishings entered on this form are accepted by the Tenant.

4. Reimbursement for any loss damage or excess wear and tear on furnishings provided to the Tenant will be deducted from Tenant's security deposit.

LIVING ROOM:

- ☐ Carpet
- ☐ Draperies
- ☐ Window coverings
- ☐ Wall coverings
- ☐ Couch   #_____
- ☐ Pictures   #_____

- ☐ Chairs   #_____
- ☐ End tables   #_____
- ☐ Coffee tables   #_____
- ☐ Lamps   #_____
- ☐ Shelves
- ☐ _____

KITCHEN:

- ☐ Tile/linoleum
- ☐ Window coverings
- ☐ Refrigerator
- ☐ Table   #_____

- ☐ Chairs   #_____
- ☐ Range
- ☐ Cabinets
- ☐ _____

BEDROOM:

- ☐ Double bed   #_____
- ☐ Single bed   #_____
- ☐ Headboards   #_____
- ☐ Mattress   #_____
- ☐ Box springs   #_____
- ☐ Bed frame   #_____

- ☐ Night stands #_____
- ☐ Lamps   #_____
- ☐ Bureau   #_____
- ☐ Pictures   #_____
- ☐ Mirror   #_____
- ☐ _____

SECOND BEDROOM:

- ☐ Double bed   #_____
- ☐ Single bed   #_____
- ☐ Headboards   #_____
- ☐ Mattress   #_____
- ☐ Box springs   #_____
- ☐ Bed frame   #_____

- ☐ Night stands #_____
- ☐ Lamps   #_____
- ☐ Bureau   #_____
- ☐ Pictures   #_____
- ☐ Mirror   #_____
- ☐ _____

BATHROOM:

- ☐ Medicine cabinet
- ☐ Shelves/fittings
- ☐ Toilet

- ☐ Shower/tub
- ☐ Shower enclosure
- ☐ _____

REMARKS:

_____
_____
_____
_____
_____
_____
_____
_____
_____
_____
_____
_____
_____
_____
_____

I agree to the terms stated above.

Date:_____, 20_____

Landlord/Agent:_____

Address: _____

_____

Phone:_____

Fax: _____

Signature: _____

I agree to the terms stated above.

Date:_____, 20_____

Tenant:_____

Address: _____

Phone:_____

Fax: _____

Signature: _____

Signature: _____

FORM 561   10-01   ©2007 **first tuesday**, P.O. BOX 20069, RIVERSIDE, CA 92516 (800) 794-0494

Minor repairs and habitability

During his occupancy, a residential tenant discovers the electrical wiring for the garbage disposal under the kitchen sink is exposed. The tenant asks the landlord to correct the faulty wiring. The landlord does nothing.

Other minor repairs later become necessary in the unit. A roof leak develops, staining a bedroom ceiling, and the water closet on the toilet bowl leaks, requiring repair or replacement. The tenant notifies the landlord of the need for the repairs. Neither the landlord nor the tenant correct any of the minor defects.

Frustrated with the landlord's lack of cooperation, the tenant stops paying rent. The landlord serves the tenant with a 3-day notice to pay rent or quit. [See **first tuesday** Form 575]

The tenant still refuses to pay rent, and the landlord files an unlawful detainer (UD) action.

The tenant defends his nonpayment of rent by claiming the landlord breached the *warranty of habitability* since he failed to repair the numerous defective conditions on the premises.

Here, the landlord did not breach the **warranty of habitability** and the tenant is ordered evicted for non-payment of rent. The defective conditions did not interfere with the tenant's ability to live on the premises for the purposes intended, despite the inconveniences.

A landlord breaches the warranty of habitability only when he fails to provide and maintain residential rental units in a habitable, that is, **safe and sanitary**, condition. [Green, *supra*]

Tenant's option to repair

When a residential landlord fails to repair minor defective conditions on the property, the tenant may exercise one of three remedies:

- repair the defect and deduct the costs of contracting for the repair from the rent [CC §1942(a)];

- make the repairs, continue to pay rent and sue the landlord to recover the cost of repairs; or

- vacate the premises. [CC §1942(a)]

However, if the premises are so unsafe and unsanitary they qualify as *uninhabitable*, the tenant can remain in occupancy and withhold payment of the rent. In an ensuing UD action, the tenant would raise the defense of the landlord's breach of the implied warranty of habitability to force the landlord to make the necessary repairs to eliminate the unsafe and unsanitary condition.

The court would then set the amount of rent due during the period of nonpayment of rent based on the percentage of uninhabitability, usually determined in the tenant's favor.

The repair-and-deduct remedy

If the leased premises is in need of repair, whether minor or major, the tenant must notify the landlord orally or in writing of the condition.

After advising the landlord of the need for repairs, the tenant can make the repairs himself and deduct the cost of the repairs from the next month's rent if:

- the landlord fails to make the necessary repairs within a *reasonable time*; and

- the cost of repairs does not exceed the amount of one month's rent, called *the repair-and-deduct remedy*.

The tenant cannot exercise the repair-and-deduct remedy more than twice in any 12-month period. [CC §1942(a)]

Also, any agreement by the tenant to waive or modify his right to repair and deduct the costs from the rent is unenforceable. [CC §1942.1]

A **reasonable time** for the landlord to repair after notice is 30 days, unless the need to repair is urgent and requires more immediate attention. [CC §1942(b)]

The repair-and-deduct remedy is not available to the tenant when the need for repair is created by the tenant's conduct. [CC §1942(c)]

Repairs exceeding one month's rent

If the cost of repairs exceed one month's rent, the tenant, while continuing to occupy and pay rent, may make the necessary repairs and file an action against the landlord to recover the cost of the repairs.

However, it may be impossible for the tenant to make the necessary repairs when the tenant:

- rents a unit in a large complex; or

- is unable to cover the cost of repairs.

If the nonresidential tenant is unable or does not want to cover the cost of repairs that the landlord failed to make, the tenant can **vacate the premises** and is relieved of any further obligation under the lease called a *constructive eviction* [CC §1942(a); see Chapter 29]

Maintaining property with care

Just as a residential landlord has a duty to repair and maintain the leased premises, a **nonresidential landlord** who retains responsibility for maintenance and repair under the lease agreement also has a duty to use care in doing so.

Consider a tenant, residential or nonresidential, who notifies his landlord a window is broken and will not stay open. The landlord begins work to repair the window, but does not complete the work. The tenant gives the landlord permission to enter the premises when the tenant is out to finish the repairs, which the landlord does not do.

Finally, the window falls, injuring the tenant.

Here, the landlord is responsible for the injuries. Once a landlord of residential or nonresidential premises undertakes to make repairs on the premises to correct a dangerous condition, the landlord must complete the repairs in a timely and proper manner. [**Minoletti** v. **Sabini** (1972) 27 CA3d 321]

Landlords of both residential and nonresidential property are also responsible to tenants, guests of tenants and members of the public for injuries caused to them by the landlord's lack of ordinary care or skill in the maintenance of his property. [CC §1714]

Nondelegable duty to repair

Now consider a nonresidential landlord who hires a contractor to repair the roof on leased property. A tenant is injured as a result of the contractor's negligence while performing the repair.

The tenant claims the landlord is liable for his injuries since the landlord is responsible for maintaining the property, and the maintenance undertaken created a dangerous condition which injured the tenant.

The landlord claims he is not liable since it was the roofing contractor's negligence while on the job which caused the tenant's injury, not the landlord.

Is the landlord liable for injuries to a tenant caused by a contractor hired by the landlord to perform repairs?

Yes! A landlord's duty to exercise care (not to be negligent) in the repair and maintenance of a leased premises is a *nondelegable duty* — it cannot be transferred or assumed by another person, such as a property manager or contractor. [**Srithong** v. **Total Investment Company** (1994) 23 CA4th 721]

Thus, the landlord is liable for injuries caused to persons (excluding the contractor's employees) during the fulfillment of the landlord's duty to maintain the property, whether the maintenance is accomplished by the landlord or by contractors he or his property manager employs.

Penalty for failure to maintain

A landlord is aware of felony crimes recently occurring in the common areas of his apartment complex and parking garage.

The tenants of the complex complain to the landlord about the crimes. The tenants request the broken doors, gates and locks be repaired and adequate lighting be provided as security to prevent the crimes from reoccurring.

The landlord fails to make the repairs or provide the security measures requested. Later, while in a common area, a tenant is assaulted and suffers injuries.

The tenant seeks to recover losses from the landlord for his injuries, as well as *punitive damages*. The injured tenant claims the landlord breached his duty to protect him from known criminal activity in the complex by **failing to maintain** and provide adequate security measures in the common areas. Further, the tenant claims the landlord is liable for breaching the warranty of habitability.

First, can the tenant recover punitive damages from the landlord?

Yes! The landlord was aware of the dangerous condition created by the lack of maintenance. By failing to correct the deferred maintenance, the landlord conducted himself with a conscious disregard for the rights or safety of his tenants. The landlord's deliberate **failure to maintain** the premises by eliminating the dangerous conditions which were known to him and over which he alone had the power to correct, exposes him to liability for punitive damages. [**Penner** v. **Falk** (1984) 153 CA3d 858]

Also, a landlord is liable for punitive damages for **failure to disclose** a dangerous condition to tenants about which he has actual knowledge. [**O'Hara** v. **Western Seven Trees Corporation Intercoast Management** (1977) 75 CA3d 798]

However, the landlord is not liable for breaching the warranty of habitability. The living quarters were habitable, and the housing complied with local codes.

Thus, the defense of uninhabitable premises for failure to pay rent based on a lack of security will fail and the nonpaying tenant will be evicted. [Penner, *supra*]

Chapter 37

Implied warranty of habitability

This chapter examines the purpose of the implied warranty of habitability and its effect on residential landlords.

Minimum quality low-income housing

A landlord, aware an apartment complex he owns is in a state of disrepair, does nothing to correct the defective conditions on the property. Due to the location of the property and its below market rents, the landlord is able to rent out units in the complex without repairing any of the defective conditions.

A tenant, fully aware of the unsafe and unsanitary conditions, enters into a lease agreement with the landlord. Soon after occupying, the tenant asks the landlord to exterminate the rodents and cockroaches in his unit. The tenant also requests that plumbing blockages, exposed electrical wiring and the collapsing bathroom ceiling in the unit be repaired.

The landlord does not correct or repair any of the defective conditions. In retaliation, the tenant stops paying rent but continues to occupy the unit.

The landlord serves a 3-day notice for nonpayment of rent and declares a forfeiture of the tenant's right to possession. The notice expires without payment and the landlord files an unlawful detainer (UD) action to evict the tenant.

The tenant defends his right to occupy, claiming the landlord failed to maintain the premises in a habitable condition, permitting the tenant to:

- retain possession; and

- pay a reduced rent set by the court.

Even though he failed to make repairs, the landlord claims the tenant must pay the agreed amount of rent since the tenant must either:

- quit the premises; or

- make the repairs himself and deduct the cost of the repairs from his rent as authorized by law.

Can the tenant continue to occupy the premises and pay a reduced court-ordered rent to the landlord?

Yes! The landlord's failure to maintain the premises in a habitable condition constitutes a breach of the *implied warranty of habitability* which all residential rental and lease agreements are subject to regardless of the provisions in the lease agreement. Not so for nonresidential properties.

Also, the **court-ordered reduced rent** will remain for as long as the landlord fails to make the necessary corrections or repairs. [**Green** v. **Superior Court of the City and County of San Francisco** (1974) 10 C3d 616]

Editor's note — Nonresidential leases do not contain an implied warranty of habitability. [See Chapter 33]

However, if the nonresidential landlord fails to make the significant repairs he is obligated to make under the lease agreement, the nonresidential tenant has two options:

- *pay for the repairs himself, demand reimbursement from the landlord, and if unpaid, file an action against the landlord to recover the cost of the repairs; or*

- *vacate the premises and file an action against the landlord for losses resulting from a constructive eviction.*

Implied warranty of habitability

The typical residential tenant under a lease agreement acquires a leasehold interest in the leased property to occupy it for a specific period of time. The tenant expects the premises and appurtenances (e.g., common areas, parking and storage) available to him to be fit for the purpose leased — to be a sanitary place in which he may safely reside.

However, a residential tenant, especially an apartment dweller, is not just acquiring an interest in real estate, he is *contracting* for, and is entitled to, a **safe and sanitary** place to live, called a *habitable dwelling*. [See **first tuesday** Form 550 §6.2]

The implied warranty requires the residential landlord to care for the premises by maintaining habitable conditions — the minimum level of living conditions for a safe and sanitary dwelling unit permitted by law. [**Hinson** v. **Delis** (1972) 26 CA3d 62; Calif. Code of Civil Procedure §1174.2]

Residential property which is not in a habitable condition cannot be rented or leased "as-is," even though defective property conditions have been fully disclosed and the substandard conditions consented to by the tenant.

The implied warranty applies to the space rented by the tenant as housing and also to common areas the tenant may use, such as laundry facilities, parking, recreational areas and storage spaces, called *appurtenances*. [Hinson, *supra*]

The public policy establishing the warranty of habitability was legislated due to landlords overreaching due to the scarcity of available low-cost housing. This economic situation left residential tenants in lesser socioeconomic neighborhoods without the bargaining power possessed by more affluent and mobile tenants when negotiating with landlords for better property conditions.

Thus, market forces cannot prevail over the higher public policy requiring safe and sanitary housing. The warranty of habitability serves to punish slumlords and discourage slum-like conditions in low-income housing.

A landlord who invests money in real estate must maintain his property. Otherwise, the value of his investment will eventually disintegrate due to competitive pressures in the rental market and court orders.

Landlord's warranty

The landlord breaches the implied warranty of habitability when the landlord fails to comply with building and housing code standards that *materially affect* health and safety. [CCP §1174.2(c)]

A habitable place to live is a dwelling free of **major defects**, not mere inconveniences, which would interfere with the tenant's ability to use the premises as a residence.

A residential dwelling is **uninhabitable** if any features of the dwelling are not properly maintained or do not **substantially comply** with building and housing codes, including:

- effective waterproofing and weather protection of roof and exterior walls, including unbroken windows and doors;

- plumbing and gas facilities;

- a hot and cold running water system with appropriate fixtures which are connected to a sewage disposal system;

- heating facilities;

- electrical lighting; and

- floors, stairways and railings. [Calif. Civil Code §1941.1]

In applying these guidelines, a leaky faucet would not render a residential unit uninhabitable, despite the inconvenience. However, a lack of running water, or no hot water, is a significant defect that materially interferes with the tenant's ability to live on the property.

At the time the rental or lease agreement is entered into, the building grounds and appurtenances, such as a pool, laundry facilities, storage areas and parking structures, must be clean, sanitary and free from all accumulations of debris, filth, rodents and vermin to meet habitability guidelines. [CC §1941.1(f)]

Further, the landlord must provide an adequate number of garbage and rubbish receptacles in clean condition and good repair. [CC §1941.1(g)]

A residential tenant in an apartment complex is not typically expected to make repairs to major components of the complex, such as a central heating system, an electrical or plumbing system or the roof.

If a residential landlord fails to make necessary repairs, and the cost of the repair is less than one month's rent, the tenant may order out and pay for the needed repairs and deduct the cost from the rent, called the *repair and deduct remedy*. [CC §1942; see Chapter 36]

However, the **repair-and-deduct remedy** is not often feasible in apartment dwellings since areas where repairs must be made are in the possession and control of the landlord.

Thus, the residential tenant must resort to other remedies, such as:

- vacating the premises, called a *constructive eviction* [See Chapter 33];

- stop paying rent and, in any ensuing UD action, prove the landlord breached the implied warranty of habitability; or

- raise and prove the defense of retaliatory eviction.

Pre-leasing maintenance program

Before renting a residential unit in a building intended for human habitation, the landlord, in addition to maintaining habitability, must:

- install and maintain an operable **dead bolt lock** on each main entry door of a unit, unless the door is a horizontal sliding door;

- install and maintain operable **security or locking devices** for windows which are designed to be opened, unless the window is a louvered window, casement window, or more than 12 feet vertically or six feet horizontally from the ground, roof or other platform; and

- install **locking mechanisms** on the exterior doors leading to common areas with access to dwelling units in an apartment complex — installation of a door or gate is not required if none existed on January 1, 1998. [CC §1941.3(a)]

A tenant is responsible for promptly notifying the landlord of an inoperable dead bolt lock, window security or locking device in the unit. The landlord will only be liable for injuries caused by his failure to correct the defect within a reasonable period of time after being notified or becoming aware of the defect. [CC §1941.3(b)]

A residential landlord failing to comply with required security measures entitles the tenant to:

- repair and deduct the cost from rent;

- vacate the premises;

- recover money losses incurred due to the condition of an uninhabitable building;

- recover losses caused by any landlord retaliation;

- file an action for breach of contract; or

- seek injunctive relief to stop the landlord from keeping an uninhabitable building. [CC §1941.3(c)]

Warranty of habitability defense

In a UD action, a tenant who successfully raises the *habitability defense* on the landlord's breach of the implied warranty of habitability by the landlord will be allowed:

- to **retain possession** of the premises;

- to **pay a reduced amount** of rent based on the uninhabitable condition of the property; and

- to **recover attorney fees** and costs of litigation. [CCP §1174.2(a)(1)]

To retain possession, the tenant must pay the rent awarded to the landlord, offset by the tenant's attorney fees, within:

- five days of the entry of judgment; or

- ten days, if the UD judgment is served on the tenant by mail. [CCP §1174.2(a)]

If the tenant fails to pay the rental amounts set by the court in a timely manner, the landlord is awarded possession of the premises. [CCP §1174.2(b)]

The landlord may or may not be ordered in the UD judgment to make all repairs necessary to return the premises to a safe and sanitary condition. When a landlord is **ordered to correct** the uninhabitable conditions by returning the premises to a safe and sanitary condition:

- the tenant remaining in possession must pay the reasonable monthly rental value of the premises in its uninhabitable condition until the repairs are completed; and

- the court retains control to oversee compliance by the landlord. [CCP §1174.2(a)]

The tenant who raises the habitability defense instead of paying the rent **takes the risk** of be-

ing evicted. The landlord's failure to make repairs may not rise to the level of a *substantial breach* of the warranty of habitability if the repairs are minor and are judged to create only an inconvenience or annoyance to the tenant.

If the landlord has not substantially breached the warranty of habitability:

- the landlord is awarded the right to possession; and

- the tenant is liable for rent accrued through the date of judgment. [CCP §1174.2(b)]

Further, the prevailing party in a UD action is entitled to his **attorney fees**, even if the rental or lease agreement does not contain an attorney fees provision. Whomever is awarded possession of the premises is the prevailing party. [CCP §1174.2(a), (b)]

Determining reasonable rental value

To calculate the **reasonable rental value** of the premises when a breach of the implied warranty of habitability exists, the court will:

- establish the percentage attributable to the tenant's diminished habitability or use of the premises due to the substandard living conditions; and

- use the percentage to reduce the agreed-to monthly rental payment. [**Cazares** v. **Ortiz** (1980) 109 CA3d Supp. 23]

When determining the percentage of habitability or useability lost caused by the landlord's failure to maintain, the criteria includes:

- the *area* of the rental unit affected;

- the *duration* of the tenant's exposure to the defect;

- the *degree of discomfort* the defect imposes on the tenant;

- whether the defect is *health-threatening* or intermittently annoying; and

- the extent to which the defect caused the tenant to find the premises *uninhabitable*. [Cazares, *supra*]

If the agreed-to monthly rent is already below market rent due to the condition of the premises, the landlord who has breached the warranty of habitability may receive only a minimal amount of rent from the tenant. The court-ordered rent properly may be so minimal as to result in a financial penalty to the landlord.

Editor's note — While this penalizing rental amount actually may be unfair to the landlord until he repairs the premises, the courts are unsympathetic. [Cazares, dicta]

The purpose of the warranty of habitability is to prevent illegal, substandard housing from having any market rental value and to encourage landlords to maintain their premises in a condition where market rents can be charged and actually enforced in a UD action.

Landlord's breach on full disclosure

The mere existence of unsafe and unsanitary conditions, whether or not they are known to the tenant, establishes the landlord's breach of the implied warranty of habitability.

Consider a prospective tenant who contacts a property manager to rent a unit in an older apartment building. The tenant inspects the unit and notices wall cracks and broken windows.

Considering the condition of the unit and the tenant's financial condition, the tenant offers to rent the premises in exchange for a reduced rent. The landlord agrees, and the property manager rents the unit.

The tenant takes possession. Soon afterwards, the tenant notifies the property manager of an inoperable heating system, electrical fixtures with exposed wiring, no hot water, and that the unit is infested with rodents and cockroaches.

The property manager advises the landlord of the need for repairs and pest control. The landlord does not give the property manager the necessary authority to correct the defective conditions in the unit.

The tenant remains in possession but refuses to pay any rent, claiming his unit has substandard living conditions making the unit uninhabitable. The tenant is served with a 3-day notice to pay or quit. The tenant still does not pay, and a UD action is filed.

The tenant claims he is not obligated to pay rent since the landlord breached the implied warranty of habitability by failing to maintain his apartment unit in habitable condition.

The landlord claims the tenant is barred from claiming a breach of the warranty of habitability by the landlord since the tenant was fully aware of the extent of the defective conditions at the time he took possession.

Here, the landlord is not relieved of his duty under the implied warranty of habitability even though the tenant was **fully aware** of unsafe and unsanitary conditions when he took possession. The state of the premises constitutes a breach of the implied warranty of habitability, not the state of the disclosures about the existence of defective uninhabitable. [**Knight v. Hallsthammer** (1981) 29 C3d 46]

Unlike the sale of property, when a landlord fails to care for and maintain his residential property in a habitable condition, he cannot rent the property "as-is" and escape liability for having fully informed the tenant about the conditions.

Landlord has no time to respond

The warranty of habitability does not entitle a residential landlord to a reasonable period of time after a tenant takes possession in which he may repair unsafe and unsanitary living conditions before the tenant takes other action, such as withholding rent.

The landlord should not allow a tenant to take possession until the premises is fully repaired.

The **warranty of habitability** is breached when the need for repairs is:

- **known** by the landlord, either through notice from the tenant or by the physical state of the property at the time it is rented; and

- the landlord fails to **immediately correct** the defective conditions.

Landlords have a duty to inspect and maintain their property and improve or correct known substandard conditions before renting it. The "no notice" and "no reasonable time to repair" rules imposed on landlords by the warranty of habitability are based on the notion that landlords are or should be aware of the condition of the physical components of the premises at the time the unit is rented. [CC §1714]

Now consider a tenant who rents a single family residence that is in a safe and sanitary condition when he takes possession. The condition of the premises is documented at the time possession is transferred.

During the tenant's occupancy, the toilet begins to leak and the linoleum floor does not repel the water. On noticing the leak, the tenant has a duty to notify the landlord and give him a reasonable amount of time to make the repairs before taking other action. [CC §1942]

However, the tenant **fails to notify** the landlord of the need for repairs. The bathroom floor rots due to the toilet leak, weakening the subfloor and eventually creating a hole. When the rent is due the tenant notifies the landlord of the unsafe and unsanitary bathroom conditions, but does not pay the rent.

Due to his refusal to pay rent, the tenant is promptly served with a 3-day notice to pay rent or quit. The landlord begins repairs on the unit.

The 3-day notice expires and a UD action is filed and served on the tenant. The landlord completes the repairs prior to the UD hearing.

At the UD hearing, the tenant claims the landlord breached the implied warranty of habitability, allowing the tenant to pay only a reduced rent to be set by the court since the rental was in an unsafe and unsanitary condition.

The landlord claims the warranty of habitability has not been breached since he did not have notice of the need for repairs until the tenant complained and refused to pay rent.

Has the landlord breached the implied warranty of habitability?

No! The tenant brought about the unsafe and unsanitary condition by failing to **promptly notify** the landlord of the need for repairs. [CC §1942]

New landlord steps into the breach

Consider a landlord of an apartment building whose tenants notify him of seriously **unsafe living conditions** in the units.

The owner is financially incapable of paying for the repairs needed and sells the complex. The new landlord inspects the building and is aware of defective and substandard conditions in the units. The new landlord proceeds to correct the conditions by renovating the building.

The new landlord notifies the tenants of the complex's change in ownership and an increase in their monthly rent to amortize his costs of renovation.

A tenants' association is organized. The tenants refuse to pay rent due to the ongoing state of disrepair in the units. The landlord serves 3-day notices on the tenants who fail to pay the agreed rent. Unlawful detainer actions are filed, and the tenants raise the breach of the implied warranty of habitability as a defense to avoid eviction and reduce rents.

The landlord claims he is not breaching the warranty of habitability since the previous owner breached the warranty of habitability, not him.

The tenants claim the change in ownership did not terminate their right to raise the warranty of habitability defense since the breach was a condition of the property that continued after the new landlord took possession, whether or not he knew of the breach or is renovating the property to eliminate the adverse conditions.

Can the tenants raise the **warranty of habitability** defense against a new owner who did not cause the existing unsafe conditions?

Yes! The tenants have a valid implied warranty of habitability defense that justifies their failure to pay rent since:

- the premises were uninhabitable during the new landlord's ownership; and

- the new landlord is attempting to evict the tenants for rental amounts due under his ownership. [Knight, *supra*]

Even though the landlord did not cause the premises to become uninhabitable and began rehabilitating the property when he purchased it, the tenants can still refuse to pay the agreed-to rent and avoid eviction.

Duty to avoid foreseeable injury

A tenant can recover more than a rent adjustment when the landlord breaches the implied warranty of habitability.

For example, a tenant inspects a rental unit and enters into a month-to-month rental agreement with the landlord. When he takes occupancy of the unit, the tenant discovers faulty electrical wiring, a clogged kitchen sink and a leak in the roof, later damaging the tenant's personal property.

The tenant notifies the landlord (and the county health department) of the **defective property conditions** and asks the landlord to make the necessary repairs.

The landlord fails to make any repairs. The tenant continues to reside on the premises. Eventually, the county health department issues a notice condemning the building as unfit for occupancy. The tenant relocates.

The tenant then makes a demand on the landlord for water damage to his personal property and the cost of relocating to a new residence since the landlord breached his duty of care to repair the defective conditions.

Here, the landlord owes a *duty of care* to the tenant, apart from the warranty the premises be up to minimum standards of habitability, to properly maintain the premises to avoid the risk of a foreseeable financial loss suffered by the tenant and caused by the landlord's failure to maintain the property.

Thus, the landlord is liable for the costs incurred by the tenant to replace damaged personal property and relocate. The costs the tenant incurred were a result of the landlord's breach of his duty of care by failing to make the necessary repairs to eliminate unsafe and uninhabitable conditions. [**Stoiber** v. **Honeychuck** (1980) 101 CA3d 903]

Additionally, the tenant can recover excessive rent paid for periods of his occupancy when the unit was uninhabitable.

Even if a residential tenant fails to raise the warranty of habitability defense in a UD action and is evicted or otherwise vacates, the tenant can later recover any excessive rent paid during the period the landlord failed to maintain the unit in a habitable condition. [**Landeros** v. **Pankey** (1995) 39 CA4th 1167]

Conditions creating a nuisance

Now consider a tenant of an apartment unit forced to relocate due to unsafe flooring and unsanitary conditions, causing the local health department to issue an order condemning the apartment complex.

The tenant makes a demand on the landlord to pay his **relocation expenses**, claiming the defective conditions in the rental unit constitute a *nuisance* since he is deprived of the safe and healthy use and enjoyment of the leased unit.

The tenant also seeks the recovery of *punitive damages* from the landlord. The tenant claims the landlord's failure to correct the defective conditions that created the nuisance was intentional and malicious.

The landlord claims the tenant cannot recover losses based on a nuisance, much less receive a punitive award for money, since his interference with the tenant's use and enjoyment of the unit is a breach of the contractual warranty of habitability implied in the lease agreement, not the tortious creation of a health nuisance.

Besides breaching the habitability warranty, the landlord has, by the same conduct, also created a **nuisance for the tenant**. The landlord's failure to make repairs and properly maintain the rental unit *substantially interfered* with the tenant's continuing **use and enjoyment** of the unit. [Stoiber, *supra*]

A **nuisance** is any condition that:

- is injurious to health;

- obstructs the free use of property; or

- interferes with the comfortable enjoyment of property. [CC §3479]

Further, the landlord's continued failure to maintain and repair the premises in a safe condition during the health department's investigation and condemnation action indicates the landlord **intentionally maintained** a nuisance on the premises — an ongoing disregard for the safety and health of the tenant.

Besides recovering his out-of-pocket losses to relocate, the tenant is entitled to an award for an additional sum of money, called *punitive damages*, since the landlord maintained a nuisance due to his intentional failure to repair. [Stoiber, *supra*]

Further, the landlord's liability to the tenant for creating a nuisance is additional to any refunds of rent and rent reduction for breaching the warranty of habitability in the rental agreement.

The tenant can also recover from the landlord any medical expenses and personal injury due to an intentional infliction of **mental distress** if the landlord's failure to maintain the unit in a habitable condition is the result of the landlord's extreme and outrageous conduct. [Stoiber, *supra*]

Chapter 38

Fire safety programs

This chapter discusses fire safety requirements for landlords, including smoke detectors, posting fire safety information and security bars.

Smoke detectors, security bars and safety information

A residential apartment building contains state-approved smoke detectors in each individual unit and in the common areas.

A tenant informs the landlord the smoke detector in his unit does not operate, even with new batteries. The landlord and his manager do not repair or replace the broken smoke detector. Later, a fire breaks out in the tenant's unit.

The tenant is injured in the fire and his property is damaged due to the defective smoke detector. The tenant claims the landlord is liable for his losses since the landlord has a duty to repair or replace the defective smoke detector on notice from the tenant.

Is the landlord liable for property damage and personal injuries caused by the defective smoke detector?

Yes! On receiving notice that the **smoke detector** is inoperable, the landlord is required to **promptly repair** or replace it. [Calif. Health and Safety Code §13113.7(e)]

Further, a landlord will be subject to a $200 fine for each failure to:

- install a smoke detector in each unit and in common areas as required; and

- repair or replace a faulty smoke detector on notice from the tenant. [Health & S C §13113.7(f)]

Tenant's duty to notify

Smoke detectors must be installed and maintained in all dwelling units intended for human occupancy, including single-family residences, duplexes, apartment complexes, hotels, motels, condominiums and time share projects. [Health & S C §§13113.7(b), 13113.8]

The smoke detector must be in operable condition at the time the tenant takes possession of the unit. [Health & S C §13113.7(e)]

If a smoke detector does not work when tested by the tenant, the **tenant is responsible** for notifying the landlord or property manager. The landlord is not obligated to investigate whether detectors are operable during the tenant's occupancy.

If the tenant does not notify the landlord about an inoperable smoke detector and the landlord is unaware of the condition, the landlord is not responsible for injuries caused by the faulty smoke detector. [Health & S C §13113.7(e)]

To repair or replace a faulty smoke detector, the landlord may enter the unit 24 hours after serving a written notice on the tenant of his intent to enter, unless the tenant gives permission for an earlier entry. [Health & S C §13113.7(e); see **first tuesday** Form 567; see Chapter 4]

Duty to install and maintain

An ordinary battery-operated smoke detector installed according to the manufacturer's instructions satisfies the requirement for both single-and multiple-unit dwellings, unless another type is required by local ordinances. [Health & S C §13113.7(a)]

For example, some local ordinances require the smoke detector to receive its power from the building's electrical system.

To determine the smoke detector requirements for a property, the landlord can contact the **local fire department** or the county fire planning department.

In apartment units and other multiple-unit dwellings, such as condominiums, smoke detectors must also be installed in the common stairwells. The apartment landlord and his property manager are responsible for **installing and maintaining** smoke detectors in both the common stairwells and the individual units. [Health & S C §13113.7(c)]

Posting fire safety information

The landlord of an apartment building must provide emergency fire safety information to all tenants if the building consists of:

- two or more stories;

- three or more units; and

- a front door that opens into an interior hallway or lobby area. [Health & S C §13220(c)]

The information must be on signs using **international symbols**. The signs must be located:

- at every stairway and elevator landing;

- at the intermediate point of any hallway exceeding 100 feet in length and all hallway intersections; and

- immediately inside all public entrances. [Health & S C §13220(c)(1)]

Further, the landlord must provide fire information to all tenants through brochures, pamphlets or videotapes, if available, or conform to adopted State Fire Marshal regulations. [Health & S C §13220(c)(2)]

If the landlord negotiates the rental or lease agreement in a language other than English, the required information provided to the tenant must be in English, international symbols and the four most common foreign languages in California. [Health & S C §13220(c)(3)]

Editor's note — A consumer-oriented brochure in English, international symbols and the four most common foreign languages is available from the State Fire Marshal. [Health & S C §13220(d)]

The State Fire Marshal has adopted California Code of Regulations Title 19 §3.09 concerning the dissemination of fire information to tenants in hotels, motels, office buildings and high-rises. Health and Safety Code §13220 addresses these issues for tenants in apartment complexes. However, information does not exist as to which four languages will be used to translate fire information.

Further, if the landlord has any questions about the enforcement or the requirements for posting and informing tenants of fire information, he should contact his local fire department or the county fire planning department. The codes and regulations are enforced on a local level, and each county or city may have different requirements for complying with the fire information regulations.

Emergency procedures for office buildings

Emergency procedures and information for office buildings of two or more stories must be provided to the building's occupants. [Health & S C §13220(a)]

The **emergency procedures information** for an office building of two or more stories may be published in the form of **literature** (pamphlets, etc.), and must be available to all persons entering the building as well as located immediately inside all entrances to the building. [19 California Code of Regulations §3.09(a)(1)]

In lieu of literature, a **floor plan** describing emergency procedures must be posted at every stairway landing, elevator landing, and immediately inside all public entrances. [19 CCR §3.09(a)(2)]

For **high-rise structures**, fire safety requirements include:

- posting emergency procedures on a floor plan at every stairway landing, elevator landing, and immediately, inside all public entrances; and

- appointing a Fire Safety Director to coordinate fire safety activities, train employees in the building, develop an emergency plan, etc. (which is also required of operators of hotels, motels and lodging houses). [19 CCR §3.09(c), (d)]

A high-rise structure is a building rising more than 75 feet above the lowest floor level providing access to the building. [Health & S C §13210(b)]

Release mechanism in security bars

Security bars on residential property must have release mechanisms for fire safety reasons. The release mechanisms are not required if each bedroom with security bars contains a window or door to the exterior which opens for escape purposes. [Health & S C §13113.9]

Also, the owner of an apartment house must **install exit signs** that can be felt or seen near the floor of the exit. [Health & S C §17920.8]

Editor's note — Any questions concerning fire safety requirements or whether an owner has properly complied with the requirements should be directed to the local fire department or the county fire planning department. Some departments provide checklists of requirements that must be met.

Chapter 39

Security to prevent crimes

This chapter focuses on the responsibility of the landlord to reduce the risk of crime through prevention when he has knowledge of criminal activity on the leased premises.

Security measures and warnings

A landlord of an apartment complex is aware of recent assaults on tenants in the common areas of the property. The landlord has also received a composite drawing of the criminal and a description of the criminal's mode of operation released by the local police.

The landlord does not undertake any of the security steps available to reduce the risk of a recurrence of the same or similar criminal activities.

The landlord later rents a unit to a prospective tenant. The landlord does not disclose the recent criminal assaults or the criminal's mode of operation. The tenant is not given a copy of the composite drawing of the perpetrator developed by the police. Further, the landlord represents the complex as safe and patrolled by security.

Later, the tenant is assaulted by the same perpetrator inside the tenant's apartment unit, not in the areas open to the public. The tenant seeks to recover his money losses caused by the assault from the landlord. The tenant claims the landlord failed to disclose the prior assaults and misrepresented the safety of the apartment complex to induce the tenant to rent and occupy the unit.

The landlord claims he is not liable for the tenant's injuries since the assault occurred within the tenant's apartment unit and not in the common areas where the prior attacks occurred.

Here, the landlord is liable for injuries suffered by the tenant inside the apartment unit. The **landlord knew** of criminal activity on the premises and thus **owed a duty** to care for and protect the tenant by either:

- providing security measures in the common areas; or

- warning the tenant of the prior assaults. [**O'Hara** v. **Western Seven Trees Corporation Intercoast Management** (1977) 75 CA3d 798]

Based on the prior occurrences of criminal incidents, the likelihood of similar future assaults on tenants is *reasonably foreseeable*. When criminal activity is **reasonably foreseeable** due to known prior criminal activity, the landlord has a duty to take reasonable measures **to prevent harm** to persons on the property from future similar criminal activities.

The landlord's conduct — failure to warn the new tenant about **known criminal activity** or provide adequate security — creates a risk that a tenant may be injured. Due to the landlord's further failure to put security measures in place to prevent harm, the landlord must compensate the injured person by the payment of money, called *damages*.

Alternatively, the landlord could be liable for the tenant's losses based on his intentional misrepresentation to the tenant regarding the safety of the apartment complex.

Editor's note — Like a landlord, a homeowners' association (HOA) has a duty to maintain the common areas since it has exclusive control over the maintenance of the common areas.

A HOA will be liable for money losses due to any injury caused by a dangerous condition created or allowed to exist by the association when it or its agents knew or should have known of the dangerous condition and the injury suffered was reasonably foreseeable. [Frances T. v. Village Green Owners Association (1986) 42 C3d 490]

Degree of foreseeability of harm

Consider a landlord of a shopping center who has exclusive control over the maintenance and repair of the common areas. Burglaries and purse snatchings have recently occurred on the premises. However, the landlord is unaware of this criminal activity in the shopping center.

At tenant association meetings, concerns about the lack of security in the center are addressed. The tenant association decides not to hire security guards on account of the expense. The tenants do not discuss or bring their security concerns to the attention of the landlord.

Later, a tenant's employee is physically assaulted and injured on the leased premises. The employee claims the landlord is liable for his injuries since the landlord failed to provide security guards to protect employees of tenants from an unreasonable risk of harm.

The landlord claims he is not liable since the assault on the tenant's employee was a type of crime that was unforeseeable.

Here, the landlord has no duty to provide security guards in the common areas. The prior crimes (theft) were not of a similar nature that would have made a physical assault foreseeable. [**Ann M.** v. **Pacific Plaza Shopping Center** (1993) 6 C4th 666]

The landlord's duty to provide protection is determined in part by balancing the foreseeability of harm against the **burden imposed** on the landlord to remove or prevent the harm. A high degree of foreseeability is necessary to impose a duty on a landlord or HOA to hire security guards.

Unless prior incidents of **similar crimes** are brought to the landlord's attention, the high degree of foreseeability required to impose a duty on the landlord to take steps to prevent or eliminate future injury does not exist.

However, **prior similar incidents** are not always required to find that a landlord has a duty to take measures to prevent future criminal activity. The *foreseeability of an injury* is determined by the circumstances surrounding the injury and its occurrence, such as the nature, condition and location of the premises, and any prior incidents of similar or related activity in and around the premises. [Ann M., *supra*]

For example, consider a landlord of an office building and parking structure located in a neighborhood known to be a high-crime area. Many petty thefts and acts of vandalism have occurred on the premises, but no assaults have taken place. The security system maintained by the landlord to monitor the parking structure is in disrepair and does not function.

A visitor returning to his car enters the parking structure while an armed robbery is taking place. The visitor is shot and killed.

The visitor's spouse seeks to recover money losses from the landlord, claiming the death of the spouse was reasonably foreseeable and could have been prevented by the landlord. The spouse also claims the landlord, who was aware of criminal activity on the premises, breached his duty to take measures to prevent further criminal activity.

The landlord claims the injury was not reasonably foreseeable since the prior criminal acts were not similar to the act causing the visitor's death.

Is the landlord liable for failing to provide adequate security in the parking structure?

Yes! The landlord's failure to properly maintain existing security features in light of prior criminal activity and the nature of a public parking structure is a breach of the duty of care the landlord owes to persons who enter the structure. Although the foreseeability of the type of criminal activity causing the death is low, the landlord is liable since the burden on him to maintain the existing security system is minimal.

Not only was the landlord aware of vandalism and thefts regularly occurring in the parking structure, the landlord knew the parking structure was located in a high-crime area. Further, parking structures by their dark and private nature tend to invite criminal activity. Thus, death resulting from a visitor's accidental disruption of an armed robbery is reasonably foreseeable, even though no other armed assaults had previously occurred on the premises. [**Gomez** v. **Ticor** (1983) 145 CA3d 622]

No liability if not foreseeable

The extent of the security measures a landlord is required to provide is dictated by the degree of foreseeability of any future harm to others. [Ann M., *supra*]

If an injury is not foreseeable since the **nature, condition and location** of the leased premises do not indicate a person entering or using the property is at risk, a landlord is not liable if an injury, which security measures may have prevented, occurs on the premises.

Consider an apartment complex where previous criminal activity has not occurred. However, the community where the complex is located is generally known as a high-crime area.

The light bulb installed at the entrance to a tenant's apartment burns out. The tenant asks the landlord to replace the light bulb. The lighting in the common area is functional.

Before the landlord replaces the bulb, the tenant is assaulted in his unit, suffering injuries. The tenant claims the landlord is liable for his injuries since the landlord has a duty to provide adequate lighting as a security measure.

The landlord claims he is not liable since the light bulb outside the tenant's unit is for the tenant's convenience, and is not intended as a security measure to protect tenants.

Here, the landlord is not liable. Prior criminal activity had not occurred on the premises that would put the landlord on notice of foreseeable risks. Thus, the landlord has no duty to take security precautions against criminal activity. Further, **lighting alone** is not considered an adequate security measure for deterring crime. [**7735 Hollywood Boulevard Venture** v. **Superior Court** (1981) 116 CA3d 901]

On-site, not off-site prevention

Tenants occupying an apartment complex have been victimized by numerous assaults and robberies in the garage area and courtyard. The landlord is aware of the criminal activity **on the premises**. In response to tenants' complaints, he promises to install additional lighting.

A tenant parks on the street instead of in the garage due to the inadequate lighting in the common areas. One night, while parking on the street, the tenant is attacked and injured. The tenant claims the landlord is liable for his injuries since the landlord's failure to provide adequate on-site lighting created a dangerous condition, forcing him to park on the street.

Is the landlord liable for the tenant's injuries that occurred on a public street?

No! The landlord does not have a duty to protect a tenant from criminal acts committed by others that injure the tenant when he is not on the leased premises. [**Rosenbaum** v. **Security Bank Corporation** (1996) 43 CA4th 1084]

While the landlord's conduct may have caused the tenant to park in the street, the tenant's decision to park on the public street imposes no duty on the landlord to also eliminate dangerous off-premises conditions. A landlord's **duty** of care is to prevent harm to others in the maintenance and management of the leased premises, not adjoining properties. [Calif. Civil Code §1714]

Prevent dangers within your control

The landlord's duty of care is derived from his *ability to prevent* the existence of dangerous conditions from existing on the **property he controls**, not adjacent properties or public right of ways over which he has not taken control. A duty of care toward tenants is owed by the landlord only when a **connection exists** between the harm suffered by the tenant and the landlord's care and maintenance of his property and any adjacent property over which he takes control.

The landlord's failure to remove or prevent the risk of injury caused by a dangerous condition over which the landlord has control must contribute to the injuries suffered by a tenant or visitor before liability for injuries will be imposed on the landlord.

While the landlord in *Rosenbaum* failed to exercise care in the maintenance and repair of his premises, the landlord **exercised no control** over the public street, nor did he create or permit the dangerous condition in the street which caused the tenant's injury.

The purpose for providing adequate lighting in the common areas of a leased premises is to help protect tenants or others against the risk of criminal attacks **on the leased premises**, not on a public street where the responsibility for lighting and security lies with government agencies. Thus, the lack of adequate lighting in the apartment complex was not the cause of the attack suffered by the tenant on the public street; it only caused the tenant to use the street. [Rosenbaum, *supra*]

Ability to control is not control

Now consider a landlord who is aware of criminal activity occurring on public property adjacent to the leased premises. A visitor leaves the leased premises at night via a public sidewalk adjacent to the premises. Lighting is not installed on the public side of the premises to illuminate the sidewalk.

While walking on the public sidewalk, the visitor is assaulted and injured. The visitor makes a demand on the landlord to recover money losses incurred due to his injuries. The client claims the landlord has a duty to protect patrons of tenants from criminal assaults on public sidewalks that provide access to the premises.

The visitor contends the landlord knew criminal activity had occurred on the sidewalk and **had the power** to exert control over the sidewalk by installing lights on the outside of the building — the sidewalk was the means of ingress and egress to the building.

Is the landlord liable for the client's injuries due to a dangerous condition on adjacent property?

No! The landlord does not owe a duty of care to anyone to take control over adjoining property and remove or prevent injury from dangerous conditions existing on the adjoining property. The landlord is not liable for failing to take steps to prevent possible injuries from occurring on a public sidewalk adjacent to the leased premises that are regularly used by tenants for access to their units. [**Donnell** v. **California Western School of Law** (1988) 200 CA3d 715]

The landlord's failure to provide lighting for a public sidewalk that the landlord **does not own or control** did not create the dangerous condition that caused the assault against the tenant's client. The fact the landlord can influence or alter the condition of the public sidewalk by voluntarily adding lighting in no way indicates he has control over the sidewalk, which would impose liability for failure to provide off-site security. [Donnell, *supra*]

Chapter 40

Dangerous on-site and off-site activities

This chapter presents the duty of care a landlord has to others, on or off the property, for dangerous on-site and off-site activities.

Duty to all to remove on-site dangers

A landlord, but his exercise of *reasonable care* in the management of his property, must prevent **foreseeable injury** to all others who may, for whatever reason, be on the leased premises. [**Rowland** v. **Christian** (1968) 69 C2d 108; Calif. Civil Code §1714]

If a person — a tenant, guest, invitee or trespasser — is injured due to the landlord's breach of his duty of care to remove or correct a known dangerous on-site condition, the landlord is liable for the person's money losses the injured person incurred due to the injury. [CC §1714]

The duty of care for others owed by the landlord **applies to all persons** on the property whether they enter the premises with or without permission or are mere social guests, unless the person is committing a felony on the property.

Conditions imposing responsibility

To **impose liability** on a landlord for an injury suffered by any person on the leased premises, several factors must be considered, including:

- the *foreseeability* of the type of injury suffered by the individual;

- the closeness of the *connection* between the landlord's conduct and the injury suffered;

- the *moral blame* attached to the landlord's conduct;

- the *public policy* of preventing future harm;

- the extent of the *burden* on the landlord and the *consequences* to the community of imposing a duty to exercise care to prevent the injury suffered; and

- the availability, cost, and prevalence of *insurance* for the risk involved. [Rowland, *supra*]

For example, the landlord with knowledge of a dangerous situation created by the presence of a tenant's dog is liable for injuries inflicted on others by the dog based on many of these factors. The landlord's failure to remove the dangerous condition from his property created by the dog is **closely connected** to injuries inflicted by the dog.

The landlord is sufficiently aware of the dangerous condition created by the presence of the dog to **reasonably foresee** the possibility of injury to others. Also, the landlord has the **ability to eliminate** or reduce the dangerous condition and prevent future harm by serving on the tenant a 3-day notice to remove the dog or vacate. [**Uccello** v. **Laudenslayer** (1975) 44 CA3d 504]

Landlord's duty to inspect

The landlord must use reasonable care in the repair and maintenance of the leased premises to **prevent harm** to others. To accomplish this level of safety through prevention of harm, the property must be inspected by the landlord whenever **entry is available** to the landlord.

Thus, each time a landlord enters into, renews or extends a rental or lease agreement, a *reasonable inspection* of the leased premises for dangerous conditions must be completed as part of his duty of care to prevent injury to others. If the landlord fails to inspect when the opportunity exists, the landlord will be **charged with knowledge** of any dangerous condition that he should have discovered had he undertaken an inspection.

Consider a landlord and tenant who enter into a nonresidential lease agreement.

The lease agreement allows the landlord to enter the premises for **yearly inspections**. Also, the tenant is required to obtain the landlord's approval before making any improvements.

With the landlord's consent, the tenant builds a roadside marketing structure and operates a retail produce business. The structure's concrete floor is improperly constructed and unfinished. Produce is often littered on the floor.

More than a year after construction, a customer slips and falls on produce littered on the floor, injuring himself. The customer claims the landlord is liable for his injuries since the landlord's right to inspect the property puts him on notice of the dangerous condition created by produce falling on the improperly constructed and unfinished concrete floor.

The landlord claims he is not liable for the customer's injuries since he had no actual notice of the dangerous condition created by the temporary deposit of produce on the floor.

However, the landlord is liable for the customer's injuries if the construction of the concrete floor:

- is a dangerous condition; or

- poses a dangerous condition when littered with produce from a permitted use. [**Lopez** v. **Superior Court** (1996) 45 CA4th 705]

A landlord is required to **conduct an inspection** of the leased premises for the purpose of making the premises safe from dangerous conditions when:

- a lease is executed, extended or renewed; and

- the landlord exercises any periodic right to re-enter or any other control over the property, such as an approval of construction. [**Mora** v. **Baker Commodities, Inc.** (1989) 210 CA3d 771]

Here, the landlord would have observed the condition of the floor had he conducted the yearly inspection of the premises called for in the lease agreement. Thus, the landlord is liable for *slip and fall* injuries when the condition of the floor is determined to be dangerous. [Lopez, *supra*]

A reasonable inspection

A landlord has a duty to inspect the leased premises when he **enters the premises** for any single purpose, such as maintenance, water damage or some other exigency causing him to make an emergency visit.

While a landlord may enter the premises during the lease term, he is not required to make a thorough inspection of the entire leased premises. However, the landlord who enters will be charged with the knowledge of a dangerous condition if the condition would have been observed by a reasonable person. [Mora, *supra*]

A landlord of a leased premises containing **areas open to the public** will be liable for injuries caused by a dangerous condition in the public area if the condition would be discovered during a landlord inspection.

However, if the landlord is not responsible under the lease agreement for repair and maintenance of **nonpublic areas**, the landlord will not be liable for failing to discover a dangerous condition occurring in nonpublic sections of a leased premises. The landlord is not required to expend extraordinary amounts of time and money constantly conducting extensive searches for possible dangerous conditions. [Mora, *supra*]

For example, a triple-net, management-free lease agreement usually transfers all responsibility for maintaining and repairing the property to the tenant.

Under a triple-net lease agreement, the landlord will not be liable for injuries to persons caused by a dangerous condition on the leased premises if:

- the dangerous condition came about after the tenant takes possession; and

- the landlord has no actual knowledge of the dangerous condition.

Editor's note — Landlords concerned about tenant maintenance of a leased premises will often reserve the right to enter the premises every six or 12 months. However, frequent inspections of a leased premises create a greater potential of liability for the landlord.

Landlords often reserve the right to conduct frequent inspections to assure that the tenant is not damaging or wasting the premises and reducing its market value. The right to enter brings with it the **obligation to inspect** for dangerous conditions. Also, the landlord may erroneously tend to overlook possible dangerous conditions he can control that are connected to the tenant's use, not maintenance, of the property.

Knowledge of dangerous conditions

Consider a landlord and tenant who enter into a residential rental agreement giving the tenant permission to keep a German Shepherd dog on the premises.

After the tenant takes possession of the property, the landlord never visits the premises and has never seen the dog.

Later, an employee from a utility company enters the yard and suffers injuries when he is attacked by the tenant's dog.

The utility company employee seeks to recover money from the landlord as compensation for the injuries inflicted on him by the tenant's dog. The employee claims the landlord should have known the dog is dangerous since German Shepherds are a breed with the propensity for viciousness.

Licensed property managers

Often, landlords employ real estate licensees as property managers.

When acting as an agent for the landlord, the licensed property manager has a duty to notify the landlord of his activities regarding the maintenance and management of the landlord's property. [CC §2020]

However, the landlord is considered to have the same knowledge about the property's condition as does the property manager with regard to the landlord's property. [CC §2332]

Further, since the property manager is the landlord's representative, the landlord will be liable for the property manager's actions performed in the scope of his representation. [CC §2330]

However, the landlord is entitled to indemnity from the property manager should the landlord be liable for the property manager's failure to properly perform his duties.

The licensed property manager will be liable to the landlord for breach of his agency duty. [CC §3333]

Is the landlord liable for the employee's injuries?

No! The landlord did not have knowledge the tenant's dog was vicious and presented a danger to others. [**Lundy** v. **California Realty** (1985) 170 CA3d 813]

A landlord's obligation to prevent harm to others arises only when the landlord is aware of or *should have known* about the dangerous condition and failed to take preemptive action.

For example, the landlord receiving complaints from neighbors about the behavior of a tenant's dog may deduce the dog creates a dangerous condition, even if the dog has not yet injured anyone.

Editor's note — The landlord's duty to protect others from an injury inflicted by a dog does not yet include asking the tenant if his dog is dangerous.

However, it is feasible the legislature could enact a law or the courts could impose a duty of inquiry on landlords when authorizing the tenant to keep a dog on the premises.

The pet authorization provision in the rental or lease agreement could include a declaration that the authorized pet is not dangerous.

Further, the owner of a dog is neither civilly nor criminally liable for a dog bite suffered by a person who enters the dog owner's property, lawfully or otherwise, unless the person is invited onto the property by the owner of the dog, is an employee of a utility company, a police officer or a U.S. mailman. [CC §3342(a)]

Landlord should have known

Now consider a landlord who leases nonresidential property to a tenant who operates a retail sales business on the property. The tenant keeps a dog on the premises and posts a "Beware of Dog" sign. A newspaper article written about the dog's vicious temperament is also posted on the premises. The landlord visits the leased premises several times a year and knows the dog is kept in the public area of the premises.

After the lease is renewed, a delivery man is attacked and injured by the dog. The delivery man claims the landlord must compensate him for his injuries since the landlord has a duty to inspect the property, ensuring safety for members of the public to enter.

The landlord claims he is not liable since he was personally unaware the dog was dangerous.

Is the landlord liable for the delivery man's injuries?

Yes! The landlord owes a duty to the delivery man as a member of the public to:

- exercise reasonable care in the inspection of his property **to discover** dangerous conditions; and

- remove or otherwise **eliminate** the dangerous condition that may be created by the presence of a vicious dog.

The injured person can recover when the landlord is **personally unaware** of the dog's vicious propensities since a reasonable inspection of the premises on renewal of the lease would have revealed to the landlord the newspaper article and the "Beware of Dog" sign. [**Portillo** v. **Aiassa** (1994) 27 CA4th 1128]

Also, it is foreseeable that a guard dog kept on a premises during business hours could injure someone.

Further, the landlord's failure to require the tenant to remove the dog from the premises on discovery that the dog constitutes a dangerous condition is closely connected to the delivery man's injuries.

The landlord had control over the condition since he could serve a 3-day notice on the tenant, requiring the tenant to either remove the dog from the premises during business hours or vacate the premises.

Editor's note — In Portillo, *the court held* **moral blame** *is attached to the landlord's conduct because of his failure to remove a condition he should have known was dangerous and over which he had control.*

Also, a landlord can often remove a dangerous condition by merely exercising his responsibility to make repairs that will eliminate the condition. However, a dangerous condition caused by a tenant's activity may require a 3-day notice ordering the tenant to correct or remove the dangerous condition, or vacate the premises. [See **first tuesday** Form 576]

On-site danger leads to off-site injury

Now consider a landlord and tenant who enter into a rental agreement for a residential dwelling. The agreement allows the tenant to keep dogs on the premises.

After the tenant occupies the residence, the landlord visits the premises monthly to collect the rent payments. During his visits, the landlord observes the dogs. The landlord is aware of the dogs' vicious nature.

One day, a neighbor and his dog are attacked and injured by the dogs tenant's two blocks away from the leased premises. The neighbor demands the landlord pay for losses resulting from the injuries. The neighbor claims the landlord owes him a duty of care to prevent injuries arising from dangerous animals the tenant keeps on the landlord's premises.

The landlord claims he is not liable since the injuries occurred off the leased premises.

Here, the landlord is **liable** for the **off-site injuries** since the landlord:

- was *aware* of the vicious propensities of dogs housed on his premises; and

- had the ability to remove the dangerous condition by serving a 3-day notice on the tenant to remove the dogs or vacate the premises. [**Donchin** v. **Guerrero** (1995) 34 CA4th 1832]

The landlord's liability for injuries inflicted by a tenant's dog off the premises is the same as his liability for injuries inflicted by the dog that occur on the premises.

While the landlord did not have control over the property where the injury occurred, the landlord did have control over the tenant's right to keep and maintain a known dangerous condition — the dogs — on the premises.

The landlord's failure to have dangerous dogs removed from the premises caused the injuries suffered by the neighbor. The injury would not have occurred if the landlord had not allowed the dogs, which he knew to be vicious, to remain on the premises he controlled. [Donchin, *supra*]

Tenant's dangerous on-site activity

Consider a landlord who is aware the tenant of his single-family rental unit occasionally discharges a firearm in the backyard. One day, a bullet fired by the tenant enters the backyard of the neighboring residence and kills the neighbor.

The neighbor's spouse makes a demand on the landlord for her financial loss resulting from her husband's death. The spouse claims the landlord breached his duty to individuals on neighboring property by failing to exercise care in the management of his property when he did not remove the known dangerous activity from the premises.

Is the landlord liable for the neighbor's death that occurred off the premises?

Yes! Even though the injury occurred off the leased premises, the landlord is liable since the landlord:

- knew of the dangerous on-site activity carried on by the tenant which inflicted the injury; and

- had the ability to eliminate the dangerous condition by serving a 3-day notice on the tenant to refrain from discharging the gun or quit the premises. [**Rosales** v. **Stewart** (1980) 113 CA3d 130]

Thus, the landlord had a duty to prevent the tenant from continuing to fire the gun on the premises. The landlord is liable for an injury resulting from a known dangerous condition or activity occurring on his property that he has the ability to remove, regardless of whether the injury from the on-site activity is suffered on or off the leased premises.

However, had the tenant left the landlord's premises with his gun and then shot and killed an individual, the landlord would not be liable. [**Medina** v. **Hillshore Partners** (1995) 40 CA4th 477]

Failure to avoid obvious dangers

Some dangerous conditions are obvious to persons entering or using the premises that impose a **duty of care** on that person to avoid injury to themselves.

For example, a person wearing cleats walks on a concrete path alongside of which is a rubber walkway for use to prevent slip and fall injuries. The person wearing cleated shoes walks on the concrete path and slips, injuring himself in the fall. A sign does not exist explaining the danger of the person's activity.

Here, a landlord has no duty to warn or guard others against a dangerous condition that is obvious. [**Beauchamp** v. **Los Gatos Golf Course** (1969) 273 CA2d 20]

While a landlord must compensate others for injuries caused by his failure to use skill and ordinary care in the management of his property, the liability has its limits.

A person, who willfully or by his own **lack of ordinary care** to protect himself brings an injury upon himself, exonerates the landlord, wholly or in part, from liability. [CC §1714]

Thus, a person has a duty of care to himself to be sufficiently observant and keep himself out of harm's way.

When the injured person's lack of care for himself contributes to his injury, recovery for his losses is limited to the percentage of the negligence attributed to him, called *comparative negligence*. The money losses recoverable by the injured person will be diminished in proportion to the percent of negligence attributable to the injured person for causing his own harm by failing to care for himself. [**Li** v. **Yellow Cab Company of California** (1975) 13 C3d 804]

Consider a trespasser who illegally enters into or onto property and fails to conduct himself with care to avoid harming himself, called *negligence*.

When the trespasser is negligent in exercising care in his conduct to prevent harm to himself while entering or moving about the property, any losses recoverable by the injured trespasser will be reduced by the percentage amount of negligence attributed to him for causing his injury. [**Beard** v. **Atchison, Topeka and Santa Fe Railway Co.** (1970) 4 CA3d 129]

Further, the landlord's liability will be limited if the trespasser was in the process of committing a felony on the property when he was injured. [CC §847]

Not a dangerous condition

Now consider a person who enters leased non-residential property and wants to look inside the building.

Next to the building, below a window, stands a vat of acid maintained by the business authorized to operate on the leased premises. The vat is covered with plywood for the purpose of keeping out dirt and dust.

In order to see through the window, the person climbs up and steps onto the plywood cover which immediately collapses. The person falls into the vat, suffering injuries.

The injured person attempts to recover money from the landlord for losses resulting from his injury.

Here, the landlord is not liable for the person's injuries since the vat is not a **dangerous condition** that presents a risk of harm. The vat of acid is an integral part of the business run on the leased premises and is not a danger to any person who conducts himself with care around the vat.

Thus, the injured person **undertook the risk** of harm to himself by climbing on top of the vat and creating the dangerous situation leading to his injuries. [**Bisetti** v. **United Refrigeration Corp.** (1985) 174 CA3d 643]

Editor's note — In Bisetti, *the injured person happened to be a trespasser.*

Consider a landlord of an apartment complex used by gang members as a hangout and base from which they commit criminal offenses when off the premises. One of the gang members is a named tenant on the rental agreement.

The tenants and law enforcement officials complain to the landlord about the gang. However, the gang members do not harm or pose a threat of danger to the tenants.

Later, a pedestrian walking past the complex in the public right of way is chased by the gang members. One of the gang members, who is not the tenant, shoots and kills the pedestrian on a street adjacent to the complex.

The spouse of the pedestrian claims the landlord is liable for the death since he failed to remove the dangerous condition, the presence of gang members, from his premises.

However, the landlord does not have a duty to protect members of the public using adjacent public streets from assaults by gang members who congregate on his leased premises. [Medina, *supra*]

The congregation of gang members on the leased premises is not itself a dangerous condition. The gang members do not pose a physical threat to others of which the landlord is aware.

Thus, the landlord's failure to take steps to prevent the gang members from congregating on the leased premises is not the cause of the off-site shooting of a pedestrian by one of the gang members.

Again, the landlord is not liable for injuries that occur off the leased premises, since the landlord has **no control over the activities** of individuals or tenants while they are on public property, only when they are acting on his property. [Medina, *supra*]

Dangerous off-site conditions

Now consider a landlord who leases a residence to a tenant. The residents of the neighboring property own a dog the landlord knows to be vicious. The neighbor brings his leashed dog onto the leased premises. The neighbor invites the tenant's child to pet the dog.

The dog breaks free from the leash and attacks the child, causing injuries. The tenant claims the landlord is liable for his child's injuries since the landlord failed to warn him of the dangerous condition created by the neighbor's vicious dog.

Is the landlord liable for injuries inflicted on-site by the neighbor's dog, which he knew was vicious?

No! The dangerous condition was not maintained on the leased premises. Thus, the landlord has no control or authority himself to remove the dangerous condition from the neighbor's property. [**Wylie** v. **Gresch** (1987) 191 CA3d 412]

While a landlord owes a duty to others to remove a dog from his property that he knows to be dangerous, he does not have a duty to warn his tenants of the presence of vicious animals located on other properties in the neighborhood over which he has no control.

The landlord's failure to protect the tenant by warning him about the neighbor's dog did not create a dangerous condition on the leased premises that caused the tenant to be injured. A landlord's duty to correct or prevent injury from dangerous conditions does not extend to the dangerous conditions that exist off the premises. [Wylie, *supra*]

While the landlord has a duty to make the leased premises safe by removing dangerous on-site conditions and properly maintaining the premises, he is not the insurer of the tenant's safety from off-site hazards. [**7735 Hollywood Boulevard Venture** v. **Superior Court** (1981) 116 CA3d 901]

Off-site injuries under landlord control

The public right of way for a street fronting a leased premises includes part of the front lawn, located between the street curb and the property line. The landlord maintains the entire lawn up to the curb.

A water meter is located on the lawn in the street right of way. Several tenants inform the landlord the water meter box is broken and needs repair.

A tenant trips on the broken water meter box and suffers injuries. The tenant makes a demand on the landlord for losses caused by his injuries, claiming the landlord has a duty to eliminate dangerous conditions located in the public right of way within the lawn maintained by the landlord.

The landlord claims he is not liable since the water meter box is not located on his property and the landlord does not own or control the meter box.

However, the landlord is liable for the injuries suffered by the tenant caused by dangerous conditions — the broken water meter box — located in a public right of way surrounded by a lawn created and maintained by the landlord. [**Alcaraz** v. **Vece** (1997) 14 C4th 1149]

Also, a landlord or other property owner who installs and maintains trees adjacent to or in the lawn area between the public sidewalk and the street-side curb owes a duty of care to avoid injuring pedestrians by hazards created by the trees he maintains.

For example, trees planted and maintained by the property owner grow and eventually produce roots that extend under the sidewalk and crack and uplift it. The owner is aware of the hazard created by the tree roots but undertakes no steps to have the hazardous condition repaired or replaced.

Here, the owner has taken control over the off-site area containing the public sidewalk and will be liable to any pedestrian who is injured due to the hazard created by the roots of trees he maintains since the trunks of the trees are located on his property. [**Alpert** v. **Villa Romano Homeowners Association** (2000) 81 CA4th 1320]

SECTION F

Nonresidential
Lease Provisions

Chapter 41

Nonresidential lease agreement

This chapter reviews a nonresidential lease agreement as the conveyance of a leasehold interest in real estate, with a term and subject to conditions for maintenance of the property.

The conveyance of a leasehold

A lease agreement is a **contract** entered into by a landlord and tenant for payment of money and care of real estate. The lease agreement also acts to **convey a possessory interest** in real estate, called a *leasehold estate*, or simply a *lease*. [Calif. Civil Code §761(3)]

By entering into a lease agreement and delivering up possession to the tenant, the landlord conveys to the tenant the **exclusive right to occupy** a parcel of real estate, or space in a parcel, for a fixed period of time. The continued right to occupancy of the real estate, the lease, *is conditioned* on the tenant's performance under provisions in the lease agreement, the contract, calling for the payment of rent and maintenance of the property delegated to the tenant.

On **expiration** of the term of the lease, the right of possession to the real estate reverts to the landlord. During the term of the lease, the landlord, as the fee owner, holds only a *reversionary interest* in the leased parcel or space.

When the lease agreement has been entered into and the tenant takes occupancy, the landlord's and tenant's **right to possession** of the leased real estate is controlled by landlord/tenant law, not contract law.

On the other hand, the rent provisions in the lease agreement **evidence the debt** the tenant has contracted to pay to the landlord over the term of the lease. The lease agreement also contains other contractual provisions establishing the responsibilities of the tenant or landlord to pay the operating costs and provide for the **care and maintenance** of the property.

The landlord may prematurely regain possession of the real estate by **forfeiting**, or terminating, the tenant's leasehold interest and right to possession, if the tenant fails to comply with, or **breaches**, provisions of the lease agreement. Under a declaration of forfeiture in a 3-day notice, the failure prior to expiration of the tenancy to either pay rent, maintain the property, or fully perform under some other material provision in the lease agreement, terminates the tenant's right to possession.

However, on forfeiture of the right to possession, the lease agreement **remains uncancelled** and in effect as a contract requiring the tenant to pay rent and other amounts for the duration of the original term of the lease. [See Chapter 20]

Conversely, the tenant's obligation to pay can be canceled prior to expiration of the term of the lease by a misunderstanding of the forfeiture provision in the notice to quit and the landlord's conduct, called a *surrender*. [**Desert Plaza Partnership** v. **Waddell** (1986) 180 CA3d 805; see Chapter 22]

Validity of the lease agreement form

A lease agreement conveying a term of occupancy exceeding one year must be written to be enforceable, a requirement of the *statute of frauds*. [CC §1624(a)(3)]

The provisions contained in a written lease agreement fall into one of three categories of activities:

- **conveyance** of the leasehold interest;

- the **lease debt**, called *rent*; and

NONRESIDENTIAL LEASE AGREEMENT
Commercial, Industrial or Office

DATE:_____, 20_____, at _____, California.

Items left blank or unchecked are not applicable.

1. FACTS:

1.1 The Landlord, _____,
leases to Tenant(s), _____,
the real estate referred to as _____
_____.

1.2 The Landlord acknowledges receipt of $_____ to be applied as follows:
☐ Security deposit $_____
☐ Last month's rent $_____   ☐ First month's rent $_____

1.3 The following checked addendums are made a part of this nonresidential lease:
☐ Additional terms addendum [**first tuesday** Form 250]   ☐ Property Description
☐ Authority to Sublease/Assign   ☐ Option to Buy [**ft** Form 161]
☐ Brokerage Fee Addendum [**ft** Form 273]   ☐ Option to Lease Additional Space
☐ Condition of Premises [**ft** Form 560   ☐ Building rules ☐ Plat of leased space
☐ Operating Expense Sheet [**ft** Form 562]   ☐ Other:_____

2. TERM OF LEASE:

2.1 The lease commences _____, 20_____, and expires _____, 20_____, the month of
commencement being the anniversary month.

2.2 The lease terminates on the last day of the term without further notice.

2.3 If Tenant holds over, Tenant to be liable for damages at the daily rate of $_____.

2.4 ☐ This lease agreement is a sublease of the premises which is limited in its terms by the terms and
condition of the attached master lease.

3. RENT:

3.1 Tenant to pay rent monthly, in advance, on the first day of each month, including rent for any partial
month prorated at 1/30th of the monthly rent per day.

3.2 ☐ Monthly rent for the entire term is fixed at the amount of $_____.

3.3 ☐ Monthly rent, from year to year, is graduated on each anniversary month as follows:
Initial year's monthly rent to be . . . . $_____, and
a. _____% increase in monthly rent over prior year's monthly rent; or
b. First anniversary monthly rent . . . . $_____
Second anniversary monthly rent. . . . . $_____
Third anniversary monthly rent . . . . $_____
Fourth anniversary monthly rent . . . . $_____

3.4 ☐ Monthly base rent for the initial 12 months of the term is the amount of $_____, adjusted
annually on the first day of each anniversary month by increasing the initial monthly base rent by
the percentage increase between the applicable CPI-U index figures published for the third month
preceding the month of commencement and the third month preceding the anniversary month.
a. The applicable CPI-U Index (Consumer Price Index for All Urban Consumer)(1982-1984 = 100) is:
☐ Los Angeles-Anaheim-Riverside, ☐ San Francisco-Oakland-San Jose,
☐ San Diego, ☐ National, ☐ Other: _____.
b. Rent increases under CPI-U adjustments are limited for any one year to an increase of _____%.
c. On any anniversary adjustment, should the CPI-U have decreased below the CPI-U for the prior
twelve-month period, the monthly rent for the ensuing 12 months shall remain the same as the rent during
the prior 12 months.
d. If the CPI-U is changed or replaced by the United States Government, the conversion factor published
by the Government on the new Index shall be used to compute annual adjustments.

3.5 ☐ Additional percentage rent equal to _____% of gross sales made from the premises during
each calendar year, less credit for other rent, real estate taxes, insurance and common area maintenance
(CAM) charges paid for the calendar year.
a. The percentage rent shall be computed and paid for each month of the lease with a signed written
statement of the gross income and percentage computation by the tenth day of the following month.

b. The additional percentage rent payable monthly to be credited for other rent, taxes, insurance, and CAMs paid by Tenant for the month.

c. Within one month after each calendar year and on expiration of the lease, Tenant shall compute and deliver a written statement of sales and the percentage rent due for the calendar year, less credit for rent, taxes, insurance and CAMs paid for the calendar year, to annually adjust the percentage rent remaining due from Tenant or to be refunded to Tenant by Landlord, which difference will be paid on delivery of the annual statement.

d. Gross sales includes all money or equivalent received by Tenant, subtenant, licensees or concessionaires, in the ordinary course of business, whether wholesale or retail, cash or credit, less credit for goods returned by customer or merchandise returned by Tenant or transferred to tenant-affiliated stores.

e. Landlord has the right, on reasonable notice, to audit Tenant's books regarding sales information.

3.6 ☐ Every _____ years after commencement, including extensions/renewals, the monthly base rent will be adjusted, upward only, to current market rental rates for comparable premises, and computation of any future CPI-U adjustments will treat the year of each current market adjustment as a commencement year for selecting the Index figures.

a. The monthly rent during any year shall not be less than the previous year's monthly rent.

b. Landlord to reasonably determine and advise Tenant of the adjusted rental rates prior to three months before the adjustment becomes effective.

3.7 Rent to be paid by:

a. ☐ cash, ☐ check, or ☐ cashier's check, made payable to Landlord.

Personal delivery of rent to be at Landlord's address during the hours of _____ am to _____ pm on the following days: _____.

b. ☐ credit card #_____/_____/_____/_____ issued by _____, _____which Landlord is authorized to charge each month for rent due.

c. ☐ deposit into account number _____ at:
_____(Financial Institution)
_____(Address)

3.8 Tenant to pay a charge of $_____ as an additional amount of rent, due on demand, in the event rent is not received within five days of the due date.

3.9 If any rent or other amount due landlord is not received within five days after it's due date, interest will thereafter accrue on the amount at 12% per annum until paid. On receipt of any past due amount, landlord to promptly make a written demand for payment of the accrued interest which will be payable within 30 days of the demand.

3.10 Tenant to pay a charge of $_____ as an additional amount of rent, due on demand, for each rent check returned for insufficient funds, and thereafter to pay rent by cash or cashier's check.

4. OPERATING EXPENSES:

4.1 Tenant is responsible for payment of utility and service charges as follows: _____

4.2 Landlord is responsible for payment of utility and service charges as follows: _____

4.3 Tenant to pay all taxes levied on trade fixtures or other improvements Tenant installs on the premises.

4.4 Should Landlord pay any charge owed by Tenant, Tenant shall pay, within 10 days of written demand, the charge as additional rent.

4.5 As additional rent, Tenant to pay _____% of all real property taxes and assessments levied by governments, for whatever cause, against the land, trees and building containing the leased premises, within 30 days after written computation and demand from Landlord.

4.6 As additional monthly rent, Tenant to pay _____% of the common area maintenance (CAM) incurred each month, within 10 days of written statement and demand for payment.

a. Common area maintenance is the cost of maintaining and operating the "Common Areas," including all sidewalks, corridors, plazas, hallways, restrooms, parking areas, interior and exterior walls and all other open areas not occupied by tenants.

b. Common area maintenance includes "all charges" for garbage removal, janitorial services, gardening, landscaping, printing/decorating, repair and upkeep, utilities and other operating costs, including charges for property management of the common area maintenance.

5. POSSESSION:

5.1 Tenant may terminate the lease if Landlord does not deliver up possession within 10 days after commencement of the lease.

5.2 Landlord is to recover and deliver possession of the premises from the previous tenant. Tenant will not be liable for rent until possession is delivered.

5.3 If Landlord is unable to deliver possession of the premises, Landlord will not be liable for any damages.

6. USE OF THE PREMISES:
6.1 The Tenant's use of the premises shall be: _____

6.2 No other use of the premises is permitted.

    a. Tenant may not conduct any activity which increases Landlord's insurance premiums.

6.3 Tenant will not use the premises for any unlawful purpose, violate any government ordinance or building and tenant association rules, or create any nuisance.

6.4 Tenant shall deliver up the premises together with all keys to the premises on expiration of the lease in as good condition as when Tenant took possession, except for reasonable wear and tear.

7. APPURTENANCES:
7.1 Tenant shall have the right to use Landlord's access of ingress and egress.

7.2 Tenant shall also have the use of _____ parking spaces for the running of its business.

8. SIGNS AND ADVERTISING:
8.1 Tenant will not construct any sign or other advertising on the premises without the prior consent of Landlord.

8.2 ☐ Landlord will maintain a directory in the lobby of the premises displaying the name and suite number of Tenant. Landlord has the right to determine the size, shape, color, style and lettering of the directory.

8.3 ☐ Landlord will provide a sign to be placed on the primary door to Tenant's suite. The fees for the cost and installation will be paid by Tenant.

9. TENANT IMPROVEMENTS/ALTERATIONS:
9.1 Tenant may not alter or improve the real estate without Landlord's prior consent.

    a. Tenant will keep the real estate free of all claims for any improvements and will timely notify Landlord to permit posting of notices for nonresponsibility.

9.2 Any increases in Landlord's property taxes caused by improvements made by Tenant shall become additional rent due on demand.

10. REPAIR AND MAINTENANCE:
10.1 The premises are in good condition, except as noted in an addendum.

10.2 Tenant shall maintain and repair the premises, except for the following which are Landlord's responsibility:
☐ Plumbing and sewers ☐ Structural foundations ☐ Exterior walls ☐ Heating and air conditioning
☐ Store front ☐ Plate glass ☐ Roof ☐ Parking areas ☐ Lawns and shrubbery ☐ Sidewalks
☐ Driveways/right of ways ☐ Electrical ☐ Other: _____

11. RIGHT TO ENTER:
11.1 Tenant agrees to make the premises available on 24 hours notice for entry by Landlord for necessary repairs, alterations, or inspection of the premises.

12. WASTE:
12.1 Tenant will not destroy, damage, or remove any part of the premises or equipment, or commit waste, or permit any person to do so.

13. LIABILITY INSURANCE:
13.1 Tenant shall obtain and maintain commercial general liability and plate glass insurance covering both personal injury and property damage to cover Tenant's use of the premises insuring Tenant and Landlord.

13.2 Tenant shall obtain insurance for this purpose in the minimum amount of $_____.

13.3 Tenant shall provide Landlord with a Certificate of Insurance naming the Landlord as an additional insured. The Certificate shall provide for written notice to Landlord should a change or cancellation of the policy occur.

13.4 Each party waives all insurance subrogation rights it may have.

14. FIRE INSURANCE:
14.1 Tenant shall obtain and maintain a standard fire insurance policy with extended coverage for theft and vandalism to the extent of 100% of the replacement value of all personal property and the restoration of Tenant improvements.

15. HOLD HARMLESS:
15.1 Tenant shall hold Landlord harmless for all claims, damages or liability arising out of the premises caused by Tenant or its employees or patrons.

16. DESTRUCTION:
16.1 In the event the premises are totally or partially destroyed, Tenant agrees to repair the premises if the destruction is caused by Tenant or covered by its insurance.

16.2 The lease shall not be terminated due to any destruction.

16.3 Landlord shall repair the premises if the cause is not covered by the tenant's insurance and is covered by Landlord's policy.

16.4 Landlord may terminate the lease if the repairs cannot be completed within 30 days, the cost of restoration exceeds 70% of the replacement value of the premises, the insurance proceeds are insufficient to cover the actual cost of the repairs, or the premises may not be occupied by law.

17. SUBORDINATION:

17.1 Tenant agrees to subordinate to any new financing secured by the premises which does not exceed 80% loan-to-value ratio, and interest of two percent over market, and not less than a 15-year monthly amortization and five-year due date.

18. TENANT ESTOPPEL CERTIFICATES:

18.1 Within 10 days after notice, Tenant will execute a certificate stating the existing terms of the lease to be provided to prospective buyers or lenders.

18.2 Failure to deliver the certificate shall be conclusive evidence the information contained in it is correct.

19. ASSIGNMENT, SUBLETTING AND ENCUMBRANCE: [Check only one]

19.1 ☐ Tenant may not assign this lease or sublet any part of the premises, or further encumber the leasehold.

19.2 ☐ Tenant may not transfer any interest in the premises without the prior consent of Landlord.

a. ☐ Consent may not be unreasonably withheld.

b. ☐ Consent is subject to the attached conditions. [ft Form 250]

20. SURRENDER:

20.1 Tenant may surrender this lease only by a written cancellation and waiver agreement with Landlord.

21. EMINENT DOMAIN:

21.1 Should a portion or all of the premises be condemned for public use, Landlord may terminate the lease and Tenant's possession. If the lease is not terminated, Tenant shall receive a rent abatement for the actual reduction (if any) in the value of the lease.

21.2 Tenant waives the right to any compensation awarded from the condemning authority for the whole or partial taking of the premises.

21.3 Any Tenant's damages shall come solely from the condemning authority.

22. WAIVER:

22.1 Waiver of a breach of any provision in this lease shall not constitute a waiver of any subsequent breach. Landlord's receipt of rent with knowledge of Tenant's breach does not waive Landlord's right to enforce the breach.

23. DEFAULT REMEDIES:

23.1 If Tenant breaches any provision of this lease, Landlord may exercise its rights, including the right to collect future rental losses after forfeiture of possession.

24. BROKERAGE FEES:

24.1 ☐ Landlord and Tenant to pay Broker fees per the attached schedule of leasing agent's fee. [ft form 113]

25. MISCELLANEOUS:

25.1 ☐ See attached addendum for additional terms. [ft Form 250]

25.2 In any action to enforce this agreement, the prevailing party shall receive attorney fees.

25.3 This lease shall be binding on all heirs, assigns and successors except as provided in section 19.

25.4 This lease shall be enforced under California law.

25.5 This lease reflects the entire agreement between the parties.

25.6 ☐ This lease is secured by a trust deed. [ft Form 451]

25.7 ☐ The performance of this lease is assured by a guarantee agreement. [ft Form 439]

I agree to let on the terms stated above.	I agree to occupy on the terms stated above.
Date:_____, 20_____	Date:_____, 20_____
Landlord: _____	Tenant:_____
Agent: _____	Tenant:_____
Signature: _____	Signature: _____
Address: _____	Signature: _____
_____	Address: _____
Phone:_____	_____
Fax: _____	Phone:_____
E-mail: _____	Fax: _____
	E-mail: _____

- responsibility for **care and maintenance** of the leased premises. [See Form 552 accompanying this chapter]

To be valid, a lease agreement must:

- designate the **size and location** of the leased premises with *reasonable certainty*;

- set forth a **term** for the tenancy conveyed; and

- state the **rental amount**, and its time, place and manner of payment. [**Levin** v. **Saroff** (1921) 54 CA 285]

Offers to lease and lease agreements

A broker, whether he represents the landlord or the tenant, should use a letter of intent (LOI) or an *offer to lease* to initiate and document lease negotiations prior to entering into the lease agreement itself. [See **first tuesday** Form 556]

An **offer to lease** entered into by both the tenant and the landlord is also referred to as an *agreement to lease*. The preparation and signing of the actual lease agreement remains to be done after its terms and conditions have been negotiated and agreed to in the offer to lease.

Consider a prospective tenant who signs an offer or letter of intent to lease property that is submitted to the landlord. The offer calls for the landlord to erect a building on the property for use in the tenant's business, but does not attach a copy of a proposed lease agreement or reference the form to be used.

The landlord accepts the offer to lease, agreeing to lease the premises to the tenant, occupancy to be delivered on the completion of the improvements by the landlord as they come due. The offer to lease also states the tenant will lease the premises for five years, commencing on completion of the improvements, when he will begin making the agreed-to monthly rental payments.

After building construction is completed, the tenant takes possession of the premises and makes monthly rental payments to the landlord as they become due. A formal lease agreement is not prepared or entered into by the landlord and tenant. Both the landlord and the tenant perform according to the terms stated in the offer to lease, except for their failure to enter into the lease agreement.

Later, the property becomes the subject of an action for inverse condemnation. Persons with an interest in the property are entitled to money, which includes the tenant's leasehold interest.

The landlord claims the tenant is not entitled to any amount from the condemnation award since the tenant has no interest in the property as he lacks a signed lease agreement **conveying** a leasehold interest to him.

The tenant claims he has a leasehold interest in the property under the offer to lease and is entitled to recover his losses resulting from the condemnation of the property.

Here, the tenant will participate in the condemnation award since he owns a leasehold (estate) interest in the property that was not limited by agreement. The written agreement entered into by the landlord and the tenant — an offer to lease on the terms stated — becomes the lease agreement when the tenant takes possession of the premises without entering into a formal lease agreement. [**City of Santa Cruz** v. **MacGregor** (1960) 178 CA2d 45]

The agreement to lease, signed by the owner, contains all the essential terms needed to create a lease, including:

- a *description of the premises* to be leased and its location — a building on the premises;

- a *lease term* — five years; and

- the *amount of periodic rent* and when it will be paid.

Since all the elements necessary to create a lease are agreed to in writing, the landlord's act of delivering possession to the tenant **conveys** the agreed five-year leasehold interest to the tenant. No part of the agreements entered into reference or limit the tenant's condemnation rights.

To record or not to record

A lease agreement need not be recorded. Between the landlord and the tenant, and all other parties who have *knowledge* of the lease, the agreement is enforceable whether or not it is recorded. [CC §1217]

Thus, an unrecorded lease agreement with a term exceeding one year in length is only void as against a *bona fide purchaser* (BFP). [CC §1214]

To qualify as a BFP, the buyer or lender must lack *knowledge* that the lease agreement exists or a tenant is in possession, and purchase the leased real estate for valuable consideration or accept the real estate as security for a debt.

However, when a tenant occupies the property at the time it is purchased or further encumbered, the purchaser or secured lender is *charged with knowledge* of the tenant's leasehold interest — whether or not the lease agreement is recorded. Thus, the tenant's occupancy puts the purchaser and lender on **constructive notice** a lease (or some other arrangement with the occupant) exists. [**Manig** v. **Bachman** (1954) 127 CA2d 216]

However, when a lease agreement is recorded, the content of the recorded agreement may be relied on by a purchaser or lender as containing **all the rights** of the tenant. The need for a tenant estoppel certificate to establish the tenant's rights in the property is eliminated by the recording.

Editor's note — An unrecorded option held by a tenant to buy the leased property or extend the lease cannot be enforced against a buyer or lender who later acquires an interest in the property when the **lease agreement is recorded,** *if:*

- *the buyer or lender have no actual knowledge of the option;*

- *the option to extend the lease or buy the property itself is not recorded; and*

- *the unrecorded options are not referenced in the recorded lease.* [**Gates Rubber Company** v. **Ulman** *(1989) 214 CA3d 356]*

The contents of a lease agreement

A nonresidential lease agreement form has five main sections:

- *identification* of the parties and the premises, and the conveyance and term of the lease;

- the *rent* and terms for payment of amounts owed;

- the *care and maintenance* of the leased property;

- *miscellaneous provisions* for circumstances peculiar to the transaction; and

- the *signatures* of the parties.

The **identification section** of a real estate lease agreement includes:

- the names of the landlord and the tenant;

- a description of the leased premises;

- words of conveyance of the leased property;

- a receipt for prepaid rents and the security deposit; and

- a list of the addenda which contain exhibits or additional terms. [See Form 552 §1]

The leasehold conveyance

The lease agreement includes words of transfer by which the landlord conveys a leasehold interest (lease) in the property to the tenant upon signing the agreement and delivery of possession to the tenant. [See Form 552 §1.1]

The **conveyance** of a lease is typically achieved with the words "landlord . . . **leases to** . . . tenant the real estate referred to as . . . ." [See Form 552 §1.1]

However, consider an owner of a department store who enters into an agreement with a tenant to occupy space in the store for three years. The tenant will use the space to conduct his business.

The agreement states the space to be occupied by the tenant will be designated by the owner at the time of occupancy. The agreement also:

- outlines the formula for the monthly **rent** to be paid for the space;

- gives the tenant the sole and **exclusive right** to conduct his business in the store without competition;

- **restricts transfer** of the tenant's right to occupy the space without the owner's consent; and

- requires the tenant to **surrender** the occupied premises on the last day of the rental term.

After the tenant takes possession, and before the term for occupancy expires, the owner notifies the tenant he is terminating the agreement and the tenant must vacate the premises. The tenant does not comply with the owner's notice to vacate.

As a result, the landlord removes the tenant's fixtures, equipment and inventory, and bars the tenant from entering the premises.

The tenant claims the owner can neither terminate the occupancy nor remove his possessions, without first filing a UD action and obtaining a judgment to recover possession since the occupancy agreement constitutes a lease which **conveyed a leasehold interest** in the occupied space to the tenant.

The owner claims the occupancy agreement is a mere *license* to conduct business in the store and is not a lease since **no defined space** was described in the agreement to identify the location of the leased premises.

Here, the agreement to occupy the space conveyed a lease, not a license to use. While the agreement itself does not identify the space to be occupied by the tenant or contain words of conveyance, the agreement becomes a lease on the tenant's occupancy of the **premises designated** by the landlord since the agreement states:

- possession of the premises is to be delivered to the tenant for his **exclusive use** in exchange for monthly rent;

- the lease cannot be **assigned** without the consent of the landlord; and

- the premises need not be delivered up to the landlord until the end of the rental term. [**Beckett** v. **City of Paris Dry Goods Co.** (1939) 14 C2d 633]

The agreement entered into by the landlord does not contain the words "landlord . . . leases to . . . tenant" as words of conveyance. However, the contents of the agreement indicate the landlord's intention to convey a lease to the tenant, and the **act of delivering possession** to the tenant of space designated by the store owner is the conveyance.

Conversely, an occupancy agreement does not automatically convey a lease just because it uses words of leasehold conveyance. The *economic function* of a "lease transaction" may actually be something quite different, that of a sale which has been recharacterized by the parties under the guise of a lease.

For instance, a lease-option agreement that allocates option money or a portion of each rental payment, or both, toward the purchase price or down payment to be made on the purchase of the property is not a lease at all. The lease-option agreement is a *disguised security device* since it evidences a credit sale by a carryback seller. Further, the lease-option agreement as a sale requires taxable profits in the down payment to be reported when it is received, and not deferred under option rules. [**Oesterreich** v. **Commissioner of Internal Revenue** (9th Cir. 1955) 226 F2d 798]

Proper identification of the parties

Each party to a lease agreement must be properly **identified**. On the lease agreement form, the identification of the tenant should indicate how his ownership of the lease conveyed will be vested, such as community property, community property with right of survivorship, joint tenancy, tenancy-in-common, sole ownership, as a trustee for himself or for someone else, or as a business entity.

When the ownership interest of the landlord is community property, both spouses must consent to agreements leasing the community property for a fixed term exceeding one year. If not, the community is not bound by the lease agreement, and, if challenged within one year after commencement by the nonconsenting spouse, the tenant cannot enforce the conveyance of the lease. [Calif. Family Code §1102]

Business entities, excluding DBAs, individuals and their trusts, that own or lease property include:

- corporations and out-of-state entities qualifying as a corporation such as business trusts;

- limited liability companies (LLCs);

- partnerships, general or limited;

- real estate investment trusts (REITs);

- nonprofit organizations; and

- governmental agencies.

When the landlord or tenant is a partnership, the lease agreement should indicate:

- whether the partnership is a limited, general or limited liability partnership (LLP);

- the partnership's state of formation, and if out of state, whether it is qualified to do business in California; and

- the name of the partner(s) authorized to bind the partnership.

With information on the partnership, the landlord and any title company insuring the leasehold can confirm through a review of recorded documents the authority of the general or managing partner to bind the partnership, such as an LP-1 for a limited partnership, or the managing member to bind an LLC.

Whether a corporation is the landlord or tenant, the full corporate name and the state of incorporation must be **disclosed**, as well as the name and title of the officer who will be signing the lease agreement.

The corporate information, along with a *resolution* from the board of directors authorizing the corporate officers to enter into the lease in the name of the corporation, will allow for confirmation of:

- the corporation's good standing to operate in the state; and

- the officers registered with the state to act on behalf of and bind the corporation under resolution by the corporation's board of directors.

Premises identified with certainty

The nonresidential lease agreement must describe the premises to be leased so the premises can be located with *reasonable certainty*. While the description may not itself be "definite and certain" as worded, an imperfectly worded description to be **reasonably certain** need only furnish a "means or key" for a surveyor to identify the parcel's location on the earth's surface or within a building. [**Beverage** v. **Canton Placer Mining Co.** (1955) 43 C2d 769]

If the premises is a building or a space in a building, the common street address, including the unit number, is a sufficient description to identify the premises.

If the premises is not easily identified by its common address, a plot map or floor plan should be included as an addendum to the lease agreement, with the space to be rented highlighted or otherwise identified. A plot map or floor plan eliminates confusion over the location of the leased parcel or space in the building, and initially establishes the parameters of the leased space.

An attached floor or plot plan noting square footage is useful if rent is calculated based on square footage occupied by the tenant, or on the percentage of square footage within a project leased to the tenant.

Also, an inaccurate or incomplete description of the leased premises will not prevent a landlord from conveying, and the tenant from accepting, a leasehold interest in a parcel of real estate for lack of certainty.

A sufficient description

A tenant signs and hands the landlord an **offer to lease** together with the proposed lease agreement for space in a retail commercial center. Attached to the proposed lease agreement is a plot plan outlining the location of the leased premises.

The lease agreement contains a provision stating the exact legal description of the premises will be prepared as an addendum to the lease agreement no sooner than 30 days after the leased premises as identified in the plot plan is occupied by the tenant.

After submitting the offer to lease, the tenant decides he would rather lease space at another location. The tenant mails a revocation letter to the landlord for the withdrawal of his offer.

However, the tenant receives the signed offer and lease agreement from the landlord before the landlord receives the tenant's revocation letter. The lease agreement does not include a copy of the plot plan addendum that was attached to the proposed lease.

The tenant refuses to perform under the lease agreement, claiming the lease agreement is unenforceable since the landlord failed to deliver the plot plan addendum that designated the size of the leased premises.

The landlord seeks to enforce the tenant's performance of the lease agreement.

Here, a lease has been entered into which is **enforceable**. The precise size of the leased premises is not crucial to the lease transaction since the location of the premises is known due to the plot plan attached to the proposed lease agreement and the lease agreement states the exact size of the premises identified on the plot plan will be determined after the tenant takes possession. [**Mabee** v. **Nurseryland Garden Centers, Inc.** (1978) 84 CA3d 968]

Also, when the premises described in a lease agreement is incomplete or inaccurate, the tenant's actual possession of the premises will set the boundaries. [Beckett, *supra*]

Further, an incomplete or inaccurate description of the leased premises which the tenant has occupied does not release a tenant from liability under the lease for the space he actually occupied. [City of Santa Cruz, *supra*]

Addenda to the lease agreement

The terms common to all nonresidential leases are contained in the provisions of a regular lease agreement form.

However, the terms and conditions peculiar to the leasing of a particular type of nonresidential tenancy, such as commercial, industrial, office, farming operation or hotel, or provisions unique to the parties and their advisors, should be handled in an *addendum* attached to the lease agreement.

The use of an **addendum** to house extraordinary and atypical provisions not in common use avoids the element of a later unpleasant (and litigious) surprise. Extraordinary provisions occasionally go unnoticed at the time the lease agreement is entered into because they are buried in preprinted copy.

Also, any handwritten or typewritten provisions added to an agreement control over conflicting pre-printed or boilerplate provisions. Should inconsistencies arise between provisions in the pre-printed lease agreement and an attached addendum, the provisions in the addendum control. [**Gutzi Associates** v. **Switzer** (1989) 215 CA3d 1636]

The use of addenda for making changes or additions to leasing provisions allows parties to tailor the lease agreement to meet their needs in the transaction, while retaining the integrity of the contents of the lease agreement form.

Addenda occasionally attached to a nonresidential lease agreement include:

- terms unique to the type of property leased;

- a property description addendum, such as a plot map or site plan;

- a structural or tenant improvement agreement;

- a condition of premises addendum [See **first tuesday** Form 560];

- a building rules addendum;

- an option or right of first refusal to renew or extend [See **first tuesday** Form 566];

- a brokerage fee addendum [See **first tuesday** Form 273];

- a tenant leasehold subordination agreement regarding a future loan;

- a non-disturbance and attornment provision;

- a signage or tenant association agreement;

- an option or right of first refusal to lease additional space;

- authority to sublease or assign; and

- an option or right of first refusal to buy. [See **first tuesday** Forms 161 and 579]

If the lease agreement is for a sublease of the premises, a copy of the master lease should be attached and noted in the agreement. [Form 552 §2.4]

The lease term

A nonresidential lease agreement is an agreement to rent real estate for a fixed term, conveying a type of leasehold estate called a *tenancy for years*. [CC §761(3)]

The lease agreement should clearly indicate the dates on which the lease term, occupancy, commences and expires. [See Form 552 §2.1]

Delivery and acceptance of possession are addressed separately from the date of the lease agreement since the transfer of possession operates independently of the date identifying the lease agreement. [See Form 552 §5]

On expiration of the lease term on the date stated in the lease agreement, the lease (right to possession) automatically terminates and the tenant must have vacated without further notice by either the landlord or tenant. [CC §1933]

On expiration of a lease, a holdover tenancy, called a *tenancy-at-sufferance*, is created when:

- the tenant remains in possession after the lease term expires; and

- the landlord refuses to accept further rent payments.

The holdover tenancy ends when the tenant vacates or is evicted, or the landlord accepts rent during the holdover period permitting the occupancy.

The lease agreement contains a holdover rent provision calling for a set dollar amount of rent due for each day the tenant holds over. The rent is due and payable when the tenant vacates or is evicted. The daily rent should be significantly higher than the fair market rate, although an excessive amount is unenforceable in a UD action since it is unreasonable. [See Form 552 §2.3]

If the amount of holdover rent is not set in the lease agreement, a fair market rate will be recoverable during the holdover (which is also the ceiling for rent awarded in a UD action for the holdover).

The landlord can initiate UD proceedings to evict the holdover tenant immediately after the lease expires. [CCP §1161(1)]

However, the landlord who accepts rent for any period of occupancy falling after the lease expires and before the tenant vacates creates a periodic tenancy. To terminate the resulting pe-

riodic tenancy, the landlord must serve the tenant with a 30-day notice to vacate the premises before he can evict the tenant. [**Palmer** v. **Zeis** (1944) 65 CA2d Supp 859; see **first tuesday** Form 571]

Delivery and acceptance of possession

Provisions in a lease agreement pertaining to the date for delivery of the leased premises to the tenant address the landlord's failure to deliver up the premises to the tenant. [See Form 552 §5]

The tenant is given the opportunity to terminate the lease agreement if possession is not delivered within an agreed-to number of days after commencement of the lease term. [See Form 552 §5.1]

A landlord sometimes fails to deliver possession to the tenant due to his inability to recover the premises from a previous tenant. To cover the risk, the lease agreement should state the tenant will not be liable for rent payments until possession is delivered. [See Form 552 §5.2]

Further, the lease agreement should state the landlord will not be liable for damages if he is unable to deliver possession. [See Form 552 §5.3]

Eminent domain

A tenant can contract away his right to receive any compensation awarded to the landlord in a condemnation action. [**New Haven Unified School District** v. **Taco Bell Corporation** (1994) 24 CA4th 1473]

Thus, nonresidential leases drafted by landlords or trade associations typically reserve for the landlord all rights to any condemnation award under the *eminent domain provision*. [See Form 552 §21]

Also, the landlord may reserve his right to terminate the lease in the event of a partial condemnation. If the landlord does not choose to terminate the lease when a **partial taking** occurs, the tenant is entitled to a rent abatement for the reduction in value of the leasehold interest.

A tenant under a lease has a right to receive compensation for his leasehold interest if his lease is terminated due to a condemnation proceeding. [CCP §1265.150]

Since the lease provisions eliminate the tenant's rights to any compensation awarded to the landlord, the tenant must look to the condemning authority to recover other losses, such as:

- relocation costs;

- loss of goodwill;

- bonus value of the lease (due to below market rent); or

- severance damages if a partial taking occurred.

Brokerage fees

Initially, the responsibility for paying any brokerage fees for leasing services is controlled by employment provisions in an authorization to lease or property management agreement entered into by the tenant or the landlord and their respective brokers.

Second, and of equal effect as a separate underlying fee agreement, is the placement of a brokerage fee provision within the tenant's offer to lease or LOI signed by the tenant.

Lastly, a provision for payment of the broker fees is included in the lease to allow enforcement in case the broker failed to obtain a prior written commitment from either the tenant or the landlord to pay the leasing agent's fee or to pay fees which will later be earned on lease extensions or purchase of the property by the tenant. [See Form 552 §24.1]

Miscellaneous provisions

An *attorney fee provision* is essential in a lease agreement if the landlord is to recover costs incurred to enforce payment of rent or evict the tenant. Regardless of how an **attorney fee provision** is written, the prevailing party, if any, is entitled to his fee. [CC §1717(a); see Form 552 §25.2]

The *heirs, assigns and successors clause* binds those who later take the position of the landlord or tenant, by grant or assignment (privity of estate), or by an assumption (privity of contract). [**Saucedo** v. **Mercury Savings and Loan Association** (1980) 111 CA3d 309; see Form 552 §25.3]

A *choice-of-law provision* assures application of California rules of law should a dispute arise with a tenant regarding the lease. [See Form 552 §25.4]

Application of California law in disputes over property located in California adds stability to the legal expectations of the landlord and tenant under the lease, produces greater commercial certainty in real estate transactions and stabilizes property values.

Also, the lease agreement must reflect the entire agreement between the parties and should be modified only in writing.

An *entire agreement clause* serves two key purposes. An entire agreement clause limits:

- the tenant's ability to imply terms into the lease based on oral statements **made before entering** into the lease agreement; and

- the **later oral modification** of lease terms and the attendant disputes over "just what are" the terms of the oral modification.

The tenant's performance of lease obligations may also be *secured* by a trust deed encumbering real estate owned by the tenant (or others) or be guaranteed by a corporate user's officer or another person. [See **first tuesday** Form 451; see Form 552 §§25.6 and 25.7]

If the tenant fails to pay rent or otherwise breaches the lease, the landlord can evict the tenant and, after a demand for payment, foreclose under the performance trust deed to recover rent due under the lease, attorney fees and costs of the trustee's sale. [**Willys of Marin Company** v. **Pierce** (1956) 140 CA2d 826]

Signatures on behalf of the parties

Individuals who sign a lease agreement on behalf of the landlord or the tenant must have the capacity and the authority to act on behalf of and bind the landlord or tenant. [CC §§2304, 2307]

When a corporation enters into a lease, the officers signing the lease agreement are given authority to bind the corporation by a *corporate resolution* from the board of directors of the corporation. [Calif. Corporations Code §300]

Unless the landlord is aware that the persons signing do not have authority to enter into a lease on behalf of the corporation, the lease entered into by a corporate tenant is valid if it is signed by:

- the chairman of the board, president or the vice president; and

- secretary, any assistant secretary, chief financial officer or assistant treasurer. [Corp C §313]

However, a corporate resolution is the best evidence of the corporate officers' authority to act on behalf of the corporate tenant.

When a LLC or LLP enters into a lease agreement, the **manager** signing on behalf of the LLC or LLP to bind the entity to the lease must be the person named as the manager in the LLC-1 or LLP-1 certificate filed with the Secretary of State and recorded with the local county recorder.

However, an LLP or an LLC will be bound to a lease agreement if a partner or member, other than the general partner or manager, signs the lease agreement and the landlord believes the partner or member is acting with the authority of the entity due to their title as chairman or president. [Corp C §17154(c)]

The economics of nonresidential leases

Nonresidential lease agreements are used in transactions involving industrial, commercial, office and other types of nonresidential income-producing property.

A tenant who acquires a leasehold interest in nonresidential real estate agrees to be obligated for none, some or all of the operating costs of the real estate, as rent due in addition to payment of the base rent and periodic adjustments.

Editor's note — A residential lease agreement usually provides for the tenant to assume no care and maintenance responsibilities for the property except for excess wear and tear which may occur during his occupancy.

Typically, the longer the term of the nonresidential lease, the more extensive the shift of ownership costs and responsibilities to the tenant, including:

- property operating expenses;

- all or future increases in real estate taxes, called *ad valorem taxes*;

- hazard insurance premiums;

- repair and maintenance; and

- the risk of an increase in interest payments on an adjustable rate loan encumbering the property.

When a long-term lease obligates the tenant to pay for all expenses incurred in the ownership and operation of the property, the tenant incurs the expenses in one of two ways:

- directly, where the tenant contracts for services and pays the cost, including taxes and insurance premiums; or

- indirectly, when the landlord incurs the expenses and then bills the tenant for payment, such as common area maintenance charges (CAMs).

The responsibility for the payment of operating costs is reflected in the reference to nonresidential leases as **gross** or **net**, with variations on each.

Leasing agents have no universally accepted definitions or guidelines for titles they use to identify the economics of a lease, and the classifications for leases are forever changing. Often, agents must clarify with each other the type of lease their clients intend to enter.

A nonresidential lease is typically called a *gross lease* if the tenant pays for his utilities and janitorial fees, but is not responsible for any other care, maintenance or carrying costs of the property.

In a lease for space in an office building, when the landlord retains the responsibility for payment of all costs of care and maintenance, including the tenant's utilities and janitorial services, the lease used is referred to as a *full-service gross lease*.

Conversely, a nonresidential lease that transfers to the tenant the obligation to pay some or all of the costs and responsibilities of ownership, in addition to utilities and janitorial services, is referred to as a *modified gross lease* or *net lease*.

A lease becomes more *net* (and less gross) for the landlord as he shifts more ownership responsibilities and operating costs to the tenant.

The modified gross or net lease is the most commonly used lease agreement in nonresidential properties, other than for multiple tenant office buildings or large multi-tenant industrial projects.

When a lease passes on the responsibility for all costs and maintenance of the property to the tenant, either directly or through CAMs, leaving the landlord responsible for capital improvements only, such as structural repairs or replacement, the lease is referred to as a *net-net-net* or *triple-net* lease in the industry.

When a tenant assumes absolutely all ownership duties under a lease agreement, and the landlord merely collects rent payments without concern for his management of the property, the lease is called a *pure net lease*.

Reformation of the lease agreement

During lease negotiations, a landlord orally assures a tenant he will enter into a lease for an initial term of five years with two five-year options to renew. Written offers to lease or LOIs are not prepared.

However, the lease agreement the landlord prepares and hands to the tenant sets the lease term at 15 years. Without reviewing the lease agreement, the tenant signs the lease agreement and takes possession of the premises.

The business operated by the tenant on the leased premises later fails, and the tenant defaults on the rent payments. The tenant then discovers for the first time the length of the lease term is 15 years. The landlord seeks to collect the unpaid rent for the 15-year period under the lease agreement (subject to any mitigation and present-worth discounting).

The tenant seeks to *rescind* the lease agreement due to the landlord's oral misrepresentation about the length of the lease term. The tenant claims the lease provisions contradict the oral agreement made by him and the landlord before the lease was entered into.

Can the tenant rescind the lease agreement?

No! The landlord's oral representations regarding the lease term prior to execution of the lease agreement do not render the lease unenforceable. The terms of the lease set forth in the written lease agreement control over prior oral understandings. [**West** v. **Henderson** (1991) 227 CA3d 1578]

Rescission of lease agreements is rare since intentional misrepresentation or other *fraud in the inducement* must be shown.

Now consider a landlord who accepts a tenant's written **offer to lease**. A lease agreement called for in the tenant's offer is prepared by the landlord. However, the lease term stated in the lease agreement differs from the term set forth in the written offer to lease. The tenant accepts the lease without review.

Later, the tenant discovers the discrepancy between the two documents. Instead of attempting to *rescind* the lease, the tenant *reforms* the lease by court order to conform it to the underlying written offer to lease on which the lease was to be based, called a *reformation action*.

Another reason for *reformation* of lease provisions arises when a significant difference exists between the square footage contained in the leased space and the square footage given in the lease for calculating rent.

Chapter 42

Rent provisions in nonresidential leases

This chapter examines the principles and application of rent provision formulas, inflation and market appreciation adjustments, and reimbursement of operating expenses in nonresidential lease agreements.

The landlord's future return

By entering into a lease agreement, a landlord conveys to the tenant a possessory interest in real estate for a period of time, called *the lease*, in exchange for a tenant's promise to make dollar payments in the future, called *rent*.

Residential leases usually are for one year and their agreements provide for a **fixed amount** of monthly rent paid in dollars during the term of the lease. In contrast, nonresidential leases are for longer periods and their agreements contain rent adjustment clauses to ensure the landlord will receive the maximum future return available in the rental market for his income property, even if the lease is negotiated during an economic downturn.

The economic function of a long-term nonresidential lease agreement for the landlord is similar to that of a note and trust deed carried back by a seller of real estate or held by a lender. The documentation in both cases, lease agreements and note and trust deeds, is almost exclusively concerned with the debt owed and the maintenance of the real estate.

Just as a trust deed note evidences the debt owed a carryback seller or a lender, rent provisions in a lease agreement evidence the debt owed to the landlord. Both the lender and the landlord are creditors of the person holding the right to possession of the real estate. The lender holds a security interest in the property until he is paid in full while the landlord holds a right of reversion until he is paid in full.

The lender's trust deed outlines the responsibilities of the borrower for the care and mainte-

nance of the secured real estate, as the care and maintenance provisions in a landlord's lease agreement do for the tenant.

If the owner of the real estate encumbered by the trust deed fails to pay on the trust deed note or breaches the care and maintenance provisions in the trust deed, the creditor forecloses. The owner loses his interest in the real estate due to his uncured default.

Likewise, if the tenant fails to pay rent or breaches the care and maintenance provisions in the lease agreement, the landlord terminates the tenant's right to possession of the property, and the tenant loses his interest in the property if the default is not cured.

The termination of these possessory rights held by tenants or owners in nonresidential real estate can be accomplished without extinguishing or canceling the tenant's or the owner's obligation to pay any loss incurred under the lease agreement or the trust deed note. [Calif. Civil Code §1951.2; Calif. Code of Civil Procedure §725a]

Setting the rent

Various rent formulas exist to meet the economics of the marketplace and the financial needs of the landlord and tenant. In all nonresidential lease agreements, a minimum amount of monthly rent is agreed to for payment, called *base rent*. [See **first tuesday** Form 552 §3.4]

Typically, the base rent is the monthly amount paid during the first year of the lease, except for percentage leases. However, in many

Rent provisions and the NOI

The base monthly rent and all other monies paid to the landlord under the lease, except security deposits, are considered rent payments.

The rent payments a landlord receives from all tenants constitute his *actual gross income* from the property.

The rental amounts and the terms of their future payment as set by the rent provisions greatly influence:

- the *market value* of the real estate;

- the availability of *long-term financing*;

- the property's attractiveness to *potential buyers*; and

- the landlord's *future return* on his investment.

The *market value* of nonresidential income property is based primarily on its net operating income (NOI). A property's NOI is composed of the property's gross income less operating expenses. Without rental income flow, improved real estate has little value.

The present and projected NOI is relied on extensively by buyers and lenders when evaluating a property.

The NOI is capitalized at the current yield sought, and sets the property's fair market value for the price (present worth) a buyer will pay, and the amounts a lender will lend.

Lenders limit loan amounts lent on property based on, among other conditions:

- the real estate's NOI; and

- the financial strength of the tenants to meet their obligations.

Likewise, buyers determine what purchase price will be offered based on, among other things:

- the property's NOI;

- a review of the tenants' financial track records; and

- the controllability of the landlord's operating costs.

Thus, the leasing agent or property manager negotiating a nonresidential lease on behalf of the landlord must make certain the landlord has considered whether the *economics of the lease* will produce rents and control costs effectively to produce maximum returns now and in the future.

short-term leases — two to five years — the base rent is paid during the entire term of the lease, without an adjustment.

A lease agreement which sets monthly rent payments at a specific dollar amount over the entire life of the lease results in what is called a *fixed-rent lease*. [See Figure 2 §3.2 accompanying this chapter]

In a rising local economy or period of general price inflation, a fixed rate of rent on a long-term lease will prove to be a financial disaster for the landlord. Fixed rent shifts the inflation hedge appreciation in the property's value to the tenant for so long as the fixed rent continues.

However, a landlord may be forced to accept fixed-rent provisions in lease agreements negotiated during an economic downturn or static rental market, if he is to keep the space occupied. To avoid a potential loss of return under a fixed rate lease during the ensuing economic recovery, a short-term lease or month-to-month tenancy should be negotiated by the landlord.

When leasing space in larger, multi-tenant retail properties, landlords often negotiate a rent provision that calculates the total amount of rent the tenant will pay as a percentage of the tenant's gross sales, called a *percentage lease*. The tenant, under a **percentage lease**, annually pays the greater of the base rent or the percentage rent. [See **first tuesday** Form 552 §3.5]

Many nonresidential lease agreements contain provisions under which the **base rent** is adjusted periodically, usually on each anniversary of the lease commencement and again every four to six years, to reflect changes in:

- **annual price inflation** affecting the property's rental value due to conditions reducing the purchasing power of the U.S. dollar, called a *Consumer Price Index (CPI) clause*; and

- **periodic property appreciation** due to economic changes in local market conditions, such as population density, age demographics, traffic count, visitors or personal income and spending habits, that increase demand and the rental value of the property, called an *appreciation clause*. [See **first tuesday** Form 552 §§3.4, 3.6]

As an alternative to the CPI, the base rent can be adjusted annually based on an agreed percentage or dollar amount over the prior year's rent, called *graduated rent*. [See **first tuesday** Form 552 §3.3]

The lease agreement rent provisions must precisely state any rent adjustment formulas to be enforced by the landlord.

Setting the grace period and late charge

The nonresidential lease agreement must, as the minimum terms of rent for enforcement, indicate:

- the **dollar amount** of the rent;

- the **time** for payment;

- the **place** for payment; and

- the **manner** of payment. [**Levin** v. **Saroff** (1921) 54 CA 285]

For the landlord to receive rent in advance, namely prepaid at a time before it *accrues*, the lease agreement must include a provision stating the tenant will pay rent in advance. [CC §1947; see Form 552 §3.1]

Rent payments not paid as they become due are not delinquent until the time has passed for a late charge to be incurred, called a *grace period*. When a late fee is not agreed to in the note, a grace period does not exist. Rent is delinquent if not paid on or before the due date, usually the first day of the month. In nonresidential (and residential) lease agreements, the grace period is negotiable by the landlord and the tenant without legal restriction regarding its length in time. [See **first tuesday** Form 552 §3.8]

Having agreed to a grace period, the landlord cannot serve a 3-day notice to pay until the grace period expires. [See Chapter 26]

The grace period may be:

- the time period stated in the lease agreement; or

- a time period set by the landlord's conduct of consistently accepting rent on a date later than the expiration date for the grace period without demanding payment of a late charge. [**Baypoint Mortgage** v. **Crest Premium Real Estate Investments Retirement Trust** (1985) 168 CA3d 818]

The landlord may provide for a late charge to reimburse himself for his collection efforts due to the delinquency of rent. The charge must be reasonably related to the landlord's out-of-pocket money losses incurred during collection efforts or the delay in receipt of the untimely payment.

Late charges are typically assessed in leases as either a percentage of the rent due or a flat rate charge. The flat rate charge should approximate the costs incurred to enforce collection and the loss of use of the rent money. In addition to dollar amounts equivalent to reimbursement of collection costs, the accrual of interest on any delinquent amount is often included to cover the loss of use of the rent. [See **first tuesday** Form 552 §3.9]

Place and manner of payment

Rent is paid in United States dollars at a set location, such as at the landlord's or leasing agent's office, either personally or by mail. [See **first tuesday** Form 552 §3.7]

However, rent does not have to be paid with money. Rent can be paid by the delivery of crops, precious metals, services, or currencies or assets other than those denominated in United States dollars. [**Clarke** v. **Cobb** (1898) 121 C 595]

The manner of rent payment also is set forth, typically cash, check, credit card, electronic transfer or other means of transmitting funds.

For checks returned for insufficient or unavailable funds, the lease agreement must include a flat rate charge in order for the landlord to shift this expense item to the tenant. [See **first tuesday** Forms 552 §3.10]

If the tenant develops a history of writing checks on insufficient funds, the landlord can require, on a written 30-day notice, payment of rent in cash or by money order. [See **first tuesday** Form 552 §3.10]

Square footage sets the rent

In nonresidential leases for industrial, commercial, office and retail space, the dollar amount of the base rent is generally agreed to as a result of multiplying the total number of square feet rented by a per-square-foot rate.

For example, a tenant leases 4,000 square feet at $2 per square foot. The base rent is set for the lease as $8,000 payable monthly.

The per-square-foot rent formula is used to negotiate the specific dollar amount of rent stated in the lease agreement. The per-square-foot formula used in negotiations usually is not mentioned in the lease agreement unless the footage is uncertain at the time the lease is entered into.

When either the base rent or additional rent, such as common area maintenance (CAMs) expenses, is based on square footage stated in the lease, the space attributable to the leased premises should be clearly defined and accurately measured. Rents determined per square foot exist in many office, commercial and industrial projects.

To avoid disputes, the landlord and tenant must agree on how the square footage will be measured:

- from the interior walls;

- from the middle of the walls;

- from the exterior of the walls; or

- to include a portion of the common hallways, lobby, restrooms or other interior areas of the structure.

Lease audits undertaken by existing tenants often establish a lesser square footage amount than the footage represented by the owner and relied on by the tenant to set the rent and share of operating costs.

The standard for determining how the square footage will be measured is negotiated through the offers and counteroffers to lease, and the competitive availability of space.

Additional rent and other sums due

As additional rent to the base rent or as future periodic adjustments in the base rent, the tenant may agree to pay some or all of the operating expenses of the leased property, called a *common area maintenance* (CAMs) clause. [See Figure 1 §4.6 accompanying this chapter]

The objective for the landlord in seeking CAMs is to provide a constant monthly **net income flow** on his investment in the property — a steady flow of income despite fluctuations in the cost of operating the property.

Property operating expenses typically include:

- utilities;

- property management;

- repairs and maintenance;

- hazard insurance premiums;

- security; and

- real estate taxes and assessments. [See **first tuesday** Form 352]

The allocation of the responsibility for operating expenses depends on:

- the type of property and its use;

- the relative bargaining positions of the landlord and tenant in the current real estate market;

- the financial objectives of the landlord and tenant; and

- the length of the lease term.

The landlord and tenant can agree the property operating expenses will be paid by the tenant directly to the provider or creditor, or indirectly to the landlord as a reimbursement.

Taxes and assessments

Tenants with long-term leases often agree to pay some or all of the real estate taxes, insurance premiums and special assessments when the leased premises is an industrial or single-use building.

Property is reassessed by the county assessor when the landlord sells his interest, even if the tenant remains in possession. [Calif. Revenue and Taxation Code §60]

Should the landlord sell the leased property and cause the tenant to face higher real estate taxes due to reassessment, the increase is caused by the owner's conduct, not by the tenant's use of the property. [See Figure 1 §4.5]

A savvy tenant will demand a **cap on any rent** increases due to reassessment caused by the landlord. When a cap is agreed to in the lease, such as a 2% annual increase, the landlord is responsible for any property tax increases exceeding the ceiling. However, the tenant should always be held responsible for the payment of assessments and taxes caused by his own improvements and trade fixtures. [See Figure 1 §4.3]

Common area maintenance

The landlord and tenant can also agree to allocate some or all of the landlord's cost of maintaining the common areas to the tenant for reimbursement to the landlord. [See Figure 1 §4.6]

The cost of maintaining the common areas when reimbursed by the tenant is **additional** rent, called *CAM charges*. Customarily, CAM charges are based on the ratio between the space leased by the tenant and the total rentable space in the project.

The term "common areas" is broadly defined to include sidewalks, corridors, plazas, halls, restrooms, parking facilities, grounds, etc.

The term "maintenance" is defined to include garbage removal, janitorial services, gardening and landscaping, repairs and upkeep, utilities and other specified operating costs.

Figure 1 *Excerpted from **first tuesday** Form 552 —*
Nonresidential Lease Agreement

4. **OPERATING EXPENSES:**

4.1 Tenant is responsible for payment of utility and service charge as follows:

_____

4.2 Landlord is responsible for payment of utility and service charge as follows:_____

4.3 Tenant to pay all taxes levied on Tenant trade fixtures installed on the premises.

4.4 Should Landlord pay any charge owed by Tenant, Tenant shall pay, within ten days of written demand, the charge as additional rent.

4.5 As additional rent, Tenant to pay _____% of all real property taxes and assessments levied by governments, for whatever cause, against the land, trees and building containing the leased premises, within 30 days after written computation and demand from Landlord.

4.6 As additional monthly rent, Tenant to pay _____% of the Common Area Maintenance (CAM) incurred each month, within ten days of written statement and demand for payment.

    a. Common Area Maintenance is the cost of maintaining and operating the "Common Areas," including all sidewalks, corridors, plazas, hallways, restrooms, parking areas, interior and exterior walls and all other open areas not occupied by tenants.

    b. Common Area Maintenance includes "all charges" for garbage removal, janitorial services, gardening, landscaping, printing/decorating, repair and upkeep, utilities and other operating costs, including charges for property management of the Common Area Maintenance.

Utility charges

The utilities provision covers the cost of utilities used in the space leased by the tenant, as opposed to the utilities required to operate the common areas. [See Figure 1 §§4.1 and 4.2]

To protect against the increased cost of utilities consumed by the tenant, the landlord who pays for utilities can negotiate to pass the responsibility on to the tenant. The landlord can determine the tenant's pro rata share, or have each leased premises privately metered to determine the charge for the tenant's consumption.

Tenants who use a lot of energy and utilities should be required to contract with the utility companies themselves.

As a practical matter, the landlord should avoid paying the utilities whenever possible, except, perhaps, for water. However, if the landlord pays the utilities and charges the tenant, the charge is additional rent to all other rent agreed to be paid.

Chapter 43

Adjustable rent provisions

This chapter discusses the various adjustable rent clauses used in nonresidential leases.

Economic goals of nonresidential landlords

Rent works to provide a yield on an investment in real estate, as does dividends and interest on stocks and bonds. A lender receives *interest* for the use of money lent for a specific period of time. Likewise, a landlord receives *rent* for the use of property let for a specific period of time.

At the end of the respective right-to-use periods, both the money and the real estate are returned.

Like interest provisions in a note, **rent provisions** in a nonresidential lease agreement should anticipate future market changes that will affect the investment (value, income, expenses and debt) by structuring the rent provisions to conform the rent income to match the anticipated changes.

Fixed-rent leases do not anticipate future changes in the investment's fundamentals. However, variable or adjustable-rent leases do anticipate changes negatively affecting the owner's net operating income or spendable income, unless shifted to the tenant by way of an equal increase in rent.

Types of adjustable rent

The three basic types of rent adjustment provisions found in nonresidential leases, sometimes called *rent escalation clauses*, are:

- *graduated rent* provisions [See Figure 1 accompanying this chapter];

- *inflation adjusted rent* provisions [See Figure 2 accompanying this chapter]; and

- *appreciation adjusted rent* provisions. [See Figure 3 accompanying this chapter]

The **economic goals** a leasing agent must review with his nonresidential landlord-client when negotiating provisions for future rents include:

- adjustments for the lost purchasing power of the dollar due to future *price inflation*;

- adjustments in rent to reflect the *rate of appreciation* on comparable properties (beyond the rate of inflation); and

- the absorption or pass-through of increased expenditures for operating expenses and interest adjustments on mortgage debt.

To protect the property's income, and in turn its value, against a loss in the **US dollar's purchasing power** due to inflation, rent can be periodically adjusted based on a price inflation clause in the lease agreement. An inflation clause calls for periodic rent increases based on figures from an inflation index, such as the Consumer Price Index (CPI) or the Cost of Funds Index. [See Figure 2]

Further, and to attain rents which reflect an increase in the property's dollar value brought about by **local appreciation**, rent can also be adjusted periodically (for example, every three years) to rent amounts received by comparable properties. [See Figure 3]

Also, increased **operating and ownership costs** can be absorbed directly or indirectly by the nonresidential tenant by passing on the responsibilities for:

- all the operating expenses, or only future increases in the expenses, by including a clause calling for the tenant to pay specific expenses; or

- a pro rata share of **common area maintenance** expenses (CAMs), property taxes and hazard insurance premiums. [See Chapter 37]

Future increases in the cost of carrying debt on the property due to **variable interest rate** mortgage financing can also be passed on to the tenant as increased rent to provide the landlord with a triple-net or pure-net lease.

With knowledge and understanding about the economic and financial consequences of the terms submitted by a tenant in an **offer to lease** or letter of intent (LOI), the landlord can make an informed financial decision whether to accept, counter or reject the tenant's offer to lease.

Graduated rents from year to year

Rents bargained for during periods of high vacancies and few prospective tenants are often below market for the initial year or two of a lease, comparable in purpose (and timing) to the initial *teaser* or *qualifying* rates for adjustable rate loans (ARMs) and graduated payment loans (GPMs).

Likewise, a **graduated rent** clause increases the initially low, monthly rent semi-annually or annually in pre-set increments. The amount of the periodic upward adjustment is set at a specific dollar amount or a percentage of the initial rent or rent paid during the prior period. [See Figure 1]

Graduated rent adjustments are not determined by use of index figures or formulas dependent on data from other sources at the time of the adjustment. The rent amounts are negotiated and set on entering into the lease agreement.

Also, any below-market rents paid in the early years are often picked up in future rents that will exceed market rents, as though the lease had a negative amortization feature taken from ARM loans.

For example, the base monthly rent might be increased, or graduated, each year on the anniversary of the lease by:

- a pre-selected dollar amount; or

- 5% of the base rent set forth in the lease agreement for the first year.

A graduated payment provision with annual rent increases can also be structured based on a *percentage* increase over the prior year's monthly rent, a *compounding of rents*.

| **Figure 1** | *Excerpted from **first tuesday** Form 552 —*
Nonresidential Lease Agreement |

3.3   Monthly rent, from year to year, is graduated on each anniversary month as follows:

Initial year's monthly rent to be $_____, and

     a.   _____% increase in monthly rent over prior year's monthly rent; or

     b.   First anniversary monthly rent . . . . $_____

         Second anniversary monthly rent . . . . $_____

         Third anniversary monthly rent. . . . . $_____

         Fourth anniversary monthly rent . . . . $_____

For example, the monthly payment during the last year of a graduated payment plan would become the base rent for annual CPI inflation adjustments to set rates annually for the remaining term of the lease.

Future rent increases after the graduated rents have reached the projected market rent amount will be set under a price inflation clause.

Percentage rents and the base rent

Now consider a tenant operating his business in a premises under a **percentage lease**. The **base rent** is a fixed monthly dollar amount during the first 12 months of the lease.

The calculations for the **alternative minimum annual rent** is set at 7% of the tenant's gross sales. The tenant will pay a total rent equal to the greater amount of the base rent or the alternative percentage rate.

The landlord and tenant also agree the base rent for each year will be increased by 2% of the base rent for the previous year, called a *compounded base rent*. Alternatively, the base rent could (and should) be increased by agreement at the rate of inflation which took place during the period prior to the adjustment. A **price inflation adjustment** to the base rent increases the floor for the least amount due as rent each year.

Thus, the annual adjustment to the base rent provides a *floor rent* for a minimum rate of return on the landlord's investment throughout the lease term should the tenant's business suffer a downturn or a drop in annual gross receipts.

Price inflation adjustments

To annually adjust the base rent to compensate for price inflation due to the dollar's continuing loss of purchasing power, a *price inflation clause* or *CPI clause* can be included in the lease agreement. [See Figure 2]

Inflation adjustments are usually made on each anniversary of the commencement of the lease. Adjustments are based on the annual percentage change in figures from the CPI for the region in which the real estate is located.

The CPI clause can be used to establish the annual rent adjustment in one of two ways:

- a base-year to current-year increase; or

- a year-to-year increase for a compounding effect.

The unpredictable cyclical movement of future price inflation both lulls and infuriates landlords. Thus, for landlords, the rent inflation clause should be boilerplate in every lease running for a period of more than three or four years — if the competitiveness of the marketplace allows for its inclusion.

Occasionally, landlords will ignore the CPI as a basis for inflation adjustments and use a set annual percentage increase of 3% or 4% in its place, which of course is back to graduated rent schedules in an effort to either out-guess or exceed inflation rates.

Periodic appreciation adjustments

If the CPI is the only rent adjustment provision used by the landlord over the life of a long-term lease, the landlord risks loss of any increase in rents in excess of the CPI that is enjoyed by comparable properties, called *appreciation*. The same risk of lost rent increases for appreciation exists when exclusively using graduated rent clauses (which tend only to cover inflation).

Value increase by appreciation is a local phenomenon, not a monetary one as is inflation. To reflect rent increases brought about by **local rental market** conditions, the landlord should consider a clause calling for periodic rent adjustments that increases the rent to meet current market rates, called an *appreciation* or *fair market rent clause*. [See Figure 3]

Figure 2   *Excerpt from **first tuesday** Form 552 —*
                                Nonresidential Lease Agreement

3.4 | | Monthly base rent for the initial 12 months of the term is the amount of $_____, adjusted annually on the first day of each anniversary month by increasing the initial monthly base rent by the percentage increase between the applicable CPI-U index figures published for the third month preceding the month of commencement and the third month preceding the anniversary month.

    a. The applicable CPI-U Index (Consumer Price Index for All Urban Consumer)(1982-1984 = 100) is:

       | Los Angeles-Anaheim-Riverside, | San Francisco-Oakland-San Jose,

       | San Diego, | National, | Other: _____.

    b. Rent increases under CPI-U adjustments are limited for any one year to an increase of _____%.

    c. On any anniversary adjustment, should the CPI-U have decreased below the CPI-U for the prior twelve-month period, the monthly rent for the ensuing 12 months shall remain the same as the rent during the prior 12 months.

    d. If the CPI-U is changed or replaced by the United States Government, the conversion factor published by the Government on the new Index shall be used to compute annual adjustments.

To make the rent adjustment, the base monthly rent is, as agreed-to in the lease, adjusted to a *reasonable amount* by the landlord every three to five years to reflect local market trends in comparable properties, or as otherwise agreed for adjustment by appraisal in the appreciation clause.

Thus, a lease agreement containing both an inflation clause and an appreciation clause assures the landlord will receive:

- an annual inflation adjustment increasing the amount of rent paid during the entire term of the lease to maintain the **purchasing power** of the rent amount received at the inception of the lease [See Figure 2]; and

- a periodic adjustment in the amount of rent to reflect any future increases in rents for comparable properties exceeding the rate of inflation. [See Figure 3]

A provision can be included in the lease agreement for an appraisal process to set the amount of the appreciated rent if the tenant is concerned about his remedies if the amount set by the landlord as the appreciation adjustment is considered unreasonable.

Setting fair market rents

Consider a nonresidential lease agreement with a **use provision** calling for the tenant to operate a movie theater on the premises for ten years.

The lease agreement contains a rent appreciation clause stating the landlord will adjust the base rent in five years to reflect the then current *fair market rent*.

At the time for the appreciation adjustments five years later, the landlord determines the fair market rent for the property by using rent amounts received by comparable properties put to higher and better uses than a movie theater.

The tenant disputes the amount of the adjusted rent demanded by the landlord.

The tenant claims the fair market rental value of the premises should be based on the present use of the property as intended by the lease, since the lease agreement does not provide for the landlord to adjust the rent to reflect a return on the fair market value of comparable properties that have been put to a higher and better use.

Here, the lease agreement states the tenant will use the property to operate a movie theater for the term of the lease. Thus, the rent can only be adjusted to reflect the fair market value of the property based on its use as a movie theater. [**Wu** v. **Interstate Consolidated Industries** (1991) 226 CA3d 1511]

Chapter 44

This chapter examines a landlord's use of rent adjustment provisions to shift the effects of inflation to the tenant.

Coping with inflation

A long-term investment goal of an owner of rental property is to generate income in the future sufficient to keep the property's value in line with market values of comparable properties, whether his property is residential or nonresidential.

Not only must the highest rate of occupancy be maintained to generate the maximum rental income, lease agreements entered into by the landlord must contain rent provisions calling for periodic rent adjustments which will maintain his **future rents** at market level during the terms of the lease.

For example, rent adjustments can be set to match the annual *price inflation* experienced in the region. Thus, rental income will increase from year to year to maintain the original purchasing power of the property's rental income over the term of the lease and extensions.

For decades prior to the mid-1970s, rent adjustments were of little concern as inflation and appreciation rates were more predictable. The 1980s saw marked increases in rents and operating costs to reflect the excessive inflation of the 1970s.

Then, rents declined and appreciation rates in California reversed in the early 1990s, stabilizing during the late-1990s. After the turn of the century, rents again began to increase, exceeding the rate of inflation as reflected in the *Consumer Price Index* (CPI), with the exception of locations with high concentrations of the information technology industry. By 2007, rent increases began to stabilize in all areas and on all types of properties, as the real estate boom years of the mid-2000s came to an end.

Unlike *appreciation* of a property which is based on the demographics of its location, consumer *inflation* is a decline in the quantity of a consumer item (square footage of space) a dollar will buy (rent) due to a general price increase for the same item (comparable space).

Inattentive landlords and those who fail to anticipate trends in inflation often saddle themselves with long-term lease agreements containing rent provisions which do not adjust rent for **inflation** or **appreciation**. Since future rents are formulated in lease agreement rent provisions, the worth of the property, and thus its equity, can be calculated at any time during the term of the lease based on the capitalization rate applied by investors at that time. [See **first tuesday** Form 552 §3]

Lease provisions establishing future rents can be economically disastrous in long-term leases and in leases with renewal options unless rent is periodically increased in a dollar amount equal to the rate of both dollar inflation and local domestic appreciation.

However, a number of methods exist to keep pace with price inflation, property value appreciation and increases in the landlord's *operating and ownership costs* occurring over the term of a lease.

CPI covers price inflation

The best method for coping with the uncertain impact of **future inflation** is to tie the amount due as future rents to figures published in the federal government's *Consumer Price Index* (CPI).

Nonresidential lease agreements typically set a base monthly rent which is constant for the first year. For the following years, annual rent is adjusted by factoring in the annual change in local or regional CPI figures. For residential rent increases, most rent control communities use a form of the CPI to allow for the amount of automatic annual rent adjustments permitted by ordinance.

Residential leases rarely exceed one year. Thus, most residential lease agreements do not need to address an adjustment in monthly rents to compensate for inflation. Rent increases are negotiated at the end of the leasing period and set based on comparable market rates or, in noncompetitive communities, as dictated by rent control.

CPI and its regions

Consumer Price Index (CPI) figures are published monthly, bi-monthly or semi-annually by the U.S. Bureau of Labor Statistics for numerous metropolitan areas across the states. The CPI is the most widely used indicator of inflation.

The CPI measures the overall price change from month to month, up or down, for a "basket" of consumer goods and services that everyday people are believed to buy or consume. The CPI-U is based on the price of food, clothing, shelter, fuel, transportation fares, charges for doctors and dentists, drugs and other goods bought for day-to-day living.

Real estate lease agreements with provisions for annual adjustments based on the **rate of inflation** most commonly use inflation figures from the regional CPI-U, the CPI for the area's urban consumers. A regional CPI-U covers the buying habits of approximately 80% of the population within the designated area.

The three CPI regions within California are:

- Los Angeles-Anaheim-Riverside (issued monthly);

- San Francisco-Oakland-San Jose (issued bi-monthly); and

- San Diego (issued semi-annually).

If property does not fall within or near one of the regions, a landlord may also use the CPI-U for a larger geographical area such as:

- the West Region CPI-U; or

- the U.S. City Average CPI-U.

Issuance date for the CPI figure

Every ten years, the Consumer Price Index (CPI) program undergoes major revisions. Part of the revisions, which last became effective January 1998, included a change from the monthly issuance date for the San Francisco-Oakland-San Jose CPI-U.

The San Francisco-Oakland-San Jose CPI-U is now issued bi-monthly covering consumer expenditures for two months — the month of issuance and the preceding month. The bi-monthly CPI-U for the San Francisco area is issued on even-numbered months such as February, April, June, etc.

Thus, the landlord with an adjustment index tied to the January CPI-U for the San Francisco-Oakland-San Jose area uses the CPI-U which comes out in February.

However, the landlord who chooses the San Francisco-Oakland-San Jose CPI-U may instead wish to switch to a larger geographical area CPI-U index which is issued on a monthly basis. For example, the landlord can consider using the West Region CPI-U.

If the landlord seeks to switch to a different index during the life of a lease, the landlord and tenant must agree to the use of the new index.

Inflationary cycles and the CPI

A few basic principles of real estate economics need to be considered when using Consumer

Price Index (CPI) figures to adjust rent to reflect the effect of inflation on the purchasing power of rental income.

First, real estate values tend to increase in excess of inflation during periods with low rates of inflation and the accompanying low long-term interest rates (and capitalization rates set by buyers) such as existed during the real estate boom of 2004 to 2006.

In contrast, real estate values go flat or decrease during periods of increasing and high rates of inflation due to the accompanying and inevitable higher short term interest rates and investment capitalization rates.

The longer the period of low or high inflation, the more distorted real estate **valuations** become, up or down, contrary to the movement of inflation and long-term interest rates, closely comparable to the effect of inflation on the bond market.

When interest rates and inflation stay high, market rents tend to rise, initially tempered by any excessive construction or speculation in the preceding 18 to 24 months. This holds true even though the property's value remains static or drops, usually due to an upward revision in capitalization rates for returns sought by investors in an effort to maintain a *real rate* of return, a margin of earnings beyond inflation.

Conversely, when rising interest rates and inflation top off and decline (generally heralding the end of a rescission), rents flatten out and tend to drop. During the following business recovery period, property resale values tend to rise, unless held down by an extended regional recession as occurred in California during the mid-1990s. The late 2000s will most likely see interest rates and rental rates receding over the short term from the 2006 levels as vacancies and foreclosures greatly increase.

Two reasons exist for a parallel movement of rent and inflation.

First, **higher long-term interest rates** which initially result from rising inflation, excessive construction and slowing real estate sales. In response, investors and brokers turn their attention to the more efficient management of existing properties which then produce more income (since the properties cannot now be sold at the price sought).

Second, since high interest rates and inflation stifle new construction, the supply of **new space** available for occupancy is cut off. Fewer starts ultimately cause rents to increase if the population remains static or increases, unless serious overbuilding has occurred which outpaced the demand for housing by households, space for nonresidential occupancy and speculators. Dramatically rising foreclosure rates throughout the state which began in 2006 will displace many households and leave even more property vacant to be purchased or rented by households.

The key to the management of rental property in times of increased inflation and higher interest rates is to produce earnings from **net operating income** (NOI), not profits on immediate resale.

On the other hand, when interest rates and inflation top off and begin to decline, real estate sales increase and less attention is paid to a property's income production. Historically, California real estate owners and brokers, driven by increasing population, tend to focus more on profit-taking from increasing values than on the efficient management of a property's income flow and operating expenses.

The long real estate recession in the 1990s up to 1996 with its declining values altered the focus from sales to property management, probably temporarily due to a general lack of hindsight among households and speculators about home ownership as evidenced during the 2004-2006 real estate boom.

When prices rise during periods of lower capitalization rates, reduced inflation and falling interest rates as happened after September 11, 2001, owners become increasingly more inclined to put their property on the market for sale, rather than bring rents into line.

How CPI works

Rent cannot be increased during the term of a lease absent an adjustment provision in the lease agreement. For instance, rent payments under a **fixed-rent lease** remain constant over the life of the lease. In contrast, rent under a month-to-month rental agreement can be increased by serving a notice of change in the terms of tenancy, which is limited in amount in cities burdened with residential rent control. [Calif. Civil Code §827]

To increase rents annually for inflation, the lease must provide a formula for calculating the rent increases.

A lease provision that calls for adjustments based on the Consumer Price Index-Urban (CPI-U) may be worded to provide a base-to-current year increase or a year-to-year increase. The resulting rent amount is the same under either calculation.

Choosing the beginning CPI month

Regardless of the method of adjustment, base-to-current year or year-to-year, the landlord will need to select a beginning Consumer Price Index-Urban (CPI-U) month.

The best month to select for the CPI-U figure to be used to compute adjustments is the **third month preceding** commencement of the lease and each anniversary of the commencement. The CPI-U figure for the third month prior to the adjustment is readily available by the time the rent adjustment needs to be calculated and the tenant is advised of the adjusted amount of rent due.

Otherwise, if the CPI-U figure chosen is for the month in which the rent will be adjusted, the landlord will need to estimate the CPI-U figure at the time of the adjustment. The actual CPI-U figure for the anniversary month to make the adjustment called for in the lease will not be available for another two months. Computation of the annual adjusted rent is either by base year CPI-U-to-current year CPI-U, or by year-to-year CPI-U.

CPI provision checklist

When the landlord decides to use the CPI method to raise rents, some basic guidelines should be followed:

- set, in advance, a base rent payable monthly during the first year of the lease which will be the "minimum" rent (floor) below which the rent will never fall;

- indicate the exact index to be used (e.g., the Los Angeles-Riverside-Anaheim CPI-U);

- indicate an alternative index should the one selected be discarded or altered;

- note the CPI beginning month for computing annual adjustments (often the third month before the commencement month and anniversaries of the lease);

- state the actual date for the adjusted annual graduations (e.g., September 1); and

- include provisions to cover future changes in the property's appreciated value and operating costs (e.g., reappraisal, CAMs, etc.).

Figure 1

*Excerpt from **first tuesday** Form 552 —*
Nonresidential Lease Agreement

3.4   Monthly base rent for the initial 12 months of the term is the amount of $_____, adjusted annually on the first day of each anniversary month by increasing the initial monthly base rent by the percentage increase between the applicable CPI-U index figures published for the third month preceding the month of commencement and the third month preceding the anniversary month.

    a.   The applicable CPI-U Index (Consumer Price Index for All Urban Consumer)(1982-1984 = 100) is:

         Los Angeles-Anaheim-Riverside,   San Francisco-Oakland-San Jose,

         San Diego,   National,   Other: _____.

    b.   Rent increases under CPI-U adjustments are limited for any one year to an increase of _____%.

    c.   On any anniversary adjustment, should the CPI-U have decreased below the CPI-U for the prior twelve-month period, the monthly rent for the ensuing 12 months shall remain the same as the rent during the prior 12 months.

    d.   If the CPI-U is changed or replaced by the United States Government, the conversion factor published by the Government on the new Index shall be used to compute annual adjustments.

Base-to-current year adjustment

Consider a lease rent provision which provides for a *base-to-current* year adjustment. [See Figure 1]

The lease commenced on January 1, 2005. The base rent is $5,000 per month for the first year. The rent is to be adjusted each January and the Consumer Price Index-Urban (CPI-U) index to be used is the Los Angeles-Anaheim-Riverside index.

The CPI-U figure for the October prior to January, the month of adjustment, is selected as the base month figure for rent adjustments. The CPI-U figure for the third month preceding commencement will be available to calculate the amount of the adjusted rent before the January rent is due. The CPI-U for October 2004 is 196.3, the base month figure.

In January 2006, the first rent adjustment takes place. The CPI-U for October 2005 is 206.9.

To calculate the base-to-current year adjustment, the formula is — the current CPI-U divided by the base CPI-U multiplied by the base rent: (current CPI-U ÷ base CPI-U) × base rent.

For the second year (2006) of the lease, the rent is $5,270 — (206.9 ÷ 196.3) ×$5,000.

For 2007, the third year of the lease, the October 2006 CPI-U is 211.4. Thus, in January 2007, the rent adjusts to $5,385 — (211.4 ÷ 196.3) × $5,000.

Year-to-year adjustment

Under *year-to-year* rent adjustment provisions, the prior year's rent, not the base year's rent, is used to set the adjusted rent. The base year's Consumer Price Index-Urban (CPI-U) is not used to make the future adjustment.

Thus, the year-to-year adjustment formula is the current CPI-U divided by last year's CPI-U, multiplied by the current rent: (current CPI-U ¸ last year's CPI-U) ´ current rent.

CPI advantages

Three advantages are provided by using the Consumer Price Index (CPI) as a basis for rent adjustments. The first and most obvious advantage is that the CPI is universally known and **easily understood**. Little room exists for the parties to disagree over the amount of a rent increase if it is tied to a government published index.

Second, the CPI is inexpensive to administer. It only takes a few minutes and a calculator to adjust the rents each year.

Third, the CPI is a widely published and recognized index.

CPI limitations on yield

Despite the advantages, the Consumer Price Index (CPI) has its limitations. The CPI bears little to no relationship to changes in the property's actual market value or rental value. The CPI only measures overall **consumer prices**, not asset values which are forged by a combination of local demographics, government programs, interest rates and supply of available units or space.

Each parcel of real estate is a unique asset. It is the location of a property which makes the primary difference since no two locations have exactly the same desirability factors affecting value.

An individual property can increase or decrease in value for a number of reasons other than inflation, including:

- traffic counts and access to the property;

- tenant demand and changes in the size and wealth of the surrounding population;

- operating expenses;

- mortgage interest rates and investor capitalization rates; and

- construction starts.

The regional CPI takes none of these local economic factors into consideration. Interest rates *charged* to home buyers are indirectly included in the CPI by using *implicit rent* as the cost of home ownership, but the *opposing effect* of interest rates on real estate values is not included. Cyclically, and in the short term, values run opposite to the direction interest rates move. When interest rates go down (decelerating the CPI), values of real estate (and other assets) accelerate even if rents remain the same, and vice versa.

Also, the CPI does not mirror actual variations in the landlord's operating costs. An owner who does nothing to maintain his property thereby reducing his operating expenses can, in a high demand location, enjoy rent increases due to the public's appreciation for the property's desirable location.

Astute tenants insist on an annual cap when rent increases are linked to CPI. For example, if the rise in the CPI figure is greater than 4% in any year, a 4% cap would limit the increase despite a greater increase in the CPI.

The key is to analyze where inflation is headed (an activity routinely performed by holders of ten year treasury notes). If inflation is expected to rise in the future, then the CPI will initially benefit the landlord. Conversely, when inflation has topped off and is dropping, the CPI will appear to benefit the tenant. Also, a shock to local rental market conditions, such as overbuilding or the exodus of a rental age or business group, can completely eliminate inflationary and interest rate effects on rent.

Alternatives to the CPI

Again, the Consumer Price Index (CPI) is a good method for controlling the inflationary reduction of the *purchasing power* of the U.S. dollar received in payment of rent.

But inflation's effect on rent amounts covered by the annual CPI adjustments is not the only concern of the property manager. Property **appreciation** and increased **operating costs** need to be managed to increase, or at worst maintain, the property's net operating income (NOI).

It is advisable to add a **reappraisal** and **rent adjustment provision** to long-term leases rather than rely solely on the CPI. However, reappraisal methods are costly, time consuming and not always without argument. Managers may feel it is too involved to reappraise the property every few years to set the new rents.

However, appraisal provisions usually call for a reappraisal and recast of the rent schedule at three-to-five year intervals or on exercise of renewal options. [See **first tuesday** Form 552 §3.6]

Some leases allow the landlord to use his judgment to set the rent for the adjustment, which must be exercised reasonably.

A provision for the periodic adjustment of rents to current rental rates is good insurance for a landlord to capture any upward shifts in rents paid in the local rental market beyond those brought about by inflation.

This periodic recast of the rent payment is economically comparable to the rollover feature some lenders include in their three-or five-year adjustable rate or rollover loans.

In addition to base rents, CPI adjustments and rollover features, **percentage rent provisions** also capture the increase in rents due to appreciation based on a change in local demographics. [See Chapter 45]

If the property is in an outstanding location, or promoted by the landlord to attract an ever greater number of consumers, which results in an increase in the tenant's gross income, the landlord should consider negotiating a percentage rent adjustment provision to "cash in" on the draw of the property's location.

Many nonresidential leases include an **additional rent provision** to reimburse the landlord for his operating expenses. Rent can be adjusted to include the operating expenses and any taxes and assessments incurred by the property, called *common area maintenance* (CAM) expenses. [See **first tuesday** Form 552 §4.6]

CAM provisions obligate the tenant to pay a pro rata share of the costs to maintain the common areas of the property including:

- utilities (water, gas, heat, etc.);
- air conditioning and venting;
- sewage;
- garbage;
- janitorial services;
- landscaping;
- security;
- insurance;
- management fees; and
- real estate taxes.

The more items included, the closer the lease comes to a triple-net lease.

Chapter 45

Percentage lease rent provisions

This chapter discusses percentage rent provisions used in lease agreements for space in high traffic retail locations.

Rental income driven by gross sales

A landlord of a newly constructed commercial building negotiates a percentage lease with a prospective tenant who intends to operate a franchised restaurant on the premises. The prospective tenant prepares an estimate of the amount of gross sales anticipated for the first 12 months of operations, based on:

- the traffic count and traffic patterns at the location of the premises;

- the volume of anticipated sales; and

- the nature of the product and service to be offered by the restaurant.

The rent to be paid by the tenant comprises a *base rent* and *additional rent*.

The landlord and tenant agree the base rent for the first year, payable monthly, will be based on 6% of the tenant's **estimated annual gross sales**. The lease agreement sets a specific dollar amount for the monthly **base rent**. The amount of the monthly base rent will be annually adjusted to conform to the rate of inflation reflected by figures from the Consumer Price Index (CPI).

Since it is a percentage lease, the lease agreement also calls for **additional rent** to be paid annually if a percentage of the tenant's gross annual sales is an amount greater than the base rent paid during the preceding 12 months.

The percentage rate used to calculate the additional rent for each consecutive 12-month period of the lease is set at 6% of the first $2,000,000 in gross annual sales and 7% on any greater amounts during the period.

Further, the additional rent to be paid will be the difference between the monthly base rent paid and the sum of the percentages of gross annual sales. The additional rent will be paid annually, within 45 days after the end of each 12-month period.

At the end of the first 12 months of business operation, the percentage rental rates are applied to the tenant's gross sales for the first year of occupancy. If the percentage amount is greater than the base rent paid, the tenant pays as additional rent, also called **percentage rent**, which is the difference between:

- the agreed-to percentage of the tenant's gross annual sales, if it is greater than the base rent paid; and

- the base rent paid each month during the preceding 12-month period.

Base vs. percentage rent

The amount of rent paid for retail space in multiple tenant shopping complexes or other **high traffic locations** is typically based on a percentage of the tenant's gross sales. Lease agreements containing a percentage rent clause are called *percentage leases*.

A prudent landlord negotiating a percentage lease includes a clause in the rent provision calling for payment of a **base rent**, a floor amount that serves as a minimum monthly rent a tenant pays during each year of the lease. Base rent is payable without regard to any amount of rent called for under the percentage rent clause. [See Figure 1 accompanying this chapter]

Generally, the base rent is set by landlord/tenant negotiations and either:

- calculated as a percentage of the estimated gross sales the tenant should receive during the first year of operations; or

- based on current rents paid for comparable premises.

The monthly **base rent** is adjusted upward on each anniversary of the lease by either pre-set increments, called *graduated rent*, or adjustments based on CPI figures, called *adjustable rent*. [See Chapter 44]

The amount of rent the tenant will actually pay monthly, quarterly or annually for the percentage rent, is the greater of either the base rent or the percentage rent.

Typical percentage rent rates for satellite tenants in a large shopping complex are 4% or 10% of the tenant's gross sales. However, the percentages for gradations of sales depend largely on the type of merchandise and services sold by the tenant, the pricing and volume of these sales and the traffic count at the location. Well known heavy advertisers, called **anchor tenants**, pay lesser rates than satellite tenants who surround the large anchor tenants.

A tenant who retails small ticket items at high volume in a high traffic area, such as a kiosk in the center of a mall, will have a high percentage rental rate, as high as 20% to 30% of sales.

Figure 1   *Excerpted from **first tuesday** Form 552 — Nonresidential Lease Agreement*

3.5   Additional percentage rent equal to _____% of gross sales made from the premises during each calendar year, less credit for other rent, real estate taxes, insurance and common area maintenance (CAM) charges paid for the calendar year.

  a.   The percentage rent shall be computed and paid for each month of the lease with a signed written statement of the gross income and percentage computation by the tenth day of the following month.

  b.   The additional percentage rent payable monthly to be credited for other rent, taxes, insurance, and CAMs paid by Tenant for the month.

  c.   Within one month after each calendar year and on expiration of the lease, Tenant shall compute and deliver a written statement of sales and the percentage rent due for the calendar year, less credit for rent, taxes, insurance and CAMs paid for the calendar year, to annually adjust the percentage rent remaining due from Tenant or to be refunded to Tenant by Landlord, which difference will be paid on delivery of the annual statement.

  d.   Gross sales includes all money or equivalent received by Tenant, subtenant, licensees or concessionaires, in the ordinary course of business, whether wholesale or retail, cash or credit, less credit for goods returned by customer or merchandise returned by Tenant or transferred to tenant-affiliated stores.

  e.   Landlord has the right, on reasonable notice, to audit Tenant's books regarding sales information.

Conversely, a tenant who retails big ticket items in low volume, such as an antique furniture store, will have a lower percentage rental rate.

When is percentage rent paid?

Typically, the tenant pays the additional percentage rent after the rental period has ended. The additional amount of the percentage rent is normally due within ten days after the end of the period used to calculate the percentage rent.

Landlords and tenants agree to a monthly, quarterly, semi-annual or annual **accounting period** for payment of the percentage rent depending on:

- whether the tenant's sales tend to be constant or seasonal; and

- the financial strength of the tenant.

Further, percentage rent paid more than once a year is typically adjusted annually in a **final accounting** to determine if any percentage rent remains due or is to be refunded to the tenant for the preceding 12 months of rental payments.

A landlord must initially rely on his tenant to, in good faith, provide an accurate accounting of his gross sales for the period.

However, in the lease agreement, the landlord should **reserve the right to**, on reasonable notice, audit the tenant's books regarding sales information and sales tax reports to the State Board of Equalization (SBOE). [See Figure 1]

Gross sales defined

The landlord and tenant must also negotiate which sales will be the subject the percentage rental rate.

Gross sales is the actual price received for all merchandise or services sold, leased, licensed or delivered in or from the premises by the tenant, for cash or on credit, as well as "layaway" sales at the time of the layaway transaction.

For the sale of **lottery tickets**, the tenant receives a 5% fee which is included in the gross sales, rather than the sales price received from the customer. [Calif. Government Code §8880.51]

Gross sales also include any sums received by the tenant for the licensing of vending machines, pay telephones, public toilet locks, etc.

If the tenant gives a vending machine operator the right to install vending machines on the leased premises for a one-time fee, called a *license*, the sums generated through the machine's sales are not included in gross sales since the tenant does not receive the sales proceeds.

Also, a periodic licensing fee received by a tenant from a vending machine operator for a license to use space is correctly considered part of the tenant's gross sales generated as a result of subleasing the premises. [**Herbert's Laurel-Ventura** v. **Laurel Ventura Holding Corporation** (1943) 58 CA2d 684]

Further, money received by the tenant from which he will receive no benefit, such as Medi-Cal funds received for direct disbursement to the staff as additional subsidized pay, is not included in the gross sales under a percentage lease. The funds did not increase the tenant's business, the tenant received no additions to sales and the funds were not for the tenant's use. [**Western Medical Enterprises, Inc.** v. **Albers** (1985) 166 CA3d 383]

The same exclusion rule applies to tips received by employees.

Items customarily excluded from gross sales in a percentage lease include:

- the selling price of merchandise returned for full credit;

- sums and credits received in the settlement of claims for damage to or loss of merchandise;

- sales tax;

- proceeds from the sale of fixtures, trade fixtures or other personal property used in the tenant's trade or business that are not merchandise;

- sales made to employees at a discount;

- refundable deposits; and

- uncollectible debts charged off by the tenant.

In practice, gift certificates are not considered part of the gross sales until they are redeemed and a sale is recorded.

Finance charges or interest on accounts receivable held by the tenant may or may not be included, depending on negotiations between the landlord and tenant, and whether the receivables are administered on or off the premises.

A fair rent for failure to use

A landlord enters into a percentage ground lease with a tenant who will build and operate a gas station on the premises. No provision requires the tenant to actually operate a gas station on the premises. The base monthly rent is set at $1,000 for the life of the lease without CPI or graduated adjustment. The percentage rent is set at 6.5% of gross sales.

The tenant builds and operates the gas station on the premises and pays additional rent since the amount of percentage rent always exceeds the base rent.

However, before the lease expires, the tenant closes the gas station. Then, the tenant pays only the base monthly rent since no sales exist. The base rent is significantly less than the percentage rent the tenant paid during the last year of operation.

The landlord claims the tenant owes him the percentage rent the tenant would have paid had the tenant continued to operate his business on the premises.

The tenant claims he owes no more than the monthly base rent since the lease agreement does not contain a provision requiring the tenant to operate the gas station at all times during the term of the lease.

Is the tenant liable to the landlord for the percentage rent the landlord would have received had the tenant continued operations on the premises?

Yes! An *implied covenant* exists in a percentage lease as a promise to continue to use the premises as anticipated by the lease agreement, when:

- the base monthly rent does not represent a fair return to the landlord; and

- the tenant decides not to operate his business on the property. [**College Block** v. **Atlantic Richfield Company** (1988) 206 CA3d 1376]

By entering into a percentage lease, the tenant is expected to continually operate his business during the lease term.

However, due to changes in market conditions, demographics, traffic patterns or other economic factors, the base monthly rent originally negotiated in a percentage lease may not always represent a fair return to the landlord — a fair rental value for the premises.

The landlord relies on the percentage rent to provide a yield on his investment that will keep pace with local rental conditions in the future.

When a tenant ceases to use the property to operate the business as anticipated by the use provision in a percentage lease, the percentage rent owed will be determined based on the amount of gross sales the tenant would have experienced had the tenant continued to use the property as permitted by the lease agreement.

The landlord should include a **use provision** in a percentage lease requiring the tenant to operate the business for the entire term of the tenancy.

Chapter 46

Nonresidential use-maintenance provisions

This chapter examines the provisions in nonresidential leases that establish the landlord's and tenant's rights and obligations regarding the use and care of the leased premises.

Shifting ownership obligations

A nonresidential lease agreement contains two basic categories of provisions establishing the tenant's obligations to the landlord:

- *rent provisions* for the payment of amounts owed; and

- *use-maintenance provisions* for the use, care and preservation of the grounds and improvements.

Rent provisions evidence the promise to pay money owed the landlord by the tenant given in exchange for the possession of the leased premises over a specific period of time. This monetary obligation is **separately enforceable** from the use and maintenance provisions.

Use-maintenance provisions in a nonresidential lease agreement establish the rights and obligations of the landlord and tenant regarding who is responsible for performing the care and maintenance of the premises during the lease term. [See **first tuesday** Form 552]

Use-maintenance obligations are unrelated to the payment of rent. Instead, they identify who will perform or contract for the repairs and maintenance of the leased premises — the landlord or the tenant.

If the landlord retains the majority of the maintenance obligations, the base rent the tenant will pay will likely be higher than otherwise. If the tenant assumes the majority of the maintenance obligations, the base rent the tenant pays will likely be lower.

Just as a tenant breaches a lease agreement by failing to pay rent, he also breaches the lease agreement when he fails to perform or acts in violation of a use-maintenance provision.

The tenant's breach of an essential use-maintenance obligation is followed by either a 3-day notice to **perform or quit** stating precisely what must be done by the tenant within three days, or a 3-day notice to **quit** if the breach is incurable, such as a use violation, the maintenance of a nuisance or waste to the property.

If the noticed breach **can be cured** and the tenant fails to cure it after notice, he loses the right to possession if a declaration of forfeiture of the leasehold interest is made in the notice. When the breach is **incurable**, as under a notice to quit, the tenant automatically loses any right to continue in possession and must vacate the premises within three days after notice.

A breach of the use-maintenance provisions by the landlord or the tenant, and the remedies available for the breach, can be litigated under contract law since the lease agreement is a contract. Not so for the separate right to possession. When the landlord involves the tenant's possessory rights in the property as part of his remedy on a breach by the use of a forfeiture election to terminate the tenancy, landlord/tenant law controls. [**Kendall** v. **Ernest Pestana, Inc.** (1985) 40 C3d 488]

Which use-maintenance provisions to include

The contents of each provision in a nonresidential lease agreement are fully negotiable when agreeing to enter into a lease transaction. The results of negotiations depend on the respective bargaining power of the landlord and the tenant, as tempered by market conditions affecting rental properties.

Also, lease provisions vary due to the type of property involved, including:

- the intended use of the property;

- delegation of operating costs and responsibility for the property's physical conditions;

- the length of the lease term.

Occasionally, the landlord or the tenant will use a lease agreement form especially prepared by their respective attorneys for repeated use, i.e., when the landlord has many properties to let or the tenant leases many locations (such as franchisors).

However, landlords more frequently use regular form lease agreements that contain provisions basic to nonresidential leases. They then attach addendums for provisions not already included in the form or contrary to provisions in the form. [See **first tuesday** Form 552 §1.3]

Editor's note — The following discussion of use-maintenance clauses refers to provisions in **first tuesday** *Form 552 —* Nonresidential Lease Agreement *accompanying Chapter 41.*

Use of the premises

On entering into a nonresidential lease agreement, a landlord and tenant agree the premises will be used by the tenant for a single, **specified purpose**, such as a retail clothing store or an auto mechanics shop, called a *use-of-premises provision*. [See **first tuesday** Form 552 §6]

If a lease provision does not restrict or specify the tenant's use of the leased premises, the premises may be used for any lawful purpose. [Calif. Civil Code §1997.210(b)]

Conversely, a lease may prohibit any change in use or set *standards* or *conditions* to be met before a change from the use specified in the use-of-premises provision may be implemented. [CC §1997.230]

If the use provision requires the landlord's consent to a change in use, but gives no *standard* or *condition* to be applied or met for the consent, the landlord must have a commercially reasonable basis for withholding his consent to the new proposed use sought by the tenant. [CC §1997.250]

The standard of reasonableness applied to the landlord's consent is the same as applied to assignment restrictions calling for the landlords consent.

In the use-of-premises provision, the tenant agrees to deliver up the premises on expiration of the lease in as good condition as it was when he took possession, less reasonable wear and tear.

Even if the tenant's use of the leased premises is unrestricted, the tenant cannot impair the premises by damaging it, creating a nuisance, engaging in illegal activities or subjecting the premises to greater wear and tear than the use contemplated when the lease was entered into.

In addition to the use allowed, the tenant agrees not to conduct any activities on the property which would:

- increase the landlord's liability or hazard insurance premiums; or

- violate any laws, building ordinances or tenant association rules, called a *compliance-with-laws clause*.

Appurtenances

Any use coupled with but not located on the leased premises for the benefit of the tenant's leasehold interest, i.e., reasonably necessary for the use and enjoyment of the leased premises, is called an *appurtenance*. [CC §662]

Leasehold **appurtenances** include rights in real estate owned by the landlord that are located outside the leased premises, such as:

- a right of way for vehicular travel through an industrial or office complex;

- parking for employees and customers;

- storage space, lobbies and restrooms; and

- access of ingress and egress from public roads to the leased premises, such as a road or driveway.

Signs and advertising

A landlord maintains the integrity of the building's physical and aesthetic appearance, and is assured all signs, advertising and addresses placed about the premises will comply with local ordinances and the landlord's policies by including a *signage provision* in the lease agreement. [See **first tuesday** Form 552 §8]

Under the **signage provision**, the landlord retains control over the size, style, content and location of signs constructed or installed on the premises to advertise the location or existence of the tenant's business.

The cost of sign installation can be charged to either the landlord or tenant as negotiated and stated in the terms of the lease.

Tenant improvements and alterations

A tenant's right to make alterations or further improve the premises **during the tenancy** is governed by the lease provision called a *tenant improvements and alterations clause*, or more simply a TI clause. [See From 552 §9]

To ensure the landlord retains control over the structures on or about the leased premises, the tenant agrees not to alter or further improve any part of the building without first obtaining the landlord's written consent. Should the landlord later consent to alterations or further improvements by the tenant, the tenant will pay all costs incurred in the construction, unless agreed to the contrary in an addendum or modification of the lease agreement.

A lease agreement for retail space, especially in malls, should include provisions which require the tenant to renovate his storefront and interior every number of years. Renovations by tenants every four to six years will help maintain a fresh appearance which is vital to the overall success of retail shopping centers.

When the landlord later consents to alterations by the tenant, the tenant must promptly notify the landlord of the commencement of construction so the landlord can post and record a *notice of nonresponsibility*. [See Chapter 5]

The **notice of nonresponsibility** is a form, releasing the landlord from responsibility for any claims made by contractors for improvements they construct on the leased premises under their contract with the tenant. [CC §3094; see **first tuesday** Form 597]

The notice bars mechanic's liens on the fee simple in the real estate and denies recovery from the landlord by unpaid contractors employed by the tenant.

Any increase in property taxes due to alterations made by the tenant are the responsibility of the tenant and will be paid to the landlord on demand.

Unless otherwise agreed, the tenant's improvements become the property of the landlord at the end of the lease term and cannot be removed by the tenant, with the exception of the tenant's trade fixtures. [**Wolfen** v. **Clinical Data, Inc.** (1993) 16 CA4th 171]

Further, when the tenant alters or improves the premises resulting in a new and different use of the premises, the tenant must, separate from the contractual duty imposed by a compliance-with-laws clause, comply with all building code requirements. If the tenant's installation of improvements violate building codes and ordinances, the tenant will be liable for the landlord's cost of conforming the new improvements to codes and ordinances. [Wolfen, *supra*]

Repair and maintenance

Of equal financial importance and effect as the amount of rent to be paid under a nonresidential lease agreement are the responsibilities for the payment of the **cost of maintenance** and repair of the premises. Ultimately, the tenant must bear them, either directly by incurring the costs himself or indirectly through the payment of basic rent or additional rent in the form of common area maintenance charges (CAMs).

The extent of the maintenance and repair obligations assumed by the tenant typically depends on the type of space leased and the length of the lease term.

The longer the lease term, including renewal options, the more likely the obligations for maintenance will be shifted to the tenant, with the exception of multi-tenant commercial and office space. The shift will be even more likely if the premises is a single-user building, such as a warehouse or bank building as opposed to a multi-tenant project.

The nonresidential tenant has a duty during the leasing period to notify the landlord of those repairs which are needed and are the responsibility of the landlord.

Some net lease agreement forms contain a *compliance-with-laws provision* requiring the tenant to make any **government-ordered repairs**, such as asbestos removal or seismic retrofitting.

If the term of the lease under a lease agreement containing a compliance clause is short, the landlord will be the primary beneficiary of the government-ordered repairs. In spite of the wording in the lease agreement placing the financial responsibility on the tenant, the landlord may be responsible for making and paying for government-ordered repairs. [**Hadian** v. **Schwartz** (1994) 8 C4th 836]

Right to enter

Once a tenant acquires a leasehold interest in a nonresidential premises, the landlord no longer has the right to enter the premises for any reason, unless agreed to the contrary or an emergency exists. However, the landlord might **reserve the right** to enter and make any necessary repairs, alterations or inspections of the premises, called a *right-to-enter* provision in the lease agreement. [See Form 552 §11]

A landlord may need to enter the premises when:

- the landlord makes necessary or agreed-to repairs or alterations, or is supplying necessary services to the tenant;

- the landlord shows the premises to a prospective tenant;

- the tenant has abandoned or surrendered the premises;

- the tenant requests a pre-termination inspection [See Chapter 19];

- a court order was issued allowing the landlord to enter; or

- an emergency exists which endangers the property. [See Chapter 3]

Waste

As would be expected in a lease agreement, the tenant agrees not to destroy, damage or remove any part of the premises or equipment, or commit waste on the premises or permit anyone else to do so, called a *waste provision*. [See **first tuesday** Form 552 §12]

If the tenant or a person permitted on the premises by the tenant commits waste on the property, the tenant commits an *incurable breach* of the lease agreement and automatically forfeits his right to possession. [See Chapter 26]

The landlord can serve the tenant who has committed or permitted waste to the property with a 3-day notice to quit, and initiate an unlawful detainer action to evict the tenant if he does not vacate. [Calif. Code of Civil Procedure §1161(4)]

Liability insurance

A landlord and tenant may agree the tenant will purchase a liability insurance policy to cover losses which might occur on the premises, including:

- property damage; and

- bodily injury.

The lease agreement should set the policy limits or minimum amount of liability insurance the tenant must obtain. These limits should be set as a result of the landlord's discussion and analysis with an insurance agent.

Typically, a tenant's obligation to maintain liability insurance under a lease is covered under the tenant's commercial general liability insurance policy which the tenant purchases to insure the business he will operate on the premises.

To protect the landlord from any dissipation of insurance proceeds by the tenant, the landlord should be **named** as an additional insured on liability and hazard insurance policies obtained by the tenant to cover the leased premises.

To be assured the landlord is named, the lease agreement should require the tenant to provide the landlord with a certificate of insurance from the carrier naming the landlord as an additional insured. [See Form 552 §13]

Under the insurance provision, both the landlord and the tenant waive any insurance subrogation rights each might have against the other. Thus, an insurance carrier cannot seek to recover from the landlord or tenant who was the cause of the injury or property damage. [**Gordon** v. **J.C. Penney Company** (1970) 7 CA3d 280]

Hazard insurance

In a multi-tenant building, a landlord obtains a hazard insurance policy and passes the cost of the premiums through to the tenant, generally by way of the monthly base rent or CAM expenses.

The landlord and tenant can agree the tenant will purchase a standard hazard insurance policy for fire losses, which also covers theft and vandalism of all personal property and the restoration of tenant improvements, including the destruction of plate glass windows.

Requiring the tenant to maintain a hazard insurance policy assures the landlord that the tenant will be in the financial position necessary to continue to operate his business if fire, theft or vandalism occurs during the term of the lease.

When the tenant is required to maintain an insurance policy for property damage resulting from fire, theft or vandalism, the landlord must be named by the carrier as an additional insured so the landlord can control the use of any insurance proceeds.

In a long-term, triple-net lease where the tenant has assumed all obligations and duties of ownership, the lease agreement shifts to the tenant:

- the obligation to maintain hazard insurance; and

- the burden of repairing any destruction of the real estate, regardless of the cause.

Hold harmless

The *hold harmless provision* covers the landlord for liability from injuries occurring on the premises which:

- arise out of the tenant's negligent use of the premises; and

- are caused by the tenant, his employees or customers due to the tenant's negligence.

Government-ordered repairs

When determining whether the landlord or the tenant is responsible for government-ordered repairs, the terms of the lease agreement do not always control.

Six factors are applied to the lease transaction to determine if the burden of complying with any government-ordered, curative actions to correct or eliminate deficiencies in the leased premises falls on the tenant or the landlord.

The six burden-of-compliance factors are:

- the ratio of the cost of repairs to the amount of rent due over the life of the lease;

- the length of the lease, including renewal options;

- whether the landlord or the tenant will benefit more from the repairs in terms of the useful life of the building and the remaining term of the lease;

- whether the repairs are structural or nonstructural;

- whether or not the repairs will substantially interfere with the tenant's enjoyment of the premises; and

- whether or not the government-ordered repairs were foreseeable at the time the lease agreement was entered into by the landlord and the tenant.

Each burden-of-compliance factor is weighed based on the circumstances surrounding the execution of the lease, the text of the lease provisions and the economic realities of the lease transaction.

For example, a landlord and a tenant enter into a 15-year nonresidential net lease agreement.

Boilerplate use-maintenance provisions transfer to the tenant all ownership duties, including structural repairs.

Less than two years into the 15-year lease, the county discovers friable asbestos on the premises and issues an abatement order to the tenant. Neither the landlord nor the tenant had previous knowledge that asbestos existed on the premises, as it was a pre-existing condition of the building.

On receiving the compliance order, the tenant seals off the contaminated area and conducts business out of another section of the building.

The costs of repairing the building is a sum roughly equal to 5% of the aggregate amount of rent due over the entire life of the lease.

Here, the provisions in the lease agreement and the circumstances under which the lease was entered into imply the duty to comply with the government order was transferred to the tenant since:

- the cost of repairs amounted to less than 5% of the aggregate amount of rent due over the life of the lease;

- the lease was for 15 years, and thus the cost of repairs could easily be amortized by the tenant during the remaining tenancy;

- the asbestos removal would most benefit the tenant since the contamination was discovered less than two years into the lease;

- the repairs are structural and the lease clearly transfers structural repairs to the tenant;

- the tenant's use of the premises would not be greatly interfered with during the abatement; and

- neither the tenant nor the landlord had reason to believe asbestos existed on the premises, yet the tenant was experienced in retail leasing and elected not to investigate the premises. [**Brown** v. **Green** (1994) 8 C4th 812]

Now consider a landlord and a tenant who enter into the same nonresidential net lease agreement but for a term of three years with an option to renew for five additional years.

The net lease contains boilerplate compliance with laws and maintenance and repairs provisions which shift all the duties of ownership to the tenant, including structural repairs.

After the tenant exercises his option to renew the lease for five years, the landlord receives a compliance order from the city requiring the leased premises to be earthquake-proofed.

The cost of quake-proofing the building roughly equals 50% of the aggregate amount of the rent due over the entire life of the lease, which is now in its fourth of eight years.

Here, even though the lease shifted the major burdens of ownership from the landlord to the tenant, an application of the six-factor test determines the landlord must bear the burden of the quake-proofing costs since:

- the cost of quake-proofing the premises was roughly equal to 50% of the aggregate rent due over the total eight-year term of the lease;

- the eight-year lease was short-term with little time remaining for the tenant to amortize the cost or the repairs; and

- the quake-proofing primarily benefits the landlord because of the short term remaining on the lease. [Hadian, *supra*]

Thus, when entering into a nonresidential net lease agreement, a landlord should consider including a provision calling for the tenant to assume the cost of compliance orders that do not regulate the tenant's use of the premises — government-ordered retrofitting or renovation.

Yet the landlord must be aware, if the economic realities of the lease agreement are not in accord with the text of the lease agreement, the landlord may still be liable for government-issued compliance orders.

Nonresidential lease agreements often favor the landlord by including a **hold harmless provision** through which the tenant holds the landlord harmless for all claims, damages or liability arising from any cause, including the landlord's negligence.

When a hold harmless clause is included in a lease agreement, the tenant needs to purchase liability insurance coverage for the risk of loss he has agreed is his — his contractual liability under the lease agreement. [See Form 552 §13]

Contractual liability insurance is separate from general liability insurance covering bodily injury and property damage.

Regardless of the type of hold harmless provision used, the landlord cannot shift responsibility to the tenant for any liability arising from his landlord's *intentional misconduct* or violation of law. [CC §1668]

For example, a landlord cannot escape liability to others for injuries occurring on the leased premises due to the landlord's failure to maintain the premises as obligated by the lease agreement, including abatement of any known dangerous conditions. [See Chapter 40]

Destruction

Initially, the responsibility for the costs of making repairs to nonresidential property when the leased premises is partially or totally destroyed lies with the landlord.

However, some or all of the responsibilities can be shifted to the tenant or allocated between the landlord and the tenant by a clause in the lease agreement, called a *destruction provision.*

In the **destruction provision**, the tenant agrees to repair and pay for any destruction to the premises:

- caused by the tenant;

- covered by insurance policies held by the tenant; or

- required by other lease provisions, such as the repair and maintenance clause.

When the tenant is obligated to carry insurance to pay for the cost of repairs, the landlord is assured the disbursement of any insurance proceeds under the tenant's policy will be used to pay for the repairs if he is named as an additional insured on the tenant's policy. [See **first tuesday** Form 552 §14]

On the other hand, the landlord agrees to repair and pay for any damage to the premises which:

- is not caused or covered by the tenant's insurance policies;

- is insured only by the landlord's policy; or

- is not insured by any policy. [See **first tuesday** Form 552 §16.3]

A destruction clause typically states the lease will not terminate due to any destruction of the premises, unless the landlord chooses to terminate it under specified conditions, such as:

- the repairs cannot be completed within 30 days;

- the cost of restoration exceeds 70% of the replacement value of the premises;

- the insurance proceeds are insufficient to cover the actual cost of the repairs; or

- the premises may not be occupied by law.

Thus, the landlord may opt to terminate the lease if the casualty is underinsured.

However, if the landlord fails to begin repairs which are his responsibility or, alternatively, terminates the lease within a reasonable time, the tenant can:

- abandon the premises due to a *constructive eviction* and be excused from further performance under the lease [CC §1942; see Chapter 29]; or

- pay rent and recover from the landlord any losses suffered due to the landlord's failure to repair. [**Ng** v. **Warren** (1947) 79 CA2d 54]

Chapter 47

Lease renewal and extension options

This chapter introduces a landlord's irrevocable offer for a tenant to remain in possession beyond the expiration of a lease.

Don't forget to exercise

A broker, acting as a leasing agent or property manager for an owner, arranges for a tenant to lease improved nonresidential real estate. The lease is for a three-year term and contains options to renew the lease for additional three-year periods.

The lease renewal options require the tenant to **exercise each renewal option** in writing at least three months before the lease term expires. Thus, renewal options, unless exercised, expire three months before the lease itself expires.

During occupancy, the tenant's business improves. As a result, he makes substantial improvements to the building with the owner's consent.

Business demands require the tenant to also lease an adjacent building. The two buildings are operated as one complex by the tenant. The cul-de-sac street fronting the building is even renamed after his business.

As the expiration date for exercise of the renewal option approaches, the tenant installs new air conditioning units, again with the owner's consent.

However, the tenant fails to give the owner the written notice required to exercise his option to renew the lease before the renewal option expires.

After the option expires, but before the lease expires, the tenant attempts to exercise the renewal option.

The owner will not waive or extend the expiration date of the option to renew. The tenant is told he must vacate at the end of the current three-year term since the renewal option expired unexercised.

The tenant claims his tenant improvement activity was sufficient to place the owner on notice of his intent to exercise the renewal option since his improvements were inconsistent with vacating the premises on expiration of the lease.

When the option to renew expires unexercised as agreed, does the lease *automatically* expire at the end of its term?

Yes! The tenant's further improvements of the premises just prior to expiration of the renewal option is not proper notice to the owner of the tenant's intent to renew. An option is an *irrevocable offer*, an agreement independent of the lease agreement, whether it is a provision in the lease agreement or an addendum to it. The option expires by its own terms, as does any offer, if acceptance is not given during the option period by exercise as specified in the option agreement. [**Bekins Moving & Storage Co.** v. **Prudential Insurance Company of America** (1985) 176 CA3d 245]

The lease term

Absent an agreement to the contrary, a lease terminates *automatically*, without further notice, on expiration of the lease term stated in the lease agreement. [Calif. Civil Code §1933(1)]

A tenant who remains in possession after the lease term expires is commonly referred to as a *holdover tenant*, legally called a *tenant at sufferance*.

A landlord subjected to a holdover may initiate an unlawful detainer proceeding to evict the holdover tenant immediately after expiration of the lease — no notice to quit is necessary. [Calif. Code of Civil Procedure §1161(1)]

Alternatively, when a renewal option does not exist and the tenant continues in occupancy and tenders rent which the landlord accepts, a month-to-month tenancy is created. Consequently, the landlord must serve the tenant with the appropriate notice to vacate to terminate the periodic tenancy created by the acceptance of rent for any period after the lease expired. [CC §§1945, 1946]

Options to renew/extend

Frequently, lease agreements contain provisions or addendums which allow the tenant to continue in lawful possession after the initial lease term expires. A prior agreement allowing continued occupancy is called an *Option to Renew/Extend the Lease*. [See Form 565 accompanying this chapter]

For a tenant, a **lease renewal/extension option** can be financially advantageous. The tenant has time during the option period to examine whether the economic and financial conditions of his trade or business at this location favor an exercise of the option and continued possession. If not, the tenant is under no obligation to exercise the option. If he does not exercise the option, he must vacate the premises on expiration of the lease.

Thus, the well-informed tenant will consider negotiating one or more renewal/extension options when entering into a lease agreement for a short term.

On the other hand, the landlord may not share the tenant's enthusiasm for a renewal/extension option since the only decision remaining seems to benefit the tenant — to renew or not to renew. With the granting of a renewal/extension option, the landlord is left in a somewhat uncertain future position as he does not know who will occupy the premises in the future. Meanwhile, the tenant is left to decide whether to exercise the option and extend the occupancy or vacate on expiration of the lease.

One solution to the landlord's anxiety about the future uncertainty of locating a new tenant is to set the **expiration** of the renewal/extension option several months before the lease expires. Thus, the expiration of the option unexercised will give the landlord sufficient time in which to locate a replacement tenant.

On the flip side of the uncertainties, the landlord also benefits from an option to renew/extend. A renewal option encourages a tenant to enter into the lease in the first place since the tenant has the right to continue in possession if the property proves beneficial to his business. Additionally, the renewal/extension option **encourages improvements** and promotion of the location by the tenant in anticipation of being able to remain in possession.

Consider a lease agreement that grants a tenant an option to renew the lease every three years at the same rental rate, without stating a date for expiration of the continuing option renewal periods. When the tenant attempts to exercise the renewal option, the landlord claims the lease is unenforceable since the lease agreement and the option grant the tenant the right to renew the lease forever — a violation of the rule against *perpetuities*.

However, the lease is valid. Nonresidential lease transactions are no longer controlled by laws governing **perpetuities**. The total term of the nonresidential lease, including extensions or renewals, if not limited by its terms, is limited to 99 years by statute. [**Shaver** v. **Clanton** (1994) 26 CA4th 568]

Renew vs. extend

A technical, but obvious, processing distinction exists between a *renewal* and an *extension* of a lease.

OPTION TO RENEW/EXTEND LEASE

DATE:_____, 20_____, at _____, California.

Items left blank or unchecked are not applicable.

FACTS:

This option to renew or extend is an addendum to the lease agreement entered into by Landlord and Tenant,

dated _____, 20_____, at _____, California,

recorded _____, 20_____, as Instrument No. _____, in _____ County, California,

regarding real estate referred to as: _____
_____

AGREEMENT:

1. Landlord hereby grants to Tenant the following option(s) to ☐ renew, or ☐ extend, the term of the lease agreement referenced above.

    1.1 The first option is for a term beginning on expiration of the original term of the lease and ending _____ year(s) thereafter.
    The rental payment schedule during the term of this renewal/extension to be:
    _____
    _____

    1.2 The second option is for a term beginning on expiration of the immediately preceding term and ending _____ year(s) thereafter.
    The rental payment schedule during the term of this renewal/extension to be:
    _____
    _____

    1.3 The third option is for a term beginning on expiration of the immediately preceeding term and ending _____ year(s) thereafter.
    The rental payment schedule during the term of this renewal/extension to be:
    _____
    _____

    1.4 Other: _____
    _____

2. Each option to renew/extend the lease expires _____months prior to the expiration of the lease term which immediately precedes the renewal/extension period provided by the option.

3. A written notice of Exercise of Option to Renew/Extend must be delivered prior to expiration of the option exercised and no sooner than _____months before expiration of the option exercised. [See **ft** Form 566]

    3.1 Exercise of each option to be delivered to Landlord by certified mail or personal delivery, or by personal delivery to broker/property manager who is:_____
    Address: _____

    3.2 Tenant's failure to timely exercise any option will cause the lease to expire unrenewed and unextended.

4. This addendum's provisions supersede any inconsistent provisions contained in the lease agreement.

5. Other provisions: _____

I agree to the terms stated above.	I agree to the terms stated above.
Date:_____, 20_____	Date:_____, 20_____
Landlord: _____	Tenant:_____
Agent: _____	Tenant:_____
Signature: _____	Signature: _____
Address: _____	Signature: _____
_____	Address: _____
Phone:_____	_____
Fax: _____	Phone:_____
E-mail: _____	Fax: _____
	E-mail: _____

An **extension** is a stretching out of the original lease term by retaining the original lease agreement and *modifying* its expiration date, extending the term for an additional period. On the other hand, a **renewal** requires the execution of a new lease on identical conditions to the original lease agreement, not a continuation of the old lease. [**In re Marriage of Joaquin** (1987) 193 CA3d 1529]

A renewal involves the preparation and signing of a new lease which creates an entirely new tenancy. The new tenancy is subject to any change in law affecting the rights and obligations of the landlord or the tenant and subordinate to any encumbrances which occurred during the term of the prior lease.

Alternatively, an extension merely **modifies** the original lease by extending its expiration date. Thus, the modified lease would not be subject to changes in the law or encumbrances occurring after the term of the original lease.

Quite often, however, everyone involved uses the terms interchangeably, neglecting to maintain clarity of purpose, legal rights and the paperwork involved.

For instance, a lease agreement granting the tenant an "option to renew" which does not specify the manner or method for exercise of the option and does not call for the signing of a new lease is considered an **extension** of the original lease agreement. As a result, the provisions of the original lease apply on exercise of the option, but with a new expiration date. [In re Marriage of Joaquin, *supra*]

Exercise of the option

To exercise a lease renewal/extension option, the tenant must notify the landlord of his unqualified intention to renew or extend the lease. The notice of exercise must be timely delivered to the landlord, unequivocal and precise in its terms for the specific period offered in the option. If not, the notice of exercise is ineffective and may be ignored by the landlord.

Consider a tenant who enters into a lease agreement which includes a provision or an attachment granting the tenant an option to renew the lease for an additional two-year period.

During the window period for exercise of the renewal option, the tenant notifies the landlord of his intention to renew the lease, but for only one year.

In this example, the tenant's notice to renew was an ineffectual attempt to exercise the option to renew the lease. The tenant's notice was a mere **proposal** to renew for a different period than the period stated in the option.

Thus, the notice was not an *acceptance* of the option to renew. The communication was an attempt to alter the original terms of the option. Here, the communication constitutes a *rejection* of the offer in the original option since it is a counteroffer calling for an alternative performance by the tenant, not an unequivocal acceptance. [**Hayward Lumber & Investment Co. v. Construction Products Corp.** (1953) 117 CA2d 221]

Also, when the renewal/extension option agreement specifies the steps to be taken and the time period in which they are to occur to exercise the option, the tenant must **strictly comply** if he intends to exercise the option. [Bekins Moving & Storage Co., *supra*]

Usually, the tenant is required to give written notice of his exercise of the option several months before the current term of the lease expires (usually three to six months).

Advance notice requirements give the landlord ample time to locate a new tenant should the present tenant elect not to renew/extend the lease.

The option should state the method for delivery of the tenant's notice of his intent to exercise the option to renew/extend. Notice of exercise should be required in writing and personally

EXERCISE OF OPTION TO RENEW/EXTEND LEASE

DATE:_____, 20_____, at _____, California.

Items left blank or unchecked are not applicable.

FACTS:

A lease agreement dated _____, 20_____, at _____, California,

entered into by _____, Landlord, and _____, Tenant,

recorded _____, as Instrument No._____, in _____County, California,

regarding real estate referred to as: _____

_____

_____

provides for renewal or extension of its term, or is subject to an option to renew or extend this lease granted by the landlord and dated _____, 20_____.

NOTICE TO LANDLORD

1. Tenant hereby elects to exercise the option to renew or extend the term of this lease following expiration of the current lease term for the additional period and on the conditions stated in the option.

2. Landlord is hereby requested to respond in writing to the Tenant regarding any further actions necessary on the part of the tenant to exercise this renewal/extension option, or implement this election to exercise the option, and result in a binding agreement for the additional term.

3. _____

_____

_____

_____

_____

_____

_____

_____

_____

Date:_____, 20_____

Tenant: _____

Signature:_____

Address:_____

_____

Phone: _____

Fax: _____

E-mail: _____

Title: _____

handed or sent by certified mail to the landlord within a specific window period of time, such as three months, which closes three to six months prior to the expiration of the lease.

If notice is to be delivered by certified mail, the risk of the notice being lost in the mail is on the landlord. When a receipt for certified mail is issued by the post office, the tenant is no longer responsible for its physical delivery to the landlord. It is unnecessary to request a return receipt. [**Jenkins** v. **Tuneup Masters** (1987) 190 CA3d 1]

Failure to **timely comply** with delivery of a written notice of exercise within the window period for exercise of the option causes the lease to automatically expire at the end of its term. To prevent an **unintended expiration** of a lease, the tenant's broker should prepare and hand the tenant an exercise of option to renew/extend lease form or make one available to the tenant during the window period for exercise of the option before the option itself expires. [See Form 566 accompanying this chapter]

An exercise of option to renew/extend lease form provides the tenant with the paperwork needed to exercise the option. The notice of exercise states the tenant's intent to exercise the renewal/extension option on its terms and conditions, without qualification or equivocation.

Typically, the broker's fee arrangement on the original lease calls for a fee on any extension or renewal. Not only is the exercise as intended by the tenant protecting the tenant, the leasing agent benefits by the exercise of the option. [See **first tuesday** Form 113]

Continued possession as exercise

A renewal option should, but need not, set forth the time period and manner for its exercise.

For example, a renewal option is silent as to the time and manner for exercise. The tenant

constructs substantial improvements on the property and remains in possession throughout the entire lease term.

The lease term expires without the tenant giving any notice to the landlord of his intent to renew the lease, yet the tenant **remains in possession**. The tenant then tenders the correct amount of rent as though he had already exercised his renewal option. The landlord refuses the tender of rent.

The landlord serves a notice to quit on the tenant claiming the tenant did not take steps to exercise the option to renew prior to the expiration of the lease and is unlawfully detaining the premises.

Does the tenant's continued possession of the property after the lease expires constitute exercise of the renewal option when delivery of a notice of intent to exercise is not called for in the option?

Yes! When the tenant has a renewal option and the time and manner for exercise is not specified, the tenant's continued possession and timely tender of rent indicates his election to renew. [**ADV Corp.** v. **Wikman** (1986) 178 CA3d 61]

Waiver of notice to exercise

A tenant is bound by the terms for exercise of the renewal/extension option, unless the landlord has, by his conduct, waived the requirements for exercise — acceptance of the option's offer to renew or extend. [**Simons** v. **Young** (1979) 93 CA3d 170]

A **waiver** is the relinquishment by the landlord of a known right, claim or privilege, such as the tenant's delivery of a notice to exercise the option to extend, by the conduct of the landlord since he holds or benefits from the right.

For example, a tenant fails to exercise his option to renew the lease as called for in the renewal option since he does not notify the landlord in writing of his intent to renew prior to expiration of the option.

On expiration of the lease, the tenant remains in possession and tenders rent to the landlord at the new rate called for in the option to renew. The landlord accepts the rent.

Later, the landlord serves a 30-day notice to vacate on the tenant. The tenant claims the renewal option has been exercised and the renewed lease bars the landlord's use of the 30-day notice to vacate to terminate possession since the landlord accepted rent called for in the renewal option.

Is the landlord's acceptance of rent when the tenant continued in possession a waiver of the written notice to exercise?

Yes! The landlord's **acceptance of rent** at the renewal rate after expiration of the lease waived his right to object to the tenant's prior failure to exercise the renewal option as agreed. [**Leonhardi-Smith, Inc.** v. **Cameron** (1980) 108 CA3d 42]

Now consider a tenant whose long-term lease contains options to extend the lease. The options will expire unless exercised in writing during a two month window period expiring 60 days prior to the expiration of the lease.

The lease agreement is entered into and dated two years prior to transfer of possession to the tenant (due to construction). The lease term is set to expire on the fifth anniversary of the date of the lease agreement.

Five years pass after the date of the lease agreement and the tenant remains in possession paying the rent due during the original term of the lease. The tenant then gives the landlord written notice to extend the lease 60 days prior to expiration of five years after the date of possession, not the date of the lease agreement as called for.

The tenant then remains in possession and pays rent at the increased amount called for in the option to extend. The landlord does not object to the notice of intent to exercise the option to extend and continues to accept rent payments.

Later, a new owner becomes the landlord.

The new landlord serves the tenant with a 30-day notice to vacate. The landlord claims the tenant's occupancy under the lease is a periodic month-to-month tenancy which can be terminated at the will of the landlord since the original lease expired without being extended due to the untimely notice to exercise the renewal option.

The tenant claims the acceptance by the prior landlord of the tardy notice of exercise of the renewal option and the rent called for in the option waived the landlord's right to enforce the conditions for exercise of the option.

Did the tenant exercise his option to extend due to a *waiver* of the notice requirement by the prior landlord when the landlord accepted rent after the lease expired and failed to object to delivery of the notice of exercise?

Yes! The prior landlord's receipt of the untimely exercise and acceptance of the rent without objection **waived compliance** by the tenant of the notice requirement for the exercise of the extension option. Thus, the lease and all its terms remained in effect for the period of extension, barring any attempts by the landlord to terminate the tenant's occupancy as a month-to-month tenancy. [**Oxford Properties & Finance LTD** v. **Engle** (9th Cir. 1991) 943 F2d 1150]

For the landlord to avoid waiving the requirement of a timely and unconditional written notice to exercise an option to extend, thus effectively extending the expiration of a lease when the tenant remains in possession and pays rent, the property manager and landlord must not accept rent from the holdover tenant unless the rent is paid under a newly negotiated lease agreement unrelated to the expired lease.

If the tenant refuses to vacate or refuses an offer of terms for a new and different tenancy, the landlord may, without further notice, begin an unlawful detainer action to remove the holdover tenant.

When the tenant neglects to properly exercise the renewal option (e.g., allowing the window period for exercise of an option to expire), the lease term will itself expire without renewal or extension. The property manager may evict the holdover tenant and relet the premises since the lease has expired and no new arrangement for continued occupancy has been agreed to, in writing or by the conduct of accepting rent for a period after expiration of the lease. [Simons, *supra*]

Finally, to exercise the lease renewal option, the tenant must be in full compliance with all conditions of the lease. Thus, the tenant cannot be in **default on rent** payments or allow any other material breach of the lease to exist at the time of his exercise of the option.

The payment of rent which is due is an implied condition which must be satisfied, in addition to any other conditions in the lease agreement, before the renewal option may be exercised. When the tenant is in default, his right to exercise his option is suspended. [**Nork v. Pacific Coast Medical Enterprises, Inc.** (1977) 73 CA3d 410]

Notice of option's expiration

A leasing agent who negotiates a renewal option **on behalf of a tenant** should arrange for the inclusion of a notice provision in the option provision that requires the landlord to give the tenant notice of the option's expiration 60 to 180 days prior to the expiration of the option.

This notice from the landlord to the tenant of expiration of the option eliminates the element of surprise for both landlord and tenant.

The tenant's inadvertent failure to exercise the lease renewal option can prove disastrous for the tenant who plans to continue in occupancy.

If the landlord will re-rent to the existing tenant despite the tenant's failure to exercise a renewal/extension option, the tenant will be forced to negotiate the terms of a new lease under the then existing market conditions. Thus, the landlord may be in a position, if availability of space is extremely tight, to take *unconscionable advantage* of the tenant, a situation the landlord must be careful to avoid. [See Chapter 48]

Renegotiation of rent and lease terms on expiration of a lease can result in increased rental rates, higher common area maintenance fees and other landlord charges, or changes in responsibilities being imposed on the tenant should the landlord choose to negotiate a lease with the holdover tenant whose option to renew expired unexercised. [Bekins Moving & Storage Co., *supra*]

Thus, a tenant's broker should inform the client as to when and how the renewal option must be exercised, and then provide the tenant with the necessary forms.

Again, if for no other reason, the leasing fee due on renewal should be a sufficient incentive to incite the broker to take action and assist the buyer to exercise the option.

Chapter 48

Lease assignments and subleases

This chapter presents the standards for a landlord's consent and the conditions for exactions under alienation provisions in lease agreements restricting leasehold assignments and subletting by tenants.

Consent conditioned on exactions

A landlord and tenant enter into a nonresidential lease agreement. The agreement contains an assignment and subletting provision, called a *restriction-on-transfer* or a *restraint-on-alienation* provision.

The **assignment and subletting** provision may either prohibit transfer of the tenant's interests or it may require the tenant to obtain landlord consent prior to assigning the lease or subletting (or further encumbering) the tenant's leasehold interest. If the provision permits an assignment or subletting, it:

- states the landlord's consent will not be unreasonably withheld; or

- fails to state a standard for objecting and withholding consent. [See Figure 1 accompanying this chapter]

Further, the lease agreement contains a *cancellation provision* allowing the landlord to cancel the lease agreement and terminate the occupancy on his receipt of the tenant's written request seeking the landlord's consent under the assignment or subletting provision.

After taking occupancy, the tenant vacates the premises and relocates his operations to another property with no intention of returning to the leased premises. The tenant finds a user who will pay rent at current market rates for the space, an amount that exceeds the rent owed the landlord on the lease, called *overriding rent*.

The tenant makes a request for the landlord's consent to **sublease** to the user. The landlord responds by canceling the lease agreement under the cancellation provision.

The landlord, having terminated the tenant's leasehold by cancellation of the lease agreement, negotiates directly with the user. The landlord enters into a lease of the premises with the user at current rental rates.

The tenant makes a demand on the landlord for the overriding rent he lost due to the landlord's refusal to consent to the sublease, claiming the landlord's consent was unreasonably withheld since no *conditions* for the consent were agreed to that entitled the landlord to the overriding rent.

The landlord claims his cancellation of the lease is valid, even though cancellation is an absolute restraint on the proposed transfer of the tenant's leasehold interest, since the tenant and landlord bargained for the cancellation provision that was triggered upon activation of the provision by the tenant's request for the landlord's consent to an assignment.

Can the landlord cancel the lease agreement even though he agreed not to unreasonably withhold his consent or condition consent on the exaction of the excess rents?

Yes! The two provisions in the lease, the consent-to-assignment provision and the cancellation provision, are mutually exclusive alternatives authorizing the landlord to take either of two separate courses of action when confronted with a request for consent to an assignment.

On receipt of the tenant's request for consent, the landlord exercised the cancellation provision, relieving the tenant of any further obligation under the lease — as well as terminating his tenancy and any potential profit from the property's appreciated rental value.

Thus, the issue as to whether the landlord refused his consent never arises. The landlord canceled the lease as agreed, thus nullifying any need to consider the request for consent.

Should the landlord choose not to cancel the lease agreement and terminate the tenancy on the tenant's request for consent to an assignment, the landlord is then **left to analyze** whether or not to consent. As a result, he is required to be **reasonable** about any objection he may have to the assignment since no other standard was set in the lease.

The cancellation provision in the lease agreement is bargained for and not the unconscionable result of an interference with an assignment of the lease. The prospective tenant did not have to enter into the lease agreement he signed or lease this premises.

Since the tenant's leasehold right to obtain higher rent had been contracted away by inclusion of the cancellation provision, the landlord did not unreasonably interfere with the tenant's right to assign or sublet by canceling the lease agreement. [**Carma Developers, Inc.** v. **Marathon Development California, Inc.** (1992) 2 C4th 342]

Transfer of any interest

An assignment or subletting provision in a lease agreement typically calls for the tenant to acquire consent from the landlord before the tenant may *transfer* his leasehold interest. [Calif. Civil Code §1995.250]

A **transfer** by the tenant includes an *assignment, sublease* or *further encumbrance* of the leasehold. [CC §1995.020(e); see Figure 1]

An **assignment** of the lease agreement transfers the original tenant's entire interest in the property to a successor tenant, leaving no interest held by the original tenant. However, the original tenant named on the lease agreement remains liable for the successor tenant's performance on the lease, even though the landlord consents to the assignment and the successor tenant becomes primarily responsible for the lease obligations, called an assumption.

For the original tenant to be **released of his liability** under the lease agreement on an assignment, a *novation* must be negotiated and entered into by the landlord and both tenants, sometimes called a *substitution of liability*. [**Samuels** v. **Ottinger** (1915) 169 C 209]

Figure 1 *Excerpted from **first tuesday** Form 552 —*
Nonresidential Lease Agreement

19. **ASSIGNMENT, SUBLETTING AND ENCUMBRANCE**: [Check only one]

19.1 Tenant may not assign this lease or sublet any part of the premises, orfurther encumber the leasehold.

19.2 Tenant may not transfer any interest in the premises without the priorconsent of Landlord.

a. Consent may not be unreasonably withheld.

b. Consent is subject to the attached conditions. [**ft** Form 250]

On the other hand, when entering into a **sublease** with a subtenant, the original (master) tenant transfers to the subtenant less than all of the master tenant's interest in the property. Also, **possession reverts** back to the master tenant on expiration of the sublease.

The master tenant granting the sublease remains obligated to perform on the master lease agreement. The subtenant does not assume liability of the master lease. However, the subtenant may not act in any way that would constitute a breach of the master lease agreement, a copy of which is attached to the sublease.

The **further encumbrance** of a tenant's leasehold interest occurs when the tenant places a lien on his leasehold to secure a loan, such as a trust deed or the delivery of a collateral assignment.

Editor's note — For simplicity's sake, the following discussion will only refer to an assignment of a lease. However, the discussion fully applies to any sublease or further encumbrance transaction.

Various alienation provisions

Leases include various types of assignment provisions, also called *alienation clauses*, which may:

- entirely prohibit any assignment of the lease [CC §1995.230];

- require the landlord's consent prior to an assignment without containing approved standards or placing any monetary conditions for the withholding of the landlord's consent [CC §1995.260];

- require the landlord's consent prior to an assignment, stating consent will not be unreasonably withheld [CC 1995.250(a)];

- require the landlord's consent, subject to *conditions* first being met by the tenant, e.g., payment to the landlord of all or part

of the tenant's gains on the assignment, a higher rental rate and an assignment fee, and an assumption by the tenant of maintenance and utility expenses [CC §1995.250(b)]; or

- contain *conditions* for a valid assignment without requiring any consent at all, such as the landlord is entitled to all or part of the consideration the tenant receives for the assignment in excess of rent due on the lease. [CC §1995.240; see Figure 1]

Standards lay out the analytical process imposed on the landlord which he must apply when making a judgment whether or not to withhold consent.

Conditions are sums of money or leasing terms that must be met by the tenant as a requisite to consent should the landlord consent to the assignment.

No standards for withholding consent

Consider a lease agreement with an assignment provision calling for the landlord's consent prior to the tenant's assignment, but devoid of any standard or condition for consent, such as consent "will not be unreasonably withheld" or that fees must be paid.

Thus, the assignment provision does not set a standard for consent or exactions to be paid as a condition for granting or withholding consent. Here, for lack of agreement to the contrary, the standards and conditions for the landlord's consent are set by law.

A lease agreement entered into on or after September 23, 1983, with **no standard** agreed to for the landlord to consent to an assignment, requires the landlord to have a **commercially reasonable basis** for his denial should he choose to withhold consent. The landlord cannot deny consent arbitrarily.

Also, **no conditions** for an exaction can be demanded when granting the consent, such as a higher rental rate, unless bargained for as a condition for consent and included in the lease agreement. [**Kendall** v. **Ernest Pestana, Inc.** (1985) 40 C3d 488]

Commercial reasonability standards

Commercial reasonability standards relate to the landlord's ability to:

- **protect his ownership interest** from property waste and financial deterioration due to the successor tenant's propensity to care for and make suitable use of the property under the use-maintenance provisions in the lease; and

- **ensure the future performance** of the lease by an assignment to a creditworthy tenant.

Commercially reasonable objections for withholding consent to an assignment include:

- the successor tenant's financial responsibility, or net worth, prior operating history and creditworthiness;

- the successor tenant's intended use, care and maintenance of the property;

- the suitability of the successor tenant's use, product marketing and management style for the property; and

- the need for tenant alterations to the premises. [Kendall, *supra*]

For example, a use provision in a lease agreement gives a tenant the right to operate a service business in a shopping center in which the landlord operates a retail business outlet. The lease agreement restricts the tenant's use to an "office use related to the business" of the tenant.

The lease alienation provision in the lease agreement requires the tenant to obtain the landlord's prior consent to an assignment of the lease agreement. The alienation provision sets **no standard** for withholding consent and provides for **no conditions** to be met (paid) by the tenant for the consent if it is granted.

Later, the tenant seeks to transfer the lease to a successor who will operate a retail business from the premises. The successor tenant's retail business will be in direct competition with the landlord's retail outlet.

Since it calls for a change in the use of the premises, the landlord refuses to consent to the assignment.

The tenant claims the landlord's refusal is commercially unreasonable since it amounts to *economic protectionism* unrelated to the landlord's ownership and operation of the rental property.

Here, the landlord's refusal is a commercially reasonable application of the use restriction in the lease agreement. He sought only to retain the use originally intended by the lease. The refusal is not due to improper economic protectionism in the management and operation of the real estate since the landlord did not seek an increase in rent or other economic benefits to enhance himself as a *condition* for his consent to the assignment of the lease. [**Pay 'N Pak Stores, Inc.** v. **Superior Court of Santa Clara County** (1989) 210 CA3d 1404]

Also, the landlord can reasonably refuse his consent to a trust deed lien the tenant seeks to place on the leasehold interest when the proceeds of the loan are not used to improve the property. [**Airport Plaza, Inc.** v. **Blanchard** (1987) 188 CA3d 1594]

Reasonable increases in rent

Consider a nonresidential tenant who agrees to pay a percentage of his gross sales as rent, but not less than a base monthly amount, called a *percentage lease*.

An alienation provision in the lease agreement requires the tenant to obtain the landlord's consent before assigning the lease. The provision does not include standards or conditions for the landlord's consent to an assignment.

The tenant enters into an agreement to sell his business and assign the lease to a new operator. The operator buying the lease (and the business) is to pay the tenant a monthly premium over the remaining life of the lease, called *overriding rent*.

The tenant requests the consent of the landlord to the assignment of the lease agreement. On investigation, the landlord determines the operator will manage the business in a manner that will not generate gross sales at the same level as the current tenant. Thus, under the percentage lease, the new operator will not become obligated to pay the amount of rent currently being paid by the tenant seeking consent.

However, the landlord agrees to consent to the assignment **conditioned** on the landlord receiving the **overriding rent premium** the tenant is to be paid for the assignment.

The tenant claims the landlord cannot condition consent on exacting the rent premium since no standards or conditions for consent exist in the lease and thus cannot now be imposed.

Here, the landlord can **condition** his consent to the tenant's assignment of the lease on the landlord's receipt of the monthly rent premium to be paid by the new tenant even though he did not contract in the lease agreement for the premium.

The landlord's conditional consent to the assignment is **commercially reasonable**. When granting consent, the landlord is entitled to preserve the rental income he currently receives from the existing tenant. The landlord does not need to accept the certain risk of a lower monthly percentage rent from the assignee while the original tenant receives a monthly premium. [**John Hogan Enterprises, Inc.** v. **Kellogg** (1986) 187 CA3d 589]

Proceeds from assignment demanded

Now consider a nonresidential lease agreement that contains an assignment provision authorizing the landlord to demand all the consideration the tenant will receive for an assignment of the lease as a *condition* for his consent to the assignment.

The landlord using the lease does not bargain for any other exaction, such as a portion of the purchase price the tenant will receive on a sale of the business that the tenant operates from the premises.

Later, the tenant agrees to assign the lease to a new operator as part of the sale of his business. The operator will pay the tenant a lump sum for the lease as part of the purchase price since rent due under the lease agreement is below market rates.

The landlord demands the tenant pass on the price paid for the lease as a condition for his consent to the assignment, which the tenant rejects.

The tenant claims the landlord's demand in exchange for consent is commercially unreasonable, and thus unenforceable, since the landlord has no lawful justification for the premium or additional rent they agreed to in the lease.

Here, the landlord may condition consent on his receipt of the payment made for the assignment of the lease.

Nonresidential lease agreements granting the landlord the right to receive any consideration the tenant is to receive related (and limited) to the *value of the lease* to be assigned are enforceable. [CC §1995.240]

Absent unconscionable or discriminatory provisions, nonresidential landlords and tenants are free to place *commercially reasonable* restrictions limited to the value of the leasehold on any assignment of the lease. [Carma Developers, Inc., *supra*]

More than rental value demanded

Again, a nonresidential lease agreement may provide for the landlord to receive all consideration the tenant receives for the assignment of the lease in exchange for his consent since these amounts are considered commercially reasonable. [CC §1995.240]

However, the consideration the landlord may receive for his consent to an assignment is limited to financial benefits directly related to the **value of the lease** assigned.

For example, a tenant occupies nonresidential property under a lease agreement.

The lease agreement includes a *profit-shifting clause* calling for the tenant to pay the landlord, in exchange for his consent to an assignment, 25% of the consideration the tenant receives for goodwill on the sale of the tenant's business which operates from the premises. Both agree it is the location of the leased property which will give the tenant's business its goodwill value.

The tenant's business is a success and the tenant locates a buyer for the business and the remaining term on the lease. The tenant seeks the landlord's consent for an assignment of the lease.

As agreed, the landlord demands 25% of the consideration the tenant will receive for his business goodwill. The tenant refuses to meet the demand and the landlord refuses to consent to the assignment.

As a result, the sales transaction does not close. The tenant makes a demand on the landlord for 100% of his lost profits on the sale.

The tenant claims the landlord's demand for a share of the profits on the sale of the business as agreed to in the lease agreement was a commercially unreasonable and unenforceable condition for granting consent to the assignment.

The landlord claims the profit-shifting provision is enforceable since all consideration received by the tenant on a transfer of the lease, even in excess of the value of the lease, can be agreed to and taken in exchange for consent.

Here, the landlord's right to receive the consideration the tenant is to receive for the sale of a business and an assignment of the lease as agreed is limited to the consideration the tenant receives for the **increased value** of the lease. For the landlord to demand the amount the tenant receives on his sale of his leasehold as consideration for the landlord's consent it must be agreed to in the alienation provision in the lease agreement to be enforceable. [**Ilkhchooyi v. Best** (1995) 37 CA4th 395]

Unconscionable advantage situations

Now consider a subtenant who must negotiate a new lease with the landlord or be evicted. The master tenant's lease agreement has been terminated by the landlord due to no fault of the subtenant.

The landlord submits a proposed lease agreement to the subtenant which differs significantly in its terms and conditions from the wiped out sublease agreement the subtenant held with the master tenant. When the subtenant attempts to negotiate a reasonable rent based on "comps" and eliminate unacceptable provisions, the landlord tells the subtenant to "take it or leave it." The subtenant is told he will be evicted if the proposed lease agreement is not signed.

The proposed lease agreement includes an alienation clause calling for a 200% increase in rent as a condition to be met before the landlord will consent to an assignment of the lease.

The subtenant signs the lease. Later, the subtenant seeks the landlord's consent to an assignment of the lease on his sale of his business. The landlord demands a modification of the rent provision to reflect the 200% increase in monthly rent as agreed, which the subtenant's buyer refuses to sign.

The landlord claims the alienation clause is enforceable since the clause was freely bargained for.

The tenant claims the provision was the result of an *unconscionable advantage* held by the landlord when they negotiated the terms of the lease since the tenant was in no position to bargain with the landlord. When the lease was negotiated, the tenant could not refuse to rent due to the goodwill he had built up for his business through a heavy investment in advertising at this location. In light of his negotiating advantage, the conduct of the landlord was unconscionable.

Can the tenant avoid enforcement of the profit-shifting clause?

Yes! The alienation clause agreed to was the result of the landlord taking *unconscionable advantage* of the subtenant's situation. The subtenant was in possession under a wiped out sublease without any power to freely bargain. He was already in possession and operating a business that had developed goodwill that would be lost if he vacated.

Collection of future rents so hugely excessive as to **effectively shift profits** from the sale of the business to the landlord for his consent to an assignment of a lease was overreaching on the landlord's part. Thus, the profit-shifting assignment provision was unenforceable as the product of unconscionable demands resulting from the advantage held by the landlord over the subtenant. [Ilkhchooyi, *supra*]

Also, any consideration the landlord seeks which is beyond the **value of the leasehold interest** or the landlord's interest in the real estate is not reasonable, whenever or however bargained for.

Proceeds from the sale of a business, or a rent amount so large in its increase as to reduce the goodwill value of the business occupying the premises, reach beyond the economics (rental value) of the lease.

Thus, the demands agreed to unlawfully shift profits that are unrelated to the value of the leasehold. The right to freely bargain is not intended to give the landlord the right to freely fleece a tenant in the name of freedom of contract. [Ilkhchooyi, *supra*]

Tenant-mitigation provisions

When a nonresidential lease agreement contains a tenant-mitigation provision and the tenant breaches the lease, the landlord may treat the lease as continuing and recover rent for the life of the lease. The provision shifts to the tenant the responsibility for leasing the property to **mitigate losses** when the tenant vacates and breaches the lease.

Under a tenant-mitigation provision, the landlord and tenant agree the tenant has a duty to find a replacement tenant, pay for any tenant improvements (TIs) and collect rent when the tenant breaches the lease and vacates the premises. [CC §1951.4]

On the tenant's breach of a lease agreement with a tenant-mitigation provision, the landlord does not have the duty to mitigate his rental losses by **repossessing and reletting** the space himself (or as an agent of the tenant) before enforcing collection of future rents due under the lease agreement.

However, if the lease agreement also provides for the landlord's prior consent to a transfer, the tenant-mitigation provision is enforceable only if the landlord's consent to an assignment is not unreasonably withheld. [CC §1951.4(b)(3)]

A landlord who prohibits assignments or unreasonably withholds consent retains the duty to mitigate his loss of rents on the tenant's breach.

Broker's role

Assignment (alienation) provisions restricting the transfer (assignment) of the leasehold interest held by a tenant become a concern of the bus-op or industrial broker when:

- negotiating the assignment of a lease in a *bus-op sale* (or negotiating a sublease or a further encumbrance);

- *relocating* a tenant whose current lease has not yet expired; or

- negotiating the origination of any lease.

A broker handling a **bus-op sale** or **relocation** of a business or industrial tenant must determine the tenant's ability and under what standards or conditions the tenant is allowed to assign the existing lease to a buyer of the business operation or other successor tenant.

The broker starts the analysis by ascertaining the type of assignment clause the landlord's proposed lease agreement contains. The broker can then determine the tenant's assignment rights.

Now consider a leasing agent who is **negotiating a lease** on behalf of a prospective tenant. The tenant's agent should limit the wording of an assignment provision to include:

- the landlord's consent "will not be unreasonably withheld"; and

- any exaction to be paid for the consent is limited to any increased rental value of the premises received by the tenant.

Any prohibition against assignment should be eliminated by including the "with consent" provision.

Conversely, the landlord's leasing agent who arranges a lease should review the assignment provision in the proposed lease agreement and include any consideration the tenant is to pay the landlord as a condition for his consent to an assignment.

For example, as compensation for consent to an assignment, the landlord may want to:

- adjust rents to current market rates;

- receive fees and costs incurred to investigate the successor tenant's credit and business conduct so he can analyze his risk of loss should he consent to the assignment;

- receive any overriding rent or lump sum payment the tenant receives that is attributable to the value of the lease;

- require the successor tenant to pay operating expenses as additional rent such as maintenance, utilities, insurance and taxes; or

- alter the terms of the lease agreement and any options to extend/renew the lease or buy the property.

Any exactions the landlord may expect or later seek for his consent must be agreed to and set forth in the lease agreement, and be related to the value of the lease to be enforceable.

Chapter 49

Nonresidential rent control prohibited

This chapter discusses the prohibition of nonresidential rent control and the narrow powers agencies have to regulate facets of business location, development and occupancies.

Legislative purpose

Residential landlords and apartment builders in California have battled local rent control ordinances since the mid-1970s.

Some judicial support for de-control is taking root since the societal objectives underlying the enactment of rent control ordinances are not being met. [**152 Valparaiso Associates** v. **City of Cotati** (1997) 56 CA4th 378]

Further, the California legislature enacted a scheme which will gradually lead to a phaseout of all residential rent control. The economics of rent control in the long term are not kind to tenants or the surrounding neighborhoods, while investment capital is unharmed since it simply locates elsewhere. [Calif. Civil Code §1954.52; see Chapter 57]

Most major metropolitan areas in California, including Los Angeles, San Francisco, Oakland and San Jose, have some form of residential rent control.

However, the city of Berkeley went beyond attempts to control only residential income properties. The city passed further rent control ordinances placing restrictions on the amount of rent landlords of nonresidential properties could change.

The stated objective supporting the Berkeley nonresidential rent ordinances was to preserve the city's older business neighborhoods without change or evolvement. Inefficient owners with improperly located shops saw their rents rise dramatically as their space was sought by better capitalized and more effective businessmen, a process called *Economic Darwinism* or *creative destruction*. Simply put, the landlords were willing to rent to more efficient and productive businesses willing to pay a higher rent.

Local historical preservation advocates asserted rent control was the only way to protect "mom-and-pop" shops which otherwise are no longer financially viable operations. Conversely, landlords felt they should be allowed to rent the space to any tenant whose business operation conforms to existing zoning ordinances.

Local community leadership is caught politically between making a policy commitment to protect inefficient, small shop owners in historic business districts or fostering an environment that encourages the growth of existing businesses or their replacement by fresh, energetic businesses in the same or newly constructed structures.

However, no California city, county or other public agency may pass and enforce nonresidential rent control ordinances. [CC §1954.25]

The California legislature felt nonresidential rent control was **economically improper** since it:

- discouraged commercial development and open market competition;

- benefitted one business enterprise over another; and

- hampered business expansion. [CC §1954.25]

Rental limit ban

The ban on nonresidential rent control also covers actions by all *public entities* who act as landlords, as well as private landlords. [CC §1954.27(a)]

A **public entity** includes:

- the state;

- all cities and counties;

- all public authorities and agencies; and

- all political subdivisions and public corporations. [Calif. Government Code §811.2]

Thus, no public entity can **control** or **limit** nonresidential rental rates, directly as owners or indirectly by ordinances. Using the power of *eminent domain* to control rents is improper.

Nonresidential real estate includes all real estate except:

- dwelling units;

- residential hotels; and

- mobilehome parks. [CC §1954.26(d)(4)]

Thus, the marketplace of available space for rent, managed by the brokers as the gatekeepers, is left to sort out **who will occupy** the space without government interference. [CC §1954.26(f)]

To meet these ends, public agencies are prohibited from designating a specific tenant with whom a landlord must negotiate to create, extend or renew a **nonresidential lease**. Any tenant may rent any nonresidential space based on negotiations unfettered by governmental interference. [CC §1954.26(f)]

The prohibition against nonresidential rent control covers all actions by local governments, whether by charter, ordinance, resolution, administrative regulations or policy statements. [CC §1954.26(f)]

Local rent control ordinances cannot establish or dictate any of the terms which might be negotiated in a nonresidential lease agreement or in the renewal or extension of the lease.

However, not all local government powers have been curbed. What has ended is government interference with nonresidential **lease negotiations** between landlords and tenants.

Remaining local powers

Local governments can still regulate all facets of business **location** and **development** such as:

- exercising eminent domain powers [CC §1954.28(a)];

- abating nuisances [CC §1954.28(b)];

- establishing zoning (use) and business licenses (policing) [CC §1954.29(a)]; and

- protecting historical resources. [CC §1954.28(e)]

Also, the ban on nonresidential rent control does not apply to **redevelopment contracts** entered into by a developer and a public agency.

Under redevelopment agreements, the developer rents to local businesses at a set or **reduced rate** in exchange for participation with the public agency. [CC §1954.28(d)]

Negotiation notice to landlord

Public agencies may establish a notice procedure for an existing nonresidential tenant to **make an offer** to the landlord, or **solicit an offer** from the landlord, negotiating for a renewal or extension of the lease.

However, the agency's action cannot interfere with rights held under an existing lease agreement. Thus, they cannot alter the lease expiration date or the attendant obligation of the tenant to vacate on expiration or be evicted. [CC §1954.31]

For example, a lease agreement exists which does not grant an option to the tenant to renew or extend the term of the lease, called a *term-only lease*.

However, the local governing agency can by ordinance create a procedure allowing the tenant to deliver a *negotiation notice* to the landlord. In the **negotiation notice**, the tenant makes or solicits an offer to negotiate an extension of the term of the lease. [CC §1954.31(a)(1)]

A tenant who has *materially breached* a significant provision in the lease agreement is not eligible to use the negotiation notice scheme. [§1954.31(b)(1)]

The negotiation notice acts as the **tenant's offer** to acquire an extension or renewal of the lease, an activity a tenant could carryout without the existence of an enabling ordinance. Of course, the tenant does not need to use a negotiation notice to contact his landlord. [CC §1954.26(j)(2)]

On the landlord's receipt of the negotiation notice, the landlord is required to respond if the notice is sent to the landlord within 270 days before the expiration of the lease. [CC §1954.31(a)(2)(A)]

However, whether or not the landlord receives a negotiation notice from the tenant, the landlord and the property manager have no duty to notify the tenant the lease is expiring at the end of the term stated in the lease agreement.

Impasse notice to tenant

If the tenant delivers the negotiation notice within 270 days before the lease expires, the landlord either:

- enters into negotiations to renew or extend the lease with the tenant; or

- delivers an *impasse notice* to the tenant no more than 180 days before the lease expires, within a time period after receipt of the negotiation notice as set by the local agency. [CC §1954.31(a)(2)(B)]

An **impasse notice** advises the tenant the lease will expire as called for in the lease and no modification of the lease will be entered into. [CC §1954.26(i)]

For example, a city passes an ordinance requiring a landlord to respond to an impasse notice within 30 days of receiving a negotiation notice, but not prior to 180-days before the lease expires.

However, if the negotiation notice is received 150 days prior to expiration of the lease, the landlord must respond within 30 days or he will be acting in **bad faith**.

The landlord is also required to send an impasse notice when he or his agent have received a negotiation notice and entered into renewal or extension negotiations with the tenant which are later broken off. The impasse notice indicates the lease will not be renewed or extended.

Also, negotiation and impasse notice ordinances cannot force the landlord to deal with a tenant or to make a counteroffer to the tenant. A landlord is not required to negotiate an additional or new term with the existing tenant and may reject the tenant's offer by use of the impasse notice.

One purpose served by the tenant's notice to the landlord and the landlord's response is to allow the tenant time to negotiate a new or extended lease with their landlord or find alternative space before the lease term expires. In practice, tenants have always knowingly borne these burdens as their possessory interest draws to an end.

On its face, and without conjecture as to unintended consequences, these ordinances appear to add nothing to the leasing environment except for the landlord's written impasse notice in response to a prior written offer from the tenant to negotiate.

However, the notice rules do not provide guidance for landlords who commence negotiations which become prolonged and continue beyond the response period set by ordinances for delivery of an impasse notice. If the landlord breaks off negotiations after the response period for delivery of the impasse notice has passed, it is too late to deliver an impasse notice unless the ordinance extended the time in which to respond.

The safest conduct for the landlord who receives a tenant's negotiation notice is to deliver an impasse notice within the response period set by the local ordinance and before entering into negotiations. If negotiations result in an extension or renewal, the notice becomes irrelevant. If negotiations fail, the landlord complied with the negotiation/impasse ordinance.

Failure to deliver notices

A landlord or property manager who fails to deliver an impasse notice and does not enter into negotiations after the timely receipt of the tenant's negotiation notice may have acted in *bad faith*. A non-response subjects the landlord or property manager to liability for the tenant's actual money losses incurred due to the **bad faith** failure to deliver the impasse notice. [CC §1954.31(a)(3)]

When confronted with a bad faith claim, the landlord should immediately deliver an impasse notice and extend the expiration of the lease to a date after delivery of the impasse notice which represents the period of time the tenant would have been given prior to expiration of the lease had an impasse notice been timely delivered. The extension avoids loss of the tenant's reasonable expectations, induced by the notice ordinance, of up to a 180-day period to relocate after receipt of an impasse notice.

SECTION G

Residential Rental and Lease Agreements

Chapter 50

Residential rental and lease agreements

This chapter distinguishes residential lease agreements from month-to-month rental agreements.

Fixed-term or periodic tenancy

Residential landlords and tenants enter into either a lease agreement or a periodic rental agreement when the landlord transfers the right to occupy property to the tenant, called *leasing* or *renting* property. Periodic rental agreements are nearly always structured as month-to-month rental agreements.

Other than the **expiration** of the tenancy conveyed by each agreement and the duration of originally agreed rights and obligations, residential lease agreements and rental agreements grant and impose on the landlords and tenants the same rights and obligations. It is the expectation of continued occupancy and the obligation to pay rent which differs.

Provisions agreed to which are not included as boilerplate provisions in the pre-printed forms used by landlords are included in an addendum to the rental or lease agreement. The provisions are entered on the addendum, and the addendum is referenced in the body of the rental or lease agreement to which it is attached.

Additional terms and conditions placed in addendums include authorization for the tenant to maintain items on the premises such as a pet, fish tank or liquid-filled furniture, or the landlord's grant to the tenant of an option to buy the property or to renew or extend the term of the lease.

A month-to-month **rental agreement** runs for an indefinite period of time since it automatically renews monthly, and on the same terms, until modified or terminated by notice. [See **first tuesday** Form 551 §2]

Month-to-month tenancies, a variety of *periodic tenancies* created by entering into a **rental agreement**, can be terminated by either the landlord or the tenant on 30 days written notice. [Calif. Civil Code §1946; see Chapter 33]

On the other hand, a **lease agreement** creates a tenancy that continues for a fixed period, called its *term*, such as six months or one year, at the end of which the tenant's right to occupy expires. [See Form 550 §2 accompanying this chapter]

Also, the lease terminates at the end of its fixed term without further notice by either the landlord or the tenant, called *expiration* of the lease. Unlike a periodic tenancy, no renewal of a lease occurs on expiration of its term, unless agreed to in an option to renew or extend.

Unlike the required use of a 30-day notice to vacate to bring a month-to-month tenancy to termination, the lease agreement contains the only notice the tenant or the landlord is entitled to receive that the lease terminates. The expiration provision in the lease agreement sets forth the day the right to occupy expires, automatically reverting the right of occupancy to the landlord.

Rental market influences

The population of tenants and the number of properties competing for these tenants, as well as the comparison of a property's location and its amenities to competing properties, create the **rental market**. It is the rental market which sets the amount of rent a residential landlord is able to charge on any given day.

Generally, tenants on month-to-month rental agreements pay higher amounts of rent for a unit than do tenants with lease agreements. Month-to-month tenants pay a premium for the privilege of being able to vacate the premises on 30 days' notice, without liability exposure for future rents. This privilege held by the tenant contributes to the landlord's uncertainty about his income and costs of tenant turnover, hence the premium rent.

Tenants typically pay lower rents when they enter into a lease. In stable rental markets, the longer the lease, the lower the rent. Rent is, however, subject to adjustments for future inflation.

Also, landlords offer lower rents on leases to persuade tenants to **commit** themselves to longer periods of tenancy. A landlord entices tenants to enter into lease agreements as part of a strategy to stabilize his income, reduce the vacancy rate and minimize turnover costs.

However, during market periods of generally high vacancy rates, price-competitive landlords favor using month-to-month rental agreements rather than leases. Therefore, when rents begin to rise landlords can adjust rents accordingly.

Just as a month-to-month rental agreement can be terminated on 30 days' notice, the amount of rent can be increased to current market rates on 30 days' written notice (except for a 60-day notice to increase rents on residential units by 10% or more within a 12-month period, and for rent control properties). [CC §827]

Lease negotiations on expiration

Conversely, a landlord cannot alter the terms of a lease agreement during the life of the lease without **consideration** and the tenant's **consent**.

The landlord desiring to keep the tenant with an impending lease expiration should contact the tenant and offer to enter into another lease agreement or a month-to-month rental agreement. Unless contacted (and the lease is renewed or extended), the tenant knows he is expected to vacate the premises on expiration of the lease.

If the tenant desires to remain in possession when his lease expires, the amount of rent a landlord can demand is limited only by negotiations and the availability of other rentals and tenants.

On expiration of a lease, the tenant has no lawful right to possession of the unit. If the tenant remains in possession and refuses to pay the amount of rent demanded by the landlord, he may be evicted immediately without further demand for possession. [Calif. Code Civil Procedures §1161(1)]

A better initial plan for retaining tenants includes the landlord entering into a lease agreement, giving the tenant an option to renew or extend the lease for a set period of months at the **prevailing rent**.

Requisites to accepting tenants

On locating a prospective tenant for a residential unit, the landlord requires him to complete a credit application so the prospect's creditworthiness can be established before entering into either a rental or lease agreement. [See **first tuesday** Form 302]

The credit application should be referenced and attached as an addendum to any rental or lease agreement entered into by the landlord and tenant. The application is part of the leasing process which persuades the landlord to accept the applicant as a tenant.

Initially, the landlord uses the authorization provided by the tenant on the application to verify the tenant's rental history, employment, credit standing and check writing history.

If a prospective tenant has a poor credit rating or no credit rating at all, yet meets the landlord's income requirements, the landlord might seek assurances in addition to the maximum security deposit allowed, such as:

- a co-signer on the lease; or

- a guarantee agreement executed by a creditworthy individual. [See **first tuesday** Form 439-L]

DATE:_____, 20_____, at _____, California.

Items left blank or unchecked are not applicable.

FACTS:

1. This lease agreement is entered into by _____, as the Landlord,
and _____,as the Tenant(s),

    1.1   regarding residential real estate referred to as: _____

    _____

    1.2   including the following:

        ☐ Garage/parking space #_____

        ☐ Storage space #_____

        ☐ Furnishings:

    1.3   The following checked attachments are part of this agreement:

        ☐ Condition of premises [**first tuesday** Form 560]

        ☐ Tenant's credit application [**ft** Form 302]

        ☐ Condition/Inventory of furnishings [**ft** Form 561]

        ☐ Rent control disclosures

        ☐ Brokerage fee addendum [**ft** Form 273]

        ☐ House/Building rules

        ☐ Option to renew/extend lease [**ft** Form 566]

AGREEMENT:

2. DEPOSIT:

    2.1   Landlord acknowledges receipt of $_____ as a security deposit.

    2.2   The deposit is security for the diligent performance of Tenant's obligations, including payment of rent, repair of damages, reasonable repair and cleaning of premises on termination, and any loss, damages or excess wear and tear on furnishings provided to Tenant.

    2.3   No interest will be paid on the deposit, and Landlord may place the deposit with his own funds, except where controlled by law.

    2.4   Within 21 days after Tenant vacates, Landlord to furnish Tenant with a security deposit statement itemizing any deductions, with a refund of the remaining amount.

3. TERM OF LEASE:

    3.1   This lease will begin on _____, 20_____, and continue until _____, 20_____.

    3.2   The lease terminates on the last day of the term without further notice.

    3.3   If Tenant holds over, Tenant to be liable for rent at the daily rate of $_____.

4. RENT:

    4.1   Tenant to pay, in advance, $_____ rent monthly, on the _____ day of each month.

    4.2   Rent to be paid by:

        a.   ☐ cash, ☐ check, or ☐ cashier's check, made payable to Landlord or his agent and delivered

            to: _____
                (Name)

            _____
                (Address)

            _____

            _____
                (Phone)

            Personal delivery of rent to be accepted at Landlord's address during the hours of _____ am to _____pm on the following days: _____

        b.   ☐ credit card #_____/_____/_____/_____ issued by _____,
            which Landlord is authorized to charge each month for rent due.

— — — — — — — — — — — — — *PAGE ONE OF THREE — FORM 550* — — — — — — — — — — — — — — —

   c. ☐ deposit into account number _____

     at: _____
        (Financial Institution)

        _____
        (Address)

        _____

4.3 Tenant to pay a charge of $_____ as an additional amount of rent, due on demand, in the event rent is not received within five days after the due date.

4.4 If any rent or other amount due Landlord is not received within five days after its due date, interest will thereafter accrue on the amount at 12% per annum until paid. On receipt of any past due amount, Landlord to promptly make a written demand for payment of the accrued interest which will be payable within 30 days of the demand.

4.5 Tenant to pay a change of $_____ as an additional amount of rent, due on demand, for each rent check returned for insufficient funds, and thereafter pay rent by cash or cashier's check.

5. POSSESSION:

5.1 Tenant will not be liable for any rent until the date possession is delivered.

5.2 If Landlord is unable to deliver possession, Landlord will not be liable for any damage, nor will this lease terminate.

5.3 Tenant may terminate this lease if Landlord fails to deliver possession within five days of commencement.

5.4 Only the above-named Tenant(s) to occupy the premises.

5.5 Tenant will not assign this lease agreement or sublet, or have boarders or lodgers.

5.6 Tenant(s) will have no more than _____ guests staying the greater of no more than 10 consecutive days or 20 days in a year.

5.7 Except as noted in an addendum, Tenant agrees the premises, fixtures, appliances and furnishings are in satisfactory and sanitary condition. [ft Form 561]

5.8 Landlord to make any necessary repairs as soon as possible after notification by Tenant. If Landlord does not timely make necessary repairs, Tenant may have the repairs made and deduct the cost, not to exceed one month's rent.

6. TENANT AGREES:

6.1 To comply with all building rules and regulations and later amendments or modifications.

6.2 To pay for the following utilities and services: _____

_____

_____

landlord to pay for: _____

6.3 To keep the premises clean and sanitary and to properly dispose of all garbage and waste.

    a. ☐ Yard maintenance included in tenant obligations.

6.4 To properly operate all electrical, gas and plumbing fixtures and pipes, and keep them clean and sanitary.

6.5 To make the premises available on 24 hours notice for entry by Landlord to make necessary repairs, alterations or services, or to exhibit the premises to prospective purchasers, tenants, employees or contractors.

    a. In case of emergency or Tenant's abandonment of premises, Landlord may enter the premises at any time.

6.6 Not to disturb, annoy, endanger or interfere with other occupants of the building or neighboring buildings.

6.7 Not to use the premises for any unlawful purpose, violate any government ordinance, or create a nuisance.

6.8 Not to destroy, damage or remove any part of the premises, equipment or fixtures or commit waste, or permit any person to do so.

6.9 Not to keep pets or a waterbed on the premises without Landlord's written consent.

    a. See attached ☐ pet addendum [ft Form 563], ☐ waterbed addendum. [ft Form 564]

6.10 Not to make any repairs, alterations or additions to the premises without Landlord's written consent.

    a. Any repairs or alterations shall become part of the premises.

6.11 Not to change or add a lock without written consent.

7. GENERAL PROVISIONS:

7.1 Tenant agrees to hold Landlord harmless from claims, demands, damages or liability arising out of the premises caused by or permitted by Tenant, Tenant's family, agents employees and guests.

　　a. ☐ Tenant to obtain insurance for this purpose naming Landlord as an additional insured.

7.2 Landlord to maintain the premises and common areas in a safe and sanitary condition and comply with all applicable ordinances and regulations.

7.3 Waiver of a breach of any provision shall not constitute a waiver of any subsequent breach. Landlord's receipt of rent with knowledge of Tenant's breach does not waive Landlord's right to enforce the breached provision.

7.4 In any action to enforce this agreement, the prevailing party shall receive attorney fees.

7.5 Notice: Pursuant to Section 290.46 of the Penal Code, information about specified registered sex offenders is made available to the public via an Internet Web site maintained by the Department of Justice at www.meganslaw.ca.gov. Depending on an offender's criminal history, this information will include either the address at which the offender resides or the community of residence and ZIP code in which he or she resides.

7.6 ☐ See attached addendum for additional terms and conditions. [ft Form 250]

7.7 ☐ See attached Notice of Illegal Controlled Substance. [ft Form 583]

8. _____
_____
_____
_____
_____
_____
_____
_____
_____
_____

I agree to let on the terms stated above.

Date:_____, 20_____

Landlord: _____

Agent: _____

Signature: _____

Address: _____

_____

Phone:_____

Fax: _____

E-mail: _____

I agree to occupy on the terms stated above.

Date:_____, 20_____

Tenant:_____

Tenant:_____

Signature: _____

Signature: _____

Address: _____

_____

Phone:_____

Fax: _____

E-mail: _____

Then, if the tenant defaults in rent payments or damages the premises, the landlord can hold the co-signer liable or collect his losses from the guarantor should the security deposit prove insufficient to cover lost rents and maintenance charges.

Condition of premises addendum

Residential landlords and tenants have a statutory duty to, respectively, maintain the property and refrain from damaging the premises. [CC §§1941, 1941.2]

To avoid disputes over who is responsible for any damage to the premises, the residential landlord and tenant should complete and sign a *condition of premises addendum* **before** the tenant is given possession. [See **first tuesday** Form 560; see Chapter 20]

Before a tenant takes possession, the landlord or his manager needs to inspect the unit with the tenant, called a *walk-through*. Together, the landlord (or resident manager) and the tenant will use a condition of premises addendum to confirm:

- the premises is in satisfactory condition;

- if there is any existing damage to the premises; and

- if there are any repairs the landlord is to make to the premises.

If the unit is furnished, the landlord and tenant will complete and sign an additional form on their walk-through called a *condition of furnishings addendum*. [See **first tuesday** Form 561]

The **condition of furnishings addendum** confirms:

- the inventory of furnishings located in the unit;

- the current condition of the furnishings; and

- the tenant's acceptance of the furnishings.

At the pre-expiration inspection to be provided residential tenants, the originally prepared condition of premises form is reviewed to help establish tenant responsibility for excess wear and tear to the unit rented.

Pet addendum

Generally, a lease agreement or month-to-month rental agreement prohibits a tenant from keeping pets on the premises.

Some landlords do allow pets, but often:

- impose restrictions on the type or size of the pet; and

- require the landlord's written consent to keep the pet on the premises. [See Form 550 §5.9 and **first tuesday** Form 551 §5.9]

Editor's note — A landlord cannot prohibit a disabled person from keeping a dog on the premises which is specially trained to assist the person. [CC 54.1(b)(5); see Chapter 53]

The landlord and tenant can sign and attach a pet addendum that states:

- the type of pet and its name;

- the security deposit to be charged for the pet; and

- the tenants agreement to hold the landlord harmless for any damage caused by the pet. [See **first tuesday** Form 563]

Waterbed addendum

Lease agreements and month-to-month rental agreements also prohibit a tenant from keeping a waterbed or other liquid-filled furnishings on the premises without the landlord's written consent. [See Form 550 5.9 and **first tuesday** Form 551 5.9]

When a tenant has a waterbed, the landlord should require the tenant to sign a *waterbed addendum*. [See **first tuesday** Form 564]

The **waterbed addendum** indicates:

- the additional security deposit the tenant will be required to provide for keeping a waterbed on the premises; and

- the tenant's agreement to maintain an insurance policy to cover potential property damage should the waterbed leak or burst. [See Chapter 19]

Brokerage fee addendum

A broker who is retained under an exclusive authorization to lease property is due a fee if the landlord rents the premises to a tenant during the listing period. [See **first tuesday** Form 110; see Chapter 12]

Likewise, a broker is entitled to a fee when a tenant has retained the broker under an exclusive authorization to locate space and the tenant rents space during the listing period. If the tenant does not provide for the landlord to pay the fee, the tenant will owe the broker the fee. [See **first tuesday** Form 111; see Chapter 13]

However, brokers often fail to insist on a written fee agreement from either the landlord or the tenant before rendering services. To be assured a fee when a prior written fee agreement does not exist, the broker should include a fee agreement as part of an offer to lease or letter of intent, lastly as an addendum to the proposed rental or lease agreement prepared for the tenant to sign. [See **first tuesday** Form 273]

Other addenda

Other information handed to a residential tenant which is made a part of a rental or lease agreement includes:

- house or building rules; and

- any rent control disclosures required by local rent control ordinances.

Also, a tenant entering into a lease agreement may have negotiated for an option to renew or extend the lease when it expires. Provisions for the option to renew or extend would be included in an addendum attached to the lease agreement. [See **first tuesday** Form 565]

A residential landlord seeking to sell the property may grant the tenant an option to purchase the property. [See **first tuesday** Form 161; see Chapter 6]

However, no portion of the option money or rent should ever be applied to the purchase price. When the terms of the lease agreement or option agreement provide for any credit to be applied toward the purchase price, or to a down payment on the purchase price, the tenant has acquired an *equitable ownership* interest in the property.

A transaction involving a lease and a purchase option calling for rent or option money payments to be applied toward the purchase price is called a *lease-option sale*, and is a sale of the property for all purposes, and not a leasing arrangement at all.

Terms of residential occupancy

On executing a residential lease agreement or month-to-month rental agreement, a landlord conveys the right to possession of the unit to a tenant, called a *leasehold estate*, or simply a *lease*.

Also, a lease agreement or month-to-month rental agreement sets forth the respective rights and obligations of the landlord and tenant for the use, care and maintenance of the property during the tenants occupancy.

A **security deposit** is usually received from the tenant to cover the cost to clean the unit or remedy any damage caused to the unit by the tenant beyond reasonable wear and tear. [See Form 550 §1 and **first tuesday** Form 551 §1; see Chapter 19]

In return for the use and possession of the premises, the tenant pays the landlord **rent** until expiration of the lease, or periodic tenancy, and possession is then returned to the landlord.

The tenant agrees to pay a **late charge** if rent is not paid within a fixed period of time after it is due, called a *grace period*. [See Form 550 §3 and **first tuesday** Form 551 §3]

Also, the number of **guests** the tenant may have in his unit and the period of time over which his guests may visit is limited. [See Form 550 §4.6 and **first tuesday** Form 551 §4.6]

The tenant agrees to comply with all building or project **rules** and **regulations** established by CC&Rs or the landlord. [See Form 550 §5.1 and **first tuesday** Form 551 §5.1]

The landlord and tenant agree who will pay or how they will share the financial responsibility for the unit's **utilities**. Landlords of apartment buildings or complexes often retain the responsibility of providing water to the units. [See Form 550 §5.2 and **first tuesday** Form 551 §5.2]

In both a rental and lease agreement, the tenant agrees to hold the landlord harmless from all liability for damages caused by the tenant or his guests. [See Form 550 §6.1 and **first tuesday** Form 551 §6.1]

Statutory rights and duties

Residential lease agreements and month-to-month rental agreements often contain provisions that restate the landlord's and tenant's statutory rights and duties.

For example, the rental agreement reiterates the landlord's statutory obligation to furnish a tenant with:

- a security deposit refund;

- notice of the right to a joint pre-expiration inspection of the unit and delivery of an itemized statement of repairs/cleaning; [CC 1950.5(f)] and

- a statement of security deposit accounting within 21 days after the tenant vacates which itemizes any deductions. [CC 1950.5(g)(1); see Form 550 §1.4 and **first tuesday** Form 551 §1.4; see Chapter 19]

Also, rental agreements often advise tenants of their limited statutory right to make necessary repairs to the premises and deduct the cost from the rent should the landlord fail to make the repairs that were noticed by the tenant. [CC 1942; see Form 550 §6.2 and **first tuesday** Form 551 §6.2; see Chapter 36]

A rental or lease agreement may prohibit a tenant from:

- using the premises for an unlawful purpose;

- creating a nuisance; and

- committing waste. [See Form 550 §§5.7, 5.8 and **first tuesday** Form 551 §§5.7, 5.8]

More importantly, a tenant who either uses the premises for an unlawful purpose, creates a nuisance or commits waste even if these activities are not prohibited by the tenant's lease or rental agreement may be evicted with a 3-day written notice to quit. [CCP 1161(4); see Chapter 26]

Chapter 51

Foreign-language residential leases

This chapter addresses California's translation requirements for real estate leases negotiated in languages other than English.

A written translation addendum

A bilingual real estate broker (or his agent), acting as an agent for a landlord of a dwelling unit located in California, negotiates a residential lease with a Spanish-only speaking tenant. The lease has an initial term which exceeds one month. Thus, it is not a month-to-month rental agreement.

While negotiations between the broker and the prospective tenant are in Spanish, the lease agreement entered into is on a form written in English.

The tenant signs the English-language lease and takes occupancy. The tenant does not receive a written Spanish translation of the significant provisions in the lease.

Later, the tenant decides to relocate to another landlord's property. However, the lease entered into with the broker obligates the tenant to occupy and pay rent for its remaining term.

The tenant hands the broker a *notice of rescission* of the lease agreement and vacates the unit. The tenant claims the lease is void since the tenant did not receive a written Spanish-language translation when he entered into the english-language lease.

Can the tenant **rescind** the lease and avoid future rent obligations based on the broker's failure to provide a written Spanish-language translation with the written English-language lease?

Yes! A written translation is required to be delivered to the tenant in the language used to negotiate a residential real estate lease at the time and place the agreement is signed by the tenant if the occupancy agreement:

- is a **residential lease** agreement for an initial term which exceeds one month; and

- is negotiated primarily in **Spanish, Chinese, Tagalog, Vietnamese or Korean** by a broker, landlord, resident manager, their employee or a person (interpreter) provided by them.

The written translation requirement to deliver a non-English language translation applies only to leases, not month-to-month or shorter periodic rental agreements, on a residential dwelling, apartment, mobilehome or other residential unit. [Calif. Civil Code §1632(b)(3)]

The **only remedy available** to a tenant who does not receive the required written Spanish, Chinese, Tagalog, Vietnamese or Korean language translation is a **rescission** of the lease. No money losses are recoverable based on the lack of a written translation. Simply put, the tenant is not bound by the lease agreement. [CC §1632(k)]

Transactions exempt from written translations

A written translation of a lease is not required if it is the tenant's interpreter who assists in negotiating the lease.

However, the tenant's interpreter must:

- be 18 years of age or older;

- be fluent in both English and the language in which the lease is negotiated; and

- not be employed or located by the broker or landlord (or their employees) involved in the negotiations. [CC §1632(h)]

Also, other real estate transactions **exempt** from the written translation requirement include:

- real estate purchase agreements;

- real estate loans, except for small private lender loans brokered under California Business and Professions Code §10245 which have their own translation requirements;

- month-to-month rental agreements; and

- home improvement agreements. [CC §1632]

Also, *addenda* ordinarily attached to leases do not need to be translated when referenced in the lease. Ordinary **addenda** include documents for the rules and regulations for the occupancy, inventories for furnishings, brokerage fees, the condition of the premises and furnishings, and waterbed and pet addenda.

Reliance on the English agreement

The terms of a lease agreement written in English set and control the **rights and obligations** of a landlord and tenant, not the Spanish, Chinese, Tagalog, Vietnamese or Korean translation of its significant provisions.

The written translation of the lease provided to the non-English speaking tenant may only be used to void (*rescind*) the English lease agreement if **substantial differences** exist between the two documents regarding **significant terms** and conditions of the English-language lease. [CC §1632(g)]

When the lease is **rescinded** by the tenant, the tenant must return the premises to the landlord and the landlord must refund any unearned rent and the security deposit to the tenant. Thus, on rescission the landlord loses a tenant, but incurs no liabilities beyond the refund.

Subsequent notices to the tenant

When a lease controlled by the translation rule is negotiated, documents later delivered to the tenant which **alter the rights** and obligations of the tenant, such as 3-day and 30-day notices, must be accompanied by a written translation in the language the lease was negotiated, whether Spanish, Chinese, Tagalog, Vietnamese or Korean. [CC §1632(d)]

However, documents authorized by the original agreement which will be delivered after entering into the original agreement and do not alter the rights and obligations of the parties do not need to be translated, such as receipts, changes in rules and regulations of occupancy and notices to enter for repairs. [CC §1632(d)]

Chapter 52

Lead-based paint disclosures

This chapter discusses the federal lead-based paint disclosure and the duty of landlords renting pre-1978 residential property to disclose their knowledge of any lead-based paint to tenants.

Pre-contract disclosure for pre-1978 housing

An owner of a residential property built before 1978 retains a broker to locate a tenant. The property is not a vacation rental, hotel, motel or elderly housing, and it is not certified as lead-based paint free.

The broker informs the owner that leasing residential property built before 1978 requires disclosure to prospective tenants regarding lead-based paint hazards that may exist on the property or are known to the owner or the broker before entering into a lease of the premises.

Based on discussions with the landlord, the broker prepares a lead-based paint disclosure form to be reviewed and signed by the owner. The lead-based paint disclosure is attached to the authorization to lease or to the property management agreement entered into by the broker and the owner. The disclosure will be handed to prospective tenants interested in renting the property.

Here, the broker has properly informed the owner, who is acting as a residential landlord, of the lead-based paint disclosures mandated by federal regulations. Lead-based paint disclosures must be provided to prospective tenants of any residential property built before 1978, other than transient and elderly housing. [24 Code of Federal Regulations §35.82; 40 CFR §745.101]

Thus, **before a prospective tenant** enters into an agreement to rent or lease a pre-1978 residential unit, unless it is exempt housing, the landlord must provide the tenant with the following:

- a **lead-based paint disclosure statement** attached to the lease or rental agreement, disclosing the presence of any known lead-based paint or related hazards on the property [See Form 557 accompanying this chapter];

- any **information available** regarding lead-based paint hazards known to the landlord or broker to exist, such as any reports determining lead-based paint exists on the property, including common areas and other residential dwellings in a multi-family housing development, if the other housing units were part of an evaluation or reduction of lead-based paint in the building; and

- an EPA-approved lead hazard information **pamphlet** entitled, *Protect Your Family From Lead in Your Home*, or an equivalent pamphlet approved for use in California by the EPA. [24 CFR §35.88(a); 40 CFR §745.107(a)]

If the disclosure occurs after an application to rent or lease has been received from a prospective tenant, the landlord must provide the disclosures to the prospect **prior to accepting** the lease application.

The tenant must be given an opportunity to either abandon the application or further negotiate in light of the newly disclosed information on the property's lead-based paint condition. [24 CFR §35.88(b); 40 CFR §745.107(b)]

However, the mandated lead-based paint disclosure laws **do not obligate** the landlord:

- to conduct an inspection to determine whether any lead-based paint exists; or

- to abate or remove any lead-based paint. [24 CFR §35.88(a); 40 CFR §745.107(a)]

Brokers involved in residential leasing transactions are obligated as agents to ensure the landlord complies with the **pre-contract disclosure** regulations. Thus, it is required of brokers to know federal rules, prepare the disclosures and inform all parties involved of known or possible existence of lead-based paint — all done before rental applications are prepared or accepted.

Lead-based paint hazards

Lead-based paint was **banned** by the Federal Consumer Product Safety Commission in 1978.

Lead-based paint is defined as paint or other *surface coating* that contains lead equal to at least 1.0 milligram per square centimeter or 0.5% by weight. [24 CFR §35.86; 40 CFR §745.103]

A **lead-based paint hazard** is any condition that causes *exposure to lead* from lead-contaminated dust, soil or paint which has deteriorated to the point of causing adverse human health effects. [24 CFR §35.86; 40 CFR §745.103]

Exempt residential rentals

Now consider an owner, broker or vacation rental operator who provides lodging on a **vacation property** for a stay of less than 100 days by a guest, called a *transient occupancy*.

Further, the occupancy agreement does not provide for an extension or renewal. At the end of the stay, the guest must depart.

The owner is concerned about the disclosure requirements of lead-based paint since the vacation property is residential real estate built before 1978.

Is the vacation owner, operator or broker required to provide the occupant of the vacation rental with the lead-based paint disclosure?

No! The lead-based paint disclosure requirements do not apply to any occupancy agreement for a period of 100 days or less, where renewal or extension of the occupancy has not been provided for. [24 CFR §35.82(c); 40 CFR §745.101(c)]

By definition, a transient occupancy by a guest automatically terminates on the expiration (departure) date and time of day stated in the occupancy agreement.

Federal Pamphlets

A copy of Protect Your Family From Lead in Your Home can be obtained from the National Lead Information Center and Clearinghouse (NLIC) at http://www.epa.gov/opptintr/lead/nlic.htm or by calling (800) 424-LEAD. Requests may also be sent by fax to (301) 588-8495 or by e-mail to ech@cais.com.

Bulk copies of the pamphlet are available from the Government Printing Office (GPO) at http://bookstore.gpo.gov/ or by calling (202) 512-1800. Refer to the complete title or GPO stock number 055-000-00632-6. The price is $50.50 for a pack of 50 copies.

Alternatively, the pamphlet may be reproduced for use or distribution if the text and graphics are reproduced in full. Camera-ready copies of the pamphlet are available from the NLIC.

LEAD-BASED PAINT DISCLOSURE
For Renting or Leasing Residential Property

> **NOTE:** For use on the lease or rental of residential property which was constructed pre-1978.

1. **Lead Warning:**

   Housing built before 1978 may contain lead-based paint. Lead from paint, paint chips, and dust can pose health hazards if not managed properly. Lead exposure in housing is especially harmful to young children. Before renting pre-1978 housing, landlords must disclose the presence of lead-based paint and/or lead-based paint hazards in the dwelling. Tenants may also receive a federally approved pamphlet on lead poisoning.

   Items left blank or unchecked are not applicable.

2. **Landlord's Certification:**

   2.1   Presence of lead-based paint and/or lead-based paint hazards:

   ☐ a. Are known to Landlord to be present in the housing (explain): _____

   _____

   _____

   ☐ b.   Are not known to Landlord to be present in the housing.

   2.2   Records and reports available to Tenant:

   ☐ a. Landlord has provided Tenant with all available records and reports pertaining to lead-based paint and/or lead-based paint hazards in the housing listed as follows: _____

   _____

   _____

   ☐ b. Landlord has no reports or records pertaining to lead-based paint and/or lead-based paint hazards in the housing.

   Date: _____, 20_____ Landlord's Signature: _____

3. **Tenant's Acknowledgement:**

   3.1   Tenant has received:

   ☐ a. Copies of all information listed above.

   ☐ b. The pamphlet *Protect Your Family From Lead in Your Home.*

   Date: _____, 20_____ Tenant's Signature: _____

   Date: _____, 20_____ Tenant's Signature: _____

4. **Broker's Certification: (When Applicable)**

   4.1   Broker certifies to have informed the landlord of his/her obligation under 42 USC §4852(d) to disclose to the tenant and agent all information known to the landlord regarding the presence of lead-based paint and lead-based paint hazards within this target housing and that all information known to the agent regarding the presence of lead-based paint and lead-based paint hazards within this target housing has been disclosed to the tenant.

   4.2   Broker further certifies that the tenant received the lead hazard information pamphlet *Protect Your Family From Lead in Your Home.*

   Date:_____, 20_____ Broker's Signature:_____

Thus, the federal regulations **exempt** all vacation rentals, hotels and motels due to their short-term transient lodging arrangements.

However, if the stay in the vacation rental is intended to extend beyond 100 days, the owner and his broker must comply with lead-based paint disclosure requirements.

Further, all landlords entering into month-to-month **rental agreements** for non-exempt residential property must comply with the lead-based paint disclosure requirements.

Month-to-month rental agreements are automatically renewable as they are open-ended tenancies. Thus, rental agreements to not require the tenant to vacate in less than 100 days since a month-to-month rental agreement will automatically continue beyond the 100-day period, unless previously terminated.

Also exempt from the lead-based paint disclosures are housing for the elderly or disabled when no child under the age of six is expected to live on the property. **Elderly housing** includes retirement communities or other housing required to be occupied by one or more individuals over the age of 62. [24 CFR §35.86; 40 CFR §745.103]

Also exempt is any **zero-bedroom dwelling**, defined as a residential dwelling in which the living room is not separated from the sleeping area. Examples include studio apartments, dormitories or the rental of an individual room in residential housing. [24 CFR §35.86; 40 CFR §745.103]

Broker compliance

All brokers who represent the landlord of a non-exempt pre-1978 residential structure must ensure the landlord complies with the lead-based paint requirements. [24 CFR §35.94(a); 40 CFR §745.115(a)]

However, residential landlords who are not represented by brokers are themselves required to make the disclosures.

A landlord's broker should begin by preparing the lead-based paint disclosures for the landlord's signature when the property management or leasing agent authorization is entered into.

Further, a landlord owes a duty to the broker to disclose any known lead-based paint hazards to the broker. A broker will not be held liable for failing to disclose lead-based paint hazards if:

- the landlord knows of the hazards and fails to inform the broker by an entry in the disclosure statement required by the broker; and

- the broker has no independent knowledge of the hazardous condition, such as the structure being a pre-1978 construction. [24 CFR §35.94(b); 40 CFR §745.115(b)]

Use of the disclosure statement

All lease agreements and month-to-month rental agreements for non-exempt pre-1978 residential property must include the lead-based paint disclosure form as an attachment. [24 CFR §35.92(b); 40 CFR §745.113(b); see Form 557]

The disclosure form must be in the **same language** as the lease agreement or rental agreement. [24 CFR §35.92(b); 40 CFR §745.113(b)]

The disclosure form must include:

- the Lead Warning Statement [See Form 557 §1];

- the landlord's disclosure of any known lead-based paint hazards or the fact the landlord is unaware of any hazards [See Form 557 §2.1];

- a list of all records or reports available to the landlord concerning lead-based paint on the property, the location of the lead-based paint and the condition of the painted surfaces [See Form 557 §2.2];

- a statement by the tenant affirming receipt of the lead-based paint information and pamphlet [See Form 557 §3];

- a statement by the landlord's broker indicating the broker is aware of his duty to comply with the disclosure requirements [See Form 557 §4]; and

- the signatures of the landlord, tenant and broker. [24 CFR §35.92(b); 40 CFR §745.113(b)]

The landlord and the landlord's broker are required to keep a copy of the disclosure statement for a period of no less than three years from the commencement of the lease or rental agreement. [24 CFR §35.92(c); 40 CFR §745.113(c)]

Rentals certified as lead-based paint free

A landlord may take steps to have his pre-1978 property certified as free of lead-based paint.

Pre-1978 residential property is considered lead-based paint free housing if no lead-based paint exists on the property. [24 CFR §35.86; 40 CFR §745.103]

The landlord of pre-1978 property does not need to provide lead-based paint disclosures with the lease agreement or rental agreements when:

- the property is inspected by an inspector certified under the federal certification program or a federally accredited state or tribal certification program; and

- the inspector has determined the property to be lead-based paint free. [24 CFR §35.82(b); 40 CFR §745.101(b)]

Editor's note — A list of statewide laboratories certified for analyzing lead in hazardous material, including paint, is available from the California Department of Health Services Environmental Lab Accreditation Program at (510) 620-3155, or from the National Lead Information Center and Clearinghouse at (800) 424-LEAD. Lists are also available on the web at http://www.dhs.ca.gov/childlead.

Lease renewal triggers disclosure

If an existing lease is **extended or renewed** and the lead-based paint disclosures were not previously handed to the tenant, the landlord must then make the disclosure to the tenant at the time of the extension or renewal.

The landlord does not need to provide new disclosures when existing leases are renewed or extended if:

- the landlord previously supplied the lead-based paint disclosures; and

- the landlord has not received any new information concerning lead-based paint on the property. [24 CFR §35.82(d); 40 CFR §745.101(d)]

When a lease expires and the tenant remains in possession as a month-to-month tenancy controlled by the old lease agreement, the lease agreement is not considered to have been extended or renewed. However, if the landlord and tenant change some aspect of the tenancy other than the extension of the occupancy, such as a rental rate, then the disclosure must be made. [61 Federal Register 9068]

Once a change in the terms of a lease occurs, other than the right to remain in occupancy, the lead-based paint disclosure rules require the landlord to then disclose any new information he may have obtained on the hazard since the original disclosure was handed to the tenant.

Failure to disclose

A failure of the landlord or the broker to comply with the pre-contract disclosure requirements does not affect the enforceability of the lease or rental agreement. However, an **intentional violation** of the lead-based paint disclosure rules by the landlord or the broker will subject him to:

- liability to the tenant for three times the amount of the tenant's actual money losses caused by the existence of the hazard, called *trebled damages*;

- civil penalties;

- court costs and attorney fees; and

- civil and criminal sanctions. [24 CFR §35.96; 40 CFR §745.118]

Chapter 53

Permitting pets and waterbeds

This chapter reviews the handling of rental applications received from tenants with pets or liquid-filled furniture.

Role of the security deposit

Landlords and their property managers are frequently confronted with acceptable, prospective tenants who own pets or liquid-filled furniture which might not be so acceptable.

However, landlords cannot automatically refuse to rent to a prospective tenant whose furnishings include liquid-filled furniture or deny an existing tenant the use of liquid-filled furniture, such as a waterbed, on the premises.

On the other hand, landlords can automatically, as a matter of policy, refuse to accept all tenants who want to occupy a unit with their pet, unless the tenant is **disabled and uses**:

- a *guide dog,* which is a seeing-eye dog trained by a licensed person to aid a blind person;

- a *signal dog,* trained to alert a deaf or hearing-impaired person to intruders or sounds; or

- a *service dog,* trained to aid a physically disabled person by protection work, pulling a wheelchair or fetching dropped items. [Calif. Civil Code §54.1(b)(6)]

Disabled persons accompanied by a specially trained dog must keep the dog **leashed and tagged** as a specially trained dog by an identification tag issued by the county clerk, animal control department or some other authorized agency.

The disabled tenant accompanied by a tagged guide, signal or service dog cannot be required by the landlord to **pay any extra** rent, charge or security deposit for the dog to be kept on the premises.

However, the owner of a guide, signal or service dog is liable for the cost to repair any damages brought about by the dog's activities. [CC §54.2(a)]

Any **public agency owning** and operating rental accommodations must permit any person over 60 years of age to keep two pets or less (i.e., dog, cat, bird or fish). The **elderly pet owner** is responsible for any damages caused by the pets. [Calif. Health and Safety Code §19901]

Pet addendum

A property manager allowing a tenant to occupy a unit with a pet should reduce the arrangement to a writing in the form of a Pet Addendum and attach it to the rental or lease agreement. [See Form 563 accompanying this chapter]

The pet addendum establishes the responsibilities of the pet owner and the acceptable behavior standards for the pet. To avoid misunderstandings as to size, type and number of pets allowed on the premises, a careful description of the pet should be given on the form.

The property manager can charge an **additional security deposit** for the pet to offset any expenses or losses caused by the pet, unless the rules for disabled persons and their trained dog apply or the security deposit ceiling would be exceeded. A typical deposit for a pet is one-third of the first month's rent, with an extra $100 to $200 for each additional pet, limited to the ceiling amount for residential security deposits. [See Chapter 13]

Thus, the **total security deposit** for an unfurnished residential unit, including the pet deposit, cannot exceed an amount equal to two months' rent (in addition to the first month's rent).

For a furnished unit, the security deposit, including the pet deposit, cannot exceed three months' rent (in addition to the first month's rent). [CC §1950.5(c)]

Also, if a pet's behavior does not conform to the terms of the pet addendum, the rental or lease agreement has been breached by the tenant. The property manager can serve a 3-day notice to the tenant to correct the activity or vacate the premises, called a *3-day notice to perform or quit*. [Calif. Code of Civil Procedure §1161(3); see Chapter 26]

Landlord liability for pets

A landlord permits a residential tenant to keep a dog on the premises. The landlord is not unaware the dog is vicious. No "Beware of Dog" notice is posted by the tenant.

A utility serviceman properly enters the backyard to check the meter. The dog attacks and injures the serviceman. The serviceman attempts to recover his losses due to the injury from the landlord.

Can the serviceman recover his losses from the landlord since the landlord allowed the tenant to keep a pet that was actually dangerous?

No! The landlord is not responsible for injury caused by dangerous domestic pets when he has no actual **knowledge of their ferocity**. Also, the landlord has no *duty to investigate* or inspect the rental unit to determine if the pet is dangerous. [**Lundy** v. **California Realty** (1985) 170 CA3d 813; see Chapters 46 and 48]

However, if the landlord has actual knowledge of the dangerousness of a tenant's pet and fails to serve the tenant with a 3-day notice to re-

move the pet or to vacate the unit, then the landlord is liable for injuries inflicted by the dangerous pet. [**Uccello** v. **Laudenslayer** (1975) 44 CA3d 504]

Also, a landlord has no responsibility to warn a prospective tenant of a dangerous pet located on a **neighboring property**, even when the landlord has knowledge of the ferocity of the neighbor's pet. [**Wylie** v. **Gresch** (1987) 191 CA3d 412]

Qualifying to maintain a waterbed

The use of waterbeds or other liquid-filled bedding in a rental unit cannot be grounds for refusal to rent to a prospective tenant. [CC §1940.5]

If the prospective tenant is otherwise qualified to rent, the landlord must rent to the tenant if the **waterbed is qualified** to be placed in the unit. For a waterbed to qualify, the landlord may establish conditions for the use of the waterbed on the premises, as long as the conditions meet the standards set by California waterbed state law.

These requirements are itemized in the waterbed addendum that is attached to the rental or lease agreement. [See Form 564 accompanying this chapter]

The **waterbed conditions** a landlord can impose on the tenant to qualify his waterbed include:

- an insurance policy against property damage;

- a special waterbed frame;

- specific methods of installation and maintenance;

- a written receipt of installation by the manufacturer, retailer or movers;

- an increase in the maximum security deposit permitted; and

PET ADDENDUM

DATE:_____, 20_____, at _____, California.

Items left blank or unchecked are not applicable.

FACTS:

This is an addendum to the following:

☐ Residential lease agreement

☐ Residential rental agreement

☐ Other:_____

dated _____, 20_____

regarding real estate referred to as: _____

The above referenced agreement prohibits pets without Landlord's prior written consent.

AGREEMENT:

1. Landlord agrees the Tenant may keep the following pet:

_____

2. Landlord hereby acknowledges receipt of $_____ as a security deposit, from which the Landlord may offset any expenses or losses caused by the pet. On termination of the above referenced agreement, the security deposit shall be refunded to Tenant with an itemization of its disposition.

3. Tenant agrees:

   3.1 Pet will not damage premises or annoy, endanger or inconvenience other tenants.

   3.2 The Tenant shall hold the Landlord harmless for any damages caused by the pet.

   3.3 To comply with all laws pertaining to the keeping and leashing of the pet.

   3.4 Pet is not known to be dangerous or to have injured individuals.

   3.5 _____

   _____

   _____

   _____

   _____

I agree to the terms stated above.	I agree to the terms stated above .
Date:_____, 20_____	Date:_____, 20_____
Landlord/Agent:_____	Tenant:_____
Signature: _____	Signature: _____

FORM 563   06-06   ©2007 **first tuesday**, P.O. BOX 20069, RIVERSIDE, CA 92516 (800) 794-0494

- requiring the tenant to comply with specific methods of installation or to remove the bed on 3-day written notice to perform (remove it) or quit. [CC §1940.5]

The floor of any residence has a limited capacity for weight centralized in one area.

Since a waterbed is considerably heavier than a regular bed, the weight of the waterbed must not exceed the weight limitation of the floor, especially if it is on an upper level.

Also, to ensure proper distribution of the weight, the tenant is required to provide an adequate bed frame specially designed to support and distribute the weight of a waterbed. [CC §1940.5(b)]

Waterbed addendum

When a tenant qualifies to maintain a waterbed on the premises, the landlord may increase the tenant's security deposit up to an additional one-half month's rent. The waterbed deposit is **in addition to** the maximum security deposit otherwise allowed. [See Chapter 19]

The landlord may also charge a reasonable **administrative fee** to cover the time, effort and money expenditures necessary to process the waterbed paperwork, such as $50 to $100. [CC §1940.5(g)]

The amounts of both the additional security deposit and administrative charges are set forth in the waterbed addendum. [See Form 564 §§2; 3]

The tenant can be required to provide the landlord with a waterbed insurance policy or certificate of insurance for property damage caused by the waterbed. The policy should name the landlord as an additional insured to eliminate any question over the disbursement of funds from a claim.

The waterbed insurance policy must be accepted by the landlord if several conditions are met, including:

- the policy is issued by a company licensed in California;

- the company possesses a Best Insurance Report rating of B or better; and

- the policy offers coverage of no less than $100,000. [CC §1940.5(a)]

The tenant must ensure the policy remains valid and enforceable throughout the period the waterbed is located on the premises. The landlord has the right to demand proof of insurance from the tenant at any time. If the tenant fails to provide proof of insurance when requested, a 3-day notice to perform or quit should be served on the tenant to deliver up the policy, remove the furniture or vacate.

Consider the insurance policy a tenant holds on his waterbed expiring two months before he vacates. The tenant does not renew the policy since he will soon be moving. The landlord fails to purchase coverage and charge the tenant for the premium or serve the tenant with a 3-day notice to get insurance, remove the bed or vacate.

Sometime after the policy expires, a liner patch from a prior leak fails. The liner ruptures, releasing its water contents. The whole apartment is flooded causing hundreds of dollars in damages as well as causing damage to the units and personal property on lower floors.

The landlord repairs the damages and demands payment from the tenant for all of his losses caused by the waterbed. The tenant claims the landlord had the responsibility to obtain coverage if the tenant did not.

Can the landlord collect the losses from the tenant?

Yes! Any damage resulting from the waterbed that is not covered by an insurance policy is the responsibility of the tenant. The landlord has no obligation to procure coverage even though he has authority to do so on the tenant's failure to provide coverage.

WATERBED ADDENDUM

DATE:_____, 20_____, at _____, California.

Items left blank or unchecked are not applicable.

FACTS:

This is an addendum to the following:

☐ Residential lease agreement

☐ Residential rental agreement

dated:_____, 20_____.

prohibiting waterbeds and other liquid-filled furniture without the written consent of Landlord.

regarding a residential unit referred to as: _____

> Possession in a rental of liquid-filled furniture is controlled by law. A tenant may keep and use liquid-filled furniture on the premises by complying with statutory conditions demanded by the landlord. [Calif. Civil Code §1940.5]

AGREEMENT:

1. Tenant may keep and use on the premises the following liquid-filled furniture:

    ☐ Waterbed described as:_____

    ☐ Other:_____

2. Landlord acknowledges receipt of $_____ as an additional security deposit, to be used to offset any expenses or losses caused to the landlord by the furniture.

    2.1 Within 21 days after removal of the furniture the security deposit shall be refunded to Tenant with an itemization of its disposition.

3. Landlord acknowledges receipt of $_____ as an additional fee to cover administrative costs incurred due to this agreement.

4. Tenant agrees:

    4.1 To maintain an insurance policy on the furniture for no less than $100,000 to cover property damage, naming landlord as an additional insured.

        a. To cause Landlord to receive at least 10 days prior written notice of cancellation or non-renewal of the insurance policy.

        b. To accept responsibility for property damage caused by the furniture should the policy expire unrenewed.

    4.2 To install the furniture according to manufacturer specifications, to operate properly all heaters and safety items, and to dispose of the liquid in a safe and sanitary manner.

        a. To give Landlord 24 hours notice of intent to install, move or remove the furniture.

        b. To provide Landlord with a written installation receipt stating the installer's name, address, and place of business when the furniture is installed, moved or removed by anyone other than Tenant.

    4.3 To strictly abide by the maintenance and safety precautions specified in the owner's manual supplied by the manufacturer of the furniture.

    4.4 Landlord may enter Tenant's residence on 24 hours notice to inspect the furniture to ensure it is being properly maintained.

        a. On lack of tenant's reasonable care and maintenance of the furniture Landlord may serve Tenant with a Three-day Notice to Perform or Quit regarding correction of the deficient care and maintenance or the removal of the furniture.

5. Other conditions: _____

6. Landlord's failure to enforce these conditions does not waive his right to an insurance claim.

I agree to the terms stated above.	I agree to the terms stated above.
Date:_____, 20_____	Date:_____, 20_____
Landlord: _____	Tenant:_____
Signature: _____	Signature: _____

FORM 564   10-00   ©2007 **first tuesday**, P.O. BOX 20069, RIVERSIDE, CA 92516 (800) 794-0494

Further, if for some reason the tenant's waterbed liability policy is canceled, expires or is not renewed, the tenant is obligated to give the landlord a ten-day notice of cancellation or nonrenewal of the insurance policy. [CC §1940.5(a)]

The notice is automatically given to the landlord by the insurer if the landlord is an additional insured on the waterbed policy — as the landlord should be.

Installation and care of the waterbed

It is the tenant's responsibility to ensure the waterbed is properly installed and maintained.

The tenant must give the property manager 24 hours' notice if he intends to move, install or remove a waterbed.

If anyone other than the tenant installs the waterbed, specifically the manufacturer, a retailer or a moving company, the tenant must provide the landlord with a written receipt that contains the installer's name, address and place of business. [CC §1940.5(c)]

To ensure safety at all times, the tenant must comply with the manufacturer's specifications for proper use of the bed. [CC §1940.5(e)]

When a landlord suspects the tenant is not meeting the provisions in the waterbed addendum, he has the right to enter the residence to inspect the waterbed and ensure it is being maintained properly. However, he must give the tenant a 24-hour notice of entry before his inspection. [CC §§1940.5(f); 1954; see **first tuesday** Form 567; see Chapter 2]

The landlord may give the tenant a 3-day notice to either comply with installation and maintenance standards or remove the bed from the premises (or vacate) if:

- the landlord finds the waterbed is not being properly maintained; or

- the waterbed has not been properly installed. [CC §1940.5(f)]

The landlord may serve a 3-day notice to perform or quit on the tenant, as long as the tenant is **given the option** of either curing the installation defects or removing the bed as performance in lieu of vacating. If the tenant fails to perform either alternative within three days, he must vacate the premises. [See Chapter 26]

In lieu of the notice to perform or quit, the landlord could serve an "advisory" letter giving notice to perform.

However, the landlord would have to later serve a 3-day notice to perform or quit if the tenant fails to either repair or remove the bed.

Finally, the landlord does not lose his right to make an insurance claim if he fails to exercise any of his rights to police the tenant's care and maintenance of the waterbed. [CC §1940.5(h)]

Chapter 54

Civil rights and fair housing laws

This chapter outlines the federal and California anti-discrimination laws and how the laws affect the management of residential and nonresidential rental property.

Property rights cannot be based on status

All citizens of the United States have the right to rent real estate, regardless of race, under the Civil Rights Act. [42 United States Code §1982]

Further, **all persons** within the United States, legally or illegally, are given the same rights to make and enforce contracts (rental and lease agreements), sue, be sued, enjoy the full benefits of the law and be subject to the same punishments, penalties, taxes and licenses, regardless of race. [42 USC §1981]

The *Federal Civil Rights Act* applies to race discrimination on the rental of all types of real estate, both residential and nonresidential.

Thus, the right of an individual to lease real estate is protected by giving all persons the right to make and **enforce contracts**, regardless of race. *Racially motivated activities* in any real estate leasing transaction are prohibited.

Federal protection against racial discrimination given under the Civil Rights Act applies to discrimination in all activities between persons, and is much broader than the protection given under the *Federal Fair Housing Act*, which is limited to dwellings.

Anti-discrimination in residential property

Unlawful discrimination in the rental or advertisement of dwellings for rent is based on status and prohibited under the *Federal Fair Housing Act (FFHA)*. [42 USC §§3601 et seq.]

A **dwelling includes** any building or structure that is occupied, or designed to be occupied, as a residence by one or more families composed of one or more people. Also included is any vacant land offered for lease for residential dwelling purposes, such as property that would hold a mobilehome unit. [42 USC §3602(b)]

Discriminatory actions of a landlord or property manager *prohibited* under FFHA are any actions a landlord or property manager may take in the negotiations or handling of a residential rental, based on a person's:

- race or color;

- national origin;

- religion;

- sex;

- familial status; or

- handicap. [42 USC §3602]

Familial status refers to the group of occupants of a residence comprised of one or more individuals who are under the age of 18 years and:

- a parent or person having legal custody of those under 18; or

- a person having written permission of the parent or legal custodian of those under 18 as the designee of the parent or custodian. [42 USC §3602(k)]

Handicapped persons refer to individuals who have:

- a physical or mental impairment which substantially limits the person's life activities; or

- a record of, or are regarded as having, a physical or mental impairment. [42 USC §3602(h)]

The term *handicap* does not include the current illegal use of a controlled substance. However, alcoholics and individuals who are considered "recovering or recovered addicts" are protected as handicapped. [**United States** v. **Southern Management Corporation** (4th Cir. 1992) 955 F2d 914]

Qualifying and processing tenants

A landlord or property manager is prohibited under FFHA **from unlawfully discriminating** during negotiations and handling of the rental of a dwelling. [42 USC §3604(a)]

Thus, a landlord or property manager may not:

- *refuse to rent* a dwelling or to negotiate the rental of a dwelling for unlawful discriminatory reasons;

- impose *different rental charges* on a dwelling for unlawful discriminatory reasons;

- use *different qualification criteria* or different procedures for processing applications in the rental of a dwelling to unlawfully discriminate; or

- *evict tenants* or the tenant's guests for unlawful discriminatory reasons. [24 Code of Federal Regulations §100.60(b)]

Different criteria for tenant qualification or processing of rental applications include a landlord or property manager using different credit standards and tenant screening approval procedures in the negotiations or handling of the rental of a dwelling. [24 CFR §100.60(b)(4)]

For example, a broker is hired by a residential apartment owner to perform property management activities. One of the broker's duties as a property manager is to locate tenants to fill vacancies.

A tenant from a religious minority group contacts the broker about the availability of an apartment.

The broker (or his agent) informs the prospective tenant of the monthly rent — a rate which is higher than the rent nonminority tenants are asked to pay for similar apartments.

When the prospective minority tenant asks the broker for an application, the broker informs the tenant a nonrefundable screening fee is charged to process the application. The creditworthy minority tenant fills out the application, pays the fee and is told the processing will take several days.

In the meantime, a nonminority tenant inquires about the rental of the same or similar apartment. The monthly rental rate the broker quotes the nonminority is lower than the rental rate the minority tenant was quoted. Further, the nonminority tenant is not charged a screening fee with his application. The apartment is immediately rented to the nonminority tenant, even though the nonminority tenant is not as creditworthy as the minority tenant.

The broker's actions, be they his own or his agents, are a violation of the FFHA. The representations made to the minority tenant are construed to be racially or religiously motivated. The broker misrepresented the availability of the apartment based on the tenant's religion by using different procedures and qualification standards in accepting and processing the tenant's application. [**United States** v. **Balistrieri** (7th Cir. 1992) 981 F2d 916]

Different terms, different privileges

A landlord or property manager may not unlawfully discriminate against a person by setting different terms, conditions or privileges for his rental of a dwelling, or by providing substandard services and facilities for the dwellings. [42 USC §3604(b)]

For example, a prospective tenant who is a member of a protected class (race, ethnicity, etc.) responds to an ad concerning the rental of a residence in a new housing development.

The property manager shows the prospective tenant the residence. The prospect informs the broker he is interested in renting the property.

The prospective tenant is then informed he cannot rent this particular unit. Due to the prospect's minority status, the property manager and the owner believe it would become more difficult to rent the remaining units in the development with this tenant occupying a unit.

The property manager offers to show the tenant a unit in another area of the development.

Here, the property manager has discriminated against the prospective tenant. The property manager improperly refused to rent the unit to the tenant due to the tenant's status as a member of a protected class of people, such as race, religion, handicap, etc. [**United States** v. **Pelzer Realty Company, Inc.** (5th Cir. 1973) 484 F2d 438]

Prohibited **selective reduction** of tenant privileges, conditions, services and facilities offered protected individuals in the rental of a dwelling includes:

- providing for different terms in a lease, such as the rental charge, security deposit and the term of the lease;

- delaying or failing to perform maintenance;

- limiting use of privileges, services or facilities to different classes of individuals; or

- refusing or failing to provide services or facilities due to a person's refusal to provide sexual favors. [24 CFR §100.65(b)]

Further, the landlord or property manager may not discriminate based on a person's status by representing that a dwelling is not available for rent in order to *steer the individual* to a particular Section 8 project or neighborhood, when the dwelling is available.

Steering involves the restriction of a person seeking to rent a to rent a dwelling in a community, neighborhood or development, in a manner that perpetuates segregated housing patterns. [42 USC §3604(d); 24 CFR §100.70]

Discrimination in advertisement

A broker making a notice, statement or advertisement when handling the rental of a dwelling unit is barred from using any wording that *indicates a discriminatory preference or limitation* against individuals of protected classes of people. [42 USC §3604(c)]

The prohibition against unlawful discriminatory advertisements applies to all oral and written statements.

Notices and statements includes any applications, flyers, brochures, deeds, signs, banners, posters and billboards used in the rental of a dwelling.

Blockbusting for exploitation

A residential landlord or property manager may not induce or attempt to induce a person to rent a dwelling to ensure the entry of certain classes of people into the neighborhood can be used to exploit discrimination, called *blockbusting*. [42 USC §3604(e)]

Further, the actual receipt of an profit is not necessary to establish discrimination provided profit was a motive for the landlord's or broker's **blockbusting** activity. [24 CFR §100.85(b)]

Examples of blockbusting activities by a broker or his agent include:

- encouraging an **owner-occupant to offer** a dwelling for rent by insinuating that a neighborhood is undergoing or is about to undergo a change in the race, color, religion, sex, handicap, familial status or national origin of its residents; or

- discouraging an **owner-occupant from renting** a dwelling by claiming the entry of persons of a particular race, color, religion, sex, familial status, handicap or national origin will result in undesirable consequences for the neighborhood or community, such as an increase in criminal activity or a decline in schools and other facilities. [24 CFR §100.85(c)]

Aiding in discriminatory activities

Landlords and their agents may not coerce, intimidate, threaten or interfere with any person from a protected class of people in their occupancy or enjoyment of a dwelling. [42 USC §3617]

For example, a mobilehome park is allowed to operate as a *de facto* "adults-only" park under local rent control ordinances. However, the park owner never legally declares the park exempt from the FFHA as a *de jure* senior citizens housing development.

Later, local rent control ordinances are amended, allowing the park management to rent vacated spaces to new residents without rent amount restrictions. The park owner then decides to open the park by renting newly vacated units to families with children.

Senior tenants currently renting mobilehome spaces in the park file an application with the city seeking a rent reduction, claiming families with children cause a reduction in available services. The city awards the tenants the reduction in rent they sought.

The park owner claims the city violated the FFHA since the rent reductions for existing tenants was a prohibited discriminatory interference since the action inhibited the owner's decision to rent to families with children.

The city claims it did not violate the FFHA since the park met the requirements of a senior citizen housing project, and was therefore exempt from the FFHA.

However, the city did interfere with the owner's rental of the mobilehomes to families with children in violation of the FFHA. The older tenants are not entitled to a reduction in rent based on the occupancy of spaces by families.

The owner's rental of mobilehome spaces to families with children cannot be the basis for reducing rent paid by tenants who do not have children. Further, only an owner, not a governmental agency, can claim the park is exempt from the FFHA under the senior housing exemption. [**United States** v. **City of Hayward** (9th Cir. 1994) 36 F3d 832]

Exemptions for some discrimination

FFHA-prohibited discrimination in the rental of a residential dwelling **does not** apply to a single-family house rented by a landlord who:

- does not own more than three single-family homes;

- does not use a real estate licensee to negotiate or handle the tenant; and

- does not use a publication, posting or mailing for any discriminatory advertisement. [42 USC §3603(b)(1)]

Thus, the FFHA prohibitions apply to all notices, statements and advertisement in the rental of a dwelling by anyone, be they an owner or a broker, who are in the business of renting dwellings. [42 USC §3603]

A person is in the **business of renting dwellings** if the person:

- has participated within the past 12 months **as a principal** in three or more transactions involving the rental of any dwelling or interest in a dwelling;

- has participated within the past 12 months **as an agent**, negotiating two or more transactions involving the rental of any dwelling or interest in a dwelling, excluding the agent's personal residence; or

- is **the owner** of a dwelling structure intended to be occupied by five or more families (larger than a fourplex). [42 USC §3603(c)]

If a broker is the agent for either the landlord or the tenant in a residential rental transaction, the anti-discrimination rules of the FFHA apply.

However, attorneys, escrow agents, title companies and professionals other than brokers who are employed by a landlord to complete a transaction do not bring the transaction under the FFHA, unless they **participate in negotiations** with the tenant. [42 USC §3603(b)(1)(B)]

Also exempt from discrimination prohibition rules in the rental of a dwelling is a one-to-four unit residential property in which one of the units is **occupied by the owner**. [42 USC §3603(b)(2)]

Religious organizations who limit the rental or occupancy of dwellings to individuals of the same religion are also exempt, provided the dwelling is owned for **noncommercial reasons**. No religious exemption exists if the religion is restricted to persons of a particular race, color or national origin. [42 USC §3607(a)]

Also exempt are **private clubs** that are not open to the public and provide their members with residential dwelling space for noncommercial purposes may limit rental or occupancy of the dwellings to members.

Finally, **housing qualified for older citizens** which excludes children is not considered unlawful discrimination against tenants with children based on familial status. However, the housing must first qualify as housing for the elderly. [42 USC §3607(b)]

Failure to comply with the FFHA

An **aggrieved person** under FFHA is any individual who claims he has been injured by an unlawful discriminatory housing practice or believes he will be injured by a prohibited discriminatory housing practice. [42 USC §3602(i)]

The aggrieved individual may file a complaint with the Secretary of Housing and Urban Development (HUD), alleging a discriminatory housing practice. The complaint must be filed within one year of the alleged discriminatory housing practice. [42 USC §3610(a)]

The Secretary will **attempt to resolve** the dispute by having the parties enter into an agreement after informal negotiations. [42 USC §3610(b)]

However, a judicial action may be required to resolve the issue of discrimination if the Secretary concludes judicial involvement is necessary. The dispute will then be resolved by an administrative law judge.

Any party to the complaint may elect to have the claims decided in a civil action before a court of law. [42 USC §3612(a)]

When a real estate broker subjected to a judicial action is ruled to have committed discriminatory housing practices, the Secretary is to notify the DRE and recommend disciplinary action. [42 USC §3612(g)(5)]

When a court determines discriminatory housing practices have taken place, actual and punitive amounts of money awards may be granted and an order issued preventing the landlord or broker from engaging in any future discriminatory housing practice. [42 USC §3613(c)(1)]

Further, if the Attorney General commences a civil action against a person for prohibited discriminatory housing practices, the court may award:

- relief preventing further discriminatory housing practices such as an injunction or restraining order;

- money losses; and

- civil penalties of no more than $50,000 for the first violation and no more than $100,000 for any subsequent violation. [42 USC §3614(d)]

The State Civil Rights Act

California's *Unruh Civil Rights Act*, an anti-discrimination law, specifically prohibits discrimination by a **business establishment** based on numerous status classifications, including: a person's sex, race, color, religion, ancestry, national origin, disability or medical condition. [Calif. Civil Code §§51, 51.2, 51.3]

However, age is a legitimate discrimination as long as the restriction is in a project that qualifies as a senior citizen housing development.

The Unruh Civil Rights Act applies to anyone in the **business of providing housing**. Brokers, developers, apartment owners, condominium owners and single-family residential owners are considered to be in the business of providing housing.

As business establishments, landlords may not boycott, blacklist, refuse to lease or rent because of the race, creed, religion, color, national origin, sex, disability or medical condition of a person, or that person's business partners, members, stockholders, directors, officers, managers, agents, employees, business associates or customers. Further, a prospective tenant may not be blacklisted or boycotted for prohibited discriminatory reasons. [CC §51.5]

Full and equal access guaranteed

A **blind prospective tenant** has a guide dog and seeks to rent an available unit in a multi-unit residential dwelling structure.

The landlord refuses to rent a unit to the blind tenant, claiming the guide dog violates the building's pet restriction in the covenants, conditions and restrictions.

The blind tenant claims the landlord is discriminating against him under California law due to his **disability** since the landlord denied him housing on account of the guide dog.

A landlord may not refuse to rent residential property to a blind tenant because of the tenant's guide dog. Landlords are also prohibited from discriminating against tenants with dogs specially trained to assist deaf and other disabled persons. [CC §54.1(b)(6)]

Fair housing for disabled persons

Disabled persons are protected from discrimination when renting or leasing California residential real estate. A disabled person anyone who:

- has a physical or mental impairment which significantly limits major life activities;

- has a record of a disability; or

- is regarded as being disabled. [CC §54(b)]

People with disabilities are entitled to full and equal access to housing accommodations offered for rent. [CC §54.1(b)(1)]

The only exception is the rental of no more than one room in a single-family residence. [CC §54.1(b)(2)]

The examples of the blind tenant and his seeing-eye dog illustrate how a landlord might attempt to avoid anti-discrimination laws. While the landlord claims to justify his behavior based on his equal application of a single pet restriction rule to pet owners (a non-protected class of people), the refusal to rent to a disabled tenant based on his reliance on a trained dog to conduct life activity is an unlawful discrimination.

Now consider a disabled tenant dependent on his spouse for financial support. The disabled tenant and his spouse seek to rent an apartment and will both sign the lease agreement. The spouse's income meets the landlord's minimum requirement to qualify to pay the rent.

However, the landlord refuses to rent an apartment to the couple, claiming the disabled tenant does not also meet minimum income requirements.

Here, the landlord may not deny housing to the disabled tenant based on the tenant being financially dependent on his spouse. The **combined incomes** of the tenant and his spouse meet the landlord's minimum income requirements for the payment of the rent amount.

The landlord's refusal to rent an apartment to the disabled tenant based on the tenant's dependency on his spouse's income is unlawful discrimination. If one tenant qualifies to rent a unit, both tenants are qualified. [CC §54.1(b)(7)]

Accommodating the disabled

A landlord is not required to structurally modify existing residential rental property to meet the special needs of disabled tenants. [CC §54.1(b)(4)]

Although he is not required to modify the structure for a disabled tenant, the landlord must allow the tenant to make reasonable modifications himself or pay the landlord to do so. The landlord may require the tenant to restore the property to its original condition when the tenancy is terminated. [Calif. Government Code §12927]

Anti-discrimination laws require new residential properties consisting of four or more units per building to be **built to allow** access by disabled persons. Required improvements include kitchens and bathrooms designed to allow access to disabled tenants in addition to wheelchair ramps.

Failure to provide the disabled with access to a newly constructed residential property with four or more units is considered unlawful discrimination. [Gov C §12955.1]

Remedies

An individual's primary remedy for discrimination based on his physical disability is to seek an injunction to stop the discriminatory activity. The injunction may be sought by the disabled person being discriminated against, or by the city attorney, district attorney or Attorney General. [CC §§55, 55.1]

Property owners who unlawfully discriminate against disabled persons are further liable for the disabled person's money losses. In addition to actual money losses, treble that dollar amount may be awarded as punitive damages, along with attorney fees. The minimum award of money damages for discrimination against a disabled person is $1,000. [CC §54.3]

Discriminatory practices, exemptions and remedies

An ethnic or religious minority tenant seeks to rent an apartment. The landlord informs the prospective tenant he cannot rent the apartment until he completes a credit check. The landlord also declines to accept a deposit from the tenant.

Later the same day, a nonminority tenant seeks to rent the same apartment. The landlord agrees to rent the apartment to the nonminority tenant without first requiring a credit check, and immediately accepts the tenant's check for a deposit on the apartment. The minority tenant is informed the apartment has been rented to another person.

The minority tenant files a complaint against the landlord, claiming the landlord discriminated against him based on his ethnicity or religion by refusing to rent him an apartment. The landlord claims no discrimination occurred since he was entitled to require a credit check of prospective tenants.

However, requiring a credit check of minority tenants, but not nonminority tenants, an unlawful discriminatory practice which allows the minority tenant to recover his money losses. [**Stearns** v. **Fair Employment Practice Commission** (1971) 6 C3d 205]

Prohibited discrimination

California law prohibits discrimination in the sale or rental of housing accommodations based on race, color, religion, sex, sexual orientation, marital status, national origin, ancestry, familial status, source of income or disability. This list of protected persons is more extensive than all others.

Discriminatory activities and conduct include:

- making a written or oral **inquiry into** the race, sex, disability, etc. of any person seeking to rent housing;

- ads or notices for rental of housing which state or infer **preferences or limitations** based on any of the prohibited discrimination factors;

- a broker **refusing to represent** an individual in a real estate transaction based on any prohibited factor; and

- any other practice that denies housing to a member of a protected class. [Gov C §12955]

The denial of housing based on the landlord or broker's *perception* that a prospective tenant, or any associates of the prospective tenant, has any of the protected characteristics is absolutely prohibited. [Gov C §12955(m)]

Income standards for tenants

Standards of conduct that a broker applies *equally to all individuals* which do not discriminate against a **protected group of individuals** are considered reasonable, and permitted to be used.

To qualify a tenant for occupancy based on his creditworthiness, a landlord or property manager may establish income ratios or standards to determine a tenant's ability to pay the rent. The higher the standard or ratio of income to rent, the less the risk of loss of rent borne by the landlord. The lower the standard, the greater the risk of loss of rent. Once set, the standard must be **applied to all equally**.

However, when renting to two or more individuals who desire to live in the same unit, whether related or unrelated, married or not, the **income of all tenants** must be considered as the total income used by the landlord to determine their collective eligibility to qualify to pay the rent amount sought.

Separately, each prospective tenant may be unable to qualify by meeting the income standard. However, if **aggregating the income** of all who intend to occupy the unit and enter into the rental or lease agreement results in total income sufficient under the ratio or standard applied to qualify a tenant or tenants for occupancy, the tenants qualify. [Gov C §12955(n)]

Also, under rent subsidy programs, such as Section 8 housing arrangements, the landlord or property manager must consider the tenant's income when assessing whether the tenant qualifies to pay their portion of the rent that is not subsidized. [Gov C §12955(o)]

The *source of income* for each occupant also includes any income claimed to be the tenant's that is lawfully received by the tenant and verifiable, whether it is directly received by the tenant or received by a representative of the tenant. [Gov C §12955(p)]

Familial status

Familial status in anti-discrimination laws refers to children under the age of 18 living with a parent or guardian. [Gov C §12955.2]

Rental policies excluding children under the age of 18 are classified as unlawful discrimination, unless the property qualifies as senior citizen housing. [Gov C §12955.9]

As with senior citizen housing, an exemption exists for religious groups. Religious organizations may give preference to other members of the same religious group when providing residential property for noncommercial purposes unless membership is restricted on account of race, color or national origin. [Gov C §12955.4]

Marital status

Consider a landlord who refuses to rent an apartment to an unmarried couple based on his religious beliefs.

The couple files a complaint with the Fair Employment and Housing commission, claiming the landlord violated fair housing laws that prohibit discrimination based on marital status.

The landlord claims he is exempt since renting to an unmarried couple violates his religious beliefs regarding the cohabitation of unmarried couples.

However, the landlord's refusal to rent to unmarried couples violates the fair housing laws since the landlord's religious beliefs do not also require him to participate in the business of renting property.

Thus, the fair housing laws prohibiting discrimination based on marital beliefs do not interfere with the practice of the landlord's religion, since he can go into a business that does not violate his religious convictions. [**Smith** v. **Fair Employment and Housing Commission** (1996) 12 C4th 1143]

Guidelines for broker conduct

The Department of Real Estate (DRE) has enacted regulations prohibiting discriminatory practices by real estate brokers. A broker or agent engaging in discriminatory business practices may be disciplined by the DRE. [Department of Real Estate Regulations §2780]

Prohibited practices include any situation in which a broker, while acting as an agent, discriminates against anyone based on race, color, sex, religion, ancestry, disability, marital status or national origin. Examples of discriminatory practices include:

- refusing to negotiate for the rental of real estate;

- refusing to show property or provide information, or steering clients away from specific properties;

- refusing to accept a rental listing;

- publishing or distributing advertisements that indicate a discriminatory preference;

- any discrimination in the course of providing property management services;

- agreeing with a client to discriminate when leasing the client's property, such as agreeing not to show the property to members of particular minority groups;

- attempting to discourage the rental of real estate based on representations of the race, sex, disability, etc. of other inhabitants in an area; and

- encouraging or permitting employees to engage in discriminatory practices.

For example, a broker is aware a licensed care facility for disabled people is located in a single-family residence near a residence the prospective tenant is interested in renting.

The presence of the facility might influence the tenant's decision to rent the property. However, for the broker or his agents to inform the tenant of the facility would be unlawful discrimination. The broker may not attempt to influence the tenant's decision based on representations of the disability of other inhabitants in the area. [73 Ops. Cal. Atty. Gen. 58 (1990)]

However, on a direct inquiry from a tenant, the broker or agent must respond based on his knowledge of the existence of a care facility.

Broker's duty to manage employees

A broker has a **duty to advise** his agents and employees of anti-discrimination rules, including DRE regulations, the Unruh Civil Rights Act, the California Fair Employment and Housing Act, and federal Fair Housing Act. [DRE Reg. §2725(f)]

The broker is not only responsible for his own conduct, but he must also ensure his employees follow anti-discrimination regulations when acting as agents on his behalf.

Disclosure of HIV/AIDS

A property manager locates a rental for a prospective tenant. The prior occupant of the property was afflicted with AIDS. Neither the property manager nor the landlord disclose the prior occupant's AIDS affliction, whether or not asked by the prospective tenant.

The tenant rents the property and later discovers the prior occupant was afflicted with AIDS while residing on the property. The tenant claims the property manager had a duty to disclose the prior occupant had AIDS.

However, the tenant has no claim against the property manager for the property manager's failure to disclose any prior occupant was infected with the HIV virus or afflicted with AIDS. No duty exists to disclose the prior tenant's affliction. [CC §1710.2(a)]

Further, California public policy prohibits a broker from responding to a tenant's inquiry for disclosure of a prior occupant's affliction with AIDS. [CC §1710.2(d)]

Also, individuals afflicted with the HIV virus are considered handicapped and are protected by the Federal Fair Housing Act. [24 CFR §100.201]

Disclosing death from AIDS

Unless the tenant makes a **direct inquiry**, the landlord's or property manager's affirmative duty to voluntarily disclose material facts to the tenant in a lease transaction does not extend to the **death** of a prior occupant occurring **more than three years before** the lease of a property.

Consider a tenant who asks the property manager if any AIDS-related deaths occurred on the property. On direct inquiry, the property manager must disclose his knowledge of the facts concerning a death on the real estate. [CC §1710.2(d)]

If the property manager is aware an AIDS-related death occurred on the property, he has a duty on direct inquiry from the tenant to disclose:

- the prior occupant's death; and

- the death was AIDS-related.

If the property manager has no knowledge of any AIDS-related deaths occurring on the property, he must disclose:

- his lack of knowledge; and

- whether or not he intends to undertake an investigation to determine if an AIDS-related death occurred on the property.

However, consider a property manager who is aware a death, from any cause including AIDS, occurred on the property **within three years** of the commencement of a tenant's lease agreement. The tenant has not inquired if any deaths have occurred on the property.

Here, the property manager will need to determine if the death on the property is a *material fact*, one which might affect the tenant's decision to lease and occupy the property.

The property manager should disclose **any death** occurring on the property within three years if he believes the fact might affect the tenant's decision to lease. On inquiry from the tenant, the property manager must disclose his knowledge of any death, including AIDS-related deaths, which occurred on the property within the last three years.

Chapter 55

Adults-only policies prohibited in housing

This chapter discusses unfair discriminatory practices in renting residential units based on familial status, and the tenant's remedies.

Familial status is protected

The landlord of a residential property may not adopt an "adults-only" or "no children" policy, regardless of the number of units on the property, unless the housing development qualifies as senior housing. A development qualifies as **senior housing** if:

- the housing units are occupied solely by persons 62 years of age or older; or

- the housing units are intended and operated for occupancy by persons 55 years of age or older and at least 80% of the occupied units have one or more people at least 55 years old. [42 USC 3607(b)(2); see Chapter 44]

To comply with state and federal anti-discrimination laws, a landlord's screening policies must not serve to prevent children from living in his rentals, called *familial status*. A screening policy must be **children neutral**, as it must also be mutual based on race, religion, nationality, etc. Conversely, senior citizen housing is exempt from unlawful discrimination based on familial status provided it meets the senior housing criteria. [Calif. Civil Code §51.2(a); see Chapter 54]

Rental policies or conduct that work to exclude pregnant women or families that contain one or more children under the age of 18 discriminate against a tenant based on *familial status*. Thus, residential policies that result in "adults-only" tenants are unlawful.

An individual submitting an application to rent cannot be discriminated against if the individual is the parent, legal custodian or a person authorized by written permission to take care of a child who will reside with the individual on the premises. [Calif. Government Code §12955.2; 42 United States Code §3602(k); see **first tuesday** Form 302]

The *Federal Fair Housing Act (FFHA)* also prohibits a landlord from using rental screening policies that discriminate against a tenant based on his familial status. [42 USC §3602]

Further, the *California Fair Employment and Housing Act (FEHA)* prohibits landlords from using discriminatory rental policies to avoid renting to a tenant based on familial status. [Gov C §12955(k)]

Additional California law, the *Unruh Civil Rights Act*, prohibits a *business establishment* from discriminating in the rental of housing based on a tenant's age, unless the property is qualified as senior housing. [Calif. Civil Code §51.2(a)]

Each of these schemes provides a variety of remedies and recoveries for a tenant who, since he resides with a child, has been discriminated against by a landlord. With the exception of senior housing, discrimination in the rental of housing based on familial status violates all three acts, and, for a landlord, property manager or resident manager, can result in civil liability, civil penalties and suspension of a real estate license.

Discrimination prohibited

Consider an owner of a two-bedroom residential unit that he rents. The unit is vacant and is advertised for rent in the local newspaper.

A prospective tenant contacts the landlord regarding the rental unit. Before agreeing to show the tenant the property, the landlord asks the tenant how many family members will occupy the unit (an inquiry which may or may not be made for discriminatory purposes).

The prospective tenant informs the landlord his spouse and child will occupy the unit with him. The landlord informs the tenant he does not qualify to rent the unit. The landlord explains families with children increase his maintenance costs by causing excessive wear and tear to the property. The tenant is forced to look elsewhere for housing.

Has the landlord unlawfully discriminated against the tenant by refusing to rent a single-family residence to the tenant based on, among other reasons, his familial status as including a child?

Yes! A residential landlord unlawfully discriminates against a potential tenant when he refuses to rent a residential unit to a tenant based solely on the fact a child will occupy the unit — a violation of FEHA. [Gov C §§12955(a), 12955(k)]

Also, FEHA prohibits a residential landlord from inquiring, as part of the screening process, into whether a prospective tenant even has children, if the purpose of the inquiry is to exclude families. [Gov C §12955(b)]

However, a landlord who targets families with children as prospective tenants is not necessarily acting in a prohibited discriminatory manner when he inquires about children. He may be intending to push advantages his property offers to tenants who have children, such as playground facilities or day care.

Whether or not an inquiry into familial status was made with discriminatory intent is shown by the landlord's **subsequent behavior**, i.e., refusal to rent, a higher security deposit, an increase in rent to anyone with children or the "steering" of families to other units or facilities.

The Unruh Act and the FFHA

The California Unruh Act prohibits a *business establishment* from discriminating in the rental of housing based on an occupant's age. [CC §51.2(a)]

Owners of apartment complexes and condominium associations fall under the definition of a business establishment for purposes of unlawful discrimination. [CC §51.2(b)]

Editor's note — Landlords of one-to-four units fall under California's FEHA, as well as the state's Unruh Act. The term business establishment under the Unruh Act applied in the broadest reasonable manner. [*O'Connor* v. ***Village Green Owners Association** (1983) 33 C3d 790*]

However, California's Unruh Act does not control mobilehome park owners. [**Schmidt** v. **Superior Court** (1989) 48 C3d 370]

A mobilehome park owner discriminating against tenants based on familial status violates federal law and California's FEHA, unless the mobilehome park is operated as qualified senior citizen housing. [CC §798.76; Gov C §12955.9; 42 USC §3607(b)]

Discrimination based on familial status does not occur under any law when the housing qualifies as senior citizen housing. [CC §§51.2, 51.10; Gov C §12955.9; 42 USC §3607(b)(1)]

Rental discrimination under the FFHA

Landlords, property managers and resident managers regularly and properly engage in discrimination for **legitimate purposes** when screening potential tenants for their rental units.

For example, a potential tenant's income, credit rating and rental and employment history are carefully considered for creditworthiness and an analysis of the landlord's risk of lost rent before a unit is rented to the tenant. In economic downturns, landlords tend to be more lenient in their rental practices by lowering rental deposits and rates, and relaxing credit requirements to keep their rental units full. They tend to accept less-qualified tenants than they would otherwise accept in better economic times. In other words, landlords become less (or more) discriminatory when analyzing creditworthiness and risk over a period of time.

Conversely, when activity in the real estate rental market turns up, landlords become more selective in the screening process to reduce the risk they take with a tenant. Landlords raise rental rates and tighten up credit standards during a strong demand for units.

However, as credit standards are raised, they must be equally applied to all prospects. Some landlords may overstep the law by cultivating an exclusive living atmosphere desired by older, more wealthy tenants, similar to criteria used in the screening process that tends to prevent families with children from renting.

Prohibited **discriminatory rental practices** toward families include both the direct refusal to rent, and the use of different rental or credit analyses or qualification criteria between competing tenants, such as:

- using different income standards;

- applying a different credit analysis;

- using different tenant screening and approval procedures; or

- imposing different rental charges. [24 Code of Federal Regulations §100.60]

Thus, a landlord cannot require tenants with children to have a higher family income or a better credit rating than tenants without children.

Also, a landlord who rents to a tenant with children cannot include different terms in the lease or rental agreements when children are involved, such as requiring higher security deposits or rental rates. [24 CFR §100.65(b)]

Any rental practice or policy that has the effect of *discouraging* or *preventing* families with children from renting a dwelling violates federal and state discrimination laws. [**Marina Point, Ltd.** v. **Wolfson** (1982) 30 C3d 721]

Discriminatory intent not required

A landlord cannot refuse to rent to families with children or adopt rental policies that **result in discrimination** against families with children. [24 CFR §100.60(b)]

Consider a landlord of an apartment complex who has a policy limiting occupancy of units to two persons. Each unit has two bedrooms and two baths. A prospective tenant contacts the property manager of the apartment complex. The tenant intends to rent a unit for himself, his spouse and two children.

The property manager advises the prospective tenant an application will not be processed even though units are available, since the complex has a policy limiting occupancy of each unit to two persons. The prospective tenant is not shown any of the units in the complex.

The tenant files an action against the landlord to recover money losses incurred in his extended search for housing, claiming the landlord violated the Fair Housing Act since he refused to rent a two-bedroom apartment to a family of four.

The landlord claims his two-or-less occupancy restriction was not discriminatory since the restriction was **even-handedly applied** to all rental applicants with the intent of preventing excessive wear to the units in an effort to reduce maintenance costs and increase the property's value.

Is the landlord liable for the costs incurred by the tenant to find new housing since the landlord's refusal to rent was based on a two-tenant occupancy restriction?

Yes! The landlord's occupancy restriction limiting use of a two-bedroom residential unit to two persons automatically results in discrimination against families with children.

A landlord's intent to discriminate against children is not necessary for him to violate the Fair Housing Act if the application of an **occupancy restriction** discriminates against families with children. [**Fair Housing Council of Orange County, Inc.** v. **Ayres** (1994) 855 F.Supp. 315]

While an occupancy restriction limiting the number of persons allowed to reside in the unit is enforceable if applied equally to all tenants, the restriction becomes an unlawful discriminatory housing practice when it has a *negative effect* on the availability of suitable rental units for families with children.

For example, a mother and her child locate a one bedroom unit she would like to rent in an apartment complex. The apartment complex has a longstanding practice of only renting one bedroom units to a single occupant out of concern for the lack of parking in the complex. Thus, the property manager refuses to show the prospective tenant the available unit. The local zoning ordinances require a minimum of 250 square feet for two persons in a unit and one bedroom unit had 650 square feet.

Here, the occupancy standard of the owner, which applied to all prospective tenants equally, violated the Fair Housing Act since it results in an **adverse impact** on a protected class of people, *family groups*. Thus, the restrictions denied the family housing for impermissible reasons — parking availability for the second occupant who was the child. [**United States** v. **Badgett** (8th Cir. 1992) 976 F2d 1176]

Number-of-occupants restriction

Now consider an owner of several single-family residences which he operates as rentals. The owner imposes a five-person occupancy restriction on some of his rentals.

On one rental unit he has a four-person restriction since it has a small yard and 1,200 square feet of living space which includes two modestly-sized bedrooms, a den opening onto the living room, a large kitchen and one large bathroom.

The unit becomes vacant and is advertised for rent by the owner's property manager. A prospective tenant is shown the rental. The prospective tenant completes a rental application, makes a deposit and passes the credit screening.

The property manager informs the owner he has located a family of five as tenants for the unit. The landlord advises the property manager he will only rent this unit to a family of four and rejects the application, claiming the family is too large to occupy the property. The tenant files a complaint with the Secretary of Housing and Urban Development, claiming the landlord discriminated against him since he had children.

The landlord claims the occupancy restriction is not intended to and does not discriminate against families with children, but is the result of a business decision necessary to prevent excessive wear and tear to property which is not designed to accommodate a family larger than three or four members.

Is the landlord liable for the tenant's losses and the civil penalty because of his occupancy restriction?

No! The landlord must only show his occupancy restriction does not unreasonably limit or exclude families with children. The landlord's occupancy restriction based on the size of the residence is a reasonable means of preventing the dilapidation of the property without barring families. [**Pfaff** v. **U.S. Department of Housing and Urban Development** (1996) 88 F3d 739]

The landlord can properly impose a reasonable numerical occupancy restriction since the purpose of limiting the number of occupants is to preserve the economic value of a property designed to house fewer occupants, occupants which may include families with children.

Chapter 56

Seniors-only housing

This chapter covers acceptable and unacceptable age discrimination in California housing.

California's fair housing laws

A landlord of an apartment complex with an **adults-only** rental policy enters into a lease agreement with a pregnant tenant. The lease contains an exclusion provision prohibiting individuals under 18 years of age from residing in the leased unit.

The tenant gives birth to a child prior to the expiration of the lease.

The landlord immediately serves the tenant with a 3-day notice to remove the child from the premises or vacate. The tenant does neither.

The landlord files an unlawful detainer action to evict the tenant since the tenant remains in possession and has failed to perform under the notice.

The tenant claims she cannot be evicted since the adults-only policy is an unlawful discriminatory practice and violates the child's civil rights.

Can the tenant avoid the landlord's adults-only policy agreed to in the lease agreement and remain in the unit with the child?

Yes! The landlord cannot refuse to rent to an individual based on age unless the individual can be excluded under senior citizen housing laws. The landlord's **adults-only** policy violates California's Unruh Civil Rights Act. [**Marina Point, Ltd.** v. **Wolfson** (1982) 30 C3d 721]

Civil rights and fair housing laws prohibit landlords, property managers and leasing agents from practicing any discrimination which is prohibited because of the *protected* status of an individual when they are locating,

negotiating with or handling tenants for property, whether residential or nonresidential. [See Chapter 54]

However, discriminatory standards practiced by landlords, property managers and leasing agents which are not based on an individual's **societal status** protected by law are valid and enforceable.

Discriminatory standards not based on a protected status include ensuring the tenant:

- is financially able to pay the rent based on equally applied creditworthiness standards;

- will not damage the property based on prior conduct as a tenant or owner of property; or

- will properly conduct himself in the use and enjoyment of the leased premises.

Senior citizen housing

Any lease or rental agreement provision that prohibits the use or occupancy of real estate based on an individual's actual or perceived age, sex, race, color, religion, ancestry, national origin, disability, marital status or sexual orientation, is *void*. [Calif. Civil Code §§51, 53]

However, if the lease provision relates to the age of occupants in qualified *senior citizen housing*, age discrimination is allowed within specific age parameters.

Senior citizen housing is housing:

- intended for occupancy only by individuals 62 years of age or older; or

- intended for occupancy by at least one person of 55 years of age or older. [CC §51.3(b)(1); 42 United States Code §3607(b)]

Landlords and owners of qualified retirement communities or senior citizen apartment complexes **can exclude children** to meet the particular needs of older individuals.

To qualify as **senior citizen housing**, the development or renovation project must have at least 35 dwelling units and obtain a public report issued by the Department of Real Estate (DRE). [CC §51.3(b)(4)]

For a housing development to qualify as **senior citizen housing** with the DRE, the project must provide:

- access throughout for individuals using a wheelchair;

- railings or grab-bars in common areas;

- bright common area lighting for individuals with difficulty seeing;

- access throughout without the need to use stairs;

- a common room and open space for social contact; and

- compliance with the Federal Fair Housing Act (FFHA) and Americans with Disabilities Act (ADA). [CC §51.2(d)]

Qualified senior citizen housing

Qualified senior housing is allowed to limit occupancy to individuals who are 62 years of age or older under an exemption from federal anti-discrimination law.

A housing project qualifies as **senior housing** by limiting the occupancy exclusively to individuals 62 or older. [24 Code of Federal Regulations §100.303(a)(1), (2)]

A housing project still qualifies for senior housing even though management employees and their families living on the premises are under 62 years of age. To be classified as employees, the **employees** must perform substantial duties directly related to the management or maintenance of the housing. [24 CFR §100.303(a)(3)]

The 62-or-older restriction excludes all individuals under the age of 62, even if one spouse is 62 or older and the other is not. [24 CFR §100.303(b)]

If a project owner elects not to qualify or cannot qualify for the 62-or-older exemption, the project may still qualify under the broader 55-or-older exemption.

The 55-or-older 80% rule

To qualify for the federal 55-or-older exemption, the housing project must have 80% of the units occupied by at least one individual 55 years of age or older. [24 CFR §100.304(b), (c)]

For newly constructed projects, the 80% occupancy requirement does not apply until the real estate is 25% occupied. [24 CFR §100.304(b)]

Development or renovation of an existing residential complex for senior citizen housing must have been put to use as senior citizen housing immediately after development or renovation to qualify as senior citizen housing. [CC §51.3(f)]

Underage occupants

An **underage individual** may occupy a residential unit in a seniors-only project, other than a mobilehome park, if the individual:

- resides with a senior citizen prior to the senior's death, prolonged absence or their divorce; and

- is at least 45 years of age, a cohabitant, or an individual providing primary economic or physical support for the senior citizen. [CC §51.3(b)(2)]

A family member or hired individual may reside with the senior citizen if they provide assistance with necessary daily activities or medical treatment. [CC §51.3(b)(7)]

Also, a child or grandchild who is disabled or who has a disabling illness or injury and needs to live with the senior citizen on account of the child's disabilities may live with the senior citizen. [CC §51.3(b)(3)]

Also, a mobilehome park cannot discriminate against a 55-or-older tenant who is or is not married to a younger occupant. Federal law does not allow any discrimination when one occupant is at least 55 years of age. [CC §798.76]

Penalties for discrimination

A leasing agent found guilty of discrimination may be liable for damages of no less than $4,000 and no more than three times the amount of the actual damages and any attorney fees. [CC §52(a)]

Chapter 57

Residential rent control

This chapter describes the nature of local rent control ordinances and California phase-out rules.

Police power and rent control

A city's or county's ability to establish rent control by passing ordinances comes from its authority as a "police power."

Police power is the basis for enacting local ordinances such as zoning, traffic, health and safety regulations, and rent control, as long as the ordinances enacted are for the public's benefit. [Calif. Constitution Article XI §7]

To be valid, *rent control ordinances* must be reasonably related to the prevention of excessive rents and maintaining the availability of existing housing. No case has yet found an ordinance lacking in purpose, no matter its inability to attain, much less come close to, its stated purposes. [**Santa Monica Beach, Ltd.** v. **Superior Court** (1999) 19 C4th 952]

Application for rent increases

Before increasing rent on residential rentals located within rent control communities, a prudent property manager must determine:

- Is this rental unit subject to any rent control ordinances?

- Does the unit fall within an exemption?

- What type of rent adjustment does the ordinance allow?

Units covered by controls

Frequently, rent control ordinances do not cover all the rental units in a city. Examples of the types of property that may be exempt from a rent control ordinance in a city include:

- owner-occupied buildings;

- single-family residences and duplexes;

- luxury apartments;

- condominiums; or

- substantially rehabilitated buildings.

Rent control ordinances may also exempt newly constructed units from regulations to stimulate construction of additional housing.

Types of rent control

Despite the complexity and variety of rent control ordinances, two primary types exist:

- strict rent control; and

- vacancy decontrol.

Under **strict rent control**, rent increases are limited across the board. The restrictions on rent amounts apply to landlords renting to either new or existing tenants. Even when a tenant vacates and a new one moves in, the rent restrictions continue to apply to the unit.

The more common type of rent regulation is *vacancy decontrol*. Under vacancy decontrol, the rent ceilings apply only to existing tenants as long as they choose to remain in occupancy of the unit. When the tenant vacates, the landlord may raise the rent and charge the new tenant market level rents.

Rent adjustment standards

Once the property manager determines a unit is governed by a rent control ordinance, the manager must then determine the type of rent adjustments allowed, *general* or *individual*.

Under a **general adjustment**, rents in all rental units in the city are adjusted using:

- an amount tied to an economic index, such as the Consumer Price Index (CPI);

- a maximum annual percentage rate increase; or

- an amount determined at the discretion of the rent control board.

However, in most rent control cities, a landlord or property manager may also seek an **individual adjustment** from the rent control board. The individual adjustment is usually determined at a hearing before a rent control board.

Adjustments are sought when the general adjustment fails to provide a fair return on the residential property.

Rent increases may be based on:

- cash flow requirements to cover mortgage payments and operating expenses;

- a percentage of the net operating income; or

- a set return on value.

Also, almost all rent control cities allow individual adjustments for capital improvements made to upgrade the units.

Reasonable expenses recovered as rent

When a rent control ordinance bases rent increases for existing tenants on net operating income, the owner's operating expenses include fees and costs incurred by the owner for professional services he used to seek the rent increases. Thus, the cost of the procedures for getting the increase in rent are paid for by the tenant through higher rents. [Calif. Civil Code §1947.15(b)]

Reasonable fees incurred by the owner in successfully obtaining a **judicial reversal** of an adverse administrative rent control decision on a petition for upward adjustment in rents will be paid by the public agency that issued the adverse decision, not by the tenant. Unrecovered fees cannot be used to calculate the net operating income on the property. [CC §1947.15(c)]

If the owner's appeal of an adverse administrative decision is frivolous, the public agency will be awarded its reasonable expenses, including attorney fees, incurred to defend against the owner's action. [CC §1947.15(h)(2)]

When an owner's petition for a rent increase is without merit and the owner is assisted by attorneys or consultants, the tenant will be awarded a reduction in the rent to compensate for the costs he incurred to defend against the owner's petition. [CC §1947.15(h)(1)]

Eviction restrictions

In addition to restricting rent increases, rent control ordinances restrict the landlord's **ability to evict** existing tenants.

In communities free of rent control, the landlord does not need to give a reason for serving a 30-day notice to vacate on a month-to-month tenant. [CC §827]

Conversely, in rent control communities, the landlord may only evict a tenant for just cause. Valid reasons for terminating a rental or lease agreement are set forth in the rent control ordinances.

Common situations that justify termination include:

- breach of the rental or lease agreement by the tenant;

- failure to pay rent;

- creating a nuisance; or

- owner occupancy of the unit.

Most other reasons (or no reason) for termination are prohibited or severely limited.

Phase-out of rent control

When a city's rent control laws conflict with state law, state law controls.

The Legislature enacted rent control *phase-out measures* to provide a more economically efficient statewide housing policy than allowed by local rent control.

The economics of local rent control have generally debilitated investment in new and existing apartments, depriving local markets of necessary housing for lack of a competitive return on investments burdened with rent control.

Since state law overrides local rent control ordinances, landlords of residential rental property may establish rent for each unit, provided the unit:

- was a newly constructed unit exempt from rent control on or **before** February 1, 1995;

- was issued a certificate of occupancy **after** February 1, 1995; or

- is a separately described parcel of real estate (single-family residence or condominium unit) or a unit in a community apartment project, stock operative or limited-equity housing cooperative. [CC §1954.52(a)]

Consider a landlord of a residential rental unit that has a separate legal description from any other lot or unit and was subject to a rent control ordinance on January 1, 1995.

The unit is now occupied by a tenant who was an occupant on January 1, 1999 under a rental or lease agreement entered into on or after January 1, 1996. Here, the landlord may establish rental rates for the existing tenant without concern for rent control. [CC §1954.52(a)(3)(C)(i)]

Also, the landlord of a single-family residence (SFR) or condominium unit can set rental rates for all new tenancies if the **prior tenant's occupancy** was entered into on or **before** December 31, 1995. [CC §1954.52(a)(3)(C)(ii)]

However, the landlord of a SFR or condo unit may not set the rental rates even though the previous tenant occupied before 1996, if:

- that previous tenancy was terminated by a 30-day notice to vacate or a 30-day notice of change of rental terms; or

- if it is a condominium unit that has not yet been sold by the subdivider. [CC §1954.52(a)(3)(B)]

Further, when any residential tenant vacates (other than on a 30-day notice to vacate from the landlord), abandons or is evicted, the landlord may establish the rental rate without concern for rent control.

A landlord who maintains a unit that has been previously cited for violations of health, fire or building codes, may not increase the rent charged to new tenants if the violation is not corrected at least six months before the unit is vacated. [CC §§1954.52(d), 1954.53(f)]

Further, the landlord may not set new rental rates if he has contracted with a local agency to establish low income housing. [CC §1954.52(b)]

State law allowing landlords to set rental rates in rent control communities does not apply to rental units that were **sublet** under a rental agreement entered into before January 1, 1996. [CC §1954.53(d)]

Demolition of residential rentals

A landlord who wants to demolish a rental building, whether or not it is under rent control, must apply to a local governmental agency for a demolition permit.

A landlord is entitled to demolish his unit since he cannot be compelled to continue to provide residential rentals if he chooses to *withdraw* his property from the market. [Calif. Government Code §7060(a)]

Before applying for a demolition permit, the residential landlord must first give a written notice of his intent to apply for a permit to all tenants in the structure he desires to demolish. [CC §1940.6(a)(2)]

A residential landlord who has applied for a demolition permit must give a written notice to prospective tenants about his application for a demolition permit before he accepts an application to rent, a screening or other fee, or enters into a rental or lease agreement, whichever comes first. [CC §1940.6(a)(1)]

The notice of intent to demolish the residential rental structure to be given to the existing and prospective tenants includes the *earliest possible approximation* of the date the demolition is to occur and the *approximate date* the tenants' occupancy will be terminated by the landlord. [CC §1940.6(b)]

SECTION H

Lenders
Considerations

Chapter 58

Leaseholds as security for loans

This chapter discusses a tenant's encumbrancing of a leasehold with a lien by granting a security interest to a lender.

Financing business expansions

A nonresidential tenant holding a long-term lease on real estate needs financing to fund the construction of tenant improvements and the purchase of equipment to accommodate his expanding business.

As a condition for making the loan, a commercial **lender wants security** in the form of:

- the new equipment;

- the tenant's inventory, tools and trade fixtures;

- existing equipment, furniture and accounts receivable; and

- a lien on the real estate.

The tenant's real estate broker assisting in arranging the loan advises the tenant to offer the lender a trust deed lien on his leasehold interest in the premises since it will have far greater value on completion of the improvements. The tenant thought only fee ownership interests in real estate could be encumbered by a trust deed as security for a loan.

The broker explains any marketable interest in real estate can be given as security for a loan, including a tenant's leasehold interest in the premises he occupies, such as a *ground lease*.

Can a loan be secured by a trust deed lien on a nonresidential tenant's leasehold interest in the premises where he conducts his business?

Yes! A fee estate is not the only real estate interest which can be encumbered by a trust deed. **Any marketable interest** in real estate which is transferable can be used to secure a loan. [Calif. Civil Code §2947]

The two operative documents used in real estate mortgage financing, also called *real estate secured transactions*, are the *note* and *trust deed*.

The **note** is evidence of an obligation to pay money to a creditor — usually a lender or carryback seller. The **trust deed** secures the money obligation by encumbering some marketable interest in real estate, be it the fee, a leasehold or a life estate, with a lien in favor of the lender.

Of course, the lender will need to determine whether the market value of the tenant's remaining term under the lease, on completion of improvements, has sufficient value as security to satisfy the lender's loan condition of a trust deed lien on the tenant's interest in the real estate.

Estates as a transferable interest

The phrase "transferable interest in real estate" is applied broadly. An interest in real estate which is transferable includes the right to exclusive possession and is legally called an *estate*.

Each **estate** in property is fully capable of being encumbered with a lien by the owner of the estate. [CC §2947]

In California, **four recognized estates** exist in real estate:

- fee simple (simply called a fee);

- life estates;

- leaseholds; and

- estates at will. [CC §761]

Each estate can be **vested** as one's sole property, or in a co-ownership such as:

- a tenancy-in-common;

- joint tenancy;

- community property, with or without the right of survivorship; or

- a limited liability company (LLC), corporation, real estate investment trust (REIT) or partnership entity vestings. [CC §682]

The fact the ownership of the estate has been fractionalized between **several concurrent co-owners** does not automatically destroy each co-owner's ability to encumber his interest in the real estate. The separately vested interests can be individually encumbered unless it is community property or property used in a partnership for the mutual benefit of all the co-owners, such as the occupancy of property by a business they co-own.

Tenants in common are often partners who hold title for the benefit of the group venture. No co-owner may individually encumber partnership assets they hold in their name.

Also, a spouse with a vested interest in title cannot encumber that interest if it is community property unless the other spouse consents. [Calif. Family Code §1102]

Even contract rights to buy an ownership interest in real estate, such as an option to buy, can be encumbered by placing a lien on the option. [**Chapman** v. **Great Western Gypsum Co.** (1932) 216 C 420]

Encumbering real estate interests

A trust deed lien on real estate encumbers only the interest in the real estate held by the person executing the trust deed.

A trust deed describing a parcel of real estate which is signed by the tenant who occupies the property under a lease **creates a lien** only on the tenant's leasehold interest in the property. The trust deed can not attach as a lien to the landlord's fee interest in the described real estate — unless the landlord also signs the trust deed and the description does not exclude his fee.

When the tenant defaults on a loan secured by his leasehold, the lender forecloses on the tenant's leasehold estate by a trustee's sale or judicial foreclosure sale in order to repossess the right to possession owned by the tenant under the lease. The foreclosing lender, as the successful bidder at the foreclosure sale, becomes the tenant entitled to occupy the property since the lender is the new owner of the leasehold interest which was security for his trust deed lien.

The lender, as the new tenant, is required to make the lease payments and otherwise fully perform under the lease to avoid a forfeiture of the leasehold interest by the landlord on a default. The lender who is now the tenant may retain the leasehold interest, sell the lease to a user of the property, or sublet the property since the lender now owns the leasehold interest, subject to the provisions in the lease agreement limiting alienation.

Occasionally a tenant holds an option to buy the leased real estate. Should a tenant with a trust deed lien on his leasehold later acquire fee title to the real estate, the fee acquired becomes security for the loan. The two possessory interests in the real estate, the leasehold and the fee, being owned by the same individual, *merge* into the greater interest, the fee. Thus, the leasehold is extinguished and the lender automatically becomes secured by the fee. [Chapman, *supra*]

On **merger**, the lender's security interest attaches to the fee since the fee is the only interest remaining in the property held by the trustor who signed the trust deed describing the real estate. [CC §2930]

Leases as security for financing

Nonresidential tenants encumber their leasehold interest with a trust deed when borrowing funds to:

- acquire an existing business opportunity together with the lease to the premises occupied by the business;

- construct improvements on vacant ground or in airspace controlled by the tenant under a long-term lease;

- expand the tenant's existing business and facilities on the leased premises; or

- acquire a home or investment property under a ground lease.

For example, an investor wants to acquire the current master tenant's leasehold position in the ownership of a shopping center.

To finance the acquisition, the investor arranges a purchase-assist loan just as if he were buying the shopping center under a grant deed conveyance.

At the close of the purchase escrow, the tenant under the master lease, acting as the seller, *assigns* his leasehold ownership interest in the center to the investor.

The investor delivers loan documents to the lender which includes a trust deed to encumber the leasehold interest the investor will acquire by assignment. The lender funds the purchase-assist loan.

The tenant and lender obtain separate American Land Title Association (ALTA) title insurance policies on their respective interests in the recorded leasehold estate.

The tenant defaults on the loan and the lender forecloses. The successful bidder at the trustee's sale becomes the new master tenant since he purchased ownership of the leasehold estate at the trustee's sale.

The foreclosure does not wipe out the fee ownership interest which remains unaffected. The fee was not security for the loan.

However, the successful bidder at the lender's foreclosure sale of the leasehold **steps into the shoes** of the leasehold tenant (as of the date the trust deed was recorded). The tenant's interest in the real estate, the right to possess and sublet to users of the premises, was sold to the highest bidder as authorized by the tenant under the trust deed's power of sale provision.

Restricting the right to encumber

A landlord can restrict a tenant's right to encumber the lease with a trust deed lien or, alternatively and less practical for the creditor, collaterally assign the lease as security for a loan. If **encumbrance restrictions** are not written into the lease, the tenant may assign or encumber his leasehold as he chooses. [CC §1995.210]

To restrict or control a tenant's ability to encumber his leasehold interest, a landlord includes a provision in the lease which defines the conditions under which the tenant may encumber the lease, called an *alienation provision*. [See Chapter 48; see **first tuesday** Form 552 §19]

In the **alienation provision** in the lease, the landlord may:

- prohibit the tenant from encumbering the leasehold [CC §1995.230; see **first tuesday** Form 552 §19.1];

- allow the tenant to encumber the leasehold subject to previously agreed conditions, such as the payment of a fee or higher rent [CC §1995.240; see **first tuesday** Form 552 §19.2]; or

- require the landlord's consent before the tenant may encumber the leasehold. [CC §1995.250; see **first tuesday** Form 552 §19.2]

If the lease requires the landlord's consent to encumber the leasehold, conditions for the payment of money contained in the alienation provision must be met before the landlord needs to grant consent. If no conditions for the landlord's consent are stated in the lease, consent must be granted unless a *commercially reasonable basis* exists for the denial of consent. [CC §1995.260; see Form **first tuesday** 552 §19.2]

Conversely, a tenant may require the landlord's consent to be subject to the standard of reasonableness by writing a provision into the lease. [CC §1995.250(a)]

It is **commercially reasonable** for the landlord to withhold consent when the encumbrance interferes with his interest, such as the tenant's:

- poor business track record;

- lack of creditworthiness;

- damage to property; or

- inadequate management skills.

Financing a business expansion

Consider a nonresidential tenant who borrows money to expand his business. The **security devices** available to secure the loan include:

- a trust deed;

- a collateral assignment of the lease; or

- a lease hypothecation, such as a UCC-1 financing statement.

When a lender agrees to accept a lease as security, the trust deed is the preferred security device used to document the lender's lien on the real estate. The secured lender or carryback

seller of a leasehold interest who uses a trust deed as the security device can foreclose on the leasehold estate by a trustee's sale.

Use of any type of security device that does not contain a **power of sale provision** will require judicial foreclosure if the tenant defaults. [CC §2924]

Financing a business opportunity purchase

Consider a buyer of a business opportunity who makes a down payment on the price. The seller carries back the balance of the price on a note secured by the business equipment and furniture, the trade fixtures, and the lease on the premises.

The buyer signs a **UCC-1 financing statement** to impose a lien on the personal property (equipment, furniture, trade fixtures and accounts receivable) and a **collateral assignment** of the lease on the premises (or a trust deed). The documents are delivered to the seller as security for the carryback note.

Later, the buyer defaults on the note. The lease and the business have no remaining value. The seller sues directly on the promissory note to enforce collection without concern for the lien of the leasehold.

Can the seller waive the leasehold as security and sue directly on the note?

No! The seller cannot first sue on the note since the debt is secured by an interest in real estate (the leasehold). The seller must first foreclose on the lease (unless it has been *exhausted* by termination of the leasehold estate on a forfeiture declared by the landlord). The lease of the premises, being an interest in real estate, requires the lender holding the lease as security to foreclose judicially to enforce collection of the loan before a money judgment can be awarded, called the *one-action rule*. [CCP §726]

Chapter 59

Attornment clauses in nonresidential leases

This chapter reviews attornment, subordination and nondisturbance clauses in nonresidential lease agreements, and their use by landlords and lenders to alter the priorities of leases and trust deeds.

Altering priorities for lenders

A lender holds a recorded trust deed lien on the fee ownership interest in nonresidential income-producing real estate. The trust deed contains a due-on provision that states the owner may not sell, lease or encumber the secured property without the prior written consent of the lender, also called a *transfer clause* or *alienation clause*.

The lender has advised the owner it will consent to new leases under the due-on clause on the condition the lease agreement contain an *attornment clause* and a *lender subordination clause*.

A tenant enters into a lease agreement with the landlord that contains an attornment clause. The lease agreement is approved by the lender.

The **attornment clause** states the tenant will recognize a buyer of the property at a foreclosure sale as the new landlord under the lease if the buyer exercises his right under the attornment clause to enforce the lease agreement. [See Figure 1 accompanying this chapter]

Later, the owner defaults on the first trust deed. The lender notices a foreclosure sale and acquires the property with a credit bid.

After the lender acquires the property, the lender mails a written notice to the tenant stating:

- the lender is the new landlord **under the lease agreement**; and

- the tenant is to pay rent to the lender.

The tenant does not pay rent and vacates the premises.

The lender claims the tenant is required to accept the lender as the new landlord under the attornment clause in the tenant's lease agreement with the prior owner since the lender purchased the property at the foreclosure sale and declared himself to be the landlord under the lease.

The tenant claims the attornment clause is unenforceable since the lease agreement that contained the clause was junior to the lender's trust deed and was eliminated by the lender's foreclosure sale.

Is the tenant required to accept the lender as the new landlord and perform under the lease?

Yes! While the leasehold interest, the *lease* held by the tenant, was eliminated from title by the foreclosure sale, the lease agreement remains enforceable. Thus, on notice from the lender, the tenant is required to recognize — attorn to — the lender as the **substitute landlord** under the lease.

The lease is *restored and reattached* to title after the foreclosure sale when the lender (or other purchaser at the foreclosure sale) exercises the right given under the attornment clause to enforce the lease agreement as the new substitute landlord. [**Miscione** v. **Barton Development Company** (1997) 52 CA4th 1320]

The attornment clause contracts around the permanent elimination of a junior leasehold interest on completion of a foreclosure sale by a senior trust deed lender. The clause allows the

---

Figure 1

Attornment clause

In the event Tenant's estate is exhausted by a disposition of Landlord's estate, Tenant will recognize the new owner who acquires Landlord's estate as Landlord under this lease should the new owner, within 30 days of acquisition, notify Tenant in writing of the new owner's election to be substituted as Landlord under this lease.

---

purchaser at the lender's foreclosure sale to restore the *extinguished* lease as though it were unaffected by the foreclosure sale.

Priority on foreclosure

A tenant's lease, whether or not recorded, has **priority on title** over an interest in the property held by another person, such as a trust deed lien or abstract of judgment, when:

- the lease agreement is **recorded** before the other interest (a trust deed) is recorded or, if unrecorded, is actually known to the person holding the other interest [Calif. Civil Code §1214]; or

- the tenant takes **possession** before the other interest (a trust deed) is recorded or the tenant's right to possession is actually known to the person holding the other interest. [**Gates Rubber Company** v. **Ulman** (1989) 214 CA3d 356]

For example, a trust deed recorded junior in time to a tenant's occupancy of the secured real estate is foreclosed. The tenant's lease, being prior in time, is undisturbed by the foreclosure — the tenancy held by the tenant under terms contained in the lease agreement remains in full effect.

Thus, the buyer at the foreclosure sale of a junior trust deed acquires title "subject to" the lease. Since the lease held by tenant has priority, the buyer must perform the landlord's obligations under the lease agreement if the tenant seeks to enforce them.

Now consider a lease acquired by a tenant after a trust deed or judgment lien is recorded on the property. Later, the trust deed or judgment lien is foreclosed.

Here, the tenant's lease is wiped out by the foreclosure of the trust deed lien or judgment lien since the tenant's leasehold interest in title is junior in time and subordinate to the lien.

On elimination of a junior lease by a foreclosure sale of the premises, the tenant loses his right to possession of the premises. [**Hohn** v. **Riverside County Flood Control and Water Conservation District** (1964) 228 CA2d 605]

After foreclosure by the senior lienholder, the tenant's continued use and possession of the property is an unlawful detainer (UD) and the tenant can be evicted. A 3-day notice to quit due to foreclosure is required to be served and expire before a UD action can be filed and the occupant, should he remain in possession, be evicted. [See **first tuesday** Form 578]

Altering the priorities

A tenant can agree in a lease agreement to allow the landlord or the secured lender to **act unilaterally** in the future to alter the priority of the tenant's lease and the lender's trust deed liens on the property. [**Dover Mobile Estates** v. **Fiber Form Products, Inc.** (1990) 220 CA3d 1494]

Nonresidential lease agreements often contain boilerplate provisions, such as an *attornment clause*, a *lender subordination clause*, a *future subordination clause* and a *nondisturbance clause*. These provisions relate to the priority of the lease against trust deeds, present and future.

The **attornment clause** allows an owner-by-foreclosure to unilaterally avoid the automatic elimination and unenforceability of a junior lease by a foreclosure sale.

The **lender subordination clause** gives a trust deed lender the right to unilaterally subordinate the lender's trust deed to a previously junior lease by written notice to the tenant. Thus, the lease would not be wiped out by a foreclosure of the lender's trust deed since the trust deed has been subordinated and the lease has priority.

Under a **future subordination clause**, the tenant agrees to subordinate his lease to a trust deed to be recorded in the future. Here, the tenant remains involved since he must sign a *specific subordination agreement* to give the trust deed priority to his lease.

The **nondisturbance clause** is coupled with the future subordination clause. The clause entitles the tenant to receive a signed writing from a new trust deed lender agreeing that the lease will remain in effect for its full term in spite of the fact the tenant concurrently signs a specific subordination agreement giving the lender's trust deed priority.

Thus, by the nondisturbance agreement, the tenant will be restored with the rights he would otherwise lose on the lender's foreclosure due to the subordination and will be able to enforce the lease agreement against the new lender.

Further, by a lender exercising its rights under the *due-on clause* in its trust deed, a lender is able to also control the terms of all future leasing of the property, except for those leases with a term of three years or less.

As a condition for the lender to give consent to each lease agreement entered into by the landlord, a knowledgeable lender will require the landlord's lease agreements to include both a lender subordination clause and an attornment clause.

The attornment clause and foreclosure

Attornment is the tenant's agreement to acknowledge the purchaser at a foreclosure sale under a trust deed senior to his lease as a *substitute landlord* who may elect to enforce the tenant's lease agreement.

To enforce a wiped-out lease, the owner-by-foreclosure notifies the tenant he has elected to be the substitute landlord under the tenant's lease. However, the new owner need not do so, leaving the wiped-out tenant with no interest in the property.

A nonresidential landlord has good financial justification to include an attornment clause in a lease agreement. Should a senior trust deed lender foreclose, it is essential for the landlord to maintain the property's value and reduce the potential of a deficiency judgment. [See Figure 1]

A financially advantageous lease agreement, enforceable by new owners after a foreclosure, will help maintain the value of the property. On the other hand, if a financially advantageous lease agreement does not contain an attornment clause, the property's market value will be lower than it would be had the owner-by-foreclosure been able to enforce the lease.

If an owner-by-foreclosure elects to enforce a lease agreement containing an attornment clause, the lease agreement remains in full effect for the remainder of its term. Thus, the owner-by-foreclosure who makes the attornment election becomes the substitute landlord and must perform the obligations of the landlord under the lease. [Miscione, *supra*]

Before the foreclosing lender or other purchaser at a foreclosure sale substitutes himself as the successor landlord, he must consider whether the leases will generate rents at or above market rates. To help make the attornment decision, the new owner should first:

- obtain the equivalent of a Tenant Estoppel Certificate (TEC) from each tenant to discover any breach of their lease agreement by the prior landlord [See Chapter 41]; and

- inspect the property to be assured its physical condition is acceptable to the new owner.

Subleases and attornment

Lease agreements allowing a tenant to sublet portions of the property to occupants of separate spaces, also called *subtenants*, contain restraint-on-alienation clauses, also called *transfer restrictions* or *assignment and subletting provisions*.

The landlord's consent is needed in order for the tenant to sublet. When setting up the guidelines for consenting to a subletting, the landlord should require an **attornment provision** to be included in the lease agreement with the subtenant. If the landlord ever terminates the master tenant's right to possession under a three-day notice and forfeiture, a process that automatically eliminates the subtenant's right to possession, the landlord may enforce the sublease agreement under the attornment clause.

The landlord electing to enforce the sublease agreement is substituted as the landlord (sublessor) under its attornment provision. Due to the election, the subtenant will continue paying rent as agreed, but to the new landlord.

No assurance of continued occupancy

Conversely, an attornment clause does not give the tenant the reciprocal right to enforce the lease agreement against the buyer at the foreclosure sale. The attornment agreed to by the tenant to recognize the buyer as his landlord is not exercised until the buyer elects to enforce the provisions.

Thus, a tenant who enters into a lease agreement with an attornment clause, whose lease is junior to a lender's trust deed, has no assurance the lease will be restored or that he will be able to remain in possession after a foreclosure sale.

Yet tenants, when agreeing to an attornment clause as a provision in their lease agreements, believe the clause states the obvious — the tenant will perform on the lease for anyone who becomes the new owner of the property. The tenant views it as a nondisturbance agreement with the lender, but it is not. The lender is not a party to the lease agreement.

However, when a junior lease is eliminated at a foreclosure sale, the new owner is unlikely to elect to enforce the lease agreement if:

- the new owner acquired the property to occupy it as a user; or

- the rents due under the exhausted lease are significantly less than the rents available in the market.

Further, a tenant will regret the inclusion of an attornment clause if rents called for in the lease agreement exceed market rates at the time of foreclosure, or if the location or premises are no longer desirable for the tenant when a foreclosure sale occurs and the attornment clause is enforced to restore the lease.

All these events typically converge during economically depressed times for all involved.

For a tenant to avoid the unilateral adverse economic impact of an attornment clause upon entering into a long-term lease under an agreement containing the clause, the tenant should:

- obtain an abstract of title or lessee's policy of title insurance to ascertain the trust deeds and other liens of record and the risk of loss they present to the tenant;

- obtain a beneficiaries statement on the loans/liens of record;

- record a Request for Notice of Default; and

- record a Request for Notice of Delinquency on the lender. [See **first tuesday** Form 412]

With the information from these documents, the tenant can take steps to protect his interest if the landlord defaults on senior liens or the underlying ground lease, long before any foreclosure sale occurs.

Notifying the tenant

A lender or other high bidder who acquires a property at a foreclosure sale, which wipes out a tenant's leasehold interest in the property, **elects to enforce** the tenant's lease agreement under its attornment clause by giving the tenant a written notice:

- stating the owner-by-foreclosure is exercising his right to enforce the lease agreement provided him by the attornment clause; and

- instructing the tenant to make all future rent payments due under the lease agreement to the buyer. [Miscione, *supra*]

A specific time period should be stated in the attornment clause within which the owner-by-foreclosure must notify the tenant of his election to enforce the attornment agreement, such as within 30 days after the foreclosure sale. [See Figure 1]

The new owner loses the right to enforce the attornment clause if:

- no time period for enforcing recognition of the new owner as landlord is specified in the clause; and

- the new owner does not elect to enforce the lease within a *reasonable period of time*.

No right to continued occupy

The owner-by-foreclosure may choose not retain the extinguished nonresidential lease by enforcing the tenant's lease agreement containing an attornment clause. Instead, he may cause the tenant to vacate. To notify the tenant to vacate and be able to evict him through an unlawful detainer action should he not vacate, a three-day notice to quit due to foreclosure must be served on the tenant. [Calif. Code of Civil Procedure §1161a(b); see **first tuesday** Form 578]

The three-day notice should be served as soon as possible to avoid conduct by the landlord or property manager that could be construed as an enforcement of the lease (by attornment) or the establishment of an unintended periodic tenancy.

For example, a new owner who elects not to enforce the lease should not accept rent from the tenant until he enters into a new written rental or lease agreement.

Accepting rent in the amount called for in the extinguished lease agreement may indicate the new owner intends to accept the lease under its attornment clause, regardless of the new owner's actual intent. [**Rubin** v. **Los Angeles Federal Savings and Loan Association** (1984) 159 CA3d 292]

If the owner-by-foreclosure accepts rent payments from a tenant when an attornment clause does not exist in the extinguished lease, a periodic tenancy is created. As between themselves, neither the tenant nor the new owner can enforce the lease agreement since the lease has been extinguished. [**Colyear** v. **Tobriner** (1936) 7 C2d 735]

Lender subordination clauses

A nonresidential lender requiring an attornment clause in a lease agreement entered into by the owner after the lender's trust deed is recorded will also require the owner to include a *lender subordination clause* in the lease agreement. The lender subordination clause allows the lender to elect, at any time during the life of its trust deed, to subordinate his trust deed lien to leases the landlord enters into with tenants after the trust deed is recorded. [See Figure 2 accompanying this chapter]

A lease agreement containing both a lender subordination clause and a tenant attornment clause allows the lender the **maximum flexibility** for preserving an advantageous lease by either:

- electing to subordinate his trust deed to the lease **before the foreclosure sale**; or

- **completing a foreclosure sale** and electing to enforce the lease agreement within the attornment election period.

Some attornment clauses are worded to state the lender must acquire the premises "subject to" the lease at the time of the foreclosure sale.

However, while an attornment clause in a lease agreement may literally state the lender is to acquire the property "subject to" the lease, the attornment clause cannot automatically subordinate the trust deed to the lease when a foreclosure sale occurs since the lender is not a party to the lease agreement. The lender did not agree to the terms of the lease agreement, even if the lender previously reviewed it and waived his due-on clause enforcement by consenting to the lease.

When the lender notifies the tenant prior to the foreclosure sale of his election to subordinate his trust deed lien to the tenant's lease, the election **need not be recorded** to give public notice. The change in priority only affects the lender, the tenant and their successors who are aware of the agreement since they are parties to it, not third parties. [CC §1217]

A trust deed that becomes senior to a lease by the lender's election to subordinate gives the lease priority over the trust deed. Thus, the lease is **not eliminated from title** by the foreclosure sale.

If the lease is not wiped out at the foreclosure sale because of the lender's prior election to subordinate, a later election under the attornment clause after foreclosure becomes unnecessary. When a lender elects to subordinate his trust deed to the lease, the high bidder at the foreclosure sale acquires the property "subject to" the lease since the lease has priority over the trust deed.

After the foreclosure sale, by either a prior election by the lender to subordinate or a later election to have the tenant attorn to the new owner, the lease agreement becomes **enforceable by both** the tenant and the new landlord. [Miscione, *supra*]

Electing to subordinate

Now consider a lender holding a first trust deed on nonresidential real estate. After the trust deed is recorded, the owner leases the property.

The lease agreement contains a lender *subordination clause* to satisfy the lender's conditions for waiver of the due-on clause in his trust deed.

During the term of the lease, the owner defaults on the lender's trust deed. The lender records a notice of default (NOD), initiating a

---

Figure 2

Lender subordination clause

Any master lessor or holder of a lien on the leased premises may elect to subordinate its interest in the premises to this lease by service of written notice on the tenant of the election, and thereafter the lease shall have priority regardless of the priorities set by law.

trustee's foreclosure sale. The lender has the property appraised and discovers the rent due over the remaining term of the tenant's lease exceeds current prevailing rental rates.

For the same economic reasons that cause the lender wants to preserve the lease agreement, the tenant wants out of the lease agreement.

The lender hears of negotiations between the owner and the tenant to modify the lease agreement. The lender does not want the landlord to alter the agreement prior to foreclosure and an attornment. The lender serves written notice on the tenant of his election to **subordinate** his trust deed to the tenant's lease, altering their priorities.

After receipt of the notice of subordination, the tenant and the landlord modify the lease agreement, granting the tenant the right to terminate the lease agreement at any time on 30 days' written notice, in exchange for the tenant paying the landlord a modification fee.

The trustee's sale is held and the lender acquires the property. The tenant is notified by the lender that he is now the owner of the property and all rent payments under the lease are to be made to the lender. The tenant notifies the lender in writing of his election to terminate the lease and cancel the lease agreement on 30 days' notice.

The lender claims the tenant cannot terminate the lease or cancel the lease agreement since the modification agreement, but not the original lease agreement, was eliminated by the foreclosure sale.

Can the tenant terminate the lease by canceling the lease agreement under the conditions stated in the lease modification entered into prior to the owner's loss of the property?

No! The original terms of the lease agreement remained unaffected by the foreclosure sale since the lender elected to subordinate the trust deed to the lease prior to the tenant entering into the lease modification agreement. Thus, the agreement modifying the lease became unenforceable by the tenant after the foreclosure sale. The modification agreement was junior in time to the subordination of the trust deed. Thus, the lease became a senior (unrecorded) encumbrance on title to the property with priority to the lender's trust deed and could not be altered without the lender's consent.

Thus, the modification of the lease agreement, but not the pre-existing lease agreement, was eliminated by the lender's foreclosure. [**In re 240 North Brand Partners, Ltd.** (9th Cir. BAP 1996) 200 BR 653]

By subordination of the lender's trust deed to the lease, the lender acted to maintain the property's value based on rents under the lease. Subordination allows the lender to avoid the effect of any later modification of the lease prior to foreclosing and acquiring ownership at the trustee's sale.

In the event the lender proceeds with a judicial foreclosure, the landlord would normally prefer the property to remain encumbered by a financially advantageous lease agreement following a **judicial foreclosure** sale to avoid a deficiency in the property's value and its inability to satisfy the loan.

Thus, the risk of loss due to a deficiency in the value of the property at the time of the remaining judicial foreclosure sale is reduced for both the lender and the landlord, but the tenant must pay.

Future subordination clauses

A **landlord's ability** to further encumber or refinance his property during the term of a lease is greatly diminished unless the lease agreement contains a *future subordination clause*. [See Figure 3 accompanying this chapter]

Like the attornment clause and lender subordination clause, a future subordination clause is an agreement to **alter priorities** on title. Under a future subordination clause, the tenant agrees to subordinate his lease (right to possession) and the lease agreement to a trust deed to be recorded by the landlord sometime in the future.

Thus, the tenant agrees to place his lease in a financially lesser or worse position on title, whether or not the lease agreement is recorded, than he enjoyed at the time he enters into the lease agreement. The tenant's lease will be subordinated to a new trust deed loan based on the terms of a new loan agreed to in the future subordination clause.

For a **future subordination clause** to be enforceable at the time the landlord arranges a new trust deed loan, the clause must specify:

- the use of the loan proceeds, such as refinancing existing encumbrances or improving the property;

- the dollar amount of the loan on the loan-to-value ratio of the financing;

- the payment schedule;

- the interest rate; and

- the due date. [**Handy** v. **Gordon** (1967) 65 C2d 578]

The clause must also contain any other terms that might be unique to the future financing that would, if agreed to by the tenant, further impair the tenant's lease.

When the landlord later arranges financing for the property on terms within the parameters agreed to in the subordination clause, the tenant is obligated to sign a *specific subordination agreement*. A title company will not insure the priority of the new trust deed over the tenant's lease without the tenant executing an agreement setting out the specifics of the loan and the subordination.

However, the tenant may refuse to sign a subordination agreement if the financing terms are not substantially similar or within the parameters of the subordination clause in his lease agreement. The tenant has not agreed to subject his lease to the uncertainties of a greater risk of loss than the risks established by the terms of the subordination clause.

Editor's note — When the landlord wants to record a new trust deed to secure a loan and the tenant refuses to sign a specific subordination agreement, the landlord's primary recourse is to serve a 3-day notice to perform or quit. If performance is not forthcoming, rather than evict, the landlord may file an action against the tenant for declaratory relief and specific performance of the future subordination clause in the tenant's lease agreement.

Nondisturbance clauses

A **nondisturbance clause** gives the tenant the right to require a new trust deed lender to enter into a written agreement with the tenant, called a *nondisturbance agreement*. The agreement states the tenant's lease agreement will remain in effect for its full term after the lease is subordinated to a new loan.

A nondisturbance clause is included in a lease agreement only if the lease agreement also

---

Figure 3	*Excerpt from **first tuesday** Form 552 —* *Nonresidential Lease Agreement*

17. **SUBORDINATION:**

    17.1 Tenant agrees to subordinate to any new financing secured by the premises which does not exceed 80% loan-to-value ratio, and interest of two percent over market, and not less than a 15-year monthly amortization and five-year due date.

contains a *future subordination clause*. The tenant is the primary beneficiary of the nondisturbance clause.

A nondisturbance clause is typically used by the landlord and leasing agents to avoid negotiating the terms of a subordination clause with the tenant while hammering out the terms of the lease.

When the nondisturbance clause and an enforceable future subordination clause are included in a lease agreement, the tenant can refuse to sign a subordination agreement unless the lender provides the tenant with a nondisturbance agreement. Any standoff between the tenant and the lender would pose a serious problem for the landlord's attempt to record financing.

Informed lenders are not likely to provide a tenant with a nondisturbance agreement when originating a loan secured by a first trust deed on property.

A nondisturbance agreement **negates** the effect of the subordination agreement by reversing the very priorities agreed to by subordinating the lease to the trust deed, a sort of *self-destruct provision*. The lease will not in effect be subordinate to the lender's trust deed if the lender agrees to recognize the continued existence of the lease after a foreclosure of the trust deed.

A knowledgeable landlord, contrary to the needs of a tenant, does not want a nondisturbance clause in his lease agreements — he wants an enforceable future subordination clause.

Unlike the purpose of an attornment clause, a lease that is subject to a nondisturbance agree-

ment will not be eliminated by foreclosure nor need to be later restored by election of the owner-by-foreclosure. The nondisturbance agreement states the lease will remain in effect for its full term without regard to foreclosure.

Since the lease by agreement with the lender cannot be extinguished by foreclosure, it cannot also be junior to the trust deed.

Thus, a subordination of the lease to the trust deed never truly occurs because of the lender's concurrent entry into a nondisturbance agreement.

Also, when a lender executes a nondisturbance agreement, an attornment clause serves no purpose. Like many clauses in some lease agreements, it becomes superfluous.

The tenant's possession and lease agreement when subject to a nondisturbance agreement remains undisturbed and continuously enforceable by both the tenant and the new owner after the foreclosure sale.

By entering into a nondisturbance agreement, the lender is **forced to become** the landlord under the lease if the lender forecloses and acquires the property.

However, a prudent lender probably wants the choices afforded him by the lender's loan subordination and attornment clauses, to accept or reject the lease either prior to or after the foreclosure.

Here, the landlord eliminates the need for a nondisturbance clause in a lease agreement by negotiating an enforceable future subordination clause outlining the loan parameters acceptable to both the landlord and the tenant when entering into the lease.

Chapter 60

Tenant estoppel certificates

This chapter explains an owner's use of a Tenant Estoppel Certificate provision in lease agreements when leased property is refinanced or sold.

Protection for buyers and lenders

A real estate broker representing an owner who wants to sell or refinance his income-producing property customarily prepares an annual property operating data (APOD) form to be included in the marketing package. The completed APOD will be handed to prospective buyers and lenders to persuade them to enter into a transaction with the owner. [See **first tuesday** Form 352]

A thoughtfully prepared APOD provides buyers and lenders with an accurate summary of financial information on the operating income and expenses generated by a property, as well as loans encumbering the property.

Buyers and lenders who rely on APOD figures should corroborate the income and other leasing arrangements prior to closing. A strategic method is to condition the closing on their receipt and further approval of *Tenant Estoppel Certificates* (TEC), one signed and returned by each tenant occupying the property. [See Form 598 accompanying this chapter]

The TEC summarizes the **financial and possessory terms** of the lease agreement, and whether the landlord and tenant have fully performed their obligations.

The objective of the TEC is to confirm the current status of:

- rent schedules;

- security deposits;

- possessory and acquisition rights; and

- the responsibility for maintenance and other operating or carrying costs.

Thus, the TEC will reveal any option or first refusal rights held by the tenant to:

- extend or renew the lease;

- buy the property;

- lease other or additional space; or

- cancel the lease on payment of a fee.

However, before the owner can require a tenant to sign and return a TEC to confirm the leasing arrangements, the lease agreement must con-

---

Figure 1   *Excerpt from **first tuesday** Form 552 —*
Nonresidential Lease Agreement

18. TENANT ESTOPPEL CERTIFICATES:

18.1 Within 10 days after notice, Tenant will execute a certificate stating the existing terms of the lease to be provided to prospective buyers or lenders.

18.2 Failure to deliver the certificate shall be conclusive evidence the information contained in it is correct.

---

tain a Tenant Estoppel Certificate provision. [See Figure 1 accompanying this chapter; see **first tuesday** Form 552 §18]

The **TEC provision** calls for the tenant to:

- *sign and return* a TEC, which has been filled out and sent to them, within a specific period of time after its receipt; or

- *waive his right* to contest its contents if the tenant fails to sign and return the TEC submitted for his signature.

Tenant response to receipt of a TEC

In addition to information regarding the rent schedule and the rights and responsibilities of the tenant, a TEC includes a statement indicating a buyer or lender will rely on the information provided by the TEC when making a decision to lend or purchase. [See **first tuesday** Form 598 §10]

The tenant's *acknowledgment* of the accuracy of the TEC contents by his signed response, or *waiver* of the right to contest the accuracy of the contents of the TEC by nonresponse, can be relied on by a buyer or lender as establishing the contents of the TEC as complete and correct statements on the terms and condition of the lease. [Calif. Evidence Code §623]

Should a dispute later arise between the buyer (or a lender) and the tenant regarding conditions covered in a TEC, the properly submitted TEC prevents any later claims made by the tenant that are in conflict with the contents of the TEC.

A buyer or lender asserts his right to rely on and enforce the terms stated in the TEC by presenting the tenant's TEC as a defense to bar contrary claims made by the tenant, called *estoppel*. Thus, the tenant is *estopped from denying* the truth of the information in the TEC or later claiming conflicting rights.

Security deposits confirmed

When lease agreements are assigned to a buyer on closing a sale, the buyer requires the seller, through escrow, to account for any security deposits collected from the tenants. The amount of the remaining security deposits to the buyer as part of the escrow process, called *adjustments*.

With a TEC, the tenant confirms the accounting and dollar amount of security remaining on deposit with the seller. Thus, the TEC avoids the transfer of insufficient amounts of security deposits on closing and establishes the extent of the buyer's liability for refunds.

If the buyer does not require a TEC to confirm the current amount of the security deposits claimed to be held by the seller and transferred to the buyer, the buyer may find himself paying tenants more than the security deposit amounts he received from the seller on closing. [Calif. Civil Code §1950.5(i)]

Any deficiency in the amount of credit the buyer received for security deposits owed to the tenants that the buyer may later be required to pay is recovered by pursuing the seller.

TEC substantiates prior representations

Use of an APOD form to present an accounting summary of the operating data on a property's income and expenses is a representation of the income flow and operating expenses a prospective buyer can expect the property to generate in the immediate future.

To establish, **prior to closing**, the rent and expenses the buyer can reasonably expect the tenants to pay, the buyer must:

- review and analyze all the lease agreements the owner has with the tenants;

- compare the results of an analysis of rent and maintenance provisions in the lease agreements to the figures in the APOD received before the offer was submitted; and

TENANT ESTOPPEL CERTIFICATE

DATE:_____, 20_____, at _____, California.
Items left blank or unchecked are not applicable.

FACTS:

This certificate pertains to terms and conditions under the following agreement:

☐ Lease agreement   ☐ Month-to-month rental agreement   ☐ Other: _____

dated:_____, 20_____, at _____, California,

entered into by_____, as the Landlord, and

_____, as the Tenant,

regarding real estate premises referred to as: _____

_____

STATEMENT:

Tenant certifies as follows:

1. The lease or rental agreement is:
    ☐ Unmodified and in effect.
    ☐ Modified and in effect under a modification agreement dated _____, 20_____.

2. Tenant is in possession of the premises, and has not assigned or sublet any portion of the premises, except:

    _____

3. If the agreement is a lease, the current term is for _____ years, ending _____, 20_____.
    3.1 Lease renewal/extension option term(s) run until _____, 20_____.
    3.2 The Tenant holds no privilege to terminate the lease prior to it's expiration.

4. The amount of monthly rent is $_____.
    4.1 No incentives, bonuses, free rent, discounts or refunds on the rental amount were given Tenant, except:

    _____

    4.2 Rent is paid through the period ending _____, 20_____.
    4.3 Tenant has not prepaid future rent, except the amount of $_____ for the rental period of:

    _____

    4.4 No Tenant liens, claims, offsets or charges exist against Landlord, except _____

    _____

5. A security deposit of $_____ is held by Landlord to cover any expenses or losses caused by Tenant's breach of the agreement.

6. Personal property in the tenant's possession and owned by the landlord includes: _____

    _____

7. Any improvements required to have been made by Landlord or Tenant have been satisfactorily completed.

8. No breach of the agreement by Landlord or Tenant presently exists, except _____

    _____

9. Tenant holds no contract, option or right of first refusal or other right to buy any interest in the real estate.
    8.1 Tenant holds no right to lease additional or substitute space in the real estate.

10. Tenant has caused no lien or encumbrance to attach to the leasehold interest in the property.

11. Tenant understands this certificate will be relied on by a buyer of the property or a lender secured by the real estate.

12. _____

    _____

    _____

BY TENANT: I certify the above is true and correct.

Date:_____, 20_____

Name: _____

Signature: _____

Phone:_____   Fax: _____

FORM 598   10-00   ©2007 **first tuesday**, P.O. BOX 20069, RIVERSIDE, CA 92516 (800) 794-0494

- confirm the rent schedules, possessory rights, maintenance obligations and expiration of the leases by serving TECs on the tenants and reviewing their responses.

Close on receipt of TECs

When signed and delivered to the buyer, the TEC statement reflects only the financial and possessory arrangements existing at the time the tenant signs and returns the TEC.

Consider a tenant who signs and returns a TEC that is reviewed and approved by the buyer. However, before escrow closes, the seller breaches, modifies or enters into other leasing arrangements with the tenant.

The seller's post-TEC activities are not noted on the TEC, and will be unknown to the buyer when escrow closes unless brought to the buyer's attention. Thus, on receiving the TECs, a buyer or lender should review them and close the transaction **as soon as possible** to avoid a change in conditions in the interim.

Consequence of no TEC

A buyer or lender may be confronted at the time of closing with a tenant who has not signed and returned a TEC. Before closing, it is good practice for the buyer and his agent to **investigate** whether differences actually exist between the owner's representations on the TEC and the tenant's expectations under the lease agreement.

Even though the buyer or lender can legally rely on the contents of an unreturned TEC when the tenant's lease agreement contains a TEC clause, an inquiry by the buyer or his agent into the tenant's failure to return the TEC is a prudent measure of prevention against future surprises.

Consider an owner of income-producing real estate who needs to generate cash. He will do so by borrowing money using the equity in his property as security for repayment of the loan.

Tenants occupy the property under lease agreements that include options to renew at fixed rental rates. The lender does not condition the origination of the loan on the lender's receipt and approval of TECs from each tenant. The lender makes the loan based on the value of comparable properties without regard for a schedule of the tenants' rent. [See **first tuesday** Form 380]

The owner defaults. The lender forecloses and is the successful bidder at the trustee's sale. As the new owner, the lender (or anyone else who purchases the property at the trustee's sale) reviews the rent being paid by the tenants.

The new owner decides to increase the rents to current market rates in order to bring the property's market value up to prices recently received on the sale of comparable properties. However, the tenants who occupied the premises before the lender's trust deed was recorded claim their lease agreements, which provide options to extend at old rental rates, are enforceable.

The lender claims his foreclosure sale wiped out the owner's rights and establishes him as a new title holder with priority over the leases and, further, the lease agreements are not recorded.

Can the tenants who occupied the property prior to the recording of the lender's trust deed enforce their renewal options even though their pre-existing lease agreements are not recorded?

Yes! The lender originating the loan on income-producing property he now owns following foreclosure, recorded the trust deed *after* the tenants were in possession of the property. Thus:

- the tenants' rights and obligations under lease agreements *held by pre-existing tenants*, recorded or not, retain priority over the lender's trust deed lien; and

- the lender is bound by the rent schedules in the pre-existing lease agreements and renewal/extension options because of the seniority of the leases. [CC §1214]

The tenants' occupancy of the premises prior to originating the loan puts the lender on *constructive notice*, i.e., the lender is charged with knowledge of the lease agreements, renewal options and rent schedules. [**Evans** v. **Faught** (1965) 231 CA2d 698]

The requirement for lender approval of a TEC from each tenant would have informed the lender of the tenants' rights and obligations to occupy and pay rent and other amounts under their lease agreements.

To be assured the owner's scheduled future income represents amounts the tenants expect to pay, every buyer or lender acquiring an interest in income-producing real estate should require tenant approval of TECs based on lease arrangements the owner/seller purports to hold with each tenant.

Signing an erroneous TEC

Consider a tenant who signs and returns a TEC on the landlord's sale of nonresidential prop-

---

Status of the lease

The TEC verifies the following:

- whether possession is held under a lease or rental agreement;

- the current monthly amount of rent and the basis for rent increases;

- the date rent is paid each month;

- the date to which rent has been paid;

- any incentives given to obtain the tenant;

- whether the tenant has prepaid any rents;

- the term of the lease and whether an early cancellation privilege exists;

- whether and in what manner the lease/rental agreement has been modified;

- whether the tenant holds any options to renew or extend, acquire additional or substitute space, or a right of first refusal to rent vacated space;

- whether the tenant holds any options to buy the real estate;

- the amount and status of any security deposit;

- any improvements the tenant must or can remove on vacating the premises;

- any landlord commitments to further improve the premises;

- whether the landlord or tenant is in breach of the lease or the rental agreement; and

- whether the tenant has assigned or sublet the premises, or liened his leasehold interest.

---

erty. The TEC is erroneously prepared, stating an expiration date earlier than the date for termination provided in the lease agreement.

The buyer relies on the TEC and purchases the property. The tenant remains in possession of the premises after the expiration date stated in the TEC. The buyer seeks to enforce the expiration date in the TEC by filing an unlawful detainer (UD) action to evict the tenant.

The tenant claims the buyer cannot enforce the expiration date in the TEC by a UD action since the TEC was not a written agreement modifying the lease, binding him to a different expiration date than actually stated in the lease agreement. The buyer claims the tenant is barred from contradicting the expiration date stated in the TEC.

Here, the new landlord can enforce the expiration date in the TEC and evict the tenant by a UD action. The TEC is a statement signed by the tenant certifying facts with respect to the lease which were relied on by the buyer. Thus, the tenant is barred from later using the contrary provision in the lease agreement to contradict the TEC, called *estoppel*. [**Plaza Freeway Limited Partnership** v. **First Mountain Bank** (2000) 81 CA4th 616]

The erroneous, unsigned TEC

Now consider a purchase agreement for non-residential rental property that requires the seller to provide the buyer with TECs for the buyer's further approval or cancellation of the purchase agreement.

One tenant's lease agreement does not state the rent amounts but contains a formula for calculating rent. The seller instructs the buyer on how to calculate the rent due from the tenant based on the provisions in the tenant's lease agreement.

The seller enters the rent amounts on the TEC based on the same calculations given the buyer

and sends it to the tenant to be signed and returned to the buyer.

The tenant refuses to sign the TEC since the tenant is not obligated under his lease agreement to provide a TEC. The seller hands the buyer a copy of the tenant's unsigned TEC to satisfy the purchase agreement condition, which the buyer accepts without further investigation and confirmation.

After escrow closes, the buyer discovers the tenant's actual rent is significantly lower than the seller's estimate. The buyer makes a demand on the seller for the difference between the actual rent paid by the tenant under the lease and the rent amounts calculated by the seller as the rent to be paid by the tenant.

Is the seller liable for the difference in the rent?

Yes! The buyer **recovers lost rent** from the seller in the amount of the difference between the seller's calculated estimate of rent and the actual amount owed by the tenant. The seller is obligated under the purchase agreement to provide the buyer with an accurate TEC, and the buyer based his decision to purchase the property on representations made by the seller, not on the rent provisions in the lease agreement. [**Linden Partners** v. **Wilshire Linden Associates** (1998) 62 CA4th 508]

A seller avoids liability for errors in the TEC prepared and sent to tenants by including a TEC clause in the tenant's lease agreement, calling for the tenant to sign and return a TEC on request. The failure of the tenant to provide the TEC as called for in the lease agreement is conclusive evidence any contrary information contained in the TEC is correct. [See Figure 1]

Thus, a tenant's refusal to sign a TEC when a TEC clause exists in the lease agreement results in the tenant, not the seller, being liable for the erroneous rent amount stated in the TEC prepared by the seller.

Chapter 61

Due-on-leasing regulations

This chapter discusses the rights of a lender under a due-on clause in a trust deed when the landlord leases any portion of the secured property to a tenant.

Rising interest rates bring lender interference

Real estate encumbered by a first trust deed containing a *due-on clause* is offered for sale or lease. A user for the property is located and enters into a two-year lease agreement with an option to purchase the property.

Does the lease agreement and option to buy trigger the due-on clause in the trust deed allowing the lender to call the loan the trust deed secures?

Yes! A due-on clause in a trust deed is triggered by a **lease agreement** that is coupled with the grant to the tenant of an option to buy the property. Thus, the trust deed lender may call the loan **on discovery** of the lease-with-option transaction, and foreclose if not paid in full. [12 Code of Federal Regulations §591.2(b)]

Interference under federal mortgage law

The **transfer** of any interest in real estate encumbered by a trust deed containing a due-on clause allows the lender to enforce the clause under federal mortgage law. Thus, by *preemption*, Californians are deprived of their state law right to lease, sell or further encumber real estate free of lender interference, subject to the lender's clearance of the buyer's or tenant's creditworthiness and property maintenance attributes. [12 United States Code §1701j-3; Calif. Civil Code §711]

For the landlord of property encumbered by a trust deed, leasing the property for a period of more than three years or entering into a lease agreement for any period of time coupled with an option to buy, **triggers due-on enforcement**.

On discovery of these leasing arrangements by the trust deed lender, the lender may either:

- **call the loan**, demanding payment in full of all remaining unpaid sums, also known as *acceleration*; or

- **recast the loan**, requiring a modification of the terms of the loan and payment of fees as a condition for the lender's consent to the triggering event, called a *waiver.*

Economics of the due-on clause

In times of rising and sustained high interest rates, lenders seize on any event that legally triggers the due-on clause as an opportunity to increase the interest yield on their portfolio. Federal policy favors this interference with the home-selling population as justified to maintain lender solvency, in spite of a shift in the risk of loss to the property owner due to the increase in payments.

As a condition for a trust deed lender to waive his due-on enforcement and allow the owner to enter into lease agreements, the lender may require the loan to be recast at current interest rates, the owner to pay a fee, or both.

Real estate interests, be they the owner's fee simple or simply the tenant's leasehold estate, when encumbered by due-on trust deed become increasingly difficult to transfer to new owners and tenants when interest rates are rising. Lender interference is then virtually guaranteed in the relentless cyclical pursuit of lenders to increase their portfolio yield and remain solvent during prolonged periods of rising or higher interest rates.

The rising inability of owners to flexibly lease their properties and retain existing financing has an adverse economic effect on real estate sales, equity financing and long-term leasing. Ultimately, as rates and lender interference rise, many buyers, equity lenders and long-term tenants are driven out of the market. The result is an increase in depressed property values due to the reduced ability to sell, lease, assign a lease or encumber real estate interests.

Unless the existing lender's consent is obtained, the possibility of due-on enforcement and a call creates uncertainty for the landlord when leasing property for more than a three-year period. The uncertainties of a call rise as interest rates increase.

To best represent landlords and tenants, leasing agents must understand which events trigger the lender's *due-on clause*, which do not, and how to avoid or handle the lender's consent.

Due-on-leasing clauses

The **due-on clause**, better known as a due-on-sale clause, is triggered when the owner of property secured by a due-on trust deed enters into:

- a lease with a term over three years; or

- any lease with an option to purchase. [12 CFR §591.2(b)]

Consider an owner with a short-term interim construction loan on nonresidential rental property who obtains a conditional loan commitment from a lender for long-term, **take-out financing**. The refinancing will pay off the construction loan when the construction is completed, providing permanent financing for the owner.

Funding of the take-out loan is conditioned on the property being 80% occupied by tenants with initial lease terms of at least five years.

The owner locates tenants for 80% of the newly constructed property, all with lease terms of five years or more. The condition is met and the lender funds the loan. The loan, containing a due-on clause, is secured by a first trust deed on the property.

The five-year leases already entered into to qualify for the refinancing precede the refinancing. Thus, the leases do not trigger the due-on clause in the new lender's trust deed.

However, after recording the trust deed, the owner continues to lease space on his property for terms exceeding three years. None of the new leases are submitted to the lender for approval. Thus, no waiver of the due-on clause is obtained before entering into these leases.

After interest rates rise, an officer of the lender visits the property or requests a rent roll and discovers new tenants. The officer learns the new tenants have leases with terms of more than three years.

The lender soon sends the owner a letter informing him the lender is **calling the loan** since "It has recently come to our attention..." that the owner has entered into lease agreements with terms over three years without first obtaining the lender's consent, an **incurable violation** of the due-on clause in the trust deed.

The owner claims the lender cannot call the loan since the lender required medium-term leases as a condition for funding the loan. Thus, the lender is *estopped* from invoking the due-on clause when five-year leases are later entered into.

Can the lender call the loan due or demand a recast of its terms?

Yes! By requiring leases with terms exceeding three years are a condition for funding the loan, the lender did not waive his right to later call or recast the loan under its due-on clause when leases with a term exceeding three years are entered into after the trust deed is recorded.

The owner should have either obtained consent from the lender before leasing, leased the property for a three-year period with options to renew for three-year periods, or negotiated the elimination of the due-on clause from the trust deed when borrowing the funds.

Assignment or modification of the lease

An **assignment** or **modification** of an existing lease agreement does not trigger the due-on clause in a trust deed encumbering the owner's fee simple, unless the modification extends the term beyond three years from the date of modification or a purchase option is added.

For example, consider an owner of real estate who enters into a lease agreement with a tenant. Later, the owner takes out a loan secured by a trust deed containing a due-on clause.

After the trust deed is recorded, the tenant assigns the lease with the owner's approval, as provided for in the lease agreement.

Here, the lender's due-on clause is not triggered by the lease assignment. The lender's trust deed only encumbers the landlord's fee, subject to the outstanding lease. The trust deed does not encumber the leasehold interest owned by the tenant. Thus, the tenant's assignment of his unencumbered leasehold does not trigger the lender's due-on clause since the leasehold assignment was not a transfer of an interest in the fee which is the lender's security and the lease provided for the assignment.

However, consider a landlord who enters into a release of liability with the original tenant, releasing the tenant from all liability under the lease agreement as part of an assumption of the lease by a new tenant. A trust deed with a due-on clause encumbers the landlord's ownership interest, whether the trust deed is junior or senior to the lease.

Here, the release of the original tenant from the lease agreement coupled with an assumption of the lease agreement by the new tenant creates a *novation*. The novation legally cancels the original lease agreement and establishes a new lease agreement with the owner conveying an interest in the secured property to the new tenant on the same terms. [**Wells Fargo Bank, N.A.** v. **Bank of America NT & SA** (1995) 32 CA4th 424]

The concurrent *release* of the former tenant from liability and *assumption* of the lease agreement by the new tenant is a two step arrangement which constituting the present transfer by the owner of an interest in the encumbered real estate to the new tenant. If the lease assumed by the tenant on the release of the original tenant from liability has a remaining term of over three years or includes an option to purchase, the lender's due-on clause has been triggered and a call of the loan is allowed.

Negotiations and conduct as waiver

Under federal regulations, lenders have the power to dictate the fate of most long-term real estate leasing transactions since most real estate is encumbered by trust deeds containing due-on clauses.

However, an owner intending to lease his real estate and avoid lender interference should consider:

- eliminating the due-on clause from the trust deed or placing some limitation on its use by the lender when negotiation the origination of the loan; or

- negotiating a *waiver* of the lender's due-on rights when entering into a lease.

Waiver agreements are basically trade-offs. The lender will demand some consideration in return for waiving or agreeing to an elimination or limitation of its future due-on rights, such as increased points on origination, additional security, increased interest, a shorter due date or an assumption fee on each consent. [See **first tuesday** Form 410]

The lender's waiver of its due-on rights would apply only to the current lease transaction under review for consent. Unless additionally agreed, any later leasing of the property will again trigger the due-on clause, allowing the lender to call or recast the loan again, due in part to the nonwaiver provision in the trust deed.

Besides obtaining a written waiver agreement, waiver of the lender's due-on rights may occur **by conduct**. By failing to promptly enforce its due-on rights when the lender has knowledge of a leasing transaction, the lender may lose his right to later enforce the clause based on that lease.

For example, a landlord enters into a lease agreement with a term exceeding three years on property encumbered by a loan secured by a trust deed containing a due-on clause. The lender is informed of the leasing arrangements by letter or during an annual audit.

The lender then calls the loan under its due-on clause based on the lease transaction disclosed or delivered. However, the lender accepts payments from the owner for 12 months after the call, stating he is unilaterally reserving his due-on rights, the landlord agrees to nothing with the lender.

Here, the lender **by his conduct waived** the right to enforce his due-on clause. The lender **accepted payments** from the owner for an extended period of time after calling the loan, leaving but one payment to be made — the amount of the call. [**Rubin** v. **Los Angeles Federal Savings and Loan Association** (1984) 159 CA3d 292]

Broker liability for due-on avoidance

Again, a lender can call the loan only when it **discovers a lease agreement** of more than three years in duration or a lease with an option to buy.

If the tenant's option to purchase is not recorded and the lease agreement is for a term under three years, the lender might not discover any transfer of an interest in the real estate has taken place that triggered its due-on clause.

However, if the lender later discovers the lease with its option to purchase, the lender's only remedy against the owner or the tenant is to call the loan due, or agree to recast the loan as a condition for retroactively waiving its right to call. The lender cannot recover any retroactive interest differential (RID) from the owner or tenant for a higher rate they would have charged for the period beginning on commencement of the lease, the triggering event, until paid. Also, if he lender calls the loan, it cannot add additional back interest (RID) to the loan payoff amount. [**Hummell** v. **Republic Fed. Savings and Loan Assn.** (1982) 133 CA3d 49]

However, an advisor, such as a leasing agent or attorney, assisting the owner or tenant to hide the lease and option to purchase from the lender for the **primary purpose** of avoiding due-on enforcement, may have wrongfully interfered with the lender's legal right to call or recast the loan. Thus, the advisor may be held liable for the lender's losses, called tortious interference with *prospective economic advantage*.

The advisor's liability is dependent upon the extent to which the advisor's actions were intended to conceal the lease agreement and prevent a call by the lender, and with the foresight that the lender would likely incur losses due to the concealment. [**J'Aire Corporation** v. **Gregory** (1979) 24 C3d 799]

The **lender's losses** caused by the advisor's wrongful interference are calculated based on the interest differential between the note rate and the market rate at the time the lease commenced, retroactive to the date of the commencement. Hence, the title of interest rate differential (RID).

Chapter 62

Gaining possession after foreclosure

This chapter presents the notices to vacate served on occupants whose possessory interest in the property has been eliminated by a foreclosure.

Notice required to remove occupants

A residential income property is encumbered by a recorded trust deed. Tenants occupy the property under rental and lease agreements entered into after the trust deed was recorded.

Payments on the trust deed note are delinquent, causing the lender to initiate a trustee's foreclosure.

Prior to the foreclosure sale, the lender employs a broker (or appraiser) to inspect the physical condition of the improvements and determine the property's fair market value for immediate resale.

Based on the broker's inspection and market review, he advises the lender to:

- complete the foreclosure proceedings;

- evict all tenants;

- renovate the property;

- relet the property to creditworthy tenants at market rates; and

- sell the property.

The lender acquires the property at the trustee's sale.

To meet the resale objectives recommended by the broker, the lender, now classified as an *owner-by-foreclosure*, wants the tenants to immediately vacate the property. The property now owned by the lender is referred to as real estate owned, or *REO property*.

The broker has each tenant served with a 30-day notice to quit due to foreclosure. [See Form 573 accompanying this chapter]

Have the tenants been properly notified and thus required to vacate the premises?

Yes! The **residential tenants** whose unexpired month-to-month rental or lease agreements were junior (in time) to the recording of the trust deed, and thus *eliminated* by the foreclosure sale, are entitled to 30 days written notice to vacate. [Calif. Code of Civil Procedure §1161a(c)]

After the expiration of the 30-day notice to vacate, a residential tenant under a month-to-month rental or lease agreement who does not vacate the foreclosed property, may be evicted by the owner-by-foreclosure in an unlawful detainer (UD) action. This general rule does not apply to rent controlled or section 8 properties.

Evicting occupants after foreclosure

A rental or lease agreement entered into after a trust deed is recorded is wiped out on completion of a foreclosure sale on the trust deed.

If a prior owner or occupant under a junior rental or lease agreement remains in possession after a foreclosure sale, the new owner-by-foreclosure can serve the appropriate notice to **quit due to foreclosure** and remove the occupants, **residential or nonresidential**, in a UD eviction action.

An *owner-by-foreclosure* is defined as a buyer of real estate which is sold at:

- a sheriff's sale on a judgment lien;

- a judicial foreclosure sale; or

• a trustee's foreclosure sale. [CCP §1161a(b)]

An owner-by-foreclosure can evict all occupants remaining in possession of the foreclosed property under a wiped-out lease or month-to-month rental agreement. However, tenants living in Section 8 housing or rent control communities are protected from unqualified termination of their occupancy after a foreclosure sale.

The appropriate period of notice to vacate due to foreclosure depends on whether:

• the property is *residential or nonresidential*; and

• the occupants are *former tenants or former owners*.

Length of notice to be given

After a foreclosure sale on a senior trust deed, a **residential tenant** is entitled to a written notice to quit for a period of no less than his prior tenancy, but no greater than 30 days. Thus, a 30-day notice will always suffice. [CCP §1161a(c)]

For example, if the foreclosed property is a residential hotel where units are let on a weekly basis, the owner-by-foreclosure is required to give each tenant no less than one week's written notice to vacate the property.

Residential tenants under wiped-out month-to-month rental or lease agreements are entitled to no less than 30s' days notice.

Unlike a residential tenant, a **nonresidential tenant** whose junior lease is wiped-out by a foreclosure is entitled to only a 3-day written notice to quit, regardless of whether the tenant paid rent monthly, quarterly or annually. [CCP §1161a(b)(3)]

A **former owner** who remains as an occupant is entitled to only a 3-day notice to quit, whether the property is residential or nonresidential. [CCP §1161a(b)(4)]

Thus, to remove a nonresidential tenant or the former owner of a residential or a nonresidential property, the owner-by-foreclosure serves them with a 3-day notice to **quit due to foreclosure**. On expiration of the three days after service of the notice and the failure of the prior owner or the tenant to vacate, a UD has been established and they can be evicted by court order. [See **first tuesday** Form 578]

Service of notice

A notice to quit due to foreclosure must be served in the same manner as a 3-day notice to pay rent or quit. [CCP §1161a(b); see Chapter 26]

An attempt at *personal service* on the occupant must first be made at both the occupant's residence and place of business, if known. [CCP §1162(1)]

If the occupant cannot be located for personal service, the server may leave the notice with a person of suitable age and discretion at the occupant's residence or business address, and mail the notice to the occupant's residence, called *substituted service*. [CCP §1162(2)]

Finally, if no person of suitable age or discretion is available at either the occupant's residence or place of business, the server may post the notice on the leased premises and mail a copy to the premises, called service by *nail and mail*. [CCP §1162(3)]

The day after the notice is served is day one of the period during which the occupant must vacate. [Calif. Civil Code §10]

UD award of rental value

In an unlawful detainer (UD) action, an owner-by-foreclosure is entitled to recover rent from the occupant in an amount equal to the *reasonable rental value* of the property for the period that the occupant resides on the property after the foreclosure sale. [CCP §1174(b)]

DATE:_____, 20_____, at _____, California.

To Former Residential Tenant: _____

NOTICE:

A holdover residential tenant must vacate and deliver possession to an owner-by-foreclosure or his agent within thirty (30) days after service of written notice to the tenant. [Calif. Code of Civil Procedure §1161a(c)]

Items left blank or unchecked are not applicable.

FACTS:

You were a residential Tenant under a rental or lease agreement

dated _____, at _____, California,

entered into by _____, Tenant,

and _____, Landlord,

regarding real estate referred to as: _____

_____

NOTICE:

1. On _____, 20_____, the real estate you occupy was sold at a foreclosure sale which extinguished your interest in the property.

2. Within thirty (30) days after service of this notice, you are required to vacate and deliver possession of the premises to the new owner-by-foreclosure or: _____

_____

3. If you fail to vacate and deliver possession within thirty (30) days, legal proceedings will be initiated to regain possession of the premises, and to recover money damages for wrongful possession and costs.

Owner-by-forclosure:

Date:_____, 20_____

Name: _____

Signature: _____

Address: _____

_____

Phone:_____

Fax: _____

E-mail: _____

FORM 573   12-06   ©2007 **first tuesday**, P.O. BOX 20069, RIVERSIDE, CA 92516 (800) 794-0494

The secured lender who acquires the premises at the foreclosure sale cannot collect unpaid pre-foreclosure rents in the UD action.

However, any rents which were due and unpaid by a tenant before the foreclosure sale belong to the lender under an *assignment of rents* *provision* in the lender's trust deed. These unpaid rents are collectable in a separate action unrelated to the UD action, called specific performance of the assignment of rents provision.

Since a landlord/tenant relationship does not exist between an owner-by-foreclosure and an occupant, a tenancy does not exist, unless the owner-by-foreclosure and occupant agree that money paid prior to foreclosure is **advance rent** for continued or future occupancy.

A matter of priority

When a tenant takes possession and records his lease agreement after a trust deed, abstract of judgment or tax lien is recorded, the tenant's leasehold interest in real estate is junior to these liens. Thus, pre-existing liens have priority and are called *senior encumbrances*.

All junior liens and junior possessory interests of the owners and tenants in the real estate are *extinguished* when a lienholder under a senior trust deed, abstract of judgment or tax lien forecloses on the real estate. [**Hohn** v. **Riverside County Flood Control and Water Conservation District** (1964) 228 CA2d 605]

On proper notice, the tenant under the wiped-out lease can be evicted. Thus, a junior lease held by a tenant is unenforceable against an owner-by-foreclosure, unless the owner-by-foreclosure makes an **attornment election** to enforce the lease. [See Chapter 59]

A tenant's leasehold interest with priority to a lien on the owner's fee title is not eliminated by the foreclosure of that junior lien.

No tenancy for wiped-out occupants

An occupant of property whose leasehold or ownership interest has been eliminated by foreclosure has no right to possession and is not a tenant.

Any landlord/tenant relationship under the rental agreement or lease which was junior to the foreclosing lienholder is wiped out at the foreclosure sale.

No tenancy in real estate is recognized for occupants who lost their possessory interest due to a foreclosure.

The wiped-out occupant, whether he is a prior owner or held a tenancy interest in the property, is not a holdover tenant, and thus is not a tenant-at-sufferance.

Also, the occupant is not a tenant-at-will since he did not occupy the property with the owner-by-foreclosure's consent.

Even though no landlord/tenant relationship exists, an owner-by-foreclosure is permitted to remove occupants from the foreclosed property by evicting them in an unlawful detainer (UD) action. [CCP §1161a(b)]

However, a buyer at an foreclosure sale does not qualify as an owner-by-foreclosure for a UD eviction of a prior occupant when the property is purchased at:

- a federal or state tax lien sale;

- a property tax lien sale; or

- a Mello-Roos sale or sale under other improvement bonds or government agency assessments.

Purchasers of property at tax sales or improvement bond sales which are occupied:

- are not permitted to remove occupants by filing a UD action; and

- are limited to filing an *ejectment action* against the occupant to recover possession of the premises.

While an **action in ejectment** and a UD action are alternative remedies for recovering possession from occupants, the UD action is faster and less expensive, and thus more desirable for the owner-by-foreclosure.

The owner-by-foreclosure who acquires title at the foreclosure sale of a junior lien takes title **subject to** the rental or lease agreement and must perform the landlord's obligations under the agreement.

On occasion, a lender may elect to alter priorities (before a foreclosure sale) under a **lender subordination clause** in the lease agreement to preserve the terms of the lease if they are advantageous. On subordination, a junior nonresidential **lease is given priority** over the lender's previously recorded trust deed lien. [See Chapter 59]

Priority is rarely an issue for leases of residential property since **residential leases**:

- are typically entered into for periods not exceeding one year; and

- those existing at the time a lender records his trust deed will have likely expired prior to completing a foreclosure.

UD action as a remedy, not a right

When residential income property subject to local rent control ordinances or a Section 8 contract is acquired by an owner-by-foreclosure, the owner-by-foreclosure must comply with the ordinances and Section 8 rules.

Consider a trust deed lender who forecloses on residential rental units by a trustee's sale and acquires the property at the foreclosure sale. The lender wants to remove the occupants who are former tenants under wiped out rental or lease agreements. The lender intends to renovate the property and resell it.

The lender, now the owner-by-foreclosure, serves each tenant with a statutory 30-day notice to quit due to foreclosure. However, the property is located in a rent control community.

The occupants claim they cannot be evicted by the lender since the rent control ordinance does not permit eviction on a change of ownership. The rent control ordinances limit the circumstances which are cause for a tenant to be evicted. Change of ownership for any reason is not a permitted basis for eviction for a tenant protected by rent control.

The lender claims the tenants can be evicted due to foreclosure since the local ordinance is *preempted* by state law allowing a tenant to be evicted after a foreclosure sale.

Can the tenants be evicted by the lender since the lender is an owner-by-foreclosure?

No! Residential tenants protected under rent control ordinances cannot be evicted after a foreclosure, except as permitted by local ordinances. The 30-day notice requirement for evicting a residential tenant after a foreclosure sale in a UD action does not preempt the local rent control ordinance.

The UD notice-and-eviction process merely provides a legal *remedy* for a lender who has *grounds* to recover possession from the tenants, in lieu of using self-help to remove tenants. Under rent control, it is the ordinance which establishes the **grounds for the eviction** of a tenant. [**Gross** v. **Superior Court** (1985) 171 CA3d 265]

Appendix A

The following represents sections of the Commissioner's Ethics and Professional Conduct Code and the Fair Employment and Housing Acts prohibiting discrimination in housing and real estate brokerage.

DRE — Anti-discrimination statutes

DRE Regulation 2780
Discriminatory Conduct as the
Basis for Disciplinary Action

Prohibited discriminatory conduct by a real estate licensee based upon race, color, sex, religion, ancestry, physical handicap, marital status or national origin includes, but is not limited to, the following:

(a) Refusing to negotiate for the sale, rental or financing of the purchase of real property or otherwise making unavailable or denying real property to any person because of such person's race, color, sex, religion, ancestry, physical handicap, marital status or national origin.

(b) Refusing or failing to show, rent, sell or finance the purchase of real property to any person or refusing or failing to provide or volunteer information to any person about real property, or channeling or steering any person away from real property, because of that person's race, color, sex, religion, ancestry, physical handicap, marital status or national origin or because of the racial, religious, or ethnic composition of any occupants of the area in which the real property is located.

(c) Discriminating because of race, color, sex, religion, ancestry, physical handicap, marital status or national origin against any person in the sale or purchase or negotiation or solicitation of the sale or purchase or the collection of payment or the performance of services in connection with contracts for the sale of real property or in connection with

loans secured directly or collaterally by liens on real property or on a business opportunity.

(d) Discriminating because of race, color, sex, religion, ancestry, physical handicap, marital status or national origin against any person in the terms, conditions or privileges of sale, rental or financing of the purchase of real property.

(e) Discriminating because of race, color, sex, religion, ancestry, physical handicap, marital status or national origin against any person in providing services or facilities in connection with the sale, rental or financing of the purchase of real property, including but not limited to: processing applications differently, referring prospects to other licensees because of the prospects' race, color, sex, religion, ancestry, physical handicap, marital status or national origin, using with discriminatory intent or effect, codes or other means of identifying minority prospects, or assigning real estate licensees on the basis of a prospective client's race, color, sex, religion, ancestry, physical handicap, marital status or national origin.

(f) Representing to any person because of his or her race, color, sex, religion, ancestry, physical handicap, marital status or national origin that real property is not available for inspection, sale or rental when such real property is in fact available.

(g) Processing an application more slowly or otherwise acting to delay, hinder or avoid the sale, rental or financing of the purchase of real property on account of the race, color, sex, religion, ancestry, physical handicap, marital status or national origin of a potential owner or occupant.

(h) Making any effort to encourage discrimination against persons because of their race, color, sex, religion, ancestry, physical handicap, marital status or national origin in the showing, sale, lease or financing of the purchase of real property.

(i) Refusing or failing to cooperate with or refusing or failing to assist another real estate licensee in negotiating the sale, rental or financing of the purchase of real property because of the race, color, sex, religion, ancestry, physical handicap, marital status or national origin of any prospective purchaser or tenant.

(j) Making any effort to obstruct, retard or discourage the purchase, lease or financing of the purchase of real property by persons whose race, color, sex, religion, ancestry, physical handicap, marital status or national origin differs from that of the majority of persons presently residing in a structural improvement to real property or in an area in which the real property is located.

(k) Performing any acts, making any notation, asking any questions or making or circulating any written or oral statement which when taken in context, expresses or implies a limitation, preference or discrimination based upon race, color, sex, religion, ancestry, physical handicap, marital status or national origin; provided, however, that nothing herein shall limit the administering of forms or the making of a notation required by a federal, state or local agency for data collection or civil rights enforcement purposes; or in the case of a physically handicapped person, making notation, asking questions or circulating any written or oral statement in order to serve the needs of such a person.

(l) Making any effort to coerce, intimidate, threaten or interfere with any person in the exercise or enjoyment of, or on account of, such person's having exercised or enjoyed, or on account of such person's having aided or encouraged any other person in the exercise or enjoyment of any right granted or protected by a federal or state law, including but not limited to: assisting in any effort to coerce any person because of his or her race, color, sex, religion, ancestry, physical handicap, marital status or national origin to move from, or to not move into, a particular area; punishing or penalizing real estate licensees for their refusal to discriminate in the sale or rental of housing because of the race, color, sex, religion, ancestry, physical handicap, marital status or national origin of a prospective purchaser or lessee; or evicting or taking other retaliatory action against any person for having filed a fair housing complaint or for having undertaken other lawful efforts to promote fair housing.

(m) Soliciting of sales, rentals or listings of real estate from any person, but not from another person within the same area because of differences in the race, color, sex, religion, ancestry, physical handicap, marital status or national origin of such persons.

(n) Discriminating because of race, color, sex, religion, ancestry, physical handicap, marital status or national origin in informing persons of the existence of waiting lists or other procedures with respect to the future availability of real property for purchase or lease.

(o) Making any effort to discourage or prevent the rental, sale or financing of the purchase of real property because of the presence or absence of occupants of a particular race, color, sex, religion, ancestry, physical handicap, marital status or national origin, or on the basis of the future presence or absence of a particular race, color, sex, religion, ancestry, physical handicap, marital status or national origin, whether actual, alleged or implied.

(p) Making any effort to discourage or prevent any person from renting, purchasing or financing the purchase of real property through any representations of actual or alleged community opposition based upon race, color, sex, religion, ancestry, physical handicap, marital status or national origin.

(q) Providing information or advice to any person concerning the desirability of particular real property or a particular residential area(s) which is different from information or advice given to any other person with respect to the same property or area because of differences in the race, color, sex, religion, ancestry, physical handicap, marital status or national origin of such persons.

(r) Refusing to accept a rental or sales listing or application for financing of the purchase of real property because of the owner's race, color, sex, religion, ancestry, physical handicap, marital status or national origin or because of the race, color, sex, religion, ancestry, physical handicap, marital status or national origin of any of the occupants in the area in which the real property is located.

(s) Entering into an agreement, or carrying out any instructions of another, explicit or understood, not to show, lease, sell or finance the purchase of real property because of race, color, sex, religion, ancestry, physical handicap, marital status or national origin.

(t) Making, printing or publishing, or causing to be made, printed or published, any notice, statement or advertisement concerning the sale, rental or financing of the purchase of real property that indicates any preference, limitation or discrimination because of race, color, sex, religion, ancestry, physical handicap, marital status or national origin, or any intention to make such preference, limitation or discrimination.

(u) Using any word, phrases, sentences, descriptions or visual aids in any notice, statement or advertisement describing real property or the area in which real property is located which indicates any preference, limitation or discrimination because of race, color, sex, religion, ancestry, physical handicap, marital status or national origin.

(v) Selectively using, placing or designing any notice, statement or advertisement having to do with the sale, rental or financing of the purchase of real property in such a manner as to cause or increase discrimination by restricting or enhancing the exposure or appeal to persons of a particular race, color, sex, ancestry, physical handicap, marital status or national origin. This subdivision does not limit in any way the use of an affirmative marketing program designed to attract persons of a particular race, color, sex, religion, ancestry, physical handicap, marital status or national origin who would not otherwise be attracted to the real property or to the area.

(w) Quoting or charging a price, rent or cleaning or security deposit for a particular real property to any person which is different from the price, rent or security deposit quoted or charged to any other person because of differences in the race, color, sex, religion, ancestry, physical handicap, marital status or national origin of such persons.

(x) Discriminating against any person because of race, color, sex, religion, ancestry, physical handicap, marital status or national origin in performing any acts in connection with the making of any determination of financial ability or in the processing of any application for the financing or refinancing of real property.

(y) Advising a person of the price or value of real property on the basis of factors related to the race, color, sex, religion, ancestry, physical handicap, marital status or national origin of residents of an area or of residents or potential residents of the area in which the property is located.

(z) Discriminating in the treatment of, or services provided to, occupants of any real property in the course of providing management services for the real property because of the race, color, sex, religion, ancestry, physical handicap, marital status or national origin of said occupants.

(aa) Discriminating against the owners or occupants of real property because of the race, color, sex, religion, ancestry, physical handicap, marital status or national origin of their guests, visitors or invitees.

(bb) Making any effort to instruct or encourage, expressly or impliedly, by either words or acts, licensees or their employees or other agents to engage in any discriminatory act in violation of a federal or state fair housing law.

(cc) Establishing or implementing rules that have the effect of limiting the opportunity for any person because of his or her race, color, sex, religion, ancestry, physical handicap, marital status or national origin to secure real property through a multiple listing or other real estate service.

(dd) Assisting or aiding in any way, any person in the sale, rental or financing of the purchase of real property where there are reasonable grounds to believe that such person intends to discriminate because of race, color, sex, religion, ancestry, physical handicap, marital status or national origin.

Calif. Business and Professions Code §125.6
Refusal to perform licensed activity

Every person who holds a license under the provisions of this code is subject to disciplinary action under the disciplinary provisions of this code applicable to such person if, because of the applicant's race, color, sex, religion, ancestry, disability, marital status, or national origin, he or she refuses to perform the licensed activity or aids or incites the refusal to perform such licensed activity by another licensee, or if, because of the applicant's race, color, sex, religion, ancestry, disability, marital status, or national origin, he or she makes any discrimination, or restriction in the performance of the licensed activity.

Nothing in this section requires a person licensed pursuant to Division 2 (commencing with Section 500) to permit an individual to participate in, or benefit from, the licensed activity of the licensee where that individual poses a direct threat to the health or safety of others. For this purpose, the term "direct threat" means a significant risk to the health or safety of others that cannot be eliminated by a modification of policies, practices, or procedures or by the provision of auxiliary aids and services.

"Disability" means any of the following with respect to an individual:

(a) A physical or mental impairment that substantially limits one or more of the major life activities of the individual.

(b) A record of such an impairment.

(c) Being regarded as having such an impairment.

Calif. Business and Professions Code §10177 Grounds for suspension or revocation of a real estate license

The commissioner may suspend or revoke the license of any real estate licensee, or may deny the issuance of a license to an applicant, who has done any of the following:

(l) Solicited or induced the sale, lease or the listing for sale or lease, of residential property on the ground, wholly or in part, of loss of value, increase in crime, or decline of the quality of the schools, due to the present or prospective entry into the neighborhood of a person or persons of another race, color, religion, ancestry or national origin.

Calif. Civil Code §51 Unruh Civil Rights Act

All persons within the jurisdiction of this state are free and equal, and no matter what their sex, race, color, religion, ancestry, national origin, or disability are entitled to the full and equal accommodations, advantages, facilities, privileges, or services in all business establishments of every kind whatsoever.

A violation of the right of any individual under the Americans with Disabilities Act of 1990 (Public Law 101-336) shall also constitute a violation of this section.

Calif. Civil Code §54.1 Unlawful discrimination due to physical disability

(b)(1) Individuals with disabilities shall be entitled to full and equal access, as other members of the general public, to all housing accommodations offer for rent, lease, or compensation in this state subject to the conditions and limitations established by law, or state or federal regulation, and applicable alike to all persons.

(6)(A) It shall be deemed a denial of equal access to housing accommodations within the meaning of this subdivision for any person, firm, or corporation to refuse to lease or rent housing accommodations to an individual who is blind or visually impaired on the basis that the individual uses the services of a guide dog, an individual who is deaf or hearing impaired on the basis that the individual uses the services of a signal dog, or to an individual with any other disability on the basis that the individual uses the services of a service dog, or to refuse to permit such an individual who is blind or visually impaired to keep a guide dog, an individual who is deaf or hearing impaired to keep a signal dog, or an individual with any other disability to keep a service dog on the premises.

Calif. Government Code §12940 Unlawful employment practices

It shall be an unlawful employment practice, unless based upon a bona fide occupational qualification, or, except where based upon applicable security regulations established by the United States or the State of California:

(a) For an employer, because of the race, religious creed, color, national origin, ancestry, physical handicap, medical condition, marital status, or sex of any person, to refuse to hire or employ the person or to refuse to select the person for a training program leading to employment, or to bar or to discharge the person from employment or from a training program leading to employment, or to discriminate against the person in compensation or in terms, conditions or privileges of employment.

(c) For any person to discriminate against any person in the selection or training of that person in any apprenticeship training program or any other training program leading to employment because of the race, religious creed, color, national origin, ancestry, physical handicap, medical condition, marital status, or sex of the person discriminated against.

(d) For any employer or employment agency, unless specifically acting in accordance with federal equal employment opportunity guidelines and regulations approved by the commission, to print or circulate or cause to be printed or circulated any publication, or to make any non-job-related inquiry, either verbal or through use of an application form, which expresses, directly or indirectly, any limitation, specification, or discrimination as to race, religious creed, color, national origin, ancestry, physical handicap, medical condition, marital status, or sex, or any intent to make that limitation, specification or discrimination.

(f) For any employer, labor organization, employment agency, or person to discharge, expel, or otherwise discriminate against any person because the person has opposed any practices forbidden under this part or because the person has filed a complaint, testified, or assisted in any proceeding under this part.

(h) For an employer, labor organization, employment agency, apprenticeship training program or any training program leading to employment, or any other person, because of race, religious creed, color, national origin, ancestry, physical handicap, medical condition, marital status, sex, or age, to harass an employee or applicant.

Calif. Government Code §12941

(a) It is an unlawful employment practice for an employer to refuse to hire or employ, or to discharge, dismiss, reduce, suspend, or demote, any individual over the age of 40 on the ground of age, except in cases where the law compels or provides for such action.

Calif. Government Code §12955
Housing discrimination

It shall be unlawful:

(a) For the owner of any housing accommodation to discriminate against any person because of the race, color, religion, sex, marital status, national origin, or ancestry of such person.

(b) For the owner of any housing accommodation to make or to cause to be made any written or oral inquiry concerning the race, color, religion, sex, marital status, national origin, or ancestry of any person seeking to purchase, rent or lease any housing accommodation.

(f) For any owner of housing accommodations to harass, evict, or otherwise discriminate against any person in the sale or rental of housing accommodations when the owner's dominant purpose is retaliation against a person who has opposed practices unlawful under this section, informed law enforcement agencies of practices believed unlawful under this section, or has testified or assisted in any proceeding under this part.

(l) To discriminate through public or private land use practices, decisions, and authorizations because of race, color, religion, sex, familial status, marital status, disability, national origin, or ancestry. Discrimination includes, but is not limited to, restrictive covenants, zoning laws, denials of use permits, and other actions authorized under the Planning and Zoning Law (Title 7 (commencing with Section 65000)), that make housing opportunities unavailable.

Calif. Health and Safety Code §35810 Unlawful discrimination by lenders

(a) No financial institution shall discriminate in the availability of, or in the provision of, financial assistance for the purpose of purchasing, constructing, rehabilitating, improving, or refinancing housing accommodations due, in whole or in part, to the consideration of conditions, characteristics, or trends in the neighborhood or geographic area surrounding the housing accommodation, unless the financial institution can demonstrate that consideration of these conditions in the particular case is required to avoid an unsafe and unsound business practice.

(b) Nothing in this section shall be construed to prohibit any financial institution from establishing a special loan program designed to engender equality in housing in accordance with the federal Fair Housing Act (42 U.S.C. Secs. 3601 et seq.) or similar state and federal laws, so long as the program promotes housing opportunities in ethnic minority or low-income neighborhoods.

Calif. Health and Safety Code §35811

No financial institution shall discriminate in the availability of, or in the provision of, financial assistance for the purpose of purchasing, constructing, rehabilitating, improving or refinancing housing accommodations due, in whole or in part, to the consideration of race, color, religion, sex, marital status, national origin, or ancestry.

Calif. Health and Safety Code §35812

No financial institution shall consider the racial, ethnic, religious, or national origin composition of a neighborhood or geographic area surrounding a housing accommodation or whether or not such composition is undergoing change, or is expected to undergo change, in appraising a housing accommodation or in determining whether or not, and under what terms and conditions, to provide financial assistance for the purpose of purchasing, constructing, rehabilitating, improving, or refinancing a housing accommodation. No financial institution shall utilize appraisal practices that are inconsistent with the provisions of this part.

Real Estate Property Management, 4th Edition Quizzes

Instructions: Quizzes are open book. All answers are multiple choice or true or false.
Answer key is located on page 469.

Quiz 1 — Pages 3-34

_____1. A(n) _____ is not conveyed in an exchange for rent.

    a. life estate   c. leasehold estate

    b. estate at will   d. none of the above

_____2. A _____ lasts for a specific period of time agreed to in a lease agreement between a landlord and tenant.

    a. periodic tenancy   c. fixed-term tenancy

    b. tenancy-at-sufferance   d. tenancy-at-will

_____3. A lease conveys a(n) _____ in real estate to a tenant.

    a. exclusive possessory interest   c. nonexclusive possessory interest

    b. personal privilege   d. irrevocable privilege

_____4. A lease and a license cannot be held by the same person.

_____5. A tenant who remains in possession of property on expiration of a lease, without an agreement or acceptance of rent by the landlord, becomes a(n):

    a. holdover tenant.   c. tenant-at-will.

    b. tenant-at-sufferance.   d. both a and b.

_____6. The characteristic(s) of a tenancy-at-will include:

    a. no provision for the payment of rent.

    b. possession for an indefinite and unspecified period.

    c. possession delivered to the tenant with the landlord's knowledge and consent.

    d. all of the above.

_____7. When a tenant holds over after a fixed-term tenancy expires and the landlord continues to accept rent, the expired agreement is _____ on the same terms except for the period of occupancy.

    a. canceled   c. both a and b

    b. renewed   d. neither a nor b

_____8. A landlord has the right to allow police to enter a tenant's unit if he reasonable believes the tenant is committing a crime.

_____ **9.** A _____ notice of entry to a tenant's unit or space may reasonably be served by posting the notice on the tenant's entry door.

a. two-week

c. 48-hour

b. seven-day

d. 24-hour

_____ **10.** A lease provision giving the landlord the right of re-entry to retake possession of a premises on the tenant's breach of the lease agreement is enforceable.

Quiz 2 — Pages 35-64

_____ **1.** If a tenant fails to make mandated improvements that are to remain with the property on expiration of the lease, the tenant is liable to the landlord for _____ incurred by the landlord to make the improvements.

a. none of the cost

c. the full cost

b. half the cost

d. none of the above

_____ **2.** Unless otherwise agreed to, tenant improvements become part of the leased property and remain with the property on expiration of the lease.

_____ **3.** _____ attached to real estate do not revert to the landlord on expiration of the lease.

a. Real estate fixtures

c. both a and b

b. Trade fixtures

d. neither a nor b

_____ **4.** A(n)_____ is a preemptive right to purchase property should the owner later decide to sell the property.

a. option to buy

c. offer to purchase

b. notice of abandonment

d. right of first refusal

_____ **5.** When options to renew or extend a lease are included in the lease terms, the expiration of the option to buy is tied to:

a. the expiration of the initial lease term.

b. the expiration of any renewal or extension.

c. either a or b.

d. neither a nor b.

_____ **6.** Entry by an owner into a purchase agreement with another party on different terms than those previously offered to the tenant does not reinstate the tenant's right of first refusal.

_____ **7.** Anyone who receives a percentage or contingency fee for continuously locating tenants or managing income properties for another:

a. must hold a real estate broker's license.

b. must hold a real estate broker's license only if the fee is greater than $1,500.

c. must hold a real estate broker's license only if the fee is greater than $2,500.

d. does not need a real estate broker's license.

_____8. A temporary manager of real estate who has a power of attorney is not required to hold a real estate broker's license.

_____9. If a lease term exceeds _____, a property manager must obtain written authorization from the landlord in order to bind the landlord to the lease.

a. six months

c. two years

b. one year

d. three years

_____10. Property managers require a(n) _____ agreement to enforce collection of their management fees.

a. written

c. implicit

b. oral

d. both a and b

Quiz 3 — Pages 65-105

_____1. Only a property owner may file an unlawful detainer (UD) action.

_____2. A property manager is required to deposit rent and security deposits into a(n)_____ within three business days of receipt.

a. trust account

c. savings account

b. impound account

d. checking account

_____3. Unless otherwise agreed to, a resident manager whose employment is terminated and refuses to vacate is not entitled to a notice to vacate before the property manager or owner may begin eviction proceedings.

_____4. Apartment buildings with _____ or more units must have an owner or resident manager living on the premises to manage the property.

a. 12

c. 16

b. 14

d. 18

_____5. Taxwise, the rental value of an apartment unit is not income to the resident manager when the unit occupied by the resident manager is:

a. for the property manager's or landlord's convenience.

b. located on the premises managed.

c. occupied by the manager as a condition of his employment.

d. all of the above.

_____6. Addresses given to residential tenants for the landlord, property manager and resident manager must be:

a. street addresses.

c. identified on a plot map.

b. email addresses.

d. clarified using a metes and bounds description.

_____7. Without a later writing signed by a client, an oral fee agreement between a broker and his client, whether a tenant or an owner, is unenforceable by the broker.

_____8. The _____ grants a broker the right to a fee if, within a fixed period after the exclusive authorization period expires, the property is leased to a tenant the broker dealt with during the listing period.

    a. right of first refusal
           c. both a and b

    b. safety clause
              d. neither a nor b

_____9. Under a(n) _____, a broker has earned a fee if the tenant enters into a lease agreement with the owner.

    a. option listing
           c. exclusive authorization to locate space

    b. net listing
              d. none of the above

_____10. An oral cooperative fee-splitting agreement between two brokers is not enforceable.

Quiz 4 — Pages 107-137

_____1. The amount of the common area maintenance (CAM) cost of a property is a(n) _____ which a broker must disclose to a prospective tenant who agrees to pay these costs.

    a. assessment
           c. material fact

    b. CC&R
           d. immaterial fact

_____2. A listing agent uses a(n) _____ to analyze a prospective tenant's current lease conditions, existing space, future needs and creditworthiness.

    a. tenant lease worksheet
           c. property management agreement

    b. offer to lease
           d. disclosure form

_____3. The identification section in an offer to lease:

    a. names the contracting parties.
    c. acknowledges receipt of a good faith deposit.

    b. describes the premises.
       d. all of the above.

_____4. An offer to lease real estate is a solicitation and cannot be accepted.

_____5. In order to form a binding agreement, an offer or counteroffer:

    a. must be accepted in its entirety and without conditions.

    b. may be accepted with minor changes in conditions.

    c. may be accepted with minor changes in conditions if both parties agree to address the conditions within 15 business days.

    d. none of the above.

_____6. Property managers do not need to identify themselves or state their purpose for seeking a prospective tenant's credit information from a reporting agency.

_____7. Credit checks on prospective tenants can only be used to establish eligibility for:

a. employment purposes.

c. the rental of a dwelling unit.

b. personal, family or household purposes.

d. all of the above.

_____8. A tenant is entitled to request a clarification by a credit reporting agency of the results of an unlawful detainer (UD) action against the tenant if the report regarding the UD is:

a. true but misleading.

c. incorrect.

b. mostly true but contains some errors.

d. none of the above.

_____9. A residential landlord may charge a fee to cover the costs of obtaining a prospective tenant's:

a. employment history.

c. financial statements.

b. former street address.

d. credit report.

_____10. A property manager must consider a prospective tenant's _____ before agreeing to lease nonresidential property.

a. race and sexual orientation

c. religion and net worth

b. business acumen and style of marketing

d. business plan and gender

Quiz 5 — Pages 139-162

_____1. A residential landlord who sets the security deposit amount based on creditworthiness must apply his credit standards equally to all prospective tenants.

_____2. A landlord _____ security deposits with other funds in a general account.

a. is prohibited from commingling

b. may commingle

c. may not place

d. either a or b

_____3. A residential landlord must give a written notice of the right to request a pre-expiration inspection to a tenant, ideally at least _____ days prior to the date the tenant is to vacate the premises.

a. 10

c. 30

b. 15

d. 45

_____4. The 48-hour notice of entry for a pre-termination inspection cannot be waived by the tenant or landlord.

_____5. Within _____ after a residential tenant vacates, the landlord must provide the tenant with an itemized statement of all deductions from the security deposit.

  a. two-weeks

  b. 20 days

  c. 21 days

  d. 24 hours

_____6. A residential landlord who fails to refund a tenant's security deposit in bad faith may be subject to a penalty of up to _____ the amount of the security deposit.

  a. twice

  b. three times

  c. four times

  d. five times

_____7. A stay-or-pay clause which calls for a tenant to forfeit his security deposit is:

  a. illegal.

  b. unenforceable.

  c. enforceable if the tenant stays less than 180 days.

  d. both a and b.

_____8. Funds received by a residential landlord from a tenant are classified as:

  a. rent, tenant screening fees, waterbed administration fees or mold inspection fees.

  b. tenant screening fees, pet deposits, rent or closing costs.

  c. security deposits, filing fee, pet deposits or waterbed administration fees.

  d. rent, tenant screening fees, waterbed administration fees or security deposits.

_____9. When a nonresidential tenant makes a partial payment of rent after receiving a 3-day notice to pay rent or quit, the landlord may accept the rent and still commence an unlawful detainer (UD) action to evict the tenant.

_____10. A residential unlawful detainer (UD) action based on a 3-day notice which overstates the amount of the delinquent rent due is:

  a. valid.

  b. invalid.

  c. valid if the amount is reasonably approximated.

  d. invalid unless the landlord holds a broker's license.

Quiz 6 — Pages 163-181

_____1. _____ in a residential or nonresidential month-to-month rental agreement may be changed on 30 days' written notice by the landlord.

  a. Addendums

  b. Provisions and conditions

  c. Clauses and terms

  d. all of the above.

_____2. Upon receipt of a 30-day notice of change in terms on a periodic rental agreement, the new terms take effect _____ after the expiration of the notice.

  a. immediately

  b. 15 days

  c. 15 business days

  d. 30 days

_____**3.** A residential landlord subject to rent control can make adjustments to rents based on:

  a. the maximum percentage of the consumer price index (CPI) as set by ordinance.

  b. the maximum percentage set by ordinance.

  c. the maximum amount previously set by the rent control board.

  d. all of the above.

_____**4.** In a small claims action for recovery against a guarantor, the amount of recovery is limited to _____ or less.

  a. $1,500   c. $3,500

  b. $2,500   d. $4,500

_____**5.** In a municipal court action, the landlord seeking to recover unpaid rents may:

  a. represent himself.

  b. be represented by an attorney licensed in California.

  c. be represented by a licensed real estate sales agent.

  d. both a and b.

_____**6.** An unlawful detainer occurs when a tenant refuses to pay rent and remains in possession of the property after the expiration of a 3-day notice to pay rent or quit.

_____**7.** A 3-day notice to pay or quit that declares an election to forfeit the lease and expires for failure to pay:

  a. terminates the lease agreement.

  b. terminates the right to possession.

  c. forfeits the tenant's security deposit.

  d. both a and b.

_____**8.** A landlord can only recover future rents if he reserves his right to collect future rents by including a default remedies clause in the lease agreement.

_____**9.** A landlord is entitled to recover _____ after the tenant fails to perform on the lease.

  a. costs to clean up the property   c. permit fees to construct necessary renovations

  b. legal fees to find a new tenant   d. all of the above.

_____**10.** A landlord cannot recover future rents if the lease agreement is canceled.

Quiz 7 — Pages 183-216

_____**1.** A tenant's failure to pay late charges is a breach which justifies the service of a 3-day notice to pay or quit.

2. Rent does not become delinquent for nonreceipt until:

    a. the expiration of any grace period stated in the lease agreement.

    b. the day following the due date if no grace period exists.

    c. five days after mailing if posted within the grace period.

    d. both a and b.

3. The purpose of a 3-day notice to pay or quit is to provide a tenant the opportunity to avoid forfeiture of his leasehold estate by paying the delinquent rent.

4. A landlord must allow a tenant to cure a material breach of the lease when the tenant is capable of curing the breached provision within:

    a. three days.   c. one month.

    b. 15 days.   d. two months.

5. A tenant may be evicted for maintaining a(n) _____ the property.

    a. unlawful use of   c. unorthodox or unprofessional business style on

    b. nuisance on   d. both a and b

6. In order to evict a tenant for laying waste to the premises, the landlord must prove the waste _____ the market value of the premises.

    a. marginally diminished   c. had no influence on

    b. substantially diminished   d. substantially improved

7. An individual who serves a 3-day notice on a tenant does not need to complete a proof of service form.

8. Personal service is accomplished when _____ signs the postal receipt acknowledging receipt of the 3-day notice in the mail.

    a. someone other than the tenant   c. either a or b

    b. the tenant   d. neither a nor b

9. A 3-day notice to pay or quit may include:

    a. delinquent rent.

    b. unpaid amounts due under the lease which are not labeled rent.

    c. both a and b.

    d. neither a nor b.

10. A late charge is only permissible when the amount is _____ cost of collecting the delinquent rent and the loss due to the delay in its receipt.

    a. greater than the   c. reasonably related to the

    b. less than the   d. none of the above

Quiz 8 — Pages 217-242

_____1. Once the 30-day notice to vacate expires and the month-to- month tenant does not vacate, the landlord may file a(n) _____ to evict the tenant without further notice.
   a. unlawful detainer (UD) action   c. offer to surrender
   b. 3-day notice to vacate   d. notice of termination

_____2. To evict a tenant under HUD's Section 8 program, the landlord must state a valid reason for the eviction in his notice to vacate.

_____3. A(n) _____ reconveys the real estate to the landlord in exchange for cancellation of the lease agreement.
   a. notice of termination   c. 3-day notice to pay or quit
   b. notice to vacate   d. surrender

_____4. A surrender may only occur by the:
   a. mutual consent of the landlord and tenant.
   b. operation of law.
   c. conduct of the tenant.
   d. both a and b.

_____5. Like surrender rules, abandonment rules only apply to residential property.

_____6. A Notice of Abandonment expires _____ days after the date the notice is sent by first-class mail.
   a. 5   c. 18
   b. 10   d. 30

_____7. A tenant, after being served a Notice of Belief of Abandonment, may stop the abandonment procedure by just reoccupying the property.

_____8. After a tenant pays storage costs to the landlord, the tenant must pick up his personal property within _____ hours.
   a. 72   c. 24
   b. 48   d. 12

_____9. Personal property worth less than _____ may be kept by the landlord if it is not reclaimed.
   a. 100   c. 300
   b. 200   d. 400

_____10. Personal property subject to a public sale must be surrendered to the tenant:
   a. at no time.
   b. two business days after receiving request for the return of the property from the tenant.
   c. 15 days after the public sale.
   d. any time prior to the sale.

_____1. A constructive eviction occurs when the tenant vacates the premises due to:

    a. waste committed on the property by the tenant.

    b. the landlord's substantial interference with the tenant's use and enjoyment of his property during the term of the rental or lease agreement.

    c. the neighbor's substantial interference with the tenant's use and enjoyment of his property.

    d. eminent domain.

_____2. When a tenant vacates due to a constructive eviction, he may recover:

    a. relocation expenses.

    b. unaccrued prepaid rent and security deposits held by the landlord.

    c. loss of business goodwill.

    d. all of the above.

_____3. A nonresidential tenant may contract to limit the covenant of quiet enjoyment; a residential tenant may not.

_____4. In an unlawful detainer (UD) action, residential tenants are allowed to raise these two defenses:

    a. breach of the warranty of habitability and retaliatory eviction.

    b. retaliatory eviction and breach of implied covenants.

    c. breach of the warranty of habitability and refusal to reimburse tenant for cost of repairs.

    d. none of the above.

_____5. Actions by a residential landlord are considered retaliatory acts if initiated by the landlord after the tenant:

    a. organizes or becomes a member of a tenants' association or tenants' rights group.

    b. exercises the statutory repair and deduct remedy.

    c. commits waste.

    d. both a and b.

_____6. After prevailing in an unlawful detainer (UD) action, a residential tenant is entitled to 120 days of protection against eviction without cause.

_____7. In addition to a tenant's actual money losses incurred due to the landlord's retaliatory act, the tenant is also entitled to recover _____ for each retaliatory act where the landlord acts maliciously with respect to the retaliation.

    a. punitive damages between $100 and $500

    b. punitive damages between $500 and $1,000

    c. punitive damages between $500 and $1,500

    d. punitive damages between $100 and $1,000

_____**8.** A landlord who fails to cure known dangerous defects will be liable under tort principles of:

    a. negligence.   c. waste.

    b. retaliatory eviction.   d. forfeiture.

_____**9.** A residential tenant has a duty of care and maintenance in the use of leased property, which includes:

    a. disposing of all waste in a sanitary manner.

    b. properly operating all electrical, gas and plumbing fixtures.

    c. using the property for the purpose it is intended to be used.

    d. all of the above.

_____**10.** A residential tenant may make necessary repairs that the landlord fails to make and deduct the costs from the rent, limited to one month's rent.

Quiz 10 — Pages 267-290

_____**1.** Part of a residential tenant's entitlement to a safe and sanitary dwelling includes:

    a. marble flooring.

    b. an external air-conditioning unit.

    c. a hot and cold running water system.

    d. new carpeting.

_____**2.** Prior to renting a residential unit intended for human habitation, the landlord must:

    a. install an operable sprinkler system if the property fronts a public street.

    b. install a washer and dryer.

    c. install a dead bolt lock on each nonhorizontally sliding main entry door.

    d. none of the above.

_____**3.** A tenant who successfully raises a warranty of habitability defense in an unlawful detainer (UD) action may:

    a. retain possession of the premises.

    b. pay a reduced amount of rent.

    c. recover attorney fees and the costs of litigation.

    d. all of the above.

_____**4.** Smoke detectors must be installed and maintained in single family residences and:

    a. apartment complexes and duplexes.

    b. motels and hotels.

    c. condominiums and time share projects.

    d. all of the above.

5. Security bars on residential bedroom windows do not need to have release mechanisms if the bedroom has a door leading out of the premises.

6. When criminal activity is _____, the landlord has a duty to take reasonable measures to prevent harm to persons on the property from future similar criminal activities.

   a. decreasing in the area

   b. reasonable foreseeable

   c. remotely possible

   d. reasonably unforeseeable

7. A landlord has the duty to protect a tenant from criminal acts committed by others that injure the tenant when he is not on the leased premises.

8. Liability is imposed on a landlord for an injury suffered by any person on the property if:

   a. the type of injury suffered by the individual is foreseeable.

   b. the injury suffered is closely connected to the landlord's conduct.

   c. both a and b.

   d. neither a nor b.

9. A landlord who is held liable for his property manager's negligence is not entitled to indemnity from the property manager.

10. When an injured tenant's lack of care for himself contributes to his injury, recovery for his losses is limited to the percentage of the negligence attributed to him, called:

   a. comparative negligence.

   b. constructive negligence.

   c. nondelegable negligence.

   d. reasonable negligence.

Quiz 11 — Pages 293-334

1. To contain all the essential terms for enforcement, an offer to lease must contain:

   a. a property description.

   b. the term of the lease.

   c. the amount of periodic rent and when it will be paid.

   d. all of the above.

2. On expiration of a lease, a tenancy-at-sufferance is created when the tenant remains in possession of the property and:

   a. the landlord posts a notice to vacate on the property.

   b. is subject to an eminent domain action.

   c. the landlord refuses to accept further rent payments.

   d. all of the above.

3. The right to receive a condemnation award on the leased property cannot be contracted away by a tenant.

4. If a tenant has a history of writing bad rent checks due to insufficient funds, the landlord may serve a 30-day notice on the tenant requiring him to:

a. vacate the property on expiration of the notice.

b. forfeit his security deposit.

c. tender payment of future rents in cash or by money order.

d. all of the above.

5. _____ are typically based on the ratio between space leased by the tenant and the total rentable space in a project.

a. Common area maintenance (CAM) charges

b. Operating expenses

c. Fair market rent

d. none of the above

6. The three basic types of rent escalation clauses are:

a. inflation adjusted rent provisions, graduated rent provisions and appreciation adjusted rent provisions.

b. graduated rent provisions, inflation adjusted rent provisions and compounding rent provisions.

c. compounding rent provisions, graduated rent provisions and reverse rent provisions.

d. inflation adjusted rent provisions, adjustable rent provisions and appreciation adjusted rent provisions.

7. Graduated rents are increased in pre-set increments on a periodic basis.

8. To annually adjust the base rent to compensate for price inflation, a _____ can be included in a lease agreement.

a. price inflation clause or graduated payment clause

b. appreciation clause or price inflation clause

c. consumer price index (CPI) clause or price inflation clause

d. none of the above

9. Under _____ rent adjustment provisions, the prior year's rent, not the base year's rent, is used to set the adjusted rent.

a. base-to-current year   c. base-to-future

b. year-to-year   d. both a and b.

10. _____ is the actual price received for all merchandise or services sold, licensed, leased or delivered for purposes of percentage rent calculations.

a. Gross sales   c. Median sales

b. Net sales   d. Total receipts

Quiz 12 — Pages 335-362

_____1. Any use incidental to the leased premises and connected to the tenant's leasehold interest is called a(n):

    a. use-of-premises provision.   c. recorded easement.

    b. appurtenance.   d. none of the above.

_____2. A _____ relieves a landlord's property from becoming security for any claims made by contractors for improvements they construct on the leased premises.

    a. notice of forfeiture   c. notice of default

    b. notice of abandonment   d. notice of nonresponsibility

_____3. If not limited by its terms, the total term of a nonresidential lease, including extensions or renewals, is limited to _____ years by statute.

    a. 99   c. 101

    b. 100   d. 130

_____4. When the term of a lease is extended, a new lease is created.

_____5. For a tenant to be released from liability on the assignment of his lease agreement, a(n) _____ must be negotiated and entered into by the landlord and both tenants.

    a. novation   c. subrogation agreement

    b. substitution of liability   d. either a or b

_____6. Unless unconscionable or discriminatory, nonresidential landlords and tenants are free to place _____ restrictions, limited to the value of the leasehold, on the tenant's assignment of the lease.

    a. commercially unreasonable   c. economically damaging

    b. commercially reasonable   d. economically unreasonable

_____7. The city and county of San Francisco may pass and enforce nonresidential rent control ordinances.

_____8. Nonresidential real estate includes all real estate except:

    a. residential hotels.   c. mobilehome parks.

    b. dwelling units.   d. all of the above.

_____9. Local governments can regulate all facets of business location and development, such as:

    a. abating nuisances.

    b. exercising eminent domain powers.

    c. protecting historical resources.

    d. all of the above.

_____10. After receiving a nonresidential tenant's negotiation notice under a local ordinance, the landlord must enter into negotiations to renew or extend the lease with the tenant.

Quiz 13 — Pages 365-386

_____1. Some landlords allow pets but frequently:

    a. impose restrictions on the type or size of the pet.

    b. require the landlord's written consent to keep the pet on the premises.

    c. both a and b.

    d. neither a nor b.

_____2. A lease or rental agreement may prohibit a tenant from:

    a. creating a nuisance.   c. committing waste.

    b. using the premises for an   d. all of the above.
       unlawful purpose.

_____3. A written translation of a residential lease agreement is required to be delivered to the tenant if its term exceeds _____ and is negotiated primarily in Spanish, Chinese, Vietnamese, Korean or _____.

    a. one year; Japanese   c. one year; Russian

    b. one month; Tagalog   d. one month; German

_____4. Real estate transactions exempt from the written translation requirement include:

    a. purchase agreements.

    b. month-to-month rental agreements.

    c. home improvement agreements.

    d. all of the above.

_____5. The mandated lead-based paint disclosure laws do not obligate a landlord to:

    a. abate or remove any lead-based paint.

    b. conduct an inspection to determine whether any lead-based paint exists.

    c. both a and b.

    d. neither a nor b.

_____6. A lead-based paint disclosure is required for all pre-1978 studio apartments which have not been certified as lead-based paint free.

_____7. A landlord does not need to provide a new lead-based paint disclosure when existing leases are renewed or extended if:

    a. the landlord previously supplied the lead-based disclosures.

    b. the landlord has not received any new information concerning lead-based paint on the property.

    c. the lead-based paint disclosures were not previously handed to the tenant.

    d. both a and b.

8. Landlords can refuse to accept tenants who want to occupy a unit with their pet unless the tenant is disabled and the pet is a:

a. signal dog.

c. guide dog.

b. service dog.

d. all of the above.

9. A landlord may charge a disabled tenant with a service dog an additional security deposit to offset any losses caused by the dog.

10. A tenant must give the property manager _____ if he intends to move, install or remove a waterbed.

a. 24 hours' notice

c. reasonable notice

b. 3 weeks' notice

d. none of the above

Quiz 14 — Pages 387-410

1. Handicapped persons refer to individuals who have:

a. a physical or mental impairment which substantially limits the person's life activities.

b. a record of having a physical or mental impairment.

c. relatives who have a record of having a physical or mental impairment.

d. both a and b.

2. A person who believes they have been discriminated against must file a complaint with the Secretary of Housing and Urban Development (HUD) within _____ of the alleged discriminatory practice.

a. 24 hours

c. one month

b. 12 days

d. one year

3. A broker found guilty of discrimination by the Secretary of Housing and Urban Development (HUD) may face disciplinary action from the:

a. Department of Real Estate (DRE).

b. local police department.

c. Department of Motor Vehicles (DMV).

d. all of the above.

4. A landlord of newly constructed four-or-more unit residential property must provide disabled access.

5. Rental policies excluding children under the age of 18 are considered _____ unless the property qualifies as senior citizen housing.

a. reasonable

c. lawful discrimination

b. unlawful discrimination

d. none of the above

6. Requiring families with children to have a better credit rating than other prospective tenants when screening rental applications is prohibited.

_____7. Senior citizen housing is property:

    a. intended for occupancy only by individuals 62 years of age or older.

    b. intended for occupancy by at least one person of 55 years of age or older.

    c. both a and b.

    d. neither a nor b.

_____8. A senior citizen and his disabled child or grandchild may live in senior citizen housing.

_____9. Two primary types of rent control ordinances exist called:

    a. strict rent control and variable rent control.

    b. market rent control and vacancy decontrol.

    c. vacancy decontrol and strict rent control.

    d. variable rent control and market rent control.

_____10. In addition to restricting rent increases, rent control ordinances restrict the landlord's:

    a. ability to enter a tenant's unit.   c. both a and b.

    b. ability to evict existing tenants.   d. neither a nor b.

Quiz 15 — Pages 413-441

_____1. In addition to fee estates, there are three other estates which exist in California:

    a. fee simple, life estates and estates at will.

    b. leaseholds, community property and fee simple.

    c. life estates, leaseholds and estates at will.

    d. estates at will, joint tenancy and life estates.

_____2. In the alienation provision in a lease, the landlord may:

    a. prohibit the tenant from encumbering the leasehold.

    b. allow the tenant to encumber the leasehold subject to previously agreed conditions.

    c. require the landlord's consent before the tenant may encumber the leasehold.

    d. all of the above.

_____3. Examples of boilerplate provisions in nonresidential lease agreements which relate to the priority of the lease against trust deeds are:

    a. future subordination clauses.   c. nondisturbance clauses.

    b. attornment clauses.   d. all of the above.

_____ 4. A _____ gives a tenant the right to require a new trust deed lender to enter into a written agreement which states the tenant's lease agreement will remain in effect for its full term after the lease is subordinated to a new loan.

  a. nondisturbance clause

  b. self-destruct provision

  c. future subordination clause

  d. power of sale provision

_____ 5. A _____ confirms the correct amount of security deposit held by the seller.

  a. UCC-1 Financing Statement

  b. Tenant Estoppel Certificate (TEC)

  c. notice of default (NOD)

  d. none of the above.

_____ 6. On the discovery of a long-term leasing arrangement which triggers due-on enforcement under the lender's trust deed, the lender may:

  a. call the loan.

  b. recast the loan.

  c. either a or b.

  d. neither a nor b.

_____ 7. The due-on clause is triggered when an owner of property secured by a due-on trust deed enters into a lease:

  a. with a term over two years or an option to purchase.

  b. with a term under three years without an option to purchase.

  c. with a term over three years or an option to purchase.

  d. with a term under two years without an option to purchase.

_____ 8. A broker who advises a buyer not to disclose a sale to a lender secured by a trust deed on the property may be held liable by the lender for the lender's right to additional interest.

_____ 9. Residential tenants under month-to-month rental or lease agreements which are wiped-out by foreclosure by a trust deed lender are entitled to no less than a _____ notice to vacate.

  a. 3-day

  b. 25-day

  c. 30-day

  d. one-year

_____ 10. Tenants in a rent control community may be evicted upon a change of ownership.

Answer References

The following are the answers to the quizzes for *Real Estate property Management,*
4th Edition and the page numbers where the answers are located.

Real Estate Property Management

Quiz 1			Quiz 2			Quiz 3			Quiz 4			Quiz 5		
1.	B	4	1.	C	37	1.	F	69	1.	C	110	1.	T	141
2.	C	6	2.	T	39	2.	A	73	2.	A	116	2.	B	143
3.	A	10	3.	B	41	3.	T	77	3.	D	122	3.	C	143
4.	F	13	4.	D	45	4.	C	80	4.	F	123	4.	F	145
5.	D	16	5.	C	48	5.	D	81	5.	A	123	5.	C	148
6.	D	19	6.	F	52	6.	A	87	6.	F	130	6.	A	150
7.	B	21	7.	A	55	7.	T	89	7.	D	130	7.	D	151
8.	F	23	8.	T	56	8.	B	95	8.	A	131	8.	D	152
9.	D	26	9.	B	59	9.	C	100	9.	D	132	9.	T	157
10.	F	31	10.	A	64	10.	F	105	10.	B	136	10.	B	158

Quiz 6			Quiz 7			Quiz 8			Quiz 9			Quiz 10		
1.	D	163	1.	F	184	1.	A	218	1.	B	244	1.	C	268
2.	A	164	2.	D	186	2.	T	222	2.	D	245	2.	C	269
3.	D	166	3.	T	190	3.	D	224	3.	T	248	3.	D	270
4.	B	167	4.	A	196	4.	D	224	4.	A	252	4.	D	275
5.	D	170	5.	D	198	5.	F	229	5.	D	252	5.	T	277
6.	T	175	6.	B	200	6.	C	230	6.	F	253	6.	B	279
7.	B	176	7.	F	207	7.	F	230	7.	D	254	7.	F	281
8.	F	179	8.	B	210	8.	A	236	8.	A	258	8.	C	283
9.	D	181	9.	C	211	9.	C	240	9.	D	261	9.	F	285
10.	T	181	10.	C	213	10.	D	242	10.	T	264	10.	A	288

Quiz 11			Quiz 12			Quiz 13			Quiz 14			Quiz 15		
1.	D	298	1.	B	336	1.	C	370	1.	D	387	1.	C	413
2.	C	304	2.	D	337	2.	D	372	2.	D	391	2.	D	415
3.	F	304	3.	A	344	3.	B	373	3.	A	391	3.	D	418
4.	C	312	4.	F	346	4.	D	374	4.	T	393	4.	A	424
5.	A	314	5.	D	352	5.	C	375	5.	B	395	5.	B	428
6.	A	317	6.	B	355	6.	F	378	6.	T	401	6.	C	433
7.	T	318	7.	F	359	7.	D	379	7.	C	403	7.	C	434
8.	C	319	8.	D	360	8.	D	381	8.	T	405	8.	T	436
9.	B	327	9.	D	360	9.	F	381	9.	C	407	9.	C	438
10.	A	333	10.	F	361	10.	A	386	10.	B	408	10.	F	441

Case Index

California Codes

Department of Real Estate Regulations

County Codes

Federal Codes

Topical Index

C

D

E

R

Race